Dead or Alive

British Horror Films 1980-1989

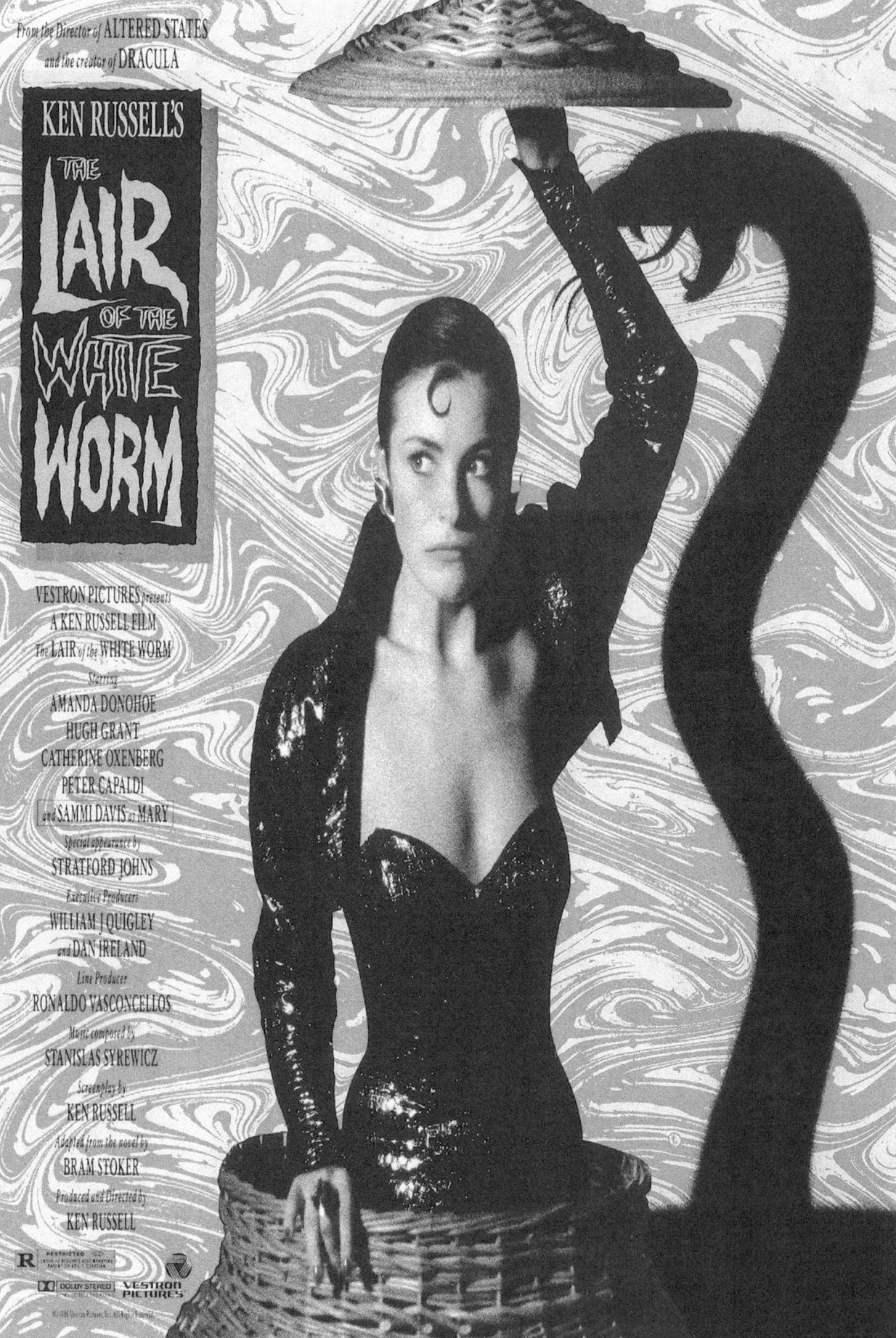

Dead or Alive

British Horror Films 1980-1989

Edited by Darrell Buxton

Midnight Marquee Press, Inc.
Baltimore, Maryland, USA

ACKNOWLEDGEMENTS

Grateful thanks are due to the following: my hardworking contributors, heroes all; plus Jonathan Rigby, Saxon Logan, Michael J. Murphy, Graham Humphreys, Phil Lyndon, Gordon Rodden, Richard Ault, Matthew Coniam, Derby QUAD, Chris Wood/britishhorrorfilms.co.uk, Kevin Lyons/eofftv.com, Carol Otter, Eric McNaughton, Stephen Volk, Gil Lane-Young and Tony Edwards (Festival of Fantastic Films), Andrew and Teresa Clark, the Cube Cinema in Bristol, Robin James and the Gothique Film Society, Stephen Longhurst, Mike Crozier, Nadia Mook, Marc Edwards, Christopher King, Steve Smith, Peter Munford, Mark Morris, Paula Fay, "Billy," Cinemageddon.net, Wayne Maginn, Paul Cotgrove and The White Bus, Dave Simpson, Charlie Allbright, Ian Bellerby, of Arrowe Hill, Sir John Hurt, Florence Dewavrin, Marcelle Perks, M. J. Simpson, John Martin, Brian Davies, Dave Gold, and Dan Leissner.

Copyright © 2021 Darrell Buxton
Interior Layout: Gary J. Svehla and A. Susan Svehla
Cover Design: A. Susan Svehla
Copy Editor: Janet Atkinson

Without limiting the rights under copyright reserved above, no part of this publication may be reproduced, stored in or introduced into a retrieval system, or transmitted, in any form, or by any means (electronic, mechanical, photocopying, recording or otherwise), without the prior written permission of the copyright owner or the publishers of the book.

Paperback black and white: ISBN 9781644301241
Paperback color: ISBN 978-1-64430-125-8
Casebound: ISBN 978-1-64430-126-5
Library of Congress Catalog Card Number 2021940438
Manufactured in the United States of America
First Printing August 2021

> "What's your pleasure …?"
> —*Hellraiser, 1987*

VIRGIN VISION PRESENTS
· A KEN RUSSELL FILM ·
GOTHIC

CONJURE UP YOUR DEEPEST, DARKEST FEAR.
THEN CALL THAT FEAR TO LIFE.

— STARRING —
GABRIEL BYRNE · JULIAN SANDS · NATASHA RICHARDSON · MYRIAM CYR & TIMOTHY SPALL

MUSIC COMPOSED BY THOMAS DOLBY · SCREENPLAY BY STEPHEN VOLK
EXECUTIVE PRODUCERS AL CLARK AND ROBERT DEVEREUX
PRODUCED BY PENNY CORKE · DIRECTED BY KEN RUSSELL

Virgin FILMS

Table of Contents

8	**Foreword** by Graham Humphreys
9	**Introduction**
11	**1980**
27	**1981**
41	**1982**
50	**1983**
60	**1984**
77	**1985**
96	**1986**
112	**1987**
124	**1988**
135	**1989**
153	**TV Movies**
189	**Appendix 1: Borderline Films/Miscellany**
238	**Appendix 2: Amateur S.O.V. Features**
241	**Appendix 3: Unfilmed Projects**
243	**Appendix 4: Short Films**
251	**Appendix 5: Problem/Peripheral Titles**
261	**Appendix 6: Hammer: The 1980s**
269	**Appendix 7: Michael J. Murphy**

Foreword

by Graham Humphreys

Is it over yet?

Big Ben struck the midnight hour and suddenly we were living in the 1990s.

I remember thinking how relieved I was to leave the preceding savage decade of shoulder pads, big hair, increasingly terrible music and of course the poisonous legacies of Thatcher and Reagan. The dawn of a new century drew closer and with it the promise of a new era of intellectual reappraisement, a world where differences could be resolved, and humans could join hands and learn to have better hair. That went well then.

Living through that decade of political turmoil, who imagined worse was to come? But on the plus side, once the embarrassment subsided and we could look back with nostalgia tinted glasses, we began to realize that far from the cultural desert the 1980s might have once appeared, the land had been rich and fertile after all.

In his 2005 book *Rip It Up and Start Again*, Simon Reynolds examines the music scene and the leaps of imagination that propelled a new bold decade of experimentation and creativity liberated by punks in the late 1970s. We thought the 1980s had been rubbish, but they had in fact been great!

In parallel to the music, 1980s horror cinema also unleashed some of its more outrageous turns. New young writers and filmmakers, inspired by the auteurs of the previous decade, poured forth—in no small part due to the rapid growth of home entertainment and VHS films previously consigned to B-movie billing and flea-pit porn cinemas finding a new proud status on the shelves.

In fact, so rapid was this growth in the UK that the government and tabloids, sensing their increasing impotence in shaping the morals of the nation, had a mutual meltdown and concocted the "video nasty" panic. Far from extinguishing the flames of matters lurid and challenging, the inferno burst forth and forged a decade so rich in diamonds that we can barely keep up. Even now, we are still rediscovering and reclaiming these gems.

The 1980s gave me a career in illustration in the brave new world of independent home cinema distribution. All these years later, many of those titles are being restored and reissued, proving that in entertainment value they are still to be counted among the best on the virtual shelves of the video shop. Meanwhile, new cinema is being crafted, directly referencing that bloody and irreverent era celebrated in these pages.

Tease up your hair, don the shoulder pads and hit "playback" ...

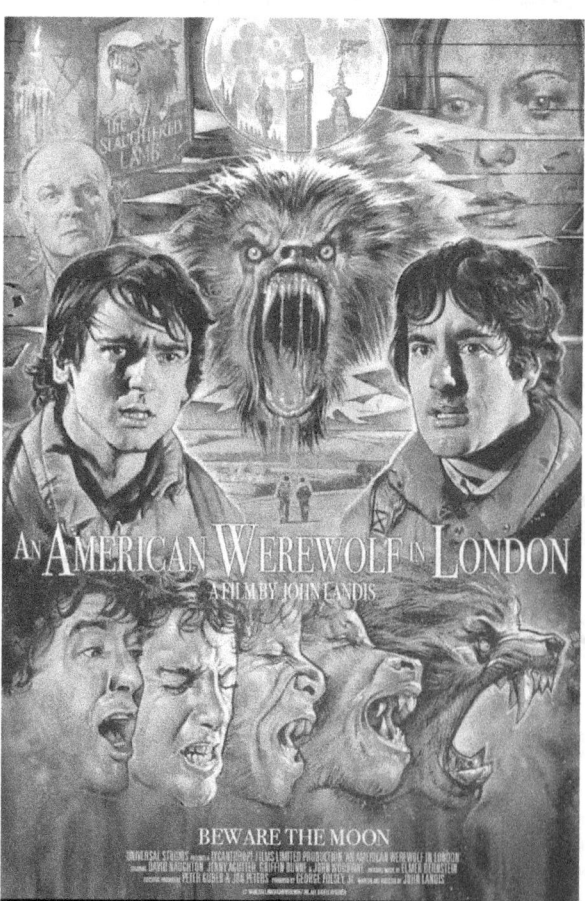

Graham Humphrey's art for *A Nightmare on Elm Street 2* and *An American Werewolf in London*

Graham Humphreys is an illustrator and designer with over 40 years experience. His bold, colourful, uncompromising style for movie posters, video packaging, and album covers helped to define the look of 80s horror, and his innovation and eye-catching graphics continue to impress new generations of fans.

Introduction

"Is Anybody There?"—tagline from *Paperhouse* poster, 1988

Aside from promoting one of the more unusual fright-flicks to emerge from the 1980s, the above might equally have rung out as an anguished cry from distressed theater managers and ushers fearing for their employment prospects, the call echoing around the UK's rapidly-emptying movie houses back then ...

Whenever I happened to mention, during the gestation period of the *Dead or Alive* project, that I was working on a book devoted to the subject of British horror movies of the 1980s, the usual response was "were there any?" After a minute or two most people managed to recall *Hellraiser*, some cited *An American Werewolf in London* but invariably added a belief that they suspected the movie might be a US production filmed here, and little else sprang to mind. All of which made me realize the need for this publication, plus the fact that the book might actually veer towards becoming a study of the unavailability and lack of awareness of the films from this era as much as it would be about the movies themselves.

Sister to *Dead or Alive* is *The Shrieking Sixties* (Midnight Marquee Press 2010), my team's earlier examination of a focus-shifting decade in British horror. Following the acclaim for that volume, including a gratefully acknowledged award nomination from the British Fantasy Society, I pondered over a suitable subject for myself and contributors to get our teeth into as a follow-up. Nineteen-seventies' British shockers had of course already been documented, more than adequately, in the pages of Harvey Fenton and David Flint's *Ten Years of Terror* (FAB Press 2001)—so the evil 1980s seemed a natural successor. On further consideration, however, it appeared to be a more complex area to tackle. With the withdrawal of the Eady levy, changes to film classification and certification systems at both the outset and close of the decade, censorship controversies including the shameful "video nasties" campaign, the very emergence of home video itself as a fresh medium of distribution and exhibition, opportunities for non-professionals to make and screen their own handiwork, the launch of Channel 4 leading to a raft of small/medium-budget film dramas screened on TV as well as in cinemas, Colin Welland's staggeringly mistimed war cry, "the British are coming!" at the 1982 Academy Awards, dwindling audience numbers, the demise of fallen-into-disrepair cinema halls up and down the land, a new breed of journalism which sought its own movie heroes and largely dismissed the past (punk style), the arrival of brash and genre-savvy newcomers such as Palace Pictures, and the continuation of US dollars pouring into the UK film economy—the story of this country's horror output during the "Thatcher years" was a potential minefield, requiring levels of research above and beyond leafing through a few books about Hammer and old copies of *The Monthly Film Bulletin*. At times I wondered if it might prove an impossible task but decided to propel myself and fellow enthusiasts headlong into the maelstrom regardless. The results, presented here, will hopefully provide a stimulating and informative guide to the many strange paths, tangents, and offshoots the terror movie bumped and weaved its way along four decades ago.

We have films directed by major US talents and by rank Brit amateurs; works by Michael McIntyre's father, Monty Python's editor, the lead singer of The Kinks, the star of *The Student Prince*, the creator of the TV show *Masterchef*, one of *Hustler* magazine's "50 most influential people in porn," and the man who dared to make a sequel to *Psycho*; while sitcom stars, soap opera regulars, comedy double acts, "Page 3" nude models, disc jockeys, and pop personalities major and minor all serve to prop up cast lists here. Subject matter includes killer monkeys, garden gnomes, the cutthroat world of advertising, women giving birth to aliens, the nuclear destruction of Sheffield, drug rehab, gourmet cooking, dyslexia, politics, the National Health Service, motorbiking, and more killer monkeys.

Rumor has it that the 1980s rather dismissed doom and gloom in favor of bright primary colors, sculpted hairstyles, MTV, legwarmers, compact discs, and John Hughes. Bear in mind, however, that British television at the outset of the period in question was awash with supernatural and psychological chills, from *Hammer House of Horror* to *Rentaghost*, *Sapphire & Steel* to *Tales of the Unexpected*. In the music world, every Duran Duran or Spandau Ballet was countered by acts daring to delve into darker territory —Siouxsie and the Banshees' 1981 album *Juju* was laced with voodoo, specters, and arcane practices; Iron Maiden frequently used classic horror references and created their own monstrous mascot, skeletal super-fan "Eddie," the "Goth" movement made inroads particularly in the North of England, via The Sisters of Mercy, Bauhaus, The March Violets and Fields of the Nephilim, and even the top-selling, radio-friendly stars of the day took genre-sprinkled items to the top of the charts (the austere, bleak "Ghost Town" by The Specials, Frankie Goes to Hollywood's controversial and aware nuclear warning "Two Tribes," even Adam and the Ants' smash-hit paean to dandyism "Stand and Deliver)." With unemployment and oppression rife among certain areas of the country and within particular communities, the looming presence of something sinister tainted the official picture being presented by the authorities, of opportunity for all, jam tomorrow, loadsamoney. (Although perhaps American filmmaker Oliver Stone fused it better than anyone, bringing an altogether Faustian/Mephisthophelean quality to his 1988 study of stock exchange culture, *Wall Street*, the "greed is good" ethos of which may just have been the most frightening movie mantra of these divisive times.)

So, enjoy a trip back to the 1980s quite unlike any other, an alternate vision of the era. With the classic manufacturers of big-screen British chills, Hammer, Amicus, Tigon and others, lying dormant or completely out of action, a new, diverse, unconnected and decidedly different wave rode in to fill the gap. Not always successfully, sure, but (especially in hindsight) with considerable ambition to bring something fresh and unique to the terror table. This book is for those who prefer the challenge of the Lament Configuration to that of Rubik's Cube.

—Darrell Buxton

Editor's Note

In researching and compiling a book on British horror movies of the 1980s, we naturally had to define the terms "British," "horror," and "film." The major year-by-year portion of *Dead or Alive* therefore includes reviews and comments on those titles that we consider fitting the full bill. *Bloodbath at the House of Death*, to take one example, is an officially British-made production, includes much horror content, and was a feature film (intended for theatrical distribution, and also later released on VHS videocassette and on DVD) and so makes the cut. Although movies such as *Aliens*, *The Shining*, *The Sender*, and *The Hills Have Eyes Part 2* may not initially seem to fit the category "British horror film," careful analysis reveals that they do in fact qualify on all three counts. Direct-to-home-video titles have also been included—ranging from cinema-worthy fare such as *The Appointment*, through rental-aimed product like *Blood Tide*, down to amateur offerings which (in the industry's desperate bid to fill video store shelves) gained BBFC certification and commercial release—e.g. *Suffer, Little Children*.

We have included appendices for single, feature-length films made primarily for television (*Artemis 81*, *Night Train to Murder*, *Jack the Ripper*, etc.); for the handful of non-commercial "home movie" amateur productions our researches have uncovered from the period; and for Michael J. Murphy, whose one-of-a-kind career is considered a unique and special case, meriting an entire section of the book. Please note that our "TV movies" appendix also includes reviews of certain episodic television serials, but only where they exist in a feature-length "movie edit" in addition to their original instalment-based form (*The Chelsea Murders*, *The Mad Death* etc. are therefore covered—while the likes of *The Nightmare Man* or *The Day of the Triffids* are omitted and relegated to brief mentions elsewhere in the book.)

Short horror films (under 40 minutes' running time), as well as the Hammer company's 1980s return to the screen via quality television production, have also been given coverage under their own individual banner headings. "Borderline" films (those

British DVD release of *Aliens*

relevant offerings that may qualify under one or two of the conditions "British," "horror," and "film" but do not seem to satisfy on all three counts) are covered in detail towards the end of the book, and we've also included a listing of "peripheral and problem" works that are deemed worthy of attention (science fiction or thriller titles with minor horror elements; episodic TV series with a running time equivalent to a feature and possibly marketed as a "film" on video, DVD or Blu-ray; one-off television plays or specials etc.)

We cannot hope to please everyone, content-wise, and if you remain unconvinced that *An American Werewolf in London* or *Britannia Hospital* deserve a place here, never mind *Whoops Apocalypse* and *Monty Python's The Meaning of Life*, then I hope you will find everything that you are seeking covered within these pages.

Please also note that some of our reviews will contain spoilers. Wherever possible, we advise you to watch the films under review prior to reading about them here. Having said that, we do also aim to introduce you to titles that you may have previously overlooked or with which you may be unfamiliar. Tread carefully!

1980

The Awakening
Blood Tide
Death Ship
The Godsend
Inseminoid
The Monster Club
The Orchard End Murder
Saturn 3
The Shining
The Watcher in the Woods

THE AWAKENING

D: Mike Newell
W: Clive Exton, Chris Bryant, Allan Scott
Starring: Charlton Heston, Susannah York, Jill Townsend, Stephanie Zimbalist

This film is based on Bram Stoker's novel, *The Jewel of Seven Stars* (presence of a second misplaced "the" dependent on which version you read, as is the ending which comes in "wedding" and "original" flavors)—a story filmed previously for TV's *Mystery and Imagination* and by Hammer for 1971's big-screen *Blood from the Mummy's Tomb*. The 1980 version, *The Awakening*, involves the discovery of an evil sorceress' hidden tomb, and how this deposed female pharaoh, called Kara, plans to return to Earth using Corbeck, the Egyptologist who unearthed her resting place, and most significantly his young daughter Margaret.

Extensive location shooting suggests a budget substantially higher than most horror films of the era. There are long establishing shots, imbuing the Egyptian-set sections with a feeling of real oppressive heat but also robbing us of some of the focus and claustrophobia you can engineer with a studio-bound production.

The artifacts of Egyptian civilization are strange, and so it's easy to believe the leap that some (von Däniken, *Stargate*, etc.) make linking Egypt with distant stars, or strange curses. Hieroglyphics, pyramids, gold-painted animal-headed gods do look freakish to our Western sensibilities; perhaps if we achieve something approaching their three millennia of existence, our cultural leftovers will seem as exotic to other eyes. It is tempting to consider other mummy films when seeking comparisons with this flick, yet perhaps an analysis using *The Omen* as a yardstick yields greater insight into this film's failings. *The Omen* adopts commonly known biblical references for its armory, and works hard to build a tangible sense of threat to all our futures by using actors with gravitas (Troughton, Peck et. al) and a compelling score that makes you feel that each death is caused by cruel satanic force. In *The Awakening* we get similar curse-caused deaths and yet we never get any sense of intelligent design behind it, simply handy convenience—nor do we learn what the returned Kara's evil schemes are. She was a pharaoh because of her bloodline in ancient Egypt, but how exactly is she planning to gain power in the modern world?

Some sparse unintentional humor includes the state of York's haircut in the opening segment set 18 years earlier, which would make any budding Vidal Sassoon or Teasy Weasy wince. Another thing I found comical was the scene involving winching—naturally when we fans see close-ups of hauling mechanisms and pulleys in a horror film we just know an unhappy event is about to occur, but what raised my eyebrows was the fact they were lifting all the Egyptian tat up a steep cliff-face when below is a road with vehicles on it! Why not put the items in the vehicles? Do they like winching? Perhaps it's Corbeck's idea; after all several times he proves he isn't the sharpest excavation tool in the box.

The film does have some good shock moments, although some of these (particularly those involving Margaret) make me question their order because minor shocks occur after major ones. This warps any escalation. At one point Margaret seeks help from a psychiatrist played by Ian McDiarmid, surely compounding any misgivings one may have about psychiatry—seeking counsel from the Emperor from *Star Wars* has to be an unwise move, seemingly proven as she starts to babble and he reaches for a convenient syringe, though provoking an attack which seems all the more brutal by the editing, which gives the impression that Margaret catches a second wind and lunges again when this shrink is busy sliding down the table with his tongue out.

Do missing or unfilmed scenes occur after Paul Witter breaks into Corbeck's house near the end of the movie? Not only is someone we never see again just behind him as he enters the house (Margaret's mum?) but he, a character the film has spent time developing, gets an implied off-screen death. This does nothing to add any genuine sense of fear. Alternatively, perhaps he should have turned up at the climax where Kara could have fried him with, say, a lightning bolt from her index finger, making the threat posed by our villainess seem more real, perhaps even bordering on the credible, thus neatly tying up this loose end.

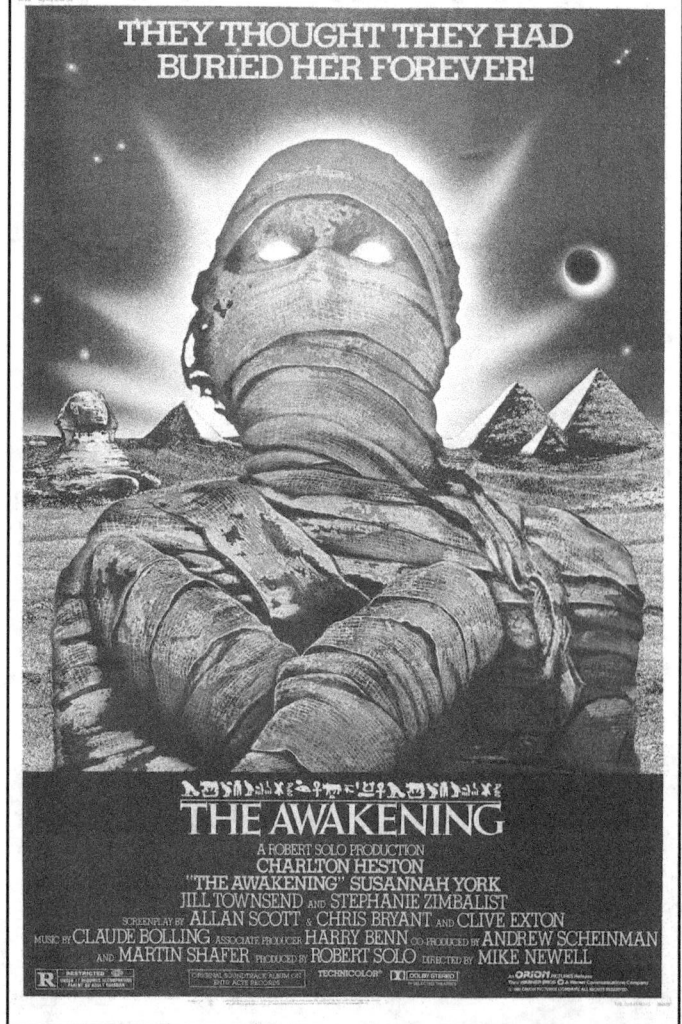

In conclusion, it is hard to like a film that undermines its genre tent-poles (e.g. the end title music seems romantic when we're crying out for apocalyptic.) However, I think Stoker's plot is a good one, and a decent story is like a fabulous jewel—it has many facets, and a different storyteller or medium will bring out varying aspects of its beauty. *The Awakening* fails to supply any sense of impending doom, making it a bland cubic zirconia of a film when we wanted a paragon diamond.
—Elliot Iles

BLOOD TIDE

D: Richard Jeffries
W: Richard Jeffries, Niko Mastorakis (with "Creative Consultant" Brian Trenchard-Smith)
Starring: James Earl Jones, Jose Ferrer, Lila Kedrova, Deborah Shelton, Martin Kove, Lydia Cornell, Mary Louise Weller

> "Before the dawn of civilization, in the early light of man's existence, life was an eternal struggle between good ... and evil"

Thus begins *Blood Tide*, a rather untidy entry in the limited field of Anglo/Greek productions. Very rarely mentioned in genre publications, and when it does get coverage it is nearly always unfavorable (See Rigby's *English Gothic*, Newman's *Nightmare Movies* and Hardy's *Aurum Encyclopedia of Horror*.)

Blood Tide has Neil Grice (Martin Kove) and his new bride Sherry (Mary Louise Weller) arrive on the photogenic island of Synanon. They are searching for Grice's sister Madeline (Deborah Shelton, who incidentally is to blame for the piss poor song at the end-titles), missing for nigh on four months.

Madeline has not been idly sunning it up on the beach during this period—she has been keeping busy restoring an icon that may pre-date Christianity. Also on the island are an archaeologist named Frye (James Earl Jones) and his main squeeze Babs (Lydia Cornell). Whereas Madeline is developing a deeper understanding of the ancient myths and traditions of the island, Frye is only interested in accumulating as many of the gold coins, discovered in an underwater cave, as he can.

Frye's character as expressed by James Earl Jones (in a role just pre-Thulsa Doom) deserves a brief mention. His dialogue seems entirely made up of lines from *Othello* (was this done by Messrs Jeffries and Mastorakis with James Earl Jones in mind or did JEJ just decide to "improvise?") Not even a diving mask and snorkel in his mouth can quell the stream of Shakespeare emitting sonorously from his lips. He also opens watermelons by punching them! Something worth seeing.

On the hunt for more coins to add to his collection, Frye blasts an ancient sealed entrance that causes the water to froth and the dry ice to get switched to 11. Frye legs it, not fully aware of the consequences but knowing that he's gone and done a Very Bad Thing indeed. What he's responsible for is to rouse an ancient evil from its slumber and now, if the tagline is to be believed, "The Myth is Alive!"

Babs is the first to go, after a briefly provocative aerobics session on the beach, followed by a nameless island woman. Meanwhile back at the icon ... Madeline's behavior is becoming odder by the minute, witness her appreciation of the perfume given to her as a present. Once fully restored, the icon displays a priapic sea demon ready to ravage a virginal young lady (Madeline's own intact status is commented on early in the film.) This sends Madeline off the deep-end and her burgeoning psychic link with the sea beast becomes fully fledged.

Now this is where we, the viewer, would expect to see some serious interspecies loving, the kind that was to prove so popular in British films around this time (see *Inseminoid*, *Xtro* and *Lifeforce*) but alas and alack we are left disappointed, stuck with Madeline doing some heavy breathing in a drippy cave, alone.

The death of Babs and the island woman, who Frye had tried in vain to save, snaps him out of his avaricious ways. After the creature has come ashore to lay waste to the island's local convent, slaughtering all the nuns save Sister Anna (Lila Kedrova), Frye decides that now is the time for direct action, taking the battle to the beastie. This leads to possibly the most hilarious groin-gripping finale of any film shot in Greece in 1980.

For many years the most widespread version of *Blood Tide* was an 83-minute cut but a pre-certificate print lasting circa 97 minutes was revived in a beautifully cleaned-up version by Arrow Video in 2020. There is some online debate as to the very dodgy incest curveball thrown in at the end when Madeline and Neil share a very un-sibling kiss. The original pre-cert print does absolutely nothing to clarify, expand or explain this scene. Maybe it's a Mastorakis thing (cf. *Island of Death*?)
—Fraser Burnett

DEATH SHIP

D: Alvin Rakoff
W: John Robins
Starring: George Kennedy, Richard Crenna, Sally Ann Howes, Nick Mancuso, Victoria Burgoyne

The Boat That Shocked? Not quite. The producers tried to hedge their bets here by mixing different genres, combining them in the hopes of better box office—a disaster Nazi horror film, Nazis being big in the late 1970s thanks to *The Boys from Brazil* etc. It does have an intriguing central idea—an interrogation ship still working 35 years after the end of World War Two.

The opening owes a big debt to *Jaws* as the ship silently scuds through the water. Its target is an ocean liner and the Death Ship is a suprisingly stealthy stalker. So stealthy that it can be in a different time zone to its prey! It manifests in sunlight while the liner is in pitch darkness. Maybe the Death Ship carries its own light like an Angler Fish ready to trap the unwary?

Anyway it rams the liner, which sinks in record time, leaving a handful of cyphers—sorry, characters—to scramble onto a bit of driftwood. The only recognizable faces are George Kennedy of *Cool Hand Luke* and *Naked Gun* fame (a dab hand at 1970s disaster fare too, which holds him in good stead here) and Richard Crenna about to embark on the *Rambo* franchise. Kennedy is Captain Ashland, unloved by his crew and on the verge of an empty retirement, while Crenna is First Officer Marshall, in line to take over his command. All the usual types are there—the hero, the grump, the annoying comic relief, the horny couple who will die, the irritating kids who should die, and the "Shelley Winters." Marshall comes complete with nuclear family. It's a bit puzzling how these lucky few, spread out across the liner as it went down, managed to clamber on to the driftwood before the others.

The Death Ship is home to some very cosmopolitan ghost Nazis. They speak German with pronounced American accents. They have pin ups of American glamour models on their bunk walls, listen to American Big Band music and watch American films. Probably not wanting to offend anyone, they display all their Nazi insignia in one room.

They also keep the ship very clean, so it's a shame no one thought to dust the radio more often, it's the only thing onboard covered in grime/cobwebs. The interrogation room must have really been a bastard to keep pristine for all those years with its gleaming white walls. I'll pass over those lifebelts and dinghy still in working order after over 35 years in a freezer.

The Death Ship doesn't waste much time in picking off the survivors in an "invisible hands" *Omen* style. My favorite is the annoying bandleader who is winched over the side, repeatedly dunked in the water and then drowned before his uninterested comrades. Other unlikely despatchings feature; for instance, having blood pumped over oneself in the shower ("It's blood! BLOOD!")—washing in the sticky red stuff won't make you clean but it shouldn't kill you! Worse still is a death by projector—one minute the guy's attacking the screen images, the next his dead body is being dropped on to the deck.

Can we have a minute's silence for director Alvin Rakoff? A man who once fought that prize ham Bette Davis. He does what he can with the piss poor script—interesting camera angles etc—but it isn't enough. The idea of a torture ship with a ghost crew carrying out redundant duties is an intriguing one. Sadly, it's not done right here.
—Gerald Lea

THE GODSEND

D: Gabrielle Beaumont
W: Olaf Pooley
Starring: Malcolm Stoddard, Cyd Hayman, Angela Pleasence, Patrick Barr

Why have horror fans been so dismissive about Gabrielle Beaumont's *The Godsend*? Is it too pastoral and not thunderous enough? Do they consider it one evil, murderous child movie too many? Is it because it is not made under a famous banner like Hammer? Instead it provides one of the few outright horrors to come in the wake of the demise of said company, with none of the house monsters, relying instead, ironically, on a more typically English lore and view of superstition. Shot in 1979 and released the following year, rather than announcing the 1980s as a decade of the British horror film in decline, along with *The Appointment* and *The Awakening*, it should have been taken as a sign that there was no reason to assume that the country would not continue to put out horror films that were professional, and played the terrors straight. Movies cast with real actors, movies that were proud of their genre and nationality.

The premise of *The Godsend* was a humdinger even in the wake of a raft of "killer kid" movies. Scripted by the actor Olaf Pooley, husband of the film's director, it was adapted from the novel by Bernard Taylor drawing on the macabre ornithological trait that sees the cuckoo, nature's worst mother, depositing its egg in the nest of another bird whereupon the hatchling will either hike the rest of the eggs from the nest or snuff out smaller and more vulnerable chicks. The original occupant will then continue to rear the single invader, accepting it. This most horrible act of nature is reproduced using a human family in this film outing.

It opens with a terrific aerial shot gliding over a verdant English countryside, a bird in flight, continuing through the opening titles and not finishing until dropping to take in a family of six crossing a stile between fields. The happy family unit is made up of the parents (Malcolm Stoddard and Cyd Hayman) and their four children, an older girl and three boys, the youngest just a baby. A stranger enters their midst, the heavily pregnant but otherwise scrawny Angela Pleasence. She is first seen through the binocular lens of the husband, an inadvertent act of "twitching" nonetheless. There is a lot of play in the dialogue as she spends the day with them and then, trapped by the downpour of rain and forced to remain while the child comes, she stays the night too.

She's not from the city. Despite her slight frame and youthfulness, she has other children that she seems to be able to report little about and she doesn't do a thing in winter except go South. When asked why so many children, she responds that it has nothing to do with want, it is in the interests of nature. The husband takes against her, and on an early attempt to escort her "home" makes a prescient point that she "mustn't leave anything behind." He wants rid of the weird cow. But stay she does and give birth she does. The doctor is called (veteran British horror film guest popper-upper Patrick Barr in one of his last appearances), but the child has already arrived. Pleasence curiously hopes to crib a cigarette and is never seen with the baby in her arms, Hayman already cradling the little thing when they arrive, and we first set eyes on the infant girl. Barr, identifying the dislike of the woman by the husband, suggests "well, you can always boot her out in the morning." In 1979 new mothers could expect five nights N.H.S. hospitality, today they hit the 24-hour countdown button the moment that arse is smacked and first cry emitted. So, our doctor has been a clinician ahead of his time.

Named Bonnie, the child wastes no time in setting up a cot death for her youngest brother and a pond drowning of the second youngest several years later. At the scene of the drowning the scratch-marks on the little blonde demon are explained away as evidence of the boy's heroic attempt to rescue his sister from dangerous waters, losing his own life in the process. The truth, of course, is that they resulted from attempts to defend himself as she drowned him. The viewer might have some concern that there is an insufficient display of grief from the parents, but the deaths evade that with passages of time, and heartache does come, as do the suspicions on the parents when a third boy dies, though it never involves the police and never becomes an investigation.

Beaumont does not want to smother her core tale with the bereavement process or suspicion but is aware enough too that she will be criticized if they are not at the very least broached. It is perhaps this element that aggravates the average viewer, but the story spans a number of years, time heals some of the wounds, and the measure of the emotional contribution to the tale is better judged than most berate it for. With the threat only upon the four children the option might have been kill, kill and kill again, followed by a repeat upon repeat false scare based around the attempted murder of the final child, but more drama is incorporated with a new pregnancy and an illness visited upon the father to ensure his future sterility.

Like *Gorgo* (1960) before it, the rules in the British horror film are that if you find a spare kid you simply take them in without any question of involving the authorities or any formal adoption process. Whereas in *Gorgo* a child lets slip her doll and it is trampled by the rampaging feet of panicked men, in *The Godsend* the plaything is left at the top of the stairs for the mother to trip over and miscarry, but it is more than a simple device to that end as the doll is spoken of as never having been played with by Bonnie, and why should it, as the little girl has inherited only her natural mother's instinctual selfishness and functional maternal brief.

The film was financed by the Cannon Film Group on a modest budget, Golan and Globus feeling a little flush following the success of their initial *Lemon Popsicle* film series. It was not their first association with Pooley and Beaumont however, having stumped up the shekels for their first film as writer and producer, the 1969 horror oddity *The Corpse* (aka *Velvet House*), directed less successfully by Viktors Ritelis. Female directors were

The three faces of Bonnie: Wilhelmina Green, Joanne Boorman, and Sarah Boorman, from *The Godsend*.

still a rarity in horror in 1980, and in the UK there were fewer examples still with only Wendy Toye and Astrid Frank held as notable—and even they had merely contributed shorts or segments of compendium features. Being the first British feature-length overt horror film from a female director was one of *The Godsend*'s several quiet achievements.

There are two distinct halves to the film, the first in the English countryside, the latter in the city and coastal towns. The greenery is about the lushest demanded of a British horror movie, matched only by Christian Marnham's *The Orchard End Murder* (1980). Shooting began in August, which was a risk, and despite reports of weather troubles, none of this shows in those scenes and it is indeed likely that the bad weather came later in the shoot when redeploying to the more built-up urban shooting locations. The risk was possibly deliberate, counting on August/September for some seasonal changes of weather, to avoid the betrayal by a sunny spell in the shifts in the storyline over an eight-year period by accidentally returning it to the same idyllic month, year in year out. Not that there is much chance normally of retaining the same weather in meteorologically unpredictable Britain.

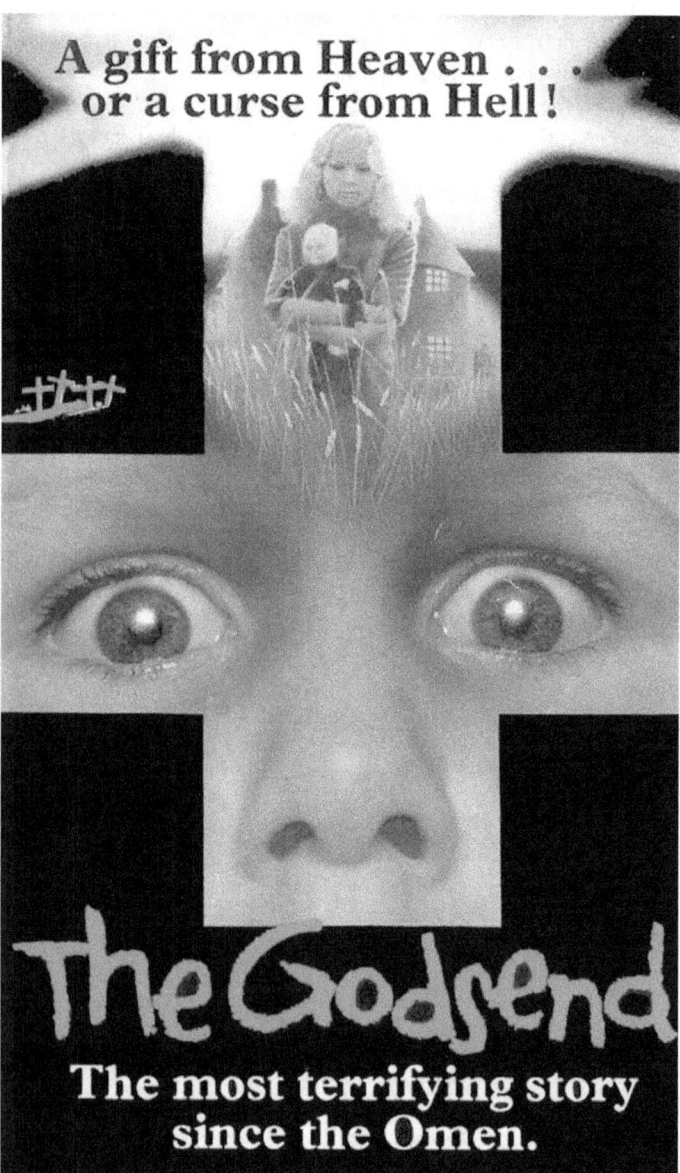

The film touches upon the rural supernatural disturbances in television plays and series over the previous 10 years, with *The Owl Service* (1969) *Robin Redbreast* (1970) *Stigma* (1977) and *Penda's Fen* (1974) among the flood. There's also a slight whiff of John Mackenzie's short public information film *Apaches* (1977) about it, with the deaths exclusively of children in countryside settings. The professional crew ensures that the film looks good though some of the location shooting is clearly on the hoof, and members of the pesky public occasionally refuse to move on and choose instead to point out the camera crew. Those less health and safety conscious days, before too long a thing of the past (possibly internationally driven by the child fatalities on the set of *Twilight Zone: The Movie*) are noticeable in both the filmmaking and the bits of background Britain sampled. On the latter note the climbing frames of the playground seem precariously high and the boy extras swing on ropes recklessly close to slides.

In depicting several ages of the children, there are a lot of juveniles called upon to play the young family members and a number of them are seemingly stranded on monuments, pushing one another, trapped in a flailing swing and most audaciously, left on a rock with the ocean waves lashing about. Viewers today would rightly assume stand-ins but here Beaumont has clearly committed both crew and children to the hazard of the odd stunt. *The Godsend* is a steady-Eddie fear flick that builds to a sickening finale. It should have stood as a signpost in the right direction for British horror films to come, alongside *The Appointment*, and *Absolution* (1978) in its belated release, mini shockers all in the absence of big money. These films were snubbed by audiences, and ill-treated by distributors—a belt-tightening decade under a government with no interest in subbing the high risk that was the average budget of a feature film left us with a pop horror pantomime parade instead. We could have had a half-decent scene. It was not to be and some of the best British horrors are the serious few that ushered the 1980s in.
—Paul Higson

The Marlowes are an upwardly mobile middle-class couple with three perfect kids. One night a heavily pregnant woman shows up and is invited in. While no classic, *The Godsend* locates the sinister side of such a fecund set-up.

My feelings for the poor couple here were ambivalent. On one hand it seemed so cruel and pointless—why does golden-tressed Bonnie need to bump off her adopted brothers and sisters? The parents are loaded and there's enough jam for everyone. The lack of reason does make her actions more disturbing, I suppose. Maybe her mother has been sent to punish complacent aspirant families?

Yet the Marlowes appear to be two of the stupidest people on the planet. They invite a pregnant weirdo into their house and take her offspring into their charge when she does a runner. They ignore the mounting evidence that this child isn't all she seems and even protect her against their own children. In a way it does serve them right for being such idiots. They only seriously get worried about their family's mortality rate when they've lost *three* fricking children! Didn't they have Social Services in 1980? Which childcare manual suggested keeping two youngsters who hate each other in the same room?

Technically it's uneven; most of the kids go in the first half hour leaving too much time for post-match analysis. The subject matter is very creepy and the images of dead children disturbing. However, the director hasn't heard of pacing.

Bonnie does sometimes look homicidally aware in her many grinning close-ups, while at other times she just gives "cute" (ahh diddums!). The actors playing the parents and the other kids are surprisingly good. The film benefits from the rent-a-trauma talents of Angela Pleasence but she's out of there in under 15 minutes. A film where she was the cuckoo in the nest (kinda like her scene-stealing turn in *From Beyond the Grave*) would've made much better viewing.
—Gerald Lea

INSEMINOID

D: Norman J. Warren
W: Nick Maley, Gloria Maley
Starring: Judy Geeson, Robin Clarke, Stephanie Beacham, Jennifer Ashley, Victoria Tennant

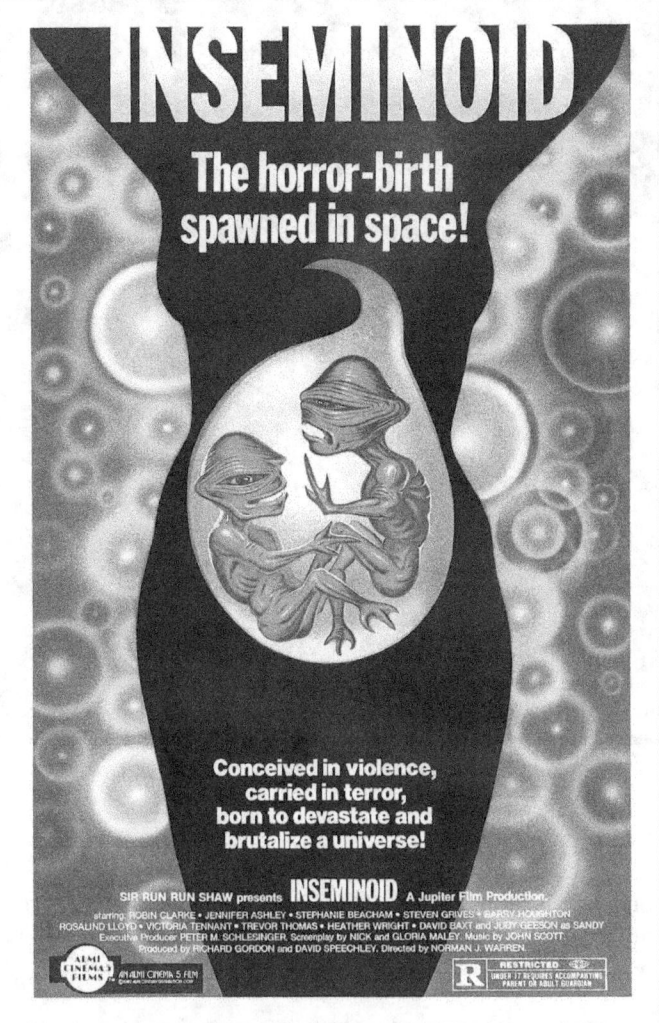

Director Norman J. Warren's second stab at sci-fi splatter, following the smaller scale character piece *Prey*, is introduced with the wondrous, once-in-your-lifetime credit "Sir Run Run Shaw Presents *Inseminoid*." This might be second only to "Walt Disney Pictures Presents a Film by David Lynch"—the opening words of *The Straight Story*—on the scale of disarming title sequence moments. More famously, it was one of two post-*Alien* European extraterrestrial gore movies to wind up on the "video nasties" list (*Inseminoid* appearing prominently on the secondary "Section 3" roll-call) though, tellingly, both it and the delightful *Contamination* are now considered goofy and tame enough to warrant uncut "15" certificate DVD releases.

Colorfully shot in widescreen by Warren regular John Metcalfe, this early effort to cash in on the Ridley Scott blockbuster prefigured an endless cycle of subsequent movies (*Galaxy of Terror*, *Titan Find*, et. al) but is more enjoyably gruesome than most of them and puts every penny of its small budget up on the screen with a refreshing lack of pretentiousness. Far from the self-seriousness of the 1979 Scott picture, *Inseminoid* is your only chance to hear Stephanie Beacham say the line "We've got to try something—there are chainsaws!"

The slim plot hook to get a bunch of Brits and token Americans up in space to be slaughtered has something to do with the discovery of a tomb-like complex on a previously inhabited planet by a group of astronauts. Characters go potty, and Beacham freaks out early on, but the film really steps up a gear when Judy Geeson gets nekkid on an inter-galactic operating table for a crude exploitation movie reworking of John Hurt's *Alien* impregnation.

Our memorably tasteless first glimpse of *Inseminoid*'s monster is through Geeson's rudely parted legs as it inserts a long tube of its unappetizing sperm (actually Swarfega, according to director Warren!) into her nether regions. From this point on, Warren's film feels more like a possession movie than an *Alien*-styled space slasher as Geeson, partly controlled by the being, turns into a cold-eyed murderess, bashing poor old Victoria Tennant's head into a wall before repeatedly stabbing her with scissors, and developing intestine-ripping super-strength. Sadly, the rough treatment meted out to Tennant still didn't spare us from *Flowers in the Attic*.

Amid all the carnage, *Inseminoid* maintains a very droll British sense of humor, typical of Warren's genre work, and notably absent from *Alien*. One character, observing Geeson's rampage with a sense of amused detachment, remarks, "That'll look great on the report: the team were terrorized by an expectant mother." Geeson's energetic, spirited performance is the stand-out among a mostly dull cast (did we mention Victoria Tennant?!), running a gamut of emotions from screaming, leg-chewing crazy bitch to hysterically sobbing sympathetic mother-to-be. She particularly gives her all during a terrific alien birth scene: the ugly sprog born conventionally rather than by the riskier Hurt method.

The movie sets Beacham up as a feisty, hammer-throwing, potential Ripley figure, but she's put out of action during the finale and all the main characters are dead by the end in a cynical fashion typical of the genre post-Romero. A cute punch line, again following the prevailing downbeat trend, features a money shot of the throat-ripping alien baby and, best of all, if you stay tuned for the end credits, you get another chance to see all the gory death scenes, set to the film's funky electronic theme tune!
—Steven West

THE MONSTER CLUB

D: Roy Ward Baker
W: Edward Abraham, Valerie Abraham
Starring: Vincent Price, John Carradine, Barbara Kellerman, Stuart Whitman, Donald Pleasence, Patrick Magee, James Laurenson, Simon Ward, Britt Ekland

Nothing fills me with quite the same profound sense of melancholy as *The Monster Club*, a tatty, patchy, childish version of a once-great subgenre of Brit horror cinema, namely the Amicus anthology movie. The book it purports to adapt isn't bad either. In fact, it was a conscious attempt by its author, R. Chetwynd-Hayes, to write something approximating the movies produced by Max J. Rosenberg and Milton Subotsky after they fashioned *From Beyond the Grave* from four of his stories. Produced at a time when the horror genre had moved on, when *Halloween* and *Dawn of the Dead* had changed the face of fright forever, it's possible that even if it had been superb it may not have been successful. As it stands, however, it's a film almost solely of interest to those who want to see the very final gasp of a very specific type of horror movie.

An Amicus film in all but name, Rosenberg and Subotsky having parted ways by the time it was made, *The Monster Club* isn't without its merits. The first story, *The Shadmock*, really isn't that bad at all, and on its own would serve as a fine last bow for Subotsky's producing style. There's a gloomy old country house, a couple of despicable attractive types (Simon Ward and Barbara Kellerman) intent on fleecing poor old lovestruck James Laurenson out of his money, Douglas Gamley providing his typically excellent spooky music in between the guitar solos, a cracking ending and a killer last line. It's even got Geoffrey Bayldon in it as a doctor in the asylum at the start (Dr. Starr?) and just writing this has filled me with enough enthusiasm to make me want to watch it again. Likewise the final tale, *The Humgoo*, is a reasonable stab at the R.C.H. story, let down by some silly teeth at the end but at least giving the great Patrick Magee one last chance to be crackers in a British horror movie (see also Magee's turn in Lucio Fulci's delirious, shot-in-England Poe adaptation *The Black Cat*.) John Bolton's artwork is employed to good effect in this one as well, illustrating how the ghouls first came to Loughville and sealed it off in its own dimension (a favorite R.C.H. idea) and Stuart Whitman, never the most personable of leads, does his best.

It's the middle story, *The Vampire*, and the linking sequences, that make the heart of even the most forgiving horror fan sink. *The Monster Club*'s director, Roy Ward Baker, himself described the film as "bloody awful" and it must have been these elements in particular that he had in mind. The vampire story isn't even in the book, but presumably the other stories were too adult for a film Subotsky consciously aimed at youngsters, not realizing that there's a big difference between children's entertainment and childishness. The framework initially bodes well, with John Carradine playing R.C.H. himself and being cornered outside a bookshop by Vincent Price's vampire Eramus. In a lovely touch the shop window is filled with actual R.C.H. books. Sadly, as soon as we get to the club itself, it's the cue for some quite awful rock songs danced to by a plethora of extras, dressed up in the rubber masks that apparently Subotsky found some milkman making before hiring him for the shoot. "They look really good if you light them properly" I remember him saying on an episode of kids' movie show *Clapperboard*. I don't think it was just the lighting that was the problem, but it certainly didn't help.

Do I hate *The Monster Club*? Not at all. I would like to love it, and I certainly love parts of it, as I hope I've conveyed above. It really was the end of an era—Roy Ward Baker never made another movie shown in cinemas, Subotsky never produced another UK anthology (though his name is prominent in the cred-

its of the 1985 American film *Cat's Eye*), Douglas Gamley never wrote horror film music again, and for many of the cast it was to be their last appearance in a horror picture. So, like I said, *The Monster Club* makes me feel melancholy. But that won't stop me watching it again once in a while.
—John Llewellyn Probert

• • •

The term "portmanteau" seems preferable to "anthology," conjuring up images of a Victorian leather case with multiple compartments containing secrets galore—something a penny-dreadful villain would clutch in a fog-enshrouded street. Portmanteau films are probably worthy of a book-sized study in their own right. Films that have excessive casts would, I feel, be wise to shift their structure from the single story to the multiple (*Pirates of the Caribbean*, take note.) I believe that this set-up represents good value for everyone. Actors get another credit with a few days' work, and if the audience doesn't take to one tale of these multi-story constructions (each bookended by the "wraparound" story), at least they will only have to wait a short while for something different. *The Monster Club* is an interesting example of the format. It is based on a 1975 book by R. Chetwynd-Hayes (henceforth R.C.H.), and that book is itself assembled in portmanteau style including wraparound, something you don't encounter in literature too often. You'd think we'd see more of these in print as it allows writers to turn short story collections (which are largely and surprisingly unpopular with the reading public) into thematic novels, a way of sweetening the medicine with the sugar of a good backdrop. Portmanteaus live or die on their "glue"; the setting must be compelling enough for you to manage to sit through one poor tale to return eagerly and expectantly. The individual stories matter slightly less, because, like buses there'll be another one along in a moment. Hours of entertainment can be achieved by asking a bunch of horror fans to create and give explanations for their own "Frankenstein's Portmanteau" where they pick and mix favorite individual existing elements. Try it!

Also based on material by R.C.H., 1973's *From Beyond the Grave* thwarted the unwritten and unwitting portmanteau tradition by not having a single lame story. *Grave*'s feel is more representative of R.C.H. than *The Monster Club* is, as its comedy is more character based than the level of juvenile humor found in its successor. The central idea of R.C.H.'s *Monster Club* book (and the film) rests on the idea of different monsters interbreeding and producing new variants of sub-monster; the majority of the book's stories feature this, making their appearance in anything but this linked printed collection difficult without explanation. R.C.H.'s work here might well have provided an ideal source for a television anthology series; perhaps to be entitled *Tales from the Monster Club*, and using a social gathering of creatures and hybrid monsters as a starting point? Much mileage is still to be had from this combination concept.

Of the three segments of the film (*The Shadmock*, *The Vampire*, and *The Humgoo*) only the Humgoo story and the wraparound are taken directly from the book. Considering the book has five stories (*The Werewolf and the Vampire*, *The Mock*, *The Humgoo*, *The Shadmock*, *The Fly-by-Night*) it's a shame more were not used. The Shadmock segment seems to be a partial mash-up of two stories from the book, the party from *The Mock* is ramped up to a posh masked ball, the Old Manor House is from *The Shadmock*, and the ending seems to be a mix of Mock and Shadmock elements—perhaps fittingly, given R.C.H.'s inter-species crossover theme!

The book's framing device of a film's opening credits for the Humgoo story is not used for the screen version, but instead this idea is shifted to the story that is the runt of the litter, the silly vampire episode based on R.C.H.'s comic offering *My Mother Married a Vampire* from a 1978 collection entitled *The Cradle Demon & Other Stories*. This distancing mechanism helps to lessen this tale's detrimental effect on the "rules" the film-within-a-film establishes.

The Monster Club is worth a look mainly for the superb Humgoo segment, but also for the charismatic and beautifully toned double act of actors Price and Carradine. Another big draw is the offbeat array of musical acts for which this film allows a unique showcase. These assorted performers—Night, The Pretty Things, The Viewers, B.A. Robertson—easily eat up screen time roughly the length of a whole additional segment. I would have liked a little variation with these interludes, featuring less music and more variety performances. The stripper is the outstanding act, navigating the tightrope walk that is the comedy/horror combination with aplomb.

Club will fall short for the modern viewer because the budget cannot live up to the vision (despite Vic Door's last minute miracles—he was apparently told to bring masks, and upon arrival realized full monsters were required), but its school report card would give high marks for effort and pushing the envelope, for example for having Carradine play R.C.H. and for the bravura striptease sequence, so fondly recalled by many fans. I also wish they'd gone for the book's punchier ending. In summary, we have here a cocktail of laughs and chills, and whether this heady mix is to your taste depends upon how much humor you like served up with your horror. *The Monster Club* as a film is worth a visit, but I for one won't be filling out a membership application.
—Elliot Iles

THE ORCHARD END MURDER

D: Christian Marnham
W: Christian Marnham
Starring: Bill Wallis, Tracy Hyde, Clive Mantle

With a background of apple trees, tiny village stations on branch lines to nowhere, high tea and cricket matches complete with warm beer and sandwiches, *The Orchard End Murder* uses its pastoral setting with effect and establishes itself in a tiny sub-genre of horror films—British Contemporary Rural Gothic (I may have just made that up), with its use of dappled daylight, and subtle subversion of genteel rural stereotypes to sinister ends.

Pauline (Tracy Hyde), tiring of watching her boyfriend playing cricket, wanders off and finds herself studying the garden of a railway crossing cottage on a sleepy Kent branch line. Initially alarmed by the hunchbacked crossing keeper (Bill Wallis), she stays for a nervy cup of tea with him and his assistant Ewen (*Casualty*'s Clive Mantle) who's clearly "not all there." Upon leaving the cottage, Pauline gets lost in a huge orchard where Ewen

Pauline (Tracy Hyde) comes to a bad end in the beautiful English countryside as Ewen (Clive Mantle) murders her. Is this in *Midsomer*? No it's *The Orchard End Murder*.

murders her before fleeing back to the crossing keeper, who helps the child-like Ewen dispose of the body—which proves more difficult than it seems—while berating the younger man for not keeping his urges in check. As Pauline's corpse is found, our deformed authority figure reveals more of his fractured and disturbed personality while positioning himself to ensure that Ewen gets the blame.

With a relatively simple narrative (and economic running time at under 50 minutes) *The Orchard End Murder* succeeds in generating both considerable suspense and some black comic moments, largely on the back of Bill Wallis' terrific performance as the sinister, sharp-minded crossing keeper and by director Christian Marnham's glorious use of the English countryside, which acts as an effective counterpoint to the grisly events. The fact that the film contains a savage sex-murder a third of the way through its running time is also quite startling, not just because it's surprisingly graphic, but also because it actually *doesn't* feel out of place in what is otherwise a fairly restrained piece. The reason why the sequence shocks but doesn't jar is because Marnham skilfully weaves an almost subliminally demented and seething atmosphere below *The Orchard End Murder*'s "Darling Buds of May" surface aesthetic—long before the vicious assault arrives, the viewer is uncomfortably aware that all is not as it seems, and the murder itself functions as graphic punctuation to the unease generated in a subtextually creepy opening 20 minutes. It also helps that Marnham treats the aftermath in a blackly comic fashion, focusing on the range of difficulties Ewen and the crossing keeper face in disposing of the body. Still, the death of Pauline is fairly grim (even watched now, with several decades of hindsight) and may be the primary reason why, even today, the film still resonates with those who saw it on original release.

The Orchard End Murder is a terrific little film, well acted, beautifully shot and with a simple but memorable story that finishes with a suitably macabre flourish. It does what good horror should do, surprises and unnerves through the twisting of familiar archetypes, and while it only delivers one genuine shock, it is constantly ominous, even when at its most chocolate-box.

The Orchard End Murder was, for a short, given fairly widespread exposure in the first half of the decade, playing as a second feature for a range of suitable (and not so suitable) main attractions. It received an "X" certificate from the BBFC in February 1982 and the distributor is listed as Marnham & Harvey Ltd. on the BBFC database—it may be that exploitation specialists G.T.O. handled initial distribution, as the film first played with Gary Sherman's *Dead and Buried* (a G.T.O. release) in the summer of 1982. Marnham & Harvey Ltd. may have been the production company and may be listed on the BBFC database because they submitted the film for certification before a distribution deal was in place, though details are hard to come by. The film then enjoyed repeated airings over the next few years—I saw it as a second feature to James Roberson's *The Witch* (aka *Superstition*) and it was also spotted supporting Stephen Frears' blackly comic thriller *The Hit* (1984). There are probably others too. It seems the film spent the first half of the 1980s pinging around endlessly between provincial cinemas as a perennial second feature, which might explain why it has retained a reputation with viewers beyond that of most other British horror shorts.

Well made, with good production values and strong performances, *The Orchard End Murder* became something of a lost gem (prior to Blu-ray revival on the British Film Institute's Flipside label in 2017)—a brief terror tale that feels just right for its running time, that carries suspense, contains one genuinely grim sequence and a smattering of black comedy. It's ripe for re-discovery. Ripe, geddit? No? Please yourselves then.
—Neil Pike

SATURN 3

D: Stanley Donen
W: Martin Amis
Starring: Kirk Douglas, Farrah Fawcett, Harvey Keitel

A troubled Lew Grade production started by director John Barry before he was abruptly replaced by unlikely choice/Hollywood musical legend Stanley Donen, *Saturn 3* (written by Martin Amis!) was unloved even by the people who made it. Composer Elmer Bernstein grumbled about the disappearance of many of his experimental score's cues and the big-name stars expressed embarrassment over their involvement—though Farrah Fawcett's next theatrical outing was *The Cannonball Run*, which should have put everything into perspective. On a particularly bum note, Barry died suddenly, at the age of 43, after his departure from the project and was not around to see its release.

Very much a product of its time, *Saturn 3* borrows freely from the major sci-fi spectaculars of the preceding years, from *Star Wars* (the opening money shot of the underside of a spacecraft) to *Alien* (the gradual appearance of the title onscreen.) It offers another riff on the homicidal-robot theme seen in everything from *Westworld* to *Demon Seed* to Tom Baker's *Doctor Who* debut "Robot." Preceding *The Terminator*, it also at times plays like a feature-length expansion of the alarming sequence in *Alien* in which android Ash turns into a would-be rapist.

Peculiar couple Farrah Fawcett and Kirk Douglas—separated by three decades in age terms—are stationed at a remote base in the asteroid fields of Saturn, overseeing food manufacture for planet Earth—a planet that Fawcett has never seen and Douglas remembers only in terms of the pollution. Suave, handsome and psychotic Captain Harvey Keitel—with ponytail!—shows up and immediately takes a shine to the comely Fawcett while expressing his opinion on dogs as something decent to eat. "You have a great body.... may I use it?" is one of his come-ons to Fawcett en route to the revelation that he is accompanied by "Hector," an eight-foot-tall demigod robot he has crafted to mimic his actions and thoughts. Drawing directly from Keitel's brain via a radio connection at the base of the Captain's skull, Hector soon starts to show homicidal impulses, killing the dog and even getting his own slasher film-era subjective camera shots.

Despite its lowly reputation, *Saturn 3* is handsome and taut. It has the significant novelty value of seeing Kirk Douglas work out, be outrageously insulted by Harvey Keitel ("You're inadequate, Major—in every way" and, to Fawcett, "Doesn't it disgust you to be used by an old man?") and show his bare butt while wrestling Keitel to the ground nude. Fawcett, who gets her own individual "hair design by ..." credit, seldom looked so good as she jogs in skimpy tops and flits about in naughty nighties. And her hair is so spectacular it deserves its own acting billing.
—Steven West

• • •

"When they want to give the solar system an enema..."

" ...that's where they stick the tube in."

How does this sound for a rather bathetic troika; John Barry—responsible for the defining look of such science fiction classics as *A Clockwork Orange*, *Phase IV*, and *Star Wars*; Stanley "King of the Musicals" Donen—director of *On the Town*, *Singin' in the Rain*, and *Seven Brides for Seven Brothers*; and Martin Amis—a hack with dental issues—pooling their talents together to create "The Ultimate Space Adventure?" Did they succeed? Well no, not really, but it is quite good fun getting there.

With an opening that manages to shamelessly crib from *2001: A Space Odyssey*, *Star Wars*, and *Alien* within the first minute, the auguries aren't too good, though thankfully things pick up quick smart ...

Grounded after failing a psychiatric assessment, Captain Benson (Harvey Keitel, overdubbed by Roy Dotrice) decides to overrule the authorities and follow his own calling. First things first he will need a spaceship, and just by luck a certain Captain James (Douglas Lambert) is required on deck for immediate take-off. Not one to look a gift horse in the mouth, Benson decides he will take James' place on the soon-to-depart ship, and after donning his ultra-stylish protective gear (giallo-killer-meets-Stormtrooper chic) Benson opens an airlock door, which sends James zooming out into space, sans flightsuit. Job done! Benson then assumes James' identity, and mission, UNKNOWN to anyone else, and before you can say "my voice has been dubbed!" he's

Japanese one-sheet for *Saturn 3*

en route to the hydroponics research station on the third moon of Saturn, aka Saturn 3.

Working at the station are Adam (Kirk Douglas) and his far, far younger colleague/lover Alex (Farrah Fawcett). It would appear that their productivity is on the slack, possibly down to the fact that all they seem to do of a day is mooch about in the nuddy, and so a brand-new droid is being brought in to improve production. This means that either Adam or Alex will now be superfluous to the station's needs.

Benson's initial attraction towards Alex rapidly increases in intensity while he constructs the android, and he makes no secret of his desire for her, but Alex rebuffs all his advances. The significance of the arrival of another, younger male on the station however is not lost on Adam, and it begins to dawn on him that an endgame is now in play.

Upon completion of the new droid (Hector) it soon becomes clear to Adam, Alex and Benson that Hector has various issues with anger, backchatting, flesh, identity, jealousy, lust, murderous rage, and playing chess. The future looks bright ... thankfully there is very little chance of stumbling into the "Uncanny Valley" with old Hector, as he makes the Mash Smash robots look like T2. Part of Hector's programming comes from a direct link-up with Benson, via some kind of wetware neck-plug, and as if to throw mud in the face of the nurturists, Hector (being made of pure unborn brain matter, from fetuses) takes directly after his old man, who in turn has issues with anger, etc., etc.

Things reach a head (almost literally in regards to Douglas' wilful nudity) when Benson attempts to leave the station with Alex in tow. Adam attacks Benson, and almost kills him before being stopped by Alex. Being the bad type, Benson uses this to his advantage, and belts Adam a sore one when his back is turned. He then begins dragging Alex to his craft, making about five yards before Hector reappears (Hector had previously been taken to pieces after killing Sally, Alex's dog, but the station's other robots reassembled him for some reason or other that passes me by ...), and promptly lops off Benson's hand, the "dragger" now becoming the "dragged" as Hector stomps away down a corridor, hauling a screaming Benson with him.

The remainder now centers on Adam and Alex's attempts to outwit and overthrow Hector, but their efforts are for nought and it isn't long before Hector has captured the pair of them. The following day upon wakening, Adam discovers that he too now has the direct link-up wetware neck-plug thing, and that Hector intends to drain him of all his thoughts, or something. After a quick check to make sure that Alex is neck-plug free, Adam sacrifices himself while blowing Hector up. It all ends with Alex traveling to earth, just in time to star in *The Cannonball Run*.
—Fraser Burnett

THE SHINING

D: Stanley Kubrick
W: Stanley Kubrick, Diane Johnson
Starring: Jack Nicholson, Shelley Duvall, Scatman Crothers, Danny Lloyd

A movie which Martin Scorsese named among the 11 scariest motion pictures of all time; which the American Film Institute selected as containing the 25th greatest cinema villain, just ahead of *White Heat*'s Cody Jarrett and just behind *Wall Street*'s Gordon Gekko; which Robert De Niro once claimed had given him a month's worth of nightmares; which disappointed source author Stephen King who described it "a domestic tragedy with only vaguely supernatural overtones"; and which our own Channel 4 declared as containing the scariest movie moment ever, in a 2003 poll.

We're talking, of course, about *The Shining*. Starring Jack Nicholson and Shelley Duvall, directed by Stanley Kubrick, based—somewhat loosely—on Stephen King's 1977 blockbuster novel, and filmed at Elstree Studios in Borehamwood. *The Shining* is a movie that managed to divide opinion at the time of its release—many fans of the novel followed King's line and wondered why Kubrick couldn't have crafted a more faithful adaptation of the book, hip horror movie buffs found it all rather tame following the onslaught of vicious teenage stalk-and-slash fare offered up during the summer of 1980 and the wave of mind-and-eye-boggling so-called "video nasties" cramming the shelves of our high street VHS and Beta rental stores, and even the film's avowed admirers had problems in interpreting the events and working them into an understandable linear storyline.

All these years on, we're confronted with—simply—an ahead of its time masterpiece. Kubrick's output has a history of being misunderstood upon release, only to be wildly reappraised and lauded with the passage of time—just think about

British Quad for T*he Shining*

the furore which encountered his swansong, *Eyes Wide Shut*, and even the long-standing Kubrick project *A.I. Artificial Intelligence*, completed after his death by Steven Spielberg, when they originally emerged. Like *The Shining*, and like *Lolita, Dr. Strangelove, A Clockwork Orange, Barry Lyndon, Full Metal Jacket*, all equally misjudged or underappreciated by many, these daring tours de force are perhaps just beginning to gain the reception and praise they deserve.

What Kubrick managed to accomplish in *The Shining*—and perhaps the main factor in the film's critical malaise over the years—was to have his cake and eat it. Brilliantly, the movie manages to work as a subtle, old-fashioned ghost story, as an affecting tale of psychological breakdown, as a brutal contemporary axe-murder shocker, and as a brain-melting mindbender. Having watched literally thousands of horror pictures during my lifetime, I've never seen another film that achieves and mingles all of the concepts and levels that this one does.

It's a movie open to endless interpretations. For instance, notice in the opening interview scene how Jack and the hotel boss Stuart Ullman are wearing very similar knitted woollen ties, knotted in the same manner. Maybe Jack's choice of neckwear might not have been entirely his own selection; that, just prior to his three-and-a-half-hour journey to the Overlook Hotel, some strange manipulative force might have already set out to guide his path. *The Shining* is filled with imagery like this, little half-noticed background elements that can easily be ignored or dismissed by the casual viewer, but which can drive *you* nuts if you focus on them too much. Why does Scatman Crothers' kindly cook character, Hallorann, exhibit huge photographs of half-naked young women with preposterous Afro hairdos in his bedroom? Why does Kubrick cast real-life *twins* Lisa and Louise Burns as the eerie child spooks haunting the hotel corridors, when the script and the dialogue pointedly refer to them as being sisters with a considerable age difference? Does Jack really spy tiny versions of his wife and son in the model of the hotel maze, and if not, why does Kubrick edit the scene to make it appear as if he does? Is the obsequious men's room attendant Delbert Grady the same person as the murderous *Charles* Grady, referred to by the Ullman character at Jack's initial interview? And even if you think you can explain all of this away, I defy you to interpret the scene where the door to the kitchen larder is unlocked, Jack's conversations with Lloyd the bartender, and the film's ending, all of which go beyond even the enigmatic and the supernatural, taking us into bold new territory for imaginative fiction.

Where does *The Shining* stand in the illustrious career of its chief acting participant? Well, any list of Nicholson's truly iconic roles would have to include *Five Easy Pieces* and *The Last Detail*, he's really impressive in supporting parts in the likes of *Reds, Easy*

British poster for *The Shining*

ing an elaborate trailer for their Kubrick season a few years back in which the camera prowled through a thoroughly detailed recreation of the set of the movie, *The Shining* continues to exert a hold on our media, with images and dialogue probably familiar even to those who haven't seen it.

Room 237, a hit at the Sundance film festival, was a 2012 documentary which examines the conspiracy theories surrounding *The Shining*, suggesting that the film may contain hidden messages and iconography pointing towards Kubrick's alleged involvement in faking the moon landings, among other way out and wacky conjecture. Stephen King's *Doctor Sleep*, his sequel to *The Shining*, was published in 2013.
—Darrell Buxton

• • •

Ever been deceived by a film? No? Then watch *The Shining*.

To begin with, not only is this Hollywood film billed as a UK/US production, it was made in the UK, maze and all, aside from scant exterior shots. The film is usually considered small in scale and claustrophobic like most haunted house movies, but it is not, for the stage is large and the players are many. At first we see numerous guests and staff (it takes a lot of employees to run a big hotel) and as they leave the cast dwindles, only to swell again as clientele and lackeys begin to appear from the grave.

Apart from one famous scene where Jack sticks his face through a bathroom door, the film is agoraphobic, being lost in the wide-open spaces. It launches with shots of grand landscapes, empty, cut off by distance and with winter increasing that isolation, the snow making the area seem even bleaker, ever more vast and endless. The hotel too, is massive. The broad corridors, a playground for Danny riding around and around on his trike; the huge maze, constructed as if some ancient monument to a giant; and the rooms, from the open meeting places, to the large dance hall, the staff quarters hidden away, and the seemingly numberless guest rooms like a stack of evil Christmas presents waiting to be opened. Even when Jack is locked away, the shouts and bangs echo far into the empty halls, into the distance.

You can add to this deception the method by which the movie cuts across the usual ideas behind the standard haunted house tale. Those of punishment or expulsion of the outsider, or like most ghost stories with a tendency to be very insular, a psychological fear preying on private concerns. Here the place is impersonal like most hotels, although by the end the ghosts are almost welcoming—as one of the guests remarks, "Great party, isn't it?" Whatever happens to control the Overlook is barely mentioned, let alone seen, and at times the ghosts seem almost incidental, an adornment, though they can whisper advice and have a physical effect.

It's based on a Stephen King novel and it appears to cover most of the Stephen King themes, as it ticks many of the Stephen King boxes. The past encroaching on the present, childhood and nightmares, psychic powers, a mysterious room with a hidden secret, an alien external force, a struggling writer, an old guru-type figure from a minority, family/friendship ties that—no matter how broken—can and do bring redemption, and of course it's set in the Northern States of the USA. As shown, Kubrick's film travels far from the Stephen King blueprint. Danny and all he brings is pretty much sidelined, as is Hallorann, and the family drifts apart in the vastness of the Overlook. King's

Rider, and *Terms of Endearment*, and even early primitive work in mid-'60s westerns *The Shooting* and *Ride in the Whirlwind* carries a mystical, difficult to capture in words charge. But as far as I'm concerned, he has never been better than in *The Shining*. Some, notably Stephen King among them, have protested that there is nowhere for this character to go, that he begins the film in a heightened state of psychosis and stays there, but that only works as valid criticism if you read this as the story of a man descending into insanity from a platform of normality. Kubrick's characters—Alex in *A Clockwork Orange*, Private Pyle in *Full Metal Jacket*, Dr. Bill Harford in *Eyes Wide Shut*, Humbert Humbert from *Lolita*, almost the entire cast of *Dr. Strangelove*—rarely follow such a path, all are deeply disturbed individuals long before the respective opening titles of their cinematic journeys begin to roll, and so crucially you need to read *The Shining* as a Stanley Kubrick movie, not as a Kubrick version of a Stephen King hit. Nicholson got that and runs with it.

The Shining has of course entered popular culture, although the film's most famous scene actually steals a slice of TV kitsch itself, with Nicholson spectacularly borrowing announcer Ed McMahon's catchphrase from long-running American talk show sensation *The Tonight Show*, and unquestionably making it his own as he leers through a shattered bathroom door at his panic-stricken spouse. From Groundskeeper Willie in *The Simpsons* discussing "The Shinning" with Bart, deftly avoiding a lawsuit from Warner Bros., to Lenny Henry aping Jack Torrance in a commercial for Premier Inns, to the British TV channel More 4 film-book ends as a monster tale as he ups the ante; there is redemption and loss. Kubrick's film doesn't, the management stays off stage, the hedge sculpture animals are missing, the claustrophobic element is lost

The basic plot remains, a man is hired to look after the Overlook hotel in the harsh winter months and we witness how it affects him and his family, but this is about all. Even the rescue doesn't comply with our expectations of a King novel. The whole film shifts focus to Jack. Danny is merely a threat to the plan due to his link to Hallorann, whereas in the book Danny is the central figure and as such the father and son relationship is crucial. So, it's not a Stephen King story, but is it a Kubrick film? It certainly has the themes, it looks amazing, there are images you will never forget, and there are endless discussions of the inner meaning to be had. It shows its film knowledge, for example the fade to white leaving a ghostly after-image that slowly dissolves beneath the next emergent scene, a technique also used in *The Innocents*. A frequent criticism about Kubrick's films is that they are frosty, remote, and unemotional. *The Shining* is far from cold in this way, the isolation, violence and lack of belonging here creates emotion. Frustration, duty, love, friendship are all present and lead to unease, anxiety and primal fear. The fades add to the unease; ominous images such as Danny's ball, the little girls, the slow and sure sound as the lift draws near and the doors open, room 237, all increase the fear. Duvall and Nicholson's performances give a full emotional clout, Crothers' warmth and desperation and Lloyd's innocence and dread add to the mix of feeling. Like most horror films it shows and comments on the taboos of society, past and present, and so opens up many interpretations.

The critical response on release was nearly all negative, at times excessive but showing a strong emotional reaction—for all the decrying of the film, it certainly hit home! Michael Powell's *Peeping Tom* was treated in a similar way, in large part due to the disdain for horror by most critics, especially when attempted by a respected director. Both films are now seen as classics. Kubrick re-edited the film within weeks of its release; originally 146 minutes, the US version is 144 minutes and the European 119 minutes. This final version cuts out background and tightens many scenes, the removal of the doctor's visit being a case in point; the only spectral aspect to be lost is that of the champagne-drinking skeletons. Kubrick actually authorized the shorter version, unusual for a director's cut. Stephen King disliked the film, stating Kubrick had "no apparent understanding of the genre," though his view may be due in part to the filleting out of many of the themes from what appears to have been a very personal novel. Now-classic moments such as Duvall's discovery of Jack's manuscript remain chilling in so many ways, however, confirming undeniably that Kubrick possessed an innate command of the genre.

As *The Shining* stands, it's not an austere Kubrick film or a populist King tale, but something in-between. The ending gives one final twist; some see Jack being absorbed into the fabric of the building (a theory supported by the recent online posting of several previously unseen script pages), while Kubrick stated re-incarnation. Either way it points to unavoidable fate. As an English film, it may be about fear of the middle class (Jack is a teacher and writer) being forced back to a working-class life (a caretaker) as only the aristocracy are not commoners.

Jack Nicholson and Shelley Duvall in *The Shining*

In the end, for all its vision and grandeur, and the equal measures of praise and rebuke heaped upon it, *The Shining* perhaps only succeeds if Nicholson and Duvall's performances work for you. Ultimately it rests on the actors' skill at deceit.
—Wayne Mook

THE WATCHER IN THE WOODS

D: John Hough (and Vincent McEveety)
W: Brian Clemens, Rosemary Anne Sisson, Gerry Day
Starring: Bette Davis, Carroll Baker, Lynn-Holly Johnson, David McCallum, Kyle Richards, Ian Bannen, Benedict Taylor, Eleanor Summerfield, Richard Pasco, Frances Cuka, Georgina Hale, Katherine Levy

Helen and Paul Curtis (Carroll Baker and David McCallum) and their daughters, Jan and Ellie (Lynn-Holly Johnson and Kyle Richards), an Anglo-American family, move into a manor—owned by Mrs. Aylwood (Bette Davis). Upon their arrival, Jan is told that she strikes a chilling resemblance to the owner's missing daughter, Karen, who vanished without a trace 30 years ago. Soon, while exploring the woods, Jan sees a strange blue light, which baffles her, and increasingly strange events cause her to find out about the real reason behind Karen's disappearance.

A family film based on the 1976 novel by Florence Engel Randall, made and released by Disney, which fuses elements of mystery, thriller, science fiction and, most certainly, horror, *The Watcher in the Woods* truly represents a classic gateway into a new decade, in spite of a troubled production history. It contains also a Hammer horror feel, managing to capture that special blend of eeriness and Englishness, with splendid use of the Gothic manor house and surrounding woodlands, where you're not supposed to wander off on your own. It was originally scripted by Brian Clemens before going through many deconstructive rewrites, because the studio found his version too scary and wanted the screenplay to be watered down to suit its traditional family orientated cinemagoers.

Directed by John Hough, the main man behind British horror gems *Twins of Evil* and *The Legend of Hell House*, who had already cranked out successful live action films for Disney (*Escape to Witch Mountain* and its sequel *Return from Witch Mountain*.) Hough did a fantastic job, but experienced major difficulties that resulted in box-office failure. Disney didn't approve Hough's original version, so the director had to re-film the ending, which became ridiculed during its first week of release. Soon, it was quickly removed from the cinema, and a new ending had to be reshot, by Vincent McEveety, without Hough's presence. When the film was finally released—a year later—the opening scene was replaced, and the Watcher's physical manifestation was depicted as a ray of light. McEveety wasn't credited for the re-shoots, due to a union rule that he needed to spend enough time on the film for a shared credit.

Another reason—major studio interference—forced Hough to abandon filming the "other world" scenes, to meet the studio's pressing demand of finishing the movie in time to celebrate Bette Davis's 50 years as an actress. Shame, because the "other world" portion of *Watcher* would have shown where Karen was, after all these years, and those visual effects would have been spectacular.

With a stellar cast of familiar faces in British horror, you have Ian Bannen (*Doomwatch*, *Fright*, *From Beyond the Grave*), Richard Pasco (*The Gorgon*, *Rasputin the Mad Monk*), Frances Cuka (*Hammer House of Horror* segment "Charlie Boy"), Benedict Taylor (Dan Curtis' *The Turn of the Screw*), Georgina Hale (*The Devils* and another segment of *Hammer House of Horror*, "The Mark of Satan") as the young Mrs. Aylwood, Carroll Baker, Eleanor Summerfield playing Mrs Thayer, and lastly Katherine Levy (*Children of the Stones*) as Karen Aylwood.

Soon-come Bond girl and former figure ice skater, Lynn-Holly Johnson, is okay as the lead character, but you wonder if it was Disney's decision to cast an up-and-coming American actress then touted as the next big thing. You also have Kyle Richards, playing Jan's younger sister, Ellie. Kyle also played little Lindsey Wallace in John Carpenter's groundbreaking film *Halloween* and, in real life, she's the aunt of Paris Hilton, another horror movie casualty.

As for David McCallum, his role has little significance, playing the British parent of the Curtis children. The house that Mr. Keller (Ian Bannen) lived in was also "Hill House" onscreen, the exact location used in Robert Wise's *The Haunting*—now Ettington Park Hotel. Bannen's portrayal is chilling and intriguing, helping to carry the movie. But the real powerhouse performances come from Bette Davis and Richard Pasco.

In 2002, Anchor Bay Entertainment decided to give *Watcher* a DVD release, hoping to feature a total of three different endings and the missing opening sequence. But Disney protested about the latter, making Anchor Bay release the DVD on 2 April 2002 without it. Also included with this edition were a wealth of extras: John Hough's audio commentary; his biography; two alternative endings; three theatrical trailers and a TV spot, together with a 20-page collectible booklet and card insert of the film's original quad. Today, this release is out of print, but you can still purchase it secondhand online, and I strongly advise you to get this version—if you're a completist.
—Jason D. Brawn

1981

An American Werewolf in London
The Appointment
Clash of the Titans
Death Shock
Dragonslayer
The Final Conflict
Venom

AN AMERICAN WEREWOLF IN LONDON

D: John Landis
W: John Landis
Starring: David Naughton, Griffin Dunne, Jenny Agutter, John Woodvine, Brian Glover

Given the amount of werewolf-based films that have come out since this was released it might be difficult for today's generation to fully appreciate the impact John Landis' production had at the time. Horror special effects were about to be "transformed" by a new wave of artists and Rick Baker was leading the way. His man-into-wolf sequence really shocked and amazed the viewer. No CGI back then, thank goodness, all done with prosthetics, puppetry and state of the art make-up. The result has rightly gone down in movie history as the finest onscreen werewolf transformation with only contemporary competitor *The Howling* coming close.

The effects work on the rest of the film is equally impressive; decaying corpses, throat rippings, beheadings and so on—this movie doesn't skimp on the red stuff. But there's a whole lot more to it than gory effects. Evident as early as the opening on the Yorkshire Moors, you can tell Landis seems to have a good feel for British life. Albeit somewhat clichéd, maybe, though with darts sessions in a pub filled with unfriendly locals, TV with only three channels and everyone's attempts to be ever-so-polite, he's not far off the mark. It's not only the fact that it's filmed in England, but the way Landis does it that makes it feel like a British film.

It's been described as a horror/comedy and I suppose that's right but on closer examination it's far more horrific than comedic. Yes, there are funny lines and much of the humor comes from their delivery, but that aside this is very much a tragic, traditional, werewolf tale. From the moment our hero is bitten, according to legend, there really is only one direction this can take, and it is to Landis' credit that he doesn't wimp out at the end.

It's filled with many standout set pieces. The early scene in The Slaughtered Lamb is great fun. It wouldn't be out of place in a Transylvanian tavern, but it's made all the more entertaining with its cozy English pub setting. The later dream sequences, which account for many of the big impact shocks, are also highly memorable, most notably the monster Nazi stormtroopers that burst into a scene of domesticity leaving a bloodbath in their wake.

David Naughton is an extremely likeable lead and it's a shame his career didn't amount to much after this. As his best friend, Griffin Dunne steals every scene he's in. He has the lion's share of the good lines, especially after he's dead, and you really accept that these two have been friends for a while. Throughout the horror and mayhem, it's their connection that allows for moments of bonding, playful joshing, even poignancy. Then there's Jenny Agutter. To males of a certain age (and I include myself) she was something special. She had graduated from child star to a nude scene in *Walkabout* [(1971), at age 21], but was still every inch the English rose. She had that "girl next door" appeal and then some. As one of the most caring and attentive nurses ever to grace the screen she earned a whole new flock of fans, especially when she uttered the line, "I'm going to take a shower. Perhaps you'd like to watch some telly...."

I vividly remember seeing the movie for the first time on its initial release and being blown away by it. The humor, pathos, special effects, everything just seemed to click into place. The only thing missing for me was that no one from my beloved Hammer Films made an appearance. It's exactly the kind of thing they should have been making but they were mired in TV production at the time.

Unlike many movies of that period it stands up extremely well to repeat viewings and part of that is due to the way it is structured. Each scene flows seamlessly to the next. None of the scenes seem labored or superfluous, and a relatively short running time keeps the pace on track.

The 1980s saw many, many horror films come out of Britain and America. It was something of an Indian Summer for the genre, but few have the longevity of *An American Werewolf in London*. I've yet to meet anyone who didn't like the movie and I think it's one of the very best the decade has to offer.
—Matthew Gemmell

• • •

I was 10 years old in the autumn of 1981 and obsessed with a film I had no chance of seeing. My older brother managed to

French poster for *An American Werewolf in London*

sneak into the Odeon, Edinburgh. All I managed was a glimpse of black-and-white stills on a display board in the foyer. But salvation lay just around the corner.

My family bought our first video recorder that Christmas: Wednesday 23, December, to be precise. It was massive, the remote control was attached by a cable, and it cost a whopping £500, the equivalent of £2,000 today. I was disappointed that it wasn't a top-loader but kept quiet.

Perhaps more than anything, the introduction of home video made me the film fan I am today. And nothing excited me more than the chance to see *An American Werewolf in London*. In those days, films did not make their way onto video for some time after their initial release, and it must have been 1983 before I finally managed to watch it, thanks to some very liberal (for which read "lax") parenting.

And what an impact it had. Much is made of the availability of cheap horror on video in those pre-VRA. days. But let's be honest, most of that was total junk. Landis's horror-comedy must rank as one of the early stars of the video age.
There is nothing cheap and nasty about the film. It's *expensive* and nasty. And the realization of David Kessler's transformation from man to beast remains one of the great special effects sequences in modern cinema. Before this, werewolves had always been a problem onscreen. Rarely convincing, usually a bit naff. Rick Baker's make-up designs were shocking, startling, funny, and above all, scary.

And that's the great achievement of this film. It manages the tricky task of being genuinely funny and genuinely chilling. Landis grew up loving the Universal and Hammer horror films and is something of an expert in the genre. It shows here; the opening scenes, on the moors and pathways of a near-mythic northern landscape, are soaked in atmosphere.

This is a director who understands the importance of pace, suspense, the Gothic flourish, and a bloody thick fog. For a nerdy Jewish kid from Chicago, he has a real feel for the unique atmosphere of British horror.

None of which is lost when events transfer to the capital. One of the pleasures here is seeing London before it morphed into the tedious, shiny, global financial metropolis so beloved of Boris Johnson and the makers of *The Apprentice*. Here it's dingy, damp, cold, the food costs too much and there's nothing on telly during the day.

So why does it make this viewer so nostalgic for the Britain of the early 1980s? Because it looks like Britain ought to. Before the country and its inhabitants and culture became so in thrall to Americana. It's a curious irony that this young American director made one of the great British movies of the period, a film where the locals are a bit surly, keep to themselves and don't like brash Yanks to the extent that, in the end, they shoot one dead in the heart of the tourist-infested West End.

Horror is often described as the most conservative genre. But *An American Werewolf in London* isn't a conservative film. It just recognizes the Brits of 1981 for what they were. And never has a film made the capital so creepy. Honestly, have any of you ever waited for a train on a quiet tube platform late at night, and not thought about *that* scene?
—Craig Williams

THE APPOINTMENT

D: Lindsey C. Vickers
W: Lindsey C. Vickers
Starring: Edward Woodward, Jane Merrow, Samantha Weysom

An unsung genre gem, forgotten and largely unloved, but probably responsible for causing fragmented emotional scars in the minds of anyone fortunate enough to catch it at an impressionable age. Lindsey Vickers' unusual and frightening film opens as it means to go on, with an implicit but genuinely creepy daylight prologue in which a 12-year-old redhead schoolgirl walks home through the "Cromley Woods" shortcut, hears unseen persons calling her and gets dragged into the bushes. This supreme opening sequence is marred only by an unnecessary voiceover that persists briefly before being dropped completely; the effect of this thankfully short-lived narration is that of a well-spoken gent sitting behind you at the cinema offering his own personal commentary and interpretation.

The girl's mysterious disappearance inspires much talk of kidnap, witchcraft, and good old-fashioned murder, but no one knows for sure—and the audience, to a large extent, is left to decide for themselves about a good deal of this film's narrative at the end. The few bones that we are thrown suggest the girl was killed via an unexplained force controlled by the troubled 14-year-old daughter of company director Edward Woodward, her relatively trivial but fittingly juvenile motive being to ensure a place in the orchestra at school. The budding adolescent musician (Samantha Weysom) has a somewhat dubiously strong attachment to her dad, and frosty mum Jane Merrow (in a disarmingly unsympathetic performance) disapproves of her "dangerous" tendencies to daydream and her manipulation of dad to get what she wants.

Both of these factors become very apparent when Woodward confesses he cannot attend her upcoming concert due to an important work-related trip. Prior to his journey, he is beset by harrowing dreams, within which he is menaced by vicious dogs and trapped in his own crashed car. With Weysom's command of said evil stronger than ever before, it becomes clear she plans to use it to take extreme revenge on her absentee father.

Weysom's peculiar and unnerving performance provides a rare British contribution to the "devil child" sub-genre, and the movie uses her well, holding unnaturally long and unsettling shots of the girl's face to chilling effect. Director Vickers, who never made another feature film, captures an eerie mood from the outset that only escalates as isolated moments of supernatural strangeness bring real shudders; cars powering on by themselves, an image of the daughter turning in an otherwise static photograph of her and her dad, post-*Omen* Rottweilers used as a manifestation of evil.

Condor is ready for his closeup Mr. Vickers!

Vickers, with extraordinary use of sound, makes this essentially three-character piece into a master class of unease via simple but superbly deployed elements. There's a cumulative sense of threat from the use of shadows, ticking clocks, dripping taps, strangely sinister empty car seats, slow pans down empty streets, vaguely surreal premonitory dreams. Kudos for the refreshing lack of "boo" scares, only one visceral moment (a discreetly nasty and oddly irrelevant demise of a mechanic in his workshop) and a measured pace, though the latter results in a good deal more shots of Woodward sleeping, eating, or reading the paper than contemporary audiences might expect or want.

The slim nature of the plot and the minimal dialogue suggest it might have made an even more remarkable 30-minute episode of a TV anthology horror series, or supporting theatrical short, but the pervasive sense of dread ensures it never gets tedious. The final section proves most memorable, with Woodward trapped in his Ford Granada, upside down and precariously balanced on top of a tree after a spectacularly staged, protracted accident set piece. The bleak, ambiguous ending has been signposted all along, but the offbeat, entrancing execution is really something special; this movie will haunt you if you stay the course. The often effective, sometimes overbearing soundtrack is by Trevor Jones, who went on to compose the eerie scores for Alan Parker's *Angel Heart*, *The Dark Crystal* and the vastly underrated *Lawn Dogs*, among many others.

—Steven West

• • •

Post-Gothic British horror had a healthy kick-start with several examples that appeared to signpost a fresh approach with new supernatural threats. *The Omen* (1976) had heralded a new British wave even as Hammer was bowing out but there was insufficient money to see out the promise. *The Haunting of Julia* (aka *Full Circle*) began the new cycle and by the 1980s *The Godsend*, *The Awakening* and *The Appointment* presented a modest trio of unnatural terrors played completely straight. It was not to last.

Lindsey Vickers had made a previous horror short, *The Lake* (1978), and might have been part of the next batch of genre herdsmen had there been the financial support. *The Appointment* might to some feel more like an overextended short subject, the story could be considered slight and the film is largely slow burn, though this is very likely as a result of a low-budget, and the need to keep the concept small and personal. "In the family," so to speak, as the bulk of the storyline merely involves Ian Fisher (Edward Woodward), his wife Dianna (Jane Merrow) and 14-year-old daughter Joanne (Samantha Weysom); the girl an only child, spoilt and, as a result, demanding.

Mr. Fisher learns that he has to stand in for a colleague at an inquest, the timing of which coincides with his daughter's violin recital. Fisher expresses his disappointment to the girl, but she refuses to accept the importance of his alternate engagement a couple of hundred miles away. Her behavior—a constant questioning and pleading—is grating, something we conclude that he normally gives in to, but on this occasion the circumstances are intractable. Mrs. Fisher, though, seems unduly agitated and irascible with the girl, albeit indirectly, and reminds her husband that their daughter is not a good mixer and subject to fantasies that are dangerous, but fails to elaborate.

Mrs. Fisher is primarily the quotidian housewife, calm and regimental for the most part. Her own frustrations are subtly registered in her warnings about their daughter's sexual awakening. She mentions it twice, latterly during a telling bed scene. Joanne, she claims, behaves differently towards Ian because he is a man. He scoffs at the idea and follows with a promise to give their child a call en route, the wife lightly admonishing him that she would like similar contact herself. While she sits in bed with a book, he rolls over asking for more bedclothes and she turns the light off, bidding him a goodnight that he fails to reciprocate. There is an air in her delivery and her back-turned position that suggests she doesn't expect him to respond. This hint of jealousy is followed by a dream sequence in which the husband and wife are in the garden talking, her hand stroking his neck. The camera slow pans and nears him until the wife is out of frame, then adopts a new angle revealing the daughter beside him, in a red dress and dolled up, the hand stroking his neck unchanged, a clever in-camera trick typical of this film's economic ingenuity.

The pace is slow but not uninvolving, and Vickers is aware that with this cool deliberation he might lose some of his audience, which is why the film begins with one of the most impressive jolts in any horror movie, one of the key reasons for *The Appointment*'s positive reputation. It opens with a narrator detailing the circumstances, to the extent to which they are known, around the disappearance of a girl three years earlier when, on May 14 at approximately six in the evening, Jenny Carr decided on the path through Cromley Woods, a common shortcut between the school and Millard Heights. The report cannot tell us what happened to the girl, who was never seen again, but we are permitted to witness the 12-year-old being wrenched violently and shockingly into the bushes by an invisible force. It does not matter how often you view this scene, the editing and the "how did they do that?" effect are electrifying. In the grass her broken violin crumples like charred wood settling in a fire. We are informed that she was feted in school as their best violinist and that she had no enemies bar the "otherwise friendly rivalries of school life." This has paved the way for Joanne to take that lauded position.

In the night three Rottweiler dogs sedately guard or quietly intrude the premises, and as the girl sleeps a photographic portrait of her and her father comes to life and she turns to look at us. We viewers have already been involved in the nightmares of the husband and wife that foresee a serious car accident on the road. In a genuinely unnerving moment Mr. Fisher appears to sense a presence and looks towards the passenger seat where the camera and viewer are placed. An edit reveals the seat empty. The camera then stares over his shoulder from the back seat and he is at once again nervous of a presence. Cutting to the back seat we are first shown the briefcase and then the flat "ghost" of a jacket hanging in the back, seemingly suggesting all is well while simultaneously sowing seeds of uneasy doubt.

The film is also renowned for its car-crash finale. The crash sequence involving a blown tire is meticulously mapped out with remarkable shots from beneath the undercarriage, and the partic-

The renowned car crash in *The Appointment*

ularly astonishing sight of the impact with the barrier that causes the vehicle to stand on its front end for several seconds before carrying on over the cliff edge. As it crashes into the barrier a suitcase flies through the window, the unworn suit free-falls, the car haemorrhages gas through the cap and the fuel gauge sinks. Sound design is a triumph throughout *The Appointment*, and this spectacular scene exemplifies the film's aural qualities, with screeching tires and scraping undercarriage caught up among something more animalistic and tortured, adding to the cacophony.

Next is a disorientating sequence with Mr. Fisher injured in the upside-down car half way up a tree, trapped in his seat-belt, his fate seemingly hexed by his own daughter—we have seen her awaken that same morning with a casual air, displaying no animosity and certainly no overarching sense of evil. Her effect on her father, on men, is a natural one. Heavy with symbolism, the accident does not occur on the way to his destination but instead after Woodward returns to a phone box where he has left a watch, a gift from his daughter, which he removed mid-call noticing that the time had stopped.

The film is beautifully shot by Brian West B.S.C., particularly in his capturing of the North Wales scenery during the journey. There should be equal praise for the entire editing and sound team. The camera often glides, sometimes a slow left to right that is followed immediately by a measured opposing movement in the next shot; and at times, the speed of other actions, like the closing of a door, is often matched with the pace of the camera maneuver. It is all intrinsically met. The music soundtrack is equally well considered. It becomes urgent and important during the opening titles and on the outset of this fatal journey. Otherwise it is subtle, relying on soft female voices and tremulous instrumentation, though the violin serves as a prescient motif, particularly in its circular warning prior to the death of the girl at the opening.

If the film has a flaw, then it comes in some half-complete thoughts. A particular problem is the audio police report, which sounds false and inaccurate, referring to a tragedy and describing the victim's end as violent at the same time as it confesses to the fact that her fate is unknown. But its faults are few, and *The Appointment* is a hugely rewarding addition to the British green belt horror film and the "deadly child" genre.

—Paul Higson

British poster for *Clash of the Titans*

CLASH OF THE TITANS

D: Desmond Davis
W: Beverley Cross
Starring: Harry Hamlin, Judi Bowker, Laurence Olivier, Claire Bloom, Maggie Smith, Ursula Andress

Clash of the Titans is the last in the cycle of fantasy adventure films to feature Ray Harryhausen's beloved stop-motion monsters, and the one which had to face up to changing trends. *Star Wars*, released a few years beforehand, had forever altered the genre, and the formula of "loosely plotted swashbuckling plus fantasy" advanced by *The 7th Voyage of Sinbad* had fallen out of favor. Director Desmond Davis and writer Beverley Cross had to come up with something fresh.

Star Wars is a fairy tale, a tight construct in which all the elements fitted together neatly. *Clash of the Titans*, by contrast, aims to be a myth: something sprawling, sometimes arbitrary, occasionally ramshackle, but—if everything goes according to plan—always grand. Its source material is the legend of Perseus, the Greek hero who rode Pegasus, slew Medusa and saved the princess Andromeda from a terrible sea monster.

That is not to say that the film is a particularly faithful dramatization. It freely interpolates elements from other sources: the sea monster is conflated with the Kraken of Norse legend; the ferryman Charon resembles medieval depictions of the Grim Reaper; the character of Caliban, from William Shakespeare's *The Tempest*, turns up under the name Calibos; and cynical viewers will say that the mechanical owl is no more than a feathery R2-D2—although Harryhausen himself denied any connection between the two.

Purists may blanch, but the script does a good job of tying together these disparate influences. And in some ways the film is true to the spirit of the Greek myths; take its portrayal of a blustery Zeus who is mocked behind his back by the goddesses of Olympus, for example. It is also worth noting that *Clash of the Titans* resists the temptation to establish a central villain in the way that, say, Disney's 1997 *Hercules* turned Hades into the hero's archenemy. King Acrisius, Calibos, the goddess Thetis, Medusa and the Kraken each serve as antagonists at one point or another, but the film never bows to the pop-fantasy convention of the looming Dark Lord and instead makes an effort to portray the network of individual motivations found in Greek myths.

A recurring problem in Harryhausen's filmography is that the monsters, as splendid as they may be, are often shoehorned into the narrative with little regard to overall story structure. *Clash of the Titans* largely avoids this pitfall and finds suitable roles for its stop-motion creatures. They come across as genuine inhabitants of this fantasy world, not merely as contrivances for set pieces. The standout scene is the battle between Perseus and Medusa, which is both a visual triumph—the Gorgon slithers through her gloomy abode, her snake-hair constantly writhing, as Perseus tries to stay out of her deadly glare—and a grand payoff to the story. That said, the limitations of the stop-motion approach are sometimes evident. Presumably to avoid the issue of lip-syncing, Calibos—one of the few Harryhausen creatures to have a speaking role—is portrayed in close-up shots by actor Neil McCarthy wearing heavy make-up. Similar tricks are used to less intrusive effect with Pegasus and the owl, but in the case of Calibos the repeated switches back and forth become so distracting that an entirely live action character would have worked better.

A more significant problem is how underwritten most of the characters are. *Star Wars* may have had a cast of stereotypes, but they were at least lively stereotypes; in *Clash of the Titans*, Perseus is accompanied by a band of interchangeable nonentities. The weakest link is Andromeda, who is portrayed as being so shallow that she fell in love with Calibos for his looks, only to reject him when Zeus cursed him to an existence with a grotesque satyr-like visage. Given that her fate forms the thrust of the film's second half, she should have been a far more sympathetic character.

Despite these weaknesses, *Clash of the Titans* is a solid adventure and a worthy epitaph to Harryhausen's career. As the poorly received CGI-infused remake testifies, they just don't make them like this anymore.
—Neil Emmett

• • •

Most of the gods that mankind has invented have the manners and morals of spoilt children—Robert Heinlein.

Yes, it's time once more for your favorite soap opera, *Olympus*—as the Harryhausen/Schneer dream team try to catch that mythological lightning one more time. The ever-versatile Laurence Olivier phones it in majestically as Zeus, grooving in front of disco lighting and constantly feuding with his reliably bitchy goddess wives, as he displays frank nepotism towards his current favorite son Perseus (hunky, bland Harry Hamlin) while the lad attempts to win the hand of the fair Andromeda (pretty, bland Judi Bowker). Giving his boy some handy plot coupons (helm of invisibility, really good sword, flying horse and—for some reason—a robot owl), he oversees Perseus' thrilling-yet-poorly-paced adventures as he attempts to secure the ultimate romantic gift—the head of Medusa, last of the Gorgons. But Andromeda's mum goes too far when she declares that her sprog is more beautiful than the goddess Thetis, and the angry deity demands the girl as a virgin sacrifice to the fearsome sea-beast, the Kraken ...

This film is, alas, something of a let-down after such genuine Harryhausen greats as *Jason and the Argonauts* or *The Golden Voyage of Sinbad*. A stellar cast of thespians and celebrities (Claire Bloom, Maggie Smith, Ursula Andress) is largely wasted, although Neil McCarthy's tragic, altered villain Calibos impresses from under his horned make-up and Burgess Meredith's luvvie poet Ammon is typically good, hammy value for money, especially his marvellous "man behind the curtain" *Oz*-style intro. And yes, Ray's contributions are as wondrous as ever. The atmospheric set piece where Medusa stalks and is stalked by our heroes, played out in dim red light and near silence, packs one hell of a punch, and a lot of that is down to Harryhausen's sinister, sinuous creation. Elsewhere, his attack squad of giant scorpions and the vicious two-headed guard dog Dioskilos are also well worth the ticket price.

But otherwise, it's so damn slow. The story plods from one encounter to another, whether it's the sub-Python comic relief of the Stygian witches, gratuitous nudity from Perseus' mum Danaë and the sacrificial bath of Andromeda, or anything that the bloody annoying robot owl Bubo ever does, down to ultimately saving Perseus' arse in his final battle with the Kraken. Some hero. Frankly, if you've got any taste, you'll be praying for poor old Calibos—an inspiration for ugly wallflowers everywhere—to redeem himself and get the girl and the glory. No such luck, sad to say.

Although heavy on fantasy, there's not much outright horror here, but what there is—whether it's the subtle shadowplay of Calibos' agonizing transformation or the eerie hunting of the merciless, petrifying Medusa—is impressive stuff, as is pretty much everything that Ray turned his supremely talented mitts to. But, in the final analysis, this is a decided whimper for Harryhausen and Schneer to present as their last cinematic offering, rather than a spectacular, memorable bang.

But in all fairness, it's a solid-gold classic compared to Louis Leterrier's 2010 monstrosity of a remake, a petty, vicious, deforming cinematic curse. Next to that, dear Calibos had it easy...
—Ken Shinn

DEATH SHOCK

D: Lindsay Honey, Bill Wright
W: Bill Wright
Starring: Linzi Drew, Bill Wright

When asked to give historic perspective to his first splatter film *Blood Feast* (1963), H.G. Lewis said: "It's like a Walt Whitman poem—it's no good, but it was the first of its type." The same thing could be said of *Death Shock*—shot on videotape for VHS release when the medium was still fairly new and long before the term "direct to video" had been coined. It's also utterly dreadful, mixing softcore sex and black magic in a way that makes Norman Warren's narratively similar *Satan's Slave* (1976) look like a masterpiece. While *Death Shock* is a victim of its own minuscule budget, it's also an early, admittedly fairly tame, example of how porn would evolve over the next 10 years, with production values, artistry (in some cases) and ambition replaced by volume and generic, unimaginative filmmaking.

The film starts with a woman on a bike being chased through the English countryside by persons unknown to a soundtrack by Mussorgsky (*Night on the Bare Mountain*—the pun probably wasn't intended) before being stripped and stabbed (there's no gore in *Death Shock*—complex effects being beyond the budgetary scope, it would seem) in a ritualistic way. We then get introduced to

Although *Death Shock* is clearly semi-professional at best, and it's therefore tempting to cut the acting and very shaky technical proficiency some slack, it's worth remembering that the 1970s was full of similar very low-budget British sexploitation fare, and even the bottom-of-the-barrel stuff (Derek Ford's *Sex Express* or Trevor Wrenn's *Erotic Inferno*) was technically better than this. With only the most perfunctory narrative, over-extended sequences of colorless actors and *Razzle* models groping each other in the most unerotic fashion, and flat, washed-out cinematography, even at 47 minutes *Death Shock* badly overstays its welcome.

The credits are short, identifying the film as a Hard Times Production, with writing and production duties falling to a "Bill Wright," a pseudonym for Frank Thring. Thring is responsible for directing over 130 hardcore porn movies, mostly in Scandinavia and Holland. *Death Shock*'s co-director is identified as Lindsay Honey, long-term partner of star Linzi Drew and probably Britain's most renowned pornography actor and director, under the nom-de-guerre of "Ben Dover." Unlike most of Honey's subsequent porn output (which is artistically worthless "gonzo" fare of the most depressing kind), *Death Shock* at least has a shred of story and makes half-hearted, ham-fisted attempts at atmosphere, although regarding this as superior to Honey's subsequent output is not exactly high praise. *Death Shock* is too cheap and unimaginative to be in any way erotic, and too obsessed with unattractive flesh in various states of undress to bother building any sense of atmosphere or dread. It's confused, ugly and even the post-credits blooper reel *It'll Be Alright on the Bed!* fails to generate much goodwill. It is, however, the forerunner of a new generation of direct-to-video sexploitation, so without the likes of *Death Shock*, there'd be no *Animal Instincts* (1992), *Indecent Behavior* (1993), Delia Sheppard or Shannon Tweed. I'll leave it up to your own conscience as to whether that's a good or bad thing.

—Neil Pike

our protagonists—two couples shagging over/around/inside their Mark 3 Granada, and a pair of lesbians, presumably for variety. When said Granada conks out, the group hitches a ride with the local Vicar (Frank Thring, giving the only turn which approximates to a performance in the whole movie) to the local Squire's place. The Squire offers them a hot meal and a bed for the night, and orders manservant Rupert and maid Dianna (1980s glamour model and Ken Russell favorite Linzi Drew) to prepare rooms for them. The next 20 minutes are taken up with various softcore couplings before one of the women is attacked by Rupert, fending off her assailant with a handy pair of curling tongs. Fleeing the scene, she comes across the Squire undertaking a black mass ritual with Dianna (which looks more like a massage than a summoning of Satan as Drew deadpans "stop, you're hurting me!") and then falls into the clutches of the Vicar, who's in on it with the Squire. The climactic black rite is then carried out intercut with yet more sex, and the botched finale is meant to suggest that the woman upon which the ritual is enacted is now Satan, or possessed, or something. It all ends with the devilish crew laughing in a sinister fashion, so I assume something bad happened, though it's not exactly clear.

DRAGONSLAYER

D: Matthew Robbins
W: Hal Barwood, Matthew Robbins
Starring: Peter MacNicol, Caitlin Clarke, Ralph Richardson, John Hallam, Peter Eyre

Sex, death, gore, violence, nudity ... so it can't be Disney! Certainly, that was the thinking as we entered the 1980s, as there had barely been a scratch of any of these in the milksop product of the House of Mouse up until that point. Disney had been consistently turning out the usual harmless live action family friendly fantasies, movies in which no character came to any genuine physical or mental harm, but cinema was changing, getting braver and so deeper waters needed to be explored. Disney's Touchstone division would later be set up to produce films with more adult leanings, whether it was the blood squibs of its disastrous dinosaur adventure *Baby: Secret of the Lost Legend* or the tantalizing nakedness of the statuesque mermaid in *Splash!* Both *Tron* and *The Black Hole* included uncharacteristic deadly threats and the studio was to court John Hough (*Twins of Evil*, *The Legend of Hell House*) as the director and Bette Davis as the star of its horror film for the entire family *The Watcher in the Woods*, also shot in England, before it would decide upon a separate production strand to separate the nominally dangerous from the unquestionably cuddly. There was one further Disney production to come before that seismic shift; Matthew Robbins' *Dragonslayer* made an almighty sidestep out of the safety zone, startling some moviegoers at the time.

Set in the sixth century, *Dragonslayer* opens with an unofficial delegation from the kingdom of Urland arriving at the castle home of a great magician, Ulrich of Craggenmoor (Ralph Richardson). The people are being terrorized by a 400-year-old dragon called Vermithrax Pejorative. To appease the beast the kingdom holds a twice-yearly lottery, as a result of which a virgin is sacrificed, chained to a post at which she will be consumed first by the dragon's flames and then its great maw. Ulrich accepts the challenge but the rebel party has been followed by loyalists to the king, led by Tyrian (John Hallam), who oppose any change to the custom lest it bring greater destruction on the realm, as it did once before their King made his "pact with a monster." It is mooted that this could be a battle too heavy for the old sorcerer who confesses, "Oh, I have no fear of it [death]. All this magic, what has it accomplished?!" The film marks its lethal bent early with Ulrich challenging Tyrian to stab a knife into him, which he does, resulting not in the promised invulnerability but instant death.

The delegation witnesses the cremation and set upon the return journey, with sorcerer's apprentice Galen (Peter MacNicol), discovering that he has inherited some of his master's power, following the band along with the curmudgeonly older retainer Hodge (Sidney Bromley). When the loyalists catch sight of Hodge with the group, they mistakenly assume he is assisting the Urland dissenters, and the deadly vibe of the movie is confirmed as they kill this comic relief too. Galen meanwhile has been for a skinny dip at the pool where Valerian, the "boy" acting as spokesperson for the faction is already bathing. The underwater nakedness confirms what we already suspected—Valerian (Caitlin Clarke) is female (and using a body-double—no way she is strapping down those puppies!). Her father (Emrys James) had hidden her gender since birth to protect her from the lottery, unfair perhaps, but as she argues, no less so than the daughters of the rich, including the King's only child the Princess Elspeth (Chloe Salaman) escaping the draw because of status or a cash incentive guaranteeing their exclusion.

On arrival, Galen wastes no time in visiting the dragon's lair, bringing down an avalanche of rocks to seal the entrance and giving the villagers cause for celebration. Valerian also doffs her boy's clothes in favor of a maiden's frock; surprisingly the locals do not take against father and daughter. Indeed, Greil (Albert Salmi) rues only not thinking of doing the same for his lost offspring. Casiodorus Rex, the ruler, is unhappy with the interference, but crooked enough to be more interested in the source of the felling magic. The talisman that all, including Galen himself, understand to be the source of the fledgling wizard's power is removed from the young sorcerer and he is jailed, but later released by the Princess after she investigates his claim that her non-participation in the draw is dishonest. Meanwhile, Vermithrax has not been put to bed at all and bursts free with great fury. As Ulrich pointed out at the beginning, the dragon is simply an aging beast and "when a dragon gets that old it knows nothing but pain, constant pain. It grows decrepit, crippled, pitiful ... Spiteful."

The priest, Brother Jacopus, challenges the dragon and in a blast of fiery breath we catch the horror of him burned black, reminding us that we are far removed from the familiar Disney fare—no *One of Our Dinosaurs is Missing*, this! The lottery is resumed immediately and is again fixed, but very differently on this occasion, by the Princess herself, determined to make amends for every time that her name was kept out of the tombola. Now she will face the fate of the many girls who went before. In a detested Royal household, her heroism does not go unrecognized by the public. The King, in desperation, returns the amulet to Galen, asking that he do his utmost to rescue the Princess.

At which point, we might expect Galen to save the Princess, slay the monster and declare his true love for Valerian, but Robbins flouts convention again. This film is far from conclusion, and Galen arrives to release the Princess but first has to fight Tyrian to the death. During the bout Galen manages to shear his magically treated spear through the Princess' chains but she has been forbidding that he release her. She insists Tyrian is correct to preserve the edict, and while busy tussling with

German poster for *Dragonslayer*

Peter MacNicol in *Dragonslayer*

Tyrian, Galen is unable to stop her walking into the dragon's lair where she will perish as food to Vermithrax's newborn brood. The horrors pile on as our hero bloodily despatches the three baby dragons.

The main dragon itself is impressive and it is to the great credit of the respective technicians that the full-size (16-foot) model, smaller hand steered puppet and the terrific Go Motion animated version all match so perfectly. Decades later it is still an unbeatable design, the perfect dragon in appearance and movement, both fearsome and tragic, but unforgiving to its victims. The attempt to kill the beast fails, and only latterly does Galen realize that Ulrich is the key, leading to a mysticism-laced climax. This mountaintop showdown is ultimately disappointing, however, particularly when compared to the subterranean battle with the creature that has preceded it, post-production parlor tricks a poor substitute for the strenuous combat that thrilled us previously.

Robbins senses this though; blood is spilled during the fight and the gruesome aftermath includes several ugly twists—the villagers turn to praise God for their delivery from the beast, and the King, a broken and pathetic figure now without heir, takes a political opportunity to plant a sword into the offal covered carcass of the enormous creature and have himself declared Dragonslayer, a great lie hidden from nobody but future history. The film's very title acts as the final irony, as ultimately it is hard to call any of the participants a true Dragonslayer, Ulrich having given the instruction remotely ensuring his own end, Galen merely crushing the amulet on command, and the eventual destruction of the beast requiring a joint effort.

The production design, effects, and costumes are all fantastic in their grungy detail and the only aspect to really disappoint is Alex North's (Academy nominated) score, sounding at times too much like a silly circus theme more suited to the Disney of another age. In attempting to hide Valerian's femininity, there also appears to have been some dubbing over or sonic play with Caitlin Clarke's voice, which persists, unfortunately but one supposes necessarily, following the reveal. The beautiful Clarke was no film regular, preferring the stage and seeing this as a frivolous sidestep into popular cinema, but relishing working alongside Ralph Richardson. She was in her late twenties when filming here and died far too young in 2002 from ovarian cancer. Sadly, Vermithrax's first beautiful blonde victim, Yolande Palfrey, also died before her time in 2011, reportedly of a brain tumor. Peter MacNicol, an unlikely heroic lead then, advanced to additional big-budget family-targeted scares with a major role in *Ghostbusters II* before becoming a very popular character actor, particularly due to him co-starring in *Ally McBeal*.

The production took up space at Pinewood Studios but also shot outside London for the village scenes, and at various locations across North Wales, Snowdonia and on the Isle of Skye. Despite the original perceived failure of the film when it was unable to match its budget in box-office receipts, still misguidedly the criteria for success or failure in Hollywood, *Dragonslayer* has always met with both critical and viewer approval—even today, it holds up considerably better than many contemporary screen fantasies.
—Paul Higson

THE FINAL CONFLICT

D: Graham Baker
W: Andrew Birkin
Starring: Sam Neill, Lisa Harrow, Rossano Brazzi, Don Gordon

The final chapter of the original *Omen* trilogy finds the Anti-Christ, Damien Thorn, now in adulthood and vying for the Presidency of the United States—the job he so desperately needs if his earthly quest for supreme, Satanic global power is to be fully realized.

Of course, being the Anti-Christ, he's not going to follow the usual paths of tireless campaigning, baby-kissing and back-handers, but rather the fast track route of subliminally ordering the American Ambassador to Great Britain to blow his own head off and then to immediately insinuate himself with the President who, of course, asks Damien to fill the vacancy. All of this ties in with one of many Biblical prophecies (of filmdom), which foretells that Christ will be re-born on the "Angel Isle," which Damien has worked out to be England.

As you would imagine, the second coming of Christ is going to prove a big spanner in the Devil's works and so, in true King Herod fashion, the plan is adopted for a massacre targeting every new born baby boy that was issued into this world on the night that Damien abruptly awakes from a particularly sweaty bad dream. Reason enough? Add to this the fact that three stars suddenly collide in the darkness and the Anti-Christ is soon putting two and two together and giving himself one major headache. A few (thousand) telephone calls later and Thorn has managed to gather all of his British constituents together on a particularly hazardous Cornish cliff face. Here, he rants that the Christ child must die and orders everyone to set to their sickening, murderous task.

Where there are Devil's acolytes, expect to find Christ's representatives here on earth as well, just to preserve the notion of fair play, and these appear in the form of a group of monks, led by the heavily accented Rossano Brazzi, who's been tasked with protecting the Holy child, while slaying the spawn of Satan in the process. Each armed with one of the seven daggers of Megiddo, they set about trying to corner Thorn at every opportunity, which provides both chills and chuckles in equal measure.

The trouble is, the monks are so inept, that the viewer (this one included) can be forgiven for egging Damien on with his use of freak-accident protection and expert grasp of animal hypnosis! The ever-diligent Brazzi turns out to be the last monk stand-

Mexican lobby card for *The Final Conflict*

ing and with the Christ child safe (though it is never explained how) it is up to Damien's deluded girlfriend to plunge the dagger home....

The Final Conflict is a film of good individual scenes rather than a satisfying whole. The cod-Biblical exposition is an unfortunate necessity, as it's a major plot device. Also, some of the key performances, particularly from Lisa Harrow as the "love interest" and Barnaby Holm as her doomed son, are one-dimensional and unsympathetic. Sam Neill, however, is perfect for Damien. He's called upon to mix insidious evil with cunning charm and pulls it off admirably.

Of course, the set pieces are the thing and it is probably the forced suicide of the original American Ambassador that the film is chiefly remembered for. It really is a true shock moment with an eerily disturbing shaky foot spasm thrown in. The deaths of the "monks on a mission" range from the ludicrously over-the-top to the incredibly tame, with perhaps the gantry slipping, foot-hanging, body burning combo as the highlight. On the other hand, it is the chilling subtlety of the murders of the infants, only hinted and intimated at, that carries the biggest impact. The baptism scene is particularly hard to stomach.

However, and perhaps disappointingly so, it is Damien's own demise which turns out to be the dampest squib. A shame, because the build-up is really quite tense and well executed, though there's the feeling that his final affront to Christ is merely an excuse for the obligatory exit line.

In conclusion, not a patch on *The Omen*, but the trilogy overall, though bending Bibledom to suit its own ends, succeeds as horrific entertainment and has certainly achieved lasting longevity.
—Nigel Smith

• • •

Possibly one of the most overlooked entries in a major movie franchise, this second sequel to *The Omen* (1976) could easily have descended into tedious theological boredom but turned out to be surprisingly refreshing. Set 18 years after *Damien–Omen II* (1978), it begins with the seven knives of Megiddo, the only weapons known to kill the Anti-Christ, being excavated from the burnt-down remains of the Thorn Museum, in some convincing Chicago-set, British-filmed scenes, with Jackson 5-alike kids running about the city streets outside the auction rooms where the knives are being stored. The blades are purchased by a group of monks led by the magisterial Rossano Brazzi, as Father DeCarlo, determined to kill the new American Ambassador to Britain, Damien Thorn (Sam Neill, using a passable American accent) after the previous Ambassador (who employs a secretary played by Ruby Wax) has been killed in a surprisingly bloody gunshot

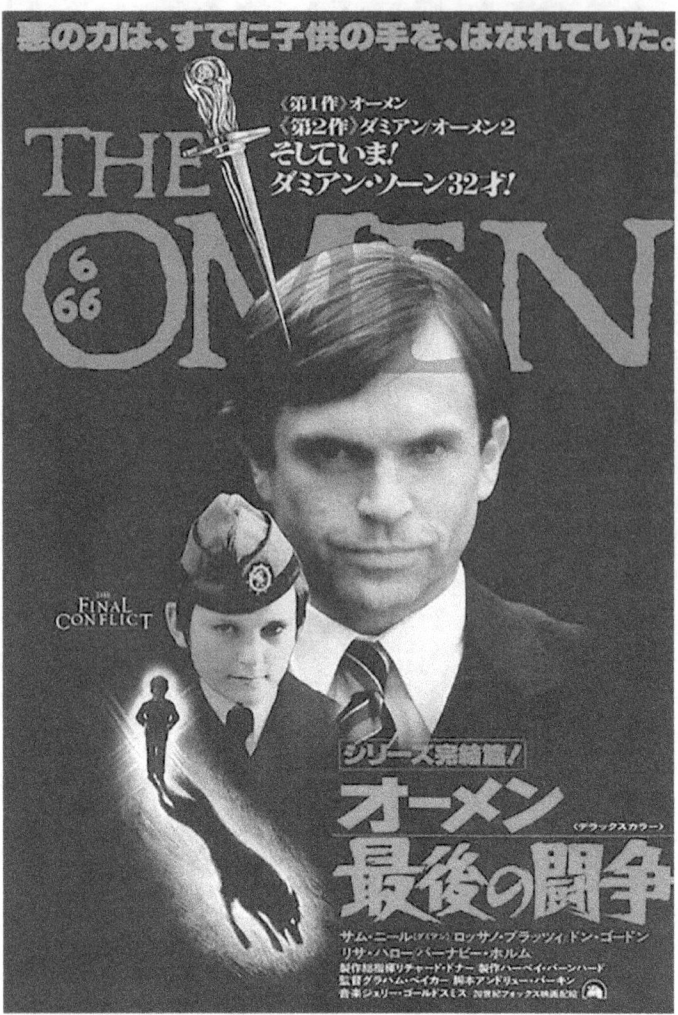

Japanese poster for *The Final Conflict*

to the head, triggered by the opening of a wired-up door. All-grown-up Mr. Thorn soon attaches himself to a political aide and his pregnant wife (Don Gordon and Leueen Willoughby) and falls in with Kate, a widowed BBC journalist (Lisa Harrow) and her son Peter (Barnaby Holm, son of Ian) who becomes the apostle of Damien, by now plotting to prevent the birth of the forthcoming Christ on March 24.

The film is an oddity. The script by Andrew Birkin oddly seems to borrow from 1977 *Omen* knock-off *Holocaust 2000* in the idea of a corporate Anti-Christ using his family position to change the world. Director Baker injects an epic feel, an improvement after the relatively pedestrian second-series entry. Wide shots of a fox hunt and Damien's country house romanticize what could have otherwise been treated as a *Jaws 3*–type conveyor-belt item, and the scenes of hundreds of unlikely Satanists (including schoolgirls, boy scouts, old ladies, farmers) in a Yorkshire quarry being called on to slaughter all baby boys born on March 24th in the name of the "one true god" echoes the Summerisle villagers in *The Wicker Man*.

The death scenes are spectacular, as usual. One scene in which a monk is torn apart by hunting dogs led by Damien may sound trashy, but Bob Paynter's cinematography lifts it, bringing the same touristy but authentically British feel he delivered in *An American Werewolf in London*. We're also presented with the epic fall of another brother into a river and the ashen, bloodied corpse of one would-be-killer cleric being hung upside down and swung across a TV studio. The film is also downbeat, seemingly joyous in scenes of infant mortality, where babies are mishandled by scouts, prams crash into black cabs, mothers burn their sons with hot irons and evil midwives are everywhere. Even the climax results in the death of both the heroic Father DeCarlo and Kate's son Peter, but the knifing of Damien (who in death seems angry and still thinks he's won), as the image of Jesus lights above, gives us a hopeful ending and suitably "praising" music from Jerry Goldsmith, again contributing a marvellous score.

In all, this is an underrated thriller, blighted by the depiction of a very 1981-like "future" and Sam Neill's slight overacting, which I'll forgive since the Anti-Christ probably needs to behave like that to make an impression and stand out from the crowd. A fitting end to the *Omen* saga, really—a 1990 TV movie sequel, *Omen IV: The Awakening*, is out of continuity.
—George White

VENOM

D: Piers Haggard
W: Robert Carrington
Starring: Oliver Reed, Klaus Kinski, Sarah Miles, Susan George, Nicol Williamson, Sterling Hayden

Piers Haggard, director of one of the UK's outstanding genre films of the 1970s, *Blood on Satan's Claw*, had the unenviable task of becoming a late replacement for imported American director Tobe Hooper when Tobe vamoosed 10 days into the shooting of *Venom*. With Hooper's name already prominent on early poster designs, the change carried with it rumors of the *Texas Chain Saw* filmmaker's apparent nervous breakdown and altercations with perhaps the feistiest member of the once-in-a-lifetime all-star cast, Klaus Kinski. Candidly referring to the shoot as being plunged into a "nest of vipers," Haggard nonetheless wound up at the helm of one of the more fascinating and entertaining Brit horrors of the 1980s. A cursory glance at the witty scene selection titles on Anchor Bay's 2004 DVD release is perhaps the best summation of the movie's pleasures, promising as they do "Severed Surprise," "Rear Entry" and, our favourite, "Trouser Snake." You normally have to rent Ron Jeremy movies for quality chapter stops like those.

Robert Carrington's script, adapted from a novel by Alan Scholefield, straddles two genres: a tense kidnap scenario based around a single house and a throwback to the popular revolt-of-nature American horror movies that were all the rage in the 1970s, a cycle that had already spawned snake-centered offerings like *Stanley*, *Rattlers*, *Jennifer* and (lest we forget) *Jaws of Satan*. International kidnappers headed by malevolently grinning Kinski (kitted out in Nazi clobber in Hooper's version), in cahoots with foxy maid Susan George (taking her knickers off without much persuasion) and triggerhappy, moustache-sporting driver Oliver Reed, plot the abduction of the sappy, asthmatic 10-year-old son (Lance Holcomb—a "cheeky little bastard" in the words of Reed) of a wealthy American couple at their plush London home. Unfortunately, an only-in-horror-movies pet shop mix-up leads to the doctor of a toxicology institute (Sarah Miles) receiving a humble African house snake while its intended owner, Holcomb, takes home a Black Mamba, the most poisonous snake in the whole world.

The genre mash-up at the heart of *Venom* inevitably sees the movie fall between the stools of not being scary enough to succeed as a pure horror picture and having too many hokey "When Snakes Attack!" set pieces to be taken seriously as a straight suspense thriller. In the realms of guilty-pleasure killer-snake melodramas, however, *Venom* is tough to beat, and with this kind of upper-tier Psychotronic cast, endlessly rewatchable. Thrown in at the deep end, into what he later referred to as a "strange psychological ballet" between Kinski ("a handful" and humorless to boot) and Reed ("a naughty boy" with a very wicked sense of fun and a fondness for winding up his co-star), Haggard captures a simmering sense of menace in the early going. As the siege scenario develops and cops amass outside the house, Susan George gets bitten on the face before the snake gets loose and Holcomb's "living legend" Granpa (Sterling Hayden) ineptly attacks innocent wires around the house despite having prior experience with mambas from his safari days. The snake, meanwhile, savages the kid's cute pets but is discerning enough to only attack the villains.

Seldom was such an eclectic cast of veterans assembled for a British horror picture. Genre favorites like Michael Gough and John Forbes-Robertson show up in minor roles while we relish the unique spectacle of Kinski (who, like all good movie villains, just wants one million pounds) slapping the intimidating and evidently pissed/pissed off Reed around. An annoying Sarah Miles is on hand purely to dispense strategically placed facts about the black mamba, like "Funnily enough, it's a gray-ish, brown-ish colour," "It's the fastest, most dangerous snake in the world," and "It's paranoid, even." Kinski, who apparently turned down a role in *Raiders of the Lost Ark* because *Venom* offered a bigger pay-day, gets to expire in slo-mo before the typically 1980s horror pan to an inevitable batch of its-happening-again snake eggs in the air-ducts of the house. The sweaty Reed, however, figures in two priceless movie highlights: one in which he's startled by a mamba in his spirits cupboard ranks alongside that Michael Aspel chat-show appearance as one of his most enjoyable 1980s media moments. It is matched only by the oddly horrifying yet hilarious sequence in which the snake slithers up the gibbering Reed's trouser leg. You will cringe, but not nearly as much as you did during Reed's grimly compelling guest spot on *The Word* some years later.

Aided by an early score from talented composer Michael Kamen—en-route to *Brazil*, *The Dead Zone* and *Highlander*, among many others—*Venom* does generate real suspense, and the snake scenes are above-average for this sub-genre. The movie's enduring curiosity factor, however, lies with that astonishing cast. The aforementioned Anchor Bay DVD (which loses at least two goodwill points by featuring a picture of a rattlesnake on the cover—doh!) features one of the most enlightening commentary tracks in memory courtesy of director Haggard. Instead of the usual self-congratulatory accounts of working with the extraordinarily talented whatshisname or a 10-minute explanation of how the camera angle on a scene involving a possessed toenail was achieved, you get an honest and hilarious recollection of an incredibly fraught set. Haggard paints a vivid portrait of Kinski and Reed constantly provoking each other out of a mutual hatred, with Reed shaking Kinski's trailer while shouting, "You fucking Nazi bastard!" being a routine occurrence. (Kinski's response? "You fucking English cunt!") Anecdotes documenting their alternatively childish and bizarre behavior—including a fight that broke out just as the investors from Guinness showed up with their families—add a whole other dimension to the already peculiar onscreen interactions between the two actors. Plus, you get a *Women in Love* story in which Haggard relates how behind-the-scenes tensions between Reed and Alan Bates prior to the filming of Ken Russell's infamous nude wrestling scene revolved around that age-old dilemma, whose willy is bigger? There's probably another gag about snakes in there somewhere but I can't be bothered ...

—Steven West

• • •

German DVD featuring *Venom*

Funny thing about this British "monster siege" suspense/horror film. Where the Americans usually have the monsters on the outside relentlessly assailing our beleaguered heroes on the inside, here the monsters—human and otherwise—are already within, and it's the good guys' job to flush them out. Tch! Contrary coves, aren't we. More tea, anyone?

All right, enough flippancy. Fun though it is (and easy) to dismiss this film as "Snakes in the Mains," it turns out—ridiculous plot contrivance notwithstanding—to be a genuinely well-crafted, suspenseful piece from the hands of the ever dependable Piers Haggard, stepping in to replace a "leaving-due-to-creative-differences" Tobe Hooper.

It's not hard to see why Hooper split. When three of your main cast are notorious hellraisers Klaus Kinski and Oliver Reed (on the side of the villains) and Nicol Williamson (allegedly on the side of the angels, but in fact more frightening than the bad guys), then you're in for a fraught shoot. It's to Haggard's credit that it got finished at all, let alone as enjoyably as it did.

Reed and his mistress (Susan George) are disgruntled bad 'uns—employed by a very rich couple to babysit their 10-year-old, snake-loving son—who hit upon the brilliant idea of helping Kinski's deranged international criminal mastermind to hold the kid for ransom inside the family home in London, in their quest for vast amounts of moolah. And they'd probably have gotten away with it too, if not for that pesky kid—and his latest snake, a deadly black mamba supplied in error by a particularly dozy pet shop owner ...

Reed's "Dave" is clearly a liability, and it's his bloody shotgun despatching of an unfortunate curious copper that calls in Williamson's frankly terrifying Police Inspector and his boys. But the baddies are as resourceful and determined as he is, and the two sides are evenly matched—until the mamba gets loose, and without even knowing it, starts tipping the balance.

The ensuing battle of wits between the dwindling band of villains and the cops becomes ever more tense and nasty, with vicious tactics being deployed by both, and Haggard ratchets up the tension superbly. A cast of dependables including Sarah Miles, Michael Gough, Rita Webb, Maurice Colbourne and John Forbes-Robertson give solid support to the psychotic leads, although Sterling Hayden's whiskery granddad is pointlessness incarnate.

And the snake is marvellous. Ridiculously contrived as its inclusion is, you'll be prepared to forgive it everything for a masterstroke of a death scene, wherein Oliver Reed learns how to sing soprano—the hard way ...
—Ken Shinn

1982

Brimstone & Treacle
Britannia Hospital
House of the Long Shadows
The Sender
Xtro

BRIMSTONE & TREACLE

D: Richard Loncraine
W: Dennis Potter
Starring: Sting, Denholm Elliott, Joan Plowright, Suzanna Hamilton

Let's be honest, even as a lifelong aficionado of Dennis Potter, it's very difficult to tackle an analysis of this film with anything approaching objectivity. Upon its release in 1982, its principal selling point seemed to be, ironically, its status as a remake (some may say a totally unnecessary one) of a play nobody had seen. The original, made as part of the well-regarded *Play For Today* series in 1976, having been, in a fit of pique and cowardice, banned by the BBC before it was even broadcast, thus immediately granting it legendary status and rendering this version (starring one quarter of the same principal cast in Denholm Elliott) the first to be viewed by almost everybody. Unfortunately, its other major selling point at the time was the casting of rock star Sting, aka Gordon Sumner, in the lead role—and that, unfortunately, has not only been proven with hindsight to be a huge error of judgment, but has dated the film badly (whereas its predecessor, starring the far humbler and more talented Michael Kitchen, has remained timeless), and left it with the unshakeable stigma of a vanity project.

Because—and let's not be coy about this—outside of his cameo as an Eddie Cochran-obsessed garage attendant in Chris Petit's *Radio On*, the Geordie bassist/vocalist is simply no actor. Yet ironically, for a man whose music is not aesthetically associated (the lyrics to *Synchronicity* notwithstanding) with horror, he seems to have spent a great deal of his "thespian career," such as it is, in or skirting around the genre, with *The Bride*, *The Grotesque*, *Artemis 81* and the Italian picture *Julia and Julia* all bearing his rubber stamp. And, as if that alone weren't bad enough, here we're also (presumably for contractual reasons) treated to a soundtrackful of trademark fretless bass-plonking, cod-reggae riddims and Jafaican lead vocals, particularly during the pointless dream sequences which seem to have been shoehorned in precisely *for* such a purpose. A purgatory from which the only blessed relief, as far as I can tell, comes in the usage of *actual* lyrics, with any "eeeyo mineeeyo bodeeeyos" conspicuous by their absence. Maybe, even in a film about the Devil, God is merciful after all ...

Given our idol's immediately obvious feet of clay (especially ironic for someone playing a character with cloven hooves) we are left to turn towards the sterling supporting cast for inspiration. Elliott, given the thankless task of playing a part he'd already mastered six years ago but with less character development (the sinister political allegiances replaced here with predictable, almost sitcom-like lustings for his secretary), manages admirably given what he has to work with, but Joan Plowright, by now into her second round of playing the mothers of mentally disabled kidults in semi-horror films with quasi-religious iconography (*Equus* in 1977 having preceded), is the real star, and shines accordingly. Sympathetic, warm, human and openly flirting with the last vestiges of her sexuality so beloved of British character actresses before the onset of early old age, she ends up being the only person (the dumbfounded Pattie excepted) you actually care about, and with whom your sympathies rest. Yet even that can't save the film.

Nevertheless, it does at least create food for thought, and in the role of Norma Bates, her relationship with the mysterious Martin Taylor (Sting) exists on two levels. Taylor bumps into husband Tom (Elliott) one night outside Waterloo station claiming to be a "friend" of their 20-year-old daughter (now paralyzed after a hit and run), before stealing his wallet, then calls to "return" it with far more dubious/ambiguous motives in mind. Prosaically, Norma is taken in by his story and rejoices in simply having some company, especially anyone representing a link to her offspring's past as an active, sentient human being. Underneath, she is also beguiled and attracted by his smart clothes and good looks (two things Sumner *does* have going for him) and subconsciously sees in him a remnant of the man her husband used to be. Although Pattie's accident is not totally to blame for that fade, and, despite being a publisher of religious books, Tom possesses certain appetites, intolerances, and at least one *very* shameful secret. It would also appear that he ceased fulfilling his vows a long time ago—which calls into question not only who is the greater "sinner" or "demon" in the household, but by what means others have been conjured ...

Thus, while we are ostensibly supposed to perceive Martin as some malign spirit, appearing randomly in the lives of commuters (including a less than co-operative Benjamin Whitrow and an all-too friendly Dudley Sutton), the *implied* truth is far more allegorical, namely that he only appears, like a demonic equivalent to The Goodies

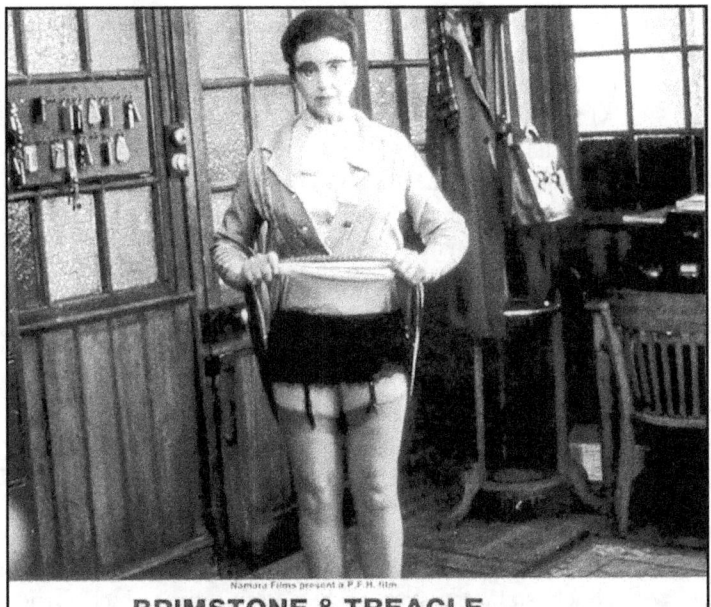

or Avengers, when "needed"—and, like Donald and Angela Pleasence in *From Beyond the Grave*, when *summoned*, consciously or otherwise—by the consciences of others. Most controversially (in the infamous scene for which the film is best remembered), by raping the bedridden girl, and thus shocking her into such blind terror that she speaks for the first time in years, he is, paradoxically, only doing his hosts what he sees as a "favor," and, like the theme says, spreading a little happiness as he goes by. This in itself, if the film were remade now, would probably see it banned all over again, but Potter's attitude to the opposite sex, from *Stand Up Nigel Barton* through to *Cold Lazarus*, was always the source of much debate, and *Brimstone* proves no exception, not only in its graphic depiction of molestation, but in the more subtle inference that, while, post-rape, Tom wishes in some way to harm Martin, both Pattie and Norma seem sad to see him gone ...

Despite the strength of the script, and the potential to appeal as horror movie, straight drama or melodrama, it's disappointing that *Brimstone* ultimately fails. Not just by casting such an inept leading man (though at least his presence ensured audiences actually turned up!), but also by dint of an inexplicable staginess, poor and pointless S.F.X., and, most inexplicably, meandering direction from Loncraine, who, after creating genuinely atmospheric masterpieces in the shape of *Flame* and *The Haunting of Julia*, seems content to sleepwalk his way through this. Despite a close working relationship with the playwright spanning several years, he seems to have far less idea here of Potter's intentions than helmer of the TV version Barry Davis, something made all the more obvious when, five years later, the original was both broadcast on BBC2 for the first time and released on VHS.

Most bizarrely of all, given its cinematic status, it looks *less* like a film and more like an extended episode of *Tales of the Unexpected*, with similar production values; while this in itself is no bad thing, the overall effect is of a failed experiment conducted by someone who didn't actually know their objective to begin with. A classic case of a wasted opportunity.
—Darius Drewe

BRITANNIA HOSPITAL

D: Lindsay Anderson
W: David Sherwin
Starring: Malcolm McDowell, Leonard Rossiter, Joan Plowright, Graham Crowden, Alan Bates, Mark Hamill

Lindsay Anderson's second feature film, *if....* was recognized as a work of genius; his third, *O Lucky Man!*, contained flashes of genius. His fourth was *Britannia Hospital*.

It still divides opinion. Either it's a brilliant, incisive examination of contemporary British society, unfairly denied recognition through being released just as the nation was swept by a wave of Falklands-victory-inspired triumphalism. Or it is a pettish *cri du coeur*, a misanthropic farce with an embarrassingly facile political analysis.

Why does it create division? On the positive side it is the work of a director, Anderson, and scriptwriter, David Sherwin, who were demonstrably capable of brilliance. It reaches for greatness, aspiring to mercilessly expose the failures of a class-ridden British society through the metaphor of a hospital (which lest we miss the point is regularly called just "Britannia.") And it has a cast of enormous and proven talent.

The idea that *Britannia Hospital* is a prophet without honor in its own (war-maddened) country is supported by the reception it received from some critics abroad. One of its great defenders was Vincent Canby of the *New York Times*, who saw in it a "mercilessly funny satire on the end of empire." But it's the negative view that is the more popular. That it's a near-criminal waste, of talent, money, and that incredible cast.

Anderson aimed for a Swiftian state of the nation satire. Yet it's impossible to watch *Britannia Hospital* without being reminded of another series of films that had also reached their nadir. It is easy to imagine this one having the title *Carry On England*, but that had already been claimed. So had the political overview, in *Carry On at Your Convenience*. That 1971 comedy featured the same bloody-minded, obstructive trade unionists. It was closer in time too to the inspiration for the later film: Industrial action by National Union of Public Employees members against the admission of private patients to Charing Cross Hospital in 1974. The time difference is important. The *Carry On* could claim some relation to then current events. Anderson's effort was based on those of almost a decade before.

It's important to remember the intensely politically polarized era that his film arrived in. Margaret Thatcher's Conservatives were in their third year of government. Factories were closing. Riots had torn across Brixton, St. Paul's, Toxteth and Handsworth. An avoidable war had been won against a right-wing dictatorship that the government had until months before been selling arms to. The P.M. was besotted by an American president who believed that nuclear war was winnable. Unemployment had tripled to three million. IRA bombings were an everyday reality (the film's use of a bomb atrocity as a throwaway dramatic device is in poor taste, to say the least.) And the opposition to all that? A disorganized and fractured left; a self-destructing Labour Party; the trade unions, reeling from government attacks and declining in membership; and single-issue protest campaigns like CND and the Anti-Apartheid Movement.

Anderson was identified with the left, with progressive attitudes, politics and ideas. At a time when lives and livelihoods were being lost and hospitals closed down (21 in 1981 alone), these were the people he turned his considerable talents against. The film's working-class trade unionists are hateful or hypocrites, the protestors a murderous mob. In a film in which everyone is a caricature, they are the worst, the most banally evil. Everyone in the story (with the curious exception of the Queen Mother character) is a grotesque, but it is the attacks on the campaigners and left-wingers that really hurt. They are the ones that leave the film's lasting impression.

Many felt betrayed. Some still do.

Britannia Hospital alienated many who might have been its supporters. That was not its only fault. It also forgot to have any heart. The contempt for humanity is unrelieved. The cinematography of Anderson's usual collaborator, Miroslav Ondříček, who would have been able to find some redeeming beauty in the hospital itself, is missing. The star, Malcolm McDowell, is briefly used in a role that denies him any chance to deploy his charisma. Bizarrely, almost equal screen time is given to an actor who personifies the bottom-scraping low point and near-death of the British film industry in the 1970s: Robin Askwith, an actor with no charisma to deploy.

Lindsay Anderson—a man never slow to criticize others—refused to admit the film's shortcomings. To his credit he rejected the Falklands defence: The fault wasn't jingoism, he repeatedly stated (including in his aptly named book *Never Apologise*) but the audience's failure to think for itself. He deserves to be remembered for better than that.

E.M.I., the film's producers, tried to recoup a little of the money they had lost on it with a hasty video release. According to this: "*Britannia Hospital* combines the anarchic fun and vulgarity of the *Carry On* films with an element of deeper social criticism ... Mind you don't die laughing!"

We were meant to be *laughing*? Ooh-er, Matron!
—Sam Dawson

• • •

Many years ago, I attempted to prompt a discussion of the merits of *Britannia Hospital* on an internet newsgroup styling itself *A Very British Horror*. Any hopes of expanding the regular debates re: Hammer's greatest hits, etc. were dashed by the moderator, who snappily informed me in no uncertain terms that "*Britannia Hospital* is not a British horror film." I beg to differ, and I'm sure Lindsay Anderson would have felt likewise.

A timely stab at a state-of-the-nation satire, which turned out to be not quite so well-planned after all (repelling the right wing, as expected, but also haemorrhaging support on the other side of the class divide by pointing the finger at restrictive and damaging union policy, and the failings of person-in-the-street protestors to coalesce), the film was widely perceived as unsuccessful at bottling the zeitgeist in the effortless manner its predecessors in the "Mick Travis trilogy," *if....* and *O Lucky Man!*, had managed.

To fans of cult cinema, however, here lay treasures galore. An early poster design for the movie, ultimately unused, controversially highlighted a roughly sketched image of a decapitated figure limply clutching our traditional red-white-and-blue Union Jack; this simple yet iconic illustration encapsulated the movie to perfection, though severe critics might argue that it did so with such forceful success that it almost made the two-hour celluloid journey superfluous.

No matter—for Anderson's voyage through the choppy waters of early Thatcherism and the wake of the Winter of Discontent is peppered with content guaranteed to appeal to the discerning gorehound! Many reviewers at the time used Hammer and the like as points of reference, but those of us who dared venture into the forbidding territory of Screen Three at our local triplex recognized kinship with the ferocious visions of Lucio Fulci and cohorts. Like Waris Hussein (*The Possession of Joel Delaney*), Stanley Kubrick (*The Shining*), and other high-profile directors uncharacteristically dipping their toes in bloodier waters, Anderson displays a surprising and more than welcome tendency to go over-the-top when using horror to butter his politics. For starters, Graham Crowden's demented Professor Millar (he of the half-man half-porker splicing in *O Lucky Man!*) is back, and this being Britain post-1979, he's kind of in charge, head lunatic overseeing the asylum. His mysterious "Genesis Project" seems to be getting everyone very excited, but the early murder of a patient (Alan Bates) sets us on edge; the lopping-off of our beloved Mick's head, two-and-a-half films into the Travis trio, provides an even more disturbing development (I watched this in sheer "you can't kill off your main character!" disbelief, mouth agape, at the cinema in late 1982), and further devilment is to come as the ex-schoolboy-revolutionary's bonce is fastened atop

a stitched-together patchwork monster of varying ethnic hues (a gross parody of the "coffee-coloured people" ideal proposed by Blue Mink's *Melting Pot*!). Crowden is a fabulous mad scientist, no surprise, but the sight of classy Anderson favorite Jill Bennett at the heart of much of the plasmatic pandemonium is gloriously rebellious. In true 1950s potboiler fashion, Britain's promise lies in the spongy furrows and ridges of a monster brain wired to a computer—Genesis climaxes *Britannia Hospital* by endlessly reciting the "what a piece of work is a man" soliloquy from *Hamlet*, to even greater import than Richard E. Grant when he repeated the trick at the affecting finale of *Withnail & I* later in the decade.
—Darrell Buxton

HOUSE OF THE LONG SHADOWS

D: Pete Walker
W: Michael Armstrong
Starring: Peter Cushing, Christopher Lee, Vincent Price, John Carradine, Desi Arnaz, Jr., Sheila Keith, Julie Peasgood

> "The old order is gone forever and we must crumble into dust."

Author Kenneth Magee (Arnaz) accepts a bet to turn out a novel in 24 hours. A crumbling old Gothic pile (a fitting metaphor for the state of the British film industry—decaying, past its prime, and reliving former glories?) is selected as his base. Supposedly empty, it turns out to be teeming with life. Old owners the Grisbane family have returned to their birthplace. They've come back to release youngest brother Roderick, locked away after a nasty misdemeanor. But he's not there … and before too long, family members start to die. Based on the play *Seven Keys to Baldpate*, the big selling point here was the chance to see the three leading men of British horror united onscreen. They had technically appeared together in the 1969 film *Scream and Scream Again*, but not all onscreen at the same time. As they arrive one by one in gloriously overblown Gothic style you can feel the excitement rising.

Cushing is wonderful as the lisping weak-willed drunk, Sebastian, who claims his automobile has broken down. His progressive state of inebriation is beautifully played, while his admission to secretary Mary Norton (Peasgood) about his nervousness and having spent his "whole life in a state of fear" is heartbreaking. His reaction to the appearance of Lionel Grisbane (Price) announcing "I have returned!" is to exclaim "Oh Lord" before hustling the others from the room as if someone had exposed himself.

Price's first appearance is unashamedly theatrical as he wanders round his ancestral home decrying the end of the old order. "Don't interrupt me when I'm soliloquizing!" he snaps haughtily when Desi tries to interject. Lee shows up as Corrigan, a mystery figure with an interest in purchasing the grand old property. That he is the evil escaped brother is very obvious, magnetic persona notwithstanding, since he's the only person over 30 who isn't a member of the Grisbane family.

They're joined by John Carradine in the best role of his later career, which had gone from B-movies all the way to Z-grade fare. Also present and more than welcome is Pete Walker regular Sheila Keith, deputizing for an infirm Elsa Lanchester. It's a rather small role, mind you, a real shame that after giving such spellbinding performances in *House of Whipcord* and *Frightmare*, her association with Walker should end on such a low note.

The unappealing Desi Arnaz, Jr. and Julie Peasgood represent the younger generation. Desi is the brash young author full of bravado and casual profanity, much to Keith's distaste. Peasgood is the winsome assistant sent by his boss to keep an eye on him. It was unwise letting them go head to head with Price or Cushing as they get acted off the screen. Desi hustles through, but Peasgood sounds like she's reading her lines off a cuecard, plus her wholesome image makes her an odd choice as the love interest.

It takes an age to build momentum, the running time is half over before the characters have assembled and the plot creaks into gear. The tension does begin rising with the manor filling up with returnee relatives and the discovery that the dangerous brother has escaped. Yet the film fails to capitalize on this, the storyline goes nowhere slowly and tension dissipates. There are plot holes you could drive a double decker through. The violence and horror is of the "weak tea" variety, some of the deaths occurring off screen. When the film was released on VHS it was rated PG, slightly dubiously because of a few gory moments but

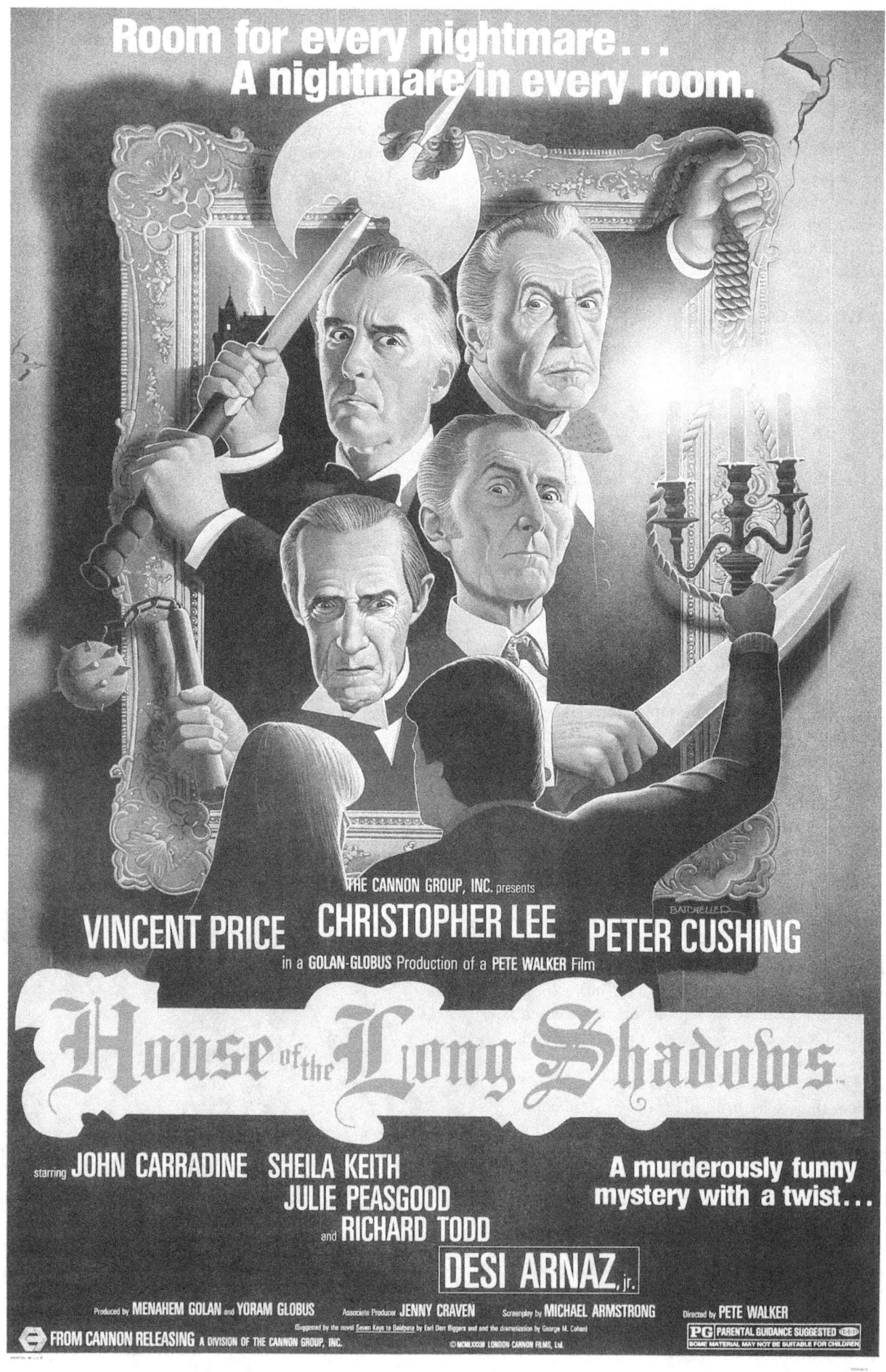

showing how out of date it was in a world of "18" certificates and video controversy.

Now for the twist. In a surprise ending, that comes almost like a slap in the face, it's revealed the whole thing was a hoax set up by the publisher. This was a bad move—despite the shoddy set up, you invest in the film because of the caliber of its cast. So, to find out you're watching something more akin to *Scooby-Doo* comes as a blow! The cheat at least lends credence to the locking up of Roderick and the inconsistencies inherent, but it does create a heap of other narrative problems. Still, once the subterfuge has been exposed, there is plenty of fun to be had watching the players discussing technique while bitching at each other in the way theatricals are prone to. The big question is, what exactly has being taking for a ride taught Desi? How will the elaborate con make him a better writer?

Maybe it's not quite the film it could have been but viewed indulgently as a finale for the Grand Old Order it is entirely fitting. As for "curtains," this was far from being a swansong for any of the vintage quartet—they each staggered on for a while after. But maybe this is how they should be remembered. Aged? Definitely. Careworn? Certainly. Still possessing that old black magic? Unquestionably.
—Gerald Lea

THE SENDER

D: Roger Christian
W: Thomas Baum
Starring: Kathryn Harrold, Zeljko Ivanek, Shirley Knight, Paul Freeman, Al Matthews, Marsha A. Hunt

A disturbed and amnesiac young man, with telepathic powers, is admitted to a mental hospital following his failed suicide attempt at a local beach. Unable to remember his own name, let alone his past, he's named John Doe #83. During his stay, his caring doctor begins to suffer a series of nightmare hallucinations, eventually causing her to make an alarming discovery about the mystery patient's real history.

Dr. Gail Farmer (Kathryn Harrold) is depicted as the sympathetic and understanding psychiatrist who is determined to save John Doe (Zeljko Ivanek), but her colleague, Dr. Joseph Denman (Paul Freeman) opposes her method and strongly believes in conducting painful experiments on their charge, which could claim his life. This plays like a typical good cop/bad cop scenario. As for John Doe #83, his vulnerability is projected to the fore, with a Norman Bates type history centering upon his domineering mother, Jerolyn (Shirley Knight), who seeks complete control of his mind. Dr. Farmer's attempts to aid are always threatened by the authority of the sadistic Dr. Denman or Jerolyn's looming, eerie presence. Even in the era of *The Fury*, *Patrick*, *Scanners* and *Firestarter*, *The Sender* stands out as a prime example of psyche-based terror.

A lack of explanation about John Doe's prior existence, and failure to clarify his relationship with his mother, may let the film down a notch or two. When dealing with a person who has lost their identity (as exemplified by the *Bourne* trilogy), their past is the key, and a way in for the audience. Obfuscation and confusion can symbolize a character's inner torment (*Memento*) but here it merely muddies the waters somewhat.

The haunting score by Trevor Jones (*Angel Heart*, *Mississippi Burning*) helps to animate the movie's crucial moments—notably the violent attack on Dr. Denman and his fellow doctors as they attempt electro-shock therapy on the deceptively passive Doe and get a high-voltage taste of their own medicine.

The ensemble of fellow patients lends a true *One Flew Over the Cuckoo's Nest* feel, and ought to have been explored further. Particular standouts are the African American Vietnam veteran, played by Al Matthews (a marine in *Aliens* and the fire chief in *Superman III*) and "The Messiah" (Sean Hewitt), who berates John. I also liked Marsha A. Hunt's brief role as the no-shit-taking nurse Jo.

Some quality special effects (courtesy Nick Allder) bring impact to the hallucination scenes: the medical fridge brimming with cockroaches, the rats swarming about in Dr. Farmer's apartment, and the car chase. Equalling any of these for shock value is the decapitation of The Messiah, though *Omen* buffs will probably rate it a distant second to the pane of glass shearing shutterbug Jennings' head from his shoulders in Richard Donner's earlier favorite.

Quentin Tarantino cited *The Sender* as his favorite horror film of 1982, on the commentary track for the DVD release of Edgar Wright's *Hot Fuzz*. The film manages to mirror, in terms of style, Samuel Fuller's *Shock Corridor*, while anticipating other horror stories set in austere asylums; *Gothika*, *Shutter Island* and John Carpenter's *The Ward*.

Despite having been largely made in England, *The Sender* strives to avoid a British feel, with many of the exterior shots filmed in Atlanta, Georgia to root the story in America (like *The*

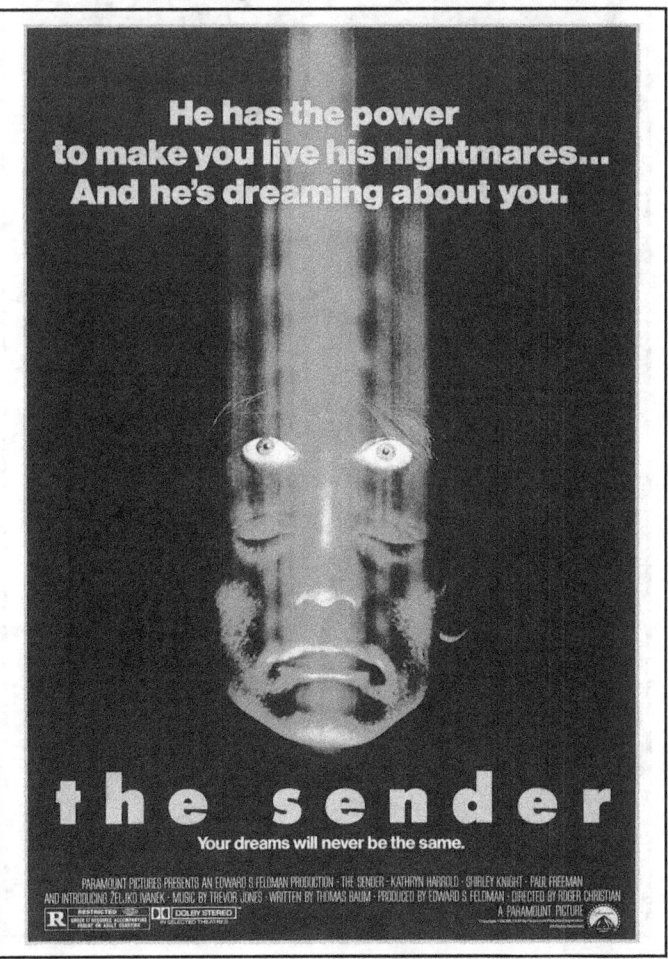

Shining, the story is based in the USA). Interiors were handled at Shepperton Studios. Director Roger Christian, who won an Academy Award for set decoration in *Star Wars: Episode IV–A New Hope*, would go on to helm the dreadful, ill-fated L. Ron Hubbard adaptation *Battlefield Earth: A Saga of the Year 3000*.
—Jason D. Brawn

XTRO

D: Harry Bromley Davenport
W: Harry Bromley Davenport
Starring: Bernice Stegers, Philip Sayer, Maryam D'Abo, Simon Nash

Anyone viewing Harry Bromley Davenport's *Xtro* for the first time today might be perplexed by the favor others show it. It's just a nonsensical if not outright silly little monster romp with a shrill synth score and was not alone in trying to cash in on the popularity of Ridley Scott's *Alien*. That much is true. But for a 16-year-old, as I was in the day, still used to catching classic British horror film on the television, aware that its golden era had come to an end in 1976 with Hammer's last satanic orgy of death and nakedness, and with a yearning for an industry revival, each new blatant Anglo terror flick was a major new hope. The 1980s was on a fantastic gore and monster roll with the steady advancement of special make-up effects technology, but it was primarily Hollywood product, and in the UK the money was not arriving as it had once before.

Xtro came out of the blue, causing some disbelief and incurring the inexplicable wrath of reviewers. Video renting gore-hounds, enjoying the newfound freedom of controlling their viewing habits, had developed a taste for the ludicrous by now and were largely accepting of the phantasmagorical carnivals suddenly available on magnetic tape. Deranged American fantasy horrors were 10-a-penny, *Fear No Evil* (1981), *Evilspeak* (1982), *The Evil* (1978), *Beyond Evil* (1980), *Mausoleum* (1983) and their ilk, but the UK had yet to place anything in theaters quite so disarmingly daft.

The most important consequence of *Xtro* is that though we may have seen oddball horror in abundance during that period, we were unaware that we were awaiting a peculiarly British version of it. *Xtro* offered a weird visionary landscape far removed from the reactionary trad fans' desires. It promised a potential new identity for British horror—but in that great British ironic tradition *Xtro* could not have existed without an infusion of American cash. Robert Shaye's New Line was moving over into film production and at the same time that it was exploring this madcap British project, it was making a comparative study in outlandish horror on the other side of the Atlantic with Jack Sholder's *Alone in the Dark*.

Further stimulation is provided by the film's very name; Hammer had incorporated the "X" certificate by proxy in the titles of its early sci-fi horror offerings *The Quatermass Xperiment* (1956) and *X–The Unknown* (1957), and by 1982 with the familiar certificate soon to depart, the X in *Xtro* paid tribute to past glories while at the same time projecting the idea of a new start in extremis for the British horror film.

Xtro was not the first British film with a barmy exploitative streak, nor was it our first *Alien* cash-in; Norman J. Warren's *Inseminoid* takes that dubious title. But it was *Xtro* that offered us those grotesque horrors foregrounded to a London landscape and the British countryside. From the outset there is an abandonment of logic; not strictly science fiction, then, but so very bizarre that it almost defies the category, possibly creating its own genre, "circus sci-fi," a berserk arena where anything can happen. The first scene sums up this crazily carefree attitude as Sam (Philip Sayer) and his son (Simon Nash) play with their dog in the oh-so-green grounds of the country home, the father casting the mutt's stick high into the sky where it crashes against something inexplicable, sparking an electric explosion turning the sky to windswept night. An alien abducts dad ...

Three years later, mom (Bernice Stegers) has moved on, with a concessionary, token American lover, photographer Joe (Danny Brainin). And the lethal extra-terrestrial is back! The first sighting of the alien banjaxes the eye and brain, easy though it is to figure out the methods used. The mime artist positions himself on his hands and feet with his back arched, abdomen in the air, while the film is reversed. The impression is that of the deformed four-legged creature caught in car headlights, dodging backwards out of the road. The alien rapes a woman seemingly squatting in the country house and in an early jaw-dropper of a sequence, the being's flesh tears open to propel a sort of webbed sex organ from the rip, attaching to the victim's mouth. Within a breakneck period of time, she gives birth to an alien reproduc-

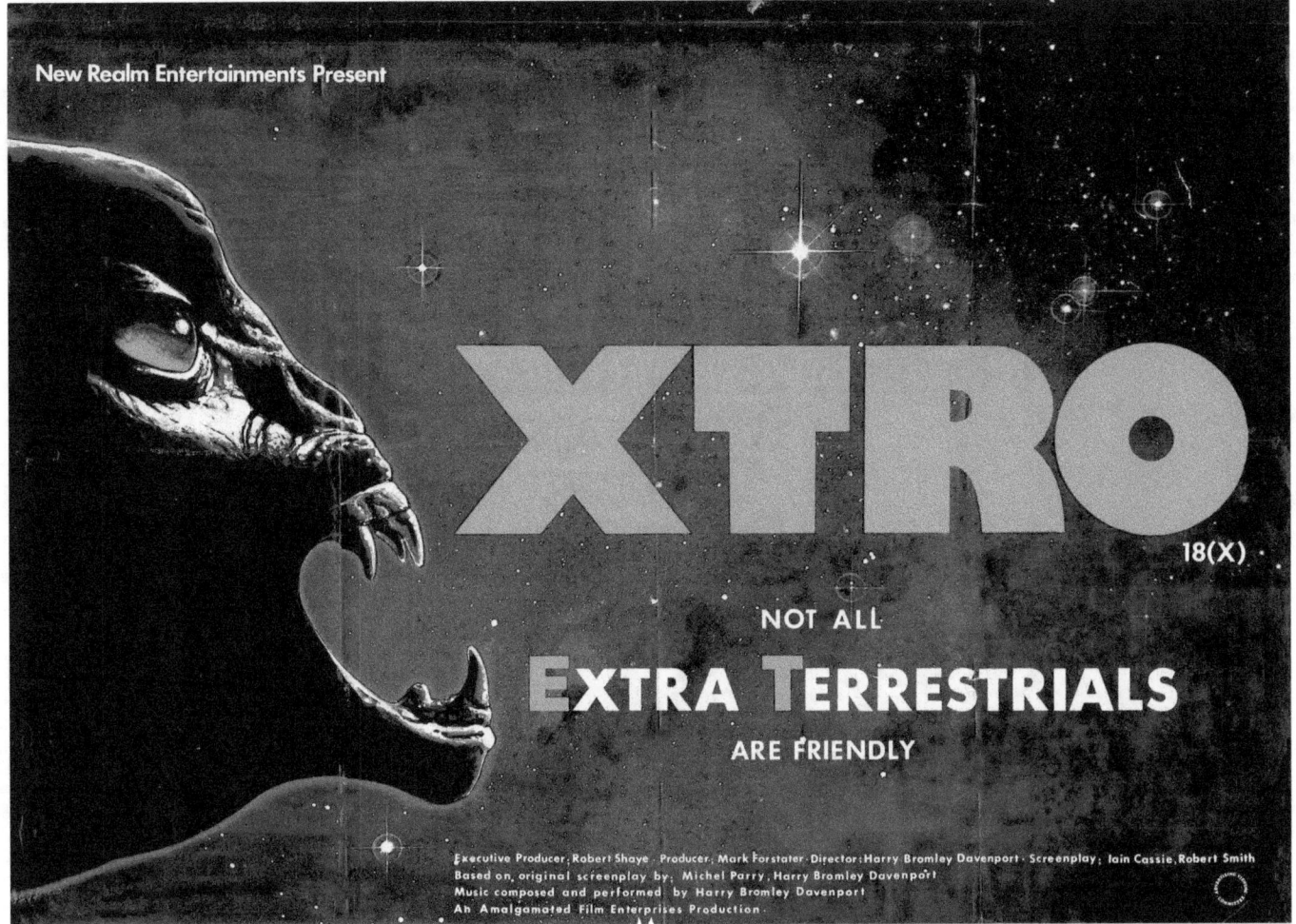

tion of Sam! He reasserts his place in the household, creating conflict, and having a nastily destructive effect on those in the vicinity. *Xtro*'s delirium continues. Before the credits roll, the son will be infected by the father, the boy will turn a wooden toy into a murderous midget clown accomplice (Peter Mandell), the caretaker will have his throat slit by a deadly illuminated yo-yo, the au-pair (Maryam D'Abo) will become an egg-popping chrysalis, with her boyfriend (David Cardy) chased by a toy tank firing real explosive ammo. The boy's newfound ability to magic up the bizarre is a theft from the *Twilight Zone* story "It's a Good Life," itself simultaneously being re-filmed for *Twilight Zone: The Movie* in more prosperous climes.

The iconic highlight comes when the unpleasant biddy on the floor below, Miss Goodman (Anna Wing, also seen in the Bromley Davenport-penned *The Haunting of Julia*) is slain for her sins by the youngster's Action Man—by now supersized into a six-foot killer. The facial/costume details of the popular Palitoy doll are re-created to perfection, lending an extra layer of shudders here prompted by nostalgic recollection among an audience all too familiar with this ubiquitous military plaything. The outsize toy soldier shears the door-chain with a big pair of cutters, mini-mines the lock, robotically stalks his way to the living room, and, omniscient regarding the old dear's hiding place, lunges in for a final bloody bayonetting through the chintz sofa. The film as a whole is often faulty and unconvincing, but no kid came away from this sequence without declaring how cool it was, and the wonder it generates ripples backwards and forwards through the movie in a confirmation of the project's spirit and imagination.

Running only 83 minutes it is a pop horror tornado, and dare we suggest, a companion to the kick-about monster marathons of Don *Nightbeast* Dohler. The fresh cast included Maryam D'Abo in her debut, the contribution of counter-culture performance artists Tik and Tok is strikingly memorable, and the crew was made up of talent that had been bopping around the studios for some time giving us every reason to anticipate a new arc of British horror film production. It was Davenport's second feature and his first to garner notable column space (they exploited, as did the later *The Company of Wolves*, the fact that its underage star was prohibited from attending the premiere; perfectly logical of course, but don't the tabloids love to report that angle as if horror movies should only hire midgets as children in their films!). Robin Grantham and Tom Harris were kept busy with the make-up and mechanical effects respectively, and Grantham would probably have been glad to put this nonsense behind him a year or two later when he was employed on matching make-up on Nicol Williamson to the Claymation effects in *Return to Oz*. Robert Shaye provided the *Xtro* bankroll but the day-to-day main producer chores went to Mark Forstater, who preferred classier fare and would follow this with the low key supernatural thriller *The Cold Room* (1984).

As for the director, his planned follow-up project, the equally demented *Near Death Experience*, went belly-up before it could begin, robbing us of the only British horror film with boxing kangaroos. Bromley Davenport took his ass and talents to America, for *Xtro* sequels and more. Our loss!
—Paul Higson

1983

**Bloodbath at the House of Death
The Hunger
The Keep
Screamtime
Slayground**

BLOODBATH AT THE HOUSE OF DEATH

D: Ray Cameron
W: Ray Cameron and Barry Cryer
Filmed in 1983, released in 1984
Starring: Kenny Everett, Vincent Price, Pamela Stephenson, Gareth Hunt, Sheila Steafel

A horror film spoof in the style of *Airplane!* seemed a natural choice for Kenny Everett, having already dabbled in cinema waters via the big-screen appearance of his TV animated star-hopping space jockey in *Kremmen: The Movie*.

It starts off fairly strongly, with a slasher movie parody every bit as brutal and menacing as you'd have seen in any film at the time. Settling down to a cozier comic tone, the early gags amuse, though not in any sustainable sense. The locals in a pub go silent when Kenny mentions the (haunted) manor, but they're actually looking at his open flies. A scene that prefigures *Shaun of the Dead* has Kenny making a phone call, yet failing to notice the bloody handprint almost right in front of him despite even resting his own hand on it. There's also a nice running joke about exposition ("Have you read all the reports?" "Yes," "Well, if you had ...")

The makers assembled an eclectic cast of the great, the good, and jobbing sitcom actors for this film—Vincent Price, Pamela Stephenson, Graham Stark, David Lodge, John Fortune, Don Warrington, Sheila Steafel, Gareth Hunt, Cleo Rocos and Barry Cryer. It's as if somebody flicked through *Spotlight* to check who was free on Tuesday. Performances are acceptable. Kenny is Kenny: loud, hammy, camp and over-the-top. He drags you along using tried and tested schtick, exaggerated limp and occasional comedy German accent. Pamela Stephenson is rather good though the script does her few favors, resorting to the "glasses on, hair tied in a bun" stereotype of repressed glamour. To pep up one brief and dialogue-heavy section where Everett addresses his scientific team, she does some neat scene stealing looking for dust on surfaces. The others are wasted—the paranormal investigators are interchangeable and none of them is given much chance to shine. One drinks, another has a *Carrie* complex and two are gay but once the obvious gags have rolled out, that's it

Price as the Sinister Man, and Stark and Lodge giving sturdy support as his disciples, have minimal screen time. It's a shame as Price displays a talent for full-blown comedy. After grandiosely announcing, "Tonight is the night of blood!" he sweeps back his arms and gives a camp "oh!" when he cuts one of his hands on an axe.

There are many easy to spot, lazy references to horror's greatest hits—with *An American Werewolf in London, The Abominable Dr. Phibes, Carrie, Jaws, The Entity, The Shining, Alien, Poltergeist* and *The Amityville Horror* definitely given the overt nod, though hard-

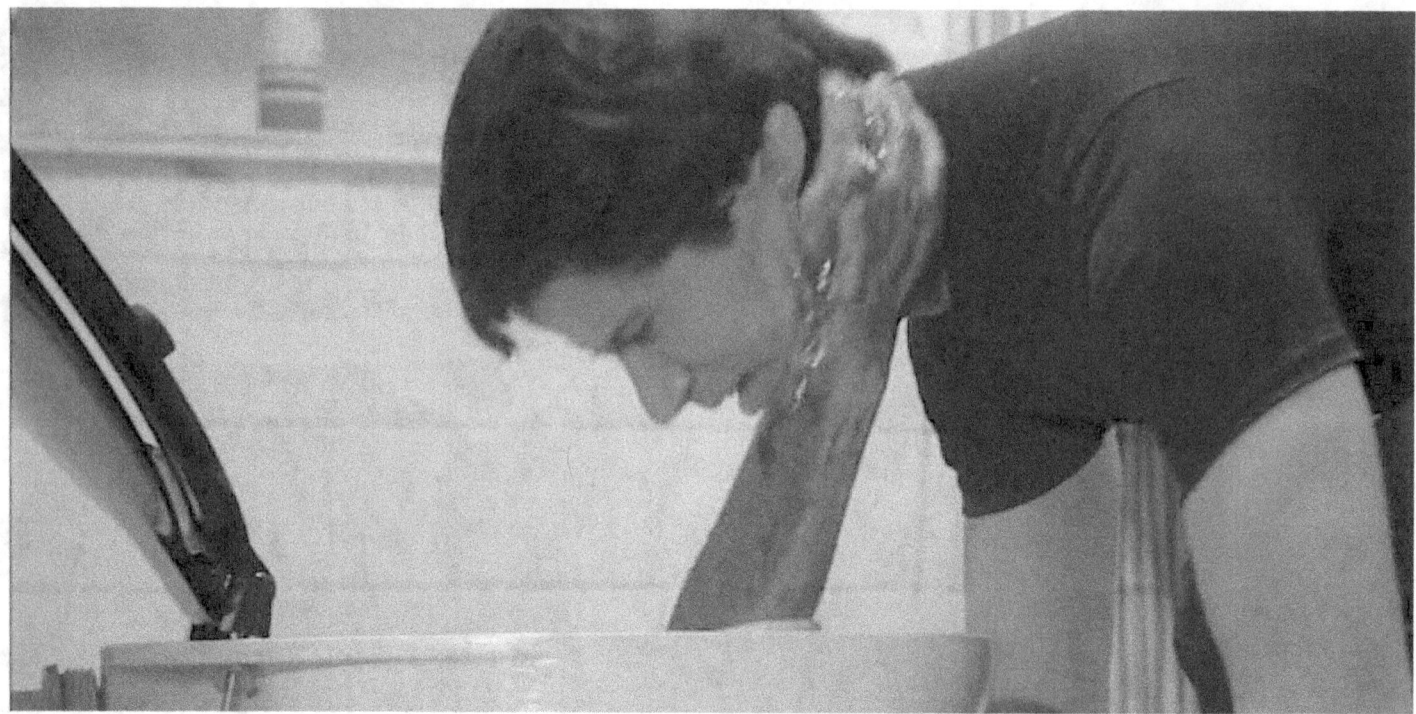
John Stephen Hill finds something strange floating in the toilet in *Bloodbath at the House of Death*.

ened buffs will likely spot (unintentional?) digs at *City of the Dead*, *The Devil's Men*, *Invasion of the Body Snatchers* and *Shivers* too.

The actors coyly swearing sound like children who've just found out saying "'shit!" can really piss off their parents. The smattering of gore is handled in the Everett style, notably a flashback to his character's days as a doctor when he becomes so enraged at his team laughing at him that he throws the patient's entrails at them. The writing is on much the same level as Everett's TV show:

Stephenson: "Look out! ... a bat!" (something falls on Everett)
Everett: "A cricket bat?" (secret door opens) "This must be an opening bat!"
Stephenson: "Let's hope it doesn't lead to a sticky wicket."

There are plenty of other fossilized old jokes, even "I suppose a fork's out of the question?" and a desperate line about burning faggots (cue fey background voice: "I don't like the sound of that!"), and star turn Price is given a rather undignified final bow in British horror ("You piss off!" & "Oh shit, my hand!") but he professionally gives it his all. The script never quite leaves the *Airplane!* runway but at least does taxi for a fair while without actually taking off.
—Gerald Lea

• • •

Like so many early 1980s horror spoofs—'twas the era of *Student Bodies*, *Wacko*, *Hysterical*, and *Pandemonium*, folks—this big-screen vehicle for an engaging Kenny Everett has a barrage of hit-and-mostly-miss gags while aiming for too many targets to guarantee any real parody bull's-eyes. Canadian co-writer/director Ray Cameron, a regular writer for Everett on his TV show (and father of inexplicable stand-up phenomenon Michael McIntyre) stages too many jokes that simply fizzle, like a bunch of Satan worshippers lapsing into a verse of "Daisy, Daisy" during a standard Satanic chant. The really limp *E.T.* joke that ends the movie makes you wonder how fellow scripter Barry Cryer (cameoing as a detective) dared show his face onscreen. At least Everett, channeling Peter Sellers as a mad German surgeon-turned-paranormal-researcher with a false leg, is a winning attention-grabbing screen presence.

Its enduring legacy is to be remembered as the movie in which Vincent Price says the line "Grab the faggots!" Alongside the gay jokes, fart jokes and even a *Star Wars* skit involving a lightsabre decapitation, the film's core is a parody of the parapsychologists-in-a-haunted-house sub-genre ruled by *The Haunting*, *The Legend of Hell House*, *The Stone Tape* and the then-recent *Poltergeist*. It opens like a slasher pastiche, demonstrating either how long the movie took to make it to the screen or how tardy Cryer and Cameron were in gauging what was then topical to lampoon in the movie world. (There's also a four-years-too-late *Alien* spoof in which Everett's chestburster-like dinner table spasms are revealed as chronic indigestion.)

A subjective camera roams around a girls' summer camp in the 1975 prologue, pinpointing "axe in the bonce" killings and screaming women in their underwear at the ominous "Headstone Manor" as the place comes under attack from robed figures. Everett and Pamela Stephenson lead the team of paranormal experts studying the house in the present day, along with ex-New Avenger and coffee-bean hawker Gareth Hunt, and pneumatic Everett sidekick Cleo Rocos. Some of the film's best moments occur during the early pub scenes in which locals warn, "Stay away from the house of death" and "Stay on the road, keep out of the woods," while a debate about previous victims winds up as a mock *12 Days of Christmas* sing-a-long. Meanwhile, as an "arch disciple of Lucifer," Price (following up the jokey *House of the Long Shadows* a year earlier) gamely mocks his now-passé camp, melodramatic genre persona. So, it's too bad Cryer couldn't feed him better lines than, "*You* piss off!"

Many of the more elaborate visual gags suffer from poor timing and staging, but Everett's gory surgical flashback and a literal, neck-biting "mole" score mild chuckles and there is a funny *Carrie*-inspired, kitchen-set telekinetic beheading of a loopy maternal figure. Stephenson suffers/enjoys a ghostly sexual encounter in her bed (in homage to Pamela Franklin in *The Legend of Hell House* and, perhaps, Barbara Hershey in *The Entity*), while several skits feel like Mel Brooks got there first, especially an old-hat bit in which frenzied strings on the soundtrack lead to the reveal of Everett frantically playing a cello (though, to be fair, *The Simpsons* was still trotting out identical fare a decade later and, to paraphrase Universal Pictures, a good gag is worth repeating.)

Not without interest and occasionally raising a smile, this has too much of the type of low, one-note humor that dominated lesser 1980s horror comedy—yep, you do get a guy pulled head first down a bloody toilet—and too little of the witty, affectionate pastiche found in clever *straight* 1980s horror flicks like *An American Werewolf in London*. Kenny and Vincent deserved far better and as for Gareth Hunt, er ...
—Steven West

(In his 2010 autobiography *Life & Laughing: My Story*, Michael McIntyre claims to have provided the voice of E.T. in this movie—ed.)

THE HUNGER

D: Tony Scott
W: Ivan Davis, Michael Thomas
Starring: Catherine Deneuve, Susan Sarandon, David Bowie

Spotlights pierce the dark of a pulsing nightclub, Bauhaus [British rock band] growl "Bela Lugosi's Dead" from behind a mesh screen. Up on a gantry, Miriam and John Blaylock (Catherine Deneuve and David Bowie) gaze with predatory eyes at the young dancing flesh below, signaling to a couple in the gloom. It isn't sex they are after, but blood to be precise ... welcome to the world of contemporary New York vampires, circa early 1980s ...

Late director Tony Scott indicated a penchant for the macabre early on with his British Film Institute-backed *Loving Memory* (1970), and his debut major studio feature *The Hunger* must hold some claim to being among the most visually beautiful of all vampire movies, though you won't find the "V" word mentioned anywhere here. Its chief concerns are with looks, (im)mortality and the disease progeria, which speeds up the body clock of anyone afflicted. Dr. Sarah Roberts (Susan Sarandon) works at a swish research clinic, and thanks to John Blaylock's rapid aging, the centuries catching up with him (cue a great scene where he waits in a doctor's lounge for an appointment and is years older before he leaves!), it won't be long before Miriam will need another partner, psychically calling out to the beautiful Sarah to provide the company she eternally aches for.

I've always had more than a soft spot for this dazzling, erotic slice of stylized horror filmmaking (indeed one review at the time memorably said that every single frame of this movie could be blown up and hung in an art gallery), but what strikes me more on repeated viewings is the sense of permeating melancholy, from the attic full of coffins that Miriam tenderly cares for—each casket containing the still living/dead, rotting remains of former lovers, either male or female—and as we watch John crumbling in the same way and being ensconced among the partners and the fluttering doves, a part of us almost wishes for Miriam to ensnare Sarah. Deneuve has never looked more elegant or been more hypnotic onscreen, Bowie is ideally cast and well served by Dick Smith's fabulous old-age makeup, Sarandon is smart and alluring, and other cast members acquit themselves well (watch out for a tiny cameo from Willem Dafoe in one of his first screen parts), but it is the sheer jaw-dropping beauty of the images captured by D.O.P. Stephen Goldblatt that sears the eyes—the gorgeous apartment house, the radiant shafts of light, the billowing curtains, sunshine or pouring rain, and the sense of a decadent time and place captured like few other genre efforts before or since. Witty too, with the aforementioned doctor's lounge scene, or the moment the vampiric seduction of Sarandon is ended with a match-cut from blood dripping down her arm to a raw steak being sliced on a plate.

Yes, homages abound to Harry Kumel's *Daughters of Darkness* (in one sequence Deneuve even has her hair done exactly the same way as Delphine Seyrig's vampire goddess from that earlier exercise in Gothic chic) and yes, many could argue that style outweighs substance, but sometimes a lesson in filmmaking technique can go a long way ... sequences appear cut like a Nicolas Roeg movie, flashbacks burst and occasionally gore erupts across the gorgeous palate, and this reviewer remains entranced with each viewing. For my money (and I await the brickbats), it's Tony Scott's best film, and one of horror cinema's most distinctive and influential entries in the overloaded vampire genre.
—Michael Wesley

. . .

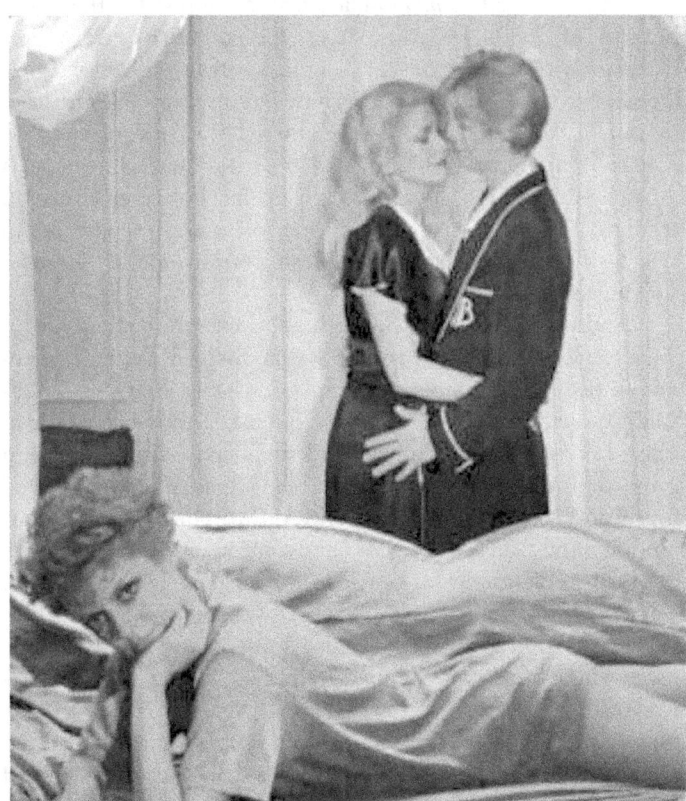

Oh Janet! Susan Sarandon, Catherine Deveuve and David Bowie in *The Hunger*

A love story not necessarily for the ages, but about them ... a film of visual sensations ... reeks with chic
—Vincent Canby, *The New York Times*
An agonizingly bad vampire film.
—Roger Ebert, *Chicago Sun-Times*

When her latest lover John (David Bowie) succumbs to age and disease, elegant vampire Miriam (Catherine Deneuve) replaces him with Dr. Sarah Roberts (Susan Sarandon).

The Hunger is *Carmilla* in black leather, suffused in the glossy imagery of 1980s TV ads. Witness the potential victim rollerskating round a ghetto blaster in a misty subway; the endless billowing curtains and flocks of white birds; the cigarettes smoked by rain-slicked windows and the gauzy tenderness of the love scenes. With the whole film seeped in a smoky haze, one expects a catchy advertising slogan to flash up on the screen every 30 seconds. This is not surprising since director Tony Scott came to this, his first commercial movie, fresh from the world of television advertising.

And yet this stylistic approach also works in the film's favor. The scenes of Miriam's rotting lovers rising from their boxes are powerful (those fluttering drapes are, here, used to good effect.) Also effective is the opening sequence: as Bauhaus perform "Bela Lugosi's Dead" in a New York nightclub, Miriam and John prowl the dancefloor in search of fresh victims. This marriage of music and montage carries a dangerous thrill and grabs the attention immediately. Elsewhere, the soundtrack makes good use of classical piano pieces, evoking the loneliness of living death: *The Hunger*'s vampires may be sexually indulgent, but they are also restless and desolate.

Diane Arbus once defined horror as "the relationship between sex and death." This definition suits *The Hunger*, for the film is at its most horrifying (and intriguing) when presenting the effects of Miriam's cruel love. Sarah is reduced to a wasted shadow of her former brilliance (although Miriam is more exciting than the doctor's dull, human boyfriend—who considers that any outward display of emotion is something you should seek professional help for), and John ages rapidly before our eyes; a scene which plays on our own natural fears of advancing years and decay. Ultimately, however, among all those her passion destroys, the most wretched victim is revealed to be Miriam herself.

While *The Hunger* may not be a wholly satisfying experience, its lingering depiction of frailty in the face of desire certainly makes it striking and worthwhile.
—Stephen Mosley

THE KEEP

D: Michael Mann
W: Michael Mann
Starring: Scott Glenn, Jurgen Prochnow, Robert Prosky, Ian McKellen

F. Paul Wilson once said that if you wrote one page a day you would have a 365-page novel by the end of the year. He made this comment because dashing off horror novels was, at that time, a second job for him, a hobby that he got some extra pocket money for. Some cruel commentators might add that this was exactly how his books read too. It would be unfair to accuse Wilson of perpetrating that of which he in part jests. The problem with Wilson's writing seemed to stem less from sketchy nightly jottings and more out of a dense narrative. If the concept was good, as it was in *The Keep*, it was sufficient, but if weak, as was the case with *The Tomb*, then there was nothing but the suspicion that his joke about 500 words a night was indeed the case. Tellingly, *The Tomb* never made it to film and to date *The Keep* is the only F. Paul Wilson title to have transferred to the screen.

Director Michael Mann had just come off his feature film debut *Thief/Violent Streets*, his stylistic approach as yet largely unknown, but undoubtedly noted by perceptive critics and audience members. Mann's film of *The Keep* would confirm his pop sheen universe, which has continued to this day in digital noir nightmares where death is cool. Reviled on its release, it stood apart from other horrors in the day, and the passage of time makes it all the smokier a curio.

The Keep holds attention for the entire running time, for reasons right and wrong, and that is surely all one can ask. One of the most enticing elements about the production, something of a surprise at the time and easily overlooked now, was that it was a supernatural horror tale set during the Second World War, 1941 to be precise. Conversation regarding horror and science fiction/western crossover films at the time could generate significant discussion but try and buddy horror with a war theme and the flow of chat would soon run dry. More commonly, of course, the military did frequent the sci-fi movies. When monsters attack, the army are normally called in—and even when the armed forces do not become involved, sides might arise and what better *Boys Own* format than the factional action adventure. With some post-war berth given, the Nazis and collaborators eventually began to pop up in sci-fi horror films again. Professor Bernard Quatermass admitted to being on friendly terms with Wernher von Braun, and at the opposite end of the spectrum, the movie title *They Saved Hitler's Brain* says it all.

From *Flesh Feast* through *The Boys from Brazil*, fiendish Nazi experimenters tried to return Der Führer but fantastic tales of horror taking place amid an actual war remained unusual. In 1969 there was the fudged supernatural fantasy of *Castle Keep* but following that we were presented with a procession of living dead stormtroopers reanimated in *Shock Waves*, *Night of the Zombies*, *Zombies Lake* and *Oasis of the Zombies*. *The Keep* was the first modern supernatural horror film to firmly root itself in the Second World War and set the ball rolling for military frights to come. In Britain, this included *The Bunker* and *Death Watch* (the latter taking place during The Great War), and it's a trend that continues to build internationally in cinema.

The Keep opens with armored vehicles, under the command of Woermann (Jurgen Prochnow), rolling into a village on the Dinu Pass in Romania, his instructions to occupy an old keep with a foggy history. The caretakers can't explain what is so worrying about the edifice, only that they must continue to maintain it, but never stay the night; we are told that travelers who have not heeded the warnings run screaming from the building before daybreak. Embedded in the walls of the keep are 10 nickel crosses. The outer walls are built with small stones and those on the interior with larger stones, which Woermann observes is something of a back to front construction, as if not to keep an enemy out but to contain something within. The treasure hunting soldiers are warned to leave the nickel crosses in situ, but when one glows in the night, two of them identify it as silver and decide to interfere with it. Digging it out releases an ancient supernatural entity that dramatically disposes of them both.

The destruction of the soldiers is inventive and startling here and throughout, and charred bodies in an agonized rictus represent only the most ordinary results. Others become desiccated ragdolls hurtling through the air, exploding dust and bone, or flesh curling into black smoke around a skull. The influence here could have been the finale of *Raiders of the Lost Ark* in which the released power likewise takes various effects on different individuals, an observation that here ensures an unpredictability and anticipation in the outcome of each soldier's fate.

A transfer request results in the posting of a smarmy young S.S. officer, Kaempffer (Gabriel Byrne), who announces his arrival demanding that the partisan action cease or five more will die for each German officer lost. Near the latest German corpses, untranslatable writing is found, and Father Fonescu (Robert Prosky) exploits the situation to have his friend Dr. Theodore Cuza (Ian McKellen) and Cuza's daughter Eva (Alberta Watson) transferred from an internment camp to the keep. This is agreed to, despite Kaempffer's impatience and dismissal of any otherworldly threat. Kaempffer will later comment that there are only two ways out of the camp; one is helping them solve the mystery, the other through a chimney ... Dr. Cuza is old, wheelchair-bound and dying, with little expectation or interest in surviving or in deciphering the keep's conundrum, his only hope being that Eva finds a means of escape.

Meanwhile, in Greece, at the moment of the ancient evil's release, Glaeken (Scott Glenn) has awoken to his ancestral task as guardian against the monster working its way through the garrison and itching to spread its malevolence wider. It is an undemanding role for a demanding actor who liked to take up a challenge with each part, whether bushido swordplay or a mechanical rodeo ride. Glaeken barely registers as human, more robotic and emotionally stiff, closer to Ash in *Alien*, and when he bleeds it is green and luminescent. The film spends less time with the unappealing Glaeken than does the book—instead, it is Jurgen Prochnow that is the emotional core of the movie, the reasonable, sensible and above all humane overseer of the unveiling horror show, he behaves and responds as we might prefer to behave and respond. There are good and bad German officers and Mann has us align and identify with this one. The second most interesting figure is also a German officer, Gabriel Byrne playing a textbook nasty. As most of Byrne's scenes pit him against Prochnow this sets up an interpersonal pact that no two other characters can match.

The evil is Molasar (the reversal of its name not mentioned in the film as it is in the book), designed by comics artist Enki Bilal and constructed by Nick Maley to look like a super-pumped-up Dark Knight. Like a sneaky Mephistopheles, he makes a bargain with Dr. Cuza, curing him of his scleroderma and returning him to youthful vitality. Molasar claims to be appalled at the terror visited upon the Jews and promises to take this up with Hitler himself. But first in order to leave the keep a talisman must be found and removed from the premises, and a deal is struck with Dr. Cuza ...

Tangerine Dream provides the electronic soundtrack, *de rigueur* for them, though it gives way to choral harmonics. Bizarrely, the film closes borrowing the theme from *The Snowman*, possibly in the expectation that the accompanying animation might never travel and would be forgotten, not become the Christmas fixture that it has done. The cinematographic range is both adventurously close and distant when it needs to be. It should be

noted that Alex Thomson was the main photographer but that even the 2nd Unit cinematographer was the highly experienced veteran Arthur Lavis, B.S.C. The movie was shot at Shepperton Studios and on location in Blaenau Ffestiniog, Wales. Special visual effects, begun by Wally Veevers who died during production, were possibly imagined along the lines of a Douglas Trumbull style spectacle, a lá the then recent *Star Trek: The Motion Picture* or *Brainstorm*. Instead they come closer to resembling a laser light show cutting through a Hot Gossip dance routine. But the rolling shining clouds, glitter storms and superimposed effects traversing deep chasms display an admirable effort from the effects team and add to the overall charm.

—Paul Higson

SCREAMTIME

D: Stanley Long (as "Al Beresford")
W: Michael Armstrong
Starring: Robin Bailey, Ian Saynor, Yvonne Nicholson, David Van Day, Dora Bryan, Jean Anderson

By 1983 Stanley Long had a reputation for naughty movies. He'd been at the heart of British exploitation cinema, including work as a cameraman on some classic shockers, but when it came to producing and directing horror, it did not appeal to him as directly as nudity and broad humor. But having set up the Alpha Film Distribution Company in 1975 he found over the following six years that there was enormous success to be had with bloody new modern terror flicks. Among the films that performed particularly well for him were David Cronenberg's *Shivers*, *Rabid* and *The Brood*, and George Romero's *Night of the Living Dead* and *Dawn of the Dead*. So, following a three-year respite from directing, he was quietly persuaded to make a short horror film, *Dreamhouse* (1981), the popular reception to which led to two more, *That's the Way to Do It* (1982) and *Do You Believe in Fairies?* (1982). As his name was synonymous with the sex film it was decided that he would adopt the pseudonym "Al Beresford" for the three shorts, which did the rounds in cinemas as supporting fodder to a main feature.

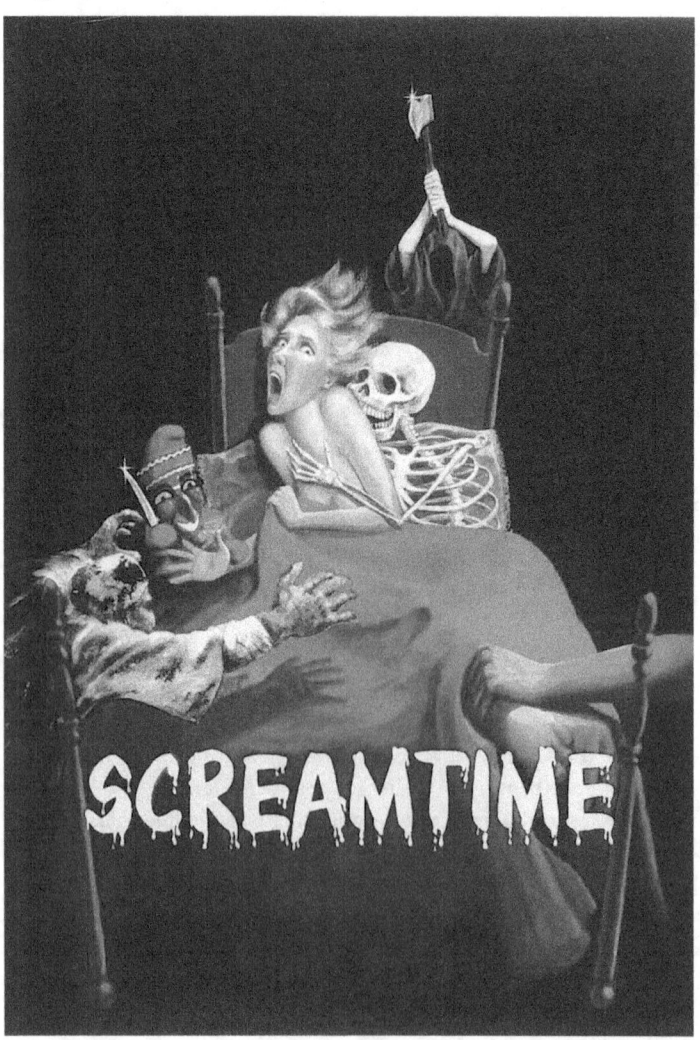

It was suggested that the three shorts be placed together as an anthology movie, but it would require a newly filmed linking device. For this Long flew to America to shoot a quick sequence depicting two thugs stealing three cassettes from the counter of a video-store. In the flat of a girlfriend, for whom we are just in time to ogle coming out of the shower, they hit the sofa to watch the trilogy of British horrors. The original shorts ran 35 minutes (*Dreamhouse* and *Do You Believe in Fairies?*) and 34 minutes (*That's the Way to Do It*) respectively and in order to comfortably fit the 87-minute feature running time, including the new wraparound sequence, each had to lose some of the original content.

The component films, each scripted by Michael Armstrong, vary in effect. *Dreamhouse* takes up the middle section and became notorious as a short and, in this compendium, as a skilfully mounted haunted house story with a shocking conclusion. Ian Saynor and Yvonne Nicholson are the couple who have been gifted one of the father-in-law's properties, only for the wife to begin experiencing frightening visions. What starts innocuously with a child on a tricycle riding in circles on the lawn builds terrifyingly, through grimmer apparitions of a knife-wielding maniac and his family of victims; none are spared. The twist in the tale is that the massacre witnessed is not a violent echo of the past but a premonition. It comes full circle when the wife is hospitalized from a nervous breakdown, and the husband, wishing the new owners of the house well in their new home, gets into his car and becomes the first victim of the predicted psychopath. Completely unexpected on first viewing, and still shocking on subsequent screenings, the murderer grabs him as he starts the engine and, all caught in a single shot, his throat is slit, a startlingly realistic injury, the husband flooring the pedal and the car doing the screaming for him.

Armstrong had always a penchant for honest brutalism and harsh deaths as seen in his debut *The Haunted House of Horror*, which he also directed (Veronica Doran, who appeared in that film, makes an appearance in *Dreamhouse* too, as the medium brought in to identify the spirits), and even more notoriously with *Mark of the Devil* and *The Black Panther*. The latter had daringly explored the actuality of the recent real-life abduction and murder of Lesley Whittle by Donald Neilson. *Dreamhouse* would get a surprising new lease of life as an unannounced remake in feature-length form in the 2009 film *Psychosis*. The feature film adaptation is an intriguing misfire, primarily because of its history as a script, but also proving that the shorter format was better for this highly effective horror tale.

Opening duty goes to *That's the Way to Do It*, a story that draws on the traditional British seaside puppet show in which a vicious hook-nosed Mr. Punch bludgeons to death a cast of wife, baby, doctor, policeman, hangman and others. The irony of a wife-beater and child murderer as a popular entertainment figure had not been overlooked in other media, Mr. Punch having been the subject of a Harrison Birtwistle opera and a song by cult pop band XTC. In that song, "Punch and Judy," Andy Partridge sang "who do we know, dear, who acts like that?" at a time when spousal violence was a newspaper headline and a rising concern, an issue no longer to be brushed under the carpet. Robin Bailey (having concluded a highly successful stint on television as Uncle Mort in the bitter sitcom *I Didn't Know You Cared*) plays the Punch and Judy man whose wife (Ann Lynn) threatens to leave for Canada. The stepson is played by Jonathan Morris (here, retrospectively seen cast against type, best known as the milksop son in another sitcom, *Bread*) giving a terrifically mean-spirited, bastard Royale of a performance taunting Bailey about the destruction of his "dolls" and then acting on it by setting fire to the tent during a performance as disturbed children look on.

Though Long would refer to the film as a story in which the puppets come to life, it is clearly the tale of an artiste who suffers a mental breakdown and adopts a role, his subsequent actions married with the story of Mr. Punch. The short form cannot make space for all of Mr. Punch's victims, but the crocodile is cleverly substituted at the end of the story by a garbage truck into which he falls and is mangled. The language of Mr. Punch is cleverly incorporated throughout, and at one point the puppet sings the familiar refrain "Go to sleep my baby," commonly associated with the show, as it slides down the stair bannister one more time to deliver savage killer blows to a visiting doctor. Renowned Punch puppeteer John Styles delivers Mr. Punch's lines via swazzle (the swazzle is the device used to create the very particular rasping squawk of the character.)

Like the following episode, *That's the Way to Do It* is moodily shot. Interiors are bordered by darkness and imposing shadows fall across the action, though there is always enough light to strategically focus our attention on the violence. It is flawed by some over-egged villainy from Morris, though this is a fault of the director rather than the actor, as some of the players here can successfully achieve the severity required, but those that need help are unlikely to get it from Long, who preferred the comic and the camp. The absurdity spreads to details like the dubiously random act of setting the Punch and Judy tent on fire with a road-works lamp, but in all it is a largely satisfying Grand Guignol episode.

Unfortunately, the connecting device and the final story ruin what was well on the way to becoming a decent portmanteau package. *Do You Believe in Fairies?* is a joke and an insult to the other two stories. David Van Day, former pin-up idol with the pop duo Dollar, makes his attempt at an acting break as the motorcycle competition rider who needs some quick money for repairs, and accepts a job as a maintenance man working for two old maids (Dora Bryan and Jean Anderson). The old dears spout on about the how the garden will require little attention as the fairies and gnomes take care of all that.

They also inform him of the history of the house and the murderous ladyship that resided there, who hid the secret of her lovers from her husband with the help of the fairies, who would bury them in the garden. The portraits indicate the 17th century but the silly story is centered round what appears to be a detached suburban house. The ladies don't believe in banks and pay in cash so Van Day, his brother and a friend decide to cut to the chase and burgle the house for a quick win. This activates the fairies, who toy with the intruders using psychokinetic tomfoolery that is so dim-witted that it would offend The Chuckle Brothers.

Plaster garden gnomes gang up on them, then a midget in a gnome costume attacks one, the zombies of her ladyship's previous lovers rise and the cute ladyship herself (future soap/sitcom beauty Kim Thomson) exits the oil painting and kills Van Day. It's too ludicrous a variation on the EC Comics revenge

German VHS cover

fable template, and is too lightweight, hardly suitable as the concluding episode in a trilogy of tales of escalating horror. But then it would have harmed the film terribly no matter where it was placed in this anthology. The linking piece is made up of a measly four minutes of footage, but has an equally damaging presence, closing with the zombies and Mr. Punch escaping the television set to assail the robbers in New York. It's a slapdash last half hour, like receiving a sickening dessert and unexpectedly hefty bill following two highly edible courses.
—Paul Higson

• • •

There really aren't enough garden gnomes in horror films. British, or otherwise. A cameo in *Funny Man*, and that's about it. A pity. Because, as we shall see, everything is better with gnomes.

When veteran *schlockmeisters* Michael Armstrong and Stanley Long made a trio of support features for UK cinematic release, they probably weren't expecting them to end up cobbled hastily together with dire American-shot linking footage and re-released as an anthology film, presumably in the hopes of profiting from fond memories of Amicus and their buddies. The said footage comes complete with a final twist so crappily-executed as to make even the ending of *Tales That Witness Madness* pack the

David Van Day meets a Victorian ghost (Kim Thomson) and deadly garden gnomes in *Screamtime*.

punch of *Unbreakable* and can be safely discarded. Basically, three New Yorkers steal some videos, watch them, take time out for sex in the shower, and ultimately die horribly. You know the deal.

No, the three shorts—*That's the Way to Do It*, *Dreamhouse* and *Do You Believe in Fairies?*—are what really matter here. Cheap and cheerful as all three are, they show those damn Yankees how horror films should be done. Oh yes.

The first two stories can be dealt with quickly. They're both good stuff, dealing respectively with small-town psychosis and

dangerous precognitive dreams, but they lack gnomes completely, although Ken Russell would probably have given his right testicle for that shot of a Punch & Judy booth in flames. No, what we really need to focus on is the last tale, all too often and wrongly dismissed as that bane of horror anthologies, "the rubbish one."

The three tales all have that winningly seediness of 1970s British exploitation cinema, but here's where we get our biggest 1980s icon to drag the tale kicking and screaming into a world of Gary Numan, Adam Ant and Rubik's Cubes. Yes, ladies and gentlemen—David Van Day, that bloke out of Dollar. Here, though, he is not nice. Here, he's a slimy wide-boy attempting to steal a shedload of cash from two old dears who believe in fairies and gnomes at the bottom of their garden. They've been reading too many Rupert annuals, presumably. Poor things.

Except ... they're right. And so, it is that, in a prolonged and suspenseful sequence, our Dave breaks into their eerily half-lit house in the middle of the night, grabs the dosh, and seems all set to get clean away. But ... what is that behind him?

In a genuine *tour de force* of creepy editing, we switch back and forth between Dave doing dastardly deeds.... and an ever-growing mob of garden gnomes observing him from behind his back. The urge to yell "behind you!," panto-like, swells as more and more of them join the ranks. Silent. Still. Staring. Accusing. What will happen next?

Alas, it turns out that stop-motion was out of the budget's reach. I'd give a lot to see a special edition of this one, with animated garden ornaments, ideally ha-ha-ha'ing and tee-hee-hee'ing, scaring the willies out of us as they approach the unsuspecting Dave. Instead, we get a sudden Attack of The Gnome Costume-Wearing Stunt Midget.

It's anti-climactic, compared to what could have been, but applause is due to Armstrong and Long for tapping into a rich vein of very British folklore. We're very fond of our tales of the faerie folk, we know that crossing them doesn't usually turn out well, and this story is a lovely, off-beat example proving the point. *Do You Believe in Fairies?*, far from being a weak link and a letdown, is—in fact—the strongest and most effective tale of the film.

And it's all down to the gnomes. Let that be a lesson to horror creators everywhere.
—Ken Shinn

SLAYGROUND

D: Terry Bedford
W: Trevor Preston
Starring: Peter Coyote, Mel Smith, Billie Whitelaw

Slayground is one of those rare things, a genre hybrid that manages to work both as a hard as nails crime drama and as a borderline horror movie. Based on the novel by Donald Westlake, one of America's finest 20th century crime writers, *Slayground* is, along with John Boorman's *Point Blank* (1967—based on Westlake's novel *The Hunter*), the best movie adaptation of his work. Its success is founded on three terrific central performances, a strong adaptation by veteran TV writer Trevor Preston, and effortless helming from Terry Bedford, his one and only theatrical director credit. His deft handling of the comic, drama and suspense elements make one wish that he'd enjoyed a longer film career and not drifted back into TV after the disappointing box-office performance of this movie.

Professional thief Stone (Peter Coyote), along with his crew, knock off an armored car in upstate New York. While making their getaway, they force another vehicle off the road, resulting in the death of the daughter of a local hoodlum. When the other members of Stone's crew turn up dead, Stone realizes that he's the last name on a short list of targets of The Shadowman (Philip Sayers), a polite but seemingly supernaturally effective hitman hired by the father of the dead girl to avenge her death. Stone hot-foots it to England to lie low in the company of Terry Abbatt (Mel Smith), a London based gangster and old acquaintance of Stone who has problems of his own, not least of which is his wife's run-down amusement park, which is going down the pan and forms the subject of interest for a couple of Scottish thugs. Eventually The Shadowman catches up with Terry and Stone, and the pair hot-foot it to Blackpool for a final showdown in the dilapidated surroundings of the park, each man facing the implications of their life choices.

Despite its hard-boiled American literary roots, *Slayground* is one of a group of late '70s and early 1980s crime thrillers that represent some of the best contemporary British filmmaking of the time. Like *The Long Good Friday*, *Slayground* takes its coolly efficient criminal antagonist and faces him off with an implacable foe seemingly beyond the reach of even their own skills and resources. For *Friday*'s Harold Shand, the enemy is the IRA, for Stone it's Sayers' Shadowman, part polite tourist, part Michael Myers. *The Long Good Friday* uses the juxtaposition of tough guy up against an antagonist he can't beat to create a Shakespearian tragedy. Bedford uses it to weave a horror thread into a crime drama, and he does it effectively, using light and shadow and the dreary background of contemporary northern settings to create a weird other-worldliness typical of a well crafted horror film.

Slayground relies on three strong performances. Peter Coyote as Stone is terrific and gets more of a chance to shine than he does in previous showy cameos in *E.T.–The Extra-Terrestrial* (1982) and Walter Hill's marvelous *Southern Comfort* (1981). Mel Smith is similarly impressive as Terry. For those more familiar with his comic work, his turn as the tough but put-upon London crime boss will be something of a revelation. He and Coyote are tremendous together and the entire second half is carried broadly on their shoulders. The most compelling performance, however, belongs to Philip Sayers. An under-used actor perhaps most familiar to readers of this tome as the other-worldly visitor in Harry Bromley Davenport's *Xtro* (1982), his turn as the almost supernaturally effective hitman (credited as "Costello," but referred to as "The Shadowman") is nuanced and brilliant, eerily calm and completely without conscience; his implacable pursuit of Stone owes as much to the realm of the paranormal as it does to the shady criminal environment, and his presence gives the film an oddness that sets it aside from its contemporaries.

It is effectively directed by Bedford, a favorite cinematographer of the *Monty Python* set. His background as a cameraman is in evidence throughout what is a beautifully shot film, his direction is sparse and economical, the drama feels rooted in its tawdry environment, and the suspense is at times pretty nail-biting. If there are faults, it's perhaps only that a couple of plot

elements seem under-developed. There's also no denying the influence of *The Long Good Friday* and Mike Hodges' *Get Carter*. It might also be the hybrid nature of the production (one friend of mine calls it "John Carpenter's *Get Carter*") that alienated critics and filmgoers at the time, as well as the title, which does make it sound like a re-branding of Tobe Hooper's *The Funhouse* (1981). Either way, it was not a success at the box office and is often ignored in discussions about those great late '70s and early 1980s crime thrillers that we Brits seemed to pull off so well.

So, is *Slayground* a horror film? Not at face value, but like much contemporary neo-noir on both sides of the water, it does weave horror elements into its structure and does so rather more explicitly than, say, John Mackenzie in *The Long Good Friday* or Stephen Frears with *The Hit*. It's a good demonstration of how important horror was in terms of international box office at the time that titles like *Slayground* were comfortable to play riffs on horror themes in non-genre films in the hope of adding box-office clout. Often this isn't successful, but when it works (the Coen Brothers' *Blood Simple* is perhaps the best example, with their *No Country for Old Men* close behind), it really works. If *Slayground* falls short of this standard, it does so only because it has such a high standard to match. Taken on its own terms, it's an effective, well-crafted thriller with elements that genre enthusiasts will recognize and welcome.

—Neil Pike

1984

The Company of Wolves
Déjà Vu
Don't Open Till Christmas
Lipstick And Blood
1984
Scream For Help
Sleepwalker
Sphere-The Spores of Doom
Suffer, Little Children

THE COMPANY OF WOLVES

D: Neil Jordan
W: Angela Carter, Neil Jordan
Starring: Sarah Patterson, Angela Lansbury, Stephen Rea, David Warner, Terence Stamp

The Company of Wolves is unique among werewolf films. With art-house sensibilities and horror at its heart, it tells us tales of wolves that lurk in every guise.

Surrounded by toys and dolls, her lips stained with blood-red lipstick, Rosaleen (Sarah Patterson) dreams herself into a fantasy world where she is no longer a child. It's the kind of lush psychosexual dreamscape only Angela Carter, queen of the Gothic fairy tale, could have written, and it is lavishly depicted onscreen by director Neil Jordan. Rosaleen's conjured imagiverse sees her coming of age in a mediaeval village filled with menace both overtly sexual and overtly male. But Rosaleen is nobody's meat. Her eccentric granny (Angela Lansbury) warns her about men whose eyebrows meet, claiming that the worst wolves are hairy on the inside. We know her advice never to stray from the path will be ignored because Rosaleen makes her own fate.

I was Rosaleen's age when I first saw the film. It was my first encounter with grown-up fairy tales, and I found it exquisite, heady stuff. I lamented that there were so few real wolves in it (even the wolfiest dog can never pass for the actual beast!) but the stories sent me running to the bookstore for a copy of *The Bloody Chamber*, which I devoured. And of course, I watched the movie again. And again.

The special effects haven't dated well, but I've always loved the transformation where Stephen Rea tears off his face to free the skinless wolf beneath. It's unforgettable. There isn't much to the second tale, where the Devil (Terence Stamp) arrives in an anachronistic Rolls Royce and gives a boy a hair tonic that makes him sprout fur and become entrapped by vines. He ends up just a howling face in a mirror. Rosaleen tells her mother a story about a girl made pregnant by a nobleman. She shows up at his wedding and curses all the guests, turning them into wolves to serenade her and her baby.

Woven throughout these vignettes as a framing device is dream-Rosaleen's own story. She dispatches older sister Alice straight away, sending her through a nightmarish forest where life-sized dolls and teddy bears clutch at her. Then Alice is in her coffin, having been killed by a wolf, and the villagers are off on the hunt. Rosaleen's father (David Warner) returns with what he swears was a forepaw when he took it for a trophy, but which is now a human hand. Rosaleen is fascinated but unafraid, reaching out to touch it. Soon she is wearing the iconic red cape and heading off into the woods to see Granny, heedless of any danger from wolves or men. Along the way she meets handsome huntsman Micha Bergese. What follows is an unconventional retelling of the familiar story. After the huntsman devours Granny and reveals his true nature, Rosaleen shoots him. She takes pity on the whimpering wolf he becomes, stroking him and telling him the story of a she-wolf (Danielle Dax), who strayed from her own path. The tale apparently transforms Rosaleen as well, and when the villagers arrive to kill the beast, they find not one wolf but two. Rosaleen has made her choice and she bounds away with her mate through the forest.

The choice forces fantasy and reality to collide and the finale is rather ambiguous, with wolves crashing through the present-day Rosaleen's bedroom while she screams in terror. I've never understood her fear at the end.

Rich with erotic imagery and gorgeous production design that belies its shoestring budget, *The Company of Wolves* is an enigmatic, poetic film. George Fenton's score is dreamy and evocative, particularly in the scene where blood drips onto a white rose, staining the hungrily opening petals. Yes, some of the symbolism is a little heavy-handed, but despite its flaws, it remains one of my favorite werewolf films. There really just isn't anything else like it.
—Thana Niveau

• • •

"Never stray from the path, never eat a windfall apple, and never trust a man whose eyebrows meet in the middle."

Wise—and oh, so quotable—advice from Granny to 13-year-old Rosaleen in the story within a story, the dream within a dream, which—onion-like—make up the layers of Neil Jordan's film adaptation of Angela Carter's short fiction. We be-

gin in the present day, with Rosaleen asleep, lips a deep glossy red, and dreaming in her room. A copy of a magazine entitled *The Shattered Dream* lies on the pillow beside her. She dreams of her older sister (herself?), running through woods, pursued by a pack of wolves. But these are stylized, thickly cobwebbed woods, where she encounters giant toys that come alive, a grandfather clock with rapidly backward running hands, obscenely overgrown toadstools, and rats emerging from her dolls' house ...

Music, lighting and the superb set design all contribute towards creating this powerful evocation of nightmare, the girl running at that languid pace typical of the dream state, while the wolves inevitably close in. From then on, the film remains pretty much in Rosaleen's dream world throughout, with the occasional cutaway to the present-day girl, still dreaming on her bed—sometimes smiling, sometimes fearful. And it's a very familiar, fairytale environment. Rosaleen and her parents are there, as mediaeval villagers, and the funeral of her older sister, killed by a wolf, has just taken place. We then meet her wise old grandmother, who tells her stories in which men change into wolves, and any bastard child born feet first on Christmas Day will meet the Devil in the woods. (Cue more wise pronouncements: "A wolf may be more than he seems" and "the worst wolves are hairy on the inside.") Later, Rosaleen tells her mother a story of her own about a wolf that's simply "different," merely seeking revenge against the man who wronged her. We are treated to a sequence of stories, including Carter's own take on *Red Riding Hood*, where Rosaleen sets off for her grandmother's cottage, clad in her red shawl, and carrying her basket ...

In our symbol savvy age, few will miss the resonances of this coming-of-age fable: pubescent Rosaleen fearing yet curious about her burgeoning sexuality, unsure of whether all men are indeed beasts, or even of her own responses. It all looks stunning—the splashes of blood on white snow; Rosaleen's red lips, the scarlet of her shawl against the winter greens and browns of the forest; the blues and silvery-grays of the night scenes. And the werewolf transformations are still powerfully effective—graphic and bloody and painful, and in this nightmare context, holding up admirably well against any present-day CGI equivalent.

The cast are all excellent, from Jordan regular Stephen Rea, as one of the werewolves, and Micha Bergese (in his acting debut) as the other, to Angela Lansbury's Granny and newcomer Sarah Patterson as Rosaleen. We even get Terence Stamp turning up in a white Rolls Royce as the Devil. There have been many werewolf films both before and since, but *The Company of Wolves* stands alone, a visual feast that bears any number of repeat viewings. This is one more film that deserves to swerve any "let's do a remake" list.
—Julia Kruk

DÉJÀ VU

D: Anthony Richmond
W: Ezra D. Rappaport, Arnold Schmidt
Filmed in 1984, released in 1985
Starring: Jaclyn Smith, Nigel Terry, Shelley Winters, Claire Bloom

Kills, chills, and ballet—yikes! A quarter of a century before the award-winning *Black Swan*, here's a glossy Golan-Globus Cannon Films presentation mashing together the diverse worlds of highbrow dance and trashy torment, in a slice of Mills & Boon tu-tu terror laden with star names but carrying a plot that could have been scrawled on the back of a discarded Covent Garden program.

Ballet is a not-infrequent bedfellow of the fright flick; Argento's *Suspiria* and the aforementioned Darren Aronofsky sensation immerse themselves in the bitchy backstage environs while traveling carefully ever deeper towards the secrets and sinister whispers awaiting revelation, while our own typically ahead of the game Michael Powell and Emeric Pressburger had immediately followed up their excursion into the troubled psyche of a dancer, *The Red Shoes*, with a one-of-a-kind fantasy/horror trilogy based upon *The Tales of Hoffmann* (a favorite film of both George Romero and Martin Scorsese, who apparently both used to obsessively rent out the same 35mm print from the New York film archive).

Anthony Richmond's *Déjà Vu* is more "Wayne Sleep" than "Margot Fonteyn," however. Jaclyn Smith, in a nicely dyed coiffure job and stylish fashions, stars as Maggie, partner of successful novelist Gregory (Nigel Terry), who inspires her companion to begin work on a movie script about the tragic history of dead-at-27 darling of the *pas de deux* Brooke Ashley. Smith has a certain bland appeal, but insufficient chops to pull off the dual role of modern Maggie and '30s beauty Brooke—even so, she looks supreme alongside the hapless Terry, who gets the lion's share of

Finnish cover art for *Déjà Vu*

screen time in his own two-part across-the-decades challenge, but is seriously wooden and one-note playing both Gregory and choreographer Michael. Check out the scene where, affected physically in a vampire-style manner when Brooke's vintage locket is dropped into his palm, he has to slowly mouth the phrase "it burned meeee ...!" Embarrassing to say the least.

A guesting Shelley Winters, at least, gets the measure of the piece with an entertainingly wacky turn as the "Wodka"-guzzling would-be psychic and surviving friend of our doomed heroine, Olga Nabokov, and Claire Bloom adds icy class late on as Eleanor Harvey, Brooke's dominant and controlling mother. It's also comforting to see Marianne Stone in a brief bit, as familiar a sight in British movies of this kind as a London bus or red telephone box. If the hiring of Pino Donaggio on scoring duties was an attempt to capture the essence of the classic De Palmas to which the composer added such texture, it failed—Pino's soundtrack isn't bad at all but is used as lush background music rather than pepping up the action and ramping up the tension.

The story flits back and forward between the 1980s and the days before Brooke's fiery demise, taking in such passing elements as the *Daily Mail*, an impaled ginger tom, a gleaming and vicious-looking carving knife, and unexplained nightmare visions of a beckoning crimson phantom floating on a bed of dry ice almost as thick as that seen during the performance of featured dance production *Sigida* earlier in the proceedings. None of it makes much sense, the climax is thrown away in a confusing mêlée of pyrotechnics and exposition, and the "women's picture" aspects sit at odds with the grubbier exploitation angle. Not nearly near enough, Nureyev.
—Darrell Buxton

DON'T OPEN TILL CHRISTMAS

D: Edmund Purdom (with Derek Ford and Ray Selfe)
W: Derek Ford, Alan Birkinshaw
Starring: Edmund Purdom, Alan Lake, Belinda Mayne, Gerry Sundquist

Don't Open Till Christmas is a Frankenstein's monster of a film, stitched together from elements of the American slasher pic and homegrown sleaze, imbued with the personalities of three different directors and let loose on the video renting public in late 1985. The man who flicked the switch that brought this shambling creation to life was American producer Dick Randall. The archetypal, chubby, cigar smoking B-movie mogul, Randall spent much of the 1960s and 1970s based in Rome and Hong Kong, producing countless trashy films in the process. The Randall back catalogue boasted every conceivable kind of exploitation, from Mondo movies to softcore frolics, to Kung Fu capers starring Bruce Lee look-alikes, to rip-offs of *E.T.* and *Superman*, and even a James Bond spoof toplining a three-and-a-half-foot Filipino midget.

At some point in the early 1980s Randall relocated to London where he would find himself producing British horror films. Appropriately enough Randall chose an office on the ground floor of Hammer House in Wardour Street as his new base of operations. This first offering from The Dick Randall House of Horror looks to have been an attempt to emulate the success of the 1982 Spanish movie *Pieces*, a Randall-produced gorefest that saw former matinee idol Edmund Purdom play a chainsaw maniac. Applying an "if it ain't broke don't fix it" logic, *Don't Open Till Christmas* shares that film's co-producer Steve Minasian and its love of ultra-violent set pieces. Edmund Purdom was also back on board, having relinquished chainsaw duties in favor of roles as the new film's director and leading man. If the rest of the credits of *Don't Open Till Christmas* are anything to judge by, Dick Randall wasted no time in finding individuals in London who were on his wavelength, with many of the cast and crew being veterans of the grubbier end of British filmmaking. Randall probably thought it was a safe bet allowing his good friend Purdom access to the director's chair, especially with all these hardened exploitation vets around to support the actor and first-time director. In reality Randall couldn't have ended up with a bigger mess on his hands if he'd installed Frank Spencer to helm the movie.

Don't Open Till Christmas sees Cliff Boyd (Gerry Sundquist) and girlfriend Kate Briovski (Belinda Mayne) drawn into a series of Yuletide murders after a masked man gatecrashes their Xmas

"enough oddity, sleaziness and mirth inducing badness to tickle the fancy of any 80's slasher aficionado"
Hysteria Lives

party. Incensed at Kate's father being dressed as Santa Claus, the disguised nutter promptly spears him through the head before disappearing in the night. Inspector Harris (Purdom) and Detective Powell (Mark Jones) are the baffled policemen on the trail of this psychopath, who has made a habit of lurking around the West End bumping off anyone dressed as Santa Claus. "It was the costume that he was wearing," Harris explains to Kate—"he was the victim of another Santa murder."

By day Cliff and Kate are buskers in the London underground, an occupation that brings them into contact with Cliff's old friend Gerry (Kevin Lloyd), a sleazebucket porn photographer. Gerry invites the couple over to his studio for tea, only it's crumpet that Gerry really has in mind. He and Cliff conspire to get Kate to pose for some topless girl-on-girl photographs with Gerry's model Sharon (Pat Astley). After all what better way to overcome the recent death of a loved one than embark on a porn career? Proper girl that Kate is, she is horrified at this suggestion, and the men's proposal really goes haywire when Gerry insensitively gets out a Santa costume for the shoot. After Kate storms out, Sharon ends up donning the festive garb and goes on to make a drunken pass at Cliff outside the studio. The evening then takes a further farcical turn when the police show up, forcing Mother Christmas and Cliff to make a run for it fearing they've been mistaken for "a couple of gays." Following a quick dash around the block Sharon escapes the police only to find herself face to face with the Santa-hating masked man. Since the mystery man only holds a grudge against male Santas, he merely touches her up with a cutthroat razor to establish she is a woman, before legging it. "His eyes, they seemed to smile" Sharon tells the police, who cart her away for indecent exposure anyway.

At this point a slovenly newspaper hack called Giles (Alan Lake) pops up to drop hints that Harris has quite a few skeletons in his closet and implies that Powell would do himself a favor by solving the crimes himself. With "only three more killing days till Christmas" (as one of Giles' tabloid headlines puts it), the cops and the killer certainly have their work cut out for them. Anticipating the Christmas rush, Santa impersonators are everywhere! One lonely department store Santa even goes to a Soho peep show dressed in his work clothes. The "Experience Santa" (as he is billed in the credits) isn't about to experience anything of interest as the peep show girl (Kelly Baker, inexplicably clad in a T-shirt bearing the legend "Ti-Ti Decontracte Diffusion No Parking") only makes bad jokes and "X"-mas themed dirty talk from behind a pane of glass. "Santa" becomes more and more nervous and frustrated. Unimpressed by her terrible dancing ("what do you expect, *Flashdance*?" she complains), this Santa is clearly intent on unloading his sack. "I'd like to have you sitting on my knee" he pervs to her, just as the killer bursts into the peep show booth and butchers him in front of the girl's eyes.

With Harris cracking under pressure, Powell goes over his head to arrange a stakeout (seemingly at a circus' toilet!) that entails two undercover policemen dressing up as "decoy" Santas. All merrily goes well with the cop Santas handing out toys to children, until the killer shows up with a blade attached to his shoe and kicks one Santa in the groin. A backup Santa gets more of the same, giving some weight to Harris' earlier observation that "Christmas is no time to be a policeman." Back at Scotland Yard the girl from the peep show (named Cherry in the film and more bluntly "Experience Girl" in the end credits) refuses 24-hour police protection and heads back to her old haunt. When Cherry's first customer turns out to be he of the "smiling eyes," a chase around London streets ensues, ending with her being dragged down into a cellar. In the process Cherry gets a good look at the killer, none other than newspaper hack Giles. "I hate Christmas, I hate everything it stands for" Giles complains, in a sinister put-on voice. Flashbacks unfold to reveal that as a child Giles discovered his Santa-suited father having sex with a blonde family friend, then witnessed this naughty Santa throwing his mother down the stairs.

Unknown to Giles, Kate has in the course of her own investigation become aware of who the killer is, and his motives. Strangely she fails to share her findings with Harris (with whom she has a dinner date) or Cliff (who enviously tries to break up said date). No matter, since later that night Giles pays Kate a surprise visit and reveals that he is in fact Harris' mad brother. "I thought I'd give him a real case to work on," Giles explains before strangling and stabbing the heroine to death. Across town Harris also reaches the end of his mortal coil when he learns the hard way why the film is called *Don't Open Till Christmas*. All of which leaves Cherry alone to face off against Giles who plans to make her "the supreme sacrifice to all the evil Christmas is."

Despite Edmund Purdom's claim to be "a born director," he clearly was nothing of the sort. In fairness Purdom can't be held solely responsible for *Don't Open Till Christmas*, and the production itself seems to have been plagued by an almost supernatural run of bad luck. Originally planned as a quickie shoot around Christmas 1983, the film eventually took over a year to make. These delays forced the cast to don wintery clothes and Santa costumes throughout summer of 1984 in order to maintain the Yuletide setting. While the cast sweated it out, the script was also re-written at one point and several roles recast, with Randall's friend—*Killer's Moon* director Alan Birkinshaw—drafted in to oversee the revision. Soon after the production ended, one of the stars, Alan Lake, gave a grim postscript to the whole affair by committing suicide. By the time *Don't Open Till Christmas* was finally completed it had not only seen off one of its actors, but also had several men fill then vacate the director's chair. According to the late Ray Selfe, Edmund Purdom made a complete hash of the film and a second director had to be found in former British sex movie peddler Derek Ford. When Ford was later fired from the project, it was left to Selfe himself to finish directing *Don't Open Till Christmas*. As the editor, Selfe also had the unenviable task of making his efforts and the aborted work of his two predecessors resemble a releasable product.

Purdom's footage—by far the most amateurish of the bunch—recalls the kind of quota quickie that Butcher's Films and E.J. Fancey had been financing more than two decades earlier. The cheaper end of the 1960s British film world is especially evoked in reoccurring exterior shots of New Scotland Yard, and scenes of Purdom and Mark Jones discussing the case in a room that has been cheaply decked out to resemble a Scotland Yard office. Such old fashioned sleuthing is in schizophrenic contrast to the very 1980s slasher scenes themselves, which find various Santas wandering on to the screen only to meet their maker at the hands of Alan Lake's psychopath (or at least the hands of Lake's masked stand-in) a few moments later. As with the chainsaw murders in *Pieces*, these sequences go hugely over-the-top in the gore department. Faces instead of chestnuts are roasted on an open fire, eyeballs are punched out, machetes embedded in heads and brains blown out. *Don't Open Till Christmas*' bad taste highlight, and the scene that no one forgets, finds a department store Santa (played by Greek pornographer Max Roman) using a urinal only to be caught short when the killer creeps out of a toilet cubicle and castrates him.

Of the three directors, it is arguably Derek Ford whose personality can be felt the most. Unlike fellow 1970s sex filmmaker Stanley Long, whose horror shorts from this period offer no clue to their director's saucy background, Ford clearly found it harder to shake off his past. As a result, *Don't Open Till Christmas* sure loves its sleaze, there is kinkiness by the bucketload here, from the dirty talk in the Soho peep booth, to Pat Astley's glamour photoshoot and the killer later threatening a semi-nude Pat with a razor. This pornographic element certainly distances *Don't Open Till Christmas* from the typical American slasher fare of the era, almost as much as the Purdom footage does. A running theme in Derek Ford's work manages to find an unlikely outlet here, thanks to Cliff's transformation from a nice guy in the early scenes to a creep who tries to capitalize on his girlfriend's grief by coercing her to appear in a lesbian photo-shoot. Hardly the typical behavior of a clean-cut horror film hero, but pure Derek Ford, whose earlier sex films like *The Wife Swappers* and *Commuter Husbands* display a deep obsession with swinging suburbia and outwardly respectable people leading hedonistic double lives.

Obsessions that, by all accounts, Ford didn't just restrict to his film work. The premise for the scene and Kate's predictably appalled reaction to Cliff's suggestion feels like someone's memory of a swingers' party gone awry rather than anything belonging to a horror film.

The casting of 1970s sex film thespians Mark Jones, Alan Lake and the always fun-to-watch Pat Astley only adds to *Don't Open Till Christmas*' overall blurring of British sexploitation and horror genres. Alan Lake is a shocker here, unshaven and with his hair reverting to its natural gray, it's all a far cry from the tanned, medallion man superstuds Lake had been playing a few years earlier. Lake's history of hellraising, alcoholism and psychotic episodes—all well documented by the tabloids during the 1970s—was clearly beginning to take its toll. So disheveled is the actor's appearance that his character Giles resembles a street person rather than the Fleet Street journalist he is meant to be. While clearly not keeping it together off-screen, Lake manages to put in a decent enough final performance. The aura of danger and unpredictability that Lake carried round with him in real life is successfully channeled into his onscreen character, bringing an authentic sense of menace to the actor's final scenes. Lake's co-star Mark Jones doesn't fare as well, having drawn the short straw of a role that puts him in contact with the film's most preposterous dialogue. Unlike Alan Lake, Jones did live to see *Don't Open Till Christmas* and reportedly hated it. Throughout, the poor

Austrian DVD cover art for *Don't Open Till Christmas*

man sports a weary expression that suggests he just wants the ground to open up and swallow him. Then there is Pat Astley, a Blackpool-born glamour model, sex-film starlet and TV extra generally relegated to playing leggy nurses and often dubbed on the rare occasions she was ever given dialogue. Here, however, Pat finally gets to shine, in her last, lengthiest big screen role before she stepped back into the anonymity of TV extra work—you even get to hear her flat Lancastrian accent in all its glory. Pat basically comes across as herself, a bubbly Northern glamour model who seems barely able to conceal her bemusement at being asked to deliver an acting performance. Nevertheless, Pat is extremely likeable and very sweet in a way that makes you want to defend her corner and turn a blind eye to her limited ability. *Don't Open Till Christmas* agreeably lets Blackpool Patricia's big screen career end on a note of triumph, as she memorably exits flashing her tits at Edmund Purdom while proudly proclaiming "I'm a professional." Indeed, she was.

As fucked up as the film is, it's hard not to admire the showman in Dick Randall and his attempts to throw anything into the mix that could save the day and endear it to a genre audience. The discovery that his friend George Dugdale was married to erstwhile Bond girl and horror icon Caroline Munro resulted in Randall talking her into appearing in the film. Munro's subsequent cameo—in which she plays herself and performs a song on stage called "Warrior of Love"—was shot in just one afternoon. It was a sequence clearly meant to be mutually beneficial to both parties, giving Munro a chance to resurrect her long dormant singing career as well as throwing Randall another name to put on the video box. It also gave the filmmakers an excuse to fling in further terrible gore effects, since Munro's performance is intercut with—what else—another Santa murder. To add to this coup, Randall managed to talk the owners of the London Dungeon into letting the filmmakers use the famous wax museum in *Don't Open Till Christmas* as well. No prizes for guessing that the Dungeon ends up as the backdrop to yet another Santa killing. Somebody who saw the latter scene from an unusual angle—namely an upside down one—was porn star Paula Meadows. A veteran of top shelf magazines and early Mike Freeman videos, Paula was roped into appearing in the scene—quite literally, as she plays a secretary who bumps into the killer during his pursuit of a Santa Claus victim, only to end up dead and hung upside down naked herself. Needless to say, it's not one of Paula's most cherished memories from her career. "The shooting of that scene was horribly uncomfortable. Once I was hanging upside-down from my feet, I began to feel dizzy and nauseous and started to panic. Derek Ford came to the rescue and held up my head in between takes" recalls Paula. "I never saw the film because I had no desire to see myself as a naked corpse with blood dripping from my throat!" For a long time afterwards the London Dungeon were said to be extremely hesitant to let anyone shoot in there again, claiming this S&M flavored scene was "a bit too much." Not that Paula would have been up for a repeat performance; "I couldn't wait to be cut down" she remembers, "I wouldn't want to enter the portals of the London Dungeon again."

This highly calamitous introduction to British horror clearly didn't put Dick Randall off continuing to fly the flag for the genre. By the decade's end he had produced three more horror films and two genre-themed documentaries. If anything, Randall could be accused of being a little too dedicated to making horror films and a workaholic lifestyle in general. As one former employee noted, the work done during this period "probably helped drive him to an early grave." Randall remains perhaps the closest the 1980s had to a Tony Tenser figure. Like Tenser, Randall was a truly large-than-life character whose producing career kept older filmmakers in work, not to mention giving new talent like George Dugdale and Paul Hart-Wilden a foothold into the biz. Of course, Randall got to line his pockets with the proceeds as well. "Artistic sensitivity was not his concern!" remembers Paula Meadows, "he was a good-natured man with an infectious smile, who just wanted to get on and make a movie in the simplest, cheapest way and rake in the most money possible!"

If truth be told *Don't Open Till Christmas* is definitely the runt of the Randall litter; his second British horror production *Slaughter High* (1985) pulls off the concept of a home-grown stalk-and-slash movie far more efficiently. So *Don't Open Till Christmas* has to settle for being a disreputable anomaly, a film released at the height of the "video nasty" hysteria in which so much stage blood is flung about that the filmmakers offer special thanks to the company that made the red stuff in the end credits. Unashamedly geared to the exploitation market as anything else with Dick Randall's name attached to it, it seems like something made in another universe away from such strands of 1980s British cinema as the period pieces of Merchant-Ivory or the social dramas of Ken Loach and Mike Leigh. None of who ever thought to include a scene of Santa being castrated in a public toilet in their work. All these years later *Don't Open Till Christmas* still retains a certain car crash fascination. Its blunt fixation with sleaze, wild outbursts of gore, and baggage retained from the tackier elements of British cinema of the 1960s and 1970s, gives it lasting, fascinating appeal to those with such cinematic interests.

—Gavin Whitaker

Caroline Munro sings in *Don't Open Till Christmas*

LIPSTICK AND BLOOD

D: Lindsay Shonteff (as "Robert Bauer")
W: Don Colville
Starring: Joseph Peters, Jane Linter, Paul Ashe

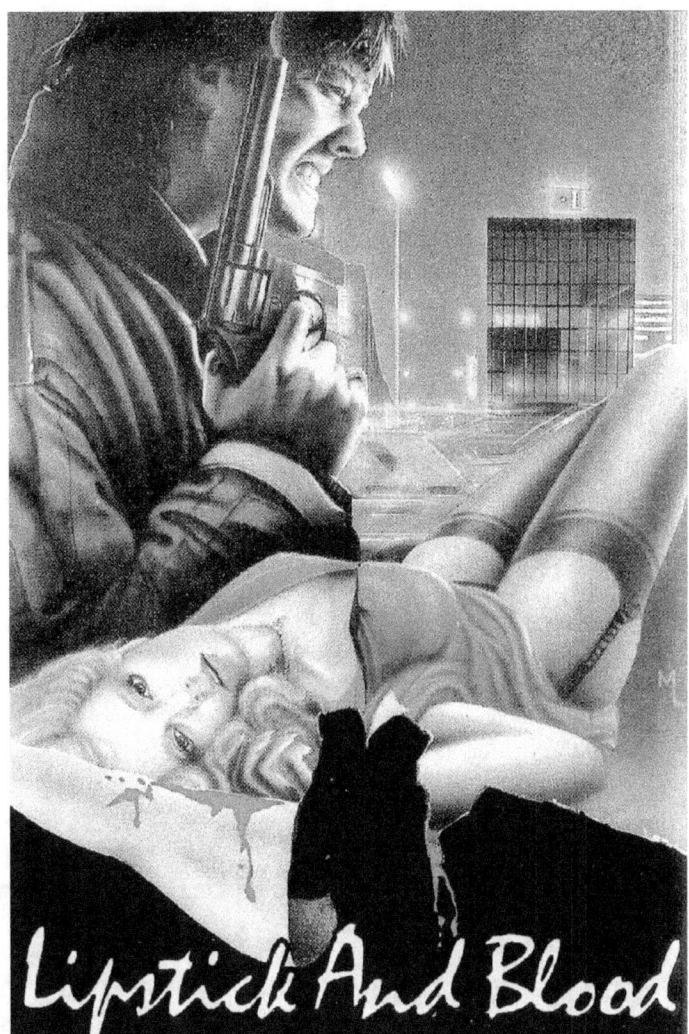

Flabbergasted isn't the word—saddened is probably closer to it. What more can I say about a film that was made by a director I admire and respect, but which represents, quite possibly, the very lowest point British horror and/or exploitation sank to in the 1980s?

Let's quantify this: Lindsay Shonteff, Canadian ex-pat turned Brit grindhouse auteur, was always a name associated with low-budget fare, often at the seedier, seamier end of the spectrum. Through his viewfinder in the '60s we glimpsed the wonderfully tacky *Million Eyes of Su-Muru*, the shameless *Dead of Night* rip-off *Devil Doll*, the unbelievable barefaced shot-in-Hampstead-pretending-to-be-Africa affrontery of *The Curse of Simba*, with its jocular descriptions of dark-skinned Africans ("I saw IT!! *IT* was in the corner of the room!!"), the clammily intense *Clegg*, which reads like a pilot for the greatest cop series that never was, and the ultimate dirty mac sex'n'terror fest *Night, After Night, After Night*—not only one of the films which helped set the precedent for the grittier, more urban and less costume-Gothic decade of horror filmmaking to come, but one which left *Archers* fans never able to think of Nelson Gabriel in quite the same way again.

As the subsequent decade unfurled, Lindsay unleashed his grubby masterpiece—the beautiful, decadent and eerie hippiesploitation epic *Permissive*—on the world, making minor sleaze legends out of prog behemoths Forever More, Comus, and Exegesis founder Robert Daubigny, before turning his hand to "naughty" martial arts cash-ins, bad adaptations of Len Deighton espionage novels, and Bond spoofs starring Tom Adams, Nicky Henson and Gareth Hunt—all Poverty Row productions, but still done with a certain degree of love, self-belief and panache, not to mention a few professional actors. His "Vietnam In Berkshire" combat schlock *How Sleep the Brave* is maybe best viewed as an eccentric misfire, but again, even by its own low standards, it retained the stamp of high ambition, and could at a stretch be claimed to have inspired Kubrick's English countryside Tet Offensive, *Full Metal Jacket*! Tragically, *Lipstick and Blood* is a step backwards, a cheapjack last-ditch attempt at zero-budget cinema (if you can call something that appears to have been shot on a portable Betamax cinema of any kind) from a tired, desperate and thoroughly depressed man, by now crushed (as was the majority of the British film industry) by the domino effect of 1980s capitalism.

It shows in the nihilism with which its central "characters" (never before or since in horror have I seen two key protagonists so thinly drawn) approach their actions. It shows in the sheer "killing for the sake of it" attitude of the psycho-baddie (a social misfit who, like the murderer in *Night, After Night, After Night*, rents space in an old warehouse and festoons his walls with pictures of scantily clad models, a pointless self-reference from the director which only serves to remind the viewer how poor this film is in comparison to its classic predecessor), the complete and utter lack of empathy one feels for the dull, wooden "heroine," and the fact that Shonteff's budget clearly didn't even stretch as far as dubbing any decent sound on, the end result hanging aurally somewhere between a wedding video and a short film made by a municipal tourist board. I think you're getting the impression by now that, even as a fan of the director, I'm none too keen on this one ...

Rather than get annoyed any further, I'll just point out the humorous bits. For instance, it's unbelievable how many chances the heroine has to either (a) escape (b) shoot her captor or (c) just wallop him, but doesn't—something that can only possibly be explained by invoking the ancient film-makers law of "BIS-SITS" ('Because It Says So In The Script'). That is, if there *was* a script—half the time it seems as if Jennie (Jane Linter) and Jay (Joseph Peters) are making it up as they go along, improvising around a rough outline. Sadly, that only works if you have talent to begin with. The plot, such as it is (psycho can't pull birds, psycho goes to club to watch birds strip, psycho becomes obsessed with one particular bird, abducts her, kills her boyfriend in front of her and then forces her at gunpoint to be his unwilling life partner—oh right, *that* old chestnut) features so many holes that it's hard to remember them all individually, but just as a taster, I find it extremely hard, if not impossible, to believe that a woman, having been kidnapped and raped (we never actually see anything—not that you'd want to, but again, I bet this was a budgetary rather than an artistic decision) several times over by a complete nutter, would (a) sit in his car with him while he spouted bollocks at her without attempting to at least do a runner, and (b) end up practically living with him in his house/hotel!! But she does.

Even more ridiculously, Jay then becomes incensed at the fact that his prisoner won't talk to him, cook for him properly or reward him with either physical kindness or polite conversation (shades of the killer in *Don't Open Till Christmas* here, but again, at least that was unintentionally funny) and storms off in a huff, leaving her by herself!! If this had been *intended* as an interesting twist on proceedings, or had been prefixed by an unexpected burst of Stockholm Syndrome, that might have at least added some texture, but it appears to have been flung in out of desperation and/or expediency, to the point where any artistic evaluation is almost redundant.

There is, admittedly, one hint at an actual story arc, whereby a gun from a botched burglary committed by the owner of the strip club becomes Linter's weapon of vengeance (*finally!!* A response at last!! Hooray!!) and some hint that maybe her wrongdoer freely accepts his fate—shot dead at point blank range from the stage, *Female Trouble*/Sid Vicious-style—as some kind of willing sacrifice for the woman he "loves," with a smile on his face—but unfortunately even that's ruined by a prolonged (as in over five minutes long) dance routine with piece in hand (obviously supposed to be both erotic and phallic but failing miserably on both counts) by the lady in question.

As either a horror film, a sex film or a thriller, *Lipstick and Blood* completely misses the boat (or should I say bad 1980s hatchback)—while there is some graphic gore, it's too infrequent and clumsy to be shocking, it's not in the *slightest* bit suspenseful, chilling or scary, there's no tension or excitement (or indeed any dynamic between the characters), people crop up suddenly in the narrative for no apparent reason other than to get killed, and there's no actual sex in it anyway, not that you'd wish to watch non-consensual intercourse involving a bargain-basement Susanne Sulley clone and a bloke with a bad Postcard Records haircut. Although, to be fair to him, he looks like he couldn't physically rape or molest a slice of cream sponge, so maybe she's safer than we think after all. It's thoroughly unlike me to give low-budget Britsploitation films a bashing, but after two viewings, the only redeeming feature I can find in this one are its locations: as a travelogue of various laybys, retail parks, Little Chefs and rural/shadowland roadsides around Berkshire (including a full close-up of a pre-redevelopment Reading Station), and thus a depiction of how truly independent, non-unionised filmmaking can operate without the constraints of having to be within a 30 mile radius of a studio, it excels. Maybe Shonteff should have just shot all that and left the rest out.

What's even more amazing is that this is only one of *two* films he made that year: the post-apocalyptic shocker *The Killing Edge*, which is marginally better depending on one's definition of the term, actually preceded this by a number of months.
—Darius Drewe

1984

D: Michael Radford
W: Michael Radford
Starring: John Hurt, Richard Burton, Suzanna Hamilton, Cyril Cusack, Gregor Fisher, James Walker, Andrew Wilde, David Trevena

> Who controls the past controls the future.
> Who controls the present controls the past.
> —Opening titles

Much-trumpeted as it neared production, this stark, brutalist and deliberately undernourished adaptation of Orwell's time-specific tale of near-futureshock was not just "the film of the year, the year of the film," it was purposely shot in the very months that form the novel.

Through this nightmare landscape—a world so very like our own but occupying a space and time to the leftfield of our known existence—wanders Winston Smith. Seen by many interpreters of Orwell's book as both an Everyman and the ultimate rebel, he is in truth the ultimate loser, crushed by authority, broken on the wheel of Totalitarianism and forced to accede to the iron fist of Big Brother. And yet ...

Hope is what drives Orwell's *1984*. The movie that emerged in 1956 bastardized the book and concluded with Edmond O'Brien (as Winston) shouting his defiance at the state. Hollywood, after all, loves a happy ending.

The world of Orwell/Winston as visualized by director Michael Radford, producer Simon Perry, cinematographer Roger Deakins, production designer Allan Cameron and their cast was altogether different to the UK-produced, Hollywoodized effort that had preceded it. This version—a

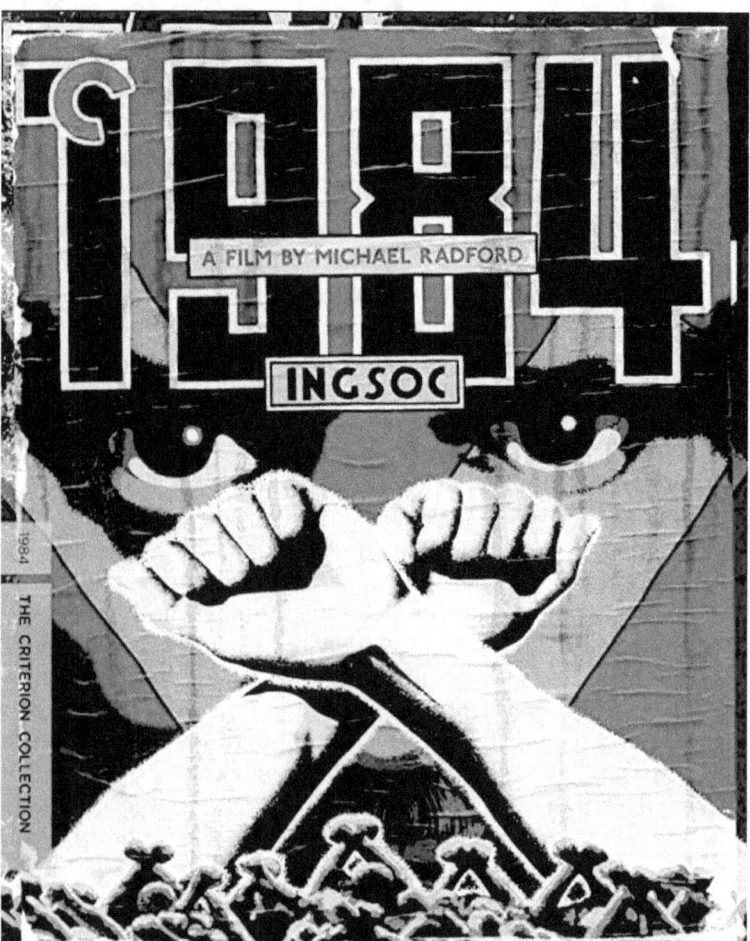

Criterion Collection DVD cover

numericalized *1984* in its advertising though credited as *Nineteen Eighty-Four* onscreen—was a chilly world of washed-out grayness in which man and machinery ground to a halt in equal measure. The stand-off between Us and Them—the Proles versus the Party—was evident in every damp cigarette, every drop of rotgut Victory gin, every broken brick in a shattered urban wasteland. If hope exists it is a needle among the rubble; love among the ruins.

Radford & company sought authenticity, and they found it in their bomb-blasted milieu. Moreover, it was given a human face by John Hurt in the role that he was surely born to play. Drawn, haggard, quasi-cadaverous like a Giacometti figure, this was not a handsome man gone to seed; instead this was a pathetic drone in an immense hive who, despite himself, managed to confound the imposed status quo by daring to think.

Hurt's hero/loser exhibits genius casting. He's perfect as the little man—representing millions of similar creatures—who worms his way through the rotten carcass of INGSOC and emerges free and defiant of conditioning, brainwashing and propaganda. In that respect the film is everything its makers wished it to be. Doubleplusgood.

Radford begins *1984* with faux newsreel of Goldstein, the hate figure, and the faithful screaming in orgasmic frenzy. Among the crowd are Winston, Julia and O'Brien, the Party inquisitor who will become the cuckoo in their lovenest.

The anonymous drabness begins to ebb away as Winston and Julia (Suzanna Hamilton) dare to begin their rebellion. But even as briefly expressed sexual abandon undermines state, telescreen and Big Brother, so images of executions and faraway warfare seep into the everyday. There is no escape.

Partly shot at Beckton Gasworks, location for the finale of Stanley Kubrick's *Full Metal Jacket*, *1984* is pervaded by a lingering, even overwhelming, mood of heavy dread. There is a sense that Winston and Julia's sexual and intellectual liberation is fleeting, and that the specter of Big Brother in the living presence of O'Brien is not just omnipresent but all-seeing.

Suzanna Hamilton is less the Eve to Hurt's Adam as she is the embodiment of the serpent. If she represents goodness, adventure and freedom—Julia is, after all, both instigator and enabler—she is also mankind's Achilles heel. She is sin, and sinning is forbidden.

Radford urged a fragile Richard Burton, in his final film role (he was cast after original choice Paul Scofield broke a leg and second choice Rod Steiger experienced slippage in a recent facelift), to eschew that glorious voice. Burton agreed and adopted a combination of stage whisper/sotto voce as the purring, seductive Party mandarin. Yet there is power in this tired old man.

A Soviet/Cold War parable made in Thatcherite Britain, *1984* speaks of parallel worlds and a terrifying dystopian future that might be. Mightily prescient on publication in 1949, it retained its power in Radford's visionary adaptation. Strangely, it is still frighteningly appropriate today.
—Tony Earnshaw

SCREAM FOR HELP

D: Michael Winner
W: Tom Holland
Starring: Rachael Kelly, Marie Masters, Corey Parker, David Allen Brooks

"I think my stepfather is trying to murder my mother ..." observes 17-year-old Nancy Drew-ish virgin Rachael Kelly in the pre-titles sequence of an astonishing (there's no other word yet created) slasher-era thriller from Michael Winner. The credentials are good. It was executive produced by *Halloween* honcho Irwin Yablans and written by Tom Holland in the wake of his excellent script for *Psycho II*, though the latter has since disowned it while politely avoiding a specific dissing of the director. In Winner's hands, this precursor to *The Stepfather* is a remarkably sleazy and unintentionally hilarious camp-fest, with an unsubtle tone set by its in-your-face God-awful score by John Paul Jones. That music simply refuses to let up and, even by 1980s standards, is hugely offensive to the human ear—though don't hate yourself if you once picked it up on vinyl at a car boot sale (... ahem).

Kelly narrates from her journals, in a uniquely squirm-inducing fashion, her suspicions towards handsome, charming stepfather (David Allen Brooks), whom she believes has married her wealthy mom entirely for her money and intends to get their lovely spacious middle-class home all to himself. Odd events fuel her paranoia. The man from the power company winds up mysteriously electrocuted, mom tumbles over some objects on the

stairs, the gas and brake pedals in her car fail with near-fatal results ... then she discovers that Brooks is sleeping with a whorish younger woman (the fabulously named Lolita Lorre) and a body count starts to build.

The first thing you notice about *Scream for Help*, other than the gratuitously exposed big knockers of Kelly's best friend (the ill-fated Sandra Clark), is that for some reason the Evil Stepfather character is constantly referred to by Christian name and surname, even in the context of a casual conversation by people who know him. A typical line is "He did this! Paul Fox!" It's almost as if someone thought we needed to be constantly reminded of our potential villain's identity. The next thing you notice is that, in the year of our Lord 1984, an Englishman made a movie in which, without any obvious signs of intended irony, the teenage heroine wears a T-shirt with the word "Muffs" imprinted in big letters on the front. Welcome to the wondrous world of *Scream for Help*.

Everything about the movie, perhaps more so than any Michael Winner picture, is amped up to 11 and then some. One early sequence has Kelly in danger in an obviously tampered-with car. It's not enough that the script reveals The Brakes Don't Work! This peril is immediately followed by The Wheel is Locked! And then: My God! A Woman in A Road with A Pram!! The escalating sequence unfolds like a *Naked Gun* skit and, had it gone on any longer, one assumes, would have also involved a nearby orphanage, a school bus, a couple of nuns and a sick puppy finally taking its big, brave steps back to normality. All of this is scored to the hilt by Jones, whose soundtrack never knows when to quit (or at least simmer down): a relatively quiet scene of Kelly overhearing Mom and Evil Stepdad fucking is scored like the big finale of an old-fashioned Hollywood thriller.

It's as mean-spirited as any of Winner's *Death Wish* movies. Sandra Clark, she of those aforementioned big knockers, perhaps has the most thankless role: immediately after announcing she's pregnant and planning an abortion ("I have my whole life in front of me!"), she's struck by a speeding car, allowing Winner to cut to a gratuitous shot of her bloody face, and then show us her anguished Mom at the hospital ("Noooo!") Kelly's suspicions of Brooks turn out to be well founded ("Not only is he an incompetent murderer, he's a total asshole!") though his actions are seen to be part of an elaborate love-triangle plot to kill her mom, involving a pair of rougher, more blue collar villains—one of whom is the often-naked Lorre, providing the majority of the movie's substantial nudity quotient.

If you've ever wanted to see Winner handle the subject of tender teen romance, you came to the right place. Approximately five minutes after Clark has been squished on the road, her boyfriend (Corey Parker, a year away from *Friday the 13th Part V: A New Beginning*, fact fans) easily persuades Kelly to give up her cherry for him in a scene scored to what sounds like an unused motif from *The Poseidon Adventure*, capped with the line "Oh my God, I'm bleeding!" This predictably queasy scene is the start of perhaps the most embarrassing adolescent relationship of 1980s cinema, sadly cut short by Kelly herself: "I don't wanna go to bed with anyone again, ever."

In its final half hour, the movie turns into an extended house siege scenario, though the acting level of the protagonists is on a par with *Neighbors* circa 1986 (Parker, who had the best career out of anyone in the film, comes off worst, especially during an awful moment of interior monologue) so the suspense is neutered. As you might expect from the director of *Death Wish II*, women are treated harshly and largely exist to be screwed, roughed up or lose their clothing. Kelly is called a "cunt" and bashed around while Holland's script provides a suitably O.T.T. climax of Wes Craven-ish booby traps and exploding bedrooms.

The outrageously contrived, bloody post-De Palma/*Friday the 13th* ending is set up by the famous last words "You'll be safe here; it's the police commissioner's house!" The perfect end to an unforgettable movie.
—Steven West

• • •

There is a good script bubbling to get out of *Scream for Help*, the writer Tom Holland having previously dared to tackle *Psycho II* (1982), with *Fright Night* on the horizon—he was also to direct the latter, possibly in response to the poor handling of his labors here by Winner. *Scream for Help* has enough elements in common with Holland's *Fright Night* to encourage the idea that he was revisiting *Scream for Help* structurally. Both have three young people, one of whom will suffer a fatality. Again, we have a high school teenager and mother threatened by the handsome new man in their lives, married to the bastard before the start of the film in *Scream for Help*, the vampire neighbor eager to cross the threshold in the other. The mother, friends and police refuse to believe the disturbed teen protagonist about the respective household threats. One gets the impression that Holland was so peeved about the treatment of his script that he was determined to show Winner how a scriptwriter and novice director could achieve what the veteran filmmaker could not.

By 1984, Winner had become one of the bad boys of British cinema, courting controversy through his movies and his mouth. His 1960s fare captured a zeitgeist without going full focus on the youth culture and it was the 1970s before he fully embraced exploitation and shock tactics (notwithstanding the daring but essentially innocent nudism of his early feature *Some Like It Cool*). By the 1980s his reputation went into further decline as the quality of the films sank, and *Scream for Help* exhibits some of his movies' worst traits with bad casting, poor performances and a botched reading of a seemingly decent script from scene to scene. The impression given is that Winner had lost interest in making films by this stage and the objective was purely to get this potboiler in the can as quickly as possible. Throughout there are discrepancies in the performance and story. Rachael Kelly shifts between overacting and responding like an automaton dependent on how ill fitting the reaction is to the scene, whereas the villains are nothing more than gurning caricatures.

It is something of a pity because the script has great potential as a sick and twisted thriller that begins as cousin to *Shadow of a Doubt* and then turns into a home invasion horror akin to *The Desperate Hours* and *Last House on the Left*. It could have settled as a cut and shunt job mingling the two common scenarios, but Holland reacts against such simplicity, throwing in a number of twists and survivalist set pieces to stir up the broth. The victims' creative retaliatory traps are of the educational variety that we came to expect of Wes Craven, though here, they are often replications of the devices originally set by the stepfather, the girl having the knowhow to reproduce the traps to despatch her tormentors. As earlier implied, the Bohle siblings are not brother and sister at all, but husband and wife who, subsequent to the murders of the mother and daughter, will blackmail stepfather Paul Fox (Brooks) to the hilt. Christie discovers this and uses it to turn the villains against one another.

The violence is tangible and brutal. A stunt person and manikin combine for one deadly hit and run as the body of the victim smacks across car and road in a painstakingly assembled sequence, each fraction of a shot taken from a new position. The stuntwoman who doubles for the mother's fall down the house stairs and cellar steps lands at an uncomfortable angle or with an almighty thump. The tight editing provides the impact.

Robert Paynter's cinematography is not outstanding but there is a generosity in the number of camera set-ups, without which the options of the editor would not have been so striking.

Italian poster for *Scream for Help*

The second half of the story also relies a lot on switches from light into black-out, and Paynter takes the image as near to darkness as possible with enough slivers and shapes of illumination or gray-light to allow easy following of the action.

Scream for Help is no less contrived than most thrillers, dependent on the plotters not acting when they could or should to kill those conspired against, whether it is the trigger finger held off a second too long or the room rigged with a gas leak not discovered until the very moment needed for it to blow up in the bad guy's face. Other directors would work meticulously on the legerdemain to draw the viewer away from those improbable but essential flaws in the tale. Likeable performers, interesting cinematography and an appropriate score commonly serve among those distractions. Unfortunately, Winner's direction is half-hearted, the performances terrible and the score ill conceived—the signposts to all that is wrong with *Scream for Help* are everywhere. It's amateurs in clogs, a pantomime thriller and a thuggish farce.

Winner had become a namedropper extraordinaire, and the more celebrity connections the better, so when in the 1980s it came to soundtracks, he began looking for rock musicians, using Jimmy Page for *Death Wish II* (1982). On *Scream for Help* he brought in Page's bandmate John Paul Jones, whose work here moves between occasional electronic urgings and full orchestral score (the arrangements by Christopher Palmer and Johnny Pearson possibly pointing to their greater influence and authorship in the latter). The music sweeps incongruously and inappropriately as if to shape some beautiful tragedy in a television weepie or bring in a musical comedy punchline to a scene that might have benefited more by a less lurching sonic accompaniment. The closing credits play out with an atrocious sub-par ditty about our heroine, "Christie," sung by Jon Anderson.

Simply credited as "filmed on Location," *Scream for Help* was shot in America and the UK but provides few clues as to actual British sites used. Several familiar expatriate American actors of the day (including David Baxt and Bruce Boa) turn up to inform us that the garage and hospital scenes were part of the English shoot.

Scream for Help is sordid and wears its awfulness like a badge. But a clever script peeks through and if any film might benefit from a remake, this is the one, preferably with Tom Holland at the helm, directly rectifying past wrongs.
—Paul Higson

SLEEPWALKER

D: Saxon Logan
W: Michael Keenan, John Varnom, Saxon Logan
Starring: Heather Page, Bill Douglas, Joanna David, Nickolas Grace

Declaration of interest—of all the minor achievements and breakthroughs I may have made in several decades' studying and chronicling motion pictures, the unearthing of *Sleepwalker* and the opportunity to present this once virtually lost title to a new and appreciative audience is perhaps this writer's crowning glory. As such, it may preclude me from any kind of objective judgement on the qualities of the film itself—however, in preparing this book, contributor after contributor stepped aside when it came to covering this particular title, graciously conceding that the Indiana Jones-like effort I'd put in to finding this missing treasure pushed me to the front of the queue.

The legend has by now been oft-told and well-traveled—my full account of *Sleepwalker*'s exhumation and glorious acceptance first appeared in the pages of *Creeping Flesh* volume one (Headpress 2003) and has been reproduced in print and around the web. For newcomers to the saga, the nutshell version is as follows: I'd read Kim Newman's review of what he described as "the most obscure horror movie ever made in Britain" in issue 10 of *Flesh & Blood* fanzine, and frankly didn't believe a word, considering the piece a playful hoax. Word eventually filtered through to the film's genuine editor Mike Crozier and genuine director Saxon Logan, who fortunately saw the funny side and adopted me as *Sleepwalker*'s official champion; between us we arranged festival screenings and one-off shows in venues nationwide, once Saxon revealed that he had a 35mm print tucked away, celluloid which had not seen the light of a projector since the mid-1980s.

Although I adore commercial cinema at its finest (my reputation as Robin Askwith's number one stalker/fan is widely known), I have to confess that I can be one of those snobby cultists who loves to track down unseen items, and that it's easy to be guilty of over-inflating their worth on initial viewing, and convey bloated opinions to other buffs before reining in the praise a while afterwards. On my first, privileged viewing of *Sleepwalker* back in early 2002, then, I fully suspected that I'd declare the

movie an undiscovered wonder—in order to bring people's attention to it—and would backtrack once word and accessibility were out. So why, all this time later, do I still regard the film as such a searing, important item?

The simple storyline sees two archly named couples, Socialist brother and sister the Britains and Tory supporting entrepreneur and long-suffering partner the Paradises assembling for dinner at "Albion," the crumbling, rain-lashed inherited pile of the former pairing. A lightning flash sends glass splinters all over the prepared spread, so the quartet adjourn to a local restaurant (encountering doddery and/or camp Bunuelian nightmare grotesques played by old stagers Raymond Huntley, Fulton Mackay and Michael Medwin.) Over a wine-fueled meal, conversation heats up and it becomes clear that there is no middle ground. The subject moves away from politics to somnambulism, with Alex Britain (award-winning Scottish director Bill Douglas, memorably grumpy here!) accused of a *Caligari*-like attempted murder while aslumber some months earlier. The bickering foursome retreat to "Albion" for a nightcap, continuing social and sexual tension, and a spot of bouncy reggae-lite—and a sleeping killer, possibly unaware of their own deadly actions, begins to slaughter the party one by one through the early hours.

Director Logan, best known as a documentarian whose work includes TV films on Dirk Bogarde and his beloved Africa, set out on his movie journey in his teens as a glorified go-fer for Lindsay Anderson on *O Lucky Man!* The political anger and rage at people's inability to connect, possessed by Anderson, clearly rubbed off on the young Saxon, who to this day continues to express hands-in-the-air exasperation at the way of the world (while enjoying a deservedly comfortable existence and peace in his own life); and it's encouraging to see that some 21st century British filmmakers have taken up the cudgel too—similarities between *Sleepwalker* and Ben Wheatley's sensational *Kill List* are palpable, while most likely entirely accidental.

The culmination of our extraordinary journey with the revival of *Sleepwalker* saw Sam Dunn of the British Film Institute contact me with a view to cleaning up and releasing the film as part of the prestigious "Flipside" Blu-ray strand. The BFI duly completed a major mastering job on Saxon's original surviving print, and the September 2013 issue of the disc brought a string of open-mouthed reviews and gratifyingly positive comment. *Sleepwalker* remains as relevant as it ever was, and the climactic sight of Bill Douglas, severely wounded, covered in blood, under intense threat, and screaming "Wake up! Wake up!"—directly at you in the audience, please note, just like Kevin McCarthy did in *Invasion of the Body Snatchers*—forms one of the most shattering finales to a movie this viewer has ever witnessed.
—Darrell Buxton

SPHERE–THE SPORES OF DOOM

D: Stephen Hilliker
Starring: Joanne Barry, Maurice Blake, John Collin, Jonathan Caplan

In the 1980s several feature films appeared on commercial video/cable circuits that didn't feel quite "right" in terms of content or component parts. That was until further investigation revealed that they were the results of film courses at major American universities. The impression given was that since film was expensive, why not leapfrog the innumerable glut of shorts and move into eye-catching feature-length production that could be marketed? I haven't had the opportunity to dig further to establish the ins and outs of this and one day fully intend to explore these films (few that they might be).

Of course, in order to accommodate every talent in a campus moviemaking team then a role had to be found for them in each film, which dependent on their area of expertise might prove dissonant in the finished work. Take animation, for example. *Zombie High* (1987) closes with several terrible seconds of 2D animation, while the carefully wrought ambience of Phillip Badger's *The Forgotten One* (1989) is marred by animated optical effects for a burst of 2D ectoplasm. In Mike B. Anderson's *Alone in the T-shirt Zone* (1986) they had to give different animators their opportunity, accounting for a spermatozoa race for the moon and a stop-motion extreme close-up of a frantic flea on the end of a pair of pincers.

Although things were opening up in other ways in the UK, unfortunately The National Film & Television School (N.F. & T.S.) was statutorily bound not to take similar advantage as its students were exactly that, not yet professionals, and did not have A.C.T.T. (the Association of Cinematograph Television and Allied Technicians union) membership. It robs us of access to a fascinating number of first films with vague description and a mere teaser of information. Films might well have seen exhibition shortly after production but allow a couple of years to pass and they were seen no more. Lloyd Phillips' 1979 N.F. & T.S. film, *Halfway Round the Circle Now*, a 16mm supernatural short starring Sophie Ward and Janet Key was screened at several festivals, in Edinburgh, Wellington and London in 1979 and Cape Town in 1981, but is unseen since.

Most of the showcase student works were short, but by the 1980s longer form projects occasionally surfaced, again possibly in a bid to reduce the outlay on costly film in a country where a career in the business seemed increasingly difficult. One of the longer-form student films is Stephen Hilliker's *Sphere–The Spores of Doom* (1984), with a running time of 40 minutes, which tells the story of a village under the power of a ruling wizard who uses magic mushrooms to enslave the locals. On first viewing it's a busy and potentially confusing broth, but repeat screenings reveal it as a straightforward and simple dark fantasy. My access to the film comes via a DVD-r taken from a videocassette owned by one of the crewmembers, supplied for the purpose of review for this book. The picture quality is not excellent but provides a decent enough representation of the original 16mm film (shot in 1:1.85). National Film & Television School records give *Sphere* a 45-minute running time, slightly longer than the film as transferred here.

The film is a tick-box of traditional movie techniques, fitting in at least one example of each. So, for instance, we get a shot taken from above ground (the branches of a tree), angled downwards. There are long shots, medium shots, medium long shots, close-ups. The camera tilts, our hero briefly goes into slow motion, the image is distorted, and there are several tracking shots, dollies and hand-held, even at ankle level. The dolly zoom (or forward zoom/reverse tracking) visual effect, famously used

Sphere-The Spores of Doom was shown at the 18th Hof International Film Festival in Germany

in *Vertigo* and for Sheriff Brody's reaction shot on the beach in *Jaws*, is also present. There are stunts with horse riding at speed captured from various positions, including point of view, and scenes with children and animals. The 17th-century setting calls for costumes and props, and special effects also account for a range of skills, including a matte, in-camera effects, optical trickery and animation, the latter a disappointing lightshow on the hill upon which sits the windmill.

The checklisting doesn't hamper the story. In exploring and reproducing techniques from elsewhere, *Sphere–The Spores of Doom* both resembles and challenges other films made slightly earlier, produced on a low-budget but with a similarly ranging adventure, like Terry Marcel's *Hawk the Slayer* and Luigi Cozzi's *Starcrash*, ambitious though short on spondoolicks. *Sphere–The Spores of Doom* has less scope to compete, though, but doesn't balk at the effort.

Opening with our romantic leads on horseback it feels like we are being thrown into an episode of Richard Carpenter's *Robin of Sherwood* television series, made around the same time. There is a similar urgency to the racing horses, swift edits from tracking long shot, to point of view, to side-on trick medium close-ups of Anna (Joanne Barry). She is distracted by a light from the windmill on the hill and knocked from her horse. In the village a cart loses part of its load of oversize mushrooms and the Preacher (John Collin) curses the outsiders for every little mishap. The story returns to the time of Anna's arrival in the village as a child (Olivia Hall), in the care of her grandparents (John Biggerstaff and Miriam Raymond), also new to the village, her parents lost. The child finds it difficult making friends when the entire population of the village is occupied in collecting the large, strange mushrooms, superb props with the deliberate color of a psilocybin, though with a more umbrella-like cap. The mushroom props were the creation of Assistant Art Director Izabella Wroczynska.

The Wizard (Maurice Blake) gives the girl attention and "befriends" her, and mistaking him for a benign presence she accompanies him to the windmill, where he attends a boiling pot of mushroom broth that is added to and sipped from by a steady stream of villagers, rendering them addicts under his power and influence. It is dark when she returns to the manor house that has been acquired by her grandparents, and the Preacher is just leaving. The Preacher makes a final request, in a manner both a little rude and threatening, for immediate access to the land where the villagers do their harvesting. When the child mentions the Wizard, the Preacher ominously intones: "Oh you must go see him. He lives on Windmill Hill. He'll be expecting you." The home-life of the girl and the grandparents is a single scene, a one-shot window of normalcy that will not be repeated as we cut back to the beautiful young adult Anna and the events immediately preceding the opening escape. The grandparents are mentioned no more.

Anna catches the eye of the new stable-lad, Dunstan (Jonathan Caplan), another outsider. He romantically pursues her, and she caves in, but it is an affair that threatens the equilibrium of the village. Dunstan does not take her too seriously when she describes the power of the old man who looks "after us all; the land, the sea, the village." Like all villagers she meets the Wizard daily and this time claims there are no mushrooms, an obvious lie as others empty sacks of fungi around them. She has always been different and shown a little resistance, and by not gathering and not sharing the broth she hopes to strengthen her resolve enough for the elopement. He warns her that she is disturbing the balance. She pleads with him to let her go, reminding him that she was always an outsider, but he threatens consequences on them both. The boy will not abate his love for the girl and in the stables, he implores her to leave with him, but the other villagers gather around Dunstan in a warning circle and he senses that it is better that he departs for now.

But they do meet, and do plan to elope, stealing horses from the stable and riding as if the Devil is on their tail. While galloping furiously through the trees Anna is distracted by a glint of light from the windmill and her head strikes a branch, toppling her from her mount, apparently dead. But although the body disappears in a cloud of silvery dust, her soul is trapped in a silver globe and Dunstan means to recover her or avenge her. Dunstan confronts the Wizard who allows him to take the heavy ball containing her soul with him. When seeking help with his burden in the village, the Preacher instead tries to strike him down with a shovel. Dunstan buries the sphere and continues on alone, arriving at the beach. But with the boy having knowledge of the village's secret, the Wizard is unwilling to allow him to take that secret with him and the film closes with the grief-stricken youth finding a mushroom in his hand, which he maniacally prepares to consume.

Robert Wynne-Simmons' *The Outcasts* (1982) was made contemporaneously and has comparable qualities, though *The Outcasts* is a more serious film with a leisurely running time more than twice that of *Sphere–The Spores of Doom*. *The Outcasts* insinuates itself upon a more adult temperament, but is of a similarly dark mythology, concerned with vulnerable people in awe at a magical figure, each playing an instrument like a pied piper. Both films end on a terrifying fate not altogether understandable. Retrospectively, *Sphere–The Spores of Doom* is as negative a tale, the Wizard living up to his powerful reputation, the young protagonists, like the rest, no match to his will or magic. The "doom" in the title is palpably correct.

The cast is well appointed and the crew competent. The locations are fitting and the costumes and props satisfactory. The child Anna carries with her a doll at all times. Created for the film by art director Catherine Greenhalgh, the cloth goblin bore a sinister expression and its creator took it home after filming. Greenhalgh confesses that the doll had a presence that finally got the better of her and a few years back it was disposed of on a bonfire. Denis Crossan, the cinematographer, met all the camera objectives set him with aplomb. Locations include the village of Brill, and the Foxhill and Fulmer Stables.

Olivia Hall as the young Anna in *Sphere–The Spores of Doom*

Though any commercial release was impossible, the closing credits state "stereo in selected theatres" as if to hail such intentions. Had it not been for union membership in UK production it could have had a commercial application as a supporting film in cinemas. *The Orchard End Murder* was still doing the rounds in secondary billing to *Dead and Buried*, *The Witch* (rerelease title of *Superstition)* and *Return of the Living Dead* and had a similar running time, but this type of mid-length fare was becoming frowned upon in 1985, support slots were shrunk down or filled with musical shorts like The Rolling Stones' *Undercover of the Night* and Julian Temple's extended music promo for David Bowie's *Blue Jean*, and the days of the featurette seemed numbered in UK cinemas.

Sphere–The Spores of Doom has had little coverage; most attention to these student films would be via festival screenings, and what was known of it to date derived from a single brief review in issue #77 of *Starburst* magazine back in the year it was made. It has since generated much interest among British horror film enthusiasts but like many productions from the students of the N.F. & T.S. it has been nothing more than a taunting paragraph or two until now, with no images to help judge it further. Let us hope that our unearthing of this title stimulates and generates further awareness, and that some way is found to release this and other long-withheld student efforts tucked away unseen.
—Paul Higson

SUFFER, LITTLE CHILDREN

D: Alan Briggs
W: Meg Shanks
Starring: Colin Chamberlain, Ginny Rose, Jon Hollanz, Nicola Diana

There are only two things you need to know about this production. One is the plot: Elizabeth, a mysterious, mute little girl is taken in by a children's home and, using her demonic paranormal powers, she gradually possesses the other children and finally causes them to attack and kill the staff. The other is the fact that the film was made by students of the Meg Shanks Drama School who, as the closing credits point out, "had no experience and no money."

So, it comes as no surprise that this is basically a home video with a storyline (a "reproduction of real events," according to the opening voiceover.) In all the formal and technical aspects of filmmaking they couldn't have got it more wrong—the camerawork, sound recording, lighting, effects, music, and editing are all as primitively inept as you would expect—imagine this as being a step down from something like Alex Chandon's *Bad Karma* and you'll get the idea. However, if you approach the film with a degree of complicity (instead of the typical MST3K take-the-piss attitude which this type of "have-a-go" effort tends to attract), then you might be pleasantly surprised. For example, the first-time amateur actors give rough but naturalistic performances and the two adult leads, who play the childrens' home managers, come over as believable and personable characters. Maurice (Colin Chamberlain) is an old fashioned, cardigan wearing, slightly authoritarian and self-important chap, but he's also well meaning and reliable, though emotionally rather maladroit. Jenny (Ginny Rose) is a more tolerant, lively, bright young thing with a social conscience and little time for a love life. So, when the bad stuff starts happening, you are concerned for their welfare, something which doesn't happen in far too many real movies, where characters are merely one-dimensional cyphers set up for the kill. Nicola Diana, the little girl who plays Elizabeth, is also rather good in her non-speaking part, being suitably creepy and evil looking.

Initially my main interest in viewing *Suffer, Little Children* was in seeing how ingenious the makers could be in overcoming the obstacles posed by severe limitations of resources and experience, but as the footage progressed, I found myself actually being drawn into the story. It doesn't matter that a scene of kids

Here's Elizabeth... — Nicola Diana in *Suffer, Little Children*

running up and down stairs is as dynamic as the film gets, or that the "sets" are confined to three rooms and a staircase at the house, a tiny back patio, and the interior of a night club, or that Elizabeth's telekinetic powers are simply conveyed by crash zooms to girl's eyes followed by a door slamming, potted plants dangling on strings, and furniture pushed around by unseen hands. The thing is, if you cut the film enough slack and can get past its amateur status, it actually starts to get rather disturbing. The sight of children, especially young girls (which most of the inmates are), brandishing hammers, knives and other weapons (including a cricket stump!) and committing sadistic and bloodthirsty acts against adults is always guaranteed to shock audiences (and upset the BBFC). One particular moment is reminiscent of *Village of the Damned*, as Elizabeth telepathically forces a staff cleaner to stab herself repeatedly in the leg with a kitchen knife,

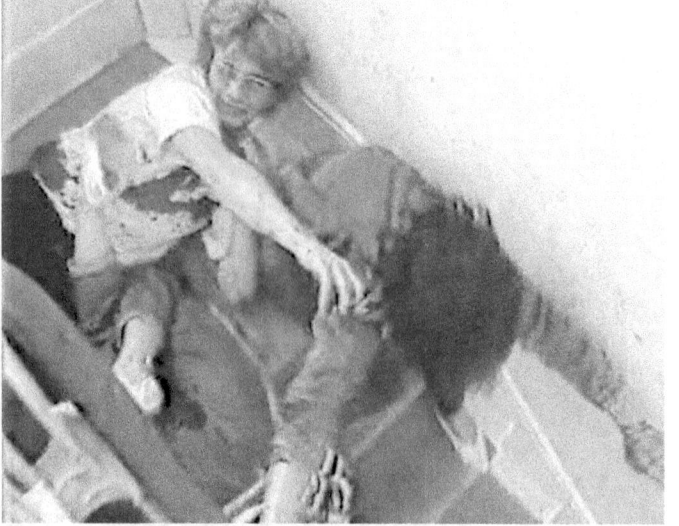

while blood sprays up the wall and the girls laugh delightedly.

Scenes of the increasingly worried adult characters talking are intercut with shots of Elizabeth and the girls in a darkened place performing candlelit satanic ceremonies, accompanied by a reverberating thrash metal cacophony on the soundtrack. This representation of innocence corrupted by evil is basic but effective. During one such ceremony the girls evoke Satan (chanting "Come, Devil, Come" in a characteristically British self-conscious, half-hearted way). Then there's an unexpectedly subtle morphing shot as Elizabeth's face is seen to transform into that of an older, dark-haired woman. "I am here" she intones in a devilish growl. The finale surprises both in its intensity and by the appearance of an unexpected antagonist. Jesus Christ himself, complete with crown of thorns, materializes to cast out the demonic spirits that possess the girls. By using strobe lighting, fast cutting, and rapid zooms, combined with the harrowing, ear splitting (electronically distorted) screams and groans of the girls seen writhing in agony as the Lord cleanses them of Evil, along with more of that overdubbed, raucous, death metal music, director Alan Briggs subjects the viewer to a sustained aural/visual assault that provides a suitably overwrought climax. The final shot could even be taken as paying homage to *Witchfinder General*—Jenny returns to the house with a doctor and, as she sees the carnage inside, the camera focuses on her horrified reaction and the film ends with a freeze frame of her hysterically screaming face.

The whole production is inevitably crude and clumsy, but it has obviously been made in earnest, unlike many amateur affairs, which try to disguise their shortcomings by taking a self-defensively humorous approach (better that people should laugh *with* your film rather than *at* it), Viewing *Suffer, Little Children* with a certain degree of indulgence helps to reinforce the maxim that an enthusiastically played game of schoolboy soccer can often be more entertaining than a lacklustre Champions League match.
—Mike Hodges

(Of all the titles caught up in "video nasty" ignominy, *Suffer, Little Children* has one of the stranger legends. Despite its stage school origins, it was picked up for video distribution by the Films Galore label; submitted to the BBFC, cuts of two minutes were requested but the police raided the distributors' premises before any re-edit could take place. The Director of Public Prosecution's office delayed proceedings for a further three months, virtually scuppering any chance this unlikely title had in an already crowded marketplace. Any suggestion from the authorities regarding alleged sex scenes or moments of extreme violence involving children, the likely focus of this misguided and panic-stricken investigation, was quietly sidelined—ed.).

1985

The Bride
The Comic
The Doctor and the Devils
The Hills Have Eyes Part II
Howling II: Stirba-Werewolf Bitch
Legend
Lifeforce
Murder Elite
Out of the Darkness
Slaughter High
Underworld
Young Sherlock Holmes

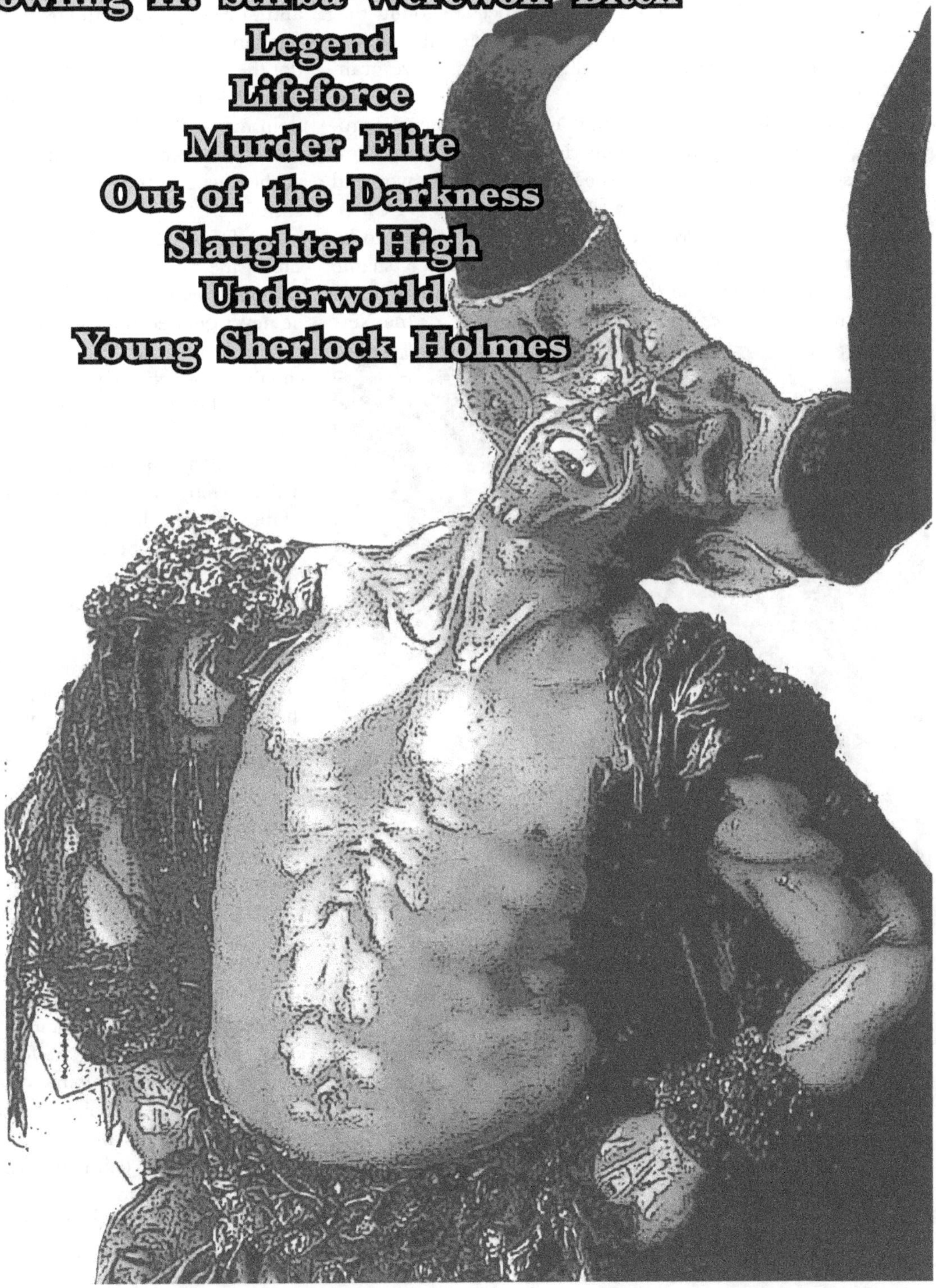

THE BRIDE

D: Franc Roddam
W: Lloyd Fonveille
Starring: Sting, Jennifer Beals, Clancy Brown, Geraldine Page, David Rappaport

Franc Roddam's take on the Frankenstein story, the 1985 film *The Bride*, has taken considerable flak over the years, and quite deservedly. Columbia stumped up $14 million, a generous budget at the time, for a two-hour fable that set out with the wrong objectives and left its few viewers adrift and unimpressed. People might return to the film infrequently and come away with the same opinion. I did, but on further inspection found that though *The Bride* was a complete failure as a horror film, it does have some retrospective curiosity value and a then rare grandiloquence.

The Bride feels like a feature-length example of the pop promos of a year or two previous, the visual extravaganzas commonly associated with Duran Duran, Elton John, Ultravox and Visage. By 1984 Arcadia's *Election Day*, directed by Roger Christian (*Black Angel*, *The Sender*), was a mini-epic proclaimed to be the most expensive music video yet made. "Nice video, shame about the song" as the *Not the Nine O'Clock News* comedy team would have it. *The Bride* was a Frankenstein movie for the New Romantic age, all splendor with little intelligence underneath. But what splendor! It was a far from a lone example, as certain directors took inspiration from the British pop video and others already adept in the form moved into feature film production taking their visionary nuances with them. *Pink Floyd: The Wall* (1982), *Dream One* (1984), *Absolute Beginners* (1986), *Give My Regards to Broad Street* (1984) and *It Couldn't Happen Here* (1987) are contemporary British films of a similar pop sensibility. Meanwhile, Russell Mulcahy, responsible for the core style, would progress to feature films with *Razorback* (1984) and *Highlander* (1986).

Roddam's overarching fault was to take a traditional fright subject and try to style it as a non-horror movie when it couldn't avoid toppling into genre traps. Filmed in le Dordogne, France and at Shepperton Studios in the UK, the film looks sumptuous throughout as the crew attach towers to existent structures, dot the landscape with crazy polystyrene statuary and make the most of studio space with elaborate floor plans for the Frankenstein manse. Shirley Russell, by that time divorced from enfant terrible husband Ken, ensures that if you are not awe-stricken at the backgrounds and backdrops then you will marvel at the costumes.

A further eccentricity in the props and casting finally subsumes the film. Roddam, the original UK film industry genre hopper, became so selfishly carried away with the details that he never queried the audience expectations or possible reaction to his playful adaptation of a popular tale. A scant handful of cinema productions pepper his eclectic career; ultimately, he achieved his biggest success with small-screen foodie smash *Masterchef*.

Roddam was wooed by a Lloyd Fonveille script that toyed with and flipped the Frankenstein tale, playfully reimagining it as a fable of friendship, love and female empowerment. In his 2002 commentary for the DVD release, Roddam states at one telling moment: "This is the point at which you can't tell if it's a fairy tale or an intellectual diatribe." I can help you there, Franc, it's definitely not an intellectual diatribe. In this version there is no subtext, only an overdressed naivety. No penis envy, just a passing procession of cameo appearances in a pantomime horror show. Not a good thing, but eventually fascinating in its own way.

The film begins with a rollicking opening laboratory sequence, as the proposed bride of the monster has life channeled back through her assembled body parts in an experiment harnessing an electrical storm. It is a wondrously elaborate and full-on Gothic horror scene, which on each viewing will pep up the viewer, momentarily raising hopes that are quickly dashed, as so much of the remainder reveals a damp squib of a movie reluctant to engage properly in nightmares. The creature (Clancy Brown) escapes the fire that destroys the lab, a conflagration that also kills both the Pretorious-like Dr. Zahlus (Quentin Crisp) and Frankenstein's physically malformed assistant (Timothy Spall). Frankenstein (Sting) and the female creation escape the destruction, and, as I have remarked in the past, if Frankenstein can raid a cemetery and piece together body parts that come out looking like Jennifer Beals then chuck me a shovel now!

The creature teams up with a dwarf (David Rappaport), and the film turns to study their developing friendship. We periodically cut back to Frankenstein and the female creature, now called Eva, but their scenes are pure mumblecore with Sting in

Japanese poster for *The Bride*

vital need of reanimation himself. Jennifer Beals will continue to look oh-so-beautiful, but simple. Her dialogue will shortly expand to try and sell us her feminist and intellectual independence, fresh and stimulating to the society into which she is introduced, but it is passé and unconvincing here.

Clancy Brown's creature is a born-again dunderhead too. It is up to Rappaport, fresh from Gavin Millar's offbeat telephone-centered horror drama *Unfair Exchanges* for the BBC's *Screen Two*, to bring some genuine acting brio into the film. His death scene is touchingly played, and as it follows an act in which he is a baby on a trapeze and Brown the mother in a headscarf, their story together concludes in a twisted Pietà, with the dwarf dying on cue in the monster's arms. Few of the many novelty performances offer anything of true import. Anthony Higgins renders cool and classy support during the "Baron and the bride" half of the story, and Alexei Sayle is a glowering, bitter circus owner of certain roistering presence. Most are wasted with little or no dialogue. Quentin Crisp, later to impress in a guest slot on *The Equalizer* of all things, could have been called on to do more here than bear witness and die. Guy Rolfe is only contracted to loiter while Geraldine Page is cursed by a role of meagre interest and no opportunity. Roddam had previous cult success with *Quadrophenia* and provided a few jobs for the boys that brought him his first hit. Phil Daniels and Gary Shail appear as circus people, Daniels communicating primarily with a scowl or a snarl before his well-earned impalement death scene. They also ensure that eighteenth century mullets abound. It looks at times like the Cult of Toyah at that circus.

The Baron is an evil blighter, sent a little doolally in the dope den of his secret room and eventually realizing that his science project is a bit tasty. The male creature inexplicably loses some of Sarah Monzani's more monstrous make-up details before he's granted an incredulous opportunity to couple off with the bride, having lobbed Frankenstein out the window to his death. The chic monster pair honeymoon in Venice "where the streets are made of water" and the viewer sits lantern-jawed. Aesthetically pleasing throughout, its beauty twinned with an innate absurdity, there is never a dull moment, and I can't deny an affection brewing for this mess with each revisit. No matter how much *The Bride* botches, it makes up for it with ample detail for any spectator to revel in.
—Paul Higson

THE COMIC

D: Richard Driscoll
W: Richard Driscoll
Starring: Steve Munroe, Berdia Timimi, Jeff Perrier, Vass Anderson

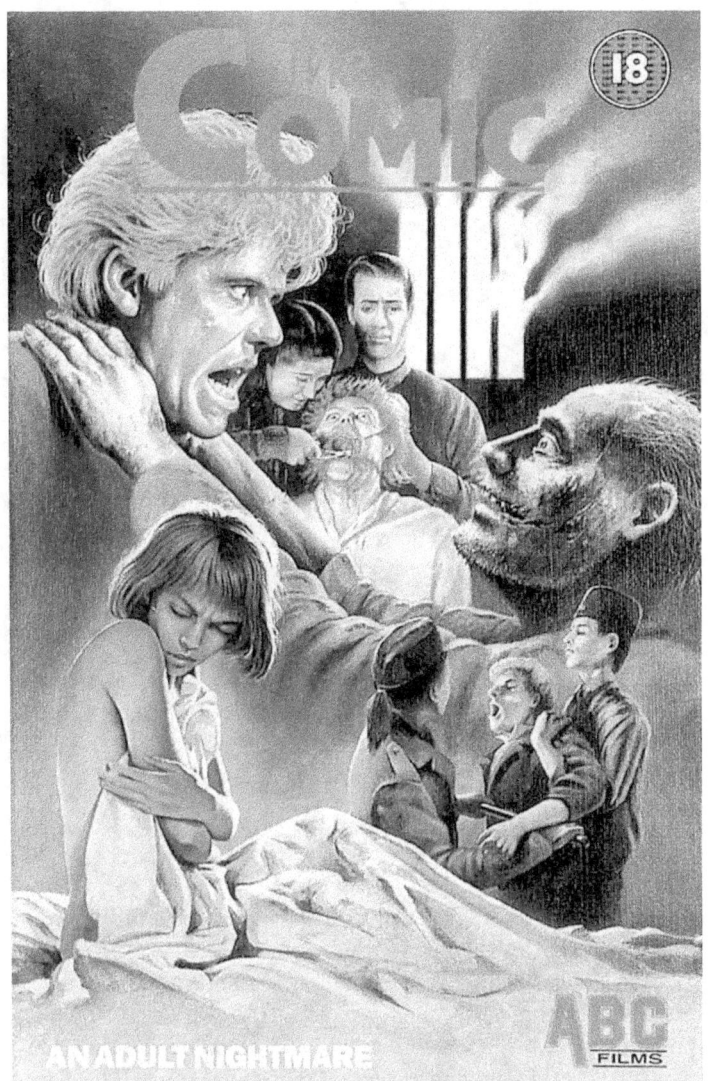

Where does one start with Richard Driscoll? A man so shameless he not only plagiarizes other directors' work (2001's *Kannibal* must have had Thomas Harris, Jonathan Demme and Ridley Scott frothing at the mouth like Anthony Hopkins in the depths of his dungeon cell), to say nothing of the yet-to-materialize *Harry and the Wizards*, *Games of the Thorns* and *When the Devil Rides Out*, but also plunders his *own* movies! To date, the woeful *The Legend of Harrow Woods*, aka *Evil Calls: The Raven*, has been re-edited and released twice; and somehow Driscoll persuaded the likes of Peter O'Toole, Daryl Hannah, Brigitte Nielsen, Sylvester McCoy, Patrick Bergin, Michael Madsen, Rik Mayall and Buster Bloodvessel to participate in his farcical *Blues Brothers*-meets-Herschell Gordon Lewis scam epic *Eldorado*, hastily repackaged as *Highway to Hell* mere weeks after its semi-legit DVD release, with a whopping half hour chopped out and all of the songs redubbed.

That Driscoll—aka actor "Stephen Craine"—ever got any films made *at all* could be a miracle in itself (his self-financed operation sometimes rumored to be the result of allegedly persuading George Lucas to accredit him royalties for a supposed minor "role" in *Return of the Jedi*): everyone always wondered not only *why* he did it, but how. His 2013 prosecution by the Inland Revenue for massive tax fraud spoke volumes and probably took us a few steps closer to the truth. But enough theorizing—on to *The Comic* itself. One of the highlights of the 1990 "Splatterfest" event at the Scala Cinema in King's Cross saw Driscoll on stage, proclaiming himself to be "the new Hammer Films" before slinking off into the cold night air clutching cans of film under his arm following an audience reception for *The Comic* to which the word "hostile" barely does justice.

Driscoll's problem—one of his problems, at least—is that he delusionally believes his work to be of great import, and thus

imbues it with so much cack-handed "gravitas" and "symbolism" that your average viewer, never mind a seasoned lover of all things crap like myself, loses patience from the get-go. In *The Comic*, for example, the (ahem) "plot" is set in a post-apocalyptic, post-nuclear world, for absolutely no discernible reason whatsoever, and seemingly all lensed on one sound stage. The film's barely seconds in when—again, for no explicable reason—an unnamed female we *never* see again delivers some rambling aphorisms directly to camera about "a world where fashion and culture are dead, and people do not survive, only exist." Ironically, if the film was made and set in Hackney nowadays, such a speech would be uncannily apposite—but in 1985, followed by an extremely overlong opening credit sequence, blaringly unsubtle incidental music (which persists pretty much throughout) and the initial utilization of one of many swathes of dry ice (again for no other conceivable purpose other than that possibly a premier smoke-machine manufacturer stumped up some dosh and requested plenty of product placement), it's simply pointless.

Oh yes, narrative. Okay, as far as I can discern: In our el cheapo post-nuclear setting, while the rest of the world has Mad Max racing other petrolheads through desert scrubland, the apex of an entertainer's career over here is to be a crap working man's club stand-up. When a greasy-ponytailed promoter won't give grumpy ginger Sam Coex a break, because there's already somebody funny in the job, carrot-top decides (after, again, some ludicrous exposition accompanied by yet more dry ice and meaningless face-paint) to off his rival and bury him in his garden, henceforth becoming very successful. Somewhere along the way, he marries a local prozzie, who then gets bribed into flitting off with the local gangland boss (real actor Vass Anderson), gives birth, develops a coke habit, and eventually burns to death in a drug den—at which point the police, mid-investigation, also find the dead rival's corpse, subsequently banging his murderer up in the slammer. Except I could have sworn he was *already* in the slammer, after being abducted earlier by futuristic drone cops. Or was he? It's honestly impossible to tell by this point, and even harder to give a shit.

Why does *any* of it happen? Where do various characters drop out of sight? What does the flashback—involving teenage Coex watching some unintroduced-to-us female relative through a keyhole as an unknown assailant murders her—pertain to? Why does his daughter appear to be about three years old less than a month after her birth? Or if more time *has* elapsed, how do we know? Who are all the rumpled figures meandering, like the *Bugsy Malone* down-and-outs, around a prison? Why, when his missus performs a sultry strip routine, and is informed by her husband "listen how well you did," is the applause *muted*? Most importantly, what bearing does the initial premise of the murder have on *any* of the subsequent events, and why, in any case, are we supposed to sympathize with someone avaricious enough to kill his contemporaries simply in order to steal their job? And, if only one murder is committed, why does it look, at the end, like a *dozen* dead bodies are rising from the graves to avenge their killer, a là William Lustig's *Maniac*?

In 2014 the *Daily Telegraph* ran a piece on Driscoll's tax fiddles, during which they named *Eldorado* as "the worst film ever," calling it "beyond bad." Their opinion of *The Comic* remains undeclared, but as choice examples of the output of Britain's most notorious film flim-flammer, the two movies would make a hell of a pairing. Maybe the *Telegraph* ought to offer Mr. D a few quid and "treat" their readers to a freebie DVD giveaway double bill …
—Darius Drewe

THE DOCTOR AND THE DEVILS

D: Freddie Francis
W: Dylan Thomas, Ronald Harwood
Starring: Timothy Dalton, Jonathan Pryce, Twiggy, Julian Sands, Stephen Rea

A bit of a slog, this one. Another variant on the Burke & Hare case, exec-produced by Mel Brooks, directed by ace cameraman and regular jobbing Brit horror legend Francis, and assembling a cast groaning with big names and, erm, Julian Sands. The major selling point here—the basis for this project was a decades-old unused Dylan Thomas script. Thomas was a wondrous poet (and wrote some nifty ghost stories in his time), but you do wonder why it didn't occur to the makers that there was a reason why this particular screenplay lay untouched for so long. In any event, another writer adapted it for 1980s consumption, so it's unclear which bits of the final product might be attributable to Thomas. The character names are, frankly, rubbish—Dr. Rock, Robert Fallon, Timothy Broom, Billy Bedlam.

It's very much of its time, despite the period trappings and the Thomas connection. Obscure subject, historical basis, everyone in fancy dress with blow-dried hair, huge wads of cash thrown at it, watch it sink. What was the deal with so much 1980s British horror of this type? *The Bride*, *Gothic*, *Edge of Sanity*, template firmly set, failure guaranteed.

This film needed so much more work on it. We instantly recognize it as Burke & Hare yet again (despite efforts to disguise the fact). There's the mandatory grimy streets, blood soaked surgeons, gutsy prostitutes and sozzled boozers. Guess what happens next. We know!! The familiar yarn rolls out for the umpteenth time, done fairly straight on this occasion without bucketloads of gore or nudity, but with lots of talk. There are at least some good performances, balanced with plenty of poor ones. Jonathan Pryce as Burke substitute "Fallon" and Siân Phillips as Dr. Rock's prudish sister are on the money. Sadly, they're in the minority.

Dalton as Dr. Rock overdoes it on the mannerisms, admittedly saddled with a difficult role as Rock spends interminable time philosophizing. Stephen Rea and Twiggy put on funny voices, Rea (as the Hare figure "Broom") overdoing the Oirish brogue while Twiggy (as the prostitute with a "heart of gold") matches him with a laughable cockney chirp.

The normally reliable Patrick Stewart gives a somewhat exaggerated turn playing a jealous colleague of Rock. And so ultimately, we turn to the enigma that is Julian Sands—wooden, and too old for his role but still he was cast! An actor who seems to have spent the 1980s featuring in one flop British horror film after another—didn't anyone notice the connection? Or perhaps there was some obscure law around at the time stating that if filmmakers were producing substandard horror then he had to be in the cast!

French poster for *The Doctor and the Devils*

Not quite a directorial swansong for Freddie Francis—he was called in to replace Ken Wiederhorn on *Dark Tower*, a Barcelona-set "haunted high-rise" affair starring Michael Moriarty and Jenny Agutter, and did an episode of *Tales from the Crypt* in the mid-'90s, but his heart remained in cinematography and the later days of his career will be celebrated more for his D.O.P. work on the likes of *Cape Fear*, *Rainbow*, and *The Straight Story* than for fag-end hack jobs like this.

—Gerald Lea

THE HILLS HAVE EYES PART II

D: Wes Craven
W: Wes Craven
Starring: Tamara Stafford, Michael Berryman, Janus Blythe, Kevin Spirtas, John Bloom

Funded largely with British money following the strong UK video performance of *The Hills Have Eyes* and released in what its director deemed to be an unapproved "workprint" version, this troubled sequel to Craven's second horror feature mundanely reworks the basic scenario of its predecessor into a predictable slasher movie format. The filmmaker has long written it off as a project he took on to keep working in the wake of the mainstream failure of *Swamp Thing*, but Craven's career is full of similarly disastrous movies born of traumatic production periods (*Cursed*), alongside misguided experiments (*Vampire in Brooklyn*, *My Soul to Take*) and simply dreadful, cynical money-making exercises (the last two *Scream* movies, *Music of the Heart*). Of course, it's still tough to be too harsh on a director who has given us at least three genuinely great modern horror films plus "that" basketball scene with Anne Ramsey in the strangely adorable *Deadly Friend*.

Hills II opens with a narrative crawl that confusingly suggests the events of the first movie actually happened in the 1970s, inspiring this film! In a way, this brings a nice sense of symmetry, given that Craven's *The Last House on the Left* may have been the first prominent modern horror to claim inspiration from real events—something which has now become *de rigueur* in an era where seemingly "found footage" is in every other genre release.

Original survivor Robert Houston is thanklessly dragged back as the previously triumphant Bobby Carter, seen at the outset telling his shrink how his life is haunted by the events of eight years earlier. Houston plays no part in the main story and his presence exists purely to shoehorn copious extant footage into the otherwise bereft script. Although not taken to the extreme of the later, flashback-dominated *Silent Night, Deadly Night Part 2*—which at least had a lot of fun with its new material—this film's inclusion of overlong sequences from the 1977 classic serves to emphasize the redundancy and ineptitude of most of Craven's update. This does, however, lead to a memorable moment of (intentional?) cinematic lunacy when returning canine hero, German Shepherd "Beast" has a vision in which he recalls savaging Pluto (Berryman) in the final act of *Hills*.

Hills Part II follows an old-fashioned trend set by *Wait Until Dark* (and rejigged for the slasher/exploitation audience with the underrated *Eyes of a Stranger*) by featuring a blind heroine played by Tamara Stafford, in her last credited acting role. Inevitably, she winds up as a crude, novelty version of the patented resilient

goon easily felled during fights with Blythe and blandly defeated, for the second time, in a rematch against "Beast." Listen out for one moment in which he laughs (distractingly) like Scooby-Doo. New character Reaper, despite his intimidating bulk, is just another mundane machete-wielding slasher flick Wildman. Of the ensemble cast of generic dead-meat, the most annoying is a stereotyped doomed, smart-mouthed black dude who hates the desert ("It ain't natural to be in a place without a disco!"), boasts about his manhood and turns out to be a big coward. Fans of *24* will get an extra kick out of the fact that his girlfriend is played by a young Penny Jerald, who bares her breasts and figures in the film's only moment of graphic gore, a throat slashing.

Craven sadly transforms the inter-family conflict at the core of *Hills* into a by-the-numbers slasher pic shamelessly aping the *Friday the 13th* movies that his *Last House* partner Sean S. Cunningham created. You get climactic scenes of bodies crashing through windows, and a last minute scare after the danger has apparently passed—plus, most blatantly of all, a Harry Manfredini score ripping off his own already derivative *Friday* soundtracks, right down to some virtually identical musical "jumps." The powerful brutality of the original is replaced by bloodless, mostly off-screen murders with no impact whatsoever, and the finale relies on our hero setting up (in record time) a super-clever trap of the kind that appears to have fascinated Craven throughout his career. All that being said, it's still a preferable movie to revisit than the majority of Craven's post-*Scream* forays into anonymous, made-by-committee Hollywood fare.
—Steven West

HOWLING II: STIRBA–WEREWOLF BITCH (HOWLING II: YOUR SISTER IS A WEREWOLF)

D: Philippe Mora
W: Robert Sarno, Gary Brandner
Starring: Christopher Lee, Annie McEnroe, Marsha Hunt, Reb Brown, Sybil Danning

final girl, feeling her way around a room full of her dead friends a là Mia Farrow in *Blind Terror*. Stafford valiantly attempts a real, non-patronizing performance, but is ill served by the script's dumb decision to give her heightened sensory powers that, at times, verge on super-heroine status and, yet, at other moments merely fit the narrative.

Stafford and rent-a-hunk boyfriend Kevin Spirtas (later, as Kevin Blair, to be the hero of *Friday the 13th Part VII: The New Blood*) set off into the desert with a bus full of Motocross fans—cue Yamaha product placement galore!—including Janus Blythe, returning as the "civilized" member of the original's primitive family. She's now called "Rachel" and again exists mostly to fill in the backstory of Jupiter and company for those who either didn't see the first film or were making some tea during this sequel's flashback interludes. The group make the mistake of taking a shortcut, and break down in the middle of nowhere so they can be menaced by the surviving Pluto (Michael Berryman) and a new character called Reaper (7 foot 4 inches Al Adamson veteran, John Bloom), the big bad brother of the late Papa Jupe.

At his best, Craven is an intelligent and sophisticated filmmaker, but you wouldn't know it from a sequel that relies on dumb contrivances (Pluto somehow knows how to ride a motorbike just so he can participate in a chase scene) and slasher movie clichés, including labored false scares, silly pranks and prowling subjective camerawork. The striking poster-boy of the first movie (and of Craven's *Deadly Blessing* for its UK video release), Berryman is here reduced to a surprisingly unfrightening

The Howling franchise recently added a bland post-*Twilight* teen horror to its brand (*The Howling: Reborn*) but is almost exclusively remembered as a series of unrelated, hideous sequels hijacking only the name of Joe Dante's deservedly beloved 1981 movie. The line-dancing lycanthropic nightmare of *The Howling VII: New Moon Rising* is 90 minutes of suffering you don't easily forget, but in retrospect each *Howling* movie achieved the rare horror sequel feat of being vastly different to that which preceded it. Most of them are messy, a couple of them are terrible, but at least the series never got stuck in a creative rut like most of its kin. You might struggle to remember which Jason movie features the guy getting split down the middle while doing a handstand (it's *Friday the 13th Part 3*, and the guy deserves it—*anyone* who does impromptu handstands deserves it) but everyone knows which *Howling* movie features Sybil Danning as Stirba, Werewolf Bitch!

Among later entries, *Howling VI: The Freaks*, a Ray Bradbury-inspired modern Gothic, is particularly inventive, while *Howling V* has moments of atmosphere, *Howling III* is batshit crazy—and *Howling II* is one of the most perversely enjoyable genre sequels of its period.

It opens marvellously, with Christopher Lee, apparently transmitting to us live from Space, reading from the Bible, mostly the bits about filthy fornications and hairy beasts. Let's face it, if you rolled over in bed late one night and were confronted with Christopher Lee proclaiming "Behold, the Great Mother of Harlots and all abominations," it would be a major turn-on, whatever your sexual preferences. Subsequently, it's Lee who provides the deepest "Amen" at an L.A. funeral where an anonymous corpse is pretending to be the deceased Dee Wallace from *The Howling*. Lee's "occult investigator" is comfortably cool donning funky 1980s sunglasses in a club where the only other genuine male talent is the unmistakable nose of *Auf Wiedersehen Pet* era Jimmy Nail, who would return to horror a few years later with *Pet* co-star Timothy Spall in the peculiar *Dream Demon*. Jimmy provides an early fatality when he's felled from above by a large wooden crate (just like in a cartoon!) as his chums are ravaged by a werewolf.

Annie McEnroe is a fresh-faced reporter assigned to cover the werewolf killings. She teams up with the brother (Reb Brown) of Dee Wallace's character to listen to Lee's impersonation of Basil Exposition. We learn of the great numbers of werewolves who live secretly among us and of their growing immunity to silver; it turns out titanium is the key ingredient to their destruction! All three of them head to the "dark country" of Transylvania—though you're not fooling us, Prague!—to pursue Stirba (Sybil Danning), the apparent reigning queen of werewolves.

Director Philippe Mora had already enjoyed a fabulously diverse career prior to the gig of *Howling II*, going head-to-head with Dennis Hopper for the astonishing *Mad Dog Morgan*, Rutger Hauer in the offbeat *A Breed Apart* and Christopher Lee as the baritone-sporting singing villain "Mr. Midnight" in *Return of Captain Invincible*. Most notably, he helmed one of the more underrated pseudo-werewolf films of the 1980s, the genuinely startling *The Beast Within*, an oft-overlooked benchmark for special make-up effects work.

Stirba eventually shows up, sporting a black dress with plunging neckline that gets promptly ripped off as she watches two werewolves go at it, while herself transforming into a terrifying creature that looks suspiciously like ... Sybil Danning with stick-on hair patches (the movie keeps returning to the scene to reveal the three snarling, scratching and whimpering at each other like some kind of forgotten lycanthropic prequel to *Wild Things*.) Meanwhile our heroes stay in Room 666 at a hotel that clearly doesn't have six floors but does have plenty of shifty staff members who creepily chuckle when you mention that fact. Although they display less onscreen romantic chemistry than Ralph Fiennes and the naked extras in *Schindler's List*, Brown and McEnroe engage in ill-timed, unlikely hotel room sex presumably in the absence of anything else to do. If that isn't enough to enjoy, around an hour in somebody gets their head squeezed until their eyeballs bloodily pop, an effect executed far better here than in the goofy, similar moment in *Friday the 13th Part 3*.

It was a nice idea to cast Lee as an unambiguous, evil-fighting representative of the forces of good a là Van Helsing, the adversary he so often battled at Hammer. It's one of his more sympathetic horror roles, and in terms of screen time one of his biggest late-period genre performances. In contrast to the glorified cameos that often arise when a horror legend is top-billed, he truly is the star of the show. Although the notoriously terse actor was quick to point out during interviews for homegrown dud *Funny Man* that he hadn't made a horror film in two decades, he allegedly took the *Howling II* gig because he had never done a werewolf movie. Of course, werewolves or not, it must have been impossible to turn down a picture offering a chance to be attacked by a possessed midget who acts like he has been adversely affected by the closing scene of *Don't Look Now*.

It's by far the goriest of all the *Howling* movies, with fake heads savaged by emerging baby werewolves, lycanthropes bloodily maimed at regular intervals and an assortment of the kind of wonderful bladder FX that dominated Mora's *The Beast Within*. If nothing else, *Howling II* is consistently busy and delivers a lively climax before its hilarious spin on the stock 1980s horror Shock Ending. And the resident punk band "Babel" are, for all their unrepentant 1980s naffness, several times more enjoyable to watch than the pretentious 2006 movie of the same name. One of them went on to pen the theme tune for ITV's game show *Catchphrase* ...

Incidentally, throughout the movie, it remains unclear just how seriously anyone is taking all this peculiar titanium-enhanced werewolf nonsense ... until, that is, its unforgettable credits sequence. Here, as any horror fan worth their salt will know all too well, Danning's disrobing is repeated ad infinitum and juxtaposed with various unrelated cutaway reaction shots taken from other scenes in the movie. This makes it look like the

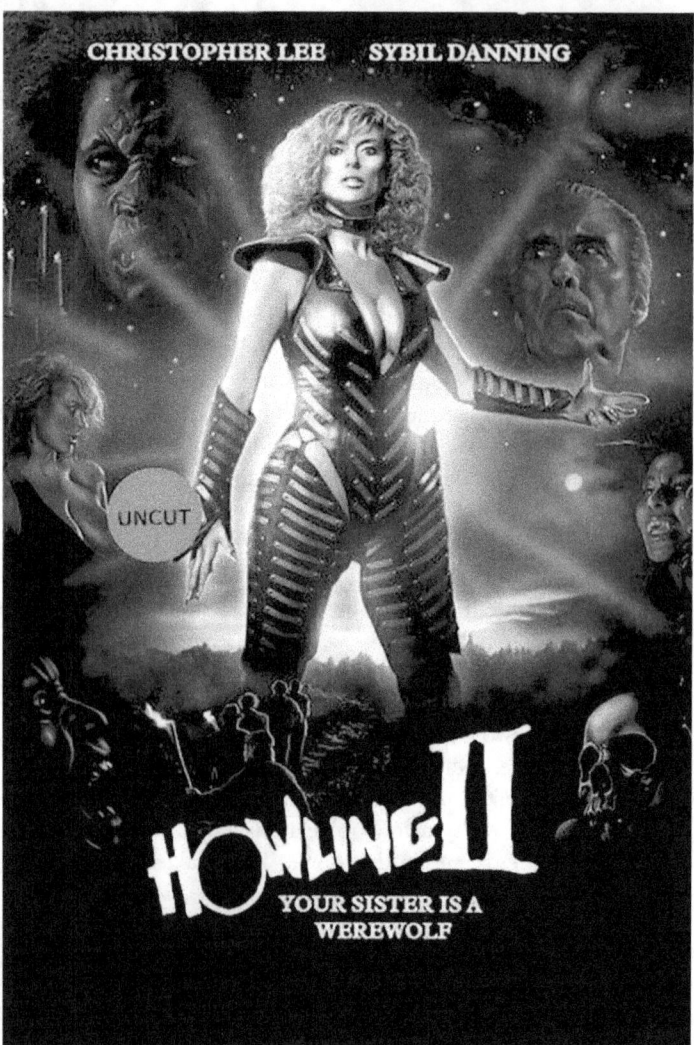

There are bad sequels and there are *bad* sequels. In discussions about the worst follow-ups of all time, people speak in awed tones about *Exorcist II: The Heretic* and *Highlander II: The Quickening*, but I think *Howling II* can stand in that distinguished company with its head held high.

Stefan Crosscoe, Occult Investigator (Christopher Lee), has uncovered proof that a sub-culture of werewolves is living secretly among us. Karen White's brother Ben (Reb Brown), and her journalist friend Jenny (Annie McEnroe) see footage of Karen's transformation and death. He hopes to enlist their aid in tracing a powerful new werewolf strain (immune to silver but not to titanium!!) to its lair in the Old Country, Transylvania …

Although the film attempts to pick up the story where the first movie left off, it becomes clear very quickly that the two will bear very little resemblance to each other. Screenwriter Gary Brandner originally set out to adapt his own novel rather than write a sequel to the first film, which might partly explain why this seems like a very different beast. But after being asked to change the story's setting twice, Brandner left the project and other hands fashioned what followed.

The rug is well and truly pulled out from under our feet when we see what is meant to be a reprise of the scene from *The Howling*, in which Dee Wallace Stone's newsreader transforms into a werewolf and is shot dead on live TV. Werewolf Karen White was one of the first film's less successful creature effects, but what we see here looks more like an escapee from *Planet of the Apes*. This may not be Philippe Mora's fault. According to Gary Brandner, there was a mix-up over costumes. There wasn't enough money to create enough new ones, so Mora asked around for hand-me-downs. Someone got their wires crossed and supplied monkey suits instead …

On top of this, producer Steven A. Lane recalls that the Czech shoot was a difficult one, with ancient equipment and a crew who were mostly drunk by lunchtime. So, in light of these difficulties, perhaps we should be grateful that the film isn't even more of a mess!

The fidgety editing style doesn't help. There's hardly a scene that doesn't contain at least one quick cut-away as though to underline the action. If someone mentions Karen White, we get a brief shot of Karen screaming in her coffin. This tends to give the film a twitchy, disjointed feel. One's enjoyment overall may depend on how one feels about Babel's theme tune, because it is repeated continually throughout.

entire main cast is reacting with exasperation/horny delight/good cheer to her norks, and it means that *Howling II*'s existence is justified if only for the Christopher Lee grin Mora edits in at one point during this riotous montage.

Lurking in the lower rungs of the cast, incidentally, is Ferdy Mayne, whose fantasy/horror movie roles range from the sublime Count von Krolock in *Dance of the Vampires*/*The Fearless Vampire Killers* through to oddities as diverse as playing God in *Night Train to Terror*, aged patriarchal figures in *Conan the Destroyer* and *Hawk the Slayer* and facing the ultimate horror: co-starring with Julian Sands (*Warlock: The Armageddon*).
—Steven West

• • •

I was very excited when I first spotted *Howling II* on the shelves of our local video emporium, back in the mid-1980s. *The Howling* had been a cracking werewolf yarn with some very effective horror sequences, a pulsating vein of black humor, and plenty of post-modern references to lycanthropic cinema of the past. The effects are variable, but Rob Bottin's transformation sequence is a showstopper, and the creature that Eddie the Mangler turns into was the best of its type that had appeared onscreen up till that point. At last, cinematic werewolves looked like the ones that had been loping through my imagination since I was a child. So, I was filled with joy at the prospect of a sequel. My heightened expectation soon faded rapidly as I started to watch the film …

The most effective horror sequence here is a *Don't Look Now* "homage" featuring an encounter between Christopher Lee and a homicidal dwarf in a red cloak. I don't want to spoil the film for anyone who hasn't seen it, but I will say that Lee fares slightly better than Donald Sutherland did ...

The cast are a rather mixed bunch. Lee works hard to lend his usual gravitas to proceedings, but his dignity is undermined when Crosscoe goes undercover at a new wave punk club dressed in a bright orange shirt and white wraparound shades. The great Ferdy Mayne (*Dance of the Vampires*, *The Vampire Lovers*) is wasted as an elderly werewolf who gets a couple of lines and a rather pathetic death scene. Sybil Danning (*Battle Beyond the Stars*) is a striking presence as the titular Stirba but isn't required to do much more than wear bizarre outfits that display a lot of cleavage. Admittedly, she does this very well. Reb Brown (*Space Mutiny*, *Yor: Hunter from the Future*) tries his best. He screeches and blasts away at the werewolves with great gusto but doesn't manage to brew up much chemistry with his female co-star. That might not be Reb's fault. Annie McEnroe (*Snowbeast*, *Beetlejuice*) wanders through the film with a fixed expression of bewilderment on her face and looks as if she is planning to fire her agent.

Marsha Hunt (*Dracula A.D. 1972*) actually manages to carry herself through the film with her poise largely intact as one of Stirba's lieutenants. This is no mean feat considering all the absurd things that she is required to do, such as participate in cinema's first werewolf threesome. *The Howling* was rather coy about its mating scene, but Mora is less bashful than Joe Dante and presents us with one of the inescapable consequences of female lycanthropy—hairy boobs.

Speaking of boobs, one cannot review this film without mentioning the end credit sequence, in which we are treated to no less than 17 repeats (yes, I counted) of the shot where Sybil Danning tears her top off, intercut with "reaction shots" of the other cast members. This was the brainchild of one of the producers, and Danning was reputedly less than pleased when she saw the results. It goes without saying that we hear Babel's *Howling II* theme again while this is going on. It's possible that this tune is played 17 times during the film too, but you'll have to tally that up for yourself.

There's a lot of fun to be had with *Howling II*, but mostly at its expense. If you approach it expecting a decent sequel to *The Howling*, you will suffer indescribable torment. But if you approach it expecting a carnival of the absurd, featuring killer midgets, were-apes, furry boobs and Christopher Lee in sunglasses, you might just have a ball.
—Paul Mudie

LEGEND

D: Ridley Scott
W: William Hjortsberg
Starring: Tom Cruise, Mia Sara, Tim Curry, David Bennent, Alice Playten, Billy Barty

The Lord of Darkness (Tim Curry) captures Princess Lili (Mia Sara) and threatens to bring eternal night to the world by slaying the last of the unicorns. Lili's sweetheart Jack (Tom Cruise) must save the day.

Ridley Scott's homage to fairy tales was not a commercial success on its first release, despite Rob Bottin's make-up earning an Oscar nomination. Bottin's varied creatures; fairies, goblins and elves (one of whom is played by veteran Billy Barty) are certainly an asset, each one displaying character and imagination in its design. Reportedly, the visage of villainous goblin Blix (Alice Playten) was patterned after that of Rolling Stones guitarist Keith Richards. There is certainly a resemblance. And watch out for Christopher Lee's Hammer stunt-double Eddie Powell as a Mummy.

Despite the film's sets being destroyed by fire before the end of shooting, no disparity shows: the fantasy worlds are clearly defined, superbly realized and convincing throughout. The world of light is awash with drifting blossoms, verdant meadows and glittering brooks. The world of darkness, however, is far more interesting, with its flames, shadows and swirling mists. Indeed, the film is at its best whenever the powers of darkness are onscreen.

Unfortunately, lethargy creeps in whenever innocence is presented—with Jack, in particular, proving an insipid hero (though I doubt that Johnny Depp, Robert Downey, Jr. or even Jim Carrey—all of whom, rumor has it, were apparently considered as leading men—could have made anything of such a bland part.)

In terms of both writing and performance, Tim Curry's horned demon fares much better. For all his raging strength and evil intentions, there are hints of vulnerability in his desire for and trust of Mia Sara's dark-eyed Princess; all of which is ably suggested by the actor, conveyed even through his bulky red prosthetics.

In his book *Behind the Mask of the Horror Actor* (Titan 2004), Pinhead actor Doug Bradley shares an insight into how Tim Curry suffered for his art. Bradley's driver for *Hellbound: Hellraiser II* (1988) had also taxied Curry during *Legend*. The driver gleefully relates to Bradley that, in anticipation of an eight-hour, head to waist make-up job, Curry grew understandably nervous in the back of the car: "The closer we got to the studio, I could see he was getting quite twitchy and restless ... he seemed to be in quite a bad way by the end of the shoot." Needless to say, the driver's banter did nothing to ease Bradley's own nerves!

Scott's finished film was cut from 125 minutes to 89 minutes for release. Even at that length, it's more than plenty. For all its longueurs, however, *Legend* is ravishing to look at, making one wonder why today's films can't look as beautiful.
—Stephen Mosley

LIFEFORCE

D: Tobe Hooper
W: Dan O'Bannon, Don Jakoby
Starring: Steve Railsback, Peter Firth, Frank Finlay, Mathilda May

Colin Wilson's 1976 novel *The Space Vampires* ended up as one of the more insanely ambitious genre movies of the 1980s: a demented Cannon Films sci-fi epic, co-written by Dan O'Bannon, that throws a loopy range of influences at the screen. The opening stretch—bored astronauts discover something extraordinary—riffs on O'Bannon's *Alien*. The nature of the central threat turns it into an offbeat vampire movie with the pre-*Species* titillating gimmick of a naked hot chick sucking the life out of willing men. It turns into an elaborate disaster movie a là Irwin Allen when a 150-mile-long needle-shaped structure starts heading to Earth, next developing into a zombie-plague picture as London descends into chaos and even plummy '50s-style BBC announcers sound alarmed. The overall effect is like watching the collected sci-fi work of Nigel Kneale on crack: if that's not a true recommendation, what is?

This is Tobe Hooper's only bona fide British movie though it's common knowledge how close he came to bringing *Venom* to the screen—ultimately missing out on the vicarious pleasures of working with Ollie Reed, Klaus Kinski and a Black Mamba (aka "Friendliest Living Thing On Set.") *Lifeforce* was Hooper's first movie since the huge boffo box-office of *Poltergeist*, a success story dogged, at least for its director, by the infamous debate about the level of input from writer/producer Steven Spielberg. It was the first of a lavish three-picture deal from Cannon Films that yielded two equally unloved but fascinating rough diamonds: the *Invaders from Mars* remake and the sublime *Texas Chainsaw Massacre Part 2*.

Amid a welter of lovably goofy straight-faced B-movie style dialogue ("It's like ... a giant umbrella ... it's enormous!"), the crew of the *HMS Churchill*—led by Steve Railsback—sent to intercept and study Halley's Comet, discover a spacecraft within the head of the comet occupied by thousands of apparently prehistoric giant bats. Oh, and nude Mathilda May is on board too, enough to make any horny femme-starved astronaut perk up ("I've been in space for six months and she looks perfect to me!") The crew is decimated, but Railsback later shows up in Texas (well, it is a Tobe Hooper movie!) and the perfectly preserved May is brought back to Earth, where she requires regular energy feeds to avoid exploding into dust—these feeds being achieved by sucking the life-force out of men-folk. Railsback develops a psychic bond with May as she heads off on a mission to find a man from whom she can draw energy, and our nation's capital overruns with a May-instigated plague.

Although overlength results in some dramatic lulls around the mid-section, the much-maligned *Lifeforce* is a pretty unique and special movie, even if it was just too damned loopy for contemporary audiences. It's a once-in-a-lifetime big-budget, latter-day B-movie dominated by respectable British Shakespearean actors, who play its wild and wacky premise totally straight, and it's filled to the brim with diverse special effects. In an age of anonymous, goofy-looking CGI by the truckload, Hooper's use of animatronic reanimated cadavers, exploding bodies, giant bats, and good old-fashioned stunts are all impressive to behold. For no extra cost you even get Patrick Stewart's head erupting into geysers of blood and a bravura city climax complete with double deckers ablaze and Chancery Lane tube station destroyed.

Often the movie lacks the distinctive stamp of its own talented helmer, missing out in particular on his mischievous sense of gallows humor. It does, however, confirm his strength at invoking mayhem, and his command of action and FX. Like *Poltergeist* before it, Hooper's career-long inspiration from EC Comics is never far from the screen, especially in the scenes of gleefully grotesque desiccated corpses sparking to unnatural life.

Of the cast, Peter Firth plays it intense, like he's in *Hamlet* or something. Frank Finlay gamely wrestles with gaudy dialogue like, "It is my belief that the vampires of legend came from these creatures!" Ill-fated Stewart presides over an asylum, May (later the star of *Naked Tango*!) is a memorably enigmatic fantasy object and Railsback (the only actor to play Ed Gein, Charles Manson and the hero in *Turkey Shoot*!) deserves points for waking up in extreme panic after a dream in which he gropes and snogs a naked Mathilda ...there are worse nightmares, man! The escalating plot, constantly heading off in fresh directions, is matched by Henry Mancini's jaunty, old-school score and the film's especially lively main theme.
—Steven West

• • •

Lifeforce attacks with more ideas than your brain can cope with. Some of the themes examined here include alien invasion, sexuality and the tracking of an entity that can jump from body to body. This latter device was central to Colin Wilson's *The Space Vampires*, the 1976 novel the film is based on. The book is an SF thriller with lots of nutty philosophy, some of it connected with male and female energies, and proposing that all living things are vampiric. Sex is advised at one point for curing illness. Ah, Colin, we'd all be rushing to get a prescription if that were true! The book and the film aren't identical, so the novel is worth tracking down even if you've experienced the movie.

This film polarizes opinion. Viewers tend to either hate it or love it, like cinematic Marmite. It has had some unlucky breaks. Its truncated appearance in cinemas, shorn of its build up, is a travesty and must have made the plot seem like an incoherent mess; with story-telling the foreplay is vital, as it is a foundation for what is to come.

Pulp-crowd pleasing elements are present, often cited in negative criticism of the film and hence the reason why you might notice a defensive tone in this essay. Okay, the Space Girl is naked, but admit it, you'd consider that too if you could change your form to look gorgeous on every new planet. And frankly it is an amazing performance, Mathilda May managing to make this uber-sexual figure so frightening. She is one of the scariest vampires on celluloid, her eyes have a hunger and she seems full of intent and barely concealed power.

One character also mentions geometric progression, years before John Sutherland's Dracula-themed 1999 essay which asked of Bram Stoker's novel, "why isn't everyone a vampire?" and discussed the exponential spread of vampirism as if it were a disease.

One of the most fantastically disturbing dialogue lines is the Space Girl's comment to Carlsen that "I'm the feminine in your mind," which explains why Carlsen seems to be falling apart at

Italian poster for *Lifeforce*

the seams—how could a man cope if all the distaff aspects of his psyche had been extracted, made flesh and put up to no good!

So many small touches make this film superior to most other invasion movies. The aliens' ecology involves zombies and vampires and bats, explaining some of our ancient superstition as a race memory of the space visitors' last rape of our planet. Clearly their intergalactic pillage is designed to take the "long game" approach. Characters think scientifically, i.e. they suggest a theory then test it, refining it as they find out more. There are also some neat touches of British humor, for example the scene with the Prime Minister, the troops enforcing the quarantine, and one soldier honorably offering his sidearm (telling you more would spoil it.)

In summary, then, for me *Lifeforce* is an ambitious British SF film. Science fiction often wears horror's clothes, and after all why shouldn't it—the future is potentially a horrifying thing, and besides the certainties of life and death nobody knows what will happen. I wouldn't want every film to be like *Lifeforce*, but I'm glad it's there, to disturb, amaze, and linger in the mind.
—Elliot Iles

MURDER ELITE

D: Claude Whatham
W: N.J. Crisp
Starring: Ali MacGraw, Billie Whitelaw, Hywel Bennett, Ray Lonnen

Kevin Francis' Tyburn Films are often the subject of conversation whenever fans of British horror cinema congregate, once excited chat about their beloved Hammer classics or Amicus anthologies has been exhausted. Particular favorites *The Ghoul* and *Legend of the Werewolf* will be cited and discussed, usually with reference to their status as the last gasp of Gothic, or in debate as to their long-time unavailability for purchase on home viewing formats. Tyburn's fondly regarded documentary celebration of Peter Cushing's career, *A One-Way Ticket to Hollywood*, may crop up too, and the more knowledgeable/adventurous buff might cautiously throw in the 1974 psychological drama *Persecution* as a topic ripe for analysis. The combination of Cushing, Roy Ward Baker and Sherlock Holmes could even bring the 1984 TV movie *The Masks of Death* to the table. Mention *Murder Elite*, mind you, and you're likely to be met with silence and a sea of blank faces.

Nobody would advance *Murder Elite* as "the great lost Tyburn film," but as a late arrival at the party thrown by past askew oddities of UK psychodrama, it shouldn't be totally dismissed. From director Whatham, whose genre credentials include episodes of *Tales of the Unexpected* and *Supernatural*, and whose *That'll Be the Day* (1973) will stand forever as a cornerstone of the British pop movie scene, *Murder Elite* has hidden depths. It might well pass for a cozy, Sunday afternoon small-screen thriller, were it not for its violent slasher movie opening and the demented revelations at the close.

That woodland nighttime opener is a vicious shocker, especially when you consider how slow most of our filmmakers had been to seek inspiration in the stalk-and-slash murder sprees that had dominated American exploitation since *Friday the 13th*. The main body of the film can't quite live up to this masked madman/glinting knife/barking dog/screaming victim startler, and so plays out as a sub-*Les Diaboliques* type plot set in and around a stableyard run by Billie Whitelaw, with imported star MacGraw as the sister scheming against her, and with former *Sweeney* regular Garfield Morgan as the copper investigating the activities of a serial killer stalking the nearby village. Hywel Bennett lurks on the sidelines throughout, in what appears to be a homage to his similar characterizations in *Twisted Nerve* and *Endless Night*; James Bernard offers a vintage music score which papers over any cracks in true Bernard fashion; and the chilling final five minutes justify sitting through all the earlier clichés.

It's a great shame Tyburn seemed to grind to a halt after this one—worth tracking down if you can.
—Darrell Buxton

OUT OF THE DARKNESS

D: John Krish
W: John Krish
Starring: Garry Halliday, Michael Flowers, Emma Ingham, Anthony Winder

In 1980 Milton Subotsky heralded *The Monster Club* as the first horror feature film made for the entire family. His previous production company Amicus had been a largely anaemic concern, and even *The House That Dripped Blood* had managed to decapitate a pair of veteran actors without spilling a drop of the red stuff. Let Hammer Films splash the blood! Part of the reason for Subotsky's reticence may have been that, as an American, he knew that back home monster movies were for kids and teenagers, so why did this damn country he'd settled in insist on rating films in a way that would deny them most of their audience? Usually the most encompassing rating a horror film could garner was an "AA" certificate (14 and over admitted), normally reserved for comedy horrors like *Young Frankenstein* and *The Rocky Horror Picture Show*, though studio power had somehow wangled Steven Spielberg's *Jaws* a general admittance "A" certificate five years earlier. *The Monster Club* too secured its "A" rating, despite the inclusion of at least one disturbing image in the finale of its first tale with a melting protagonist.

Prior to 1980, The Children's Film and Television Foundation (previously the Children's Film Foundation) had produced a number of Saturday matinee items with a supernatural angle or featuring monsters or ghosts of a benign bent. Meanwhile on television, children's shows were scaring the bejesus out of British youngsters every bit as much as the classic horror filling the late evening film slot might be spooking their parents. In a cash-strapped country, with initiatives for the film industry being sidelined and government support for British Cinema on the wane, the Children's Film and Television Foundation's days as a production outlet were numbered in the 1980s. Toward the end they put out a couple of atmospheric and so potentially more disconcerting titles, in Andrew Bogle's *Haunters of the Deep* (1984), a haunted tin-mine tale, and John Krish's *Out of the Darkness* (1985), a ghost story drawing on the events that took place in the village of Eyam in Derbyshire in 1665 (previously the subject of a BBC Birmingham play *The Roses of Eyam* in 1973, directed by Don Taylor). The Black Death had arrived in Eyam in a parcel of unclean clothing, and the inhabitants voluntarily cut themselves off from neighboring settlements, in a self-sacrificial act, allowing the village to die and preventing the plague from spreading. In *Out of the Darkness*, set in the modern day, the haunting originates from the violent death of a child whose parents had tried to save him from the plague by smuggling him out of the doomed village. He stays in nearby Stonewell with a family of three who shortly thereafter die from the plague, of which he is seemingly now the carrier. He buries the family in the garden and his subsequent unfortunate end is to be revealed at the end of the film.

The story and dialogue is fairly humdrum and of its type, familiar from a number of children's television shows over the previous decade in which events from the past visit the present, with a suggestion that they are as much slippages in time as they are actual ghosts; the resonances ceasing only when a message is received and the truth known and recorded. A cottage is bequeathed in a will and the beneficiary mother, her two children, Mike (Michael Flowers) and Penny (Emma Ingham), along with Mike's best friend Tom (Garry Halliday), travel to Stonewell to inspect what could become a weekend retreat for the family. Unlike today's film and television, in which the casting of the children focuses on the pixie cuteness and good looks, the C.F.T.F. went for ordinariness, inviting all (at least able bodied) kids to relate to the protagonists during their adventures. The siblings here fly the ginger flag at a time when it was a curse and a half to be a copper top child in the school playground. Tom meanwhile looks like an underdeveloped Cadpig [Cadpig is the smallest Dalmatian puppy in *101 Dalmatians*] version of Mark Lester. Unfortunately, it is also 10 minutes before you realize that one of the three is a girl, Penny looking more boyish than the other two.

The cottage is clearly uninhabitable, but they stay the night in rooms at a village guesthouse. During the first night the 300-year-old ghost of the Eyam boy traipses around the garden, alerting Tom to his presence with the jingling of a bell fastened around his neck by the blacksmith. Tom does not go to inspect so the ghost appears at his window, 10 feet up, in a shot that has clearly been stolen from Tobe Hooper's *Salem's Lot*. Effective nevertheless! The children persuade mum to allow them to stay an extra night at the guesthouse, during which they will continue to investigate the haunting. Mother has no qualms about this, but her being within earshot at all was already something of a rarity in the C.F.T.F. universe, where children generally got up to many unsupervised escapades and high jinks. They return to the cottage, where Penny this time has an out of body experience and witnesses the phantom removal of a coffin at the bottom of the stairs.

Local historian and ghost-hunter Julian Reid (Michael Carter) regales the children with Derbyshire legends, and given their new links with the property, will look to them to solve the mystery of the ghost and its continuing visitations. During a trek into the

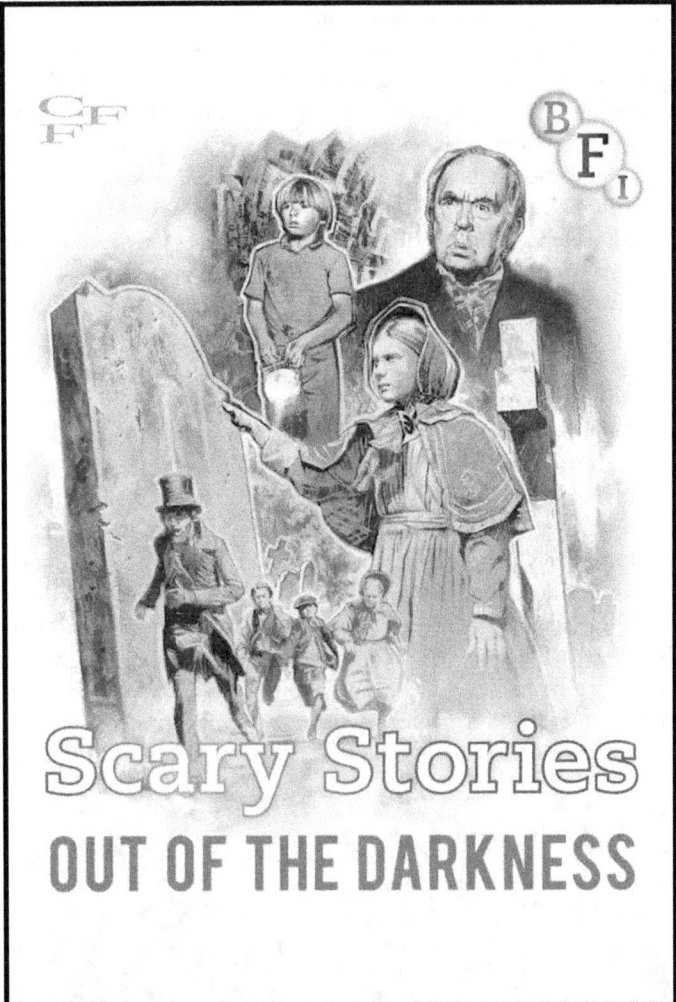

hills and valleys he recounts a tale of two hundred years earlier when five men murdered a couple, the culprits soon themselves to die mysteriously one by one, the final one confessing his guilt before his own demise. The telling of this bleak anecdote is unfortunate for the movie, because this simple horror story might be considered preferable, by some viewers, to the milquetoast offering set before us.

Returning to the main thrust, we are told that a terrible violence was visited on the 17th-century lad, and mists fall and reopen to visions of the angry villagers in the boy's pursuit. The final revelation is that there was no group bludgeoning of the boy, but that the guilt carried down through generations had been misspent. The villagers had stood guard over Eyam to prevent anyone from leaving, but they had also done their utmost to keep the boy away from their own without physically harming him. This could have been grim indeed, the populace driving him to return to a corpse-ridden village and likely into starvation. But the boy's actual death comes not at their angry hands, but as a result of a rock-fall accident caused by the only person prepared to help him. The incident is re-enacted with Tom spending the night with the ghost boy trapped under the toppling rocks, before being dug out by the mountain rescue team and reunited with his friends.

Out of the Darkness was shown at the London Film Festival in 1985 as part of a junior film program sponsored by Capital Radio. Based on the novel *The Ivy Garland* by John Hoyland, it has atmospheric moments, particularly in the empty cottage, with voices escaping the walls and in striking shots overlooking the guesthouse garden, but that ambience dissipates with the departure from the former location and the less unearthly appearance of the ghost in new places, as the tale descends into an adventure with time-slip clichés. It culminates in an overly sappy ending, bringing together the whole village in a kitchen in celebration as Ed Welch's hitherto subtle soundtrack gives way to a cringeworthy synthesizer party tone.

In the London Film Festival program, John Krish asks who would not try to protect their child and transport them out of a danger zone. Krish had been 16 at the outbreak of the Second World War and compared the smuggling of a child out of a plague village to the evacuation of children to the countryside away from prime bombing sites. Krish witnessed the dissociative effect that the separation would have on youngsters when finally, they were returned to their families. Krish may have tried to capture this allegorically in the story, but for most it would be too vague an allusion to the experience, and it is a subject worthy of more direct investigation in a separate fiction or documentary. Krish had made two Children's Film Foundation programers prior to this in *The Salvage Gang* (1958) and *Friend or Foe* (1982) but his feature film career was spotty—unfortunately so, given the cult popularity of his sole SF/horror noir offering *Unearthly Stranger* (1963) and his talk-of-the-school-playground gorefest Public Information Film *The Finishing Line* (1977), the latter serving to educate children against playing on railway tracks.
—Paul Higson

SLAUGHTER HIGH

D: George Dugdale, Peter Litten, Mark Ezra
W: George Dugdale, Peter Litten, Mark Ezra
Starring: Caroline Munro, Simon Scuddamore, Marc Smith, Gary Martin, Carmine Iannaccone

As awful a film as *Slaughter High* proves, this reviewer felt it important that it ought to be given the once-over by at least one graduate of an American high school, yours truly. A grimy cringe-fest in which primarily British actors run around British locations with a British crew pretending that the kind of crumbling Victorian edifice which Wackford Squeers might have patronized is a Rydell-like place of education. *Slaughter High* probably merits some kind of health warning. It's a great piece of evidence for those who take the view that British horror films, and the British film industry in general at the time, found themselves in a headlong rush of synthesizer-accompanied, Quantel-animated decline, despite the number of cases against that assessment elsewhere in these pages.

Marty (Simon Scuddamore, tragically to commit suicide after the film's release) is a geek who could have leaped into a live-action world straight out of a *Simon* cartoon. He's dragged into the locker rooms by Carol (legendary 1970s icon Caroline Munro, who might have thought it wiser to go into suspended animation during these painful years.) At first glance, Carol looks like she might have been a guidance counsellor of some kind; on viewing *Slaughter High*, the gradual realization that the character was supposed to be a student elicited a series of now-amusing, increasingly desperate verbal denials from the present commentator. Carol's apparent interest in Marty is really part of a cruel hoax (fittingly taking place in a shower, which is what viewers will sorely need after the film.) Understandably distracted by his genuinely distressing hazing (on his birthday, and April Fool's Day, no less), Marty gets absentminded later during a science experiment and disfigures his face with nitric acid. The accident itself is a hilariously convoluted affair—the bullies' majestically comical reaction, though understandable in the ludicrous circumstances, pretty much condemns them all to their eventual fates.

Several years later, the Doddsville County High reunion is announced, and the pranksters return to the scene of their crime, belatedly discovering that they're the only ones there, save the outdated Stepin Fetchit-style black janitor. After finding a personalized spread laid before them (alongside their old lockers, no less), they begin to realize something's not quite right, then people start getting killed off, and none too frickin' soon. Skip (Iannaccone) helpfully reveals the plot around this time (while quaffing Colt 45 and Pabst Blue Ribbon—no expense has been spared), i.e. that Marty's experiences have turned him into a vengeance-crazed killer. He thinks it's a joke, and in a way, it really is. It would be a lot funnier if it didn't last an hour and a half. Thankfully, the action winds down, after some occasionally creative deaths, and the film fittingly ends with one of those in-

sultingly nonsensical flourishes that certain directors apparently believed an acceptable substitute for artistic quality.

Slaughter High was presumably intended to cash in on the regrettable avalanche of American high school slashers of the period, but it's difficult, even considering the era's loathsome standards, to see what appeal was intended. It's neither scary nor arousing, and the imitation American high school flavor is equally annoying and mystifying to moviegoers used to the real thing. Which leaves us grasping desperately at a few frequently amusing minor touches. The *Simpsons*-like evasion of geography (Skip's car looks like it has Minnesota plates, but the radio station amusingly lacks a "W" or "K" at the beginning), one of the jocks is wearing a letter jacket emblazoned with a "T" at a place named Doddsville High, the sight of "$E=mc^2$" on a chemistry lab blackboard, the breathtakingly grotty Stella-Joe-Frank love triangle, and Caroline Munro doing push-ups by thrusting her groin at the floor. If you're into that, then apparently *Slaughter High* was good for something.
—Wendell McKay

• • •

It took three writers and three directors to concoct this tacky, highly entertaining British-but-pretending-to-be-American slasher. It emerged very late in the 1980s slasher cycle courtesy of legendary producer Dick Randall—the mogul who helped birth Lynda Day George's cry of "Baaaaarssstarrd!" in *Pieces* and arranged a Caroline Munro cameo in the sublime *Don't Open Till Christmas*, that has been known to make grown men hide behind the sofa in embarrassment. *Slaughter High* steals brazenly from *Terror Train* and *Carrie* for its lengthy set up before a main scenario cribbed from the creepy *The Redeemer/Class Reunion Massacre*, but, after around 45 minutes of meandering, it comes into its own with memorably nasty deaths and loopy twists.

Thirty-six-year-old Caroline Munro, admittedly in good shape, is the bitchy "schoolgirl" who, at the outset, seduces obnoxious geek Marty on April Fool's Day/his birthday, during a De Palma-influenced girls' locker room humiliation sequence featuring a surprising amount of full-frontal male nudity. His trauma gets her and her bullying buddies in trouble, so they retaliate with science lab prankery resulting in Marty suffering acid burns and almost dying in an explosion. A decade later, the stock American slasher movie characters involved are invited to a mysteriously arranged reunion at the now-abandoned school. Broadly divided into generic categories like Slut, Bully and Jock, they are given appropriate names like Skip, Stella and Ted. Munro has become an actress fond of wandering around at home in sexy nighties and turns down offers from sleazy agent Manny (played by—hey!—Dick Randall, gratuitously plugging *Pieces*!). Much joint-smoking, beer-guzzling and fake shower scare hijinks ensue while we learn that, after many months of failed skin grafts, Marty's mind collapsed: "He still roams the nuthouse, ever hopeful for that chance to escape." More importantly for cinema history, this is your one and only chance to see Caroline Munro snort coke, folks! (well, onscreen, at least.)

The abundance of fake American accents (everybody, including Munro, is pretty dreadful) and ridiculous caricatures (welcome, Surly Football Coach, Bespectacled Nerd and Ageing Black Janitor—the latter brought in just for cheap false scares) strongly suggest this one was conceived as a semi-spoof. Dialogue exchanges like, "Look, my gloves! I lost them on Prom Night!"/"That's not the only thing she lost!" reinforce this suspicion. Composer Harry Manfredini, who came up with an appropriately catchy/earworm recurring theme for the jester-masked killer, sends up his own *Friday the 13th* scores, including a direct homage for a faux fright involving a hockey mask ("Who'd you think I was, Jason?!")

Whatever the intentions, the movie hangs together better than most, with a fun double-twist shaggy-dog ending helping to excuse many earlier illogical moments, including Marty's typical super-slasher ability to appear everywhere and to bounce back from mortal wounds. Sub-genre clichés are followed to the letter, complete with a Steadicam that impressively pursues Munro through corridors and up and down staircases as she finds her pals nailed to doors and so forth in the final act. Shoulder pad enhanced fashions and haircuts-from-Hades all add to the pleasure.

In retrospect, *Slaughter High* also has some of the finest show-stopping moments from this relatively barren stage of the slasher movie cycle. You won't forget the idiot who unwittingly downs a beer can of acid, causing his stomach to graphically explode, or the small-boobed Josephine Scandi reduced to a gaudy *House on Haunted Hill*-style skeleton after taking an acid bath. You also get a marvelous tendon-slashing car-splattering possibly influenced by *Happy Birthday to Me* and one of the best coitus-interruptus dual-death scenes, involving an electrified bed and a fried nekkid woman.

It's amiably brash in its approach to the conventions of the day. The aforementioned twist end involves two major fake-outs; the killer hounded to his doom by zombie-like vengeful victims (c.f. *Don't Go in the House* and *Maniac*) and the all-a-dream revelation (a là *The Slayer*) that leads to a *Dead and Buried*-style hypodermic-in-the-eye shock. All told, 28-year-old Simon Scuddamore, in his sole movie role before apparently committing suicide soon after completing his work as Marty, is a memorably unhinged slasher villain.
—Steven West

UNDERWORLD

D: George Pavlou
W: Clive Barker, James Caplin
Starring: Denholm Elliott, Miranda Richardson, Steven Berkoff, Larry Lamb, Art Malik

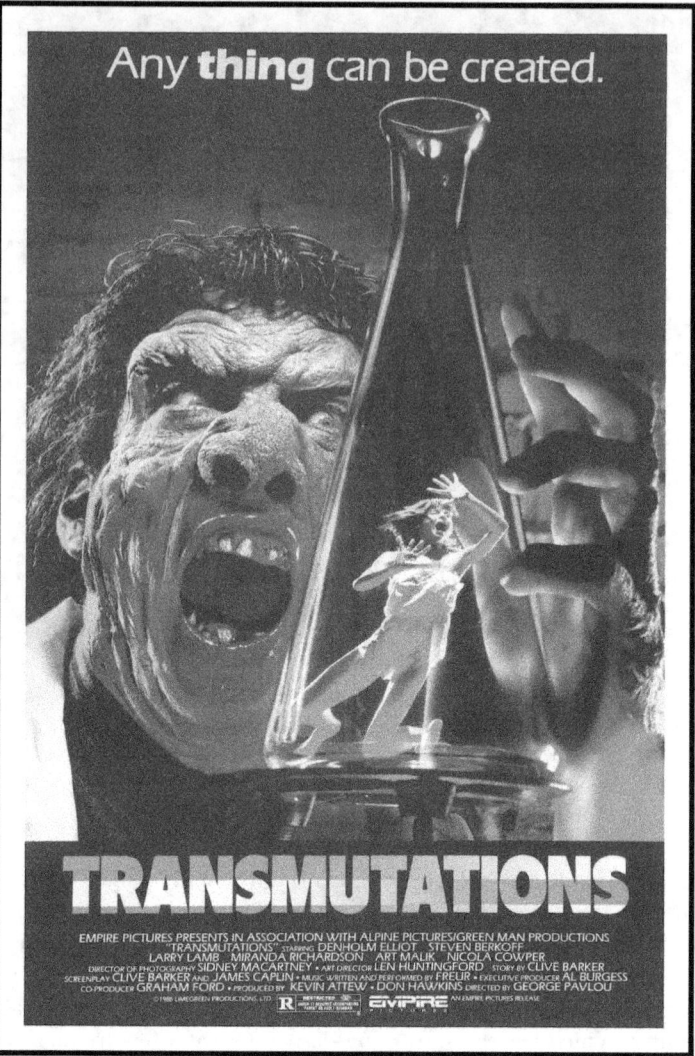

Underworld was released as *Transmutations* in the US, France and parts of Canada.

In the opening scene of *Underworld*, we see a number of black clad figures furtively springing, crouching and sprinting their way through an urban wasteland at night. In fact, precisely like we've seen countless times in movies involving covert F.B.I. operations, commando sorties or terrorist attacks. But there is absolutely no reason why these men should move so secretively; the streets are both poorly lit and, more importantly, totally deserted. This immediately gives away what kind of film this will be—a pointless montage mimicking scenes we've seen numerous times in other (and usually better) films. *Underworld* sets out to be a genre bender, mixing horror and sci-fi elements with a film-noir style Private Dick investigation. Thus we are subjected to one tired cliché after another; the heavies dispatched to escort the retired operator to his former employers; the boss arguing with the reluctant ex-agent before finally persuading him that he's "the only man for the job"; the discovery of the clue overlooked by everybody else; the come-ons from hot chicks; the turning-the-tables-on-the-would-be-ambusher, and so on.

Doctor Savary (Denholm Elliott) has invented a new and powerful hallucinogenic drug, nicknamed "Whitemare," which somehow makes dreams "take root" in the user, whatever that's supposed to mean. Long-term use has the terrible side effect of transforming anyone addicted into a Rondo Hatton look-alike, with gross facial disfigurement and a bad attitude. The only person who has failed to suffer any side effects is high-class prostitute Nicole (Nicola Cowper), who works at the upmarket brothel run by Madame Pepperdine (an embarrassingly bad performance from Ingrid Pitt). The girl is kidnapped by the mutating junkies and taken to their secret lair in the sewers. Pepperdine's associate, ex-crime boss turned legitimate business tycoon Hugo Motherskille (Steven Berkoff) sends for Roy Bain (Larry Lamb, here displaying less charisma than his Toytown namesake), Nicole's one-time bodyguard and ex-lover. Motherskille persuades Bain to abandon his tranquil retirement, painting watercolors in his studio by the Thames, to track down the missing tart. This he does, after a quick visit to Savary's clinic, before winding up in the Underworlders' decrepit hideout, comprising a couple of tunnels and a six-foot-square Ops Room implausibly complete with working telephones, dentist's chair, neon strip lights (curiously identical to the ones in Bain's apartment), and a wall-sized map of the world. Only then does Bain realize that Motherskille isn't as legit as he claims, and that he's been using him to locate the Whitemare "victims" with a view to their extermination.

If the plot seems basic, the film manages to pull off the seemingly impossible feat of making it even more simplistic, while simultaneously rendering it practically incomprehensible. First of all, what was Savary's motive? Some reviews mention that his new drug was developed to "cure" heroin addicts. Although that doesn't make the slightest sense, none of the rest of the story does either, although, in fact, this particular point is never mentioned in the film, as far as I could tell. It would appear that the Doc's motives were purely financial, judging from Elliott's reprise of his stock greedy/cowardly character. Again, Bain's motivation for taking up the case despite his initial reluctance was that he was still secretly in love with Nicole. Savary was also an avid client of hers, and likewise proclaims undying passion for the girl. But Nicole (as played by the truly clueless Cowper) has considerably less personality and sex appeal than the tree trunk that Michael Jayston had the hots for in that infamous instalment of *Tales That Witness Madness*. Then we have the fastest ever case of Stockholm Syndrome, when Nicole, after approximately half a day with her disfigured abductors (most of which time she spends unconscious), refuses to be rescued. "This is my new home. These are my friends" she whines. A natural preference I suppose, after years as a pampered, high earning, bejewelled, luxury mansion-dwelling maîtresse. Barker's message that monstrousness is only skin deep and that we are the real monsters, later unsubtly hammered home in his self-directed *Nightbreed*, is already on view here. Just why Motherskille and his Merry Men wish to wipe out the Underworlders isn't made clear (now there's a surprise), especially considering that the drug takers are their clients—or so I deduced; it seems that Motherskille was in cahoots with Savary all along, though, again, it's never made explicit by word or action. There is some vague suggestion about the Mafioso being worried about "the threat of exposure," thereby meaning the junkies must die.

There follows a cut-price shoot-out between the mutants and Motherskille's men at a derelict house (reasonably well handled despite the obviously low-budget), then the gangsters chase their quarry underground to pick off their leader and a couple of extras. As three of the "monsters" are still alive, our Hugo barks the order "gas the bastards!", which chief henchman Fluke (Art Malik) proceeds to do (using a portable *nebelwerfer* which appears to have been knocked up by Valerie Singleton using Fairy Liquid bottles and sticky backed plastic), despite the fact that the pursuers are bristling with semi-automatic weapons and standing at point blank range from their targets.

Visually and stylistically, the film screams out its mid-1980s production date. Cheesy sax'n'synth music combines with horrendous fashions, those ubiquitous blue neon strip lights, a *Miami Vice* palette of pastel pink, blue and yellow hues, and rumbling ventilation ducts. Not forgetting Fluke's habit of wearing wraparound shades at all times, even at night and/or underground. How cool is that? There's even a couple of one-liners, and occasional sparklingly witty dialogue like "This is Dudu"/"My friends call me Shitface." And of course, being the 1980s, there has to be an exploding head somewhere down the line, so, in the penultimate scene, Nicole confronts Savary as he's slipping out the back passage. Her eyes glow like those of the kids in *Village of the Damned* and she mumbles "show me your dreams!" This is where the makers dropped the ball (or more likely ran out of cash), as gory dream sequences were another staple of 1980s horror, but here all we get is Elliott doing a few facial contortions. A couple of pulsating veins later, he's blown his mind, in a blink-and-you've-missed-it shower of meaty morsels. Nicole dies (possibly of boredom) and Bain exits the Underworld through a handy manhole cover.

Underworld is nicely shot, in a typical 1980s music video style, and the cinematography manages to evoke a modicum of Gothic atmosphere in a handful of scenes. Suspense is generated when a mutant attacks Nicole's prostitute pal in a lift, and the film just about manages to keep up a certain momentum through to the finish. Despite the incoherent script, indifferent make-up and special effects, and uninspired camerawork, it's an undemanding watch. Unfortunately, "undemanding" seems to have been director George Pavlou's approach to eliciting decent performances from the totally wasted cast, who have probably (hopefully!) never done anything worse than this.
—Mike Hodges

YOUNG SHERLOCK HOLMES

D: Barry Levinson
W: Chris Columbus
Starring: Nicholas Rowe, Alan Cox, Anthony Higgins, Sophie Ward

Let's be perfectly honest, we're not talking about a classic here. No one would claim this is a great Sherlock Holmes film. It's not even a very good one. But it does have its moments and incidental pleasures.

First though, let's get the problems out of the way. For a start, it's a typical product of that period in the 1980s when Spielberg's name was attached as Executive Producer to apparently every other major film that came along. On the plus side in that respect, the same year brought us *Back to the Future*, which is magnificent. In the debit column, however, is *The Goonies*, which no amount of ironic retro-praising can save from being a shrieking pile of over-produced pap.

If Steven was watching these films closely and happily signing them off, you have to assume that for this period at least, he was suffering from the world's greatest sugar buzz, and a bad case of A.D.H.D. *Young Sherlock Holmes* is similar to *The Goonies*, in that they're very glossy, obviously hugely expensive, too fast and too noisy. As you sit today through the depressing sight of Michael Bay's latest *Transformers* entry, you may wonder where it all began to go wrong. I have a strong suspicion it was here.

Another problem is the main actors. Have you kept up with the careers of Nicholas Rowe and Alan Cox? Me neither. A more wooden, plodding, humorless and flat-footed couple of leads it's harder to imagine. They manage to kill every line and nuance (such as they are) stone dead, utterly fail to gel onscreen, and offer no hint of the Holmes and Watson we're waiting for them to grow into. In short, they're rubbish.

So, what, then, are the pleasures? There is no doubt that the film looks absolutely lovely. There is something of the early steam-punk aesthetic about *Young Sherlock*, from the marvellous mechanical gadgets to flying machines, which any fan of Alan Moore's *League of Extraordinary Gentlemen* comic books will recognize and love. Add to that some beautiful snowy settings, and a first-rate realization of a Victorian London that we all know never really existed, and there's no doubt you're in for a visual treat.

It's also surprisingly scary. The plot centers on a hallucinogenic drug used to kill old codgers, which allows for some fantastic early CGI attacks by roast pheasants, gremlins and a stained-glass knight. These all play much better than they sound. There's also some entertaining business involving the titular pyramid, lending the piece the feel of a Victorian Gothic.

But the greatest pleasure comes from the ripe turns by a string of our best-loved British character actors. Michael Hordern, as an aging Watson, delivers occasional narration. In a lovely touch, Nigel Stock, once Watson to Peter Cushing's Holmes, returns in his cinematic swansong as a rather batty old teacher, the wonderfully named Rupert Waxflatter, with a past full of secrets. His flight around the rooftops of the school in a prototype airplane is perhaps the most famous aspect of the film, and the bit you would have seen excerpted on *Wogan*.

Of course, all pales next to a typically fruity appearance by the magnificent Freddie Jones, as the equally splendidly named Cragwitch. His exposition of the back-story from Egypt is surely the inspiration for his similar turn in the 2000 *League of Gentlemen* Christmas special, and is the undoubted highlight here. It's just a shame he's prevented from murdering the rather annoying boy leads, because he certainly seems to be enjoying himself, and you can't fault his judgement.
—Craig Williams

• • •

Looking back on *Young Sherlock Holmes and the Pyramid of Fear* (to give it it's full title) with hindsight, one can still see a film that looks good and had more than a pretty penny spent on it. But a youth today might have some difficulty determining just how big a deal it was in its day. It was of little consequence that Barry Levinson directed it, because to the media it was a Steven Spielberg production and although the adventure film had reached a new level of guile, only the "Spielberg" or "George Lucas" brand was the true mark of quality as far as the layman was concerned. Lucas had dabbled outside of *Indiana Jones* and *Star Wars*, but Spielberg was unbounded, bouncing around from one hit project to another with an unpredictability of genre, and a success ratio that could dismiss as a blip his disastrous war comedy, *1941*. So, whether he directed a particular project or not, all he had to do was spit on a set and it became "a Steven Spielberg movie."

Young Sherlock Holmes was a big deal and a major investment, and every dollar showed onscreen, in set design, costumes, effects and period detail. It could even pass for a new film today, lavish as it is, though half of what is up on display in *Young Sherlock Holmes* would now be created on computers. So impressive-looking was it and so incident crammed that it won me over too, any minor irritancies endurable. It continues to hold up very well now, though the sloppiness of the scripting is more apparent—the devices which introduce Holmes to the catchphrases and motifs by which he would become popular are sledgehammered in, while the underdeveloped dialogue and meager characters of the younger Holmes and Watson deny them both the real intelligence and the comprehensible connection that kindled the friendship in the first place. Why should Holmes strike up an on-the spot bond with such a drab, unintelligent fellow pupil?

But *Young Sherlock Holmes* is an important and unusual film that needs to be placed into perspective. By 1985, the Spielberg machine had ruthlessly identified potential box-office across numerous genres and themes. As a subject Sherlock Holmes seemed like a safe bet, but here they were approaching him sans Conan Doyle, speculating instead on how Holmes and Watson could have met earlier as boys. There had been a phenomenal response to the Indiana Jones escapades and *Poltergeist* (1982), and so adventure and horror would also here be important to the mixture, with the subtitle of the movie, *Pyramid of Fear*, invoking Indy's *Temple of Doom*, as do the bald-pated idolaters. *Young Sherlock Holmes* was formula piled on formula. It couldn't fail.

The horror emphasis was curious as this family-orientated production was shooting in a country whose politicians, police and classification board were in the middle of a full-scale war against grotesque screen content, this despite a tradition of great spooky children's television. In the UK only a few homegrown movies had dared to fully explore horror for a family audience, *The Monster Club* and *The Watcher in the Woods* among the frontrunners. But *Young Sherlock Holmes* was advancing in its shock tactics, as engendered via two of the plot's main strands, the visual representations of a hallucinogenic drug driving people to their death and the practices of the Egyptian cult in the story.

The victims (including Patrick Newell and Nigel Stock) are variously attacked by a pheasant dinner, animated coat stands and gas lamps, a stained-glass knight, and an ornamental harpy that causes them to bring about their own destruction, whether it be to dive through a window, run under the wheels of a carriage, or stab themself to death when fending off an imaginary monster attached to their person. Watson (Alan Cox), Holmes (Nicholas Rowe) and the Great Detective's young love interest, Elizabeth Hardy (Sophie Ward) survive their encounter with the drug though they too are assaulted by nightmarish visions, the most striking of which are those that befall Elizabeth as she imagines falling into an open grave with skeletal hands grabbing at her, then views another skeleton chiselling her name into a gravestone.

The cultists are scarily painted as murderously obsessive, and in one of the most gruesome scenes we see a young, female victim bound like a mummy and waterboarded with what appears to be liquid silver, her cry of horror and pain chilling. Cavalier in its lethal atmosphere, the film also sees off Holmes' cuddly eccentric mentor, retired schoolmaster and perpetual inventor Waxflatter, played by the aforementioned Nigel Stock. (Elizabeth is his orphaned granddaughter, explaining her pres-

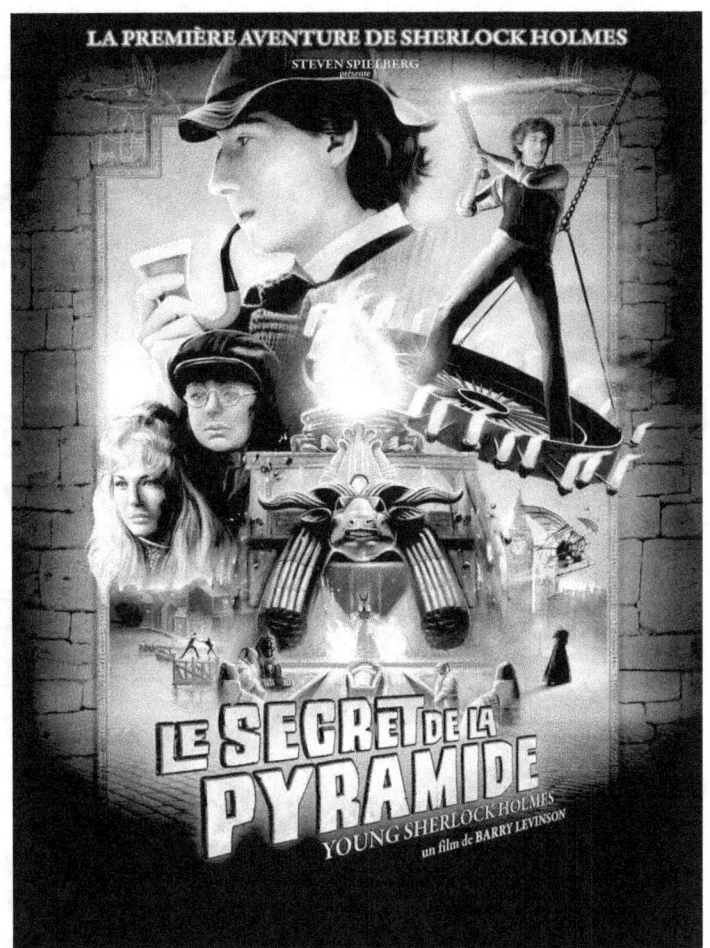

French poster for *Young Sherlock Holmes*

ence in the boys' school.) In a move even more shocking at the time, Elizabeth too dies before the end, at the hands of the lead villain Rathe (Anthony Higgins), sacrificially taking a bullet for our hero, freeing him to a mournful, less vulnerable future as a detective largely unfettered by cumbersome romance.

The imagery would also dredge up—or anticipate—other horror films. *Dr. Phibes Rises Again* (1972) is a perceptible influence in the Egyptiana and the barmy construction of a hidden pyramid (beneath London), while the breaking of the ice underfoot as Holmes and foe clash is reminiscent of the finale from *Dracula, Prince of Darkness* (1965). The killing of people using drugs that facilitate horrific visions, or some other state of being, propelling them towards suicide would feature in *Bad Dreams* (1988) and in Danny Boyle's *Inspector Morse* investigation "*Cherubim & Seraphim*" (1992).

Special effects are often impressive, with a mix of approaches, from Go Motion to Stop Frame, plus a significant early assignment for Pixar. The presence of both David Allen's stop-motion and incoming upstarts Pixar (with John Lasseter on the team) makes the film an interesting counterpoint in special effects history. The weakness of the normally quaint stop-motion, here stuck with the embarrassing job of bringing life to the silliest of hallucinations as Watson is attacked by cream cakes, is just asking to be put out to pasture when compared to Pixar's stained-glass knight stalking the priest in the church aisle, dazzling in its day and still standing up to scrutiny.

—Paul Higson

1986

Aliens
Bloody New Year
Frightmares
Gothic
The Housekeeper
In the Shadow of Kilimanjaro
Into the Darkness
Link
Moonstalker
Nightmare Weekend
Rawhead Rex

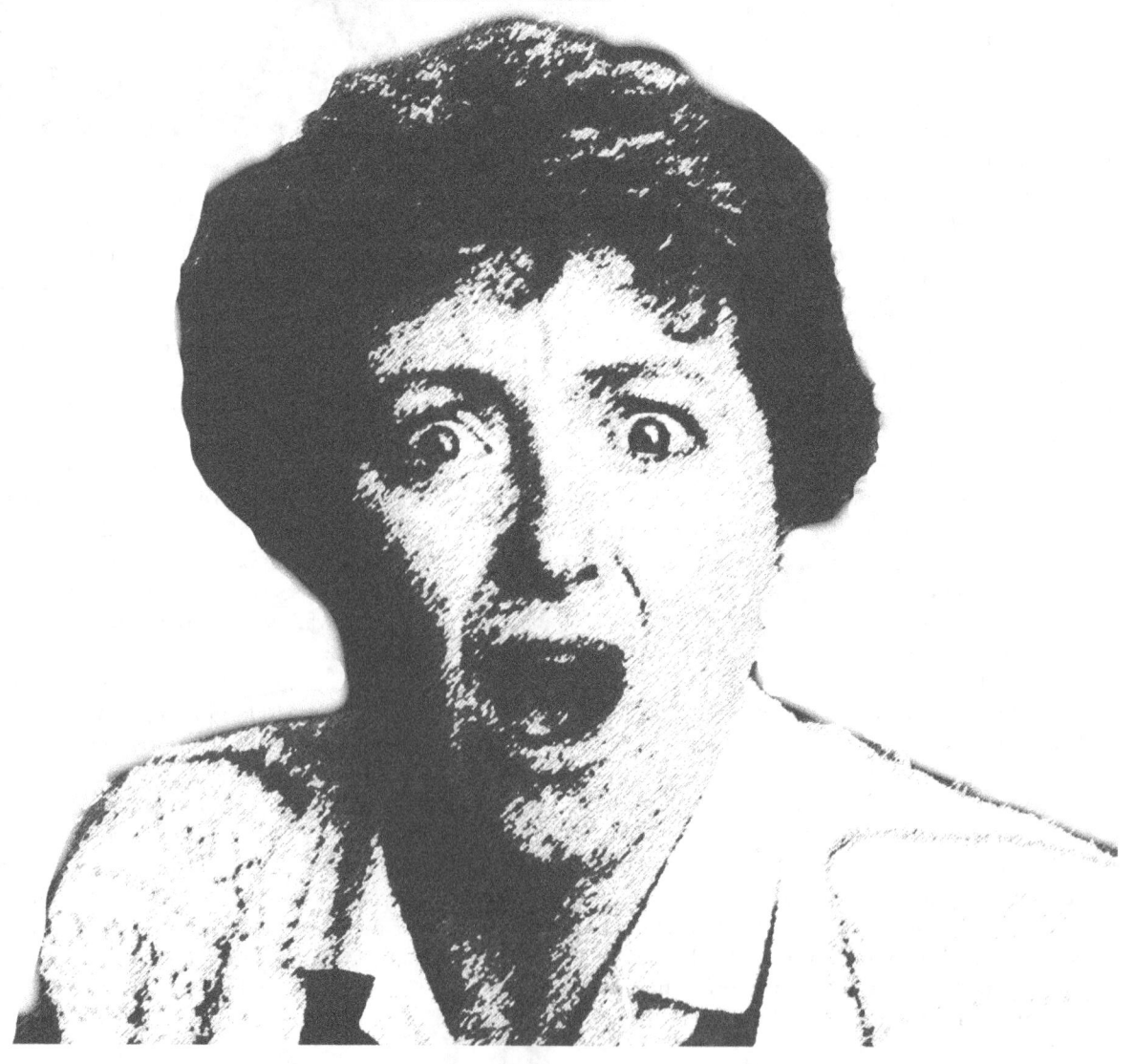

ALIENS

D: James Cameron
W: James Cameron
Starring: Sigourney Weaver, Michael Biehn, Jenette Goldstein, Carrie Henn, Bill Paxton, Lance Henriksen

Look at the list of all-time highest grossing movies and James Cameron's two most recent action-packed directorial projects—*Avatar* and *Titanic*—hold second and third place, pipped only by Marvel's *Avengers: Endgame*. By the standard which Hollywood most values, he is by some way the most successful living film director, and probably the most successful in history. So why is it that he died creatively after *Aliens*, which was only his third film, and a sequel for which he was essentially the hired help?

The answer lies in the fact that everything which once made Cameron an exciting talent reached its peak in this film, and everything he has done since is a pale imitation. His love and feel for military types is repeated almost beat-for-beat in *Avatar*, as is his interest in seeing a technologically more advanced super-power come off worse against a force of nature (arguably, that's also the main theme of *Titanic*.) And then there's missing parents being replaced by a surrogate. Just as Ripley takes over in place of Newt's mother, so the T-800 in *Terminator 2: Judgment Day* becomes father to John Connor. Only in the director's later films, these themes are handled at much greater length, and in a much more lachrymose, much less affecting manner.

Nothing Cameron has made since *Aliens* captures its thrills, dread, horror, humor, or sheer dirty, sticky, bloody gruesomeness. All these years on, it feels like one of the last hurrahs of the pre-CGI age, with physical effects caught in camera and on set, and so much the better for it.

It doesn't have the creeping dread of *Alien*, nor the originality of design and tone. But faced with the choice of which one to watch on Blu-ray, I suspect almost everyone would pick *Aliens*. It's a genuinely thrilling ride and re-wrote the way the genre operates. Watch the final drop ship sequence, as Bishop picks up Ripley and Newt to escape the planet. The cutting and the music beats must be among the most imitated in modern action cinema. It's a masterclass.

How British is it? Onscreen, it's not very British at all. While *Alien* had a multi-national cast, with John Hurt and Ian Holm perhaps the most memorable members (Weaver aside) of a brilliant ensemble, there's none of that here. This is a *very* American film. In fact, in many ways it's one of the most Reaganite-American films you're likely to see. Remember, it's made by the man who wrote *Rambo: First Blood Part II*. There was a time, before he began hugging trees and diving to meet sea creatures, when Cameron was seen as a right-wing filmmaker. It's certainly the sensibility of the film under review here. Yes, it's mildly critical of corporate culture, but it loves its grunts. It fetishes the military, even when they fail in the face of a terrifying natural predator. Yes, these marines may get their asses kicked all over the planet, but the film honors their code, their corps d'esprit. It is this above all else which gives *Aliens* its very American feel.

But there is a certain pride to be had in the way British craft and filmmaking skill brought Cameron's vision to the screen. And even more pride to be had in the knowledge that he so hat-

Japanese (top) and Polish (bottom) posters for *Aliens*

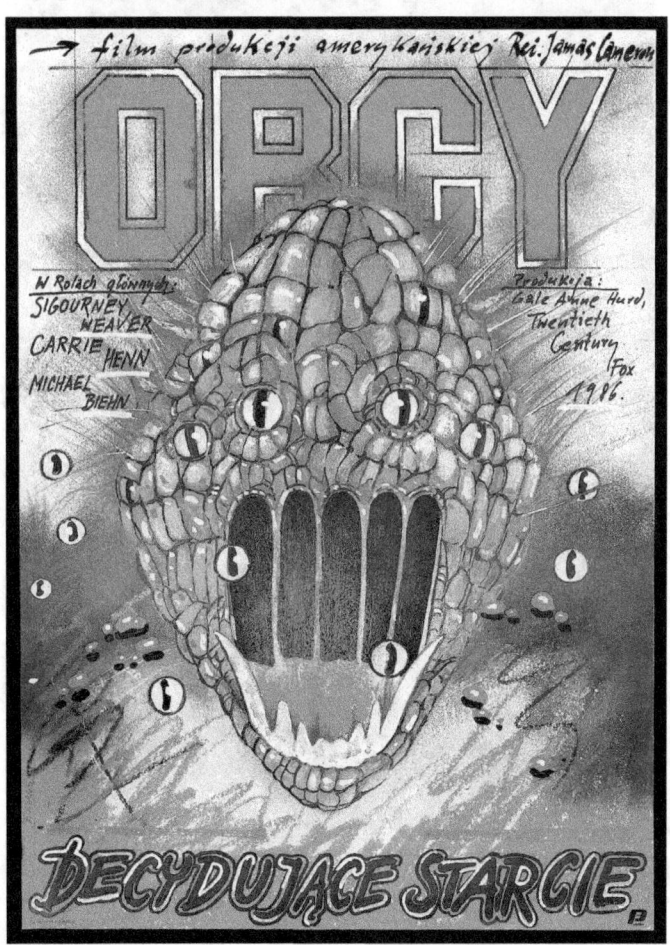

ed the British crew and their working methods (especially their fondness for tea breaks and cheese rolls) that he never worked here again. Cameron took the rest of his sorry oeuvre to other, less bolshy, cheaper parts of the globe. Something about filming in damp, dark old England brought out the best in him. Nothing he has made since even comes close
—Craig Williams

BLOODY NEW YEAR

D: Norman J. Warren
W: Frazer Pearce
Filmed in 1986, released in 1987
Starring: Suzy Aitchison, Nikki Brooks, Colin Heywood, Mark Powley

On the cusp of 1960, at the Grand Island Hotel, a seemingly normal New Year's Eve celebration will be interrupted by two curious happenings: a downed military plane in the woods carrying an experimental anti-radar device capable of shattering time and changing the molecular structure of people and objects, and the even stranger occurrence which sees a young reveler pulled through a mirror while checking her attire! Cue present day, and a group of youngsters flee a fracas at a local funfair and later abandon their scuttled sailing boat, to pitch up on the unhealthy island shown in the prologue, for a less than relaxing sojourn within the walls of its time-warped hotel ...

Deliciously paying cheeky respects to *The Shining*, *Carnival of Souls*, *Friday the 13th* and many others, revered UK exploitation director Norman J. Warren's swansong feature is a low-budget, high-concept and strikingly achieved little party piece, hampered by many production difficulties and, with the exception of Mark Powley who plays Rick, a lackluster cast. However, don't let that put you off, for this little-seen curate's egg of a film swiftly develops into a veritable blizzard of imaginative set pieces and near surreal, Argento-esque detail: ghostly maids slip quietly down stairways, vintage rock bands play in limbo to non-existent audiences, in-house cinemas screen *Fiend Without a Face* on an endless loop, sad ghosts voyeuristically watch young lovers from the imprisoned depths of wall mirrors, pool balls magically rearrange themselves out of sight of our doomed protagonists, and beware fishing nets, carved stair ornamentation and, in one huge "jump" moment, even tables, as they are all at the beck and call of the trapped forces on the island.

In one striking shock sequence, a black-and-white film in the cinema comes alive and the sheikh on display leaps from the celluloid a là *The Purple Rose of Cairo*, to kill an innocent; and with the re-entry of the angry, burly, carny workers into the mix, plus much zombification and supernatural subterfuge, the scene is nicely set for a pell-mell half hour climax where our final damned pair of lovers will square off against resurrected (and mutilated!) friends, living snooker tables, intense colored lighting and cackling fiends, giving this the air of a British *Evil Dead*—and don't expect a happy ending either, as in a beach-set pay-off and a haunting little coda, we end up very much as we came in.

Throw in dead airmen exploding into bloody clouds of dust in the woods, lifts metallically reaching out to ensnare the unwary with Freddy Krueger-like glee, and more imagination than most 10-times-budgeted films can fling a ghoul at, and this is well worth owning a copy of!
—Michael Wesley

• • •

Forewarned is forearmed, so don't watch this expecting to see a "serious" horror movie. That's to say that Norm and company didn't set out to "push the envelope," "redefine the genre for a new generation" or any of that pretentious B.S. that certain filmmakers are wont to expostulate. Instead they came up with a cut-price pastiche of the cliché ridden, effects heavy contemporary horror movies which were endlessly borrowing from (or ripping off) each other throughout the decade, from the USA to Bollywood (think *A Nightmare on Elm Street*, *The Evil Dead*, *The Beyond*, et. al), and gave it an indubitably surreal and very British twist—which didn't stop a guy on the IMDb from writing the following while listing his reasons to love this movie: "9. It's Australian. 10. No American could ever make a film this good." I'm sure Mr. Warren would have been gratified to hear such an accolade, especially in view of the fact that he always seemed rather dismissive of this, his last feature film. And he wasn't alone in that, to be sure.

Five teenage pals go to a fun fair and save an American girl from three bullies who are working the Waltzer and they have to run away when the bullies try to get them back and they take a rowing boat but it hits a rock and then they're stuck on an island where there's this hotel, but it's all covered in Xmas decorations and a banner that says "Happy New Year

Pakistani movie poster for *Bloody New Year*

1960," but that's weird, because it's really 1986 and it's summertime. Then they put on 1950s outfits they find in the hotel because their own clothes got wet in the sea, and then strange stuff starts to happen; there's this maid who gives the American girl a blanket, but then she disappears like a ghost, a Father Christmas decoration starts to move by itself, balls rearrange themselves on a snooker table and the TVs in the rooms suddenly come on and there's this program with a brainy bloke talking about an experiment with an RAF plane taking place that night which is December 3, 1959 but the kids don't take any notice and the hotel has got its own cinema and they're showing *Fiend Without a Face* and then another film starts and a sheikh comes out of the screen and kills one of the kids, then the other kids run away and one of the girls is attacked by a poltergeist-propelled fishing net in an empty cottage, two kids get chased around the island by invisible people, it suddenly starts snowing inside a house, a tablecloth turns into a green plasticine monster, a killer pinball machine trundles after another teenager in the hotel's games room, one of the thugs chasing the last two kids into the kitchen gets dissolved in a vat of boiling water, the walls of a lift melt and swallow a girl, a wooden dragon thing at the end of a staircase comes alive and bites a person, all the people at the 1959 New Year's party materialize as ghosts, the kids who were killed come back as zombies. In the end the survivors try to get away from the island in another boat ... but there's a twist ending.

That synopsis, written in a style intended to evoke the film's brisk pace as well as the rather unelaborate and perfunctory mise-en-scene, is pretty much all there is to this movie—a simple succession of bizarre and on the whole poorly realized scenes of "spooky things attacking kids." Norman and co-scriptwriter Frazer Pearce have included some deliberate touches of humor, such as a horny girl repeatedly attempting to seduce her unwilling boyfriend (well, it makes a change) and the baddie who skids on a tray and plunges (upwards) into the aforementioned vat of boiling liquid—the lid slams on him and he thrashes around for a few seconds, then the lid opens to reveal only his undigested boots as we hear a sonorous comedy belch. Another amusing touch, possibly unintentional, occurs when two of the teens are pursued by unseen people, their presence being represented by a TV sitcom laughter track.

Due to the paucity of resources, the blatantly nonsensical script, the inexperience of the cast and the tacky SFX, *Bloody New Year* will most likely be enjoyed by aficionados of trash flicks and predictably dissed by those seeking a "proper" scary movie. But if you stick with it, you'll find that the sheer accumulation of random weirdness and almost total lack of logic help the film to finally build up a certain dramatic momentum, as well as that incoherent atmosphere of unreality and W.T.F-ness that pervades many a bad dream ... or a good nightmare.
—Mike Hodges

FRIGHTMARES

D: Shani Grewal, Clive Paton, Alain Berberian
W: David Fleming, Clive Paton, Ethen Cetintas, Alain Berberian
Starring: John Hurt, Ron Berglas, Edward Hardwicke, Philip Mackenzie, Richard Atkin, Rebecca Pauly

Nothing whatsoever to do with Pete Walker—*Frightmares* is a 1987 VHS video release (according to the onscreen credits, that is, the back of the box says 1986!), comprising three assorted 1985 shorts, all hosted and introduced by John Hurt, no less, sitting in a plush armchair on the stage of a deserted theater. The video cover is a thing of wonder—the main artwork depicts Mr. Hurt in a smoking jacket, enjoying a cigar, while a clawed demon lurks menacingly behind him and four monstrous hands reach out from the back of his leather chair as smoke from Hurt's stogie curls around them. "Worse than your worst nightmares," suggests the tagline, possibly coming unintentionally close to the truth. Hurt is described as "the Master of Suspense" on the reverse of the sleeve ... Shani Grewal directed the most professional looking of the trio, *Vengeance*—not a terror yarn, but a fairly gripping thriller in which Edward Hardwicke plays an accountant who stumbles upon some McGuffinesque secret documents. There are hints that the IRA and the British secret service might be involved. Grewal went on to a career in features and British television, remaking *Vengeance* as an expanded big-screen version, *Double X: The Name of the Game* in 1992.

Holiday for Three, directed by Clive Paton, is an insubstantial tale about three lads in a holiday cottage—chucked out of the local pub for chatting up the landlord's missus, and bored with playing practical jokes on each other (including one of their numbers being sent to the off-licence after dark, and the others spooking him and leaping out on him as he walks back through a graveyard), they decide to hold a Ouija session—the message "Death Upstairs" is spelled out in the cards, and this prediction is fulfilled by the story's end. The third film is very odd—entitled

The Short Night, it's a *Thriller*-like lady-in-peril episode, and I'm not entirely sure where it originates from, as all of the credits are in French but the actors seem to be speaking undubbed English. Directed by Alain Berberian, it contains a creepy hulking psycho and has a few effective surprise moments among all the talk and would-be "suspense."

All in all, it's pretty wobbly, and despite being packaged as a horror anthology, it really only has fleeting moments of genre material, but as a rarely-discussed title and a chance to experience a variety of short subjects from an era not noted for this type of production, it certainly is of interest. The grand old tradition of the portmanteau film took a bit of a bashing during the 1980s, with Brit offerings tending to be thrown together in the manner of this shoddy compilation (see also Stanley Long's *Screamtime* and the obscure video 1992 release *Nightmares*, which features a couple of unrelated British shorts from the 1980s)

I was lucky to chat briefly in person with John Hurt about this mish-mash on a couple of occasions, and took the opportunity to ask how much he might have been paid for what seems to amount to a morning's work reading his intros off cue cards. "Not enough, dear boy, not enough!" came the stock industry response! One can't add anything to that.
—Darrell Buxton

GOTHIC

D: Ken Russell
W: Stephen Volk
Starring: Gabriel Byrne, Julian Sands, Natasha Richardson, Myriam Cyr, Timothy Spall

Gothic has a big problem, since it's well known what happened that infamous night in Geneva when the 19th century British literati gathered at Villa Diodati. They sat around reading stories to each other and that's about it. Maybe there was fornicating, maybe drug taking, but that doesn't fill out 90 minutes. There's a feeling that the script wasn't finished. There are many scenes where it feels like we're watching actors workshopping, jumping about and talking bollocks [trash].

Strangely we never see the celebs sit down to write or recite their stories, which is after all the reason why the weekend is so famous. There are some rather leaden hints at the genesis of Mary Shelley's classic, most memorably from a naked Sands squatting on the roof informing us, "Lightning is the fundamental force of the Universe!" See kids, drugs can be boring.

Gabriel Byrne is miscast as sexual dynamo Byron, looking more like a fading matinee idol wearing what has to be a wig. Julian Sands is ... well, Julian Sands, nice enough to look at so long as he keeps his mouth shut and stays perfectly still. Timothy Spall is the standout, outrageously camping it up and stealing

the show. The late Natasha Richardson, in her film debut, gives an earnest performance with, you suspect, greater effort and research than the others.

There's a second tier cast of servants mirroring the main performers including Andreas Wisniewski (Necros in *The Living Daylights*) and Dexter Fletcher. They appear onscreen for no more than a few minutes, though that's time enough for a scene featuring a maid suggestively milking a goat while Andreas shells peas!

The 1980s is largely a forgotten era of British cinema. While a few big-budget epics were being produced, most of our investors were queuing up to give away money to maverick directors making films no one wanted to see. Our man Ken is a great example of this—long gone were the glory days of shocking the highbrow via delirious biopics of famous composers, his career was in a downward spiral which was ultimately to lead to him grinding out home movies in his back garden. Visually *Gothic* feels so much like a music video that you keep wondering whether Iron Maiden or Queen might pop up. There are lots of striking images thrown in merely because they are striking. Dead babies, fish flopping on a sundial, leeches in food, an imp who comes alive in a dream sequence and vanishes, a suit of armor with a big codpiece, a robotic dancer and eyes replacing nipples

It feels like there's a clash between writer and director, since Stephen Volk's intimate script, maybe written with TV in mind, contains tight little atmospheric shocks while Russell ladles on the flamboyant and trippy imagery. It's all rather jaded—Russell has spent so long trying to shock that he's forgotten how to entertain. Amazingly Russell here has become relatively coy about sex and nudity, *Gothic* offering a quick flash of flesh every so often either behind gauze or in long shot. There's some quick coupling by the two couples, while the voyeuristic Spall gurns wonderfully.

It all winds up with some sightseers wandering round the same grounds seen earlier and, as the tour guide repeats most of the same patter we heard at the beginning, Russell focuses on the corpse of a baby floating under the waters of the lake. Russell makes a direct correlation between 19th century gawpers and modern tourists—what does that say about us, I wonder.

Oddly, several other film productions set around the events at Villa Diodati emerged at about the same time as *Gothic*—namely *Haunted Summer*, *Rowing with the Wind*, and the slightly later Roger Corman comeback/Brian Aldiss adaptation *Frankenstein Unbound*.
—Gerald Lea

THE HOUSEKEEPER

D: Ousama Rawi
W: Elaine Waisglass
Starring:, Ron Petty, Tom Kneebone, Shelley Peterson, Jackie Burroughs

Nothing to do with Zsa Zsa Gabor (you know the old joke, married nine times, always keeps the house ...), this Toronto-lensed offering is an adaptation of Ruth Rendell's 1977 novel *A Judgement in Stone*, the famous opening line of which manages to tell all while keeping you hooked and gagging for further enlightenment: "Eunice Parchman killed the Coverdale family because she could not read or write."

Rendell's work has not been served well by the big screen—the author herself rated Claude Chabrol's acclaimed 1995 version of *A Judgement in Stone*, *La Cérémonie*, as a rare case where a filmmaker got it right. I doubt if her verdict on this earlier attempt would have been as positive, although it has certain merits.

Rita Tushingham does her thing once again, the mousy, put-upon maiden who leaves home to experience the wider world. Hammer Film Productions' *Straight on Till Morning* (1972) beautifully exploited her '60s wallflower persona, throwing this figure fresh from *The Knack* and *Smashing Time* into the disturbed vicinity of that other popular stereotype of the time, the delusional and dangerous psychopath. Eunice here captures elements of both within the same character—dyslexic, the focus of childhood torment at school, and embittered at her life of drudgery in London looking after her ailing and constantly complaining father, she does in the old man one day with an EC Comics flourish ("Here's your pillow, dad!") and wangles a job as an au pair for a well-to-do American household—an early indication of her twisted ways comes when she double-crosses the friend who has concocted a glowing fictional reference to assist her employment chances.

Ensconced in the huge family home of the Coverdales, she succumbs to nightmare fantasies which build as the story progresses—a clutching hand glimpsed in the convex reflection of a kitchen kettle, the zombie-like lumbering of her late father gasping her name as he staggers into her room, an odd sequence where she seems to butcher the family's prize pedigree hound before cremating it *Something to Hide/Apt Pupil* style, and, unforgettably, a *Shining*-like gusher of blood pouring from the parson's nose of a cooked Xmas turkey!

Despite her loner qualities, Eunice unavoidably hooks up with a handful of locals (each laboriously introduced by name, occupation, brief pen-picture describing their foibles, etc. in the manner that only ever happens in movies)—most notably she befriends religious reformed hooker, grocery store proprietor, and post office overseer Joan (Burroughs), who displays embarrassing confessional fervor at church meetings, steams open all of the local mail, and is revealed in the last 20 minutes to also be an Armageddon-obsessed survivalist with a closet full of provisions and loaded arms! All of which leads to bloody double-barreled mayhem at the New Year's party climax.

Hints of semi-incest lie beneath the surface of the story, with the standard sweet teen romance here tainted since the participants in the relationship are the respective son and daughter of the second-time-around Coverdales. It's an uncomfortable detail but one that could have added an extra layer of subversion to this piece—lamely, instead it's all glossed over and accepted with a few guilty glances and cheesy grins. Much better is the way the screenplay makes constant, nagging references reminding us about Eunice's inability to read—every other scene seems to take a dig, which serves to force the viewer into the housekeeper's state of mind and her increasingly desperate bids to cover up her educational failings. We're not allowed to forget this, and so we come to realize that she must have thoughts of the deficiency buzzing through her head all day, every day. Very effective.

Too glossy and too much of a soap opera, with performances ranging from by-the-numbers to abysmally amateur, *The Housekeeper* plays like a Sunday afternoon TV movie with occasional bursts of added violence or fractured psychology. There are points of interest—one early scene sees Tushingham accidentally losing a tea towel to the sucking mechanism of a waste disposal. Instead of responding with the expected panic or discomfiture, a fascinated, child-like Eunice immediately reaches for an egg and pops that fragile item down the chute too, grinning gleefully as the shell crushes. More of this, less of the broader strokes and cartoon characterizations, and this one could have been a keeper.
—Darrell Buxton

IN THE SHADOW OF KILIMANJARO

D: Raju Patel
W: T. Michael Harry, Jeffrey M. Sneller
Starring: John Rhys-Davies, Timothy Bottoms, Irene Miracle, Michelle Carey, Leonard Trolley, Don Blakely, Calvin Jung

"Violent death was the easy way out!"

The year is 1984 and Kenya is undergoing its most severe drought in 10 years. The majority of the wildlife has died or migrated to less arid regions, but not the baboons. In an unprecedented move the Olive and Yellow baboons have put aside their differences and are teaming up in their search for food and water. The residents of the small town of Namanga and the workers at the nearby Sinya Mining Company are about to discover

Danish movie poster for *In the Shadow of Kilimanjaro*

that they are now on the menu, or so *In the Shadow of Kilimanjaro* would have us believe.

Enter stage right Game Warden Jack Ringtree (Timothy Bottoms), a Great White Hope in the Heart of Darkness. Quick on the uptake, Jack needs only the discovery of one mauled corpse to realize that some bad shit is going down. Cue hard-headed clashes with disbelieving authority figures and rough-diamond mine-manager Chris Tucker (John Rhys-Davies), as Jack tries to evacuate the townsfolk and miners from the onslaught of 90,000 pissed-off primates.

Into this mix is thrown Jack's wife, Lee (Irene Miracle), who arrives just in time for the action. That she seems more appropriately dressed for a Helmut Newton shoot than a few weeks in the Kenyan bush is neither here nor there, at least she looks pretty.

Whether the baboons are actually killing people for food, for available sustenance or for just plain evil ape reasons is never made explicit as they appear to be motivated by all the above—Gagnon (Jim Boeke) is attacked to be eaten, the driver of the provisions lorry is attacked to gain access to his cargo and Lucille Gagnon (Patty Foley) is attacked by a baboon that has the insight to sneak aboard a plane and stay hidden until the craft is airborne and maximum havoc can be caused ...

Before you can say animals on the rampage, the townsfolk and miners are forced to take a last stand in the schoolhouse as the baboons descend en masse, and only the combined whiteness of Jack and Chris—or a downpour—can save the day. I won't spoil the ending.

Kilimanjaro may not be the best British Killer Monkey film of 1986 (see *Link*), nor the most shocking Kenyan/British exploitation title of the 1980s (that's the severed-heads-in-the-fridge sleaze classic *Rise and Fall of Idi Amin*) but it is a diverting enough way to spend 92 minutes. Fun can be had watching Timothy Bottoms struggle with facial hair continuity and Rhys-Davies battling to keep a straight face.

My one complaint with the movie is in its lack of credit for the non-white actors. Linda, the local schoolteacher, has a more involved and significant role than many of the white crew but she remains uncredited in both the opening and closing titles, as do all the other "natives." This issue is addressed by the excellent BlackHorrorMovies.com website, which also suggests "*Red-Assed Terror*" as an alternative title to the more "artsy-fartsy" genuine article!
—Fraser Burnett

• • •

A "based on a true story" revenge-of-nature horror flick notably filmed on location in Kenya and heralded by typically sensationalistic publicity trumpeting an onslaught of 90,000 baboons that went crazy during a severe drought in 1984. In case we'd forgotten the promises made by the ads, hero Timothy Bottoms keeps reminding us that there are 90,000 of them out there. We stopped counting at around 37 or so.

"Anything can happen when animals are starving ..." Conservationist park ranger Bottoms becomes aware of the impact the drought is having on the behavior of animals, somewhat reminiscent of the ozone-depletion that made various beasts aggressive and caused Leslie Nielsen's shirt to fall off in *Day of the Animals*. There are cool scenes of elephants and rhinos assaulting his 4x4 but only the baboons—previously a passing cinematic threat in *The Omen*'s safari park set piece—have turned into bitey pink-assed monsters.

The first scene is typical of the sub-genre: A fake threat (rattlesnake) is overcome before an extra's demise is tracked by subjective camera. Subsequently, John Rhys-Davies represents the mining company, refusing to act on Bottoms' insistence on evacuation, while Irene Miracle (whose 1980s genre career spanned from the all-time-high of Argento's *Inferno* to the don't-tell-the-relatives low of *Watchers II*) shows up as Bottoms' estranged wife.

As usual, attempts at dealing with the rampage—including the killing of dominant males to leave the carcasses as food for the others—fail miserably, and every few minutes, minor characters have their legs torn off or sustain grisly flesh wounds. Director Patel proffers lots of close-up shots of snarling mandrill mouths to try and distract from the fact that, much of the time (including the many shots of slo-mo baboons running), these creatures look too cute and carefree to be the super strong, ravenously hungry, flesh-ripping beasties the script attempts to convince us they are.

The score, predictably enough, imitates the classic chords of *Jaws*, though on occasion employs some dramatic drums that are alarmingly similar to your everyday *EastEnders* cliffhanger. It also provides knockabout comedy motifs for the resident drunk Brit comic-relief character, just in case we hadn't picked up on the jokiness, and some mushy stuff for when Miracle shows up.

It's a watchable, fairly well paced flick with not too many lulls, and plenty of material for those with a fetish for ogling

Thai movie poster for *In the Shadow of Kilimanjaro*

Irene Miracle running and tumbling in slow motion (you know who you are.) It climaxes with a familiar siege scenario, before a sudden heavy shower saves the day as abruptly as the *deus ex machina* finale of *War of the Worlds*. John Rhys-Davies sums it up with a terse yet relieved and typically British lament of "bloody rain!" Meanwhile, a coda reassures us the film's "monsters" were treated extremely well during the production, a relief in a Euro-shock era when hairy and non-hairy creatures alike were routinely molested to provide gory goods while we waited for John Morghen to get his cock chopped off.
—Steven West

INTO THE DARKNESS

D: David Kent-Watson
W: David Kent-Watson, John Saint Ryan, Brett Sinclair (as "Michael Parkinson," "John C. Barker," and "Paul B. Hutchinson" respectively)
Starring: Donald Pleasence, Ronald Lacey, Polly Jo Pleasence, John Saint Ryan

> She's dead. You can't get any older than that.
> —David Beckett (Donald Pleasence)
> in *Into the Darkness*

In 1986, David Kent-Watson made what would be the first of two feature films away from his creative partner Cliff Twem-

Spanish VHS release of *Into the Darkness*

low. Despite the lack of involvement from Cliff, many of their other Manchester-based collaborators were on board for this formulaic stalk-and-slash picture.

Into the Darkness begins in a small town in Malta, with a young boy learning that his mother is a prostitute. We cut to London, England "some years later," and follow a mysterious figure being escorted to a bedroom by a young hooker. Once they reach the bedroom and she begins to undress, we cut to a shot of a knife. Freeze frame. Titles. The main story that follows is a world apart from this opening (or is it?)

As with Kent-Watson's later film, *The Assassinator*, *Into the Darkness* features John Saint Ryan (here credited as "John Ryan") in the lead. Ryan plays struggling actor Jeff Conti who—after some persuasion from his agent—reluctantly accepts a modeling assignment in Malta. The classically trained actor, who is not without ego, considers modeling of any kind to be beneath him. The photographer for the swimwear ad shoot is Steve Sutton, played by Brett Sinclair (credited as "Brett Paul.") Sutton has quite the ego of his own, and immediately butts heads with Conti. They are joined on their Malta trip by four glamorous young models, and a pair of assistants. During their stay, Conti takes a shine to Debbie, one of the models new to the business. Debbie notices that the group are being followed around by a mysterious older man (Donald Pleasence), and soon afterwards members of the group start disappearing one by one, falling victim to an unknown killer.

Ultimately, after many a red herring, the slayer's identity is revealed and the connection to the opening sequences becomes clear. *Into the Darkness* channels *Halloween* and *Peeping Tom* throughout, but especially so for their famous pre-title set pieces that offer the viewer a glimpse into the origins of the psycho, and even assumes their POV.

The incredibly misogynistic motivations of the killer (mother was a whore, all women are whores, must murder all women) are decidedly trite, and lend a nastier tone than the film deserves. While viewers are never encouraged to empathize with such a figure, as for example *Maniac* demands, it certainly leaves a sour taste.

Despite being shot on VHS, like the rest of David Kent-Watson's output, the production values of *Into the Darkness* are considerably higher than most of his work with Twemlow. The exotic locations certainly assist tremendously. The filmmakers had connections in Malta, which provided them access to many impressive sites. Possibly the most surprising contribution comes via half an album's worth of Chris Rea songs that permeate the soundtrack, particularly the aptly titled "Out of the Darkness". The songs are sourced from two Rea albums that predate the film by several years, and events leading to this odd musical adoption remain a mystery. Nevertheless, these tunes add to the wonderfully 1980s vibe and lend to the overall polish of the finished product.

The screenplay is credited to "John C. Barker," "Paul B. Hutchinson" and "Michael Parkinson," but reportedly these were pseudonyms for John Saint Ryan, Brett Sinclair and David Kent-Watson. The story they crafted, though wholly unoriginal, is at least coherent. The quality of the dialogue and acting seems to be a cut above most of the Kent-Watson/Twemlow canon; of course, that might not be saying very much. Perhaps it was the presence of the distinguished and dependable Donald Pleasence that prompted the writers and actors to raise their game. Certainly, the company of such a prolific actor was a big boost to the production. But Pleasence does seem to be phoning in his performance, which at least allows the rest of the cast to hold their own with him during shared screen time.

Into the Darkness includes a few genuinely creepy and imaginative moments. In particular, there's one scene in which the hand of a dead body is seen between some rocks, before the camera moves out and away from the appendage. We see just how minor that detail is in the landscape as many passers-by, predominantly tourists, are oblivious to the horror around them. But quality moments such as this are few and far between, and as for the film's ability to instill fear in the viewer ... well, it takes a special kind of motion picture to feature a swimwear mogul as an antagonist!

—Stephen J. Crompton

LINK

D: Richard Franklin
W: Everett De Roche
Starring: Terence Stamp, Elisabeth Shue

Before we get to Richard Franklin's orangutan-on-the-loose horror film, a word about Cannon. Every decade had its go-to studio for exploitation hi-jinks. In the 1950s it was American International Pictures, with their beach parties, giant mutated insects and bikers. In the 1960s it was Hammer, with their buxom vampires, gore and period nastiness. In the 1970s we could rely on New World for slime and hot rods and girls in halter-tops and cut-offs (if you were lucky, such gear would be covering the curves of Claudia Jennings or Jocelyn Jones.) In the 1980s Messrs. Golan and Globus kept the tradition alive. Who else would have been convinced they could make septuagenarian Charles Bronson the action star of the era? Who else would throw $70 million at Tobe Hooper? Who else would think that the next big thing in international cinema would be Chuck Norris?

Cannon, that's who.

Golan and Globus were responsible for jaw-droppers like *Invasion USA*, a film so reactionary it makes *Rambo III* look like it was directed by Ken Loach. Another Cannon favorite, *Revenge of the Ninja*, is a film that pits mafiosi against ninjas in Salt Lake City and throws in standard ninjas, little old lady ninjas, kiddy ninjas, half-naked blonde ninjas, electronic ninjas and shop window dummy ninjas. When they didn't think that was enough ninja-nonsense, we got films with possessed ninjas, ghost ninjas, gold lamé ninjas and laser-toting ninjas. However, alongside such drive-in fare as *10 to Midnight* and *New Year's Evil*, they also made excellent films like Andrei Konchalovsky's *Runaway Train*, one of the very best thrillers of the 1980s, and the marvellous visual feast *Powaqqatsi*. In their time, Menahem Golan and Yoram Globus jumped from art-house to documentary, to splatter film, to martial arts, to period drama, to sex comedy, to action movie and back again. Much (but by no means all) of what they made was rubbish, but it was usually entertaining rubbish, which when it came to Hollywood in the 1980s was about as much as you could expect. Did I mention *Invasion USA*?

Anyway, as you can tell, I'm rather fond of Cannon and the vast majority of their output (we'll draw a veil over *Death Wish II*—every barrel of apples has the odd rotten pippin), so the fact that the Cannon logo appears at the beginning of *Link* automatically gets the old exploitation gland twitching. Throw in the fact that it's directed by Australian Richard Franklin, responsible for *Road Games*, a funny, original, creepy Antipodean suspense thriller, and *Psycho II*, a shamefully under-rated film which your humble reviewer considers one of the best horrors of the 1980s, and all the stars are in alignment for this, the world's first monkey-slasher.

Elisabeth Shue stars as Jane Chase, who has secured the post of research assistant to Dr. Steven Phillip (Terence Stamp, in a role turned down by Anthony Perkins), a scientist working on primate intelligence and who lives in a big dark house in the lonely English countryside. With Phillip are two gifted chimps learning sign language and an old orangutan called Link, who Phillip rescued from a circus and who now functions as a sort of ape-about-the-house, dressed in suits—a monkey-butler if you will. When Phillip starts talking about putting Link to sleep, the orangutan begins to act oddly, and one morning Jane wakes up to find her boss has completely disappeared and that Link is running the place now, becoming more aggressive and refusing to let her leave, as well as dealing with visitors to the house, settling a few scores with Phillip's favored chimpanzees, and going through Jane's boyfriend and his mates like a dose of salts. Eventually it boils down to Jane and injured beau versus Link in a monkey/starlet three-round slapdown.

Now I know what you're thinking. Monkeys, old dark houses, murder, Cannon, Richard Franklin—how can this possibly go wrong? This is the exploitation motherlode, right? Unfortunately, not. *Link* is all over the place, it's a creepy horror movie, then it's a black farce, then it's an over-the-top comedy, then it's a daft thriller. Technically it's reasonably well made, and Shue, to her credit (in a very early role) plays it straight and comes off as quite an agreeable heroine, but the film doesn't really know what to do with itself once past the half-hour mark. In essence, *Link* is effectively a slasher movie featuring a young woman in an isolated old house surrounded by mysterious deaths and disappearances—albeit at the mercy of a mad monkey. Franklin is no stranger to this type of thing—hell, in *Road Games* he made sitting in the seat of a truck seem sinister, and *Psycho II* is a master class in this kind of claustrophobia, but here Franklin dispenses with his usual careful craft, delivering a flabby film that never really scares or generates any sustained tension. He's not aided by Jerry Goldsmith's uncharacteristically awful score, while Link's

French poster for *Link*

likeability (even when the beast stands on the roof of a burning house smoking a Havana) also fails to turn the tide. The deaths are effectively bloodless and even the twist ending feels out-of-place. There's also a scene in which Link ogles Shue up and down as she's about to take a bath which is more than a bit queasy, even for the time, and looks positively dodgy by today's standards.

So, there we have it. Cannon and Richard Franklin drop the ball on this one. If you want a better killer primate movie, check out George Romero's *Monkey Shines*, which covers similar ground in a much more effective and considered way, or Dario Argento's *Phenomena* in which at least the monkey is the good guy. If you want British horror the Cannon way, go to our "1985" section and peruse the reviews of *Lifeforce*. As for *Link*, well, let's just say it apes a horror film, but not a good one.
—Neil Pike

• • •

Link has very respectable credentials for a mostly forgotten/derided 1980s psycho-horror flick. In truth, it's far from the strongest of screenwriter Everett De Roche's cycle of (largely Australian) genre movies, which was at its apex when dealing with hostile forces of nature (*Long Weekend*, *Razorback*). Nor is it the best remembered from the oeuvre of his fellow countryman Richard Franklin, the man who made the strongest of a surprisingly decent slate of *Psycho* sequels. In retrospect, however, it is an oddly appealing addition to the curious 1980s pop-culture fascination with employing primates as a source of easy amusement (hence the Clint Eastwood/Clyde partnership and the PG Tips commercials) and as an object of fear and threat (it came out soon after *Phenomena* and preceded *Monkey Shines*.)

Accompanied by one of Jerry Goldsmith's most playful scores—with echoes of *Gremlins* that prove appropriate when the exposition notes how the chimps follow four distinct "rules"— the movie sets out its stylistic stall early on. Franklin, as evidenced from his attention-getting early films *Patrick* and *Road Games*, was a Hitchcock acolyte fond of ominous point of view shots, dramatic overhead angles, extended takes et al. Here, he relishes the chance to indulge his classical thriller skills and exploits De Roche's scripting gifts; chiefly, a central cliff-top mansion and a bunch of well timed melodramatic storms.

Sexy Elisabeth Shue—just a couple of short years away from *Adventures in Babysitting*, folks!—is a zoology student named Jane (geddit?) at London's Science College who gets a job at the remote coastal home of eccentric Terence Stamp. The reclusive inventor has trained two apes to communicate with computers and develop considerable I.Q.s. Link, who is old enough to be Shue's father, performs chores around the home though Stamp is quick to emphasize that neither he, nor his fellow hominid Imp, should ever be treated as equals. Stamp, by turn, treats Link as a disappointing/naughty child, a loyal servant and an entertainer—the latter in reference to Link's circus days as "Master of Fire."

While Shue disapproves of Link wearing clothes and smoking cigars, notable shifts in his behavior alert her. The creature begins with minor Gremlin-ish mischief (microwaving the phone), escalates to Norman Bates-ish voyeurism (checking out Shue at bath time) and styles himself as a knight in furry armour by saving the young woman from a vicious rottweiler attack (smashing the dog against a fence) and against a threatening human visitor. When it becomes clear Stamp's intentions were to put Link down, a bodycount accumulates, commencing with Stamp himself.

The show is predictably stolen by the menacing Link and heroic Imp, both trained to perfection by Ray Berwick, but with Stamp taking an easy pay cheque and an early exit, it's Shue who carries most of the movie as the only onscreen human. She's very appealing—and flesh-hounds will appreciate the brief ogle of her naked form, a refreshing alternative to the baggy jumpers she dons throughout the rest of the flick.

This overlong movie ultimately turns into a gimmicky variant on the usual stalker/slasher scenario, developing an earlier discussion about apes being just as capable of acts of violence and war as man. Link terrorizes final girl Shue with the kind of resilience you might expect from an anonymous masked psycho in a generic knife-kill movie. He pursues her in and around the house, crashing through windows, riding atop moving vehicles and surprising minor characters in "Oh! It's You!" type shock moments that were obligatory for this era. Franklin's technique and inventive use of the huge house give it vivid production value, and the full-blown Gothic fiery finale is fun, with Link falling to his doom after one final, defiant puff on a cigar. "Only civilized humans know about fire, Link, and you're a stupid animal" dismisses a feisty Shue in a moment that hardly would have helped the movie's lasting popularity with its monkey demographic.
—Steven West

MOONSTALKER
(PREDATOR: THE QUIETUS)

D: Leslie McCarthy
W: Leslie McCarthy, Cliff Twemlow (as "Mike Sullivan")
Filmed in 1986, released in 1988
Starring: Cliff Twemlow, Cordelia Roche, Paul Flanagan, Darryl Marchant, Brian Sterling-Vete

The late, great Cliff Twemlow was a true working-class renaissance man who—until his death in 1993—tried his hand at everything from stints as a nightclub singer, library music composer, bouncer and horror paperback writer, finally settling on a dual career as an actor and DIY filmmaker. Twemlow's best known film *G.B.H.* (1983), the violent story of a Mancunian nightclub bouncer—autobiographically played by Cliff himself—was a fondly remembered rental from the early days of British video. Its ballsy claim to be "more brutal than *The Long Good Friday*," non-stop action, and one-liners worthy of Gene Hunt himself, easily won audiences over, despite *G.B.H.*'s humble, shot-on-videotape origins.

Actual stories about the so-called "Beast of Exmoor" proved to be the inspiration behind 1986's *Moonstalker*, which adds horror elements to Twemlow's tried and tested *G.B.H.* formula. "The Beast," if you remember, was all over the newspapers in the 1980s thanks to constant tabloid speculation that a high amount of sheep deaths was the result of a giant, panther-like cat being loose in the countryside. Clearly not even this was sensationalist enough for *Moonstalker*'s writer/producer/leading man Twemlow nor its director Leslie McCarthy, who instead use the film to posit the idea that the offending creature was in fact a werewolf!!!

Given such a spin on the story, it's no surprise that a New York newspaper dispatches ace reporter Kelly O'Neill (Cordelia Roche) to a little village in England to investigate the apparent werewolf attacks. The paper also hires big game hunter Daniel Kane (Twemlow) in order to provide the back-up brawn to her brains. Clearly taking no chances, Kane arrives in the UK carrying with him machine guns and "an image that's as wholesome as sewerage." The fact that you are not exactly allowed to run around the English countryside tooled up like Rambo is cheekily dismissed by a line claiming that Kane has been granted a special permit to bear arms by the freemasons!! "Charles Bronson eat your heart out," wisecracks one character.

Kelly's initial scepticism starts to crumble when Mr. Rooney and Mr. Clancy, a pair of old Irish drunkards, start feeding her stories about the werewolf's exploits. The sozzled duo's merry demeanor and habit of injecting exclamations of "bejesus" and "Mary, mother of God" into their conversations quickly endears them to Kelly. "That's real Irish charm," she tells Kane. Kelly inadvertently gives Rooney and Clancy a flash of inspiration as to how they can settle their bar tab when she mentions the cash reward on offer for the werewolf's capture. This sets into motion several attempts to find the werewolf by the Oirish double act, whose well-pissed antics provide the film's idea of comic relief.

The werewolf itself occasionally surfaces to polish off livestock and a few minor characters as well as scaring a pair of randy teenagers out of having a quick bonk in a field. Just to add to the village's problem of having a lycanthrope on their doorstep, a local biker gang have started throwing their weight around ... as well as the odd Molotov cocktail. Sporting names like Weasel and Badger and looking like they've escaped from the set of *Death Wish III*, the motley motorcyclists are naturally destined for a run-in with a certain big game hunter.

As if the film didn't have enough eccentric support characters, we also get to meet the delightfully named Wilbur Sledge (Darryl Marchant), a strange young man who appears to know more about the werewolf than he is letting on. Wilbur serves as a mouthpiece for a surprisingly poetic side to Twemlow's screenwriting, and the script offers him plenty of opportunity to wander about the countryside delivering odes to trees and passing rabbits. "You are such a statuesque tree, proud and mighty," Wilbur proclaims, "why did you anger the Lord of lightning?" Wilbur also gets to give a Dracula-like "Children of the Night" speech about the werewolf as it howls away in the distance. "The beast is lonely" explains Wilbur to a rabbit, "it needs my friendship." An utterly unique character played by an equally distinctive-looking actor—imagine Gary Numan reciting Edgar Allan Poe while dressed as a farmer.

Initially built up as a likely werewolf suspect, Wilbur instead ends up taking on a friend/spiritual adviser role to Kane. After the beast injures Kane, Wilbur even volunteers to stitch him back up with a needle and thread, a scene that acts as *Moonstalker*'s one real stab at gore. It probably would have been more advisable for Kane to have gone to hospital, but as it turns out Kane is impervious to pain anyway having mastered "jungle law," so that's all right then!!! A fairly impressive menace finally

takes center stage in the expected Kane vs. Werewolf climax; all slightly bungled by post brawl revelations that initially suggest a *Scooby-Doo* type twist, only to renege and opt for a genuine "monster on the loose" explanation instead, presumably sparing Twemlow and company the wrath of any believers in the real life Beast of Exmoor in the process.

Moonstalker gives the impression of having more money and ambition behind it than the average Cliff Twemlow vehicle, with shooting done on film instead of the usual Twemlow medium of videotape. The film makes a decent attempt at bamboozling the audience into thinking the opening scenes were shot in New York, thanks to some N.Y.C. stock footage and shots of actors roaming what in reality were the mean streets of the North West of England rather than the East Coast of America. Yet for all of the upgrade to film and illusory "overseas location" work, *Moonstalker* still retains the hallmarks of Twemlow's small-scale but enthusiastic output. Twemlow's eye for action scenes and ear for *bon mots* are evident. Obscure areas of Twemlow's beloved North West are predominantly offered up as background scenery, *Moonstalker* being largely filmed in the sleepy village of Chipping and an off-season scout camp in Worsley. The cast includes such Twemlow regulars as Maxton G. Beesley and Brian Sterling-Vete, adding to the strong sense of a close-knit filmmaking troupe at work. As if to prove that his films were a real family affair, Cliff also called upon the services of his sister Ethel to do the catering on this one.

Behind the scenes stories portray Twemlow as a dedicated trouper who'd seemingly do any deal and tackle any obstacle in order to see a film get completed. According to Brian Sterling-Vete, Twemlow's encounters with the supernatural weren't just confined onscreen. Sterling-Vete claims a real-life ghost was causing mischief during the production of *Moonstalker* and that the troublesome spook can—allegedly—be briefly seen in the film itself!! Given such hair-raising production troubles, a quick title change at the last minute (the original title *Predator–The Quietus* being unusable when it emerged that Hollywood was about to unleash a *Predator* of its own) must have seemed a comparatively minor problem for Cliff. Another moment of low-budget ingenuity saw Twemlow talk a local Fiat car dealer into providing transport for the production, in return for some obvious product placement in the finished film. That handshake resulted in poor Kane having to spend the movie searching for a werewolf in a Fiat Panda, a less than macho mode of transport that characters unconvincingly insist is a jeep.

In the event, the miscast vehicle fits in conveniently well with Twemlow's habit of giving his characters quirky traits that play against audience expectations. In *G.B.H.*, Twemlow had shown his tough guy bouncer sharing a bed with a giant teddy bear, and in *Moonstalker* he makes Kane a strict teetotaller. There's a priceless onscreen moment when Twemlow—a man built like a brick shithouse—goes to a bar and orders "a glass of orange juice please." Scenes such as this illustrate Twemlow's ability to gamely take the piss out of himself in a way that the egos of far bigger Hollywood action heroes would never permit. Well, when was the last time you saw Chuck Norris or Steven Seagal in bed with a giant teddy bear?

Twemlow quickly followed up *Moonstalker* with 1988's *The Eye of Satan*, another hybrid of gung-ho action and horror that once again saw him stepping into the role of Kane. Although whether *The Eye of Satan* was intended as a direct sequel to *Moonstalker* is a moot point, since Kane sports rather different characteristics in his second outing—namely an allegiance to the Devil and glowing green eyes!! (He managed to ditch the Fiat in between films as well.) *The Eye of Satan* also features several *Moonstalker* actors in different roles to the earlier film, indicating that Twemlow actually envisioned the two films as being unrelated to each other, save for their recurring central character

Perhaps this was just as well, given that while *The Eye of Satan* was afforded a limited video release and a few satellite TV airings, a dispute with a film developing laboratory in Yorkshire initially resulted in *Moonstalker* being left on the shelf. In the early 1990s, Hemdale Film Corporation, a company that had been set up by the actor David Hemmings and his agent in the 1960s, acquired the rights to the film. When Hemdale went bankrupt in 1995, *Moonstalker* and the rest of the Hemdale library ended up the property of the Hollywood giant M.G.M. To everyone's great surprise M.G.M. chose to re-master *Moonstalker* in high definition, subsequently broadcasting an H.D. version several times on American television in 2010. Quite an achievement for a previously unreleased item, starring nobody anyone in America will have ever heard of, and featuring locations and accents that are equally obscure to a US audience.

Back in the UK, *Moonstalker* had its belated British premiere—nearly 25 years after it was made—as part of the 2010 Salford Film Festival. In typical Cliff Twemlow fashion, the premiere was held above an old pub located just outside of Manchester City Centre. If the true litmus paper test of a film's entertainment value is how it plays before a live audience, then this one passed with flying colors. Proving a real crowd pleaser, *Moonstalker* had its audience laughing along with its knowingly implausible storyline, and cheering when Cliff's face first appeared onscreen, while even the slightest hint of an upcoming action scene was greeted by enthusiastic yells of "Go on Cliff!!" Methinks Mr. Twemlow would have approved.
—Gavin Whitaker

NIGHTMARE WEEKEND

D: Henri Sala
W: George Faget-Bernard, Robert Seidman
Filmed in 1984, released in 1986
Starring: Debbie Laster, Dale Midkiff, Debra Hunter, Wellington Meffert

"George to Apache!" Movies with the word "weekend" in the title have a pretty decent hit rate. There's Godard's paean to the car-wreck, *Weekend* itself; Ozploitation cultists have often sung the praises of Colin Eggleston's creepy man-vs-nature skirmish *Long Weekend*; there are those who rate *Weekend at Bernie's* as the finest work director Ted Kotcheff ever offered to cinema. And then there's *Nightmare Weekend* …
In October 2004, a pseudonymous "beilttog" posted a review—more like a confessional—at the IMDb, declaring himself the on-line producer and person responsible for casting *Nightmare Weekend*. His own candid description of this notorious howler read "may be the worst movie made of all time," and he went on

to provide a little explanatory background. According to his account, French and English producers were due to put up half of a $750,000 budget for a Florida shoot, but no cash materialized. Instead, all the American partners received was a French film crew, a director rumored to have been involved in Thai pornography, and a really poor screenplay written entirely in French. The script was redrafted, but producer Bachoo Sen (one of the project's tenuous UK connections, previously known for the early films of Norman J. Warren) insisted on another re-write by the original French author. By the time filming got underway, no one had much of a clue what was happening, the young cast were leaping in and out of bed with each other onscreen and off, and eventually, with 80-plus minutes of incomprehensible garbage in the can, the movie was released onto an unsuspecting video market eager for any old rubbish bookended by opening and closing titles (of which this movie's are barely legible).

So, what can one say about *Nightmare Weekend*? Balls. Ball bearings, to be precise. They're the focus of this ridiculous little bit of nonsense. A professor and his attractive but mean female assistant are working on a computerized program, by way of which they somehow fire steel spheres into the mouths or bodies of selected human subjects, in order to create a higher form dubbed "neuropaths." The crooked sidekick has other ideas and rejigs the program so that the metal marbles become lethal, causing their targets to expire in a variety of complicated (and frankly, indescribable) ways. One such death involves an unlucky guy choking on a pair of his girlfriend's discarded silk panties, another has a terrified arachnophobe collapsing at the sight of a hairy-legged tarantula which then crawls around her lower jaw for a few seconds. In one scene an attractive young lady consults the computer for tips on meeting men, and is advised that hitch-hiking has a 66% success rate ("discos" come top of the list, as indeed they ought); she duly hitches a ride, only to be promptly raped by a horny motorcyclist, who somehow is traced by the Apache computer which fires a ball bearing (across some considerable/impossible distance? None of this is made at all clear) into him, causing him to thrash around in a foot-deep lake for as long as it takes for us to register that he's a goner.

Nightmare Weekend is celebrated, if for nothing else, as being the film in which "George" appears. George? Well, he's a green-haired, green-nosed, heart-shape mouthed cloth puppet. He seems to operate entirely independently, talks in a really annoying speak-and-spell voice, is somehow integral to the Apache program, and looks to be chiefly responsible for selecting the targets and firing the spheres. How? Why? W.T.F.? More unanswered queries.

A couple of cast members waded out of the morass and moved to better things. You'll recall Dale Midkiff from the excellent film adaptation of Stephen King's marvellous *Pet Sematary*; meanwhile, Andrea Thompson survived her low billing here to play a prostitute in *Wall Street* before establishing a solid supporting career in American TV, with the likes of *Falcon Crest*, *NYPD Blue*, and *24* on her resumé.

Another IMDb contributor popped up in December 2008, this time one Andre Sala, revealing himself as the director's nephew and concurring that *Nightmare Weekend* "is indeed one of the worst movies of all time." Andre says that he spent years seeking a copy of the film, eventually found one, and proposed that he was going to dish DVDs out to all his relatives as Xmas gifts that year!
—Darrell Buxton

• • •

Ocala, according to the US Census Bureau, has a population of 60,786, making it the 49th largest city in the state of Florida. It's the seat of Marion County, and an important center for the breeding of thoroughbred horses, as well as the home of the Funking Conservatory, a professional wrestling school and training center, and you've got to be impressed I made it to the end of the sentence without making fun of that name. Alongside this short list of achievements, Ocala was also the location where seemingly all of *Nightmare Weekend* was shot. The motto of the city is "God be with us." I'm assuming they adopted it at some point in 1986. I know how they feel.

The film opens with two bikers trying to sabotage a weird piece of electronic equipment at the behest of someone called Julie. Unfortunately for one of them, the device seems to have an element of computer protection, as a sort of black marble object is programed to shoot out and hits one of the bikers in the head, making his face fall off. We're only five minutes in and already this is making no sense. Cut to the University of Central Dumbass, and two aerobics students are talking about an experiment underway that very weekend. One of the students is the daughter of the scientist and she's off to see Daddy, whereas the other just wants the $500 fee. Meanwhile, the surviving biker is sad at the loss of his buddy, and we get a flashback to hap-

pier times when they were almost run over by a truck. Julie, who turns out to be the assistant to the scientist, drags our biker out of his *"The Way We Were"* moment and reminds him it was all an accident, which, given that his pal had his face taken off by a magic marble, stretches the definition of the term somewhat.

In her room, the daughter, who we've now established is called Jessica, is having a conversation about picking up guys with her Daddy's computer. He's called George and is the same protection program that marbled the biker dude to death. Did I also tell you he was a frigging hand puppet with fluorescent Homer Simpson hair? No? No idea how that slipped my mind. Jessica isn't wearing very much at this point, and the whole scene seems a bit creepy in a *"Muppets* meets *Demon Seed"* kind of way, but George is happy to help out and suggests that if she wants to meet a guy, she should try hitch-hiking, because that always ends well. She does, and gets picked up by Robert Burke, one of several future name actors slumming it (he was *RoboCop* once Peter Weller had had enough.) Burke's bad boy tries to rape her, but Jessica is saved by a combination of the repentant biker and another one of the deadly marbles that George dispatches—which makes Burke's head explode.

Three bimbos are brought to the house of dodgy experiments in a limo (!), and Julie is waiting for them. She's already established herself as the villainess by shouting at the hired help and having a *Dynasty* haircut. She confirms her bad girl status, selling her boss out to some unknown bloke on the phone and turning his experiment (and I still don't have a clue what it's actually supposed to be) up to 11, which apparently changes our bimbo guinea-pigs into dribbling mutants who then dispatch most of the rest of the cast, though the closing two minutes, which may or may not contain a twist ending, are so dark that it's almost impossible to establish what happens. It's then topped off with a power ballad called *"Nightmare Weekend,"* the only conceivable capper for what we've just experienced.

Now I know what you're thinking. You're thinking of your humble reviewer "Neil, are you on medication? None of that makes any sense whatsoever." You'd be right, it doesn't. Admittedly, I left a few tidbits out, like the scenes at a bar where they serve no booze which seemingly serves no narrative purpose either, and a couple of softcore couplings so poorly lit they look like randomly moving dark shapes in fog, but essentially the story is there in the three paragraphs above. It genuinely seems like it was made up on the spot. Now I'm no fan of the Medved Brothers, and their sneering *Golden Turkey Awards* garbage, but occasionally something is so bad that it transcends its own ineptitude and becomes perversely compelling, and *Nightmare Weekend* fits this category perfectly. Thirty minutes in, I'd gone past boredom, frustration and anger to the point where I found myself actually trying to re-edit the damn thing in my head to see if it made any more sense. I was still doing this at the end, which meant I was thinking about it a lot more than I did with the last Hollywood blockbuster I saw. It's so awful that it actually engages you. What's most impressive is that clearly some money was spent on it, the effects are passable, and the score, intrusive though it is, has a certain professional sheen—and yet even then, it's all so abysmally lit, shot and edited, it almost defies belief.

Shot in the States by a French porno director, with a mix of American and French technicians, *Nightmare Weekend*'s British credentials come from its financing (in part) and the fact that it was produced by British film mini-mogul Bachoo Sen, a former cinema owner who branched out into production. Sen made sexploitation pictures, was the producer of *Her Private Hell*, an early softcore flick by future British horror film director and general nice guy Norman J. Warren, and perhaps his best-known credit is mid-'70s sex thriller *Erotic Inferno*. *Nightmare Weekend* is a departure from his previous raincoat-friendly output and for the life of me I have no idea what he saw in the project, but let's be charitable, and put it down to a troubled shoot. The script was, apparently, subject to multiple major re-writes (presumably in Esperanto, Mandarin and Klingon) and the international nature of the funding and the mix of nationalities on the technical side made the filming extremely difficult, at least according to some bloke on the internet. To be honest, there's not too much information out there about the production, and that's probably just as well. In the only fitting finale to the whole sorry tale, Troma bought the rights to the movie and released it on video, presumably because they didn't want *Troma's War* to be the shittiest film in their back catalogue.

In all conscience, I can't recommend *Nightmare Weekend* to anyone. It takes a special kind of love of zero-budget horror films, or a self-flagellating streak, to inflict it on yourself, never mind encouraging someone else to see it. That said, there is a sort of underlying challenge in trying to figure out what the fuck is supposed to be going on, and a certain sense of awe when you discover how spectacularly it goes off the rails—so if you really must, then go forth and experience it for yourself. Just keep the motto of that fine city of Ocala at the front of your mind as you do so. And don't blame me.
—Neil Pike

RAWHEAD REX

D: George Pavlou
W: Clive Barker
Starring: David Dukes, Kelly Piper, Niall Tóibín, Ronan Wilmot

With dialogue highlights including "Jesus Christ, it's a bloody massacre!" it's fair to assume that screenwriter Clive Barker—adapting a much gorier *Books of Blood* short story—doesn't emphasize *Rawhead Rex* to a great extent when compiling his CV [resume]. It was his second feature film foray after the equally forgotten *Underworld* from the same director Pavlou, and the writer was just a year away from the release of his career-making *Hellraiser*. *Rawhead* is a silly but thoroughly enjoyable monster picture boasting an atmospheric rain-drenched misty Irish backdrop and an above average level of apparently unintended camp, even for the 1980s.

We don't learn much about the eponymous eight-foot-tall humanoid creature except that it was around before Christ, before civilization in fact ("He was King here!"). Rawhead, with his massive muscular torso, wild mane of black hair, glowing hypnotic red eyes and fresh drool dripping from huge jaws looks like a washed-up former star of TV's *Gladiators*. He's played by 6' 11" actor Heinrich Von Schellendorf. Maybe with a name like that, playing Rawhead Rex is an inevitability, who knows? It's too bad the lame "shock" coda of this film (someone says: "It's all over" right before ... ah, you guessed it) didn't lead to a franchise, because Von Schellendorf could have become the Kevin Peter Hall of the low-budget British monster scene.

The late David Dukes is the obligatory imported American hero, a historian writing a book about the proliferation of sacred sites in the Irish countryside, much to the chagrin of his bratty kids and annoying wife (Kelly Piper). She just wants to go shopping in Dublin: "This is the land of your forefathers!"/"Yeah, and they left!" runs a typical familial dialogue exchange.

During a cheap bout of optical FX that looked shite even in 1986, a workman inadvertently unearths Rawhead and soon the beast is offing the obligatory pair of 1980s amorous young lovers in the woods. Dukes has to convince the coppers of the unlikely menace while Guinness-supping locals share tales of Rawhead Rex sightings. A crazy ranting priest, played to the hilt and beyond by Niall Tóibín, seems to know a lot about the monster, and after being pissed on by Rawhead (!) this man of the cloth actually utters the line "Get upstairs fuckface, I can't keep God waiting!" with some degree of conviction.

This cheerfully cheesy movie is several times more entertaining than nearly every Oscar winner for "Best Picture" from its decade and is surely overdue for rediscovery as some kind of forgotten gem. It deserves recognition and Blu-ray shelf space for all sorts of reasons, starting with the decent cinematography by veteran genre lenser John Metcalfe, who gave the likes of *Xtro*, *Inseminoid* and *Satan's Slave* more production value than they might otherwise have had. It has a show-stopping moment in which Rawhead fatally munches down on the hero's pleasantly doomed pre-pubescent son (only downer: it's sadly offscreen, like too much of the gore); Pavlou shows flair staging a bravura caravan park rampage that includes both a gratuitous explosion and the tits-out-for-the-lads spectacle of a girl's blouse being ripped open as Rawhead drags her out of a broken window. Moreover, it's a monster movie not afraid to give lots of screen time to its marvellously ferocious, unrepentant monster.

The reliably daffy climax of *Rawhead Rex* involves a destroyed church, sundry people on fire, a splendidly splattery death for Tóibín and a heavily contrived resolution in which Piper, who has been useless for the entire film, unconvincingly saves the day. It's arguably not a very good picture in conventional critical terms, but it's totally impossible to dislike.
—Steven West

1987

American Gothic
Goodnight God Bless
Hellraiser
Howling IV: The Original Nightmare
Love Potion
The Stepfather
White of the Eye

AMERICAN GOTHIC

D: John Hough
W: Burt Wetanson, Michael Vines
Starring: Rod Steiger, Yvonne De Carlo, Janet Wright, Sarah Torgov, William Hootkins, Michael J. Pollard

"Ah don't wanna jump rope!"

If it looks like a duck, walks like a duck and quacks like a duck then the chances are pretty good that it is a duck. *American Gothic* looks American, feels American, sounds American, and has the word "American" in the title, but it isn't American. It is in fact an Anglo/Canadian production. Ahhh, the 1980s.

Described by Jonathan Rigby as an "imitation backwoods slaughter saga," and compared unfavorably to *Mumsy, Nanny, Sonny and Girly* by Nigel Burrell (see *English Gothic* and *The Flesh & Blood Compendium*), *American Gothic* is the ever-busy John Hough's stab at the stalk-and-slash genre.

Hough was no stranger to the horror field, having already directed the classic *Twins of Evil* for Hammer in 1971, as well as fan favorite *The Legend of Hell House* in 1973. His filmic forays into the forbidden continued into the 1980s, with the distinction of helming Disney's first attempt at a horror *The Watcher in the Woods*, which could have been a winner if the Disney execs hadn't shit themselves and cut/edited out any sense of dread or terror. His disappointment at this treatment may go some way to explaining the monster/rape antics that followed in his next feature *Incubus*. Or maybe not.

American Gothic opens with Cynthia (Sarah Torgov—in her final role before giving up on the acting game) being released from a one year staycation at the local booby-hatch after the negligent/accidental drowning of her child, emerging to the forgiving embrace of her annoying-looking husband Jeff (Mark Ericksen). Jeff plans to aid Cynthia's recovery with a visit to the island where they honeymooned. Along for the trip are two other couples, Rob (Mark Lindsay Chapman) and Terri (Caroline Barclay), and Paul (Stephen Shellen) and Lynn (Fiona Hutchison). Experiencing engine problems en route, they are forced to land their plane at the nearest island and set up camp there. The following morning, Jeff announces that he is unable to repair the plane and that they will need to explore the island for a new engine or something ... Paul, who seems unlikeable but doesn't get much of a chance to prove it, is assigned by Group Leader Jeff to stay behind and keep an eye on the plane while the rest of them go off on an exploratory yomp.

It doesn't take a deal of location shooting before our hapless bunch discover a cottage inhabited by a family of incestuous religio-nutjobs, namely Ma (Yvonne De Carlo), Pa (Rod Steiger) and their three "children," Fanny (Janet Wright), Woody (Michael J. Pollard) and Teddy (William Hootkins). Fanny must be in her late forties and Woody looks older than his Pa! This however doesn't stop them acting like big children, and Fanny is keen to let the new arrivals know that she will soon be celebrating her 12th birthday!

While appearing outwardly welcoming it's not long before the family's true murderous nature rises to the surface. Rob is the first to buy the farm (although this may not actually be the case,

as it is never made clear precisely when during the proceedings Paul receives a hatchet to the face), dispatched by Fanny and Woody on a swing that would make Health and Safety officials cringe. Next up for a serving of death is Lynn, getting trussed up and hung by a set of children's skipping ropes courtesy of Teddy, Woody and Fanny, who don't seem too sympathetic towards her pleas about not wanting to play.

Fanny casts an eye in Jeff's direction, and after a brief spying session comes to the conclusion that if she cannot have Jeff then no one can. Fanny tackles this dilemma by sticking a lance from an ornamental knight-on-horseback into his eye. Ma, seeing that Fanny has only done half a job, finishes Jeff off with a couple of knitting needles plunged into his back. This leaves Cynthia and Terri—two final girls!—though the latter only lasts for another five minutes before Teddy catches up with her for a little spot of neck-breaking/post-mortem rape.

Following Terri's death Cynthia's already tenuous grasp on the here-and-now loosens completely, and before you can say total assimilation, Cynthia is done up in an identical gingham dress to Fanny and accepted wholeheartedly into the family fold; the clan give her a tour of the cellar where the bodies of their victims (previous and recent) hang from meathooks. And thus, it would stay were it not for the touchy subject of bathing Fanny's ossified baby. The site of Fanny preparing her bassinet for baby's bath time sends Cynthia into full blown psycho-mode, and after a quick tug-of-war over the dessicated tot, resulting in said infant being broken in half, Cynthia picks up the bassinet and duly staves Fanny's skull in. It's fair to say that Fanny has had it coming. "Naughty Woody" and "Naughty Teddy" don't have to wait too long for their rewards either. Proving that you can never get too much of a good thing, Cynthia re-employs the horseman figurine, jabbing Woody through the ear. A sickle that has seemingly remained offscreen throughout is instrumental in Teddy's demise as he takes one in the neck for the team. And in another pay-off to an earlier bit of foreshadowing, Ma has a close encounter with her knitting needles.

Returning from rabbit hunting, Pa discovers that his family has been wiped out—Fanny's death seeming to upset him most—and he begins to renounce God in a most actorly fashion, although which God he felt he was serving by killing anyone that landed on their island is open to question. One barrel-load from his shotgun, emptied into his back by Cynthia, would appear to represent the deity's prompt judgment. Ending with Cynthia alone on the island and lost in her head, *American Gothic* is an enjoyable piece of fluff from Hough.
—Fraser Burnett

GOODNIGHT GOD BLESS aka LUCIFER [UK]

D: John Eyres
W: Ed Ancoats
Starring: Emma Sutton, Frank Rozelaar-Green, Jared Morgan, Jane Price, Alan Roland, Alistair Meikels

John Eyres is a familiar name to those haunting the fringes of the film business, having eked a living out of fast buck sci-fi and monster movies in America since the outset of the 1990s. Yet there have always been clues, in the names of several of his limited partnership companies, to point towards Eyres' roots in the UK. Take as two examples Ed Ancoats Films, Ltd. and Miles Platting Films, Ltd. Ancoats and Miles Platting are neighboring areas of Manchester, immediately north of the city center; once notorious areas of deprivation. I should know, I worked there for six months in 1995. It had the highest pregnancy rate among under-sixteens and the highest ratio of rats per resident to anywhere else in the country. Six months there could provide you with a thousand stories. Eyres was raised in Manchester but never filmed there, and it is with some disappointment that such eventful council estates didn't influence and inspire his work more (the high incident content of Channel 4's *Shameless* is a pointer to what could have been.) Instead he seemingly avoided realism, character and horrific farce in favor of more escapist and uncomplicated fare.

Eyres' film career in the UK was brief before his move to America, completing only one film here, *Goodnight God Bless* (aka *Lucifer*). His Stateside move could hardly be branded another case of a great talent jumping ship, as what we largely came to expect from him in time were rote adventures and unimaginative fantasies. The films (mostly under the Nu Image banner) are bland and even fail to provide unintentional laughs, but with this early work he threw himself unabashedly into the moviemaking process—rewarding fans of bad cinema with a psycho thriller rich in embarrassments!

Eyres did have the common sense and foresight to engage a professional cinematographer in Alan M. Trow, who must have been asking how he got roped into this farrago. The British horror scene was struggling but persevering, via a wide and disparate number of individuals in the wake of a film industry that had by 1987 all but abandoned the genre.

Eyres' film couldn't even garner adequate publicity upon its release on the Mogul video label. Following the Hungerford massacre, violent, bullet-riddled action and horror films came under attack and in the immediate week of Michael Ryan's deadly rampage, Bob Clark's *Black Christmas* (1974) and Harley Cokeliss' *Battletruck* (1982) were among the titles withdrawn from the television schedule at a time when the UK only had four terrestrial channels. The Video Packaging Review Committee, responsible for monitoring sleeve advertising images, ruled that you could carry a gun on a video cover, but you couldn't be seen to be pointing it at anyone. School-ground slayings would have seen a similar media backlash and *Goodnight God Bless*, which opens with such an event, was released in the immediate aftermath of one such tragedy in the States. This playtime slaughter sees what appears to be a priest enter the gates and ram a knife into a teacher before pulling out a handgun, shockingly opening fire on the little ones. The children mill around endlessly in a montage depicting the panic, some of them dashing before the camera several times back and forwards, as if participating in a game of British Bulldog. When we return to the scene with the

detectives, the victims are covered by spotless white sheets and seem to have been gunned down in a small, tidy radius, which is at least handy for the shot.

It is impossible to synopsize *Goodnight God Bless* without picking niggling fault in virtually every set-up and action. The blunders are everywhere, in the story, behavior, and procedure. The latter is particularly inexcusable given that the policework is center-stage, but the writer's idea of a crime investigation hub has the officers housed in an inadequate open plan office—the sole W.P.C. even has her locker in the same room. You half wonder why they don't have a *Barney Miller*-style barred holding cell in the corner of the room, though the budget probably wouldn't stretch to it.

For some reason the unit has an American cop seconded to it, namely Joe Yamovich (Frank Rozelaar-Green) who is teamed with John Brett (Jared Morgan) to track down the killer. One hundred of the fleeing kiddies failed to witness anything in the melee but one little girl, Mandy (Jane Price) hid behind the bins and got an eyeful of what was taking place. Phew, a witness! The detectives visit her mother, Lisa (Emma Sutton)—the widow will become the nonplussed American's love interest, and he the family's protector, for the duration of the film.

Meanwhile, the killer priest is striking again, as a nightclubbing couple squabble in the early hours of the morning, the girl then becoming his victim. The newspaper hoardings report the murder and although one stands in the entrance to the police station, blaring the headline, Brett has to break the news to his colleague when he pulls up in a car. A young woman walking her dog in the woods is careful not to let the mutt off the leash until its cue to be stabbed to death by the maniac, but he takes his sweet time about doing the same to her, hovering over this fresh prey, his crucifix dangling in front of her face. This allows her to be rescued, but leaves her a hospitalized, hysterical mess. The killer returns to the central mother and child, breaking into their house but failing to go in for the kill at the right time. There is a further attempt on the little girl's life when they go to the cinema, which is a weird enough experience even without this looming threat. Eyres seems to have been unable to secure a legitimate film for them to see, so settled for some amateur footage of a fairground, at which they laugh insanely as children are projected on routine rides and a helter-skelter. This all to a comic musical soundtrack, complete with whistles and flutes.

The killer priest turns his attentions to the police, and with the achieving of feature-length in mind, the sequences become prolonged as Yamovich and an unpleasant detective named Daniels (Alan Roland) pursue the now almost supernatural menace to a warehouse, where a deadly trap awaits Daniels. Mother and daughter are now under protective custody in a hotel, but when the American returns, he finds that his fellow officers have been disposed of. All leads to a final run-in with the priest before Joe blasts him out of the window. The film closes with a confessional sequence that feels like an add-on as the penitent is revealed to be an apparently demon-possessed priest ...

Modern fears are referenced in a particularly hamfisted manner. The nightclub couple split following an argument and having trotted out an accusatory "wrong time of the month?," the boyfriend follows with that old chat-up zinger, "Hey, you think I got bleeding AIDS or something?" The anxiety in the day was real and ignorance admittedly high, but here the expression is part of a constant immaturity. The Troubles are lobbed in when an Irish officer defending Yamovich is jokingly branded as having IRA connections. The schoolboy standard of the script becomes pitifully random at times. When idiot detective Morris (David Charles) deliberately mishears "condoms" the Irish detective calls his associates a bunch of wankers. "Exactly," responds Morris, "that's why we need the condoms." I picture a put-upon Alan Trow on set, surrounded by a crew made up of a bunch of secondary school boys in blazers carrying their satchels and sniggering.

Curiously, a lot of the sound is captured on location, and as the girl is interviewed in her back garden, the birds twitter and what sounds like a dual carriageway over the fence almost drowns out the conversation. Emma Sutton puts on a good show, and tries to earth the performance in the reality of a mother fearful for the safety of both her daughter and herself, but it's a losing battle and nobody else questions the ludicrous material or tries to showcase any acting talent they might possess, possibly because of the futility in trying to salvage the project as it sags under such wayward authorship and direction. Adversely, however, it perhaps remains Eyres' most interesting film, if only because its guffaws are preferential to the inconsequential body of work that followed.

—Paul Higson

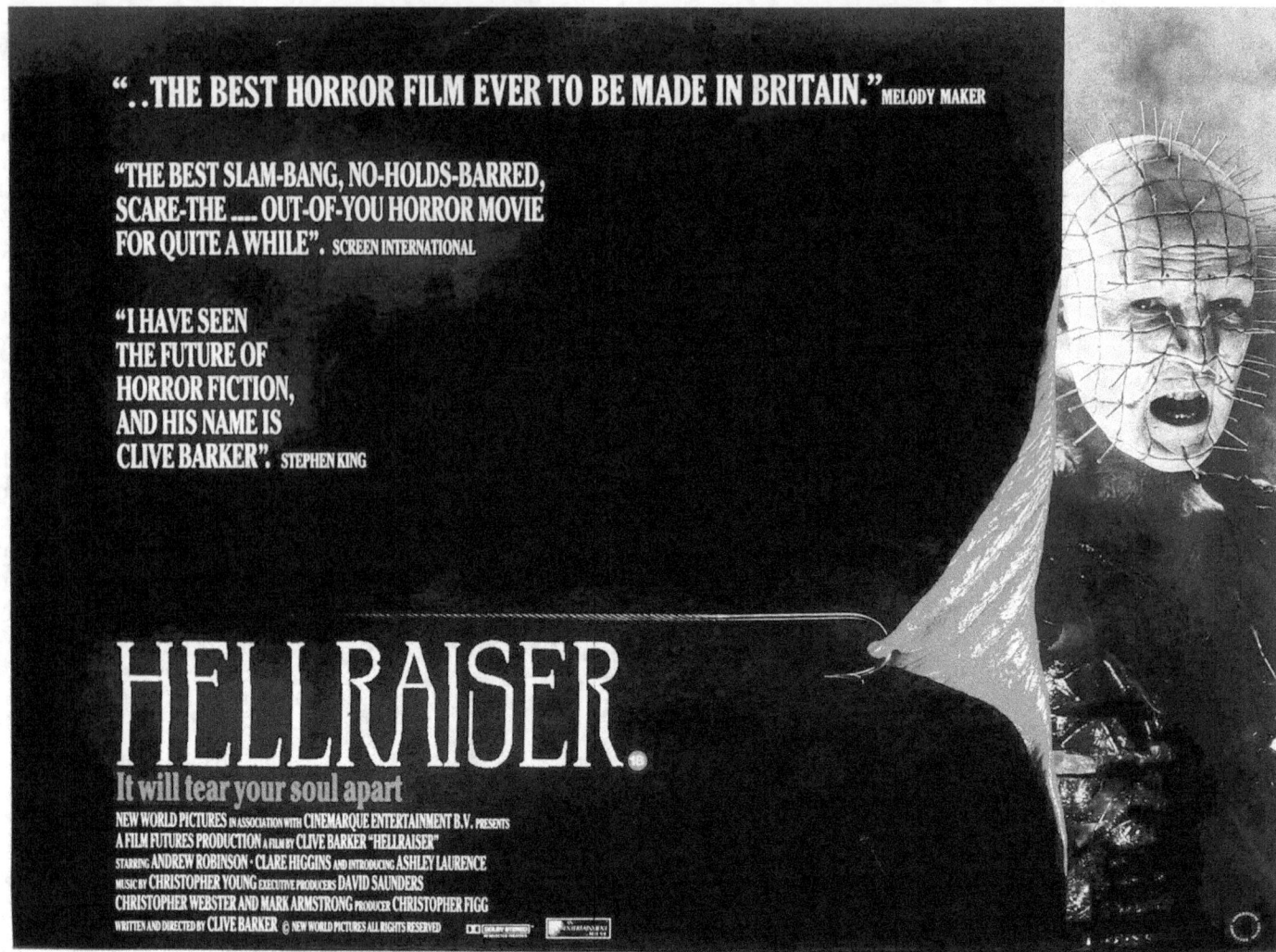

HELLRAISER

D: Clive Barker
W: Clive Barker
Starring: Clare Higgins, Andrew Robinson, Ashley Laurence, Doug Bradley, Sean Chapman, Oliver Smith

Larry (Andrew Robinson) and Julia (Clare Higgins) move to "the old homestead" in the UK, hoping to start afresh and patch up their indifferent marriage. The house on Ludovico Street had been previously occupied by Larry's dangerous, perverse, thrill-seeker of a brother, Frank (Sean Chapman), who has done a bunk, and Julia remains haunted by the torrid, often violent sexual affair she had been involved in with him. Larry's daughter Kirsty (a beguiling Ashley Laurence) from his first marriage is in town, working in a pet store, so the scene is set for a stormy homecoming for all ... oh, and have I mentioned the Cenobites, "demons to some, angels to others," who have designs on not-quite-dead Frank, reaching out for him from another dimension—a realm of pleasure and pain ...

It's hard to believe that horror/fantasy author Clive Barker's directorial debut is well over 30 years old now. I have to confess being a little indifferent to it on its initial 1987 release, but like a fine wine it has matured with age, a dark claret of sweaty storytelling, shocking gore and some genuinely iconic images, none more so than in the lead Cenobite, Pinhead, essayed with dark bravura by Doug Bradley in the role that has given him a shot at immortality. However, there is much more to the film than scattered moments, innovative make-up effects and fetishistic costume design, as for me *Hellraiser* is driven along by two major components—a rousing, occasionally overwhelming score by Christopher Young, and a truly detailed and disturbing performance from acclaimed stage actress Higgins as the devious and deadly Julia; driven by a need to bestow flesh to the bones of her illicit lover Frank, holed up in the attic since spilled blood began his messy resurrection from under the floorboards. As our initially reluctant temptress lures horny young men to the house to despatch them and "feed" them to Frank, here is a tellingly fine piece of screen acting, moving from timid and neurotic to dangerous and thrilling as the goal moves ever closer, her initial feelings of revulsion at killing soon giving way to a glorious wallow in the dark delights of death! One superb shot, simply staged, just shows Julia sipping a drink, her face positively glowing with memories of her evil deeds.

Other performances are not so effective, sadly. Robinson comes over as weak and annoying as the doting, frustrated Larry, while the less said about the actor (?) playing Kirsty's boyfriend, the better! Also, it has to be said that for a fine writer, Barker does put some ridiculous dialogue into the mouths of his set of characters here, my two favorite examples being Larry's incredulous "what the hell is that!!?" at the simple sound of a phone ringing, or Julia's enquiry "is it deep?" regarding a cut on Larry's hand caused by a rusty nail, while witnessing positively Fulci-esque levels of gore spraying from the wound across the attic floorboards! (It is this spilled plasma that of course begins Frank's "rebirth")

Elegantly photographed by Robin Vidgeon, making great use of shadows in the eaves and in the corners of rooms, essaying real flair in the messy, flesh-ripping, metal-strewn lair of the Cenobites, and backed up by brilliant sound design (just listen carefully to the constant background noises in the house), *Hellraiser* spawned a slew of lesser sequels that overused Pinhead, making him the focus of the tales, whereas in the original he is used to sparing but startling effect. One can forgive the first-time-out-of-the-gate directorial flaws (even the clunky, rubbery Engineer monster that chases Kirsty down a long scary corridor can almost be embraced with hindsight!), as the overall mood and tone is so well judged ... and where else can you see a film with truly fantastic ideas such as the Lament Configuration box that summons the demons (a sort of cosmically evil Rubik's Cube), startling and original genre characters like the pain/pleasure-dealing Cenobites, and a man intoning "Jesus wept!" through stretched lips as he is torn apart by hooks!? One of the most striking horror films of the 1980s, *Hellraiser* genuinely looks better each time you view it over the passage of the years, warts and all. If by some small chance you have never seen it, give yourself a treat.

—Michael Wesley

• • •

"Pain and pleasure ... Indivisible."

Hellraiser is a godless film, which is just as well considering how often the characters take His name in vain. In an early scene, cheap religious trinkets are dumped outside the front door—signaling an absence that is later confirmed as total by a brief shot, during the climax, of Jesus hiding in a cupboard. In this spiritual vacuum, the characters are able to indulge themselves in selfish pleasure, free from notions of morality, guilt or abstinence.

Frank Cotton (played by Sean Chapman with skin, and Oliver Smith without) does exactly that; he is a man so dedicated in his pursuit of sensory experience that he has become completely detached from humanity. Frank's extreme hedonism brings him to the attention of the Cenobites who demonstrate that while there is no Heaven, there's definitely a Hell. And in this particular version of Hell your torment may be eternal, but it will also be exquisite.

So entwined are pleasure and pain—and more specifically sex and death—that it's tempting to read *Hellraiser* as yet another conservative horror movie, in which those who indulge in casual and extra-marital sex are mercilessly punished. However, I think that in making clear that his film has banished religion, Barker is telling us that such conventional mores do not apply. Instead I suggest that Barker is positing a world without any governing morality, religiously derived or otherwise.

The film's aesthetic backs up that suggestion. It would be easy to view *Hellraiser* today and dismiss it as looking dated, but in rooting his film so explicitly in the 1980s—with its appalling designs and tasteless fabrics, not to mention the dehumanizing make-up sported by Julia (a riveting turn from Clare Higgins)—he is inviting the viewer to make a connection between the amorality of the characters and the ugliness of the world in which they live.

It's difficult not to recall the dark days of Thatcherism and Reaganomics in this gruesome tale of greed, predation and self-interest. In a neat metaphor, Frank is resurrected by the "trickle down" effect—in his case, his own brother's blood. Reborn, he grows stronger by preying on the hapless men Julia lures back to the house, literally sucking them dry. But Julia too is being exploited: Her repulsion at what Frank asks her to do is exceeded only by her lust for him, and she'll do anything to get what she wants. In this film one character's pleasure is always gained at the expense of another's pain, which encapsulates Barker's condemnation of the dominant right-wing politics of the 1980s.

Much has been made of the film's bizarrely muddled setting: the locations are clearly British (thanks to the clarity of Blu-ray, you can spot signs in the pet shop showing prices in pence) but many of the characters speak with an American accent and indeed some (most notably Frank) have been dubbed with American voices. It's undeniably jarring and was almost certainly done with an eye on transatlantic markets but having said that it does fit with the political interpretation. In the mid-1980s the "special relationship" between the two countries was probably at its strongest, so setting his film in a curious amalgam of the two is apposite on Barker's part.

Ironically for a film which is so explicitly critical of the mood of its time, *Hellraiser* went on to become a very successful

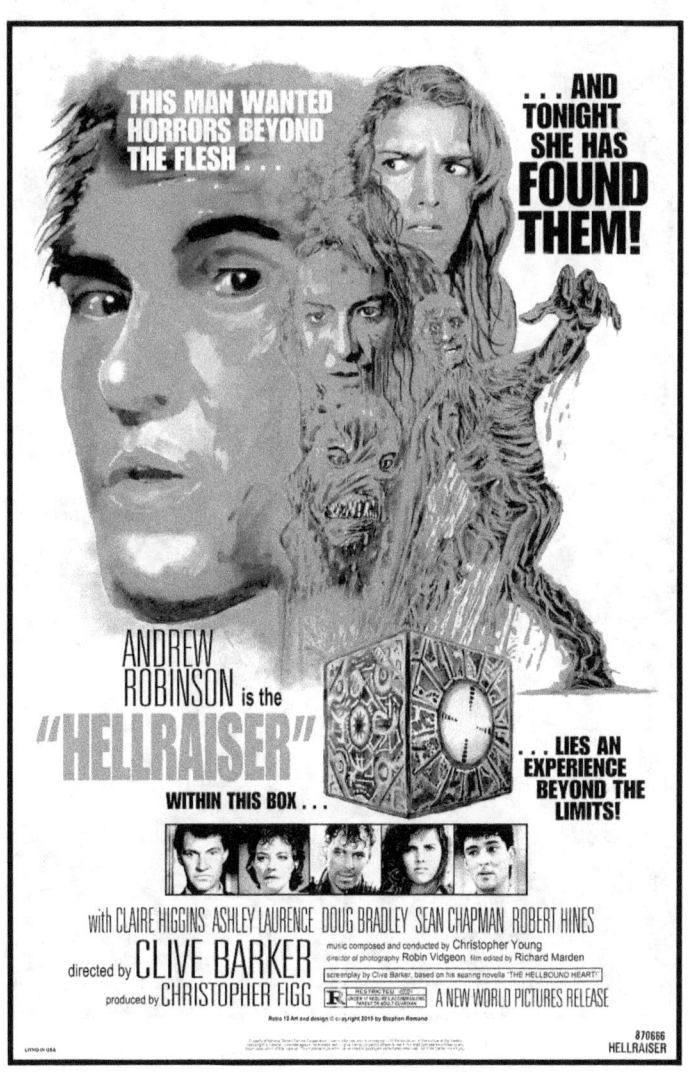

franchise, one in which Pinhead—the *de facto* leader of the Cenobites—developed into a horror icon to rival Freddy Krueger. It's easy to forget that in the first film the chief villain is actually Frank; the Cenobites are fleetingly glimpsed characters who actually punish Frank, inflicting the comeuppance he so richly deserves. However, as the series developed, Barker's input declined, the Cenobites moved center stage and social comment didn't so much decrease as disappear altogether. Perhaps in the long-mooted remake, we might discover what he makes of mankind in the 21st century
—Daniel King

HOWLING IV: THE ORIGINAL NIGHTMARE

D: John Hough
W: Clive Turner, Freddie Rowe
Starring: Romy Windsor, Michael T. Weiss, Antony Hamilton, Susanne Severeid

There's something oddly appealing about the *Howling* franchise—ironic considering it tends to rank alongside things like the *Leprechaun* series in the annals of fan-despised long-running genre brands. Sure, most of the sequels to Joe

French VHS for *Howling IV*

Dante's witty, satirical 1981 movie have been dreadful on many levels—but no two are close to being similar, and most of them cheerfully roam free from any sense of formula, hurling assorted wacky ideas and images at the screen in the hope that some will stick.

The Prague-shot *Howling II: Stirba–Werewolf Bitch* (the movie in which Sybil Danning's chest out-acted a characteristically unamused Christopher Lee for the only time in cinema history) set the tone for a genuinely unique run, and led you to wonder if the legendarily grumpy star had a secret DVD copy stashed away under the mattress! If you kept up with the series, further rewards included demented Australian spoof *Howling III: The Marsupials*, the surprisingly intelligent Ray Bradbury homage, *Howling VI: The Freaks* and the line-dancing trouser-wearing werewolves in the outright embarrassing *Howling VII: New Moon Rising*. At least you can tell them apart, something which you might struggle to do with the majority of second-verse-same-as-the-first horror sequels.

Howling IV, which errs closest to the story and structure of Gary Brandner's entertainingly trashy original novel, was going to be directed by co-writer Clive Turner (who stayed on to direct *New Moon Rising*) until financing fell through and—gawd bless him—Harry Alan Towers stepped in with a cheque. Shot in South Africa, this British-funded movie wins the 1987 "bloody cheek!" award for boasting the subtitle *The Original Nightmare*, though the word "nightmare" turns out to be appropriate in relation to its jaw-dropping Justin Hayward theme song. Entitled

"Something Evil, Something Dangerous," it has the erstwhile Moody Blue trilling "On the borders of my consciousness, something dangerous! Something eeeeevvvvill, something dangerous ..." until members of the audience start sharpening their popcorn boxes to sever their ears.

"Original" is a harder moniker to live up to in a film that reworks the plot of *The Howling* while throwing in a recurring ghostly nun seemingly on hire from *A Nightmare on Elm Street 3: Dream Warriors* and a couple of dream sequences blatantly ripping off *An American Werewolf in London*. The movie's awkward production history—much of it was shot silent and dubbed later—results in a bizarre mixture of accents and peculiar performances, though its biggest failing is to strand an underrated, talented director with mostly unworkable material. John Hough's eclectic movie career encompassed the liveliest of the Hammer Carmilla trilogy (*Twins of Evil*), the still-terrifying *The Legend of Hell House*, the gloriously tacky Patsy Kensit/Jack The Ripper farrago *Bad Karma*, mainstream hit *Escape to Witch Mountain*, "Dark Disney" offering *The Watcher in the Woods* and a couple of overlooked but interesting 1980s horrors, *American Gothic* and the genuinely creepy *Incubus*. In latter years, thanks in particular to Tarantino, Hough has had a cachet of cool restored due to the enduring cult of *Dirty Mary Crazy Larry*. In his oeuvre, *Howling IV* probably ranks alongside the Barbara Cartland adaptation *A Hazard of Hearts* and the ill-fated *Biggles*.

It starts out in L.A., where screwed-up novelist Romy Windsor is in dire need of a break due to her fragile mental state. Her doctor's advice is that she go somewhere where her imagination won't run riot ... so what better vacation home than a creepy, mist-enshrouded woodland cottage in the strange little town of Drago, complete with claw marks on the front door?! What, were all the cabins taken at Camp Crystal Lake? Drago is full of generic American movie characters like a genial pair of shopkeepers who refer to each other as Mr. and Mrs. O, and a dopey hiking duo who exist solely to be torn apart in a feeble, cheesily scored attack scene representing the only (mild) horror in the movie until the last reel. That is, unless you count lycanthropic local harlot Eleanor, meant to be an alluring husband-stealer like Elisabeth Brooks in *The Howling*, but in comparison a repellent hag with too much make-up.

Much of this tortuously slow movie consists of Windsor ploddingly discovering the town's secrets while bored hubby Michael T. Weiss roughs it with the (cough) sultry Eleanor, probably due to Drago's exceptionally poor assortment of quality crumpet. Sadly, Windsor can't carry the movie and has all the range of Rachel Ward, struggling to offer any variation on her single expression even when her husband's flesh melts off his bones and his remains regenerate themselves into werewolf form. This fairly novel variant on the typical transformation sequence instigates a finale showcasing some gory, rubbery Steve Johnson make-up effects, which, although good, are too little too late. The fiery bell tower climax, again cloned from *The Howling*, and the patented clumsy last minute 1980s "shock" also fail to take the movie into the beyond-comprehension enjoyable nuttiness of its two predecessors.
—Steven West

LOVE POTION

D: Julian Doyle
W: Julian Doyle, Mark Ezra
Starring: Nancy Paul, John Rowe, Robert Ashby, Norman Chancer, Ian Barritt

Shot in the winter of 1987, Julian Doyle's *Love Potion* is one of the least-known British horror films of the decade. I became aware of the film as a result of frequent screenings on Sky Movies circa 1992, and there was a UK video release around the same time under the title *Shock Treatment*. The video release was unannounced, but it did hit the shops (I once saw a copy in Preston), and one copy of the British videocassette was spotted on eBay, with a hefty asking price.

The film was the feature-length directorial debut of Julian Doyle, an accomplished editor and cinematographer with the experience, skills, circles and contacts to help bring in a low-budget movie at a time when the industry was struggling. People often talk about a "seventh" *Monty Python* member, be it Carol Cleveland or Neil Innes. Doyle is one of the several "seven" contenders, having worked closely with the entire team both on Python films and individual projects. He was the editor on *Monty Python's Life of Brian* and *The Meaning of Life*, Terry Gilliam's *Time Bandits* and *Brazil* and Terry Jones' *The Wind in the Willows*, with second unit work on Jones' *Erik the Viking*. Of interest to Kate Bush fans, prior to *Love Potion* he had also directed the *Cloudbusting* promo video featuring Donald Sutherland.

Julian Doyle: "*Love Potion* was private money raised by a financial advisor, £500,000. We filmed under the title *Love Potion Number 9* and were selected to run at the Toronto Film Festival. Suddenly we got a call from either Jerry Leiber or Mike Stoller who originally gave us permission but now a US film had asked to use the title. Our producers got cold feet and pulled the film from the festival. We did a deal for the rest of the world (not US) with Interaccess that was a branch of Vestron. They did the deal with Sky but then Vestron went into liquidation blocking further deals. Not only that but the production company of the film (Flying High) went bankrupt and one of the creditors (Metro Labs) blocked the negative. It was a stupid move

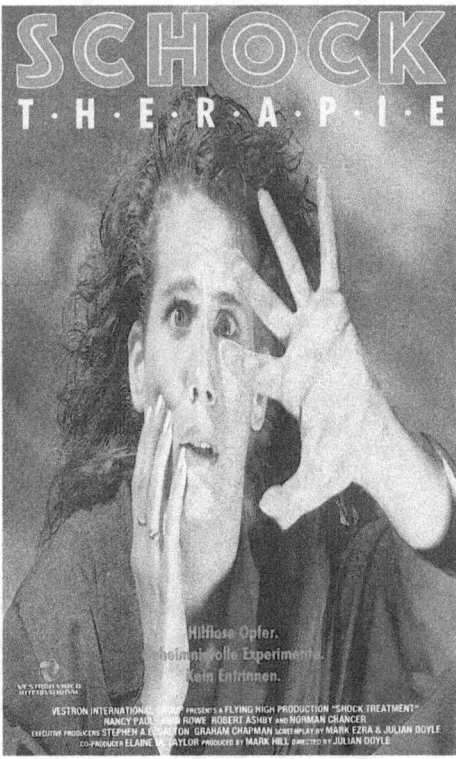

German VHS for *Love Potion*

German DVD for *Love Potion*

because we could not release the film in the US and make money. So, the film got paralysed."

Love Potion opens in New York with Delaware (Nancy Paul, who resembles a cross between a young Samantha Eggar and JoBeth Williams) attending the launch of her brother's book. The book is titled *Chemical Wedding* which Doyle insisted on as a predictive in-joke, as he intended in time to make a film called *Chemical Wedding*. When that second horror movie (Doyle might prefer not to think of it as such) surfaced two decades later, with a plot outline very different from that considered back in 1987, it did get noticed, and is a lot of fun, with an entertaining script by Bruce Dickinson and starring Simon Callow as a revived Aleister Crowley.

Delaware's brother dies of a drug overdose during the launch and she reacts over time by becoming a drug addict herself. It's a year later that we catch up with her as she is escorted to Bath in England by her father (Norman Chancer). They pass the spot where Eddie Cochran died and she is registered into the Avesbury Clinic, an experimental rehab center for young people with a recent history of drug use. There are nine other patients, five of each gender, all there for the cure. The clinic is run by Dr. Samphire (John Rowe) who has a disturbing resemblance to British politician Iain Duncan Smith, the last person you would entrust with the care of others.

Delaware has smuggled drugs into the clinic, even using them in the plane toilet, joining a very different kind of "mile high" club. The treatment includes Dr. Badel's (Robert Ashby) education program, during which they will learn everything about drug addiction, though it is unclear how that is intended to work and the audience is duly inattentive, except when they watch gruesome Mondo footage of victims of the Mexican drug trade, focusing on a bloated corpse and explaining how one young dependent's mutilated hand is the result of eating his own fingers in his drug-induced madness. They are given daily doses of Vicepton, which will in time be replaced with Methadone linctus. The movie's first half hour is largely given over to the treatment with only the occasional hint of the direction it will take into horror; the suspicious behavior of members of staff, an unseen mystery "designer" drug user tucked away in a room in the basement, and ominous talk of losing one of the patients when we have just seen a second experience a violent fit.

During a review meeting with Delaware as the subject, the staff discuss heart problems in the girl's family, stepping up the "treatment," how she continues to romanticize drug-taking and, in a kill or cure move, how to diminish the idolatrous image she has of her brother which is bringing her to mimic his behavior and join him. The patients sneak downstairs in the night to party on drink and drugs raided from respective cabinets, and during the revelry Chrissy (Samantha Phillips) does a full strip. Cut to the morning and the bedroom that the two of them share, Delaware awakens to find Chrissy dead.

There is an increase in the inexplicable incidents. Ben (Ian Barritt) disappears through a door, which is suddenly locked from the inside. Lloyd (Neil Conrich), sneaking some poppers, has a serious nosebleed and when Delaware and Sarah (Shelley Pielou) go for assistance in the basement treatment rooms, Sarah becomes trapped behind a door. In the frosted glass of the door, a second unidentifiable figure grabs her and Sarah's blood splashes across the glass. Things spiral until Delaware and Gary (Kevin Carr) are seemingly the last two patients, discovering all the other bedrooms stripped of bed linen and personal effects. Gary leads Delaware in a proposed escape route that ends up in the treatment corridor just as they are wheeling another of the girls into the room, delirious on a gurney. Gary is not one of the patients but one of the conspirators. "You may not have a use for your body, but we do," Delaware is told by Samphire, revealing that the clinic is the center of an organ farming operation. She takes the opportunity to flee, taking her past other victims—including Sarah, pleading to her for help, part of her arm surgically opened exposing the muscle.

The film is reasonably well made but given the houseful of patients and staff there is difficulty differentiating them in the space of a single viewing. There is some irony in this when considering one small fact about the story that I have yet to reveal. Despite this there is an attempt to provide each actor with a quota of screen time. The dialogue among the patients is a little bland in the first half hour, filler and unfunny wisecracks, but this is bypassed once the thrills set in. The dialogue could have done with the hand of a David McGillivray, and it does remind one of a Pete Walker horror film, though with less sex and gore. The script is co-written by Mark Ezra (*Slaughter High*, but don't let that put you off) with Julian Doyle, from Doyle's own concept.

There are several performances that help the movie considerably, like that of Jean Leppard as Nurse Rached, of whom Doyle rightly favors close-ups as he dares the viewer to read good or evil in her face. She somehow channels both concern and malevolence in the same expression. As for Nurse Bill … it's time I came clean and discussed the final twist now that I have provided the curious with enough to go on.

*** SPOILER ALERT! ***

Yes, the movie has a twist, changing everything that has preceded it. Following Delaware's escape, her father places a call to Dr. Samphire at the clinic. He leaves his office, walks the empty corridors and opens a door into … a dressing room, occupied by the rest of the cast … that is to say, the theatrical company formed to pose as staff and patients to scare one client out of his or her addictive tendencies. Yes, I know, it falters in theory. But it remains a bold move. Retrospectively, we see how brazen Doyle has been with some of the clues. In losing the character of Denise (Mary Cornford), she wasn't being pulled out of the program by her sponsors, nor was she too far gone, nor was she going to die, but had in fact secured a place with the Royal Shakespeare Company. Chink of glasses! This also explains a mysterious delivery of Shakespearian verse in the toilets, during what we take to be Delaware in a fever dream comedown.

Nurse Bill and Patient Ben is the most outrageous stunt as they are the same actor, Ian Barritt, a jittery long-haired hippy conspiracy theorist when a patient, coldly cynical with a pronounced accent when a male nurse. His features are the most distinctive among the cast members and it should have been an easy read, but Doyle is cocksure of his aural and visual legerdemain and fooled this viewer. Due credit to the actor, too! The cinematography of Brian Herlihy is unfettered and somber. There are a couple of "magic hour" shots such as the moment when Delaware is captured at the window like a pre-Raphaelite beauty, a curling red mane framing her wistful face.

"We made it in 1987 and shot in winter—most in an elaborate country hotel just outside Exeter," Doyle reports. "I think it was originally a private house owned by W.H. Smith of the bookshops. As it was winter, we almost had the whole place to ourselves—staying and working in the same place."

Whereas the rest of the *Python* team went on to great success—including Gilliam's directorial career, Cleese's creation of Basil Fawlty and Palin's globe-roaming adventures for the BBC, Graham Chapman's personal projects were prone to failure, cut all the more cruelly short by his early death. That same curse came to *Love Potion*, restricting its release, though Chapman was an enabler for the production.

Doyle: "Graham Chapman helped in several ways—he knew Ronnie Wood and suggested we use Jo (Mrs. Ronnie Wood) in the film. He also allowed us to use his house to film a scene that was supposed to be in the US, but we cut it out." Jo Wood appears in the film as a patient, performing under her maiden name of Jo Karslake. "She is one of the inmates who is a very quiet girl but suddenly comes out of her shell at the party where she starts a competitive stripping dance (which she loses). She was on set for the full time and Ronnie came and spent a week down with us on the set." The film mentions Keith Richards with a sly rumor that he was a previous attendee of the clinic, and there is a love of rock and roll in the soundtrack with popular standards like "Three Steps to Heaven" and "In the Year 2525" cannily placed for effect.

The opening credits list the songs, the closing credits detail the artwork in the background. An examination of the paintings used, escapist dreamscapes and nightmare visions by Wyeth, Dadd, Poussin, Blake and Bosch among others, and their correspondence with the themes in the film is probably worthy of an article in itself.

—Paul Higson

THE STEPFATHER

D: Joseph Ruben
W: Donald E. Westlake
Starring: Terry O'Quinn, Jill Schoelen, Shelley Hack, Charles Lanyer, Stephen Shellen

The US horror thriller *The Stepfather* might seem like an odd inclusion in a book about British movies but warrants its place here thanks to being the 56th entertainment film from Lord Lew Grade's ITC (Incorporated Television Company), first found-

British VHS for *The Stepfather*

ed in September 1954 and intended to be a contractor for the then newly created ITV in the UK Despite becoming more renowned for glamorous cult crime-busting shows such as *The Saint* and *The Persuaders*, ITC introduced film co-production from the 1970s onwards with such familiar titles as *Capricorn One*, *The Eagle Has Landed* and *The Boys from Brazil*. Co-produced with New Century Vista, *The Stepfather* was released on January 23, 1987 and offered far more than a by now hackneyed slasher script or a trite "by-the-numbers" variation on the "cuckoo in the nest" theme.

There were two obvious benefits to this sleeper success. The first was the script by Donald E. Westlake, the legendary crime writer who, under the pseudonym of Richard Stark, created the popular Parker character made famous on celluloid by the likes of Lee Marvin in *Point Blank* and Jason Statham in the eponymous *Parker*. Well known for sparky dialogue plus intense and believable characters, Westlake invests potentially clichéd psycho situations with a low key, almost mundane quality as a damaged man strives to becoming the all-American hero dad by insidiously worming his way into a single parent family. Although capable of violence and even murder, Jerry Blake (played by the other big hit of the production, Terry O'Quinn, in his pre-*Millennium* and *Lost* breakthrough role) has a clarity of purpose that is understandable and touching, even if his methods leave much to be desired. A scene in which he watches a perfect family unit from a distance offers beautifully judged pathos. The little girl of the family waves, and so does he in return, before smiling and almost crying. Prior to this, the opening sequence cleverly sets out the film's stall as O'Quinn enters a bathroom as a bearded, bespectacled and blood-spattered figure then gradually and calmly transforms himself into a clean-shaven man in a suit. Looking neat, tidy and professional he then descends the stairs and calmly walks past the murderous carnage that he has visited upon the family home.

He has already prepared his next nest and the bulk of the plot details his infiltration of the lives of Susan and her daughter Stephanie. The blandness of Shelley Hack and Jill Schoelen respectively is fortunately insufficient to blunt a witty script, one that spends more time allowing O'Quinn to internalize his mania than dwelling on body count histrionics. The introduction of such homely trivialities as a "dinner in 15 minutes" is enough to bring the character back from the brink, but not forever.

Things unravel at a believable pace and in a naturalistic way. The fine moment when Susan realizes that her new man is not who he claims to be is sublimely judged by O'Quinn as he calls himself "Hodgkins," only to stop in puzzled bewilderment and say aloud "Wait a minute ... who am I here?" Chilling stuff.

Westlake cleverly juxtaposes meaningless family banter with violence and suspense: "You're a very bad girl" he says to Stephanie before chasing her with a knife, and another character is dispatched following the passive aggressive: "Next time Jim, call before you drop by!" before the killer pay-off in which he stands with a knife entrenched in his chest before whispering: "I love you" and falling down the stairs. A final sawing down of a phallic birdhouse by his triumphant stepdaughter perfectly sums up the cheerfully macabre wit of the text.

—Ian Taylor

WHITE OF THE EYE

D: Donald Cammell
W: China Cammell, Donald Cammell
Starring: David Keith, Cathy Moriarty, Art Evans, Alan Rosenberg, Marc Hayashi, Alberta Watson, China Cammell

White of the Eye is possibly the most fully realized articulation of cult auteur Donald Cammell (*Performance*, *Demon Seed*) and his key pre-occupation and obsession, namely the duality of the soul. That the most recent biographical study of Cammell (*Donald Cammell–A Life on the Wild Side* by Rebecca and Sam Umland) fails to connect Cammell's Scottish heritage, with its rich cultural lore of duality, double walkers, fetches and changelings, to his own alter-ego issues—uncensored Don was his own personal Jekyll—seems like a missed opportunity.

And so to the film ...

I don't think that I am giving too much away by saying this is less of a whodunnit and more of a when-will-they-find-out-he-dunnit, but with *White of the Eye* Cammell has created a searing and obviously very personal desert song. A world where everything you think you know about somebody can be turned upside down in the time that it takes to find a trophy bag hidden behind bathroom fixtures, a world where idle affluence is met with ritualistic brutality.

The story concerns the relationship between prosperous Paul and Joan White, how they met and where they are now, 10 years down the line. It seems that they are still in love and doing very well, thank you very much, Paul (David Keith) is kept busy with his carpentry/sound system business—he has a human-tuning-fork capability of finding the ideal site for positioning hi-fi speakers—and Joan (Cathy Moriarty) appears content with her role of housewife and mother to their nine-year-old daughter Danielle (Danielle Smith), but amid this idyll something is rotten in Globe, Arizona.

There has been a series of murders—posh totty eviscerated in their designer desert homes. These assaults are presented in striking fashion—the body-spin head-slam has stayed with me since I first saw this, decades ago—and their juxtaposition of languidity and violence enforces yet another aspect of the duality at the heart of this film.

Into the proceedings steps Charles Mendoza (Art Evans), a detective investigating the murders. Paul is one of four people whom forensics have fingered as being a key suspect—by way of his tire tracks—and it is now only a

Austrian DVD for *White of the Eye*

matter of time before truths present and past rise to the surface in an explosive finale.

Moriarty as Joan, and Alberta Watson as the seductive Anne Mason, both turn in sensitive and balanced performances—the same alas cannot be said for Alan Rosenberg, who plays Mike, Joan's original boyfriend prior to him being cuckolded by the more rugged and manly Paul. Rosenberg seems to be channeling the spirit of a rat for his motivation. This may however be down to Cammell's "complete control" on set ...?

But let's face it, this film is all about one person—who is two people—and one person only, and David Keith manages to convince us regarding his dual nature with a qualified ease.
—Fraser Burnett

1988

Dream Demon
The Eye of Satan
The Girl in a Swing
Hand of Death Part 25: Jackson's Back
Hellbound: Hellraiser II
High Spirits
How to Get Ahead in Advertising
The Lair of the White Worm
Paperhouse

DREAM DEMON

D: Harley Cokeliss (as "Harley Cokliss")
W: Harley Cokeliss, Christopher Wicking
Starring: Jemma Redgrave, Kathleen Wilhoite, Mark Greenstreet, Jimmy Nail, Timothy Spall

Nik Powell and Steve Woolley's Palace Pictures arrived in the age of video with a reputation for acquiring quality cult cinema and distributing to the rental marketplace. Come their move into film production, the common expectation was that Palace would make pictures of a similar verve and intelligence, in which art and exploitation came conjoined, stylistic with a shock value, similar to the films they hawked on tape: *The Evil Dead* (1981), *Basket Case* (1982), *Diva* (1982), *The Loveless* (1981), *Female Trouble* (1974) and *Aguirre, the Wrath of God* (1972). Instead, Palace gave us *Dream Demon*.

The company may have plunged in with the noble hope of rescuing the British horror film, and to that end roped in Christopher Wicking on co-authorship. Wicking was a writer with a history in British horror and had been identified by *Sight and Sound* at the outset of the 1970s as one of the fresh wave of talent in the bloody new British cinema. Unfortunately, despite prominence, his screenplays rarely earned favor among critics or fans.

Dream Demon was accused of jumping on the *A Nightmare on Elm Street* bandwagon, taking on themes in which the dream domain bleeds dangerously into the real world. The concept naturally lends itself to surreal and potentially frightening imagery if done properly, ridicule and confusion if not.

Bride-to-be Diana (Jemma Redgrave) starts to have sleepless nights upon moving into her new London flat. Her psychologist palms the nightmares off as an ordinary enough deep-seated anxiety about sexual relations, the fears of a virgin, which she happens to be, and that she might fail to consummate the marriage. Her future husband (Mark Greenstreet) is a Falklands hero so upper class that he begins his sentences with an "I say, awfully ..." Their upcoming wedding is the subject of a deal of press attention, though the inadequacy of the budget limits this to two grotesque reporters (Timothy Spall and Jimmy Nail) who loiter and harass the young debutante, and even trespass into the building if the opportunity arises. Spall and Nail are a casting novelty, a tailored attraction for the British audience, house names at the time as two of the stars of Franc Roddam's then hugely popular series *Auf Wiedersehen Pet*.

A token American, Jenny, is thrown into the mix because, as everyone knew in the 1980s, Americans would not watch British films unless there was one. (Curiously, American films did not feel the need to reciprocate, unless perhaps they needed a villain with an accent you could understand.) It is a role for the then budding geek pin-up Kathleen Wilhoite, who one year earlier had stood out in a distinctive character spot in Kevin Tenney's *Witchboard*. Seeing Diana under great duress undergoing the dual assault of gutter press and perturbing dreams, Jenny offers to stay with her. She ends up accidentally popping into one of Diana's dreams, discovering a very real threat from the denizens of the haunted and taunted heroine's sub-conscious.

Diana's dreams abduct the pressmen, the obnoxious double-act appearing increasingly repugnant in future nightmare-land encounters. Before Paul (Nail), the muckraking reporter, disappears he reveals to Diana that her beau has money troubles and "doesn't need a bride, he needs a bank he can bonk." The girls' collective situation can be rectified, but the revelations—which elaborate upon and explain Jenny's own connection with the property in which they both reside—are hardly worth the wait.

Dream Demon is a dismal failure that never takes hold. Unlike *A Nightmare on Elm Street* or *Dreamscape* (both 1984), it doesn't have the compelling backstory that paves the way for the dream domain sequences and is an unsatisfactory and confusing non-experience short on imagination or any real surprise. Dialogue rings a constant false note. This is a film about insecurity and yet is itself pieced together from insecurities. The grab-bagging from here and there is too focused on predicting what elements might appeal to the audience, instead of concentrating on an interesting angle and allowing a story to tell itself. Director Cokeliss is left driving pegs into wrong-shaped holes.

Curiously, and more interestingly, the writers do tap into the real media circus that circulated the Royal Wedding of 1981, again possibly going for the heritage audience, though that obviously never became clear in the film's publicity which was based more on the pus and mutation of Nail and Spall. Redgrave's protagonist is named Diana and is a kindergarten teacher. She even wears similar clothes to Lady Diana Spencer, including that ruff-like collar. People became protective of the royal Diana after

she approved a simple newspaper snapshot and her shapely legs became silhouetted by the sunlight through her thin skirt, causing a furore and a frenzied media circus. Today, more unsettling than the supernatural premise of *Dream Demon* is the role of the film's paparazzi, as a despicable intrusion and even a threat to life, particularly when set alongside tragic events which were to take place less than a decade later in Paris.
—Paul Higson

• • •

Diana (Jemma Redgrave) is a young woman who is engaged to marry a dashing Falklands war veteran. She has a string of nightmares about what could go wrong at the wedding, and an encounter with a pair of crass and intrusive tabloid reporters named Peck and Paul (Timothy Spall and Jimmy Nail) only adds to her stress levels. A cheeky but well-meaning American named Jenny (Kathleen Wilhoite) arrives at Diana's door. Although she grew up in Los Angeles, Jenny spent her early childhood in London but has no memory of this period of her life. She is convinced that she once lived in Diana's current home, however, and has come in an attempt to jog her memories

After meeting Jenny, Diana's nightmares grow worse. She is now accosted by monstrous versions of the two reporters, and also has inexplicable visions of a man on fire and a little girl dressed as an angel. Her own dreams are overlapping with Jenny's repressed childhood memories, and the only way to end it all will be to find out what really happened to her new friend.

The success of the *A Nightmare on Elm Street* series inspired a flurry of imitators: 1988 alone saw the releases of *Bad Dreams*, *Deadly Dreams* and *Dream Demon*. Helmed by journeyman director Harley Cokeliss and co-written by Christopher Wicking in his last job as a movie screenwriter, *Dream Demon* was a British contribution to the cycle. But while *A Nightmare on Elm Street* based itself around the communal memory of a child murderer, this film taps into the personal theme of suppressed childhood trauma.

Despite its limited resources, *Dream Demon* does a good job of creating an imposing set of unreal landscapes through off-kilter camera angles, stark lighting techniques and a few well-paced special effects. The film portrays the dreams of Diana and Jenny less as a state of being, and more of a tangible location, as the heroines freely stumble from the real world into their joint psyche simply by walking through a door. At its heart, *Dream Demon* is a haunted house film: its main setting is a place that is riddled with painful memories, some of which are prone to crawling back to the surface.

The film has a very different cultural backdrop to the small-town teenage America of *Elm Street*. With her cut-glass accent, pearl necklace and Prince Charming soldier fiancé, Diana fits into the "Sloane Ranger" stereotype that arose in the Britain of the 1980s; she even shares her name (and paparazzi harassment) with the most famous Sloanie of all. Jenny, meanwhile, sports heavy black eyeliner, messy black hair and a mostly dark wardrobe, all of which associate her with the Goth subculture— another scene that developed in 1980s Britain.

Playing on the idea that everyday anxieties can be amplified in nightmares, the film tries to turn the uncouth reporters Paul and Peck into demonic villains. The two shifty geezers get sucked into Diana's dreamscape, causing them to undergo transformations: Peck turns from a pervy voyeur into a rapist and finally into a decomposing revenant, while Paul takes on a distorted, snake-like aspect. These two characters make effective antagonists at first but, like Freddy Krueger before them, quickly become self-parodies—Spall being the worst offender, as he plays Peck as something like a pantomime henchman.

It is also hard to miss the snobbish subtext as the upper-crust heroine is pitted against a working-class antagonist who becomes, literally, a subhuman monster. The film even makes the bizarre decision to exaggerate Peck's cartoonishly gross eating habits as he bores deeper into Diana's psyche, as though the audience is expected to be genuinely frightened by poor table manners.

Despite these narrative and conceptual weaknesses, *Dream Demon* did not deserve its fate of ending up in horror history as a mere *Elm Street* knock-off. On the whole, the film is a spirited and sometimes inventive take on the haunted house subgenre that avoids slasher clichés in favor of something a little more thoughtful.
—Neil Emmett

THE EYE OF SATAN

D: David Kent-Watson
W: Cliff Twemlow (as "Mike Sullivan")
Starring: Cliff Twemlow, Ginette Gray, Maxton G. Beesley, Brett Sinclair, John Saint Ryan

By 1988, Cliff Twemlow, David Kent-Watson, and their crack team of DIY VHS filmmaking collaborators, had developed into a solid production crew. *The Eye of Satan* was easily their most audacious project to date, and in their entire canon only 1991's space bound sci-fi actioner *Firestar: First Contact* would surpass it for sheer ambition. A true renaissance man, Cliff Twemlow wrote the screenplay, produced, and starred in *The Eye of Satan*. His screenwriting credit as "Mike Sullivan" is typical of a tactic he would employ, presumably to increase the apparent scale and legitimacy of the production.

In this particular film, Cliff plays Kane, a Satan-worshipping gun-for-hire who may or may not be a giant panther, and who becomes embroiled in a gangland dispute. Kane is hired by the shady Bronstein (Paul Flanagan) to protect Christine (Ginette Gray), the daughter of gangster Stringer (Leo Atkin), from her father's former client, an arms dealer called Camille (John Saint Ryan). There is an awful lot of double crossing throughout the film, and when Kane takes the brunt of it, he seeks bloody revenge and the bodies start piling up. Meanwhile two police detectives, Peters (Brett Sinclair) and Chase (Maxton Beesley), follow Kane's trail of carnage, which leads them them to a priest who tells Chase that he believes Kane to be a member of the Panthertari, an occult sect who "cohabit with the Devil" and worship the black panther. With the tensions escalating, the film leads to a climax where all roads meet, and few survive.

Paul Flanagan, who plays Bronstein, recalls *The Eye of Satan* as being "a little bit of a horror thing, but it's more like a thriller as well, and then, of course, there's the gangster stuff." That it manages to find a corner for itself as a truly unusual cross-genre affair makes it distinct from earlier Twemlow films, which had either been strictly crime (*G.B.H.*) or horror (*Moonstalker*). Yet, unsurprisingly, it also seems very confused.

The film includes solid performances from Flanagan and John Saint Ryan, but their efforts are weighed down by an abundance of clunky dialogue, and a plot that makes little sense even within the scope of its own intentions. It is no surprise that Flanagan and Saint Ryan have continued to work as performers long after the Twemlow band went their separate ways following Cliff's tragic death in 1993. The rest of the acting is considerably less impressive but works for what it is; pure schlock.

There is no credited composer for *The Eye of Satan*, and the soundtrack, which consists largely of stripped-down synth and keyboard pieces, often comes across as a sporadically shifting selection of library music. As Cliff and director David Kent-Watson were themselves prolific producers of library music in the 1970s, that may well have been the case.

The make-up effects are limited and are one area in which the lack of a budget really shows. Like so many films of the 1970s and 1980s that sported video covers and poster artwork promising so much more than was actually delivered, the promotional imagery for *The Eye of Satan* repeatedly shows Kane as half man, half beast. This is a transformation that is only—inadequately—represented during the course of the film by the occasional green glowing of Kane's eyes, and at one point by a jump cut (or "jump cat," as might be more appropriate).

The Eye of Satan lacks the strength of conviction necessary for any real scares. To that extent it fails as a horror movie even when compared to Kent-Watson's previous *Into the Darkness*. Despite its many shortcomings in the company of far more accomplished fare reviewed in this book, *The Eye of Satan* is a surprisingly enjoyable experience. If one prefers their horror firmly tongue in cheek or has any interest in "badfilm" or cult cinema,

there is a strong chance they will find much to appreciate in this quirky picture. For anyone curious about the exploits of Cliff Twemlow and his remarkable contributions to British film, this would also be a fantastic place to start.

Although the movie did receive a VHS release, like the rest of Cliff's creative output, it remains unreleased on official English language DVD (*Firestar* received a badly dubbed DVD release in the Netherlands.). The original VHS is hard to come by, and the film is usually obtained in bootleg circles on DVD-r sourced either from a low-grade VHS screener, complete with timecode, or a much better quality subtitled Dutch VHS release. Carrying an 18 certificate with the British Board of Film Classification, it is the only film associated with either Cliff Twemlow or David Kent-Watson to be listed in the BBFC archive, illustrating just how limited the distribution of their work has been.
—Stephen J. Crompton

THE GIRL IN A SWING

D: Gordon Hessler
W: Gordon Hessler
Starring: Meg Tilly, Rupert Frazer, Nicholas Le Prevost, Elspet Gray

Animation producer Martin Rosen had meted out harrowing treatment to two Richard Adams novels with his celebrated

versions of *Watership Down* and *The Plague Dogs*, both of which resolutely avoided becoming too child-friendly and retained the pessimism and harsh realities of the original sources. The first live action feature to be based on an Adams book saw genre veteran Gordon Hessler (*Catacombs*, *Golden Voyage of Sinbad*, *Scream and Scream Again*) take up the reins on *The Girl in a Swing*, a decidedly "adult" offering at face value, rather than camouflaged, this time out.

Adams' 1980 publication proves difficult to transfer to film, not because of its storyline—stuffy English antique dealer falls head-over-heels in love with ethereally beautiful German secretary who is revealed to have a troubled secret past—but due to the rarefied world of ceramics, auction houses, country piles, globetrotting travel, etc. failing to mesh with the strong supernatural elements quite as well onscreen as it all effortlessly does in print. Meg Tilly impresses as Karin, the clerical employee who whirls into the dull life of pottery expert Alan Desland (Frazer in the type of role Hugh Grant and Colin Firth would later claim as territory), but her freewheeling spirit and aura stand out amid the genteel Home Counties tea-and-cakes environment this style of production never quite seems able to shake or expand.

Adams' plot beautifully stirred shuddery disquiet into the world of the well-to-do English folk, and Hessler's movie is at its most successful when adding little upsetting stabs to puncture the apparent bliss—Karin's brutal mercy-killing of an injured gull before a crowd of appalled bystanders, executed with cold efficiency, being particularly effective. During an intimate dip at the local swimming hole, Karin claims to have seen a body at the bed of the lake, and she displays a vampire-like aversion to things holy, churches and religious ceremony. There's also some business with Frazer envisioning a circular green padded cushion on a chair as a large toy tortoise, the suggestion of which sends Karin into panic. Tilly's crumbling topple towards hysteria is a highlight of her performance, yet sadly throws the one-note playing of the remainder of the cast into sharp relief.

Where the novel escalates to a devastating finale, this screen version tumbles into confusion—creepy enough when focusing upon the eerie sounds of a child sobbing and screaming in the wooded gardens of Desland's property, but with a poorly handled beach climax featuring one of the film's several unconvincing sex scenes and a very dodgy optical effect atop the crashing waves. Unless you're familiar with Adams' book, much of this will seem rushed and make little sense.

As for the strange title itself? Well it refers to a porcelain rarity that Karin picks up at auction for a bargain £30, as part of a pots-and-pans job lot; transpiring to be worth a cool £200,000, it seems to offer financial stability for the couple, but the figurine works on Desland's nightmares and imagination in odd ways, leading to weird occurrences (or fantasies?) set within the domed ornamental garden feature where Karin is often seen relaxing. Her ghostly reappearance on the swing at the very end ought to provide a shiversome post-script to the piece, but again is shot and scored in such a way that many viewers will find comforting rather than disturbing—that's assuming they're not already scratching their heads in bewilderment. An excellent horror-infused novel has been transformed into something that, stray fleeting moments aside, you could comfortably put before your maiden aunt.
—Darrell Buxton

HAND OF DEATH PART 25: JACKSON'S BACK

D: Anders Palm
W: Mark Cutforth
Starring: Gregory Cox, Fiona Evans, Edward Brayshaw, Debbie Lee London, Kim Fenton

"Even my mum's a lush! We're all like that, me and my friends!" speaks an ill-fated, drunk character at the start of this engaging no-budget London-set slasher movie pastiche. She, and a bunch of equally inebriated mates, fail to heed the advice of a Crazy Ralph-style prophet of doom: "Don't go in that house! None of us is safe!" After a bout of sex talk ("Last night, I had an orgasm!"), booze and intercourse, the pals are brutally murdered by a figure wearing a Jason-esque hockey goalie mask and a long black overcoat. Characters go for a piss, or split up from the group, and get their hearts ripped out and faces torn apart. A couple shagging against a wall have a spear driven through them in patented *Bay of Blood* fashion, and one woman offers a blowjob to the killer if he spares her; instead she receives a broken lamp to the skull.

The killer is Jackson (Gregory Cox), a quite charming English gent who has offed so many people that 25 movies have been made about his exploits. Beaten and abused as a child by his drunken, serial killer father, he moved to America to become a camp counsellor (!), allegedly "drowned" in an accident and ultimately lived in the wild for years. Now back in his native England, the disfigured Jackson wants to quit the murder lark and make a clean start when he falls in love with a quirky blind woman named Shelley (Fiona Evans). Although alarmed by her vast collection of dildos and female inflatable dolls, he grows to love her optimism and her non-judgemental attitude, while she likes him because he talks to her, is sincere and does the washing up. Inevitably, however, Jackson is driven back to killing again, partly due to his dad (played by Edward Brayshaw in his final movie credit after three decades of roles in *Doctor Who*, *Rentaghost*, and alongside two incarnations of *The Saint*) whose eyeball he squeezes out in a moment of anger.

In the wake of *Scream*, itself a collage of post-modern concepts found in bona fide 1980s slasher movies like *He Knows You're Alone*, self-referential stalker movies became fashionable. *Hand of Death Part 25* inventively prefigured witty takes on the genre like the faux documentary *Behind the Mask: The Rise of Leslie Vernon*, which shares a key joke characterizing the killer as a perfectly affable and charismatic chap just doing his "job." It also foreshadows Julian Richards' chilling *The Last Horror Movie*, which expands upon the unforgettable "home-movie" murder interlude in *Henry: Portrait of a Serial Killer* with coal-black humor and an inspired subversion of psycho movie clichés.

Considering the direction the sub-genre was forced to take in order to stay fresh and trendy, *Hand of Death Part 25* plays better today than it ever did. It's more consistent than earlier 1980s cheap-and-cheerful slasher movie spoofs like *Student Bodies* and *Wacko*, both of which lacked the courage of their convictions. Crucially, it more confidently balances graphically gory murders (pitchforks in stomachs, cleavers to the face, screwdrivers in the head, all courtesy of Image Animation) with an endearing central characterization and an often-funny demolition of slasher codes and conventions.

There are obvious-but-cute parodies of genre standards, like the sequence in which Jackson chases a girl through the woods, helpfully advising, "No sense trying to run for it. You'll get 10 feet maybe, run into a branch or stumble over a root ..." The best laughs come from the more offbeat comic scenarios, such as Jackson getting recognized in a pub by obnoxious tourists who make a toast to Ronald Reagan and Mark Chapman before being stabbed ("That's what I hate about those Americans, no fucking manners!"). The understated delivery of the Byron-quoting Cox sells a lot of the dialogue, from his solemn reflections of losing his virginity to a camp counsellor (Shelley, misunderstanding his lament of "She was dead," responds with a sympathetic, "I suppose we're all a dead lay now and again!") to his proud description of the "friends" he has in the movie business.

After decades of hackneyed vulnerable blind characters in slasher movies and thrillers, Evans undermines expectations by making her Shelley feisty and wonderfully dirty, and her initially absurd romance with Cox is played well enough to make it feel surprisingly genuine despite the context. Although flatly shot and unevenly paced, *Hand of Death Part 25* also earns goodwill points for being affectionate in its humor where the worst of the *Scream* sequels were smug and arch. It is also unapologetically British, with its references to Thatcher and *EastEnders*, and sometimes disarmingly sweet: The moment in which Shelley dons an identical goalie mask just to make Jackson feel better is a heart-warmer, for sure.

Unlike a lot of genre-specific spoofs, the movie also has a satisfying punchline perfectly puncturing the dominance of endless cash-in sequels throughout the 1980s. Realizing there is no escaping his fate as a killer and Shelley's as the inevitable victim, Jackson slashes her throat before being confronted by the ultimate horror: A cinema marquee displaying the title *"Hand of Death Part 26: Jackson Returns."* "Nooooooo!" he screams, dropping to his knees with all the rage and resigned panic of a 21st century film fan seeing a poster for, say, a new *Resident Evil* movie on the side of a passing bus.
—Steven West

Japanese video poster for *Hand of Death Part 25*

HELLBOUND: HELLRAISER II

D: Tony Randel
W: Peter Atkins
Starring: Clare Higgins, Ashley Laurence, Kenneth Cranham, Imogen Boorman, Doug Bradley

"And to think … I almost hesitated."

Certain sequels—a precious, revered handful—attain the reputation of being better than the originals. *The Godfather Part II*, *Star Wars Episode V: The Empire Strikes Back*, *Bride of Frankenstein*, *Hellbound: Hellraiser II*….

…. wait, *what*?

Okay. To be fair, it isn't a majority opinion. The original *Hellraiser* is largely regarded as a classic of horror films full-stop, while *Hellbound* is often dismissed as a scrappy, unfocused mess. And both of those statements contain a lot of truth. However, a small but significant minority will champion *Hellbound* as the better film, myself included—so, why do we?

Well, I prefer *Hellbound* for its sheer broadening of scope. The original small, intimate story has its strength, true, but this is Hell that we're talking about! What's needed is Big Stuff, wild ideas, and an almost operatic sense of scale and vision. Which is where *Hellbound* really comes into its own.

Following straight on from the first film, we follow Ashley Laurence's Kirsty as she embarks on a determined quest to save her father's soul, the trail leading to a sinister mental institution, home to the enigmatic, puzzle-solving Tiffany and the frankly too-obsessed-with-Hell-for-his-own-good Doctor Channard—and, once the evil Julia has been resurrected, onwards to Hades itself … Hell on a budget has both its strengths and weaknesses. Leviathan, an immense, possibly sentient Lament Configuration box hovering over the labyrinth of the underworld, is a great image—appallingly blue-screened. And Tiffany and evil Uncle Frank's torments—stupid, non-scary clown faces cackling in lines and a chorus line of shrouded fornicators on roll-away IKEA beds, straight out of a particularly crass Meat Loaf video—really don't add up to much. But the imagination—the wish to think big, to go further—still shines through. The enthusiasm to venture outside of the box, to give us increased spectacle with greater potential.

The performances are strong, at times even over-ripe, covering some of the cracks that the budget can't; Laurence's winning Kirsty, Imogen Boorman's silently-expressive Tiffany, Kenneth Cranham's dangerously-driven Channard and of course Doug Bradley's dignified, imposing Pinhead—whose human side, all-too-briefly seen here (and ignominiously defeated, along with his cohorts, far too easily by the new improved Channard Cenobite) has a sad nobility captured in a single, wordless smile of gratitude.

Everything wants to be grander, more epic, but the peanuts budget prevents it from attaining true splendor too often, while much of the imagery is thrown in heedlessly in the often-misguided belief that it will look scary, regardless of what it adds to the plot. Which is usually nothing.

But, in the end, two things make this film an improvement on the original, and a small treasure to be cherished. The dedication and skill of its cast, with not a bad performance in sight … and its sheer ambition. This film wants to show us that there *is* more to Heaven and Earth than is dreamt of in our philosophies. And it tries its best to do so.
—Ken Shinn

HIGH SPIRITS

D: Neil Jordan
W: Neil Jordan
Starring: Peter O'Toole, Steve Guttenberg, Daryl Hannah, Beverly D'Angelo, Liam Neeson

I'll admit, despite him being a one-time resident of my hometown, Bray, Neil Jordan has never tickled my fancy. He's been too pretentious for my liking. This film, an Irish-UK-US co-production filmed for $15 million with interiors at Shepperton Studios and exteriors in Dromore Castle, Co. Limerick, with effects by the legendary Derek Meddings, is an attempt for the mainstream, with a kind of "Bank Holiday morning on ITV" feel to it. It has a sterling cast including Steve Guttenberg (the most unlikely British horror star, yet his CV includes roles in this, *The Boys from Brazil* and one of Richard Driscoll's myriad monstrosities), Liam Neeson, Daryl Hannah, Beverly (Mrs. Jordan) D'Angelo, Peter O'Toole and Jennifer Tilly, and Irish stalwarts

such as Donal McCann, Ray McAnally, Tom Hickey (star of the Irish soap *The Riordans*, which was the influence for *Emmerdale Farm*), and the singer Mary Coughlan, a neighbor of Jordan's in their seaside terraces in Bray, who looks perpetually awe-struck in her mannish, dumpy, flame-haired form and even warbles and plays the harp at one point in her distinctively dreary style. This is leveled with a sprinkling of British actors such as a pre-*Royle Family* Liz Smith, the US-born Connie Booth and Preston Lockwood. O'Toole plays local Anglo-Irish gentry, Peter Plunkett (with Smith as his elderly Granny Addams-esque mother) who has turned his disused ancestral abode into a bed and breakfast, to offer employment to the local villagers, to drum up publicity, and to pay a loan owed to an American businessman. He fakes ghosts in order to attract tourists, but then Martin (Neeson) and a badly-accented Mary (Hannah), who happen to be real ghosts, materialize, alongside McAnally's Plunkett, Sr., all of whom sport pale flour-covering makeup and white hair.

The film feels like a grimmer, slightly more adult *Rentaghost* for the *Ghostbusters* generation, with terms such as "shagging" used instead of the f-word ("what the shagging hell are you doing up here?") and Guttenberg telling D'Angelo, "sex is out of the question." Smith is quite likeable as the talkative mother, and O'Toole has some choice lines: "Mr. Brogan, if I cannot send your payment, how on earth do you expect to transport an entire castle across the sea? The number of stamps alone is mind-boggling!" However, stereotypes are retained by the Irish director. 1950s-style buses are held up by sheep. There is well-labored slapstick via the paddywhackery of the eccentric locals in flat caps and tweed, manning Heath Robinson machinery to fake the hauntings, as faux-headless knights fidget in the background, dummies fall, and farmers talk to horses in the rain. Guttenberg is in full *Police Academy* goofball mode, getting Ireland confused with Scotland, and namechecking the Loch Ness Monster. D'Angelo is cranky. Neeson is mumbly, screaming repeatedly, "What have I done?" The romantic subplots are labored and unrealistic. The ending is confusing, suggesting bigamy. In all, it is a mess, sporadically entering but mostly feeble. Neil Jordan struggles once again with a populist subject.

—George White

HOW TO GET AHEAD IN ADVERTISING

D: Bruce Robinson
W: Bruce Robinson
Starring: Richard E. Grant, Rachel Ward, Richard Wilson, Jacqueline Tong

Super-stressed advertising executive Denis Bagley (Richard E. Grant) is approaching the crest of a nervous breakdown over his inability to blitz an effective ad campaign for an upcoming pimple cream, due to be launched on the market! His long-suffering wife Julia (Rachel Ward) and boss Mr. Bristol (Richard Wilson) are bearing the brunt of his escalating hysteria, and soon Denis is developing a nasty boil on his neck, as if his body is revolting, Cronenberg-like, under the stress, and giving him what he fears most ... things get worse, far worse, when the boil starts to speak, grow a moustache, argue violently with him, and attempt to turn him into the main thing he despises—a suave, fully committed slave to the altar of consumerism and advertising ... truly a deal with the Devil!

Writer/director Bruce Robinson's follow-up to cult favorite *Withnail & I* is arguably the greater film, but far fewer people are aware of Richard E. Grant sprouting a second head and becoming Ad Man Incarnate than they are of him arguing with Uncle Monty or ordering fine wines in a teashop! Yet this delirious combination of monster movie, psychological breakdown, and brilliant satire on the two-faced (or headed?) world of advertising, fused with a modern spin on Jekyll and Hyde, remains a potent, surreal and dare I say it, important work of cinema all these years on. This reviewer vividly recalls seeing this blackly hilarious and disturbing gem at the late, lamented Lumiere cinema in London in '89 in the company of a small handful of bemused punters, who by the halfway mark seemed to be clearly wondering what they had purchased a ticket for ...

It's rare that a movie can be acutely funny, politically relevant, often touching, upsetting and disturbing in a prophetic way all at the same time, but there are moments here that astound in their reach; Denis trying to incorporate the boil's amusingly bland ad jingles into a dinner conversation with his wife ... his first sight of the boil's face in the bathroom mirror, throwing him into a mad frenzy, screaming and running around the ample grounds of his house, being chased by a doctor brandishing a syringe ... his pathetic attempts to record a personal view of an impending global holocaust to a video camera, while having to wear a wine carton over his head so the sleeping boil won't waken and argue with him ... and after the stunning hospital transformation, where the boil has fully grown into a leering facsimile of Grant's face and takes over in a blizzard of clever editing and fine acting, the slow realization by the various other characters in the tale that Denis Dimbleby Bagley, Esq. has become a different person altogether—super smooth, sexually voracious and a fully functioning, near demonic exponent of "sell, sell, sell!"

Grant has never been better than here, a whirling dervish in the first half, manic and hilarious and utterly awful to watch all in the same breath, and exuding real, dark power in the closing scenes with his wife Julia and the exhilarating Sermon on the Mount finale. The usually dire Rachel Ward overcomes some early scene indifferences and becomes genuinely touching as the story progresses, and Richard Wilson is deadpan hilarious as Bagley's boss ... but it's the nightmarish scenes with the boil and the personality changes, coupled with some alarming predictions on the state of the world, that linger (the idea that in the future so much of the world's vegetation will have been destroyed that the Brazilians will be able to fix oxygen prices, in the same way that Americans fix oil, being one such grotesque scenario!) Watch too for an early screen appearance by Sean Bean in the opening scene, being berated by Bagley, Jacqueline Pearce from Hammer's *The Reptile* as, erm, a rather reptilian and pushy secretary, and Hugh Armstrong, who in the previous decade had played the cannibalistic London Underground dweller in Gary Sherman's magisterial *Death Line*. *How to Get Ahead in Advertising* has survived to remain a funny, scary and potent mix of nightmare, horror and satire, and one of the genre gems of the 1980s.
—Michael Wesley

THE LAIR OF THE WHITE WORM

D: Ken Russell
W: Ken Russell
Starring: Hugh Grant, Catherine Oxenberg, Amanda Donohoe, Peter Capaldi, Sammi Davis

"Do you have children?"
"Only when there are no men around!"

Hooray for Ken Russell. Love him or loathe him (and at the height of his career the camps were probably pretty evenly divided), the films he's made have never been less than attention-grabbing. *The Lair of the White Worm* is no exception—a playful, sexy bit of insanity that only he could have created from Bram Stoker's source novel. Working with a tiny budget courtesy of a deal with Vestron, and shooting at Knebworth and in Thor's Cave, Staffordshire, it's difficult to think of anyone doing a better job with the resources available. Archaeologist Peter Capaldi has found the remains of a Roman temple and an enormous snake skull in the garden of the country cottage he's staying in. The find coincides with the arrival back in England of Lady Sylvia Marsh (Amanda Donohoe in a career-best performance) who happens to be the immortal high priestess of a snake cult. Lady Sylvia's looking for a sacrifice to the big wobbly rubber serpent she keeps under the house and thinks Catherine Oxenberg

(dubbed and looking distinctly uncomfortable at playing in this sort of film) will do the trick. Catherine's boyfriend is floppy-haired Lord James D'Ampton, played by floppy-haired Hugh Grant before he became famous. With Lady Sylvia sprouting big fangs and Hugh setting up some massive speakers atop his stately home to blast out snake-charming music, the scene is set for an appropriately daft climax.

Only the most humorless of reviewers could fail to like *The Lair of the White Worm*, a film that starts as it means to go on with a crash of ominous music at the sight of a curled-up hosepipe. There's some utter silliness with a snake-possessed policeman and some bagpipes, a selection of deliciously over-the-top outfits for Ms. Donohoe to look fabulous in, and even Stratford Johns pops up, rather the worse for wear as Hugh Grant's butler. In fact, the tone of the entire piece is so light and frothy that some typical Russell attempts at weird dream sequences actually end up seeming misjudged—as do the videotaped scenes of Romans attacking nuns, amid sundry shots of the undraped Lady Sylvia. Similarly, Hugh's dream about stewardesses cat-fighting on board an aeroplane is almost too wild even for this movie, but can be forgiven since so much more of what's on offer is gloriously entertaining. Bob Keen's special effects giant worm isn't terribly special either but fortunately it is glimpsed only briefly at the climax.

But let's not dwell on the movie's shortcomings—revel instead in the spectacle of the future star of *Notting Hill* cutting a snake-possessed old lady in half with a sword, in Amanda Donohoe's P.V.C.-clad seduction of a boy scout being interrupted by a ringing door bell, by the bagpipe-playing kilt-wearing Mr. Capaldi being chased around the grounds by a policeman who comes to a sticky end on a sundial. Lots and lots of fun, and even more so if you can get hold of the Blu-ray with Ken's audio commentary that provides an entertainment package all of its own.
—John Llewellyn Probert

PAPERHOUSE

D: Bernard Rose
W: Matthew Jacobs
Starring: Charlotte Burke, Glenne Headly, Elliott Spiers, Ben Cross, Gemma Jones

A child's pencil moves across a white page, drawing the outlines of a simple house, surrounded by a fence and standing stones, as the opening credits superimpose themselves over the

image. The child is Anna, she's at school and it's her birthday, and she is soon in trouble ... a fainting fit in the school corridor sees Anna "awaken" into a dream world where the house in her picture is real, alone in a vast empty field, complete with that sketched boundary and ancient megalithic markers. Coming down with glandular fever, Anna is soon confined to bed, where she adds more detail to her drawing: a boy's face at the window. The next time she falls asleep, she encounters a real boy looking out of the same window. His name is Marc, and he cannot come out and join her because there are no stairs, and—besides—he cannot walk. Anna's doctor, who prescribes a prolonged rest, mentions another patient of hers, a little boy who's been in bed for a year ...

The structure of the film then follows a straightforward pattern: Anna draws, dreams, then draws again. Each alteration to the artwork is reflected in the dream world, so Anna puts in furniture, toys, an orange tree and flowers outside. When the children ponder the question about their own presence in this "other place," Marc considers that he must have done something wrong, and that "they left me here." Anna, however, rejects this explanation with regard to herself. Back in our world, Anna briefly attempts to deny the "paperhouse" and its lonely disabled occupant, but later accepts responsibility, and tries to put things right.

The film offers no convenient rational explanation for the events; Anna and Marc simply exist together in each other's dreams, without ever coming together in reality. But it's the physical creation of Anna's imagined world that makes for such a powerful and emotionally convincing film. The walls of the house do indeed resemble paper, the rooms look out of perspective, with outsized furnishings and crudely drawn appliances. Even the orange tree looks plastic, and the standing stones like painted polystyrene. When Anna returns to the dream, having defaced the drawing and thrown it out in the rubbish, the house is wrecked, toys and furniture broken, the walls brown and tea stained. Anna's father is absent (working abroad, but also suffering a drinking problem), so when Anna puts him in her picture, and then tries to cross him out because she made him look angry, he returns in her dream as the monster, blind and murderous. This is a genuinely frightening sequence, from the first sighting of Dad, silhouetted against the night sky, to his relentless attack on the house and Anna, claw hammer in hand.

The children escape to an isolated cliff-top lighthouse and enjoy a brief interlude of carefree happiness. There's not a happy outcome for Marc in the real world, of course, but for Anna, there is reconciliation and her family are reunited. Charlotte Burke as 11-year-old Anna acquits herself well (despite a dodgy tantrum scene by the rubbish bins and having never appeared in anything subsequently). Glenne Headly as Anna's mother appears strangely distant, but Gemma Jones and Ben Cross give sterling performances. Greatest credit here, though, must go to director Bernard Rose, bringing a wonderful vividness and stark clarity to the images of Anna's fantastic vision. Rose would later go on to direct another powerfully visual supernatural "other" world in the excellent *Candyman* (1992).
—Julia Kruk

1989

Black Rainbow
Cold Light of Day
The Cook, the Thief, His Wife & Her Lover
Don't Scream It's Only a Movie!
Edge of Sanity
Hardware
Howling V: The Rebirth
I Bought a Vampire Motorcycle
Living Doll
Murder on Line One
Nightbreed
Stepfather 2: Make Room for Daddy
The Urge to Kill
The Witches

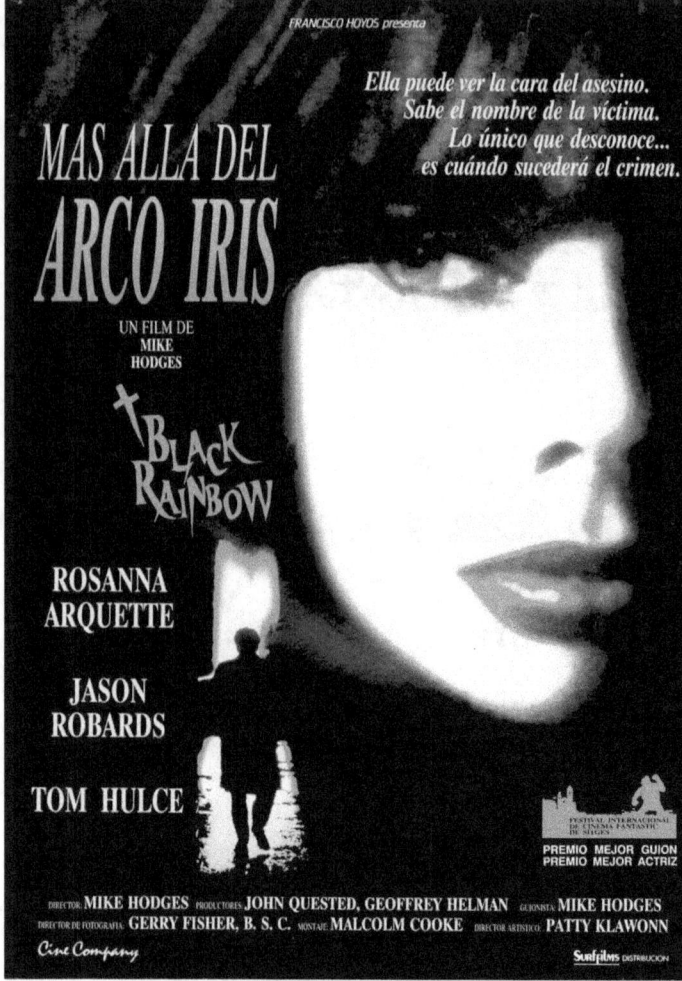

Spanish video poster for *Black Rainbow*

BLACK RAINBOW

D: Mike Hodges
W: Mike Hodges
Starring: Rosanna Arquette, Jason Robards, Tom Hulce

I must be one of the few Brits to have actually seen Mike Hodges' 1989 supernatural horror in a cinema. Never properly released either side of the Atlantic, he brought it and star Rosanna Arquette to the Edinburgh Film Festival in 1990 in an attempt, as he put it, just to get the film seen. It had by then acquired something of a reputation as a troubled project, having languished on the shelves for more than a year thanks to a legal dispute. Since then it has virtually disappeared, which is a shame as, while no classic, it has its moments and could certainly be used to teach today's horror auteurs something about mood, atmosphere and ambiguity.

Arquette stars as Martha Travis, a medium at the center of a traveling spiritualist show hosted and managed by her drunken sot of a father, played to type by Jason Robards. As is the way of these things, Martha claims to put members of the audience in touch with their dead loved ones. There is much gospel singing, the Lord is praised, and people generally go home comforted, if possibly conned. But then something new and troubling happens; one night in an unnamed southern town, she seems to make contact with someone who isn't actually dead. Or at least he isn't dead yet. Because later that night, the man she described is murdered in what appears to be a professional hit. So, has Martha begun to see the future? And why has this suddenly started happening now? What follows is a mixture of mystery and corporate conspiracy, with journalist Tom Hulce trying to work out what's going on both in the nearby industrial plant, and in Martha's increasingly tortured mind.

Hodges has always been a great director of actors, and Arquette is superb in the central role. She was always beautiful, but usually dismissed as "kooky." Here, she is wild, sexually predatory, damaged, and in the end destructively malicious. As she spirals into despair, struggling to make those around her take her gift seriously, she is utterly chilling. It's a brilliant performance, especially in the scene where she foresees a death close to home.

Is Martha for real? Hodges never reveals his hand. Everything is ambiguous, all the way to the genuinely baffling ending. At the Q&A after that Edinburgh screening, he refused to pin down what happens, saying he was playing with ideas, and didn't want to tell the audience what to think. Although that could be annoying, it works well here. The ending piles ambiguity upon ambiguity. Watch the reporter's car in the final shot. How did it get into that state?

It's obviously low-budget, but the locations are well used, and there's an effective sense of unease conveyed. It's slow moving, but this really pays off at the climax. The conspiracy element is less well realized, and the journey of a killer coming to town to close down the events around Martha is dull. In fact, it feels a little as though this was used to introduce the "ticking clock" so beloved of script editors. But Hodges has been an intermittently superb director. Everything he has made is worth seeing, from *Get Carter* and *The Terminal Man*, through the glorious *Flash Gordon*, to this. In the years since, he has enjoyed late critical acclaim and modest commercial successes with Clive Owen in *Croupier* and *I'll Sleep When I'm Dead*. But *Black Rainbow* hints at what he could have achieved had he worked more in the horror genre, and it's a tantalizing, frustrating glimpse.
—Craig Williams

COLD LIGHT OF DAY

D: Fhiona-Louise
W: Fhiona-Louise
Starring: Bob Flag, Martin Byrne-Quinn, Jackie Cox, Andrew Edmans, Geoffrey Greenhill

> I'm moving in the Colherne, with the leather
> all around me, and the sweat is getting steamy,
> but their eyes are on the ground, they're just
> hanging around... hanging around.
> —The Stranglers, 1977

An unintentionally ironic lyric quote, maybe, especially given the method of killing chosen by the subject of this film, but also an apt one—describing an open-minded straight man's experiences in a gay pub in mid-'70s London, when homosexuality was still, to many, a taboo. Unknowingly, when they wrote it, The Stranglers not only described the experiences of the murderer (albeit prior to any crimes), but of the majority of his potential and actual victims—to say nothing of the social climate in which they occurred. And some still dare to say life doesn't imitate art ...

In 1983, police called at an attic flat in Cranley Gardens, Muswell Hill, and quizzed its occupant, an unassuming, quiet civil servant based at Kentish Town Jobcentre, about what appeared to be several particles of human remains found in the drains below the building—divided, like many three storey houses in North London, into rented flats. Within an hour, he had confessed not only to the murders of three men on the premises, but a further 13 to 15 at his previous residence in Cricklewood. The man was one Dennis Nilsen, born in Scotland in 1945, soon to be infamous as Britain's most prolific multiple murderer, and this film is his story. Well, almost.

To clarify: From my own recollection of the late 1980s, a proposed film about the so-called "Muswell Hill Murders"—an inaccurate description, seeing as most of them took place over five miles away in NW2, but that's human perception for you—was to be called *Killing for Company*, named after the book examining the crimes, but it never materialized. A short of that name, based around the same subject, was finally made in 2013, David Attwood's 1990 BBC1 drama *Killing Time* centred upon Pip Donaghy's Nilsen-like character (renamed "Martin"), and a Nilsen-inspired ballet, *Dead Dreams of Monochrome Men* was released on video in the 1990s, but to date, the only other significant dramatization of the events remains this slightly-fictionalized account, released in 1989. I say "fictionalized" simply because, while the story is indeed a graphic, realistic and extremely bleak retelling (with very little window-dressing or attempt to smooth the rough edges) in which a thirtysomething, bespectacled, gay man befriends several young companions before murdering them at home, masturbating over them, dissecting them and then shoving them either under the floorboards or down the bog, there are still several deviations, either intentional or accidental, from real life.

For a start, Nilsen's name is changed here to Jorden March (of all possible names, one ponders the reason for that peculiar choice) and the street renamed Langley Gardens, while the fate of the man he shared a two-year relationship with (and who in truth left Nilsen years before his first murder even took place) blurs into that of his first victim. With even greater inaccuracy, the film makes the suggestion that all the murders occurred at one address rather than two. Elsewhere, March/Nilsen visits a female prostitute in Soho, something he was extremely unlikely to ever do in real life, and perhaps most glaringly of all, the interrogations that actually took place, documented in *Murder Casebook Vol. 2: The Muswell Hill Murders* (1989), in which the killer is described as being "so co-operative, friendly and wryly humorous that the police found it hard to say they disliked him" are replaced by the standard shouty encounter of many a Brit crime show, complete with an angry bald copper (Geoffrey Greenhill) leering into camera. So much for "docudrama" or "factual reportage," then ...

Yet, even if a little more consistency in the reality stakes wouldn't go amiss, it should be stressed that none of the above actually dulls the effect. Shot on a modest budget with the barest of lighting, its modest origins convey the inherent fallibility of humanity, the sad, cold and particularly "icky" nature of the slayings, and the circumstances around them, far more effectively than any big-budget treatment could, to the point where structural shortcomings take secondary importance. For this reason alone, presumably, *Cold Light of Day* won several awards at festivals throughout the early 1990s (its 79-minute running time making it difficult to place in "standard" theatrical screening slots): indeed, it's still highly regarded today by a coterie of fans and writers.

All of which seems even more remarkable when a cursory glance at the credits informs us that production was handled by the infamous Richard Driscoll, noted exploitation auteur, plagiarist and con-merchant par excellence (although in his case, "excellence" isn't really the word one would usually choose.) Thankfully for all of us, his trademarks (atrocious acting, nonsensical plotlines, poor SFX, obtrusive music and unsubtle foley, plus a misguided belief that his work is of some Wellesian cinematic significance) are absent, presumably because, for once, he merely provided the money necessary to make the damn thing, and handed over the directorial reins to the far more capable Fhiona-Louise. If only he'd done this *every* time he wanted to make a film, there might be a whole different story to tell ...

Yet quite bizarrely the director, whose only other credits are in the form of acting roles in low-budget shorts, has not seemingly put eye to viewfinder or fingers to clapperboard since—which is a great shame, as here, despite the aforementioned inaccuracies, she shows extreme promise, not only in her handling of the sort of cloying, confined tension Peter Collinson used to convey so well, but in her choice of angles, shots and perspec-

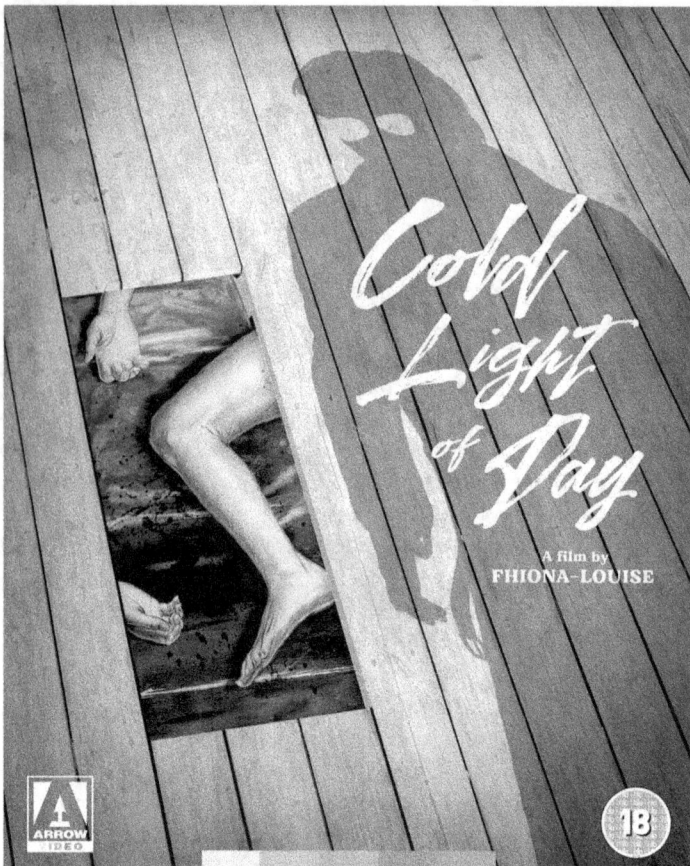

tive. Also, Bob Flag's portrayal of the so-called "kindly killer" is extremely convincing, constantly hovering both sides of the line between empathy and utter disgust. Whether this was the director's or actor's doing is a matter of conjecture, but whereas many players cast in the role of real-life serial killers tend towards caricature, Flag, like Dickie Attenborough before him, gets it just right.

Yes, he murders people and then does unspeakable things to their corpses, but conversely, he babysits his neighbor's cat without harming it (even if he does shout at it when it disrupts one of his burials), and cares sufficiently for his senile neighbor to buy him groceries, and to change his pyjamas after a bout of incontinence. From this, the impression we begin to derive, particularly when he finds one soon-to-be-victim slumped in a heroin stupor in his neighborhood (something which actually happened) is that his overriding motive, as well as a need for company based on an inherent loneliness, denial of his true sexual nature in early life and repressive Scots upbringing, is actually rooted in a compassionate desire to see human suffering of all kinds ended.

After all, in real life, Nilsen was heavily involved, as he continued to be within his maximum security prison, in trade union activity and radical libertarian politics: at least two people of my own acquaintance who claimed benefit in North West London in the early 1980s were signed on by him, and they confirmed, as also described in *Killing for Company*, that his interest often lay on the behalf of the client rather than the government (he wouldn't last five minutes under today's administration) to the point of making himself unpopular with his workmates. He also loved and cared for his own dog Bleep, sadly destroyed after his arrest, in a manner suggesting another side to his nature entirely. Mind you, Hitler had a pooch too.

Whatever your own perspective, though, these very contradictions also quashed Nilsen's plea of manslaughter via diminished responsibility. As one who could feel a variety of emotions from anger (strangling Malcolm Barlow because he was "in the way") to pity (reviving another victim after four failed killing attempts because he simply felt sorry for him, then sending him home), he was considered "unstable and unpredictable," yet this very discretion also revealed him as more sane than contended, and able to see humans as people rather than the "objects" he claimed. Almost as notoriously as the murders themselves, the trial dragged on interminably while lawyers and doctors passive-aggressively reproached each other in couched jargonese, something that might have made a decent screenplay in itself ...

"Far from home now, waiting by the telephone, there's a new world, you can make it on your own, are you still proud of your little boy? Don't be afraid, you don't have to hide away ..." "Hideaway," Erasure, 1987.

A commendable effort. Bloody hell, you mean I actually partially enjoyed something Richard Driscoll was involved with? If this keeps up, I might end up strangling *myself* and flushing my own remains down the loo ...
—Darius Drewe

THE COOK, THE THIEF, HIS WIFE & HER LOVER

D: Peter Greenaway
W: Peter Greenaway
Starring: Richard Bohringer, Michael Gambon, Helen Mirren, Alan Howard, Tim Roth

A crude, violent, jealous thief, Albert Spica (Michael Gambon), lords over and terrorizes the cook (Richard Bohringer) and staff of a plush, haute cuisine restaurant, while unaware that his downtrodden wife Georgina (Helen Mirren) is carrying on a charged affair with her lover, the bookish Michael (Alan Howard) right under his nose ... things do not end well!

Peter Greenaway's state of the nation address, circa 1989, decked out in glorious Jacobean tragedy-style vestments, remains one of arthouse cinema's most dazzling, emotional and shocking achievements; from its grotesque opening scene, wherein Albert and his cronies beat, strip and force feed dog faeces to a luckless soul in the restaurant car park, right through to its enforced cannibalistic climax, no stone of shock impact, high drama or sheer arresting visual brilliance (color-coded costumes and art direction) is left unturned.

Powered by an extraordinary, career-best turn from Michael Gambon as Albert, played as a vile, petulant, vicious, overgrown man-child, spouting some of the cinema's most memorably coarse, ear-bashing dialogue, and anchored by a quietly authoritative Helen Mirren as "Georgie" (superb—watch for her amazing to-camera monologue in the final act), the perennially abused wife, it's all here—iconic Michael Nyman score, the late, great Sacha Vierney's elegant camerawork and lighting, stunning sets (and sex! Prudes, look away ...), forks rammed into faces, knee-to-groin action, torture of young choirboys, and yes, the aforementioned cannibalism (complete with steaming vegetables!) for its satisfyingly revengeful *coup-de-grace*.

Greenaway has never made a better film, though his awesome and controversial religious parody *The Baby of Mâcon* comes pretty close. A wilful, wonderfully pretentious artist allying his masterly, painterly visual skills to a solid, often sordid, three act saga of love, death, retribution and food ... memorably performed, stylishly shot and edited, rhythmic in visual tone, an optical and aural feast that works as a graphic horror film, high art, at times high camp, and is arguably the best British film of the 1980s. Like vintage wine, time has been kind to this masterclass in artful horror, and while other contemporary films may have fallen by the wayside, Greenaway's two-hour stunner just keeps looking better and better as the years since its release fall away. For those with the stomach for it, this is a packed four-course feast of a film. Pass the menu!
—Michael Wesley

DON'T SCREAM IT'S ONLY A MOVIE!

D: Ray Selfe
W: none credited
Starring: Vincent Price

Yet another shoddy product from the Dick Randall/Steve Minasian stable, *Don't Scream It's Only a Movie!* is notable only for Vincent Price's final onscreen appearance in a British horror-related affair. Price narrates this ragbag of jumbled excerpts from

a variety of public domain titles or Randall/Minasian-connected fare, which unlike the earlier *Terror in the Aisles* (1984) has no discernible thread or purpose to it.

Within the first 90 seconds, Vincent has posed the question, "What am I doing here?," something which viewers might also be asking of themselves. He promises us "a tour of terror, torture, and naked fear," and amazingly for once Messrs. Randall and Minasian do deliver—we kick off with the outrageous acid bath scene from *Slaughter High* (not the last lengthy clip we'll see from that opus—in fact we virtually get to revisit half the damn movie) and are later offered gory highlights from the likes of *Pieces*, *Mother's Day*, and *Don't Open Till Christmas*, with chunks of footage from the first two and a greatest hits montage of many of the Santa Claus murders from the latter.

Price rather embarrassingly interacts with Boris Karloff across a distance of a quarter century, via shots from Karloff's intro to Mario Bava's *Black Sabbath*, and the same director's *Bay of Blood* is excerpted too, as is the hit American film which stole several of its best ideas and moments, *Friday the 13th Part 2*. The *Friday* scenes segue in from a green-tinted version of the shocking "reveal" in 1925's *Phantom of the Opera* (Randall reissued that Lon Chaney classic at around this time), with Price awkwardly attempting to link the two while babbling about unmasked killers.

At times Vincent's spiel seems to be leading us towards sections on werewolves, the Frankenstein monster, etc., but oddly we soon veer off at strange tangents to allow for yet more *Don't Open Till Christmas* clips to be paraded before us. A spectacular beheading scene from Georges Méliès' *Le Borreau Turc* (aka *Decapitation in Turkey*) has Price reacting by informing us that "these days special effects are much more believable," this pronouncement immediately being proved suspect as the ridiculous 'flying severed head' episode from Indonesian camp-fest *Queen of Black Magic* is rolled out before our disbelieving gaze.

Price does get to deliver the occasional line with some of his old-time relish—the witch-burnings from *Mark of the Devil* lead in to a shot of him purring, "these days, electricity replaces the firebrand," lusciously elongating every vowel and syllable, though the effect is rather killed when Ray Selfe cuts to yet another *Slaughter High* scene, this time the electrocution of a couple in the throes of passion. Ancient movies such as *The Ape*, *The Devil Bat*, *The Thirteenth Guest*, *The Cat and the Canary*, and *The Lost World* mingle for our attention with the likes of *An American Werewolf in London* (the processes via which Randall and company gained permission to screen the Piccadilly transformation and ensuing car-crash mayhem from the John Landis picture are probably better left undiscussed), and portions of the Christopher Lee-narrated documentary *In Search of Dracula* are presumably included to make us believe that the *Don't Scream* producers have, in fact, hired *two* horror greats to help relate this madcap history of the genre. Paul Hart-Wilden's late 1980s short *Horrorshow* even turns up at one point, as does that very entertaining 1948 "old dark house" mystery for kids, *Who Killed Doc Robbin?*

Like Randall's contemporaneous *The Urge to Kill*, *Don't Scream It's Only a Movie!* does not appear to have ever been given an official release (I recall reading a review of the compilation in an edition of Stefan Jaworzyn's fanzine *Shock Xpress* circa 1990)—a chunk of it was uploaded to YouTube by an anonymous donor in January 2013, but you'd honestly be able to devise a more ac-

curate look back at the story of terror in the cinema by pulling a few stray DVDs from your own shelves at random.
—Darrell Buxton

EDGE OF SANITY

D: Gérard Kikoïne
W: J. P. Felix, Ron Raley
Starring: Anthony Perkins, Glynis Barber, Sarah Maur Thorp, David Lodge

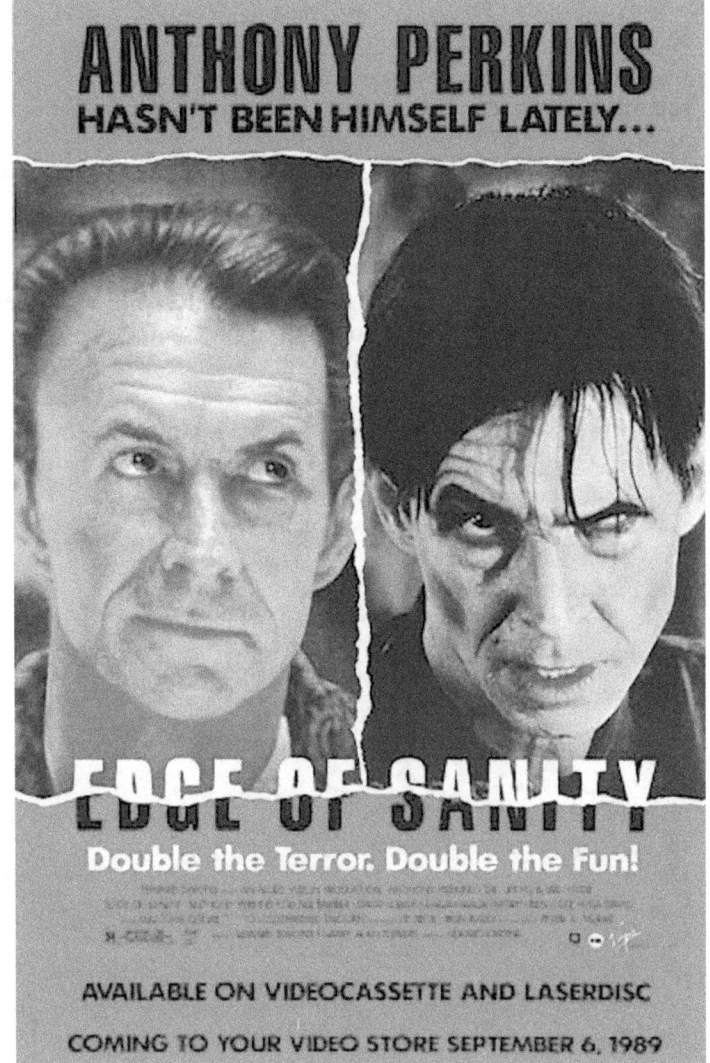

Off his rocker, more like. Harry Alan Towers was still bouncing around the world fleeing creditors, exploring tax breaks, and running out of countries to film in, when his 1989 variation on *Dr. Jekyll and Mr. Hyde* surfaced. The resultant film was met with a mix of derision and cult favor, certain naysayers claiming insufficient departure from R.L. Stevenson's text, others grumbling there was too much outrageous tinkering with the tale. Somehow *Edge of Sanity* achieves both! It is highly representative of my own theory that this was the decade of the schizoid British pop horror film. This is a stylish, stylized, anachronistic work, a period film with an injection of the rude modern.

Edge of Sanity is a contradictory magic trick pulled off with considerable élan. Admirably perverse without becoming too vulgar, it is a sexy and daring horror that owes a light nod to Ken Russell. Infused with color, it opens with a striking shot of a boy working his way through the rafters of a barn in order to spy on a writhing wench (Sarah Maur Thorp). There is a dubious perspective to it, as she appears to be directly flirting with the child peeping tom—but there is another adult presence in the barn, a male lover, the subject of her come-hither gestures, and the couple proceed to have sex. The boy slips from his vantage point and ends up suspended upside down. The two mock him and the man flogs him, whacking the child's bare backside. It is implied that this nightmare of Doctor Jekyll's (Anthony Perkins) is an actual memory, and as he falls victim to a spillage of chemicals in his laboratory that will periodically change him into the monstrous Mr. Jack Hyde, then the elements of his prepubescent humiliation will become part of the parcel of his murderous id's activities.

Maur Thorp takes on a dual role, returning as a whore who becomes central to both Jekyll and Hyde's lustful fantasies. But unlike most adaptations there is no graduation in the menace and violence. This is a 1980s film, and more immediate horrors are called for, so Jack Hyde embarks on a bloody killing spree from the outset, Stevenson's Edinburgh replaced by London so that he can gain notoriety as Jack the Ripper (this sprint into the murderous may have been inspired by Walerian Borowczyk's equally baroque *Docteur Jekyll et les Femmes / Bloodbath of Dr. Jekyll*, from 1981.) The domestic life is one of Victorian homeliness and somber décor, but the world on the Hyde side of his id is transformed into something out of a new romantic pop video. The prostitutes dress like Hot Gossip, and the camera might lopside or angle down or fisheye or point of view at any moment. These visual affectations are used economically, and for the most part the photography is shot in judiciously and effectively mounted orthodox manner with great clarity, leading the viewer with ease through its phantasmagorical cavalcade of color and kinkiness. One of the bigger, meaner shifts is that Jekyll becomes an increasingly willing collaborator to his id's heinous crimes, leading to a shocking fate for Mrs. Jekyll.

Stevenson's original dialogue earths the story with a necessary intelligence, whereas the added material brings a knowingness befitting more uninhibited times, no less aided by Kikoïne's reputed experience as a director of pornographic films. The moment most evocative of that "blue" background comes when the first of the prostitute victims is forced to bend over a table, excitedly squeezing her buttocks and murmuring, "Look at them! Look at them!" She lifts her head to reveal an expression that betrays a nonchalant acceptance. It is a shot familiar from porn films, the face that accompanies the question "are we done yet?" where even the sexually extraordinary becomes routine. Kikoïne is surprisingly conscious of all of his players, providing them with a swathe of emotions and opportunities. Even supporting players and minor characters are given little traits and actions to enliven shots just that bit more. Sadly, some of the dialogue is misjudged, particularly the plain daft musings of the police investigating the murders.

Shot in the UK and, chiefly, Hungary—there were at the time rumors that Kikoïne was a pseudonymous Jess Franco, but I would have been astounded if Franco, by then the messiest of hack directors, could have delivered anything quite so technically adept. Gerry O'Hara confirmed that, as an associate of Harry Alan Towers, he had reason to briefly visit the set, and informed me that it was not Franco on set but a younger Frenchman. The supporting cast includes many beauties including Glynis Barber as Mrs. Jekyll and Claudia Udy as one of the prostitutes. The veteran character actor David Lodge is roped in for his own sterling presence.

The film generated something of a cult following, at a time when too many of the new horror films were undisciplined, ridiculous rubbish. In the early 1990s I received a videocassette including, among its varied content, several home-made pop promo videos by Jim McLennan, editor of the fanzine *Trash City*. The first two promos sampled footage and off-air recordings from news, manga, film and other stray sources, but one—possibly set to a Front 242 track—was composed entirely from visuals taken from *Edge of Sanity*, the music synchronized with great deliberation to the movements of the camera or the actions of characters in-camera. It was good editing practice for Jim, results that sold his ability using no more than a couple of VCRs, but it also emphasized the quality of the composition of the images in the original film.
—Paul Higson

HARDWARE

D: Richard Stanley
W: Richard Stanley
Filmed in 1989, released in 1990
Starring: Dylan McDermott, Stacey Travis, John Lynch, William Hootkins

The city lies in ruins. Away from the more prosperous financial center, which has shored up its defences to protect the wealthy few inside, the wreckage of once thriving industries presents itself along the banks of the grimy river as a series of huge abandoned edifices, fronted by enormous twisted hulks of broken metal machines, once functional, now discarded. The buildings house groups of shadowy denizens, living under the threat of imminent nuclear attack, who pillage the decaying structures, re-using the metal they find to construct machines of their own, machines with a purpose known only to those who make them.

Sounds like the opening of a cheap science fiction novel, right? Wrong. It's fact, it's London in 1989, and it's the genesis of Richard Stanley's film *Hardware*.

Looking back, late 1980s London feels like another country. So used are we to seeing the now familiar luxury apartments and canyons of glass that front the city's riverside, it's hard to believe that at that time the area was a derelict shadow of its former bustling dockyard workplace, with dismantled cranes, cavernous empty warehouses, and a residue of bomb damage from the Second World War. The area became a bit of an anarchist playground around then, populated by tribes like the Mutoid Waste Company. M.W.C. were a performance art collective that tapped into cultural sources like the comic *2000 AD* and the emerging acid house scene, creating their own sci-fi world, a bridge between fiction and real life, populated with giant metal sculptures of their own design, often imbued with some crude animatronic movement. M.W.C. would take over empty spaces—anticipating late 1980s rave culture—for their "happenings," realizing a dangerous but exciting environment utilizing the junk available to them. All of this would provide rich visual source material for *Hardware*'s vision of the future.

Richard Stanley, a self confessed comics fan who had cut his teeth shooting music videos as well as an ill-advised foray to film aspects of the Afghan war, borrowed the rather uncomplicated story of *Hardware* from a short strip entitled *"Shok!"* which appeared in the *2000 AD* comic some years earlier. He may also have seen *The Terminator* once or twice. The plot involves the discovery of a robot in the desert, which is quickly broken down for parts and sold. The head ends up in the possession of Jill, a sculptor of metal, who finds a practical use for it in one of her pieces. It turns out that the robot is a M.A.R.K. 13 self-repairing military droid, which proceeds to do just that by draining the power from Jill's flat to switch itself on, then plundering bits of her sculptures to rebuild itself. M.A.R.K. 13 trundles around, killing some people including Jill's boyfriend Mo (who was involved in the original sale of the droid parts), until Jill traps the droid in the bathroom and, learning of its vulnerability to water or humidity, turns on the shower, short circuiting it. As the film closes, we learn that M.A.R.K. 13 has been deemed a success and the Government has approved its mass production, presumably for the decimation of countries without rainfall only.

Hardware is a film that, until recent DVD and Blu-ray releases, had been more slagged off than actually seen. It's a film that people queue up to actively dislike. Part of this can be traced to the film's visual aspirations, originally conceived to reflect its rather low budget, which became considerably expanded with the input of money (and American lead actors) from Miramax, but not necessarily with any additional coherence. It looks like a small film with too much cash spent on it, and the robot is still basically a head on a stick. The quasi-religious/metaphysical imagery caused by the droid's injection of a lethal toxin into its victims (making them hear Pavarotti—argh!) feels clumsy and forced, whatever Stanley's original intentions. Tacking on opening and closing scenes shot in Morocco doesn't help. Their widescreen vistas jar horribly with the other material, which was claustrophobically shot on one set (in the then abandoned Roundhouse in London, now a performing arts space).

The performances are also decidedly mixed. Stacey Travis turns in a bold appearance as Jill, suffering convincingly when menaced by the droid, but she plays against a block of wood called Dylan McDermott as Mo. McDermott, a so-so actor in titles like *Steel Magnolias* and *Twister*, reduced his performance to a level just above catatonia supposedly as a result of being dumped by the actress Julia Roberts immediately before filming began. It was a situation that led Stanley to comment that he seemed "deeply traumatized by the whole experience," so much so that McDermott initially refused to participate in a sex scene with Travis! Eventually he compromised and let Travis take the "top bunk" so he had less to do—how gallant of him. Casting-wise, *Hardware* subscribes to the then fashionable inclusion of a range of cameos, including Iggy Pop as D.J. Angry Bob, Lemmy from Motorhead as a taxi driver (who apparently was paid in bourbon—the drink, not the biscuit, I'm assuming), and Fields of the Nephilim's Carl McCoy, playing, well, a guy in a stupid

hat really. Oh, and Stanley himself crops up as the voice of the talking lift.

On the plus side, the color palette is great—Stanley is an admirer of Dario Argento and Mario Bava and it really shows—although rather pretentiously Stanley also claimed inspiration from the color wheel of the Hopi Indian tribe.

Watching *Hardware*, I was reminded of the fate of *Hellraiser*, reviewed elsewhere in this book, which similarly started off as a more domestically based film and which was Americanized to increase its box office potential. I'd have liked to have seen *Hardware* made as originally intended, with its Britishness intact (the original idea had been to set it on a council estate of the future) with a lower budget necessitating invention and economy. In fact, Stanley's 1985 Super 8mm student short *Incidents in an Expanding Universe* hints at the film he should have made. There's still enough in the movie, from the seedy London-based locations (including the lobby of the then vacant Finsbury Park Rainbow and parts of the East End) to its nods to counter culture (it includes footage loaned by Throbbing Gristle's Genesis P-Orridge) to get a sense of a darker film beneath the Miramax gloss, but it would have been interesting to have seen a gloomier alternative script for *Hardware*, developed but shelved by Stanley, in favor of the finished item.

"No one makes films like this in England," claims Stanley on the director's commentary for the Blu-ray release. And he's right of course. I like to think that Britain just wasn't ready for its first authentic cyberpunk film, but now that technology has caught up and the future is here, with its clean lines and smooth edges, I rather suspect the moment has passed.
—David Dent

HOWLING V: THE REBIRTH

D: Neal Sundstrom
W: Freddie Rowe, Clive Turner
Starring: Phil Davis, Victoria Catlin, Elizabeth Shé, Ben Cole

The fourth sequel to Joe Dante's most celebrated movie is routinely described as a remake of the 1974 Amicus film *The Beast Must Die*. Indeed, a brief summary of the plot reveals a major similarity: A disparate group of individuals are invited to an isolated house. One of them is a werewolf and one by one the other guests fall victim to its murderous attacks. Who is the lycanthrope, and will its identity be discovered before everybody else is ripped apart? The earlier movie even included the gimmick of the "Werewolf Break"—the action stops while a clock ticks off 60 seconds so the audience can ponder their answer to the question "whodunnit?" (or rather "whoisit?"). *The Beast Must Die* is generally held in a certain degree of contempt as being an embarrassing misfire within the Amicus catalogue. Conversely,

Howling V is often considered to be a pretty decent entry in what is indisputably a rather lackluster franchise.

The stylish pre-credits opening scenes are set inside a castle in 14th century Hungary. A traveling shot reveals the bloodied corpses of several people strewn around a banqueting hall. A distraught nobleman and his lady commit suicide by impaling themselves together on a broadsword. Before drawing his last breath, the man hears a monstrous baying coming from within the castle and gasps "It was all in vain!" This sequence, accompanied by *Omen*-esque soundtrack music, certainly provides an intriguing and atmospheric prologue to the main narrative, which is unfortunately (but unsurprisingly) set in the modern day.

The somewhat contrived and nonsensical plot reveals that several people, hailing from different countries and various walks of life (a B-list actress, an anthropology professor, a well-known photographer, an unctuous lounge lizard, etc.), have each received an invitation to attend the re-opening to the public of the castle seen in the prologue. They assemble at a Budapest hotel and embark on a coach journey in the charge of their host Count Istvan (played by English actor Philip Davis, later acclaimed for his portrayal of Wilfrid Brambell in *The Curse of Steptoe*.) After apparently running over a mysterious beast that springs into the road on the way, the vehicle disgorges its passengers at the castle gates, just a few hours ahead of a raging blizzard. It's clear (and just in case it's not, the ominous "chan-choon" musical motif spells it out) that most of them will not be coming out alive.

In the majority of the movies in this particular horror film saga the werewolf is only ever seen briefly onscreen, and *Howling V* is no exception. In fact, it may be the *Howling* movie that shows the least wolfman action of all. Many of the creature shots are extreme close-ups of the monster's jaws and teeth. The only time it is seen full on is in a lightning-fast shock effect in which the lycanthrope bursts out of a snowdrift to attack its hapless victim unawares. But despite the paucity of monster action and although the story is convoluted and illogical, the film has atmosphere to spare, making the most of the sense of isolation with howling (ho ho) winds and snowstorms battering the ancient fortress, while assorted characters search spooky underground passages by the flickering light of flaming torches. There are one or two decent shocks along the way to a corpse littered finale (and a rather impressive and unexpected beheading), culminating in a suspenseful confrontation between the final girl and the two remaining suspects. Which of them is the monster? Suffice to say that if you have been paying close attention to the plot ... it won't help you in the slightest!
—Mike Hodges

I BOUGHT A VAMPIRE MOTORCYCLE

D: Dirk Campbell
W: Mycal Miller, John Wolskel
Starring: Neil Morrissey, Amanda Noar, Michael Elphick, Anthony Daniels, Daniel Peacock

Central TV's series *Boon* was a surprise ratings hit during the late 1980s, with Michael Elphick hitting a popularity peak as the easy-going private investigator ("Anything Legal Considered.") One equally surprising unofficial tangent arrived on UK cinema screens and home video in 1990 in the shape of *I Bought a Vampire Motorcycle*, a ramshackle horror comedy made by members of the *Boon* cast and crew in their spare time during 1989.

Neil Morrissey, leather-jacketed sidekick "Rocky" in the TV show, took the lead role in *Motorcycle* as "Noddy," purchaser of a Norton Commando 850cc machine that, unknown to its new owner, is possessed by evil and thrives on blood. Other *Boon* alumni involved included Elphick himself, as "Inspector Cleaver," handily reeking of garlic and expressing a firm belief in things supernatural; David Daker, who plays a police desk sergeant here; and even Dean Friedman, curly-haired New Jersey hit maker of the 1970s (*Ariel, Lydia*, and *Lucky Stars*) who penned incidental music and faux-country numbers for the series and who got roped in to perform similar duties on the movie, here rocking out on the likes of *"She Runs on Blood ... Not Gasoline."* Anthony Daniels made a rare non-*Star Wars* appearance as a biker priest, while Danny Peacock, a familiar face on the British alternative comedy scene, memorably played Morrissey's pal Buzzer—he is decapitated by the bloodthirsty Norton early on but his severed head features in a later nightmare sequence, and he pops up as a talking turd in a toilet bowl during a revolting fantasy episode, propelling himself from the crapper and into Noddy's mouth!

The vampire motorcycle is chiefly out for revenge against a gang of Hells Angels who have murdered an occultist with a crossbow—but once this rowdy mob has been effortlessly dispatched, the out-of-control hog proceeds to cause mayhem in a hospital and to sway an attempt at exorcism. The bike's aversion to light may be its only weakness—one exploited by Noddy, the inspector, and co. in their bid to defeat the revving chrome beast.

Morrissey and his then-wife Amanda Noar carry the movie adequately as Noddy and sassy girlfriend Kim, propped up by an experienced supporting cast. The world-weary Elphick could do this stuff in his sleep, it's great to watch Daniels outside the confines of his golden C-3PO droid suit for a change, and the likes of Graham Padden and Ed Devereaux provide ample assistance. Even well-known newspaper movie critic (and author of many seminal books on horror films) Alan Frank became heavily involved with the production and got to cameo as an ambulance man. When Burt Kwouk pops up as owner of a Chinese takeaway restaurant inevitably named "Fu King," you know all you need to know about this particular movie. Watch it with a chow mein, washed down with a few pints of Strongbow cider.
—Darrell Buxton

LIVING DOLL

D: Peter Litten and George Dugdale
W: George Dugdale and Mark Ezra
Starring: Mark Jax, Katie Orgill, Gary Martin, Eartha Kitt

Directors Peter Litten, George Dugdale and Mark Ezra had disgraced themselves with *Slaughter High* but were to have another stab with *Living Doll*, with the script by Ezra and Dugdale based on an original story by Paul Hart-Wilden. Dick Randall, producing again, tried to camouflage the British shoot behind American accents and with a snippet of misdirection location shooting in New York. Films carrying a necrophilia theme could be expected to operate on the side of extreme, with little chance of a UK release at the time, but the team seemed aware of this, carefully tailoring their grim love story and ensuring a balance between the controversial and the conventional. They quite deliberately nabbed the title of a big Cliff Richard hit, playing up the humorous value and recognition factor, similarly aiming for wit over outright comedy in the movie itself.

The film also cast Katie Orgill, a Page 3 Girl, in the role of hospital florist Christine. Orgill was a nude model in the British redtop *The Sun*, and the popular tabloid was more than happy to help with the publicity on the horror flick, with a "before and after" feature on one of their house beauties—"full torso putrescence" and "unblemished topless original" comparisons, over the collective readership's breakfast tables!

Anything can happen on a Dick Randall film, and this one provided an early assignment for future Oscar winner Dave Elsey, who had been asked by Paul Catling to turn up and assist with the application of Catling's designs to the rotting girl. When Catling did not appear, Elsey found himself on set starting from scratch and acquiring an unexpected special make-up effects credit. Catling's no-show was as the result of a fight outside a pub the night before, which put him in hospital with a pulped face that was no effect. Unable to see through swollen eyes, his mouth "like a duck's beak made of liver" (Dave's description), he would spend as long in hospital as Dave did on set.

The story is tight, with Howard (Mark Jax), a troubled mortuary assistant at a New York hospital, developing a crush on Christine, the flower girl stationed in the reception area, his unrequited love not abating even after her death in a car accident. Her boyfriend Steve (Marcel Grant) is responsible for the crash but places Christine's body behind the wheel on her demise. Howard cadges some of her belongings, accessing her apartment where he finds a medical emergency card advising that she suffers from catalepsy, which is all the damaged fellow needs to "prove" that she is still alive—despite him having attended the autopsy.

His landlady (Eartha Kitt) already has an intense dislike for the strange young medical student, perpetually late paying his rent. She regards his keeping of a pet axolotl as breaking the conditions of his tenancy agreement but is more displeased by the appalling reek that permeates the house once Howard's beloved is sharing his bed. In his eyes Christine is alive and beautiful, but in his arms she putrefies. It's intriguing that Howard works with the irreparable dead, while domestically he studies a reptile that has self-healing properties, a regenerative ability that may have elementally fed into his perceived wish-fulfilment for the return of Christine following the shock of her death.

Purchasing new clothes for his corpse companion, he finds himself without rent money, but with the girl of his dreams now across the threshold he is emboldened to palm off debtors and turn to theft. Having kept her keys and other personal possessions, he returns to Christine's flat, sneaking back out when Steve arrives to occupy the dwelling following his successful motor insurance claim. Howard steals money from another "dead on arrival" and appears blasé to accusations and the trouble he has caused for his only friend and fellow morgue worker Jess (Gary Martin, the sole returnee from *Slaughter High*). The stench in Howard's flat draws unwanted attention, and he transfers his beloved to the morgue, easier to access following the surprise coronary attack death of his unpleasant boss Ed (Freddie Earl); "He had a heart?" exclaims Howard.

His dead bride is talking to him now, instructing him to collect Steve to keep her company—he kills her ex at the questionably acquired apartment. Kissing her festering mouth awakens Howard to her putrid condition and he flees, taking up instead with a striptease transsexual whore who he murders.

This sleazy pitstop feels as if it has been ushered in from the other Spectacular Films production from that period, Derek Ford's execrable *The Urge to Kill*. The sequence appears to be jammed in to provide some unnecessary "bonus" boobs and blood to pad out the running time, betraying the relatively solid composition of the rest of the film as we reach the climax.

The leading performers are all well cast. Jax as the pathetic Howard is a British successor to other fictional flat-dwelling social misfits of New York like the murderers of *The Driller Killer*, *Ms. 45* and *Maniac*. Katie Orgill's participation should not be underestimated, despite the early death of her character—dead Christine is more demanding than the live cypher, her required stillness can't have been easy to achieve, plus she is called upon to rouse from that lifelessness to momentary animation on cue, as a living dead illusion of Howard's mind.
—Paul Higson

MURDER ON LINE ONE

D: Anders Palm
W: Anders Palm
Starring: Emma Jacobs, Peter Blake, Andrew Wilde

> "I know this sounds crazy, but I've just got home, and I found an eye on my doorstep."

Having seen his inventive and mark-hitting slasher spoof *Hand of Death Part 25* fall foul of the then-prevalent censorious trend, Anders Palm managed to follow up that late-in-the-decade VHS favorite by squeezing in one more offering before we bade farewell to the 1980s. And in attempting to skirt around the snipping scissors of the powers-that-be, he crafted a little-known, little-seen drama that rather anticipated the type of fare that was to become popular on mainstream TV in the United Kingdom over the following decades. Our commercial channel ITV has often used its "post-watershed" midweek 9 p.m. slot to offer series pitched as detective thrillers or forensics-focused fare, using these as cover to bring extreme violent content to the masses in palatable doses; the BBC followed suit with the likes of their two-part *Messiah* shows, featuring crazy Phibesian murder plots with a religious slant. By concentrating on aftermath, on "reveal" killings rather than depiction of the events themselves, and by having professional Quincy wannabes carving up cold corpses in close-up in place of perpetrators committing the deeds which created those cadavers, these small-screen shockers somehow got away with content that Lucio Fulci would have pulled somebody else's eyes out to achieve. The great British public may have been conditioned by our media and authorities to howl with protest at unknown Spaniards or Italians lopping off limbs; but seemed perfectly happy to stomach familiar faces like Robson Green being confronted by the grisly results of such actions.

Murder on Line One (known under a variety of titles, including *Deadline*—I especially favor the French *Le Boucher de Notting Hill*) anticipates the popular trend, and at an extended and well-structured 106 minutes could have easily been hacked down the middle to form a telly two-parter itself. Video packaging highlighting the cold stare of a psycho wielding a big blade tried to sell it as a late-period slasher, but Palm instead sets the template for viewer-friendly acceptance by centring upon journalistic sleuthing, with a side order of police procedural, and Agatha Christie guessing games. Within a "wrongly-convicted innocent" storyline we are offered severed heads, cut-out eyes, torsos with oozing red canal lines sliced across them, words like "Bitch" etched in crimson across every available surface, but all presented as clues in a puzzle, never as a depraved climax to in-view butchery. This may have harmed the movie's chances at the time, but in retrospect shows it as cannily predicting the genre's future, "getting away with it" by pretending not to be a "horror" presentation at all. Ultimately it also pulls something of a *Scream* trick, seven years early, too.

Adding to the diversionary tactics, our killer's selection of implement is not the glinting carving knife glimpsed on the box art, but more often, a very un-British baseball bat, used to stove in the heads of victims. We first see this bit of sporting equipment in use during a no-nonsense opening as a middle-class family unit is battered to oblivion in their everything-in-its-place home; more conventional strangulation, and some disturbing gunplay, features later on but the big wooden bat is never far away from the death-dealer's grasp. "This is probably the work of some students studying to be film directors," snaps a trenchcoated police investigator at one point, not a judgment on Palm's aptitude but a comment on a videotape kindly provided by the slayer—John McNaughton's *Henry: Portrait of a Serial Killer* was in the can by this point but was unknown to British viewers until its acclaimed premiere at the Scala Cinema's notorious "Splatterfest" in early 1990, so the presentation here of a psycho filming their activities

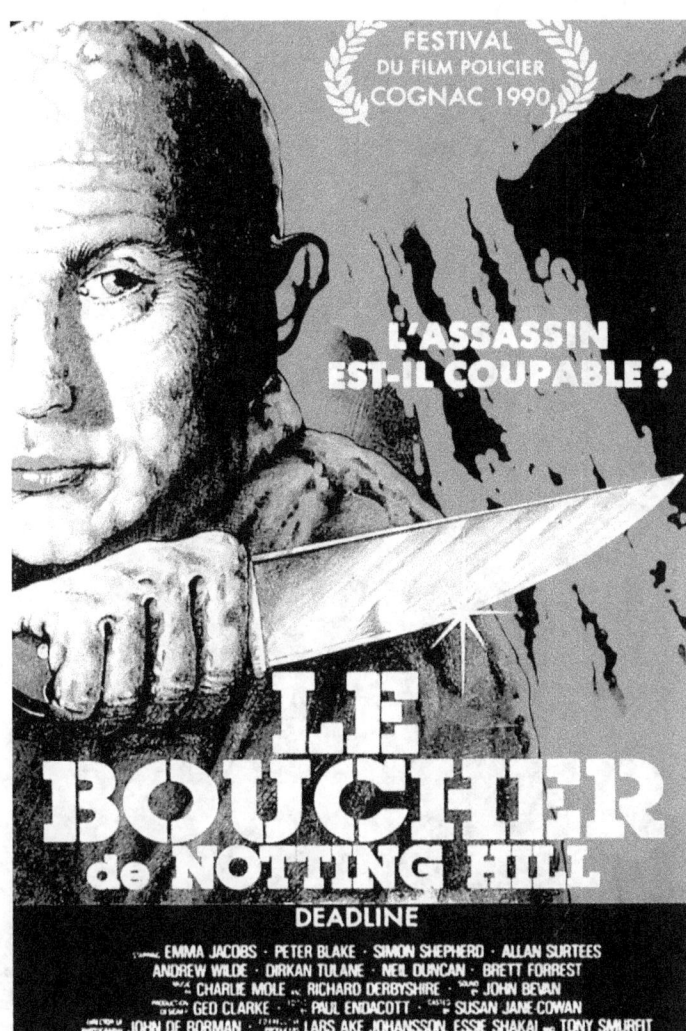

French poster for *Murder on Line One*

(and not simply for personal use, but packaged in padded envelopes and posted off to bait our protagonists) might have come as an additional layer of frisson to anyone happening across this one at the time—not that many took much notice. A shame, really, as Palm's brace of late 1980s shockers display range, intelligence, inventiveness, and an ability to riff on prevailing trends but, in doing so, to point in new directions.
—Darrell Buxton

NIGHTBREED

D: Clive Barker
W: Clive Barker
Starring: Craig Sheffer, Anne Bobby, David Cronenberg, Charles Haid, Hugh Quarshie, Hugh Ross, Doug Bradley

"Then don't say it …"

Clive Barker had made quite the name for himself in the world of horror by the late 1980s. With his ground-breaking *Books of Blood* series, his critically-acclaimed debut novel *The Damnation Game*, and his strong involvement in turning his novella *The Hellbound Heart* into the iconic *Hellraiser* film franchise, the Liverpudlian wunderkind seemed to have the kingdom of a

new strain of fear truly at his feet, to do with as he would. What, a growing crowd of followers wondered admiringly, would he do next?

Well, he wrote a lean, focused novel titled *Cabal*. He seemed extremely enamored of this work, even as a large number of his fans started to complain about it not being what they'd really wanted. Which must have left them even more bewildered when Clive threw himself whole-heartedly into making a big-screen version of the tale, already talking gleefully of sequels to both the book and film. Whether the fans wanted it or not, the *Nightbreed* were coming to a cinema near you.

Although set in America, the story had a very strong British feel, both behind and in front of the cameras. Clive brought such old British friends as Doug Bradley, Simon Bamford, Catherine Chevalier and Nicholas Vince with him to fill out the enormous cast of characters. And he was still a sufficiently Big Name so that all looked set for the film to be both made, and released, by the end of 1989.

Then things started to go awry. Rumors started to spread of general dissatisfaction with what was being created, of re-shoots mounted in a desperate attempt to pull something decent together. Although Barker himself remained a staunch supporter of what he was doing, both the fans and their favored publications became more concerned, as did the backers. When the finished item finally made it to the screens in early 1990, it did so with an ill-advised publicity campaign which seemed intent on selling it as some generic slasher, with initial trailers focusing on the bloody slayings committed by the story's enigmatic serial killer, The Mask. No one, general punters or fans, seemed entirely sure as to what to expect. Then, the film unspooled in the fleapits, and a large body of opinion solidified. With the best of intentions, it stated, Barker and his friends had produced an embarrassing mess. *Nightbreed* failed to become the box-office smash that had been hoped. Barker carefully stopped mentioning follow-ups to either the book or the movie. Finally, swiftly, it disappeared from the cinemas to the limbo of video rental release, and a lot of people seemed happy to see it vanish from the record.

In hindsight, they were badly wrong. *Nightbreed* is a frightning work, but it's also fascinating. Fantastic. A very different core of compassion lurks at its horrific heart, a powerful cry for tolerance. If it had any failing at all, it was that it was simply not the right film for the time.

Its story is simple. Boone, a young man with a history of mental issues, becomes worried that he is the killer responsible for a series of brutal slayings, and his sympathetic psychiatrist Decker agrees, urging him to give himself up. Instead, after a shocking encounter in a hospital, he goes on the run, eventually arriving in the mysterious, isolated mausoleum city of Midian, home to a whole community of literally inhuman rejects and outcasts, where he undergoes some traumatic changes—and discovers that he isn't the killer, and that Decker knows a lot more than he's saying. With his lover Lori attempting to track him down, and with the forces of Darkness, guided by Decker, intent on stamping out Midian like particularly brutal pest-exterminators, the stage is set for an apocalyptic confrontation that will alter Boone's life even more radically, for ever after …

There's still so much to enjoy, in either the film as initially released or its subsequent director's cut. Bob Keen and his team of special make-up geniuses produce an entire city of believable and amazing monsters, almost all—thanks to well-judged characterizations by the players—rounded figures. Danny Elfman provides a score which ranges from the eerie to the epic. The turns range from the unexceptional-but-adequate likes of Craig Sheffer and Anne Bobby as Boone and Lori, to the genuinely marvellous performances of Hugh Ross as the crazed-but-likeable Narcisse and David Cronenberg, on the other side of the camera from usual, providing a chilling portrayal of oh-so-reasonable Evil as Decker. It does remain a shame that Suzi Quatro didn't end up playing "a monster" as pre-release scuttlebutt suggested (apparently she did film a scene that was eventually excised), but hey, nothing's perfect.

The main problem remains that the audiences were expecting another bloody and shocking battle between Good and Evil, and that they got it. Just not in the way they expected. "You've made the monsters the heroes!" yelled the indignant executives. "But that's the whole bloody *point*!" riposted the exasperated Barker (or words to that effect). It's not much of an exaggeration to say that American filmmakers—and audiences, come to that—wanted nice, simple Good Guys back then, your Rockys, your Rambos, your Riggses and McClanes. And the foreigner— the *outsider*—was always the Bad Guy. The Monster was there to be evil, and to be destroyed. Barker's message—"but who are the *real* monsters?"—was hardly the most original of lessons, but that didn't mean that it wasn't well worth repeating: however, the clear-cut multiplex ideology of the day didn't want that.

Hollywood wanted Boone to be the Bogeyman. Barker wanted him to be Moses. That clash of beliefs was never going to have a neat, tidy outcome. And so, Boone, Lori, and the survivors of Midian set off to find a new home, with (depending on which version you watch) some combination of the resurrected Decker, the brutal police chief Eigerman, and the tormented, transmuted ex-priest Ashberry hot on their heels… but, bar an interesting, short-lived comics series from Marvel's "adult" Epic line, that was that for the Breed.

A great pity. *Nightbreed*'s plea for tolerance, for acceptance and even celebration of the different, remains as valid as it ever has—arguably, more than ever. Somewhere out there, Midian endures. Long may it do so.

Shangri-La on dope, we love it!
—Ken Shinn

STEPFATHER 2: MAKE ROOM FOR DADDY

D: Jeff Burr
W; John Auerbach
Starring: Terry O'Quinn, Meg Foster, Caroline Williams, Jonathan Brandis

As was always common practice, wherever a hit appeared a sequel was sure to follow and by the late 1980s it was sure to have a digit attached to it. The second *Stepfather*, again co-produced by Lew Grade's ITC, opened in US cinemas on November 3, 1989 despite the original intent that it would be a straight-to-video release. The implausible return of Jerry Blake (wait, who is he here?! Shouldn't that be "Gene Clifford"?) extends little further than him getting away with this palaver for a third time in two movies. Though there was clearly no credible way that he could have survived the denouement of the first film! Still, at least Terry O'Quinn is present in the titular role and he puts in just as convincing a performance the second time around. He just about manages to overcome the unlikely comeback and convince the audience that he might just possibly escape an insane asylum and set himself up in marriage guidance—the perfect guise for meeting single parent mothers.

The decision to aim for a cinema audience regrettably necessitated (in the producers' eyes) the need for a more slasher-orientated approach, and in taking this route the smarter, more steadily paced and believable aspects of the tale are thrown aside. The tagline "Tonight Daddy's coming home to slice up more than just the cake!" sums up just how much of the intelligence of the first *Stepfather* has been jettisoned, and it is no surprise that the almost sympathetic qualities of this wannabe Best Dad are lost. It can't have helped that the option to spice things up was declined by the director Jeff Burr (who would go on to suffer yet further directorial interference with his next production *Leatherface: Texas Chainsaw Massacre III*). O'Quinn also opted

out of reshoots, leaving a generally mismatched feel to the new scenes in the "enhanced" story.

The frustrating thing is that daddy's new family are infinitely better played than their predecessors. The ever-reliable Meg Foster turns in a typically confident performance as the new love interest Carol Grayland, while the ill-fated Jonathan Brandis avoids irritating as her son Todd. Caroline Williams of *The Texas Chainsaw Massacre 2* also offers strong support as Carol's friend and neighbor but none of them ever quite manage to lift proceedings above that of a fairly unnecessary retread. O'Quinn steals the show once again but was wise in his decision to jump the train at this point and avoid *Stepfather III* and the horrors of diminishing returns.

—Ian Taylor

THE URGE TO KILL

D: Derek Ford
W: Derek Ford
Starring: Peter Gordeno, Jeremy Mark, Tiga Adams, Sarah Jane Palmer, Sally Ann Balaam

After the debacle of *Don't Open Till Christmas*, Derek Ford embarked on a busman's holiday to Europe, eventually surfacing in Sweden as assistant director of *Blood Tracks* (1985), a horror cheapie that pits a hair metal band against a family of mutant cannibals. Back in London by the end of the 1980s, Ford once again hooked up with the irrepressible film producer Dick Randall. This renewed association resulted in the odd unproduced screenplay and Ford then finding himself writing and directing *The Urge to Kill*, a sort of low-brow, gender role reversal on the 1977 Julie Christie shocker *Demon Seed*.

Showbiz veteran Peter Gordeno plays a Stock, Aitken and Waterman era record producer. A man whose success in the charts is equal to his success in the bedroom, Gordeno's character, the bizarrely named Bono Zorro, is never without a sexy girl on his arm, or two more in his hot tub. When he is not being pursued by groupies eager to sleep with him in return for a step up in the music biz, Bono is partying with call girls, exploits he records for posterity on CCTV. Such is Bono's sex appeal that his hi-tech computer set-up—a "Central Environment Control System" or "CECSY," pronounced "SEXY"—develops the hots for him, and quickly becomes jealous of all the flesh and blood women he keeps bringing home. His latest conquest, wannabe singer Melanie, is easily seduced by all the mod cons in Bono's house and vague promises that he'll listen to her demo tape ... at some point. While Melanie marvels at his gadgetry, Bono heads off to his friend Jane—a high-class call girl—in an attempt to talk her into a threesome. In the meantime, Melanie proves to be a fast mover herself, and invites a female friend over to Bono's house, ending up in bed with her. Since hell hath no fury like a jealous female computer, "SEXY." begins turning all of the house's devices against Bono's girlfriends, playing havoc with Bono's sex life in the process. Quite literally turning up the heat on Melanie, "SEXY." roasts her in the shower. A far more outrageous fate awaits Melanie's friend when "SEXY." causes the poor woman's breasts to explode under a sunbed.

Bono returns home to find Melanie missing and the house's gimmickry malfunctioning. Computer-operated doors fail to re-open, keeping him and Jane shut in the house, and the computer itself gives Bono an almighty electric shock. Parts of the CCTV recording have also been deleted by "SEXY." removing the evidence of the murders, but thoughtfully retaining the CCTV recording of Melanie's earlier sexual encounter. Thus, allowing Bono to ogle the sight of the two women in bed together; "kids these days," he quips to Jane. With the planned afternoon romp with Melanie now a non-starter, Jane calls up Tiga and Susan, a pair of fellow call girls, to provide the fun and games. This turn of events doesn't go down well with "SEXY.," who dispatches the prostitutes at the first available opportunity, boiling Susan in the hot tub and turning an electric toothbrush against poor old Tiga. "SEXY." then mischievously attempts to fool Bono into believing that the women's disappearance is all part of a blackmail plot by Jane and the other sex workers. Just to add to the record producer's mounting problems and paranoia, "SEXY." also begins materializing in the form of a naked woman, and not just any naked woman either, but one with green skin, a computerized voice and kabuki style make-up and wig!! A truly spectacular sight to behold, "SEXY." in human form offers up competition to "exploding breasts in a sunbed" as the film's most unforgettable image.

Believe it or not, the plot gets weirder and wilder in the final act, which sees "SEXY." wipe Bono's memory, leaving the green lady free to try and bump off Jane. "SEXY." also rings up two more call girls, this time from the "Cat Calls Agency," to act as a distraction for Bono. And what a distraction this pair are! Dressed in fishnet body stockings, the duo's routine consists of playing Bono a video of a mud wrestling competition (the clips are actually taken from the 1983 British sexploitation film *Hellcats: Mud Wrestling*) and tearing each other's clothes off while making feline sounds! Jane's subsequent attempt to put an end to "SEXY.," combined with *Hellcats* footage, results in a climax that can boast to combine a bloodbath with a mudbath.

Originally filmed under the schlocky title *Attack of the Killer Computer*, Dick Randall decided on calling the movie *The Urge to Kill* instead. The retitling was motivated by the fact that Randall owned the rights to a very 1980s pop song called "Urge to Kill" and felt it would fit right into the film (sample lyrics: "I've got the urge to smash, smack, break and crack ... it's unbearable, I must fight back ... I've got the urge to kill.") Never one to miss a trick, Randall then persuaded Peter Gordeno's son to record a slightly different version of this ditty for the film after discovering that Gordeno, Jr. was a budding musician (he went on to play keyboards in Depeche Mode.)

The Urge to Kill is, if anything, more of a low-budget affair than *Don't Open Till Christmas*. Derek Ford shot the film over just one week, mainly at Dick Randall's house in central London with some additional shooting done at Randall's office, as well as in Peter Gordeno's own abode in Weybridge. "The budget was about £1.50," a crew-member later joked. Ford just about manages to pull off the trick of evoking the moneyed, decadent world of Bono Zorro and his gal-pals on extremely slim resources, chiefly due to having shot the film at Randall's expensive looking home. Not only does chez Randall convince as the pad of a wealthy music industry player, it also illustrates that there was clearly a few bob to be made from producing B-movies too! As with the earlier Randall/Ford film, *The Urge to Kill* is very much a piece of old-school exploitation, with stage blood and bare breasts being the fuel that drives this particular project's wheels.

Derek Ford really goes hell for leather here, reflecting both his sex film background and his off-screen interests, by throwing in all manner of kinky behavior. This really has it all, finger sucking, women in leather, pole dancing, catfights, mud wrestling and a high amount of nudity from the female cast. While such a colorful display of exploitation incident is to be expected from a work bearing the names Derek Ford and Dick Randall in its titles, it is more of a surprise to see Peter Gordeno headlining such a venture. Gordeno was predominantly a dancer and choreographer, with secondary careers as a singer and actor, and was best known to cult TV fans for his supporting role in Gerry Anderson's sci-fi series *UFO*. Viewers more familiar to witnessing Gordeno save the world from alien invaders might raise an eyebrow at seeing him here sharing a hot tub with two naked starlets, baring his own arse at one point, and comparing women to Kleenex tissues—"use 'em and throw 'em away." Should anyone consider holding a competition to find the seediest character to ever have been envisioned as a horror film hero, then Bono Zorro—a sexist womanizer, male nymphomaniac and compulsive voyeur—has to be in the running. Still it is hard to deny that Bono is perfectly suited to a film that is equally driven by sex and cheap thrills.

Gordeno's co-stars were mostly plucked from the world of pornography and found themselves dubbed "a host of centrefold girls ... who die in the strangest manner" by the movie's trailer. Small roles are taken by the likes of Marie Harper and Susie Silvey, both prolific glamour models and bit part actresses since the late 1970s. Marie's career had previously seen her being filmed in a coffin for the bad taste documentary *Mary Millington's True Blue Confessions* (1980), in which she played Mary Millington's corpse! Susie, meanwhile, is familiar to British horror buffs as the woman who gives birth to a fully-grown man in *Xtro*. A sizeable role went to Sally Ann Balaam, a popular Page 3 girl who was being dubbed "the new Sam Fox" at the time the film was made. For a non-actress/glamour model Balaam is given quite a bit to do as the ill-fated Melanie, but just about convinces, even pulling off an American accent, seemingly a requisite for cast members in latter day Randall productions like *Slaughter High* and *Living Doll*. On account of its nubile and frequently undressed cast, *The Urge to Kill* found itself the recipient of some free publicity when it became the subject of a tits and bums themed article in the *Daily Star*.

So why, you may ask yourself, have you probably never heard of this one before? Well, much to the disappointment of Peter Gordeno, British horror aficionados and possibly a few *Daily Star* readers, *The Urge to Kill* was never released, anywhere, anytime or anyplace. Well, at least not officially. After sitting on the shelf for well over two decades, a hooky copy of Ford's film surfaced on the collector's circuit in 2011. The time code on this version suggests it derives from a VHS screener copy, meant only for the eyes of a distributor but likely to have fallen into the hands of an unscrupulous bootlegger at some point. Prior to this "leak," the public had seen only fleeting glimpses of *The Urge to Kill* since it was made. A couple of seconds, culled from its trailer, appear in *The Wild, Wild World of Dick Randall*, a 2005 documentary on its producer. Curiously, a decade earlier, TV viewers had been treated to some uncredited clips from *The Urge to Kill* when Jonathan Ross incorporated footage from it into a comedy sketch for his 1995 BBC series *Mondo Rosso*.

Dick Randall had one final horror film left to unleash on the general public in the form of *Living Doll*, which was in post-production when *The Urge to Kill* was hastily put together. This busy schedule proved beneficial to *Living Doll*'s original writer Paul Hart-Wilden, who got an extra gig from Randall when he was hired as assistant director on *Urge*. For Derek Ford, however, *The Urge to Kill* was to prove his cinematic swansong. With the recession of the early 1990s looming and little work in the film industry coming his way, Ford abandoned directing soon afterwards, instead concentrating on a writing career and going on to "officially" pen two books before his death in 1995. In retrospect, the 1980s were a tough time for Ford and the other British exploitation filmmakers still active during the era. The dissolving of the Eady fund during the decade provided a lethal blow to the sort of sex and horror themed low-budget filmmaking that Ford specialized in. Ford's ambition to progress to bigger-budget films never really amounted to anything, and the 1980s would see him struggle to find work even in the exploitation field, a rapidly disappearing genre by that point. The lyrics of a song in Ford's 1970 sex film *Groupie Girl*— "you're yesterday's hero in a world of today, as you crawl down the narrow lanes like you never get the time of day" now seem sadly prophetic of Ford's decline in the 1980s. "He did have some imagination and sensitivity but lacked the clarity of vision and practical expertise to bring off a major project" remembers Ford's friend Paula Meadows, adding that "consequently he was probably, inside, a disappointed man who felt he had never achieved his full potential."

Post *The Urge to Kill*, there remains a further footnote to the career of Derek Ford, one that is equally amusing and tragic. In the final few years of his life Ford found himself a career sideline writing erotic novels for women, for the Black Lace company. As

Black Lace only published erotica by female authors, Ford went to great lengths to disguise his real identity in order to pass these books off as being the work of a woman. Eventually a female associate was found to lend her name as a "front," only for Ford to pass away soon after they were published, leaving the credited authoress free to not only take acclaim for the books but abscond with the royalties as well. Never in a million years could Black Lace's female readership—lured to the books by the company's claim of publishing "world leading erotic fiction for women by women"—have imagined they were actually reading the literary output of the director of *Attack of the Killer Computer*!
—Gavin Whitaker

THE WITCHES

D: Nicolas Roeg
W: Allan Scott
Starring: Anjelica Huston, Jasen Fisher, Mai Zetterling, Rowan Atkinson, Bill Paterson, Jane Horrocks, Brenda Blethyn

This film is a joy. It is a children's picture by the man behind *Don't Look Now*, based on a Roald Dahl novel, with Anjelica Huston as the Grand High Witch of a truly grotesque coven who wear realistic masks concealing their true hide, and who plan to rid the world of youngsters. The hags, under the guise of the seemingly charitable Royal Society for the Prevention of Cruelty to Children, convene at a Rowan Atkinson-managed seaside hotel where a young boy, Luke (Jasen Fisher) is staying with his Norwegian grandmother (Mai Zetterling). She has encountered the witches before, they having trapped a friend of hers in a painting, and has warned her orphaned grandson, who was previously visited by a snake-wielding witch, but knew what his granny told him. At the hotel, he meets a gluttonous boy named Bruno, an English equivalent to Dahl's own Augustus Gloop, and his worrisome cat-loving, mouse-hating parents, played by Brenda Blethyn and Bill Paterson. The two boys hide at the conference, Luke knowing that the delegates are witches, but both lads are turned into mice (Jim Henson creations, some of the last work Henson would do hands-on), and with the aid of Luke's grandmother have to prevent the evil schemes of the Grand High Witch (Huston clearly relishing the part, thick European accent and all.). However, at the end, with Anjelica defeated, her assistant (a frightfully young Jane Horrocks) manages to display a kindlier side and transform the mice back into boys, unlike the book's rather dark ending with the narrator speculating that he will poignantly live as long as his grandmother, as he is now a mouse, and that Bruno will probably be eaten by his mother's cat. It was these changes that enraged Dahl, who died shortly afterwards, though he was ecstatic when his personal favorite for the Grand High Witch, Huston, was cast, partially making amends for his reported anger that Spike Milligan had not been chosen to play Willy Wonka two decades previously.

This film is enjoyable. The changes to the ending are, yes, slightly saccharine, but still there is a lot to love. The seaside hotel adds a touch of "Findus Gothic" to the idea of witches—not the pointy-hatted sort, as Dahl points out, but those of Norwegian mythology, scabby-scalped troll-like creatures who can pass themselves off as normal women. Although most of the featured speaking witches are played by attractive or feminine actresses such as Huston or Jane Horrocks, many of the extras at the R.S.P.C.C. conference were played by men in drag, one of them rumored to be a cameoing Michael Palin, in a green floral print dress in the fifth row.

Among the notable performances, Zetterling is wise and knowledgeable and authentically Scandinavian as the grandmother, Blethyn is good as the screaming, mouse-phobic mother, and Atkinson does his best as a comedic manager, Mr. Stringer. In all, this film—one of several that bewitched my horror-loving side as a child—is an expert union of three geniuses, Henson, Dahl and Roeg.
—George White

TV Movies

The Anatomist
The Curse of King Tutankhamen's Tomb
Dr. Jekyll and Mr. Hyde
The Dybbuk
Artemis 81
The Chelsea Murders
Les Contes d'Hoffmann
The Secret of Seagull Island
The Hunchback of Notre Dame
Ruddigore
The Bad Sister
The Case of the Frightened Lady
The Hound of the Baskervilles
The Mad Death
Frankenstein
The Masks of Death
Night Train to Murder
Rainy Day Women
Threads
Unfair Exchanges
Daemon
Titus Andronicus
The Canterville Ghost
The Gourmet
Mr. Corbett's Ghost
Born of Fire
The Magic Toyshop
Duke Bluebeard's Castle
Jack the Ripper
Under the Bed
Star Trap
The Woman in Black
The Yellow Wallpaper

THE ANATOMIST

1980
D: Julian Amyes
W: Ronald Mavor
Starring: Patrick Stewart, Elizabeth Millbank, Lorna Heilbron, James Coyle

> It is how everyone speaks of Dr. Knox. He is horrible. He is conceited. He is overdressed. He is ugly. He is pompous. He's rude. He is a married man and he is forever dancing attendance on unmarried females. And everyone knows he is hand in glove with the sack-'em-up men! (BBC publicity, July 1980.)

The Burke and Hare saga has been one of the most frequently dramatized penny dreadfuls in British film and TV. *The Greed of William Hart*, *The Flesh and the Fiends*, *Burke & Hare* (1971), *The Doctor and the Devils*, *Burke & Hare* (2010) have all directly brought the gruesome historical yarn to our screens, with a decent success rate to boot. Bodysnatching was also the focus of *Corridors of Blood*, while Hammer's *Dr. Jekyll and Sister Hyde* features Messrs. B & H in cameo, and *The Vault of Horror* ingeniously pitches the stars of London Weekend Television's popular *Doctor ...* sitcom, Geoffrey Davies and Robin Nedwell, into spoofing the graverobbing shenanigans of their infamous predecessors, along with Arthur Mullard doing the spadework! In June 1939 a live broadcast of James Bridie's stage play *The Anatomist* was televized by the BBC, starring Andrew Cruickshank and featuring W.G. Day and Harry Hutchinson as Burke and Hare; 1956 saw Diarmuid Kelly and Michael Ripper take up the bodysnatching duties in another TV adaptation of the Bridie play toplining Alastair Sim and his protégé George Cole (this one was reportedly released to American audiences in the early 1960s)—Ripper had portrayed Hare in an earlier 1949 BBC TV retelling alongside Sim's Knox, with Joel O'Brien responsible for transferring Sim's West End stage revival of the play to the living rooms of those fortunate enough to have access to television. While 1980 saw BBC Scotland revive the drama for an 85-minute remake starring a pre-*Star Trek: The Next Generation* Patrick Stewart as a Doctor Knox for a whole new generation.

Screened on BBC1 at 9 p.m. on July, 27, this production for the *Play of the Month* slot was directed by Julian Amyes, scripted by Ronald Mavor (Bridie's son), and overseen by producer Pharic MacLaren. Micky O'Donoughue was Burke and James Coyle Hare on this occasion, while the cast also included Lorna Heilbron (familiar to horror fans from *The Creeping Flesh* and *Symptoms*), and Gregor Fisher (some years before becoming a household name as the mighty dole-queue philosopher Rab C. Nesbitt.) It seems that *The Anatomist* has fallen off the radar—copies of the 1956 transmission abound but this 1980 show from the Beeb seems more difficult to come by. Luckily, our spies at BBC Scotland advised "the good news is that the program still exists, the bad news is that there are no viewing copies in the BBC archive, only a Digital Betacam master and a couple of D3s (older format)." Remarkably, a rare copy did wing its way along during the preparation of this book, for which we are exceedingly grateful, and so I can report that it is a fine addition to the list of Knox/Burke & Hare retellings. Patrick Stewart plays Knox as a pompous, brash, obnoxious fellow, and this and the generally over-ripe feel to the production lends it a quality that really suits the subject matter. A couple of the female characters even speak in what must be an impenetrable dialect to anyone south of Berwick—I barely understood a word but found that the local color all added to the piece rather than detracting. Lorna Heilbron proves a formidable adversary to Stewart, and the always-welcome Fisher features as the landlord of B & H's local grubby tavern. The action shifts from lavish drawing room to seedy bar and grim morgue, a beautiful contrast really pointing up the understated "haves" and "have nots" aspects of the historical hysteria, and for all Stewart's puffing and pontificating, his Knox is a rather battered and beaten figure by the close—it would be nice to think that the actor's subsequent superstardom may help lift this one out of the vaults at a future date, as his portrayal of the notorious doctor takes more than a few chances and exhibits Stewart's willingness to tackle flawed and dislikeable characters, as also seen in darker roles later in his career (*Dad Savage*, *Green Room*).

Radio versions of *The Anatomist* had been frequent as part of the BBC Home Service programming. 1951 brought a 70-minute audio restaging with James McKechnie as Knox and Paul Curran and Roddy McMillan as the graverobbing duo; a 1965 show under the banner *Repertory In Britain* had Iain Cuthbertson as Knox in a production by Glasgow's Citizen's Theatre Company; previously, October 1937's version starred the splendidly-named Helbert Tatlock as Knox, with W.G. Day and Fred O'Donovan supplying the corpses, while Alastair Sim had an earlier stab at the Knox role in 1944 with Nicholas Parsons as Augustus Raby, Edward Byrne as Burke and Harry Hutchinson as Hare (there was a 1952 broadcast featuring Sim, possibly a repeat of this?). And on June 21, 1953 Dilys Powell presented *The Doctor and the Devils*, a talk on Dylan Thomas' "experimental film scenario" based on the Burke & Hare case (and of course eventually brought before the cameras by Freddie Francis in 1985—in which a demoted Patrick Stewart played Professor Macklin, with Timothy Dalton as the Knox-esque Dr. Rock.)

—Darrell Buxton

THE CURSE OF KING TUTANKHAMEN'S TOMB

1980
D: Philip Leacock
W: Herb Meadow
Starring: Eva Marie Saint, Harry Andrews, Robin Ellis, Raymond Burr, Tom Baker, Angharad Rees, Wendy Hiller

It goes without saying that they don't make them like this anymore: What is more surprising, to be honest, is that they were still making them like this then.

Almost as if two films have collided, this made-for-TV trifle combines a straight, nicely detailed (if largely fanciful) account of the discovery of Tutankhamen's tomb with a nutty *Boys' Own* adventure subplot featuring Raymond Burr as devilish Egyptian villain Jonash Sebastian. Burr, stirring up political intrigue and intent on securing the treasures for himself, has his bulk clad bizarrely in a massive wraparound garment and loose, floppy turban that constantly changes color, as if Peter Greenaway were among the screenwriters and each hue was intended to convey some archaic symbolic meaning (in one scene it's a fiery pillar-box red, in another deep midnight blue.) Boot-polished and bellowing all the while, he seems to have strayed in from a Hanna-Barbera cartoon. Long before Tom Baker turns up as his henchman halfway through, delivering his usual florid performance through matching layers of axle grease, some viewers may begin to smell parody.

As with the later *Jack the Ripper* (1988) what we have here is a hybrid: A reasonably sober British production (from HTV West, something of a fantasy specialist at the time) that went bananas when Columbia turned up with American money. Which is a pity, because a lot of this, when you scrape the excess paint off its canvas, is fine. Harry Andrews and Robin Ellis are good as Carnarvon and Carter, the latter stepping in at the 11th hour to replace an injured Ian McShane (the casting of Ellis has the pleasing additional result of re-teaming him with Angharad Rees, his co-star in the TV series *Poldark*. She's as charming as usual—and born to wear 1920s fashions—as Carnarvon's daughter Lady Evelyn Herbert.). The scenes in England, the preliminaries of the planning and digging, the thrill of the accidental discovery when all seemed hopeless, and then the tension and wonder of the tomb unearthing are all conveyed nicely. Excellent use is made of the locations, and atmosphere is well sustained.

But given the potential of the tabloid-angled account of the excavation itself, already so dependent on wild conjecture and exaggeration, why anyone felt the need to go further even than contemporary journalists, and create entirely new characters and events out of whole cloth, is hard to imagine. We have an international conspiracy of occultists, exploding airplanes, berserk clairvoyants rasping out coded warnings, and a top-billed Eva Marie Saint contributing almost nothing to the plot as a sympathetic journalist, grafted in seemingly only to provide a little fictitious love interest which then, even more oddly, comes to naught. It takes more than a sober, National Geographic commentary in the reassuring tones of Paul Scofield to convince us that we are watching anything more than a jovially insincere romp. But then, TV movies were a law unto themselves in this, their golden age.
—Frank James

DR. JEKYLL AND MR. HYDE

1980
D: Alastair Reid
W: Gerald Savory
Starring: David Hemmings, Lisa Harrow, Ian Bannen, Clive Swift, Toyah Willcox, Roland Curram, Diana Dors

You couldn't move without bumping into The Duality of Man in the early 1980s. Ken Russell's *Altered States*, Walerian Borowczyk's *Docteur Jekyll et les Femmes*, a flood of exciting new werewolf movies, several potion-quaffing spoofs including *Dr. Heckyl and Mr. Hype* and *Jekyll and Hyde...Together Again*, even Sydney Pollack's *Tootsie*, Barbra Streisand's *Yentl*, Woody Allen's *Zelig*, Carl Reiner's *All of Me*, and Blake Edwards' *Victor/Victoria*. Just ahead of the game came this near-two-hour production from the BBC, scripted by Gerald Savory, basking in the plaudits for his first-rate adaptation of Stoker's *Dracula* starring Louis Jourdan.

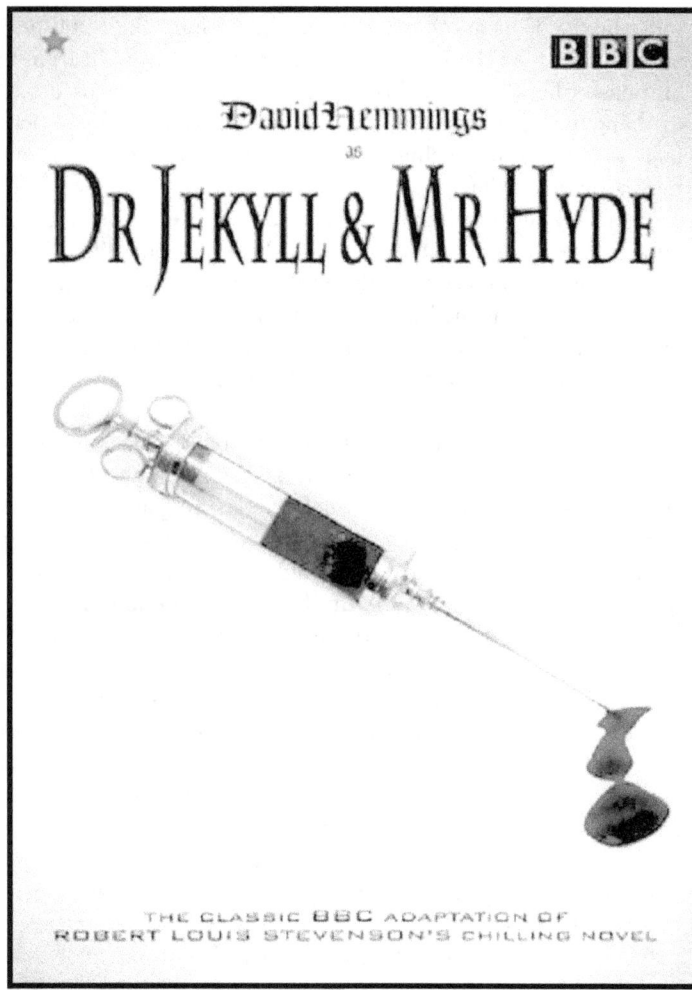

Distinguished by its ever-roaming, highly kinetic camerawork, sufficient to induce vertigo among unwary viewers, Alastair Reid's version of R.L. Stevenson combines standard Victorian costume drama cliché with attempts at something a little more daring, mostly to great effect. The production thieves the "gruff hirsute Jekyll/clean shaven upbeat Hyde" concept from Hammer's hugely underrated *The Two Faces of Dr. Jekyll*, and casts most of the folk you'd expect (dour Caledonian lawyer Ian Bannen, colorful and saucily brash madame Diana Dors, new kid on the block Toyah Willcox, and the obligatory Clive Swift), but brings enough of its own to the party to make it worth your while.

Hemmings manages the unusual and infrequently achieved feat of making both Jekyll and Hyde into watchable figures full of character. As the "good" half of the pair (penchant for visiting pox-ridden dominatrices notwithstanding), he grumps along, immersed in his quest to locate man's darker aspect, yet not so obsessed that he can't find time for his matchmaking friends and his charity work. As Hyde he is playful, happy and smiling, but almost immediately reveals pedophilic tendencies (an early scene where he approaches a *very* young "flower-seller"—"well Mary, you take off all your clothes, and I'll tell you what I'm going to do to you"—is perhaps even more disturbing to 21st century eyes than it must have been on original broadcast) and seems to take over and dictate the path of Jekyll's experiments and theorizing, with a particular eye on bringing forth the hidden side of the females who exist in the doctor's orbit.

The transformation scenes were to become passé within months, but have a charm and invention to them—the opener is a truly creative mélange of close-up, point of view shot, odd stock footage, and chroma key effects, initially depicting the emergent Hyde as a hulking shadow before the startling sight of the boyish Hemmings appears before us in a mirror, sans Jekyll's unruly mutton chops and Jimmy Edwards 'tache. A second makeover is played out beneath the light-dark-light of a swinging overhead lamp, again with considerable impact in its orthodox method, though it has to be said that the interim ape-like stage has Hemmings rather resembling a cross between Robin Gibb and Brett Anderson—this prior to the beautifully grim touch of Jekyll spitting out three or four teeth into his palm. Other simple but well-handled indications of "the change" occur with Hyde awakening beneath Jekyll's bedclothes at his early morning breakfast call, or Jekyll clambering into a hansom cab at the start of a journey and Hyde alighting from the passenger door once the destination has been reached.

Dr. Jekyll and Mr. Hyde is at its very best under Savory's watch when it most tantalizes. Swift's seeming denunciation of Calvinism during one dialogue exchange requires no development to tell us everything about the nature of his character; the hints that Willcox's illiterate maidservant may have been impregnated by Hyde add frustratingly undeveloped possibilities to the familiar storyline (Hyde takes great naughty glee in spelling out the letters "D-R-E-A-M-S" to the maid, from a container labeled "mescal" ...;) and Lisa Harrow's performance is deceptive, as she appears to be all starch, cheekbones and embroidery throughout but is unleashed in a terrific, eventful closing sequence, rising to the challenge of playing the range from "seductive" and "scandalous" to "gibbering wreck" almost within seconds.
—Darrell Buxton

THE DYBBUK

1980
D: Jane Howell
W: Sholom Anski
Starring: Giselle Wolf, Louis Hammond, Harold Goldblatt, Simon Callow

Jane Howell is one unsung figure in TV British horror, and TV in general—specializing in adaptation of source material familiar by name but rarely the subject of actual production. Jane dabbled in single and episodic dramas but had a penchant for the past and for reviving ancient fare consigned to memory. She was appointed to the *BBC Television Shakespeare* team, directing a number of the Bard's plays for that ambitious project, including *Richard III* and a highly controversial *Titus Andronicus*.

The Dybbuk director Jane Howell

1980 was a busy year—for the Christmas schedules Jane helmed a new three-part version of the old Tod Slaughter barnstormer *Maria Marten or Murder in the Red Barn* (Pippa Guard in the title role, supporting cast including Kevin McNally, Tenniel Evans, Shane Briant, Peter Benson and Christopher Fairbank), while February had seen the broadcast of *The Dybbuk*, a two-hour-plus restaging of the old Yiddish play by S. Ansky. Best-known, if at all, in its 1937 Polish feature film incarnation directed by Michał Waszyński, Ansky's take on classic Jewish folklore is often mentioned as being a forerunner of *The Exorcist* and the demon-possession trend that peaked in cinemas during the mid-1970s. Leah, a young bride-to-be, is declared to be inhabited by a dybbuk when her veil is lifted during the ceremony, and all attempts at ridding her of the evil spirit fail. A climactic exorcism conducted by a holy man eventually forces out the entity, but the cleansed Leah rejects her intended groom and elects to spend eternity with the ghost of a young student, her true love, who had died unexpectedly during the play's first act.

Howell's BBC presentation of this material, adapted by the director from Henry Alsberg's translation of Ansky, and produced by Louis Marks, aired on BBC1 at 8.05 p.m. on Sunday February 24, 1980. The blurb in the *Radio Times* ran: "According to Jewish legend, a dybbuk is the wandering and anguished spirit of a dead person which takes possession of a living body in order to find a resting place. It can only be expelled by exorcism, but even this does not always work." This production only appears to have aired once, and unfortunately seems to be unavailable to view at present.

That online resource, the BBC Genome, reveals that a 1937 TV broadcast of "scenes from" Ansky's *The Dybbuk* (by the Habima Theatre from Tel-Aviv) was screened at 3.20pm on November 19. Almost inevitably, Rudolph Cartier produced a version, aired at 8.30 on October 21, 1952 starring Yvonne Mitchell. As for radio, the BBC's Third Programme presented *Il Dibuk*, Lodovico Rocca's opera based on the story, on October 30, 1953; while Radio 4 transmitted *The Dybbuk* in audio form on March 30, 1979, starring Angela Pleasence as Leah.
—Darrell Buxton

ARTEMIS 81

1981
D: Alastair Reid
W: David Rudkin
Starring: Hywel Bennett, Dinah Stabb, Dan O'Herlihy, Sting, Roland Curram

On a distant twin-sunned planet, angels Asrael (force of evil) and Helith (representing light and goodness) clash, with Asrael awakening vengeful Earth-mother Magog to wreak havoc on humanity. On a cross channel ferry, numerous passengers will come into possession of an artifact recalling the image of Magog, and once having landed, will commit suicide via various methods (drowning, immolation, asphyxiation).

Also traveling on the ferry are Gwen Meredith (Dinah Stabb) and celebrated musician/organist Albrecht von Drachenfels (O'Herlihy), both of whom will play a major part in the oncoming metaphysical war. Meanwhile, an emotionally impoverished, closeted gay writer (and friend of Gwen's) called Gideon Harlax sits at his typewriter and begins to tap out his latest novel of the paranormal. On the screen appear the characters "... ARTEMIS 8 .. 1.."

Artemis 81 was shown just once by the BBC on December 29, 1981 (and no, the title does not refer to the year it was made/screened), and eventually released on DVD in 2007. Directed by the late Alastair Reid and scripted by celebrated English playwright and screenwriter David Rudkin, it will be nigh impossible in a short review to get over the sheer complexity, visual *élan* and thematic depth of this staggering three-hour production, but if my comments encourage anyone reading to seek it out, job done! Don't be put off by the epic length, because it engrosses from the off, the eerie series of suicides prompting Gideon to begin research for his book, unaware that he will soon meet (and fall in love with) Helith, who literally decends from the sky in a helicopter to save Gideon after an accident near a cliff face. Throw into the mix numerous filmic references, Hitchcock's *Vertigo* being cleverly used, first via a lecturer friend of Gideon discussing it in his class, to Gideon having his own belltower moment with a hanging woman (a bravura set piece!), as well as his own "Jimmy Stewart/Kim Novak" episode, the camera encircling his embrace with Helith in a 360 degree movement. Watch also for the library scene, which showcases a very young Daniel Day-Lewis in one of his earliest roles, not to mention Ingrid Pitt as an alarming "Hitchcock Blonde!"

It has to be said in minor detriment that human beings do not talk the way all the characters do here, but Rudkin's dialogue is so "readable" and philosophical/poetic that I find it only takes a very short while to adjust to the literary artifice—which actually makes more sense when you watch it again; Gideon is a successful novelist, and as the very first shot is of him sitting at his desk and preparing to write, adjusting his glasses and appearing to concentrate intensely, one possible reading could be that everything you see stems from his typewritten endeavours rather than occurring for real. The whole piece is open to myriad interpretations.

Artemis 81 contains superb performances from the great Dan O'Herlihy as von Drachenfels—a haunted, powerful, larger than life figure—plus Dinah Stabb as Gideon's friend and confidante Gwen, a luminous turn from Sting as the beautiful Helith, Roland Curram as his dark alter-ego, and possibly a career best from the often underused Hywel Bennett as Gideon. There's no shortage of splendid set pieces too, particularly a powerful stretch when Gideon is briefly "returned" to witness an alternate view of the world, now a city of sickness and plague, people coughing up blood on doom-laden tram rides, smoke and death all around, a glimpse of what-might-be should evil prevail, and visually resembling a dark, Terry Gilliam-like delve into the void! Above all the wealth of ideas, and often arch but magnificent dialogue/pronouncements, gives *Artemis 81* the edge over lesser TV fantasy in intellectual terms. It eventually climaxes with an exciting, challenging finale in a church, and even finds time during its resolution for Gideon to break the fourth wall and speak to us, the audience—a moment that in some ways is more startling than a lot of the more outré elements.

If you didn't see this on TV all those years ago, do yourself a favor and hunt down the DVD, it repays multiple viewings. One sad fact to ponder is that in the current age of totally dumbed-down 21st century television, if David Rudkin were to present his exact same script to any broadcaster currently operating in the UK now, I guarantee it would be turned down flat for being too ambitious and confusing. Thankfully this unimpeachable work was made in a more tolerant and enlightened time. One to set alongside Rudkin's equally astounding TV play from the 1970s, *Penda's Fen*.
—Michael Wesley

THE CHELSEA MURDERS

1981
D: Derek Bennett
W: Jonathan Hales
Starring: Dave King, Christopher Bramwell, Miranda Bell, Michael Feast

ITV's popular *Armchair Thriller* had a brief but fondly-remembered run in the late 1970s and through 1980, showcasing episodic dramatizations of contemporary crime novels with occasional hints of the macabre or supernatural. Most renowned and fondly-recalled of the bunch were the *Armchair* versions of Antonia Fraser's "Quiet as a Nun" and Patricia Highsmith's "A Dog's Ransom" (that particular yarn being handled for telly by John Bowen, notably), but in total the show offered 12 tales adapted across four or more 25-minute instalments.

Only 11 of these were broadcast in their intended form, for *The Chelsea Murders* was filmed as a six-part series during 1979 and promptly shelved. It eventually appeared on British TV screens towards the end of December 1981, re-edited into a 104-minute feature without the *Armchair Thriller* banner attached. (The original individual episodes have since been issued as part of the Network label's DVD box set of the show.). Based on a book by Lionel Davidson, it centers upon a series of assaults and killings in London, with the initials of the victims corresponding to the initials of famous poets commemorated on English Heritage "blue plaques" attached to their historical former residences. Involved in the mix are a team of investigating coppers (entertainingly clichéd!), an ambitious female journalist, a local librarian and an arty group of experimental filmmakers desperate to find funding to complete their Ripperesque throwback silent movie. That production's cast sport outlandish costumes finished off with garish plastic masks, and the maniac at large is reported by witnesses as dressing in the same manner. A couple of murders have taken place before we join the story, and others follow, some depicted, some glossed over, some attempts even unsuccessful. The high point arrives midway with a shocking chloroform/cleaver attack and decapitation as the masked assailant forces their way into an innocent Dutch female student's room, in the show's most vicious and violent scene—worthy of an American slasher flick.

That whole "matching up of initials" concept comes over as somewhat forced, but bear in mind that even acknowledged prestige productions have similarly struggled with that kind of caper—*Exorcist III* and its plethora of Ks, for example—and that the *Psycho*-style authoritative info-dump we're treated to at the

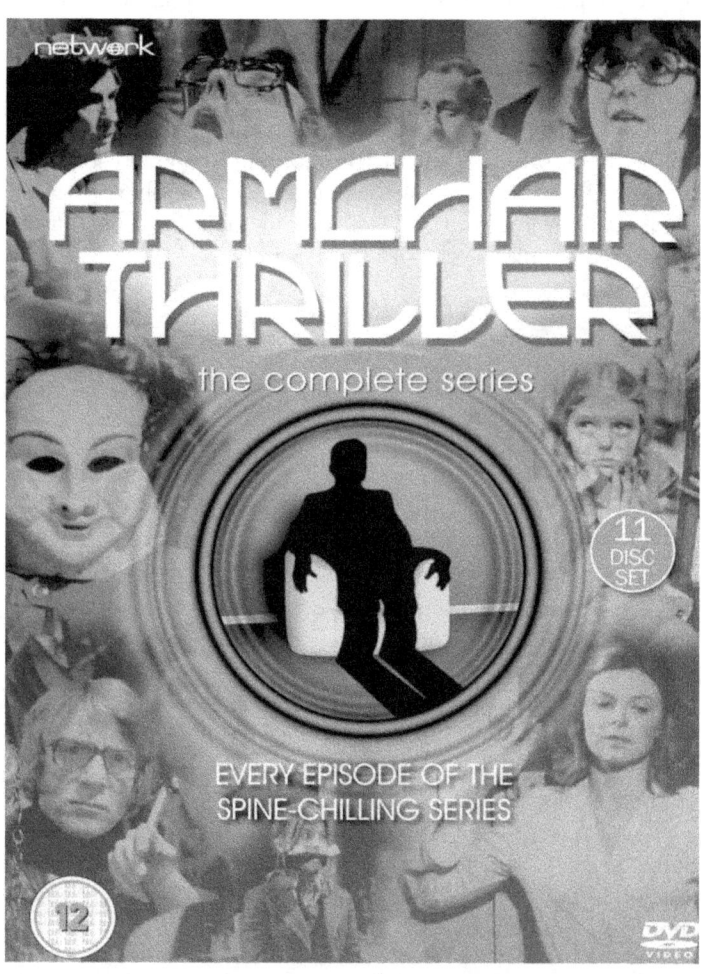

end here does go some way towards convincing the viewer about the pattern. Likewise, the poetry quotations and their connections to each method of murder just about achieve a *Theatre of Blood*-style balance, feeling justified although constantly on the verge of toppling into absurdity—one memorable moment has an investigating detective recognizing a line from *Matilda who Told Lies, and was Burned to Death*, and loudly announcing "that's Belloc's!", leading to a raised eyebrow and a "pardon?" from his superior officer.

Dependable and instantly recognizable character players pop up throughout to bolster the piece—it's always a pleasure to see the likes of Ishaq Bux, Robin Parkinson, or Lucy Griffiths doing what they do. As for the major players, Dave King is a joy as the grumpy Superintendent Warton, very much in the *Sweeney* tradition (dismissing Chelsea early on as being a "lousy area ... full of troublemakers. Bankers, politicians, judges, Mrs. Thatcher"), while David Gant's extraordinary Withnail-esque turn as chief suspect Frank, sobbing away about porridge or cackling heartily to a joke somewhere inside his own head, may not necessarily be acting at its finest but is certainly attention-grabbing.
—Darrell Buxton

LES CONTES D'HOFFMANN

1981
D: Brian Large
W: Jules Barbier, Michel Carré
Starring: Plácido Domingo, Luciana Serra, Agnes Baltsa

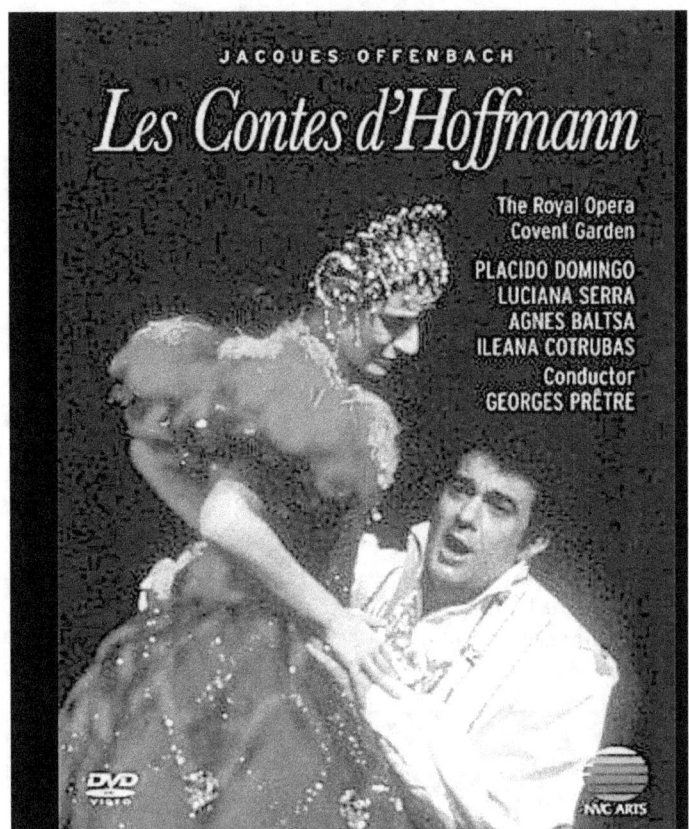

I have to confess a great fondness for the daft comedy romp *Honky Tonk Freeway*, released in 1981 and widely regarded as John Schlesinger's first major flop. After two decades as a director, during which time he had delivered *Midnight Cowboy*, *Marathon Man*, *Billy Liar*, *Darling*, and *Far from the Madding Crowd* among a genuine variety of critical and audience successes, Schlesinger's financial disaster here (a $2 million return on a budget more than 10 times the size) gave me a great time when I paid to see it at my local cinema, and had me chuckling once more when I rented it on home video a few months later.

Schlesinger's movie career never again reached his 1960s and '70s heights, but he found acclaim and awards coming his way via television, with *An Englishman Abroad* and *A Question of Attribution* both receiving BAFTAs. Never seen as a Renaissance man as such, perhaps he deserved a greater reputation along such lines, since he also worked in theater, directing for the Royal Shakespeare Company, as well as staging George Bernard Shaw's *Heartbreak House*; in 1992 he even directed a Party Political Broadcast that helped John Major to an unexpected election victory. He made several documentaries including *Terminus* (1961), and from 1980 he began to dabble in opera too.

Schlesinger's first venture into the world of tenors, sopranos, and "fat ladies singing" was a new production of Jacques Offenbach's *The Tales of Hoffmann*, performed at the Royal Opera House in Covent Garden. The venue's own website describes it as "sumptuous" and "a classic in the Royal Opera's repertory." And, in the same year as *Honky Tonk Freeway*, a live recording of *Les Contes d'Hoffmann* was captured on camera for broadcast by BBC2, and simultaneously on Radio 3.

Schlesinger received the producer credit, while Brian Large directed the telecast. Large is regarded by aficionados as one of the major figures in the world of televised opera, having worked in that capacity for the BBC from the mid-'60s to 1980 and then filming for the Royal Opera thereafter. *Les Contes d'Hoffmann*, right on the cusp of that career change, stars the globally renowned Spanish tenor Plácido Domingo as dark fantasy writer E.T.A. Hoffmann himself. Previously and unsurpassably filmed for cinema in 1951 by Michael Powell and Emeric Pressburger as *The Tales of Hoffmann*, the Offenbach work features a boozy tavern-set extended prologue, leading to three separate fantastical episodes each detailing the experiences of a particular target of the scribe's affections—Olympia (a mechanical dancing doll), Antonia (a suffering beauty who may die if she sings) and Giulietta (who attempts to steal the author's mirror reflection).

Large manages to keep this a lively and interesting two-and-a-half hours even for the uninitiated, with the somber, unobtrusive sets being effectively captured by his cameras, and the on-stage action being nicely framed (and not always merely head-on from the front stalls either). Even as something of a philistine when it comes to "the classics," I have to admit that Domingo's powerful performance and striking voice hit home, and it's also pleasing to find Robert Lloyd (later to star in Leslie Megahey's chilling *Duke Bluebeard's Castle*) in a featured role as Lindorf.

The *"Olympia"* episode, based on Hoffmann's *"Der Sandmann,"* features a heavily made-up Luciana Serra as the performing automaton, stitched into a detailed meringue frock and whirling about the stage, as do a handful of male robot minions. Her dismemberment at the climax (a stunning moment in the Archers' 1951 movie) is rather thrown away, though the image of Domingo desperately clutching at her faceless, *Westworld*-like mechanical "corpse" (while a laughing Lindorf's clockwork heart pops out on a spring!) is pretty indelible.

A sinister turn was taken by Schlesinger and his set/costume designers for act two, *"Giulietta,"* Siegmund Nimsgern's Satanic Dapetutto arrives done up like a Gothic glam rocker, and yes, he wants Hoffmann to be in his gang—or the writer's essence, at least, promising courtesan Giulietta (Agnes Baltsa) a jewel upon the capturing of his reflection. The lure of the glittering gemstone is a pull strong enough to entice her into the nefarious scheme, and Hoffmann's image is duly ensnared. Skulls, skeletal figures, crimson drapes, faceless assistants clad in dark robes, all set the tone for 35 minutes of operatic eeriness, also featuring a drifting gondola and offering the opportunity for Plácido to display his fencing skills!

We conclude with *"Antonia,"* the tale of a young woman who loves to sing but seems cursed to die, fading with every note she warbles. Her late mother had suffered a similar terrible affliction; can the domineering, vampiric figure of Dr. Miracle assist, or might he in fact be the root cause? Miracle is played by Nicola Ghiuselev; lank-haired, in chunky boots and a lengthy leather overcoat, he anticipates the "Goth" fashions of the mid-1980s while also having something of John Barrymore's 1920 Mr. Hyde about him.

John Schlesinger tried his hand at horror cinema in 1987 with the lukewarm *The Believers*. Avoid that one but do expand your horizons and give the splendid *Les Contes d'Hoffmann* a try.
—Darrell Buxton

THE SECRET OF SEAGULL ISLAND

1981
D: Nestore Ungaro
W: Jeremy Burnham, Augusto Caminito, Nestore Ungaro
Starring: Prunella Ransome, Nicky Henson, Jeremy Brett, Pamela Salem

Originally made as a five-hour mini-series, this Italian/British co-production is more frequently seen (where available) in its cut down film version. Obviously, the loss of several chunks of story leads to a few massive gaps of logic here and there, but the upshot is a pacy film that rattles along on its own sort of barmy momentum.

The plot as it stands sees young Brit abroad Barbara Carey searching Italy for her lost blind sister. With worrying tales circulating about young girls turning up murdered, she enlists the help of a nice young man from the British consulate to find out just what is going on. Their investigations lead them to l'isola del gabbiano (the titular Seagull Island) and its suspicious inhabitants, notably "archaeologist, anthropologist, collector" David Malcolm. Strange things are afoot, and before you know it our heroes are engaged in a desperate fight for their lives.

There are moments of genuine excellence within the film, scenes comparable to examples from other highly regarded Italian works of the 1980s such as Dario Argento's *Tenebrae*. The most affecting and visually impressive image is that of an eyeless body weighted down to the ocean floor. This vision is perhaps all the more powerful because of the choppy editing: among all the 1970s-style chase sequences and terrible swimwear, suddenly there appears this moment of vivid horror, beautifully filmed, all the stronger for its incongruity with the lack of outright shock effect elsewhere in the picture. Other memorable moments include a blind woman throwing herself to her death at the sound of seagulls played on tape, and an attack on a diver with depth charges. Indeed, the below-surface shots throughout are top notch, betraying the fact that director Nestore Ungaro was better known as an underwater photographer.

On the acting front, *Seagull Island* contains a surprising amount of talent for such a B-picture. Taking the lead with wide-eyed determination is Prunella Ransome, whose appearances in this and Spanish picture *¿Quién Puede Matar a un Niño?* (*Would You Kill a Child?*) are both incredibly well judged and underrated. She is ably supported by Nicky Henson as her confidante and guide. Despite his appalling fashion sense, Henson makes for a charming hero (quickly picking up "James Bond" as a nickname), and the two share an engaging chemistry. Leading them to the island is Jeremy Brett as Malcolm, who rides the knife-edge between intensity and pastiche with aplomb. When they get to the charmingly named location they find none other than Pamela Salem, bringing an incredible sheen of class to her tiny role as Malcolm's sister, imbuing their exchanges with depth and meaning (quite what the meaning is remains unclear, but that isn't her fault.) The quality of the cast helps to maintain the British feel among the spaghetti horror hi-jinks.

Due to the film's truncation, the story as it stands today is rather thin and nonsensical. But this is a vintage-era Italian production, and as such the fact that it is a case of style over substance should not be seen as a minus. For despite its shortcomings this certainly is a stylish exercise, with echoes of both the high fashion horror of Dario Argento and the classical Mario Bava whodunits. Perhaps, in the end, the "secret" of Seagull Island is something of a letdown, but the journey to its discovery is so enjoyably daft and well executed that you will not be disappointed.
—Martin Parsons

THE HUNCHBACK OF NOTRE DAME

1982
D: Michael Tuchner
W: John Gay
Starring: Anthony Hopkins, Lesley-Anne Down, David Suchet, Derek Jacobi, Robert Powell, John Gielgud

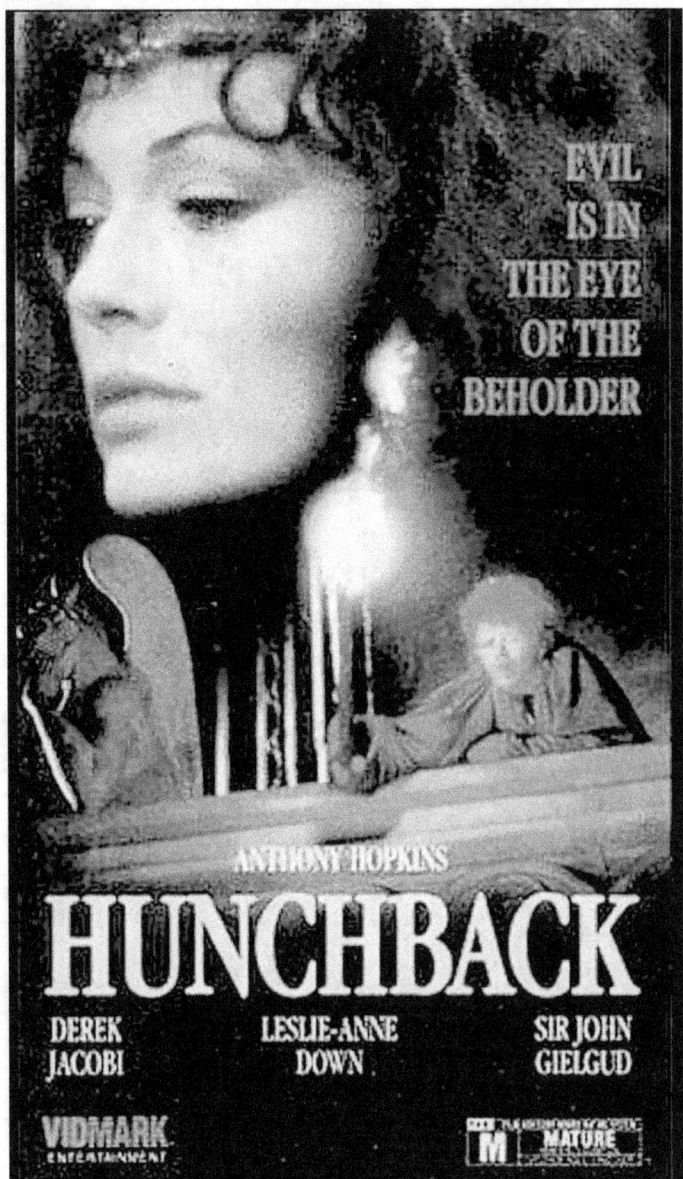

The umpteenth remake of Victor Hugo's classic novel of romance, despair and campanology. This one, a TV movie shot at Pinewood, sticks pretty closely to the book, only veering off to give us an obligatory happy ending. It's strange to think how many classical works are better known through the additions and revisions of subsequent generations. Sometimes there's so much tinkering that experiencing the original story, free from any amendment, can come as quite a shock.

There are visual echoes of previous versions here, with some scenes, like the candidates putting themselves forward for King of Fools, copied exactly.

It has a starry cast headed by Anthony Hopkins giving a fine performance as Quasimodo, almost unrecognizable underneath masses of make-up and a 1980s mullet. As in Disney's later animated version, the hunchback seems sympathetic rather than hideous here. There are echoes of Charles Laughton's vintage 1939 portrayal, but Hopkins' take is more carefree and less introspective. He manages a fine balance, not letting the characterization get out of control and go over-the-top. Initially almost monosyllabic, he becomes quite garrulous once he gets Esmeralda to himself.

The real star of the show is Derek Jacobi, a class act, as the troubled, obsessive Frollo. He is a villain but manages to invest the character with humanity. His hopeless attempts to romance Esmeralda reveal what a tortured individual Frollo is, torn between his calling and uncontrollable passion for the Gypsy girl. The inner tension boils to the surface when Esmeralda runs out on him, underscoring his command for Quasimodo to "Bring ... her ... back!" Every move is like an acting masterclass—his stunned, "What ... ?" when he learns that the object of his desire is "married" to Pierre is wonderful. His hesitant pondering on the nature of the couple's sexual relationship is neatly underlined by Jacobi dipping his quill pen into an inkpot.

Lesley-Anne Down (familiar to a generation of TV viewers from Upstairs, Downstairs) is a pretty forgettable Esmeralda. She doesn't exude much sensuality and seems careworn. Her dancing is unenticing, and it defies belief that she could make a living from such shuffling about. The weakness of her performance is especially enhanced when sharing the screen with Jacobi—in one scene he's acting her off the screen while she merely pouts and cries. Gerry Sundquist is handsome but limp as Pierre Gringoire. Maybe he should have swapped roles with Robert Powell, miscast as the self centered Phoebus, focus of Esmeralda's adoration.

The supporting cast is full of recognizable faces. David Suchet is Clopin Trouillefou, King of Beggars. A brilliant actor—this role came a few years before Poirot, which would make his name and define his career. It is amazing to contrast these two totally different performances. Tim Pigott-Smith, soon to play the oily Captain Merrick in The Jewel in the Crown, appears as Frollo's assistant, the equally oily Philippe. There are also cameos from Nigel Hawthorne and Sir John Gielgud as merciless Inquisitors, not to mention future EastEnders Pam St. Clement ("Pat Butcher") and June Brown ("Dot Cotton") playing two women in the cathedral gossiping over the baby Quasi.
—Gerald Lea

RUDDIGORE

1982
D: Barrie Gavin
W: W. S. Gilbert
Starring: Vincent Price, Keith Michell, Sandra Dugdale, John Treleaven

Brent Walker's 1982 filmed-for-television production of *Ruddigore* (or to give it the full onscreen title *Gilbert & Sullivan's Ruddigore or The Witch's Curse*), starring American horror legend Vincent Price and BBC TV's favorite King Henry the Eighth, Australian Keith Michell, is a gleeful send up of the Victorian school of barnstorming, penny dreadful melodramas, recounting the tragi-comic story of the Murgatroyds, Baronets of Ruddigore, in Cornwall, who have been cursed by a witch to commit a crime every day of their lives or else suffer an untimely and excruciatingly painful death. Said malediction has been passed on down several generations and now resides with Sir Despard Murgatroyd—played by Price.

The production, filmed at Shepperton Studios, is divided into two acts, the second of which is set almost entirely in the classic Gothic horror milieu of Ruddigore Castle, a gloomy stone fortress atop a barren mount, bedecked with cobwebs and replete with leering gargoyles, ancient suits of armor, human skulls and the indispensable glittering candles, secret passages and, of particular relevance in this case, somber portraits of generations of villainous aristocratic ancestors.

Despite receiving mainly negative contemporary and latter day reviews (several deviations from the source material seeming to be at the root of the bad notices), it really is a splendidly entertaining adaptation of one of the musical duo's "minor" operettas—and equally a joy to behold Price relishing the chance to spoof the "tormented aristocrat" parts which had formed a staple of his screen work (mainly through his roles in A.I.P.'s Roger Corman-directed Poe cycle). Although his singing is rather rudimentary, it is perfectly serviceable, and well suited to tricksy lyrics such as, "Avoid an existence of crime, or you'll be as ugly as I'm."

His next assignment, also filmed in the UK the same year, *House of the Long Shadows*, along with the earlier *The Monster Club*, are the only substantial feature-length horror performances given by Price in the 1980s, making his participation in *Ruddigore* a doubly welcome treat.

Mezzo-soprano Ann Howard's Mad Meg is a hoot, by turns batty and beguiling, and principal soprano Sandra Dugdale portrays the lead female character, Rose Maybud, as suitably sweet but not especially discriminating. Dugdale possesses an impressive singing voice, while the way she plays the somewhat dotty damsel sometimes brings to mind Angela Douglas in the *Carry Ons*. Cornish-born tenor John Treleaven is terrific as the not-as-simple-as-he-looks sailor Richard Dauntless, and the bridesmaids of the chorus are both pretty and vivacious.

The sets are very well realized, evoking the Victorian village, Cornish seaport and gothic castle/graveyard with economy and creativity. Indeed, the latter are highly reminiscent of the fairy story feel of the studio-bound exteriors that Hammer Films sometimes favored over their customary Black Park location shoots. The opening credits sequence, comprising a leisurely concatenation of panning shots through the overgrown cemetery with its fog enshrouded gravestones, sinister crypt and imposing mortuary effigies could well have been appropriated from one of Hammer's more atmospheric gothic outings.

The direction is remarkably fluid for a filmed operetta—the work of former film editor and BBC music program specialist Barrie Gavin. The obvious enthusiasm which the whole cast and crew bring to the production results in a fast moving, uplifting, amusing and thoroughly enjoyable two hours of solid entertainment. One of the highlights is undoubtedly the quick-fire patter ditty "It Really Doesn't Matter" (later added by Joseph Papp to his 1980 Central Park production of *The Pirates of Penzance*) sung with great panache by Price, Howard and Michell.

Ruddigore manages to be far wittier—and more fun—than many of the films that similarly set out to spoof the Gothic genre such as *Dance of the Vampires* or the Frankie Howerd vehicle *The House in Nightmare Park*. As a parody of Victorian melodrama it comes across as an even more over-the-top version of Tod Slaughter's penny dreadful, moustache-twirling, potboilers such as *Maria Marten* or *Crimes at the Dark House*, with added humor

and musical numbers. And if that's not sufficient recommendation, what is?
—Mike Hodges

THE BAD SISTER

1983
D: Laura Mulvey, Peter Wollen
W: Peter Wollen
Starring: Dawn Archibald, Kevin McNally, Matyelok Gibbs, Marty Cruikshank

Of all the events to stir up the British media during the 1980s, the emergence of Channel 4 in late 1982 caused more impact and controversy than most. In *An American Werewolf in London*, visiting Hollywood wag John Landis gleefully sent up the deficiencies of our television in the scene where David Naughton idles away an afternoon, at one point turning on the tube to discover that early 1980s England has access to a mere three TV channels, and that the available selection is a trade test pattern, a saucy ad for the *News of the World*, and a darts match.

The introduction of a fourth channel had been mulled over for many years, and the 1980 Broadcasting Act set operations in motion for the establishment of a new commercial outlet to rival the by-now firmly rooted ITV. Although the revenue model was similarly based in attracting funds from advertisers, the program output of the new Channel 4 was to prove markedly different from its competition. Early successes included *The Comic Strip Presents....*, a showcase for the best of the burgeoning "alternative comedy" scene to display their talents under the guiding hand of Peter Richardson; afternoon brain-teasing words-and-numbers puzzle *Countdown*, an enduring hit to this day; and the Australian import *The Paul Hogan Show*, which proved that if lowbrow comedy was funny enough, it was "art" and therefore deemed acceptable as a component of this brave new venture.

Our home film industry seemed to die at the very moment a buoyant Colin Welland proclaimed: "The British are coming!" during the 1982 Academy Awards. With investment in UK cinema haemorrhaging, Channel 4 stepped in to fund a string of experimental and/or low-budget productions designed for airing on the small screen and for brief runs in arthouse cinemas. Neil Jordan's *Angel*, Michael Apted's *P'tang, Yang, Kipperbang*, Stephen Frears' *Walter* and above all Peter Greenaway's striking exercise, *The Draughtsman's Contract*, caught the attention of many, and for one brief flicker it seemed Welland's promised tidal wave might be surging in from a rather unexpected direction after all.

Channel 4 failed to sustain the initial success of its film program, and it was probably works such as *The Bad Sister* that helped put paid to the endeavor. For each populist attention-grabber or surprise highbrow crossover, there was an incomprehensible, over-indulgent, arty ramble by some pseud or other. *The Bad Sister* aired on Channel 4 in February 1983, was to my knowledge never repeated, and seems rather elusive all these years on, with only stray clips, stills, or comments to be found on-line. Based on Emma Tennant's novel, the shot-on-videotape feature has two program-makers discussing their dramatization of a double murder case in which a Scotsman named Dalzell and his daughter Ishbel have been killed, possibly by a second (illegitimate) daughter, Jane. Following much pretentiousness, cutting between the TV producers and the collected interview footage, home movies, photos etc. they are assembling and editing, we see a flashback of Dalzell's murder (a hammer to the eye socket), committed in tandem by Jane and her mother, both working as domestic servants and driven to the grim act following a disagreement over a wages deduction. Elements of classic film noir, including "good/evil sibling" type movies, are mixed with familiar horror tropes (exhumation, vague suggestions of vampirism, traded souls) but all done in such a pompous, self-important way that any casual viewer would soon consider switching to one of the UK's other three television channels, in the hope that *Starsky & Hutch* or the football highlights might be on offer as a more entertaining alternative. Soft Machine's Mike Ratledge and Karl Jenkins provided the soundtrack for *The Bad Sister*, the unavailability of which is probably of rather greater concern than the scarcity of the movie itself.
—Darrell Buxton

THE CASE OF THE FRIGHTENED LADY

1983
D: Christopher Menaul
W: Victor Pemberton
Starring: Virginia McKenna, Warren Clarke, Tim Woodward

"This place is like a mausoleum.
It stinks of death out there."

The Lebanon family has a problem or two. Lady Lebanon is desperate to live to see the continuation of the family line, her chinless wonder of a son may harbor murky secrets about his past in India, their heavy-handed brusque American servants don't exactly fit the *Upstairs, Downstairs/Downton Abbey* stereotype, and there's the small matter of a traditional locked room somewhere within this orthodox old dark manor house. To cap it all, a series of strangulation murders are plaguing the surrounding woodland area.

The unique style of death dished out by the Thugee in 19th century India has featured in many movies varying from Hammer's heated *The Stranglers of Bombay* to Ismail Merchant and Nicholas Meyer's colonial *Boy's Own* take on the theme in *The Deceivers*. Falling somewhere in between, both in terms of chronology and content, the BBC's 74-minute TV adaptation of Edgar Wallace's stage play *Case of the Frightened Lady* adds to the screen roster of Thugee terror, and follows two earlier UK cinematic attempts at the Wallace warhorse (directed by T. Hayes Hunter in 1932 and George King in 1940), plus the inevitable German krimi *Das Indische Tuch/The Indian Scarf* (Alfred Vohrer 1963). It wasn't even the play's small-screen debut, since the BBC had already televised a version as early as July 1938.

Director Christopher Menaul's take on the material remains rather faithful to the Wallace original, perhaps surprising at a time when British television was enjoying a particularly daring and experimental period in the wake of Channel 4's arrival into our living rooms. This was sturdy stuff, overly talky and largely played out on a main interior set with the occasional shift to another part of the house or an excursion into the local forest. The stagy nature of the production makes it appear a little sluggish in comparison to early 1980s telly's more vibrant and groundbreaking fare, but it's an enjoyable enough romp through Wallace's dialogue and contains surprises throughout, not to mention a few frissons towards its climax. Virginia McKenna is well cast as Lady Lebanon, initially a clichéd matriarchal cut-glass faded aristo, but with the actress finding depth within the character as her anxieties and troubles begin to gradually reveal themselves. Warren Clarke, ever welcome, steals the show as investigating detective superintendent Tanner—channeling John Thaw's "Jack Regan" somewhat, as did many TV cops of the era, while also looking forward to his mid-'90s role as the top-billed half of *Dalziel and Pascoe*. Clarke's banter with uniformed subordinate Totty (William Maxwell, giving as good as he gets) is an undoubted highlight. It all livens up no end in the closing 10 minutes, the twists proving effective despite their familiarity from earlier versions and, it has to be said, from plenty of similar novels, plays, and movies. This would have all seemed rather staid and dull in 1983, but the passage of time allows us to view *The Case of the Frightened Lady* on its own merits today, and it stands as a solid piece of quality filler TV drama.
—Darrell Buxton

THE HOUND OF THE BASKERVILLES

1983
D: Douglas Hickox
W: Charles Edward Pogue
Starring: Ian Richardson, Donald Churchill, Denholm Elliott, Martin Shaw, Nicholas Clay, Glynis Barber, Connie Booth, Brian Blessed

An ancient curse; a spectral hound; mysterious deaths; an escaped murderer; set on a deadly, mist shrouded moor. The elements of a murder mystery and supernatural thriller, present and correct.

Not only is this the most famous case of Sherlock Holmes, it is also the most cinematic and melodramatic of all the Holmes' tales. For all the ingenuity of the Conan Doyle yarns, most are set after the crime has taken place—in this piece Holmes enters as the young Baskerville arrives from the States and the crime is building again as the threat to his life grows.

There are several flaws in *The Hound of the Baskervilles*, that don't hamper the book but which are magnified in the visual telling. Holmes is absent for much of the story, as well as onscreen, and of course there's the issue of the dog. On the page this isn't a problem but on film it really shows.

With Holmes missing for so much of the running time, it all depends on Watson. Richardson is a charming Holmes, with a delightful smile that seems to show how much fun he finds the investigative process, amusing him no end. His Holmes is in the Basil Rathbone mould—sadly Churchill's Watson is in the Nigel Bruce style. A more bumbling Watson than in the stories, but a lot less tolerant and arrogant to boot. He comes across as a Colonel Blimp character—he even harrumphs. As Watson takes up such a large part of the middle section it weakens the film.

The dog causes a quandary in two ways: First, its attacks are not consistent. In the initial attack, the hound does not actually

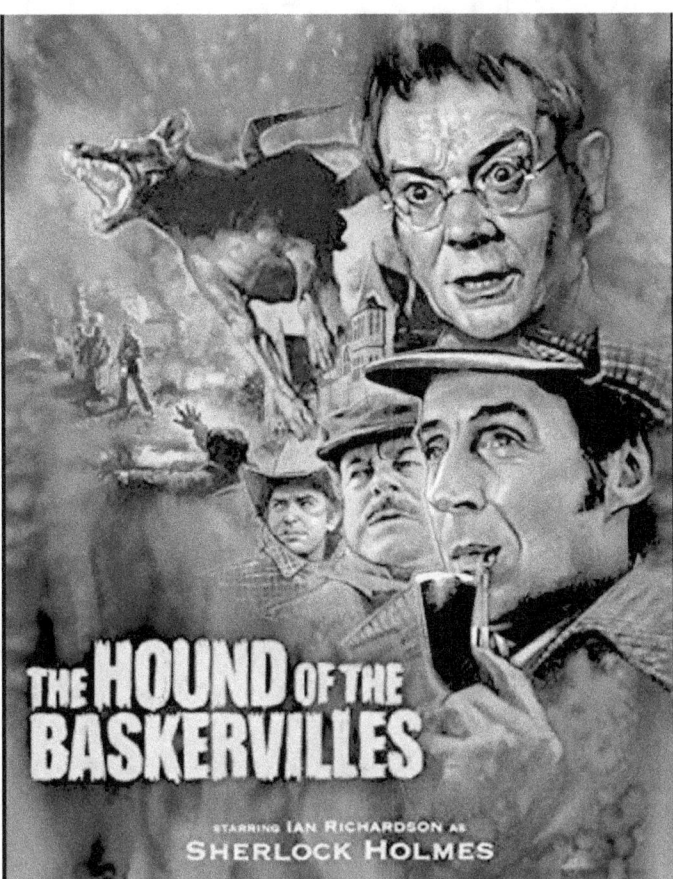

assault Sir Charles Baskerville but is frightening enough to cause his death, while later encounters with victims do see emergent savagery. The second problem is simply the dog itself—as noted, a creature that instills terror. When seen, however, it is never as fearsome as everyone describes it (a giant spectral beast that glows in the dark), and so causes an anticlimax. Sadly, this is true in all the screen versions of the tale. We are so used to seeing dogs of all types as pets that even wolves do not seem to hold as much dread as they ought.

The film itself looks fine on the whole and is set in the original period, although some of the sets give testament to its TV film origins, seeming poky and a little on the inexpensive side. Note that the title sequence also includes parts of its companion piece *The Sign of Four*, lending to the suggestion that this has small-screen ambitions rather than stand-alone grandeur at heart. Hickox presents some excellent shots and thankfully does not film things in the flat way television often demands. The image of Dr. Mortimer as he goes to read the Baskerville manuscript with Holmes and Watson at Baker Street is a tad cramped, but shows an eye for depth and a director trying to create interestingly composed scenes.

The strength of the film is in the cast, a strong roster of wonderful British character actors. Standouts are Ronald Lacey as Lestrade who even in his brief part displays different facets of the Inspector, Eleanor Bron and Edward Judd as the mysterious and creepy servants, and Brian Blessed who captures both the belligerent and vulnerable sides of the artist he plays.

In all this is a good version of an old favorite tale with a splendid, strong British cast—if you like Basil Rathbone-style Holmes you'll find plenty to enjoy here.
—Wayne Mook

THE MAD DEATH

1983
D: Robert Young
W: Sean Hignett
Starring: Robert Heffer, Barbara Kellerman, Richard Morant

Originally screened in three parts in 1981, Sean Hignett's adaptation of Nigel Slater's novel (not, I'm assuming, the TV chef) is an odd mix of cozy catastrophe science fiction (in the BBC tradition of *Survivors* and *Day of the Triffids*), public information film and melodrama. For a generation of 1980s teenagers, the series represents an example from a particularly bleak period for British broadcast TV containing as it did *Threads*, *Boys from the Black Stuff*, *A Very British Coup* and, for me at least, most episodes of *World in Action*. Revisiting the mini-series in the present day is an instructive example of the emotional power of memory—far from being the mix of *Panorama* and Guy N. Smith novel I vaguely remembered it to be, *The Mad Death* is instead a talky, rather dull melodrama with occasional flashes of "PG"-rated horror.

For those unfamiliar (or who had forgotten in the intervening decades), *The Mad Death* follows an attempt by the British government to stem the spread of rabies, introduced when a French woman smuggles her cat through customs and it meets its Waterloo at the hands of a Scottish fox. Before long, Ed Bishop is having aquatic-themed hallucinations, half of Scotland is going Manson Family on their own pets and the Army are out in the fields blasting away at anything with more than two legs.

The Mad Death makes uncomfortable viewing for animal lovers, and there are a few sequences that are effectively chilling, but with much of the running time taken up with concerned-looking scientists spouting great leaden chunks of exposition to each other, it quickly starts to drag. Much was made on first broadcast of the scientific accuracy of *The Mad Death*, but I remain unconvinced—after all, rabies occurs on mainland Europe and we don't see French commandos out in the Dordogne undertaking the Pedigree Chum equivalent of *The Purge*. As a young conservation officer in the 1990s I had a copy of our local rabies plan sat on the shelf gathering dust, and while it certainly contained provisions for the control of foxes and badgers, it was hardly on the scale portrayed in *The Mad Death*. For all the fuss made of its army of scientific advisors, *The Mad Death* is essentially horror melodrama and as such, it's rather less effective than contemporary mini-series such as *Quatermass* (1979) or *The Nightmare Man* (1981), which take much pulpier material and somehow manage to make it more mature and affecting. It stands to reason that, as a nation of animal lovers, British viewers will be affected when a farmer takes a shotgun to his dog, or when pets are routinely rounded up, and while these scenes are undoubtedly upsetting they also feel like cheap shots. The sense that *The Mad Death* is more sensationalist than serious is underlined by some distinctly underwhelming performances from familiar square jawed TV actors that wouldn't look out-of-place in an episode of *Survivors*. There's also a very dated sense of class snobbery at play under the surface, with the working classes largely portrayed as stupid, cruel or unable to help themselves—this is another hangover from the tradition of popular British post-war dystopian science fiction that is the real progenitor of *The Mad Death*, regardless of how many scientific advisor credits appear at the end. If you don't believe me, pick up a copy of John Christopher's *Pendulum* or John Wyndham's *The Kraken Wakes* and spot the similarities.

The Mad Death was repeated once in 1985 by the BBC before an edited version was released on home video in the mid-1980s. A DVD containing the three original episodes eventually saw release via Simply Media in 2018. I haven't seen the movie version (this review is taken from the mini-series) as it's extremely difficult to track down—if it cuts down on the endless scenes of scientists gassing about death rates and quarantine zones then it might at least move a bit quicker than the TV series does. Not having seen the edited VHS release, it's difficult to compare the qualities of the two versions; however, *The Mad Death* is probably too much of a lost cause to be saved even by brutal editing, and for my generation is probably best left as a disturbing memory.
—Neil Pike

FRANKENSTEIN

1984
D: James Ormerod
W: Victor Gialanella
Starring: Robert Powell, David Warner, Carrie Fisher, John Gielgud

Televised on December 27, 1984, this made-for-television film from Yorkshire TV was part of my Christmas chiller choice as a child in front of the telly. Like the Mary Shelley novel, it

***Frankenstein* German DVD**

tells the story of a brilliant scientist, bent on creating life, but whose success is met with tragedy. Robert Powell's portrayal of Victor Frankenstein is flawless, reminding me of Peter Cushing's overzealous version in *The Curse of Frankenstein* (1956)—Powell not only shares his dark secret with his childhood friend, Henry Clervell (Michael Cochrane), but also asks for his scientific help.

A veteran of Brian Clemens' *Thriller*, director James Ormerod's version of this familiar material is first rate, while not entirely sticking precisely to the book. For example, in Shelley, Henry has no interest in science, but instead possesses great morals that contradict Frankenstein's agenda. In Victor Gialanella's teleplay he is seen to be a fellow student of medicine. Purists may protest, yet it works well as part of the narrative, and I don't think that the experiment as presented here would have been successful without Henry's aid. Previously, Gialanella wrote the Broadway stage play (1981), with John Carradine as DeLacey—the blind hermit.

The film begins with the memorable Yorkshire TV ident, before taking us to the scene of two robbers, one of them played by Edward Judd (*The Day the Earth Caught Fire*), who plunders corpses for their client, taking us right back to another Peter Cushing film, *Frankenstein and the Monster from Hell* (1973), with its stunning *mise-en-scene* that encapsulates the 1970s British Gothic look.

The score by Alan Parker is chilling and atmospheric. The composer later went on to write music for another British horror flick, *American Gothic* (1987). Special make-up effects (courtesy Jim Gillespie) on the creature are fittingly gruesome, and successful in demonstrating a face of the creature's own tortured soul.

David Warner plays the rather sympathetic creature, who, after losing his educator/father figure (DeLacey), longs for companionship. But the moment he meets his creator, he is instantly rejected, after Victor learns that he's accountable for the accidental deaths of his youngest brother, William (Graham McGrath) and Henry's inamorata, Justine Moritz (Susan Wooldridge).

Warner gives an excellent performance, as does Carrie Fisher, in her post-*Return of the Jedi* (1983) role, playing Victor's love interest, Elizabeth Lavenza, who later meets her doom on her wedding day. But it's Sir John Gielgud who steals the show as DeLacey, the only person who sympathizes with the creature's unhappiness and offers him shelter.

As the story progresses, the protagonist begins to lose his close ones and later spirals downward to loneliness, much like his creation. The theme covers not merely alienation, but also suggests how we should take full responsibility for our own doing, with the title character's own dangerous pursuit of knowledge at the heart of this adaptation.

Filmed entirely in North Yorkshire at Ripley Castle and Rudding Park Estate, with a stellar cast, and special effects kept to a minimum, this film is largely forgotten and deserves a re-release for fans of retro British Gothic. Like an earlier celebrated small-screen version, Jack Smight's *Frankenstein–The True Story* (1973), this is one of the best takes on Mary Shelley's classic novel.
—Jason D. Brawn

• • •

Victor Gialanella's 1981 stage adaptation of *Frankenstein* is one of the great legendary Broadway flops, famously (or, rather, infamously) opening and closing on the same night. It was the recipient of some spectacularly harsh reviews, which makes one wonder how and why it was to fetch up on British television a few short years later.

Scripted from his own play by Gialanella, *Frankenstein* was presented by Yorkshire Television when the UK's regional TV stations were still free to offer up independent drama. A much truncated, pared-back and concertinaed version of Mary Shelley's Promethean opus of 1818, it represents an odd and unwieldy entry into the horror sub-genre of Frankensteinian fare.

The cast is impressive. Robert Powell, having dallied with a film career in *Asylum*, *The Asphyx*, *The Thirty-Nine Steps* and *The Survivor*, was able to effect a comfortable segue into principal roles on television. And after a sensational star-making performance as the titular *Jesus of Nazareth* what self-respecting leading man would turn up the chance to play Mary Shelley's misunderstood Man/God? If he lacks the single-minded drive and manic energy of Peter Cushing (and his 1980s bouffant hairdo is a glaring error) then Powell at least plays Victor straight, making the most of a limited (and limiting) script.

There is little to do for Carrie Fisher, a very contemporary transatlantic heroine clearly out of place in period garb. She shares top billing with Powell. Hiring Princess Leia herself was clearly a producer's dream—the commercial possibilities were endless, the reality rather less sparkling. Thus the magic of the ensemble comes via the inclusion of John Gielgud, empathetic and gentle as the blind hermit, DeLacey, and killed off after contributing an extended cameo; Edward Judd as grasping grave robber, Metz; Terence Alexander as Victor's blinkered father and, top of the heap, David Warner as the monster. For this thing from the grave is truly monstrous, but also a pitiful manifestation of man's hubris and ego. His meeting with Frankenstein, in which he confesses to the accidental killing of a child, is the film's emotional pinnacle and points to the obvious stage origins of the piece. As led by Warner, a theater veteran of power and grace, it lifts the film, albeit momentarily, above the merely mediocre.

There are some niggling plot holes, not least when Frankenstein's creation stumbles off into the night, leaving his formerly preoccupied creator to focus on his previously abandoned ladylove. And there is a smattering of Hammer flourishes, including the use of place names such as Carlsbad, an ever-present element in any number of Cushing/Lee adventures.

Shot on location in Yorkshire—Ripley Castle provides the backdrop for Frankenstein's stately pile—it is confined to a limited (and patently English) landscape that underlines a beggarly budget. Clearly the hard cash was lavished on Powell, Fisher, Warner, Gielgud and company, with costumes provided in-house just as locations were to be conveniently found on the studio's doorstep.

Carrie Fisher as Elizabeth in *Frankenstein*

Yet it has merit as a filmed record of an aborted production, with original theater director Tom Moore receiving a giveaway credit. What it lacks in depth it makes up for in the fragmentary glimpses of magic witnessed in the final reel: the death of Elizabeth (Fisher), the grief of Henry Clervell (Michael Cochrane) and the creature's desperate yearning for humanity ("Why did you not give me a soul?" he wails.). But it's not enough to buoy up an anorexic script and the film misses the overtly Gothic manifestations of the Universal and Hammer series.

Frankenstein rattles along to its unsatisfactory denouement—Victor's lab burns, conveniently consuming father and bastard child following an all-too-brief discussion on the Bible, creation and the Almighty—in less than 80 brisk minutes. In that time, we have witnessed an unnatural birth, the consummation of a long-held dream, multiple deaths and the dawning realization from Victor and his creature that loneliness is arguably life's ultimate curse.

The entire production feels undercooked, as if whole sections of the script were tossed away due to budgetary restraints. In truth the money was probably never there, forcing workhorse director James Ormerod, active in TV since the late 1950s, to cobble together what he could. If *Frankenstein* clomps along in the leaden footprints of its theater outing as a TV flop, then it is an honorable one.
—Tony Earnshaw

THE MASKS OF DEATH

1984
D: Roy Ward Baker
W: Anthony Hinds, N.J. Crisp
Starring: Peter Cushing, John Mills, Anne Baxter, Ray Milland, Anton Diffring, Gordon Jackson, Susan Penhaligon

Everything about *The Masks of Death* screamed "Noooooooo!" Yet, against the odds, it emerged as a viable and plausible entry in the ever-expanding canon of Sherlock Holmes pastiches.

It was 1984. The Channel 4 winter schedule was released and within it was a project that had the public and the press equally salivating and scratching their heads. The ingredients were impeccable. Returning to the role of the ultimate consulting detective was Peter Cushing. As Dr. Watson, enter John Mills. Hammer and Amicus veteran Roy Ward Baker was in the director's chair. And the remainder of the cast and crew was a phalanx of talent that collectively amounted to well over a century of filmmaking experience.

Few of the actors that had made their reputations playing Arthur Conan Doyle's creation actually succeeded with an authentic and accurate portrayal. Successive producers wrested the stories from their roots and amended and adapted to suit modern audiences. Even Jeremy Brett, arguably the purest of the modern purveyors of Holmes, saw the character evolve beyond the canon. And Peter Cushing suffered more than most.

From Hammer's sexed-up Byronic Holmes battling a monstrous, demonic dog amid a mist-shrouded Devonshire mire to the BBC's hurried, harried and deeply unsatisfying struggles with Victorian villains and 1960s TV budget cuts, Cushing had never had his moment in the smog. Suddenly, aged 71 and evidently frail (he had been diagnosed with prostate cancer and had lost a significant amount of weight that his thin frame could ill afford), he was back.

The Masks of Death, penned by N.J. Crisp, was at once an original piece and a loose adaptation of "His Last Bow." Cushing may well have seen something in Conan Doyle's title there—treating this as a last hurrah and possibly a final chance to crack a role that had been with him for 25 years. The story takes Holmes and Watson from London to a country park to investigate the disappearance of a European princeling. Holmes soon discovers that he has been duped and that a wily aristocrat, Graf

Italian poster for *The Masks of Death*

The Masks of Death starring Peter Cushing and John Mills

Udo Von Felseck (played with a Teutonic glint in the eye by the ever-reliable Anton Diffring) is at the heart of a nefarious plan to poison the British capital.

Producer Kevin Francis, the man who had launched Tyburn Films as a late rival to Hammer and Amicus in the mid-'70s, saw *The Masks of Death* as "a genuflection." The piece was grounded in Hammer-esque mood and atmosphere—a deliberate move that benefited from the tag team of Cushing and Mills, from Baker's steady and studied direction, and from an ensemble of superannuated players that nonetheless delivered gravitas and believability in spades. Alongside Diffring were Ray Milland, Gordon Jackson, Russell Hunter and, in a particularly pointless (but lovingly presented) cameo, Anne Baxter as Irene Adler.

Crisp soaked his script in period trappings. Of course, Cushing wears the deerstalker. He also potters along with a walking stick—a nod to his advanced years. But Cushing is also to be glimpsed as the even older Holmes, a testy nonagenarian reluctantly reminiscing about adventures of long ago as prodded by Watson.

The Masks of Death is alternatively gentle and plodding, nasty and forward thinking. Russell Hunter's hoarse warnings of nocturnal creatures roaming London's dark streets—"They had holes for eyes!"—preface the rolling clouds of mustard gas that would engulf British troops on the killing fields of the Somme. Cushing brings his customary discipline to Holmes's scurrying investigations and there is superb interplay between him and Mills, the latter introducing a no-nonsense aspect to a character too often (and mistakenly) played for easy laughs.

A modest budget is satisfactorily spent with studio sets and locations matched well and with intelligence. Crisp packs his screenplay with a sufficiently layered representation of classic and accessible Holmesian elements, allowing Cushing to immerse himself fully in a world that Hammer and the BBC had previously botched. There is genuine simpatico between Cushing and Mills, and between hero and villain as Holmes duels with Von Felseck. Even the introduction of "the woman," potentially the clunkiest aspect, is carried off with confidence.

The film's primary flaw is Cushing himself. The actor is superlative, channeling all his accumulated knowledge of the character of Holmes, his era and milieu into a near-perfect portrayal. Yet the man is so patently, palpably feeble and delicate, so evidently older than his years, that his fragility almost sinks the production. Almost ... but not quite.
—Tony Earnshaw

NIGHT TRAIN TO MURDER

1984
D: Joseph McGrath
W: Eric Morecambe, Ernie Wise, Joseph McGrath
Starring: Eric Morecambe, Ernie Wise, Margaret Courtenay, Fulton Mackay, Pamela Salem, Kenneth Haigh, Lysette Anthony

So, what exactly constitutes a "Christmas film"? It's a fair question. Does it have to be set at Christmas? No. Does it have to be something regularly shown on TV during that season? Possibly. It definitely helps if you, the viewer, first glimpsed it during that time of year—helped by some kind of innate

warmth, cozy yet eerie, aesthetically radiating and resonating through environs of twinkling lights, fir trees and ye olde gas lamps, and best viewed through a haze of port and mincemeat gluttony. That would certainly be fair criteria in my house.

Night Train to Murder, however, bears the dubious honor of being a film that easily ticks all those boxes, and has thus secured itself a special place in the hearts of some—while others (not that I'm one of them, I hasten to add) believe it scrapes several barrels and represents the career nadir of its stars. To cap it all, it commits the grievous sin of being a film initially made exclusively for television (always a stigma back in my day—"oh, it's one of those *TVM*s," my Mum was oft heard to mutter, vocally italicizing her disapproval before settling down to watch the movie in question anyway!), and is notorious principally because it represents Morecambe and Wise's last onscreen outing together before Eric's death not long afterwards. Plus, general public consensus tends to lean toward the belief that as final throws of the dice go, it really isn't very good.

Well, I won't bullshit you, chaps and chappesses, it definitely ain't no classic. Indeed, it's a strange, stilted feature, uneven, and laden with an anachronistic theme tune (over which the mirthsome twosome interject several slightly repetitive jokes) more redolent of a 1970s cop picture than the mid-'40s in which it is actually set. In fact, as either a horror movie or a thriller, the film's very existence seems anachronistic—its subject matter and style, as well its supporting cast (boasting bit parts from Britcom stalwart Frank Coda, former dollybird Penny Meredith and horror/SF/public information film veteran Edward Judd), all belonging somewhere between 1961 and 1975 rather than the Voorhees-addled early 1980s.

It's also one of the few movies I can think of which manages to seem both overlong and too short at once, often featuring jumpstarts, longueurs, padding and paucity all within the same scene. Yet somehow these quirks, idiosyncrasies and shortcomings make it all the more fascinating, as if its flawed nature were in some way a reflection of the pair's tumultuous friendship. And with its blend of scares and jokes, its country house setting (a staple of so many great thriller-chillers), and the requisite amount of antique furniture on show, I think it more or less qualifies as "atmospheric" if nothing else. Plotwise, it's no great deviation from the tried and tested Old Dark House formula—an elderly relative of Eric's dies, meaning several family members are summoned to hear the reading of the will, after which strange disappearances, unexplained sudden deaths and elaborate "accidents" abound, with secret panels, eyes behind paintings, clanking suits of armor and femme fatales (the pairing of Lysette Anthony and Pamela Salem in this case) aplenty—except that directorially, while he may have excelled at episodic television, McGrath is no James Whale or even William Castle.

Be fair, though, he probably wasn't asked to be—remember, *Night Train* is simply another vehicle for Eric and Ernie, so anyone expecting cinematic gold or Ealing-worthy genius is probably barking up the wrong tree. Ergo, when Morecambe's eligible, très glamourous niece (Anthony) is approached by Fulton Mackay, playing a family solicitor called, surprise surprise, "Mackay" (did he ever play anyone called anything else except in *Fraggle Rock*?) and asked to visit said mansion, the plot doesn't exactly thicken—in fact, it's pretty thin to begin with and reaches somewhat of a plateau 30 or so minutes in—but as homages go (in this case to a genre the duo must have been particularly fond of, hence their ongoing comedic usage of Peter Cushing throughout their series), it's pretty spot on. And, despite my earlier remarks about anachronism, there is just enough nastiness and grue, particularly in one scene involving blood dribbling out of an eyeball, and another which sees the hanging/impaling of yet another relative (Richard Vernon) on something sharp and pointy, to occasionally distract the viewer from the cosiness.

As expected, M & W play themselves all the way through—only this time it's 1946 and they're an ailing music hall act on their last legs and treading the boards on an endless circuit taking in the delights of Carlisle and Darlington. "Changing trains at Crewe" a lá Tod Slaughter himself, calling all pianists Ambrose or Geraldo and staying in a litany of down-at-heel hotels. They share a bed , clad in striped pyjamas, without appearing campy. Only this time their asexuality is made even stranger by the fact that Salem clearly wants Eric to give her one and isn't afraid to blatantly say so—and vice versa!

And you know what, though Morecambe's frailty is visible, and not all the gags work, when they do—look out for the faulty gramophone, and that old classic number "Charlie Chan, You're a Different Man (Since You Backed into the Electric Fan)"—they're hilarious. On the horror and suspense fronts, there are several sudden jolts and scares that would have given me the willies at a tender age. And that's to say nothing of a fiend in a mask so creepy he even frightens himself looking into a mirror, an eerie 6' 7" Karloffian butler (Roger Brierley) whose voice echoes for no apparent reason, a "man of a thousand faces" worthy of Lon Chaney, a truly surreal false reality gag involving the comedians relating the story of the death of the actor playing "Big Jim," and a supposedly haunted Scottish mansion (probably actually in Berkshire or Middlesex, but again, that's all part of the magic), all thrown in as a bonus.

In fact, sometimes, watching *Night Train to Murder* almost makes you feel as if you were conducting your very own search for a hidden inheritance, digging for treasure 'neath its unfathomable, half-TV, half-movie veneer—but if you take off your analytical head and commit yourself to the principle of sheer enjoyment (difficult in these cynical times I know, but give it a whirl), while retaining an eye and ear for the absurd, you're guaranteed to find something of interest, and the more you sit back and let its strangely detached atmosphere wash over you, the more of a uniquely dreamlike experience it becomes—possibly because by all laws of logic, such a film shouldn't exist, and you still can't quite comprehend that it does, in the same way this writer (as a teen in the 1980s) couldn't believe the amount of rare Beatles and Monty Python footage from the tail-ends of their careers that kept cropping up, or the unseen material inserted into the legendary BBC Moviedrome screening of *The Wicker Man*. Seriously, we're approaching that level of clandestine strangeness here—plus, if you're a Bonzo Dog Doo-Dah Band aficionado, or just a lover of vintage popular song, there's also a quite macabre rendition of "Little Sir Echo" to look forward to, though I won't tell you how it figures as part of the storyline. All I'll say is that the Bonzos' head honcho Viv Stanshall, if he happened to see it, would probably have chuckled ...

I shall also refrain from revealing the ending, disclosing the decidedly odd final few jokes, or throwing in a handful of the oblique references which make this a goldmine for culture-spotters. Frankly, I think I've gone into enough detail to alert you to the film's merits and warn you of its pitfalls (although I will add that for ironic incongruity, nothing quite matches watching two people, one soon to die and the other now also long-departed, singing the line "we're really glad to be alive" to an audience designed to look as if they're not even glad to be in the room ...).

If it is a Christmas film, it's quite an unconventional one, even within its own nostalgic paradigm, but on reflection, I like my festive season to be a strange, haunting and unclassifiable experience. All these years on, it's apparent that *Night Train to Murder*, while not particularly good, isn't all that bad either: There are a lot worse things you could watch at this time of year, most of them on television, and whatever its faults, it's probably the most offbeat, unpredictable, perplexing, and thus interesting, coda to any double act's career I can think of. Old chaps, your legacy remains safe and unsullied.
—Darius Drewe

RAINY DAY WOMEN

1984
D: Ben Bolt
W: David Pirie
Starring: Charles Dance, Cyril Cusack, Suzanne Bertish

One of the neglected masterpieces of British TV—Mark Lawson, *The Guardian* 2008.

"That summer, the countryside had suddenly become an unknown world ..."

David Pirie carved out a career in Gothic-tinged television during a period when such a notion had become rather unfashionable. The successful series *Murder Rooms*, detailing the surmised sleuthing performed by a young Conan Doyle and his mentor, Dr. Joseph Bell, may have been his biggest hit but Mr. Pirie has also managed to adapt such noted titles as *The Woman in White* and *The Wyvern Mystery* to the small screen. The majority of the "monster kid" generation will of course be familiar with his publications *A Heritage of Horror* and *The Vampire Cinema*, penned while in his early twenties and regarded to this day as essential and opinionated guides to their subjects (respectively, the British horror film, and the screen bloodsucker from *Nosferatu* through to Hammer and beyond.)

A constant champion of Hammer Films and a major defender of the company's number one director Terence Fisher, Pirie has often aimed at recapturing that unique Bray Studios flavor in his own work, and *Rainy Day Women* (scripted for the BBC's landmark *Play For Today* strand, at the time in its death throes) provides early evidence of that influence. Ostensibly it's a wartime drama set in 1940, pitting imported "Land Girls" against the hostile and suspicious local Home Guard, but the combination of Pirie's adoration of Gothic styles (in print and onscreen) with Ben Bolt's assured and in-tune direction, and Stanley Myers' often moody and menacing score, lends the production an air of disquiet and seething tension not unlike that of,

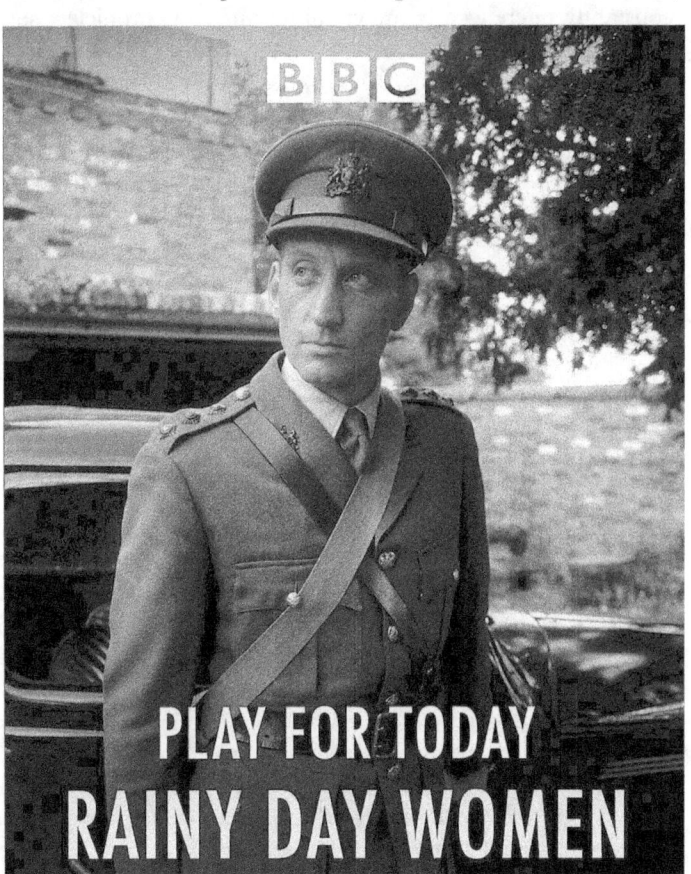

say, *The Reptile* or *Quatermass 2*. A voice-over line early in the proceedings describes the tale as "a ghost story without the ghosts," and the author remains true to his promise.

Charles Dance plays a shell-shocked military captain, temporarily absent from service due to his post-Dunkirk condition but still sufficiently able to undertake a mission for the Ministry of Information—he's sent to the tiny, remote hamlet of Darton to investigate reports of possible spy activity emanating from the region. His journey along near-deserted country lanes to his destination is almost as fraught with imagined peril and sinister encounters as Janet Leigh's flight from her employer in the opening section of *Psycho*. Once he arrives, we're in *Wicker Man* territory by way of *Straw Dogs*—he's unpopular with the natives, but not half as much as are the relocated young women toiling on the village farmland. The girls are billeted with Alice Durkow, a feisty and uninhibited individual once married to a German and believed to be a witch by most in the surrounding area. Anti-Nazi feelings run riot, and, coupled with misogyny and sexual tensions, create a powder-keg of emotion. As the ineffectual Dance fumbles and blunders his way towards uncovering the truth, and as the male population of Darton bid to crush the liveliness and spirit of the outsiders, we reach a truly shocking finale—tellingly, the "Rainy Day" of the title is said to be official Ministry code describing "something so threatening to internal morale during invasion that it is simply obliterated," as an appalled Dance spits towards the close.

Pirie's subsequent TV work has never quite achieved the sheer rage and anger of *Rainy Day Women*—indeed, he's barely attempted to do so, choosing instead to move in more traditional directions. By no means a conventional "horror film", and yet so wrapped up in the genre's tropes and machinery that it is constantly referenced by movie historians and chroniclers specializing in the field, it's a bitter, political cry perhaps muted only by its period setting. Even so, the Falklands War would of course have been fresh within the memories of a contemporary audience—one wonders how many viewers might have linked the obfuscation and maneuverings of the powers-that-be here with similarly shady and secretive activity before and during the spring of 1982. It's a game that continues to this day.
—Darrell Buxton

THREADS

1984
D: Mick Jackson
W: Barry Hines
Starring: Karen Meagher, Reece Dinsdale, Jane Hazlegrove, Rita May, David Brierly

Threads emerged at the height of a mini-cycle of early 1980s Reagan-era nuclear paranoia movies, the tone of which was typified by two American TV productions: *The Day After* and Edward Zwick's astonishing faux-news report *Special Bulletin*. The ominous sense that we were all potentially on the brink of a nuclear catastrophe crept into mainstream cinema, from teen action flick *WarGames* to one of the best Stephen King adaptations, *The Dead Zone*, in which melancholic psychic hero Christopher Walken sacrifices himself in order to destroy the career path of sleazeball senator Martin Sheen that will lead to World War III.

The Dead Zone and *WarGames* exploited contemporary fears, while offering optimistic resolutions in which the most positive facets of humankind triumph over the destructive impulses of those who might bring about its end. *Special Bulletin* offers the harrowing climactic sight of seemingly unflappable TV anchorman Ed Flanders crying, "There's gotta be something we're supposed to *do!*," live on air as the realization dawns that a nuclear device has been detonated in South Carolina, causing thousands to perish while hopeful viewers awaited a happy resolution to the unfolding crisis. *Testament* (for which Jane Alexander achieved a surprise Oscar nomination), the UK's *When the Wind Blows* and the extraordinary *Miracle Mile* present even less hope, the latter bowing out with its doomed romantic leads resigning themselves to the fact that "It's the cockroaches' turn" as the world they knew gets obliterated in seconds.

All of these movies have supremely powerful moments and images, but the BBC production of *Threads* from writer Barry Hines (in a nod to Hines' *Kes*, the central male character is a bird fancier) might be the one that ingrained itself the deepest on the psyche of impressionable viewers. For a certain audience, it is probably responsible for as many enduring nightmares as any of the obvious selections for Scariest Moments Ever you can care to name—including the hand-holding bit from *The Haunting* and the "*Dark and Lonely Water*" public information film employing Donald Pleasence's dulcet tones to loosen the bowels of prepubescents across the nation.

Told in an unsentimentalized fashion with straightforward narration (from the BBC's Paul Vaughan) and documentary-style onscreen captions informing us of the escalating carnage and devastation, *Threads* has its origins in an even more controversial BBC production from a different but equally fraught era. Peter Watkins' *The War Game* is the terrifying grandfather of the British Nuclear Nightmare film, its closing images of suffering and hopelessness set to "Silent Night" representing TV of any age at its most potent. First broadcast on BBC2 in September 1984, with a repeat showing the following year (as part of a season that also included the first broadcast of hitherto unscreened *The War Game*) representing its last UK transmission until two decades later, *Threads* and its black-and-white predecessor remain impossible to shake off.

The build-up to chaos is devastatingly effective. *Threads* consciously avoids the disaster-movie style ensemble of familiar actors that threatened to tip *The Day After* over into nuclear soap opera. Although the US equivalent to *Threads* was admirable, somehow seeing familiar faces like John Lithgow, Jason Robards and (whisper it) Steve Guttenberg face the End of All Things takes the edge off the authenticity, reminding us that at least one of them will be signing up for another *Police Academy* sequel during the last commercial break. *Threads* offers no such comfort: The cast is filled with unknowns and the personal stories are subdued in favor of an authentic depiction of humdrum working-class life slowly invaded by faraway events. One blissfully ignorant character mistakes the Middle East for the Far East, noting optimistically, "It's far enough, isn't it?"

The setting is Sheffield, fifth largest city in Britain, and one of the victims of the country's traditional recessions. The script gives us a young couple (Reece Dinsdale, Karen Meagher) whose prior-

ities are centered on the unplanned baby they will soon be producing. News of a Soviet coup in Iran is met with a muted response. Normal folks switch over to the football results instead, while Dinsdale and Meagher are more nervous about the imminent meeting of their respective parents than they are with the barely registering escalating tensions between Moscow and Washington.

When the British Prime Minister shows his support for American action against the USSR, everyday life begins to change. Supermarkets start looking like it's Christmas Eve, albeit with the unwelcome bonus of tinned goods shooting up in price as demand and panic grow. Protestors take to the streets to remind us, "You cannot win a nuclear war!" Looting begins in earnest while schools close, non-essential phone lines are disconnected and the motorways jam with traffic as families frantically head for Lincolnshire and Wales.

If you happened to walk in from the pub halfway through *Threads*, your evening's TV entertainment would have been dominated by the sight of Sheffield turned into a wasteland following nuclear exchanges between The Powers, resulting in 2 megatons falling on the UK. Millions are killed in the blast itself—including Dinsdale—and subsequently *Threads* follows the survivors as they struggle to avoid starvation, cope with the effects of fall-out and try to eke out an existence in a world where night and day are now indistinguishable.

With no music, naturalistic performances, and a camera that doesn't flinch, *Threads* offers no hope or respite from its foregone conclusion. Stark images of horribly charred bodies, dead dogs, burned babies, corpses in bin liners and characters screaming, sobbing and feasting on raw, contaminated meat from dead sheep dominate the second half. The methodical preparatory measures followed by local government and detailed in the early part of the film prove futile, as we realize the practical impossibility of treating and feeding the walking wounded. The survivors simply regress to a primal survival-of-the-fittest state, with death a blessed release when it happens.

The disquieting faux-documentary approach this film shares with *The War Game*—complete with montages of monochrome stills depicting the carnage—is now a familiar one, but it adds an extra layer of uncomfortable authenticity to *Threads*, barely diluted by the sometimes grating deployment of the BBC newsreader-style narration. Likewise, the sight of mushroom clouds above Sheffield is such a staggering image to behold that you barely have a moment to consider the obvious use of superimposed stock footage.

In the context of a typical evening's TV entertainment from an era when shocking people wasn't such a nigh-on-impossible task, it is even more impressive. If it was made today, the harrowing final scenes, of Britain's population reduced to four million and our dead heroine's mentally deficient daughter suffering a still-birth, would probably be completely ruined by an onscreen caption violating the screen to remind us that something along the lines of *"Britain's Fattest Grandmas"* starts in five minutes. Incidentally, *Threads* joins the ranks of a select few TV shows and movies to recognize the power of silence: the screen freezes on an image of despair before the credits roll eerily without a sound.
—Steven West

• • •

After 15 years of détente, in which the Third World War had diminished from the grim all-too-possible nightmare of *The War Game* or *Fail Safe*, to a colorful piece of background for re-

venge fantasies (*Mad Max*) or action and adventure (*The Ultimate Warrior, Damnation Alley*), the period 1979-80 saw the Cold War turn pretty hot again. With the arrival of Margaret Thatcher and Ronald Reagan on the world political stage, 1970s concerns about fuel prices, three-day weeks and Three Mile Island suddenly turned back to matters of mutually assured destruction. Reagan, in particular, had made the Soviet threat, and the re-arming of America, an election issue, and his incendiary dialogue didn't abate upon his entering office. The invasion of Afghanistan, the overthrow of the Shah in Iran, and increasingly violent conflicts in Southern Africa woke the world up to the fact that perhaps there was more to our imminent annihilation than using it as a production design choice in science fiction thrillers, and cinema again turned its attention back towards the possibility of global nuclear conflict in the real world.

The first post-Reagan stab at a non-science fiction nuclear war movie was actually a TV mini-series. *World War III*, directed by David Greene and Boris Sagal, and broadcast by NBC in 1982, is essentially a re-tread of *Fail Safe*, with Rock Hudson in the Henry Fonda role. It's an effective film, miles above the usual US standard of the time, but with its focus on the military and political implications of the Cold War, it feels conventional compared with what was to come. In the following 24 months, four TV movies would be produced, three of which would eschew the *Fail Safe*/*On the Beach*/*Dr. Strangelove* politico-military view of global nuclear conflict re-hashed in *World War III*, and instead focus on the effects of Armageddon on the lives of farmers, painters and decorators, housewives and office workers (the exception being HBO's *Countdown to Looking Glass*, an earnest variation on *Fail Safe*, told from the perspective of a CNN-like cable news channel.) These three films were hugely important, and all three directly influenced the policy of the countries that produced them. They were *Testament*, *The Day After*, and *Threads*.

Testament and *The Day After* were American TV productions. *Testament* was produced by PBS and based on Carol Amen's novel *The Last Testament*. It's a quiet, dignified, somber movie, beautifully directed by Lynne Littman and written with an overwhelming sense of melancholy by John Sacret Young. It is the best of the three films by some margin, but perhaps because it avoids the overt politics and the more graphic elements of both *Threads* and *The Day After*, it is the least well known of the trio, despite a limited theatrical release and lead actress Jane Alexander's 1983 Oscar nomination. *The Day After* was similarly a TV movie, made for the ABC network, which was also subject to a limited theatrical release, mainly overseas. Written by Edward Hume (best known as the writer/developer of *The Streets of San Francisco*!) and directed by Nicholas Meyer, the film is almost exactly the opposite of *Testament*. Through the use of stock footage and, ironically, US Air Force training films, it paints a vivid portrayal of a growing superpower confrontation in its first third, then proceeds to follow the nuclear chain of dominoes that fall after a set piece destruction of Kansas City and surrounding areas which opens its second act. Unlike *Testament*, which replaces suspense and tension with regret and despair, *The Day After* is graphic and genuinely suspenseful, and from halfway through, deeply depressing.

Threads, made the year after both *Testament* and *The Day After*, owes rather more to the latter. Its other obvious debt is to Peter Watkins' 1965 docudrama *The War Game*. Written by Barry Hines and directed by then documentary filmmaker Mick Jackson, the film concentrates on the effects of a nuclear attack on the city of Sheffield. Like *The Day After*, *Threads* attempts to create a contemporary and realistic political lead up to war, but unlike *The Day After*, it does so via text onscreen, underpinning its docudrama approach. The film follows the lives of two Sheffield families—the Kemps and the Becketts. Ruth Beckett is pregnant, and father-to-be Jimmy Kemp agrees to marry her as the two plan a life together, even though Ruth is keener on the prospect than Jimmy is. In the background, tensions in the Middle East increase, with a Soviet invasion of Iran, and the US mobilizing its rapid deployment force to defend Iran's southern oil fields. A naval conflict explodes in the Persian Gulf, and both the Soviets and the US use tactical nuclear weapons to defend their respective bases.

For a day or two, tensions plateau. However, as news of the nuclear exchange in the Gulf becomes known in Britain, panic breaks out. Looting and supply-hoarding take hold, and the Government enacts the Emergency Powers Act, arresting "dissidents" (including peace activists and trade unionists), closing down ports and airports and ordering local authorities to man their emergency bunkers. Sheffield City Council has a cramped facility under City Hall, and they comply with instructions, albeit reluctantly. Both Jimmy and Ruth comment casually on the increasing tensions, but with awkward family dinners to get through, as well as decorating their new house, the events in Asia are really only abstract to them.

On May 26, Sheffield City Hall receives Attack Warning Red and a couple of minutes later, a Soviet ICBM warhead explodes high over the North Sea. The electro-magnetic pulse it delivers knocks out most electrical equipment over Britain and North West Europe. Within a couple of minutes, a nuclear weapon explodes over the RAF base at Finningley in Lincolnshire, 20 miles east of Sheffield. As sirens go off in Sheffield, and the mushroom cloud from Finningley appears over the horizon, the population of Sheffield panics. Jimmy, on a job in the city, seeks shelter under his van, whereas Ruth tries to follow the advice in the *Protect and Survive* leaflet in order to build a fallout shelter for her and her parents. A few minutes after that, Sheffield itself is attacked and effectively destroyed.

The remaining film follows two different stories (Jimmy is forgotten and presumed killed in the initial attack.) It examines the aftermath of the blast on Ruth and her family, and the futile efforts of the civil servants under Sheffield City Hall trying, and failing, to provide succour to the city's dwindling populace. As we follow Ruth and her daughter through the months, years and eventually to a decade beyond the devastating event, the film strays closer to *Testament* in that it becomes a series of sketches depicting the reversion of Britain to a medieval agrarian society, finishing on a particularly chilling freeze-frame.

Director Mick Jackson was handed the job on *Threads* based on his 1982 BBC *Q.E.D.* documentary *A Guide To Armageddon*. The story, indeed even some of the footage, was recycled for *Threads*, and it certainly seems on viewing both, that Jackson, rather than Hines, may have been the primary driving force behind *Threads*. Although both Jackson and Hines deny it, *Threads* is a political film, just as Peter Watkins' earlier *The War Game* was, just as *The Day After* was (director Nicholas Meyer famously said of *The Day After*: "They [ABC] gave me millions of dollars to go on prime-time TV and call Ronald Reagan a liar.") By documenting the failure of the policy of deterrence, *Threads* is clearly and blatantly political. Like *The Day After* (often compared by critics to an apocalyptic episode of *Little House on the Prairie*, thereby getting and missing the point simultaneously), *Threads* uses a familiar TV trope (here the kitchen sink drama) to package its message. It is, in essence, propaganda, and is amazingly successful selling its viewpoint. Duncan Campbell and Bruce Kent could have written it. By avoiding name actors, and making a virtue of its tiny budget, *Threads* has the same strengths as *The War Game*, which is high praise indeed, though it is a more straightforward narrative, and lacks Watkins' subtextual games with the nature of the medium.

Threads is so effective it feels debilitating just watching it. On first broadcast it was genuinely terrifying and, more than any other film in this book, it lives in the collective consciousness of a generation of Britons who grew up four and a half minutes from a Soviet SS-20 captain's phone call to his theater commander in Czechoslovakia. What is most remarkable about the film is that with 30-years-worth of hindsight, *Threads* has lost little of its power to shock and appal. In that sense, *Threads* is perhaps the most effective horror film of its era, albeit one which avoids the traditional comforting landmarks and signposts of the genre.
—Neil Pike

UNFAIR EXCHANGES

1984
D: Gavin Millar
W: Ken Campbell
Starring: Julie Walters, David Rappaport, George Lapham, Robert Kingswell, Ken Campbell

In the Spring 1971 issue of *Sight and Sound* magazine, David Pirie wrote on the "New Blood," in which he speculated about the incoming directorial talent in the UK horror genre. In identifying Stephen Weeks, Peter Sasdy, Gordon Hessler and Peter Sykes, plus giving a nod to screenwriter Chris Wicking along the way, his predictions were semi-successful, as horror fans continue to recognize these names today. Others joined them, most noticeably Pete Walker and Norman J. Warren. A decade later, with funds running dry, the few that were still able to attract a budget were itchy about touching the genre, and those who did make fright flicks moved country if they wanted to produce more, or found themselves resigned to journeyman work in television, well away from the monster fun. As the 1980s came to a close, I recall considering what might have been, and how the "next generation" fright pack might have been a more conceptual group avoiding the accepted tenets. Few of the filmmakers that came to mind could have been considered young guns but might have been a presence had the industry been more solid

and robust. They included Richard Loncraine, Lindsey Vickers, Gabrielle Beaumont, Herbert Wise, Peter J. Hammond and, in particular, Gavin Millar.

Millar found opportunities to delve into the bizarre in several movies and professed an interest in working in the genre when I contacted him in 1992 about *Unfair Exchanges*, his 1984 offering made for the BBC's *Screen Two* series of television films, a strand instigated by producer Kenith Trodd. He encouraged me to seek out another of his BBC offerings, the equally difficult to see *The Russian Soldier* (1986), in which a family are nightmarishly confined to their remote valley farm when their livestock fall prey to a mystery disease. His *Dreamchild* (1985) went into cinemas and presented us with an elderly Alice Liddell, who as a child had inspired Lewis Carroll's inquisitive adventurer, now subject to visits by particularly grotesque inhabitants of that Wonderland in a seemingly worrying onset of dementia. In 1999 came his film of Iain Banks' *Complicity*, receiving a limited theatrical release in Scotland, which somehow failed to capture a full-on horror tone despite a succession of bizarre deaths that Dr. Phibes would have approved of. The fates of the victims included an arms dealer disarmed, that is to say upper limbs wrenched from the torso, a fox-hunter with explosive charges attached to his shins blasting them to blood and bone before the hounds are turned on him, and another well-to-do forced to drink an entire cask of wine funneled into his throat. In one scene Jonny Lee Miller is awaiting a contact at an arranged meeting place, out front of a butcher's shop in the middle of the night; when the contact is late he turns and realizes that his whistle-blower has been turned into prime cuts for display in the butcher's window.

Unfair Exchanges was the first film *Screen Two* made to go for horror. It was written by Ken Campbell, who appears in a supporting role and also provided the voice of the March Hare in Millar's *Dreamchild*. Julie Walters, fresh from her *Educating Rita* Oscar nomination, plays Mavis, who works for a feminist publication called *Today's Lady*. She has a young son and is living apart from the gay father, Ronnie, but the two are on good terms. She resides in a terraced building where the fellow occupants are an agitated writer and an eccentric dwarf called Arthur, played by David Rappaport, in blistering form. When the ground floor tenant falls unusually quiet, Mavis collects the spare key from under a pot in the garden and discovers him dead, apparently blasted in the face by an electrical discharge from the phone.

In the opening scenes a yellow telephone van is either parked nearby, or seen following her, and strange telephonic activity and phenomena pursue her throughout. Already curious and now dissatisfied with the official police approach (they surmize that the victim was killed by lightning), Mavis launches her own investigation, which brings her into contact with several people with an interest in the Fortean.

Celebrated actor-writer Campbell laces the 67-minute film with his trademark wit and inventiveness. Arthur has made his flat a tribute to all the things that he doesn't believe in, listing them at some length: "I don't believe in saving energy or saving whales and I don't think Jesus is saving much anymore ... I don't believe in banning fox-hunting and I think animal experiments are okay as long as they're for a good cause like making women look prettier." It is Arthur who first comes up with the notion that might explain what is happening: The telephone system is alive. "The way people use the network has charged it to make a living brain." The emotions expressed within calls, and the fear/horror/grief/joy/anger that accompany the emergencies and desperate situations in needs-must usage have breathed life into it, and the information shared by everyone nationally provides the knowledge that packs this electronic consciousness. But the network does not possess the intelligence to combine knowledge with feelings, and is instead is a mischief-maker tormenting phone users, particularly anyone with an inkling of the network's sentience or awareness.

Mavis is terrorized by the telephone system. Ronnie calls her in the middle of the night to express concern that there might be an intruder, but when she next speaks to him, he claims there was no such call. Nor does she have any recollection of an earlier conversation that she is supposed to have had with him. On another occasion a voice jumps in on their chat to disturbing and comical effect. "I'll ring back," suggests Ronnie. "I'll still be here," taunts the voice, "I've decided to live here." While at her father's Maria is subjected to nuisance calls heightened with maniacal laughter and contacts the police to have them trace the call. She keeps the line open until the police warn her to get out of the house; "he's on the extension." Shades of Fred Walton's *When a Stranger Calls* (1979)! She runs out but has to return for her son, though not before arming herself with a large axe. There is nobody there, and the police even claim later that there was no conversation or trace.

As a result of the disturbing events, Ronnie agrees to stay the night, but he has stock to collect for opening shop the next day, and alone again she takes a call—this time from Mavis. Yes, from herself (and I will try here to avoid conjecture that this suggests the imaginings of her own fractured psyche), warning her not to go to Arthur for help. She finds Arthur dead on the floor of his shower, a cubicle designed to resemble a red telephone box, the showerhead fashioned as a telephone receiver. Time to retaliate—Mavis pops her son in his tansad and sets off into the streets, first disabling the receivers in phone booths with a pair of wire cutters, and then trespassing the Telephone Exchange, disembowelling it of circuitry.
—Paul Higson

DAEMON

1985
D: Colin Finbow
W: Colin Finbow
Starring: Susannah York, Bert Parnaby, Arnaud Morell

While it was the objective of the Children's Film Foundation (CFF) to provide a quota of movies that appealed directly to youngsters, the Children's Film Unit (CFU) was a charitable organization that was set up in 1981 to not only enable children to act in front of the camera but to provide them with the opportunity to gain experience on the technical side too. It was the brainchild of Colin Finbow who would go on to direct many of the films made by the unit, normally shooting during the six-week summer holiday period, picking up on shots and completing post-production over subsequent weekends. While the CFF had often tackled sci-fi/fantasy subjects, most spectacularly in the eight part 1962 serial *Master of Venus* starring a young Robin Stewart and Zienia Merton (who would later play Sandra Benes in *Space: 1999*), the CFU responded more to the tastes of youngsters as it had stood for over a decade, as found in the popular teatime shows of the day and paperback purchases from the Armada imprint. To whit, their penchant was for eerie tales of the supernatural, of phantoms that might be ghosts or innocents lost in time, of history and lore bubbling into the present and of ancient gods still influencing events today.

Even the Children's Film Unit stories that did not feature the supernatural often contained a threat one notch above anything that the Children's Film Foundation ever dared to approach. *A Swarm in May* (1983) included a ghost, *Under the Bed* (1988) a monster that is the adverse result of an ill-kept room, *Doombeach* (1989) a nuclear power station leak, and *Emily's Ghost* (1992) retells that old chestnut of girls from both the past and present mistaking one another for spooky visitors to their own time. *Survivors* (1990), *Nightshade* (1995) and *The Gingerbread House* (1996) each offer tales of danger and the macabre. *Dark Enemy* (1984) was a rare burst of British post-apocalypse, in which a group of children, in a world where all the adults are dead, survive in an idyllic valley, while a mysterious threat looms in the form of mutated others. *Dark Enemy* is considerably grimmer than *Daemon* (1985) which was screened on Channel 4 over Christmas in the year that it was made. That is not to say that *Daemon* does not have its edgier moments, if anything it contains more such material than any other film out of the two production stables, including an onscreen shock death of a character.

Not that children's television shows were shy of death. *Doctor Who* tended to kill most of its guest characters over the serialized adventures, and in *The Changes* (1975), based on a trilogy of books, a vicious, murderous gang are slain themselves by the combined forces of a village and a Sikh community armed with forks and scimitars. The CFU was bringing 25 years of CFF expectations with it, and that was a universe in which there were threats aplenty, but the resolutions were bloodless and death free.

Daemon begins with a family moving into their new home, the parents bizarrely errant, working outside the country and leaving their three children, Nick Foster (Arnaud Morrell), Clare (Donna Glaser) and Jenny (Sadie Herlighy), under the supervision of the new Swedish au pair, Helga (Faith Steemson, playing the character to unfunny comedy effect, is older than many of the cast and a former pupil of the Sydenham Girls School used for one of the locations.). Nick has had to change schools and is befriended by Sam (Orlando Swayne), but is vulnerable to the bullies. In scripture class Mr. Crabb is perpetually teaching The Ten Commandments, and the pupils, constantly side-tracking to the fact and fiction of Graham Baker's *The Final Conflict*, ask if it is possible for evil to reside in an ordinary Joe. Crabb (Bert Parnaby) encourages them and arrives at somewhat disturbing theological conclusions. "I have come to feel that the balance is healthy, that the struggle between good and evil is the sole reason for our existence."

At home Nick takes delivery of an Apple computer, a "moving in and sorry we're absent" gift from his parents, though before he can finish setting it up, there is a ghost in the machine and the words "Help Me!" appear in Westminster font on the screen. The house creaks and the cavities rustle with unidenti-

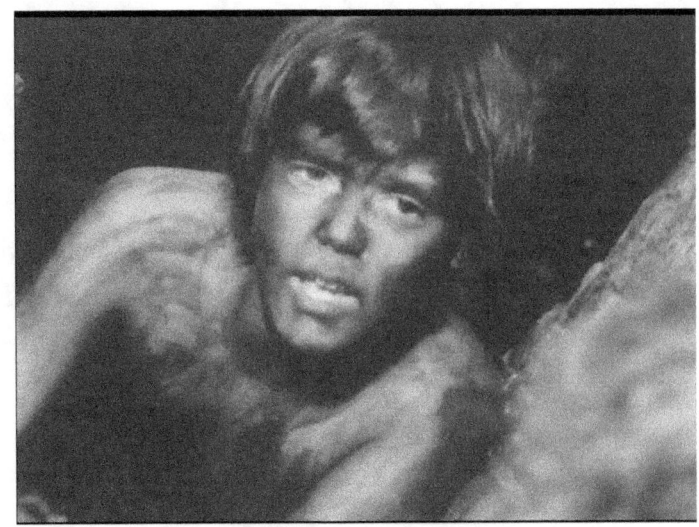

Neil Walker in *Daemon*

fied activity. He develops blisters on his feet and scratches on his elbows. Coming down with a fever while at school, the sudden illness is mistaken for chicken pox and he is kept there overnight, with Mr. Crabb overseeing his containment. He is referred to child psychiatrist Rachel (Susannah York, then a patron of the CFU) who was his sister's medical specialist when the girl was diagnosed with a personality disorder—it's all go in this family—and his symptoms are blamed on auto-suggestive physical reactions to the recent changes in his life.

Things become more ominous when the boys at school begin to refer to the appropriately named Nick as a harbinger of evil, confirmed for them when Mr. Crabb is found dead at the bottom of the school stairs. The boys begin to propose the murder of the new boy, to rid the school of this great evil before it comes for them. Sam is due to sleepover at Nick's, the two alone, the girls and the au pair out on dates. The other boys intend to invade the house and kill Nick, but they are scared off by unexpected events as the supernatural activity resumes. Nick breaks through the wall into a forgotten chimney, into which he climbs until reaching the trapped ghost of a boy sweep from the 19th century. The boy recounts his never-ending, nightly repeated fate, before Nick is able to dislodge him, dragging the skeleton back down with him.

Daemon occasionally plays against expectations and a prominent twist here is the death of Mr. Crabb in the stairwell. It is a necessary shock as it sets up the dreadful air of menace that follows, that others can and may die, that this could be the work of the supernatural element tormenting Nick, or that the threat of murder from his classmates (shades of *Unman, Wittering and Zigo*) is no child's play. This is a film that could not have been made in this way eight years later following the Jamie Bulger murder, a crime blamed on a horror movie at the time, *Child's Play 3*.

Hence the softening of the CFU style by the time of the later *Emily's Ghost*. The murder plot among the boys is quietly disturbing as Sam tries to persuade them against it, but they are immovable and determined ("You're not going to hurt him"/"No, we're only going to kill him.") Other gruesome details crop up in the conversation with the ghost of the boy sweep, who has mistaken Nick for the young master of the house, and relates not only his experience but the fate of other children in a "horrible histories" lesson to his rescuer. When he became fast in the chimney, the brutal master sweep had set a fire under him to encourage him to move, but that only blistered his feet, the stigmatic message later visited on Nick. The nastiest of the tales he recounts is the fate of another boy sweep as he speculates how they might "tie a rope to my leg. They did that to Valentine Brown and pulled his leg clean off."

The music of David Hewson apes Pino Donaggio and John Carpenter, emphasizing the genre from the opening shot. But for all the inherent shudders, the film disappoints. Contradictory to the horror is the lame comedy of the dim-witted au pair and moments such as the sisters dyeing their hair and emerging with ridiculous multi-colored Jonathan King-style wigs. The acting of the children, who make up the majority of the cast, and dominate over most of the 65-minute running time, is generally stilted and poor, made all the worse by the presence of Susannah York, her naturalistic performance by comparison heightening the weakness of the child actors; a real person in the middle of a puppet show. Although the episode in the chimney is well conceived and executed, the remainder is unimaginative, full of simple shots useful for educating the children in set-ups, but with an absence of anything too elaborate, ensuring that the shoot is completed on time yet leaving the whole thing feeling rather one-dimensional.
—Paul Higson

TITUS ANDRONICUS

1985
D: Jane Howell
W: William Shakespeare
Starring: Trevor Peacock, Eileen Atkins, Edward Hardwicke, Brian Protheroe, Hugh Quarshie

The 1996 publication *The BFI Companion to Horror* contains no entry for William Shakespeare, while Leslie Halliwell's *Filmgoer's Companion* describes The Bard in typically abrupt manner as, "British playwright and dramatist whose plays have received plenty of attention from filmmakers." When the splendid Mr. Jonathan Rigby generously offered to pen an afterword for my own publication *The Shrieking Sixties*, however, coverage of the Stratford scribe took up more than half of the piece he presented. Indeed, the particular work Jonathan referenced was *Titus Andronicus*, which he pointed out remained unproduced for more than three centuries ("because it's a horror play!", he concluded—adding the exclusive that Robert Hartford-Davis' proposed and aborted film version circa 1970 would have starred Christopher Lee and Lesley-Anne Down.)

In the mid-1970s producer Cedric Messina pitched the idea to the BBC that all 37 of Shakespeare's plays should be captured for the small screen. The resulting *BBC Television Shakespeare*, as the project became known, was crafted and aired between 1978 and 1985 and remains a popular collection and a valuable archive record to this day. Messina's successors Jonathan Miller and Shaun Sutton expanded the brief beyond the original concept, encouraging freedom and experimentation, and the series attracts praise and renown both for its authenticity and its more challenging aspects. As any schoolboy knows, the oeuvre is packed with sex, violence, and other controversial material (as well as those Shakespearian "jokes" your English Lit teacher was always so fond of pointing out), and of course *Titus Andronicus* is considered by many to be the biggest offender—some experts go so far as to say it is Shakespeare's worst offering, occasionally expressing doubt that it is his work at all. Because it's a horror play, probably.

As Messina had committed to a full run at the outset of the extensive BBC program, naturally this runt of the litter had to be included at some point. Years passed, no *Titus*—until, finally, director Jane Howell tackled the material, filming it in eight days during mid-February 1985 for transmission at the end of April. The 167-minute production arrived several months later than planned, due to a 1984 strike having prevented the scheduled shoot, though rumors were rife that the Beeb were nervous about the play's content. Indeed, *Titus* happened to be one of only four Shakespeare works that had never been previously adapted by the BBC prior to this '70s/1980s run.

It's a stunning piece of work in the 1985 version, not stinting on the gory details and possessing an awareness of screen violence quite unlike most other British fare at the time. The infamous set pieces—poor wretched Lavinia having her hands and tongue bloodily severed, Chiron and Demetrius getting their throats slashed, Tamora tucking into a decidedly dodgy meat pie—are all present, and staged in ways which might have had highbrow viewers reaching for a bucket but may well have grabbed the attention of any passing Freddy Krueger Fan Club members (one can imagine Steve Pemberton's celebrated video store regular "Henry Portrait," from the Beeb's hit black comedy *The League of Gentlemen*, tuning in halfway through and sleazily delivering his patented, "'Ow many killings?!" catchphrase). Director Howell

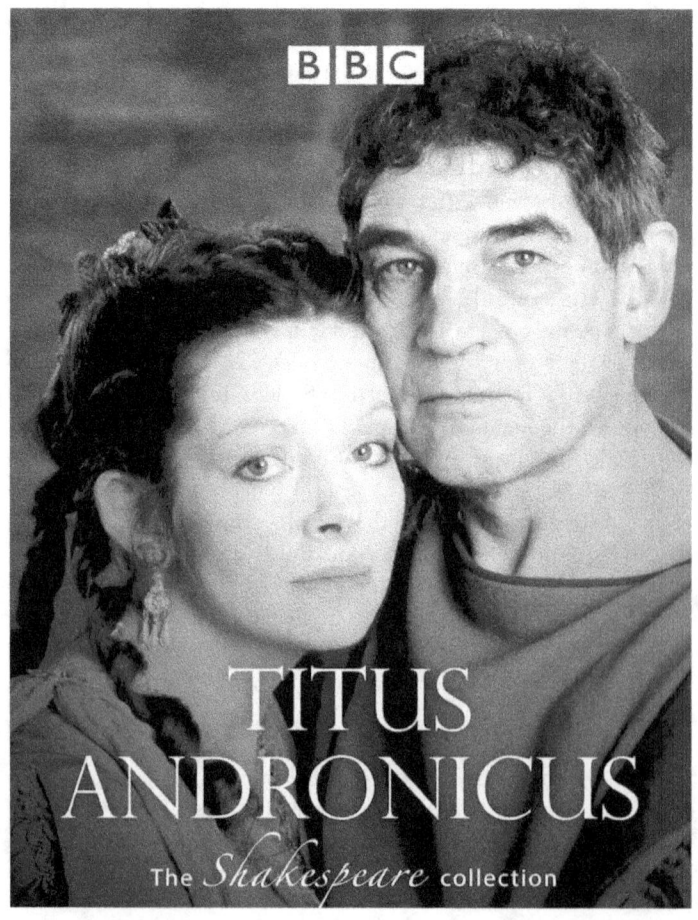

had initially intended to re-set the story in modern-day Northern Ireland but finally settled for period; one innovation, however, was to take up a "what are we doing to the children?" theme, involving use of the boy Lucius as a focal figure, present in many scenes and often significant even when off-screen. Right from the beginning, his face is superimposed alongside mist-swathed shots of skulls, and Lucius plays a prominent part in the climactic dining hall bloodbath too. The demise of Tamora's sons echoes *The Long Good Friday* in having them strung up alongside sheep carcasses, while Anna Calder-Marshall's impressive, quietly vengeful turn as Lavinia wouldn't have been out of place in one of the batch of late-1970s *Carrie* clones.

Titus Andronicus has remained one of the least favored and rarely filmed of The Bard's works—Julie Taymor directed an acclaimed cinema version, *Titus*, in 1999, influenced considerably by the BBC adaptation but adding extensive anachronisms and a mixture of ancient and modern as further texture. If you're going to pick just one of the tiny handful of movie or TV productions, however, this Jane Howell/Shaun Sutton take on Shocking Shakey is certainly the one to opt for.

—Darrell Buxton

THE CANTERVILLE GHOST

1986
D: Paul Bogart
W: George Zateslo
Starring: Sir John Gielgud, Ted Wass, Andrea Marcovicci, Alyssa Milano

What do Charles Laughton, Patrick Stewart, David Niven, Bruce Forsyth, and Bernard Cribbins have in common? Well, they and many others have played Sir Simon de Canterville, Oscar Wilde's cursed and spiteful spirit, in various film or TV adaptations of the 1887 novella *The Canterville Ghost*. Wilde's story is one of those that seems to be newly presented for each successive generation, yet oddly has never quite entered the public consciousness with the same love and affection people hold for, say, *A Christmas Carol*. The 1980s brought at least four fresh versions to the small screen, two American (a 1985 TV movie and a 1988 24-minute animation), one South African (1983), and a feature-length offering co-produced by Britain's HTV channel, one of the ITV network's most ambitious franchise outlets, and veritable fantasy/horror specialists over the years.

Produced by Peter Graham Scott, himself no slouch when it came to visual magic and mainstream-friendly chills, HTV's *The Canterville Ghost* plays on its Transatlantic status by having an American family traveling to the UK to take up residence at the stately home they have inherited (filming took place at the sumptuous Eastnor Castle in Herefordshire.). Harry Canterville is a recently unemployed company man whose job loss has happily coincided with his windfall, leading him to transport his second wife Lucy and daughter Jennifer (from his first marriage) over to Blighty. Sir Simon, played in something of a casting coup by Sir John Gielgud on this occasion, wastes little time in materializing to cause havoc, green-hued, booming ("I shall soon make short work of these brazen, impudent upstarts"), and rattling his chains. The castle's resident specter also conjures up a creeping tarantula to traumatize Harry and Lucy as they canoodle on their bed, later ejecting that same bed outside and dumping it in a nearby marsh as the couple sleep! Other tricks see the ghost causing uproar at a dinner party, his head taking the place of the main course when the lid of a silver salver is lifted, with the victuals and champers exploding messily across the dining hall. There's also a *Poltergeist*-inspired shock, toned down but effective nevertheless, where Marcovicci experiences a brief flash vision of herself as an old hag in the mirror while applying make-up.

Things take a *Stone Tape/Legend of Hell House* turn when spook-hunter Cook arrives, fully equipped with a buzzing, clicking, whirring array of electronic gizmos to attempt to lure and expel the unquiet and unwelcome presence. Bill Wallis makes a game attempt at establishing a vivid character here, but you can't help imagining that a broader, more boastful figure like Willie Rushton or Freddie Jones would have grabbed this role with both hands and turned it into something truly special. Indeed, Gielgud himself battles to impose and dominate the proceedings, but does so by rather channeling Christopher Lee, who might have been a more comfortable fit. Sir John seems to find much of the playful ghostliness beneath him, but does at least relish bellowing about "the torment of perpetual purgatory" and the like; he and Wass also get to share one glorious scene, cracking open a 1625 bottle of vintage wine and choking in unison on taking their first sips ("smooth!")

—Darrell Buxton

THE GOURMET

1986
D: Michael Whyte
W: Kazuo Ishiguro
Starring: Charles Gray, Mick Ford, David Rappaport. Alec Mango

Manley Kingston is the gourmet of the title, played by a perfectly-cast Charles Gray for this 45-minute slice of the supernatural, screened by Channel 4 and fondly remembered by its TV audience over the years. *The Gourmet* inevitably hit YouTube, but not until the spring of 2019, and proved to have retained its elegance and originality over the decades. The storyline from the pen of Kazuo Ishiguro (who went on to nab a handful of very prestigious credits later in his career) tells of a quest for the ultimate varied diet, and establishes in simple strokes an entire strata among the bored rich who strive to consume the most exotic foodstuffs—no lists are given but one can well imagine these wealthy connoisseurs having tasted okapi, polar bear, remote island plant-life, even human flesh, in their time, never content, never satisfied, always looking ahead to their next unique meal. Kingston's encounter with rival delicacy-hunter Mr. Rossi (Alec Mango) some years ago confirmed that Rossi had eaten a ghost, and that the taste was "exquisite" beyond belief; a nine-year quest to tick this item off his own menu card seems achievable when Manley is ushered into the inner sanctum of fellow gastronome Dr. Grosvenor (a rather effectively dubbed David Rappaport) and informed about how he might trap and devour a spirit.

That excellent and under-appreciated actor Mick Ford provides fine support for Gray during his bid for ghostly game, as our *bon viveur* finds himself in a soup kitchen queue at the gates of the grand premises to which he has been directed (possibly an accidental wrong turn, perhaps all part of the subterfuge.) The shabby, shuffling homeless unfortunates awaiting their bread and baked beans are treated with some courtesy by Kingston, though we sense that he has only one real focus—and Ford engages him in conversation and winds up as a reluctant partner in the scheme.

Ghost for lunch anyone? *The Gourmet*

Does Manley ensnare his ectoplasmic prey? Does he sautée a spook? And if so, does it taste as glorious as has been promised by his foodie forerunners? Find out for yourselves, by giving this decidedly delicious little delight a look. And revel in Gray's detailed, mannered, cultured performance—I honestly cannot call to mind any other actor who might have come anywhere close to convincing in this tailor-made role.
—Darrell Buxton

MR. CORBETT'S GHOST

1986
D: Danny Huston
W: Gerry Wilson
Starring: Paul Scofield, John Huston, Mark Farmer, Burgess Meredith

With Gothic horror and the ghost story having largely disappeared from cinema and television screens by the middle of the decade, Christmas was considered the last bastion for the odd phantom manifestation or weird happening, but even that expectation was waning. One would scour the pages of the bumper fortnight Yuletide edition of the *Radio Times* for seasonal menace and happen upon something distantly chiming of possibility. Actually experiencing the broadcast, however, seemed to bring only disappointment—Alastair Reid's take on Robert Louis Stevenson's *The Story of a Recluse* turned out to be a weak post-modern experimental intrigue, and David Pirie's *Wild Things*, a modern mystery in a hotel under the leer of close circuit cameras, was low in chills and slim of resolution. The directorial debut of Danny Huston, *Mr. Corbett's Ghost*, during Christmas 1987 promised a period piece ghost yarn, and this time delivered in style.

Adapted by Gerry Wilson from the Leon Garfield novella and running a compact 55 minutes, it takes place on New Year's Eve 1767 in Gospel Oak. Local apothecary Thomas Corbett (Paul Scofield), a pedant for hard work and cleanliness, is tormenting an apprentice. Benjamin Partridge (Mark Farmer) is eager to join the revelry and a family meal beforehand, but his boss is deliberately postponing his festive participation. Just as the lad perceives himself released from duties, a greater tormentor enters through the shop door, ordering a peculiar mixture that must be made up and delivered that night. Preying on the boy's small ire, the sinister interloper—played by John Huston, no less—offers him a strange contract on delivery of the potion, to give up a quarter of his earnings, in perpetuity, in exchange for the demise of the one causing his misery.

On his return from the delivery, Master Partridge encounters Mister Corbett in the woods, fleeing in fright from something unknown and dropping dead on the spot. Fearing the rope if found with the corpse, young Benjamin determines to distance himself from the body, but is discovered by a band of murderous thieves who encourage him to accompany them to the cemetery, where they intend to offload their own victims. On arrival he is short of a coin to complete the burial and is given the choice of flight or a cut throat. He tries to disguise the body as an accident beneath the wheels of a passing coach, but the carriage carries none other than Huston, leading our protagonist into an even deeper trap with yet more constricting terms binding his own future.

Scofield is given the opportunity of portraying two very distinct Corbetts. The living version is a curmudgeon and a tyrant, though we will discover that he was also a loving father and great family man. Borderline Dickensian in character, haughty and expressive, his catchphrase is the appendage of the words "... when there is work to be done" as a challenge to any notion of an extracurricular activity or emotion, and to whom a "promise" to family, at least his employee's family, "must stand in line." The spectral self is altogether different, a sorry and pathetic sight, ashen, cold and nowhere near the figure he cut while alive.

Mark Farmer, a familiar face from *Grange Hill* at the time, is required only to play Partridge as a put-upon boy, never quite coming across as vengeful or spiteful enough to order the death of his manager. It is a role that might have better suited someone like Phil Daniels or Philip Davis, were they not already too old by then; actors who would have been able to convey a fleeting malevolence followed by a heartfelt apology, although Farmer displays a touching tenderness when trying to protect the ghost from onlookers, fruitlessly trying to help him obtain warmth from a blazing hearth. Familiar faces pop up, ever-impish Burgess Meredith in one all-too-brief scene, plus 1980s celebrities like Alexei Sayle as a good-natured gatekeeper and Jools Holland as a bandit attired as a defrocked priest (and more than a little touched in the head). Scofield's Corbett is the only detailed character; most are hastily drawn caricatures. The piece relies much more heavily on the highly entertaining dialogue.

A playful film, it looks towards a happy resolution over a more classically terrifying conclusion, closer to the ultimate assurances of Scrooge than the climactic shudders found in M.R. James. Robin Vidgeon's cinematography is an attractive chiaroscuro, and the production seems to have had the pick of Berman's costume warehouse. Set dressing is good, particularly the details of the apothecary shop. Tantalizing, dark moments pepper the film, from the instruction to catch a fragment of a ghost in a bottle to a villain's comments on a rotten corpse on a gibbet, "his remains make fine decoration for the festive season." At a time when money was scarce for film production in the UK, Huston's financial backer here was one of the richest people in the isles, J. Paul Getty. The film is dedicated to Huston, Sr. and actress Zoe Sallis, or, as Danny might have referred to them, mom and pop.
—Paul Higson

BORN OF FIRE

1987
D: Jamil Dehlavi
W: Rafiq Abdullah
Starring: Peter Firth, Suzan Crowley, Stefan Kalipha, Oh-Tee, Nabil Shaban

With a fractured narrative, extraordinary, hypnotic visuals and a fevered sense of magic, *Born of Fire* amazes and frustrates in equal proportion. A re-telling of the Faustus legend filtered through Islamic mythology, *Born of Fire* is probably the least British-feeling British horror movie in this book, but it's a tremendous film, if you buy into its surrealist approach.

Paul Bergson (Peter Firth, terrific, and not a D-Notice situation in sight!) is a concert flautist troubled by terrible visions he doesn't understand, but which seem to point to a world consumed by fire. A chance meeting with an astrologer (Suzan Crowley) who shares his visions, and a deathbed confession from his mother, lead Bergson to Turkey in the footprints of his father who went to learn the flute from a mysterious Master Musician—the world's most extraordinary flautist and a Shaytan (a devil in Islamic mythology) as well as someone, Bergson comes to believe, who is seeking to bring about the end of the world through the power of his music. With help of The Silent One, a local mystic, he tries to stop the Master Musician from completing his apocalyptic task.

Born of Fire is probably the closest that British cinema has ever come to the mysticism of Alejandro Jodorowsky. Director Jamil Dehlavi ties his visually arresting set pieces together with minimal conventional narrative, and it's a strategy that alienates as many viewers as it attracts, but if you hook into the style, the power of Dehlavi's imagination drives the film supremely well. To this end, he's helped by some inspired casting, particularly of the enigmatic Oh-Tee as the Satanic Master Musician and Nabil Shaban as The Silent One, both of who manage to give remarkable performances without uttering a word.

It's stuffed full of eye-popping images. Alongside Jodorowsky's influence, the bleak, Cappadocian landscapes against which the majority of the film is set recall the final haunting vistas of Fulci's *The Beyond*. Surrealistic body horror and the fate of Crowley's character remind the viewer of Andrzej Zulawski's *Possession*. A sun is eclipsed by a human skull, a murderous moth-

like creature born from menstrual blood grows in a cocoon and a vulture smashes through the windscreen of a car driving through a rain-swept London night. Eventually the power of Dehlavi's visual delirium seeps into the viewers' subconscious and lends the whole exercise an atmosphere of magic and oddness so that, in the context of its own weirdness, Born of Fire kind of makes sense. It also generates a gloomy sense of impending doom, an out of the ordinary apocalypse for sure, but the end of the world, nonetheless.

The story itself will be familiar to anyone who knows the Faustus legend, or the Charlie Daniels Band song "The Devil Went Down to Georgia" (and by extension, Walter Hill's movie Crossroads) and anyone expecting a Turkish version of Hill's film (such a beast would surely have starred Kunt Tulgar in the Joe Morton role!) would probably walk out after 25 minutes, but if you can stick with it, Born of Fire is a unique experience for the British horror film aficionado. Mixing avant-garde European art-house tropes with eastern mysticism, Born of Fire is certainly not everyone's cup of tea, but it is unique and worms its way into your subconscious by the power of its visuals alone, and one has to admire a project that takes the demonic horror film and entirely re-shapes it from a non-Christian point of view. Top stuff, for those prepared to buy into its symbolism and who aren't too wedded to a linear, conventional narrative.
—Neil Pike

THE MAGIC TOYSHOP

1987
D: David Wheatley
W: Angela Carter
Starring: Tom Bell, Caroline Milmoe, Patricia Kerrigan

Angela Carter fever hit the UK movie scene for a brief, flickering moment in the 1980s. Neil Jordan's bid to capture Carter's peculiar brand of magic, fairytale, and Gothic in 1984's *The Company of Wolves* caused the biggest stir, but many admirers of that movie and the author may have been unaware of an earlier short film version of Angela's *The Bloody Chamber*—starring Terence Stamp and a debuting Rupert Everett, this take on the Bluebeard legend hit British cinemas in support of Walter Hill's *48 Hrs.* in late 1982, in something of a mismatched pairing.

A third Carter adaptation arrived from Granada and was aired initially on television before achieving a brief theatrical run. *The Magic Toyshop* seems to have fallen into obscurity, with no official home-viewing release, and an army of devotees holding fond memories of TV screenings or catching it at the local art house. If you loved *The Company of Wolves* you'd probably fall for the charms of this one too, and it does admittedly feature a shattering horror climax in its final five minutes—but it's a pretty laborious journey, if truth be told, and the memorable shock finale is rather un-earned.

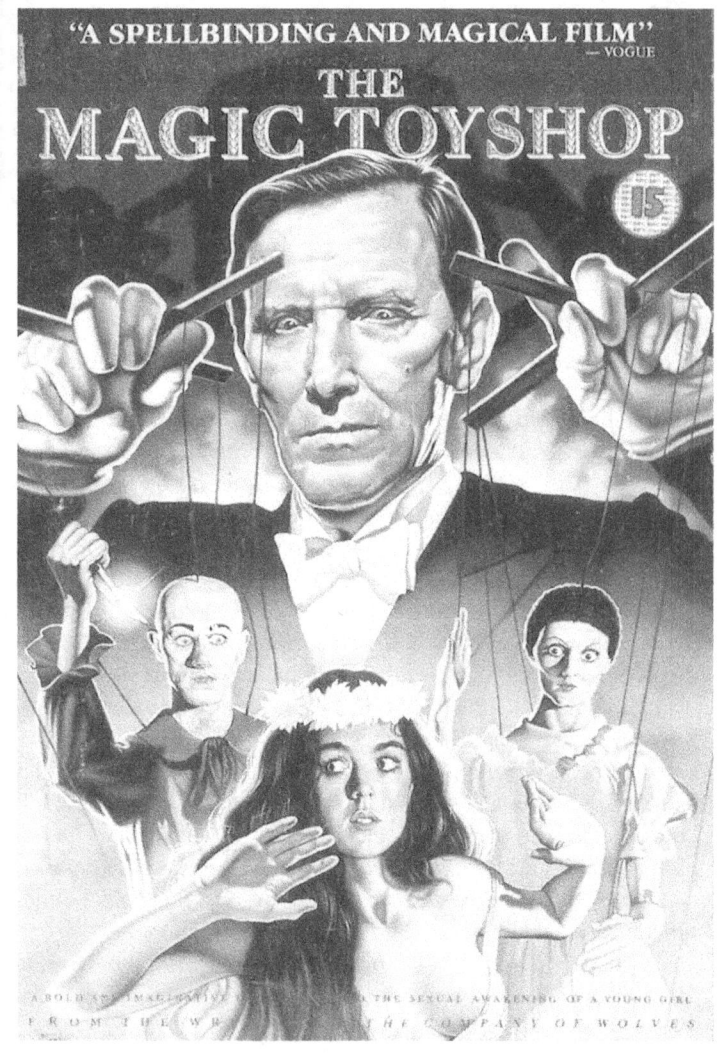

Once again, a pubescent female is at the center of the story, the braided-haired Melanie (24-year-old Caroline Milmoe, playing a decade younger.) Discovering her femininity and sexuality, Melanie's reveries concerning her developing body and her burgeoning desires are rudely interrupted when she and her orphaned siblings are farmed off to reside with Uncle Philip (Tom Bell). He runs an old-fashioned toyshop and spends his days carving and constructing the produce, from miniature vehicles to life-sized marionettes. He also takes the possessive view that "I don't like children playing with my toys." So far so Scrooge, and the ever-gruff Bell would seem ideally cast here—yet something is lacking, he never quite lives up to his fearsome reputation and as a result the nightmarish fate that befalls him comes over as unmerited.

The Magic Toyshop will play satisfyingly to the light fantasy crowd—the Melanie character is an archetype with proven appeal, and the film's universe is one in which the mystical and unexplained exists alongside a recognizable reality. A bull terrier jumps into a painting of itself, figures in photographs become animated, Melanie's room somehow temporarily exists on another plane with the furnishings appearing on a sandy beach with waves washing across the floor, those huge person-sized puppets perform shows where it is unclear who is pulling the strings or, indeed, whether they are dolls or living, breathing entities. Despite Carter herself authoring the screenplay, it's all rather flat and crucially fails to mesh the fantastic with the mundane. Those last few terrifying minutes are worth the wait for the horror audience, though even then at least one of the surprises (concerning a bonfire party and the lack of a "guy" atop the flaming heap) is signaled prematurely, weakening the revelation a little. *The Magic Toyshop* would like to consider itself in the same league as Powell and Pressburger's *The Red Shoes* or *The Tales of Hoffmann*, or in the realm of classic British dark fantasy, but it falls some way short of Harry Potter and comes nowhere near Dennis Potter.
—Darrell Buxton

DUKE BLUEBEARD'S CASTLE

1988
D: Leslie Megahey
W: Béla Balázs
Starring: Robert Lloyd, Elizabeth Laurence

What's Opera, Doc? The BBC's remit as a public broadcaster has taken a rather convergent and diminished direction during the 21st century, yet during the golden era of the 1960s, 1970s and 1980s, the Beeb was a veritable haven for challenging, experimental, and downright arty writers, directors, producers and performers. Where else might unsuspecting viewers have experienced *Schalcken the Painter* (1979), for example? Leslie Megahey's *Omnibus* documentary on a lesser Dutch portrait painter, with a prominent mention for Queen Elizabeth II in its credits, took a turn for the dramatic—not to mention the hideous—as it lurched from its hushed museum reverence to out-and-out zombie ghastliness. Charles Gray's contribution as narrator ought to have given the game away, in hindsight, but this beautifully shot, stately item lodged in the minds of its deliciously appalled audi-

ence for decades and has been officially exhumed by the BFI as one of their cult "Flipside" Blu-rays, bringing fresh acclaim and rediscovery its way. Highly merited too.

But what of Megahey's other major bid to marry the ultra-highbrow with the bloodsoaked? *Schalcken* may have had its profile elevated and its reputation cemented, but 1988's *Duke Bluebeard's Castle* would seem to have bypassed most horror fans upon original BBC2 broadcast (evening of March 12, 1989, simultaneously also run aurally on Radio 3) and has remained virtually unknown. Based on Béla Bartók's operetta, this take on the legend of the spouse-slaughtering hirsute aristo was given a VHS tape release in the early 1990s and has found a home on YouTube, but in comparison to most other cult horror TV of its era, has largely been ignored. Within a fan scene where many of us constantly dig deep to retrieve hidden nuggets and bring them to prominence, here's one that has lain undeservedly buried—perhaps its operatic origins disguised its impressive genre content, or proved off-putting to those who prefer their chills without soprano shrieks or tenor terror. In short, this is one of those rare horror productions that may well have held greater appeal for classical-loving parents or grandparents of the 1980s gore generation rather than the children of Freddy/Jason/Michael themselves.

Duke Bluebeard's Castle is a riveting two-hander, displaying all of the skill, eerie period dressing, expert mood-lighting, set/costume design, and ability to combine frights with culture, shown by its predecessor *Schalcken*. The opening shot immediately marks this as the work of Megahey—an extreme close-up with the facial features of the Duke (Robert Lloyd) filling the 4:3 frame could have been lifted directly from the earlier production, accompanied by a cold, chilly silence which again echoes the director's prior endeavor. We proceed to enter the world of the Duke and his latest unsuspecting conquest, and although 64 minutes of subtitled warbling within sets at once cavernous and minimalist may sound a daunting prospect, your patience and attention will be rewarded in spades.

Megahey reteams here with his *Schalcken* cameraman John Hooper and boy does it show, as *Duke Bluebeard's Castle* achieves a noticeably similar ambience and visual quality. The air of classiness that pervades the entire enterprise is often neatly and effectively undercut by scything moments of sheer dread, or unnerving minor details that pass in an instant, leaving traces of something fearful in their wake—the revelation that a shimmering liquid pool is filled with tears, the outsize plant-life populating the indoor garden, and so on. The grand set pieces are quietly stunning—our heroine Judith (Elizabeth Laurence) wandering into a white-tiled torture chamber where streams of blood pour down the porcelain walls before her shocked gaze, or the ultimate confrontation with the previous brides at the climax, where she stumbles into a secret hall to encounter their motionless forms (Hypnotized? Preserved? Stuffed and mounted?) garbed in gorgeous finery, glacial facial expressions and tilt of head reminiscent of Universal's 1934 *The Black Cat*. These truly disturbing figures, beautiful in their stasis, wouldn't be out of place in a Russell T. Davies or Steven Moffat-era *Doctor Who* yarn, either, frankly.

Megahey decamped to America soon after, embarking on a lucrative career in script-doctoring for the Weinstein company and leaving his BBC travails far behind. He remains best-known for *Schalcken* and for his odd 1993 theatrical feature *Hour of the Pig*, a somber examination of insane mediaeval justice (with the titular beast put on trial, like *Witchfinder General* gone even crazier); but *Duke Bluebeard's Castle* is of equal fascination and well worth an hour of your time. Try it on a double bill with Aronofsky's *Black Swan* or Argento's *Opera* sometime.
—Darrell Buxton

JACK THE RIPPER

1988
D: David Wickes
W: Derek Marlowe, David Wickes
Starring: Michael Caine, Armand Assante, Ray McAnally, Lewis Collins, Susan George, Jane Seymour

Filming had already begun on a low-budget series based on the Jack the Ripper murders when producer/director David Wickes secured a better deal with Euston Films and Thames Television. The series, which featured Barry (*Van der Valk*) Foster in the role of Inspector Abberline, was effectively scrapped in favor of this much bigger and glossier mini-series with Michael Caine taking the lead role. At the time, the producers claimed that extensive research and access to Home Office documents promised that the teleplay would disclose Jack's true identity. Such a revelation could only ever be conjecture, but it served as excellent publicity for the production. There's no way the Ripper could have been the Queen's physician Sir William Gull, the alleged culprit here, but that didn't stop *From Hell* using the same plot device years later.

This is certainly a lavish production that benefits from all the money thrown at it. Victorian London looks superb, even if Whitechapel and its prostitutes are a bit too clean to ever be convincing. It sticks very much to a police procedural approach in telling the tale, with a few side stories thrown in. There's a love interest for Abberline in Jane Seymour, and a subplot involving an actor (Armand Assante) who's in town with his production of *Dr. Jekyll & Mr. Hyde*. I would have preferred these diversions to be absent, but it was very much the style of TV films from this time to inject some glamour into the story—even if wasn't required.

When it focuses on Jack and the search for him, it's first class. Michael Caine fills the role of Abberline like no one else before or since. Despite his tendency to shout his lines, it's a convincing performance of a dedicated policeman on the hunt for a seemingly unstoppable killer. He's ably assisted by his sergeant, as played by Lewis Collins in one of his few post-*Professionals* roles. I always liked Collins and was surprised he never went on to bigger and better things. The two make an engaging pair as they try to put the pieces together in fogbound London town.

As it's made for TV, the gorier side of Jack's work isn't fully represented on camera. Considering the subject matter, that might be considered a bit of a cop out, but it's done so well that it never presents itself as a problem. The murder scenes are quite faithfully recreated, and the injuries are discussed in full by Abberline and the pathologist. Besides, if they had gone down the bloody special effects route it would never have aired. This was terrestrial TV, remember, not cable!

There are bound to be many liberties taken with such a well-worn story, and this version is no different, but it's not a documentary despite its attempt at unveiling the killer. It's a glossy two-part TV drama that does exactly what you would expect of it. It entertains and engages the viewer while presenting enough real facts to give a decent account of the events in 1888 Whitechapel.

The last half hour certainly kicks into high gear as the chase for Jack intensifies. We are presented with the main suspects who are all preparing for something major, and there is a sense of a "ticking clock" to the proceedings. Will the police be able to stop Jack before he kills again and who exactly is the Ripper?

Formulaic it may be, but it's slickly done. As stated, the unmasking of Jack doesn't bear close scrutiny but that's not the point. If every movie about Jack the Ripper stuck to the facts it really would be a bore. There's a reason the legend has grown and shows no sign of abating. Jack was never identified, and that very fact has allowed novelists and filmmakers free rein to an extent. I've lost count of the amount of theories on the Ripper's identity, but that, coupled with the backdrop of Victorian London, lends itself to the imagination. I feel the ultimate Jack the Ripper movie has still to be made—there are many contenders for the title, and a lot of fun can be had with *Murder by Decree*, *Dr. Jekyll and Sister Hyde*, *From Hell* and so on, but for my money, this is the best of the crop to date.
—Matt Gemmell

UNDER THE BED

1988
D: Colin Finbow
W: Laura Beaumont
Starring: Thomas Arnold, Nicola Stewart, Charlie Dore, Maria Charles

> "I've been meaning to have a word with you about your room, George."

A cautionary tale concerning tidiness, *Under the Bed* announces itself under the credit banner "Scary Tales by Laura Beaumont and Bill Oddie," though sadly no further instalments of such a series appear to have arrived. A Channel 4-backed production of the Children's Film Unit, a project designed to allow under-16s to make movies targeted at a juvenile audience, this followed the earlier post-apocalyptic *Dark Enemy* and the creepy *Daemon* as a further fantasy entry among the CFU's output. As hinted at by Oddie's prominence, this is a more light-hearted offering than its predecessors, yet *Under the Bed* contains a few effective chills amid its comedy.

Brother and sister George and Felicity have their mum tearing her hair out with their lack of cleanliness and order. It's reached the point at which they don't even own sufficient crockery on which to serve meals, as used plates, dishes and cutlery have been left lying about the house and have mysteriously vanished (we witness George attempting to eat a sausage in a cup using a teaspoon in an early tone-setting scene.) The bickering family begin to accuse one another of hiding house-

A trash monster named Heap haunts *Under the Bed*.

hold items and personal possessions, but eventually all becomes clear when—via a literal smoke-and-mirrors effect—a trash-beast formed from the various undiscarded or forgotten bits and pieces rises up to startle the pet cat and launch its bid to gobble up the garbage. The beast, named "Heap" by Felicity, telekinetically pulls objects beneath the divan to add to its expanding mass (though it's choosy, firmly rejecting Felicity's tentative experimental offer of a *My Little Pony*!), awaiting the point where it can confidently reveal itself to the world and continue its refuse-chomping campaign.

An initially overjoyed Felicity collects rubbish and dirty laundry to sate the entity's vast appetite, Heap greedily and noisily slurping away at the grubby offerings—but when she herself falls victim to the creature's voracious hunger, her brother picks up his toy lightsaber and plastic shield, launching into defensive action as the beast looms large. Meanwhile, a security-obsessed busybody neighbor from next door is keeping her eyes peeled, her ears open, and her private CCTV and audio recording systems in full snoop mode ...

In classic monster movie tradition, Heap is kept hidden for a substantial part of the running time—but once he emerges, oozing out from hiding to reveal himself in full glory to George, *Under the Bed* really takes off. The messy behemoth is a mass of putrid food scraps, used cartons, plastic packaging and other detritus (even a copy of Jackie Collins' *Hollywood Wives* dangles from his formidable form!), all topped with the missing space helmet George has been seeking for ages. George employs a handy can of Glade air freshener to temporarily subdue the marauding threat, and finally manages to see off the funky fiend—although a supremely scary twist ending, beautifully staged and catching the viewer unawares, suggests otherwise.

Besides its pleasingly simple moral and its clever take on monster clichés, *Under the Bed* contains plenty of incidental delights. Former Alexei Sayle associate David Stafford raises laughs as a cheesy pub landlord staging increasingly naff theme events at his hostelry ("very Roy Rogers, I must say," comments a sarcastic punter on "Cowboy Night"!); chroniclers of fake horror films will revel in a detailed over-the-bar discussion about *The Night of the Big Green Wobbly Things*; George is an ardent devourer of comic books, so we see him eagerly leafing through issues of D.C.'s *House of Mystery* and Marvel's *Fantastic Four*—he also has a *Creepshow* poster tacked to his bedroom wall, though this indication of good taste is tempered by the sight elsewhere of a felt-tipped drawing of Timmy Mallett; but best of all has to be director Finbow's dream coup, as in the lead-up to the big finale he manages to corral Oddie, Tim Brooke-Taylor, and Graeme Garden for a brief *Goodies* reunion! The legendary trio play council binmen in a lovely scene to gladden the hearts of any cult TV viewer, reveling in the opportunity to adopt atrocious "working-class" accents and deliver a routine in which they fantasize about taking alternative employment (Graeme suggesting medicine, Bill ornithology, until Tim concludes that they ought to form a comedy team—"We could be the new *Young Ones*!" suggests Garden, to which Bill responds "I wouldn't mind being the old *Young Ones*!")

The credits confirm the participation of many school-age children among the crew, with their respective ages (ranging between 10 and 15 years old) appearing alongside their names. Bill Oddie was the script editor, while, oddly, he, spouse/co-writer Beaumont, and 12-year-old Christopher Heath are credited with special effects. Maybe Bill spent a couple of evenings preceding the shoot rifling through his dustbin ...
—Darrell Buxton

STAR TRAP

1989
D: Tony Bicât
W: Tony Bicât
Starring: Nicky Henson, Frances Tomelty, Jim Carter

In the same year that ITV adapted Susan Hill's *The Woman in Black* as one of their rare stand-alone small-screen offerings, this Zenith production for London Weekend Television also filled a couple of hours on the commercial network. It opens with a vicious knife-murder, committed within the ring of an ancient stone circle by a jester-like figure sporting a devil's mask ("carnival shop job—what kids wear at Halloween.") The victim? A prominent reactionary right-wing Member of Parliament, Sir John Fortescue. Local investigation of the case is aided by Adam Blunt (Nicky Henson), ex-police detective and best-selling author of pulp crime novels. Blunt lives up to his name, being a no-nonsense sort of boorish but somehow likeable figure—as if he's one of Henson's familiar 1970s Neanderthal "medallion man" characters, grown-up—and in a scene that ideally captures his persona, he's heckled, booed, and chased into the night by a bunch of outraged feminists midway through delivering a lecture about his work as a paperback hack.

Director Tony Bicât seems to have had a sparse career in film and television—his experimental 1972 BFI-funded venture *Skinflicker*, also centered around the gruesome murder of a high-ranking politician, is certainly worth your time, though he largely worked in theater. It came as quite a surprise to see his name pop up on this one in the late 1980s, and *Star Trap* exhibits a frivolity and broadness at odds with much of Bicât's other output. It almost plays like a pilot show for a prospective series, perhaps along *Midsomer Murders* lines, and although it isn't of sufficient quality to have prompted a longer run, one can well imagine Henson and Frances Tomelty continuing their bitchy relationship in future episodes.

Anticipating the likes of *Hot Fuzz*, *Star Trap* sees a number of rural types skulking about after dark, holding meetings at which assignations and events are discussed in secretive tones, committing foul deeds, and donning robes and other satanic finery. The lugubrious Jim Carter, always a welcome presence in this type of fare, plays Dr. Wax, a respected local personage who gives the impression that he actually believes in the powers of darkness—confronted by the two segments of a cracked/reassembled "witch's mirror," he reacts with alarm and lapses into a trance state (Bicât inserts a whirling 360 degree whip pan here, which proves to be one of the more memorable moments of the show), and he's later witnessed (by us) apparently offering his soul up to his "Master." A second brutal killing at the standing stones is captured on camera, but all may not quite be what it seems, and the over-involved plot resolves with a *Theatre of Blood*-style fencing finale interrupting a stage performance of *Richard III*, with Blunt and R.S.C. Shakespearian star Basil Underwood (Philip Sayer) as the blade-flashing participants. The title comes into play here too, with Tomelty fac-

Below: TV listing for *Star Trap* and its competition

Thu

EVENING

7:00 ⓶ **48 Hours** A report on the historic December 1st Moscow summit between Soviet leader Gorbachev and Pope John Paul II. (In Stereo) ▫
⑤ **Cosby Show** Tempers flare when Denise's in-laws visit the Huxtable clan. (In Stereo) ▫
⑦ **Mission: Impossible** Members of the IMF use modern technology and old-fashioned superstition to uncover a dishonest arms dealer in the Northern Ireland conflict. (In Stereo) ▫

⑨ **Movie** "Ordeal by Innocence" (1984) Donald Sutherland, Faye Dunaway. A research scientist in England sets out to unravel the mystery behind a woman's murder. Based on a novel by Agatha Christie. (2:00)
⑪ **Chicago Tonight** With John Callaway.
㉖ **Rebelde**
㉜ **Movie** "The Godfather" (1972) (Part 2 of 2) Marlon Brando, Al Pacino. A mafia patriarch finds that ruling his volatile family is his biggest challenge. (2:00)
㊳ **700 Club**
㊿ **Movie** "Star Trap" (1989) Nicky Henson, Frances Tomelty. Two writers put aside their mutual disdain of one another to locate the brutal killer of a Parliament member. (2:00)
㉚ **Movie** "Last Embrace"

(1979) Roy Scheider, Janet Margolin. A former undercover agent finds himself being pursued by an unknown killer. (2:00)
(ARTS) Victory at Sea The little-known islands of Peleliu and Anguar were the sites of some of the most bitter fighting in the Pacific.
(BRAVO) South Bank Show "Joseph Heller" A discussion about Joseph Heller's fourth book, "God Knows," featuring interviews with Heller and his close friends.
(DIS) Best of Walt Disney Presents "In Shape With Von Drake" Goofy and Ludwig Von Drake demonstrate comical calisthenics.
(NICK) Bewitched
(SHOW) Jimmie Walker and Friends II Taped in Las Vegas, the veteran co-

median introduces three newcomers -- The Amazing Jonathan, Ron Richards and Carol Siskind. (R) (In Stereo) ▫
(TMC) Movie "Midnight Run" (2:02)
(TNN) Conversation With Dinah Scheduled: Wayne Rogers. (In Stereo)
(USA) Christmas Adventure Animated. Santa faces a dilemma on Christmas Eve when his reindeer master disappears.
(WWOR) Remington Steele Laura and Remington are hired to find out who murdered an artist.
7:05 (WTBS) Movie "Rescue From Gilligan's Island" (1:40)
7:30 ⑤ **Ann Jillian** (Series Premiere) Comedy. A New York widow moves to California and does her best to

accustom herself to the new surroundings. (In Stereo) ▫
⑪ **Sneak Previews Goes Video** (In Stereo)
(ARTS) Eagle and the Bear Tensions rise when the Soviet Union backs North Korea in the conflict with South Korea.
(AMC) This Is Your Life: William Bendix (R)
(NICK) Mister Ed Mr. Ed convinces Wilbur to let a swaybacked horse stay with them.
(TNN) Crook and Chase Featured: actor Jimmy Stewart's new book "Jimmy Stewart and His Poems." (In Stereo)
7:50 (DIS) Disney Salutes the American Teacher First lady Barbara Bush hosts this collection of profiles of America's top teachers. (R)

Nicky Henson and Frances Tomelty in *Star Trap*

ing a fiendish fate trapped beneath the pulverizing counterweight of the theater's trapdoor mechanism.

Nowadays a little dated—the lame would-be "humorous" spots involving a pair of comedy-relief Japanese tourists, the score by Bicât's brother Nick being dominated by *In the Air Tonight*-style percussion overlaid with synth swathes—*Star Trap* passes the time nicely enough, but ultimately fails in its aim of combining devil worship and "folk horror" tropes with a more ITV-friendly manner. An unengaging comedy thriller which comes up short on both laughs and excitement.
—Darrell Buxton

THE WOMAN IN BLACK

1989
D: Herbert Wise
W: Nigel Kneale
Starring: Adrian Rawlins, Bernard Hepton, David Daker, Pauline Moran

Transmitted originally by ITV on Christmas Eve, 1989, this adaptation of Susan Hill's 1983 novel revived fond memories of the BBC's late lamented *A Ghost Story for Christmas* and, until *Ghostwatch* came along three years later, was arguably the most frightening British TV movie of its era. Its credentials were certainly impressive: Director Herbert Wise was a TV veteran who helmed episodes of *Out of the Unknown*, *Man in a Suitcase* and, most notably, the classic "Royal Jelly" (among eight others) from *Tales of the Unexpected*. Mid-'90s Oscar winner Rachel Portman contributed the score, the strong cast includes small roles for Hammer veteran John Cater and future Brit horror hero Andy Nyman, and in charge of the adaptation was screenwriter Nigel Kneale, already the force behind perhaps the finest British TV ghost story of the 1970s, *The Stone Tape*.

Now better known for its long-running stage version and a 2012 Hammer Films remake, *The Woman in Black* makes for a splendidly eerie and beguiling small-screen ghost story, ideal for a chilly winter's night or a crisp Christmas Eve by the fire with some sloe gin. It's old fashioned in the best way and full of classical elements, drawing us effortlessly into its traditional old mansion setting surrounded by misty salt marshes, with the ever-present sound of howling wind and a mysteriously locked room that, at one key point, is suddenly found with portal ajar. The mark of its success is that such a modest detail as an open door proves far more powerful than the leagues of bathroom mirror/hand on shoulder jump-scares that came to dominate post-*Scream* American horror.

Adrian Rawlins is a charismatic presence, as a sceptical solicitor with a loving family and a new baby, who is sent by his employer to tend to the affairs of a recently deceased woman in a quaint market town full of shifty-acting locals. With only a (short-lived) cute dog named Spider for company, Rawlins stays at the dead woman's house and is soon haunted by the eponymous ghost—a silent, funereally-garbed pasty figure with reddened eyes whose demise he hears repeatedly. Further investigation reveals the woman's bastard son was taken away from her—desperate to get him back, both she and the child perished in a marsh "accident".

Pauline Moran's brief appearances as the Woman in Black haunts this movie just as she plagues its central character. Initially appearing as an unearthly but low-key background presence, she is afforded a stark close-up half an hour in, though her most alarming appearance forms the core of the film's best scare. Awoken by a (dead) child's voice, Rawlins is confronted by the malevolently grinning Moran looming over his head. As if it wasn't already hard enough to sleep on Christmas Eve when you're 11, this movie only added to the juvenile festive insomnia ...

Until the final scene, this is the most overt fright in an admirably understated though consistently creepy movie. Director Wise knows what makes an effective ghost story, punctuating the

steadily unfolding tale with subtle foreshadowing (prefiguring his own demise, Rawlins saves a Gypsy girl from falling logs) and quiet spine-shivering chills involving a child's ball bouncing by itself (shades of *The Changeling*) or a dog barking intently at nothing visible. Aside from the hackneyed use of piercing *Psycho* strings, Portman's somber score fits the mood nicely and Rawlins, who has to carry hefty portions of screen time by himself, is a sympathetic hero responding believably to the intense situations. His reaction after seeing the Woman in Black initially is to retreat to his own house and swiftly turn all the lights on.

As with most ghost stories of its kind, the ending brings little in the way of comfort, though this one bows out on a startlingly grim note. Enjoying a day out on the lake with his family, Rawlins sees the Woman standing on the water right before a falling tree capsizes their boat and sends everyone to their doom. Ah, dead children and terrifying ghosts invading your bedroom at night ... Merry Christmas, kids!!
—Steven West

THE YELLOW WALLPAPER

1989
D: John Clive
W: Maggie Wadey
Starring: Stephen Dillane, Julia Watson, Carolyn Pickles, James Faulkner, Dorothy Tutin

Amid a world of lawn croquet, piano recitals, meringues, and society gatherings, the fragile Charlotte's plight is played out before us. A disturbed young woman, but with the fortune to be married to a doctor specializing in her particular illness of

Creepy eyes watching you in *The Yellow Wallpaper*

the mind, Charlotte (Julia Watson) is whisked away to a country retreat for recuperation—but her barred and sparse room, furnished with a brass bedstead steadfastly nailed to the floorboards, and decorated with peculiar primrose wall covering which holds a magnetic allure, becomes as much a focus for inner torment as is the interior of her cranium.

This BBC adaptation of the feminist short story by Charlotte Perkins Gilman is a riveting piece, largely forgotten today but really perhaps only a notch or two down from the classic psychological/supernatural combos brought forth from the likes of Nigel Kneale or Lawrence Gordon Clark. The central performance by Watson is captivating and affecting, and John Clive's careful directorial approach proves constantly significant and arresting. Note the pre-credits scene, a simple close-up of Charlotte traveling to her destination by carriage—on one hand it conveys this basic information, yet the quiet intensity, the monotony, the nodding of her head (caused merely by the vehicle's movement? Or something more internal?), even the quilted padding of the inner door, are immediately suggestive of the poor woman's struggle against her demons.

Cameraman John Hooper is one of the major unsung heroes of British horror, having worked marvels alongside Leslie Megahey in the justly-feted *Schalcken the Painter* and the equally impressive *Duke Bluebeard's Castle*, and on duty again here Hooper pulls some startling tricks—the eerie shots of Charlotte's visions, possible phantoms represented by a white-frocked child pedaling a bicycle and a truly unsettling, hideous crawling figure garbed in bright yellow, evoke the genre's past while perhaps looking ahead to the beyond-creepy imagery of late 1990s Japanese and Korean horror, and the film's unforgettable, sensational set piece in which a pair of unattached, isolated eyes spring open within the pattern of the wallpaper itself is preceded by a foreboding, agonizing camera crawl taking we viewers on a hypnotic journey into the heart of the design—as effective a moment of audience/character identification/crossover as you could experience.

While the seasoned aficionado may well guess the eventual outcome, this particular viewer did not; telegraphed or otherwise, the concluding images in the wrecked room add a final frisson or two which ideally cap this exercise in low-key, high-effect mental fright. Highly recommended to admirers of period "costume chills" and those who appreciate their horrors hushed and reserved.
—Darrell Buxton

APPENDIX 1:
BORDERLINE FILMS/MISCELLANY

Besides the entries featured in the main body of *Dead or Alive*, our editor and team considered many other titles for possible inclusion—discarding plenty on the basis that they were not fully or partially official British productions (despite appearances), that they were not sufficiently "horrific" (maybe leaning more towards the thriller or fantasy genres, for instance), that they were not "films" (we've included qualifying cinema releases plus features aimed at the home video market; and we've included a separate section for "movies made for television" but have been selective in distinguishing between TV "films" and one-off small-screen dramas, giving certain titles a full entry but relegating others to our "peripheral and problem" appendix, sometimes based on running time, sometimes on nothing more than a gut feeling).

In making our choices, however, we felt that some of the titles we'd ditched might be worthy of fuller coverage. Some contributors even submitted speculative reviews of particular favorites—foreign horrors shot in England, macabre comedies, genre-straddling TV plays, etc.—and we also decided to select a few of the stronger semi-British, semi-horror, or semi-"film" contenders for the full review treatment. This "Borderline" section contains reviews of the assorted 1980s productions that maybe don't quite fit the remit of *Dead or Alive*, but which possess an appeal all of their own for those horror buffs who have seen all of the conventional fare and are maybe seeking to expand their shock-film horizons. Not quite "British Horror Films of the 1980s," then, but the following titles probably deserve the attention of fans of that scene and that era. All are missing an element, or maybe two, excluding them from the main body of the book (*Haunted Honeymoon*, for example, is a "film" and is "horror" but isn't actually "British" despite being shot in England with a home-based supporting cast) but we think they all ought to be of interest to anyone reading this.

This appendix also features substantial reviews of two of the titles from our British horror shorts listing, namely *Chimera* and *Incident at Romans Court*.

APARTMENT ZERO

1988
D: Martin Donovan

Six years after the Falklands conflict, here's a welcome show of Argentinean/British unity—or perhaps not, as *Apartment Zero* is in fact the result of a team-up between production houses in Buenos Aires and Jersey, a decidedly odd partnership even in the increasingly strange world of cinematic "puddings" of this nature.

The content displays "mash-up" tendencies of a similarly unexpected variety, mingling Polanski-style isolation/enclosure/psychosis with a political/terrorism bent (Pablo Larrain's masterpiece *Tony Manero* achieved a similarly outré mix of slasher-film bodycount and Pinochet bodycount two decades later, throwing in *Saturday Night Fever* for good measure!) Colin Firth has gradually usurped the likes of Hugh Grant to corner the market in bumbling babe-magnet bachelor types, but has by no means been averse to taking roles in more disturbing fare, with *The Turn of the Screw* (1999), *Trauma* (2004), *Dorian Gray* (2009) and *Devil's Knot* (2013) on his resumé, and *Apartment Zero* represents the earliest occasion on which his career took a turn for the bleak. He plays Adrian LeDuc, a flat-dwelling loner whose only outlets seems to be working part-time in a local cinema (we meet him projecting *Touch of Evil* while standing in front of an *Eyes of Laura Mars* poster) and paying visits to his insane mother, being cared for in a nearby nursing facility. In need of cash, he takes up a suggestion to rent out ma's room—but is the James Dean-cool, brash, outgoing new tenant Jack Carney (Hart Bochner) also the efficient assassin terrorizing the neighborhood and piling up corpses hither and thither? ("Victima Numero 12," scream the newspaper headlines.)

In the absence of 1980s Roman Polanski contributing a new layer of lodging-house lunacy in echo of his *Repulsion*, *Rosemary's Baby* and *The Tenant*, here director Martin Donovan steps in to offer a claustrophobic thriller filled with menace, tension, hints

of homoeroticism and suggestions of doppelganger identity confusion, and best of all, a truly Polanski-like gaggle of grotesques congregating on the landings and stairwells, a rancid Greek chorus of decided disapproval, led by the superbly seedy McKinney sisters (Dora Bryan and Liz Smith, doing what they do best!) Firth's attempts to ingratiate himself with his new room-mate extend merely to a showboating "game" in which he claims to be able to identify any motion picture via the naming of three cast members (sample: Yul Brynner, Edward G. Robinson and Vincent Price), leading to his anguished cry of, "You ruined it all with Art Garfunkel!" at one point. The extended running time of 125 minutes does unfortunately mean we get padding aplenty, though this often proves noteworthy in itself—the comic cat-rescuing episode half-an-hour in, for instance, which dissipates the grim tone but carries pleasures of its own, all spoof-Leone extreme close-ups of facial features in rapid succession set to jaunty violin accompaniment.

Apartment Zero (so named because one of the numbers adorning Firth's front door has come loose) skirts around fear and fright throughout, instead emphasizing repression, sexuality (or lack of), paranoia and politics, but the threat of murder lurks constantly in the background and emerges fully-fledged towards the close, with bodybag splitting, cadaver-dumping, and a fleetingly-glimpsed but indelible "crazy person interacting with stuffed corpse around the dinner table" moment to round everything off in a suitably macabre manner.
—Darrell Buxton

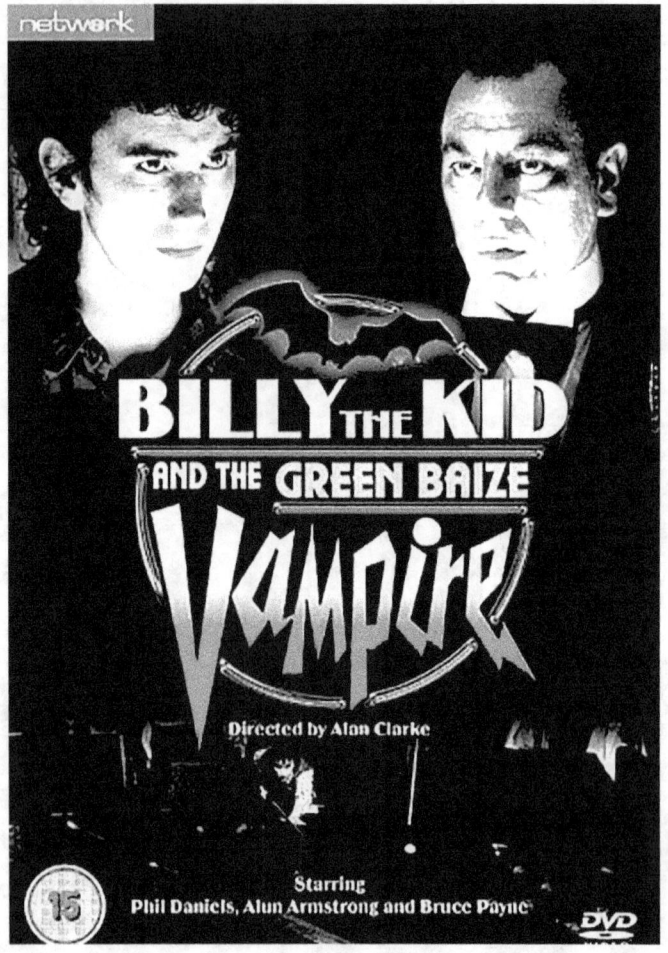

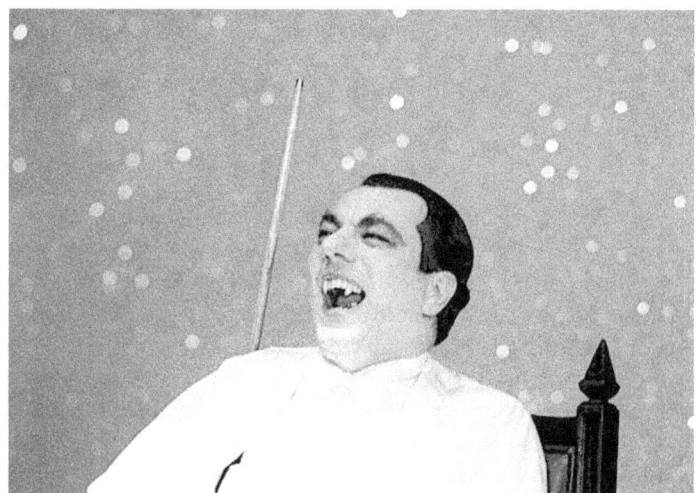

***Billy the Kid and the Green Baize Vampire* is an Alan Parker musical featuring a pool-playing quasi-vampire.**

BILLY THE KID AND THE GREEN BAIZE VAMPIRE

1985
D: Alan Clarke

People did some strange things in 1985. Perhaps buoyed by the recent success of an arthouse horror film—Neil Jordan's *The Company of Wolves*—the bright sparks at ITC Entertainment decided to see if they could bottle the lightning a second time. They hired some genuine acting talent—Phil Daniels, Alun Armstrong, Don Henderson, Zoot Money—and even secured the services of *Company*'s composer, George Fenton. As icing on the cake, they nabbed Alan Clarke as director—a man whose extensive television and cinema output featured such hard-hitting, at times artistic, pieces as *Scum*, *Made in Britain*, *Elephant*—dealing with the troubles in Northern Ireland in terrifying manner—and *Rita, Sue and Bob Too*. For television, he directed such seminal works of fantasy and heightened realism as *Penda's Fen*, *Psy-Warriors*, and the highly acclaimed, David Bowie-starring adaptation of Brecht's *Baal*. And with the scripting help of Trevor Preston, who'd done such great, off-kilter work on ITV's fantasy adventure series *Ace of Wands*, all seemed set for a film that would at least be interesting.

So, what went wrong? The sad answer is, almost everything. tensions between Clarke and Preston plagued the production—the latter wanted an exuberant, colorful, location shooting-filled piece, the former a shadowy expressionistic collection of extremely minimal sets (which he got). A good many of the usually excellent cast frequently seem to be phoning it in, grimly lowering their head and bulling towards the wrap party and pay cheque. Fenton's musical score shows none of the atmosphere, beauty or menace that he brought to *Company*.

And the whole film suffers from an identity crisis. Our titular snooker-loopy hero is at first seen as a kindly, Robin Hood figure, donating the winnings from his tournaments to the disadvantaged—the poor, the elderly, the sick. With his reigning champ opponent characterized as a wannabe-posh social climber, hiding his obnoxiousness under a sneering upper-class veneer, all seems set for some good old socialism versus capitalism action. Maybe not original, but at least enjoyable.

But then it throws that all away. The big final confrontation has Billy's supporters depicted only as would-be edgy kids wearing artfully proto-grungy ensembles that doubtless cost as much as the tuxes and twin sets sported by the Vampire's upper-class, stuffy cohorts. The old, the sick, the truly needy, aren't there cheering Billy on. They've vanished, and the whole thing becomes a shabby riff on the old "the kids are all right" theme. By the time that the only true hints of the supernatural in the whole film appear, with the not-a-vampire Vampire using telekinesis to suspend Billy's winning ball over the pocket, and Billy responding by whipping out a magic gun and shooting the ball into the hole, it's hard not to feel as though we've been sold an almighty pup. This impression is only strengthened as we don't even get a decent victory celebration scene, but simply smash into the end credits as Bruce Payne, playing Billy's manager and giving the only committed performance in the thing, belts out one more number looking a lot like the younger, sharper Adam Faith.

Because yes, this film is a musical. However, it's a totally forgettable one. None of the many songs here would pass Old Grey's famous whistle test. If anything, the Faith comparison perhaps points the way—this would have probably worked a lot better as some splashy, cheery Cliff Richard vehicle from the mid-1960s, with the colorful location work that Preston, in this case, had been right to request. Instead, the whole film is a dreary oddity, and an unfortunate misstep by the usually shrewd Clarke. A musical with uninteresting songs, a film whose title promises horror but delivers only the most token of fantastical gestures. It's sad to say that this one's been all but forgotten, but maybe the stake was through the heart before the first frame was shot.
—Ken Shinn

THE BLACK CAT

1981
D: Lucio Fulci

Filmed in England by one of the Italian horror greats, in the wake of his classic "zombie" period, *The Black Cat* also toplines two debatedly "British" actors, Northern Irish legend Patrick Magee in one of his last roles, and New Zealand-born but British-based one-time Hammer thesp David Warbeck, by this time a star in Italy, as, respectively, a mad professor who believes cats are evil (similar to Peter Cushing in *The Uncanny*; Cushing turned down the role here) and a Scotland Yard inspector. All hell breaks loose in the sumptuous yet somehow alien-looking English countryside, "Italianized" as only Fulci could, making a quintessentially English village look out-of-step. Cars crash, hilarious "meowing" noises are set to POV shots from a moggy's eyes, the feline kills suspiciously Latino-looking locals, and Warbeck's Inspector Gorley and American photographer Mimsy Farmer (in a role perhaps better suited to British Fulci regular Catriona MacColl) have to stop it. It plays like a giallo with a cat as the killer! Mad, beautifully shot and with an unrestrained, towering performance by British horror veteran Magee, this wild, loose Poe adaptation may only be partially shot in Blighty, with interiors done in Rome, but manages to capture an odd kind of Agatha Christie quality, albeit in that gory Fulci style. See it!
—George White

BLACK CANDLES

1980
D: José Larraz (as "Joseph Braunstein")

> "I'm sure you've never seen a billy-goat mounting a woman—and later coming inside her."

By the early 1980s things were certainly more "Jesús Franco" than "General Franco" in the newly liberated Spain. New freedom of expression onscreen may have ultimately paved the way for Almodovar, Alex de la Iglesia, and Alejandro Amenabar, but true to exploitation form, the immediate effect was a welter of titles taking up the nation's love of cinematic sex and violence, expanding these within fresh and more lenient boundaries.

José Larraz, famously a resident of Tunbridge Wells but flitting between England's Home Counties and Barcelona in crafting a string of exciting, attention-grabbing horror and thriller productions, had coasted a little since his 1974 peak which unleashed the classic British fright flicks *Vampyres* and *Symptoms*. *Violation of the Bitch* (1978) offered a striking return to form, and in 1980 Larraz set and shot *Los Ritos Sexuales de Diablo* (aka *Black Candles* or *Hot Fantasies*) in and around London, this simple study of a sex-crazed Satanic cult furthering the director's penchant for mingling shocks with bare flesh. The nudity and bedroom antics take precedence here, with a number of artily-shot couplings dominating the running time—horror elements are confined to a post-coital voodoo demise during the prologue, a grim climactic sword impalement (via anus!) towards the close, and lots of ritual gatherings, use of pagan imagery, and that aforementioned spectacle featuring a performing goat and a game young actress. Speaking of "game," Euro-veteran Helga Line heads the cast here, and, aged almost 50 at the time and looking a knockout, throws herself into the sexual melee with abandon, going topless without a second thought (though reliant on a body double for anything more risqué and energetic.)

Black Candles is mainly presented in tight shots and cramped tableaux, possibly to disguise its thinly spread resources, though it still looks pretty cheap. The frequency of the sex scenes at least prevents an over-reliance on tedious and trite dialogue. Pundits seem to be divided with regard to the "all a dream/it's happening again" closing scene, but students of Larraz ought to rejoice, as this wasn't the first time the director had employed such a conceit. The director himself, hugely self-critical, is said to rate only *Symptoms*, *El Mirón* (1977) and the TV series *Goya* from his own oeuvre; quoted in Cathal Tohill & Pete Tombs' study of Euro-horror, *Immoral Tales*, his viewpoint on *Black Candles* was, "I don't like that film ... I'm very interested in sabbatical things and witches. To do a good film about this you need a lot of money and good actors and actresses, and you don't go so far with the sex. No one in that film could act. So, what do you do with them? You put them in bed and have them jump on each other."
—Darrell Buxton

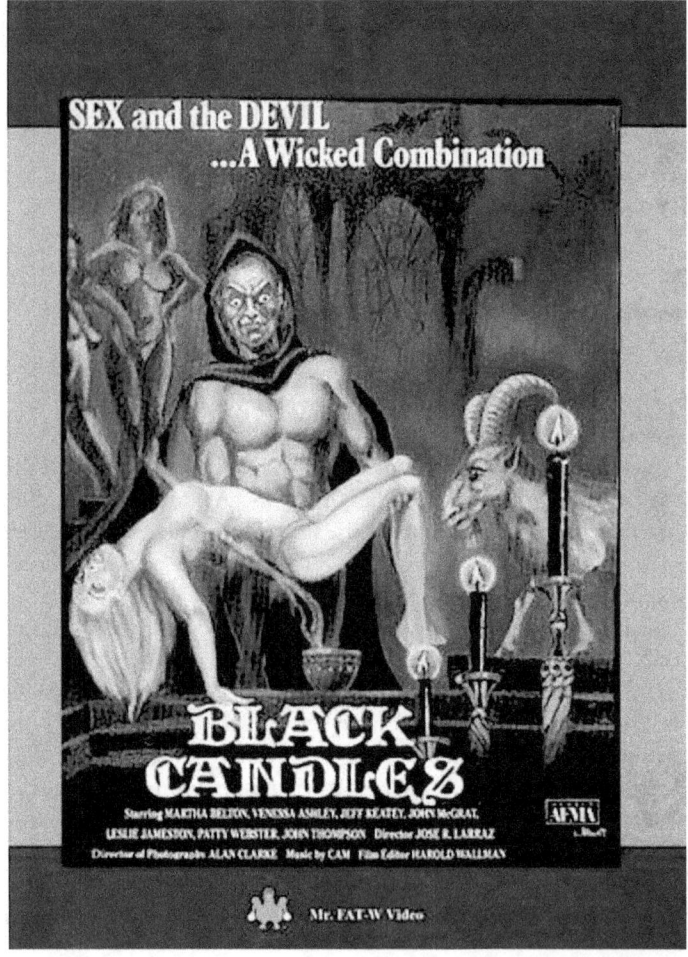

BLOOD TRACKS

1985
D: Mats Helge (as "Mike Jackson") and Derek Ford (uncredited)

For a man who once claimed rock and pop made him physically sick, Brit exploitation supremo Derek Ford certainly spent a lot of time working with musicians who played it. His own masterpiece, *Groupie Girl*, pits a non-existent rock combo fronted by Donald Sumpter against real-life hopefuls Opal Butterfly and English Rose; *Don't Open Till Christmas* allows Hammer Glamour superstar Caroline Munro a crack at pop stardom with her brand of sex-laden white funk before inevitably bringing her face to face with a sliced-up corpse (cue scream); while this rarely-seen curiosity, shot in Sweden with a primarily Swedish cast but with considerable British involvement, goes one better by actually acting as a vehicle for native glam metallers Easy Action (referred to in the film, for the benefit of anyone who digs Bolan references, as "Solid Gold"), who even by the standards of that genre are as low-rent as the film itself. And trust me, as one who grew up listening to this stuff, I'm being complimentary ...

Put it this way: Hanoi Rocks they weren't, although their playing is relatively professional compared to some of their contemporaries (like Poison, who blatantly stole the melody from a song included in this very movie for their hit "I Want Action" a year later), their obscurity ensures them a certain underground credibility, and guitarist Kee Marcello later achieved worldwide fame with Europe. But the music isn't the problem: sadly, while said song *("We Go Rockin'")* and the title track appear several times throughout, more focus is actually given to their acting skills—which, in all honesty, are dismal, although Marcello manages a comical "mwahahaha" while dicking around joke-scaring his girlfriend/groupie before, of course, *actually* getting killed in gory and painful fashion.

Allegedly, during shooting, the entire band, particularly singer Zinny Zan, were so terrified of reading lines on cue, that both directors decided to resolve the problem by getting them so pissed they no longer cared. It shows, although to be honest most Scandinavian (or indeed British) sleaze-glam merchants I've encountered behave like that anyway. Likewise, their bimbo model-dancers, presumably not hired for their thespian abilities (but, hey, when were glamour girls in horror flicks *ever* hired for such reasons?), splutter through their lines with little conviction—or at least we assume they do, as the film appears to have been shot in phonetic "Swinglish" then dubbed into more easily saleable Yank accents by people who *also* can't act. The key to enjoying the film, therefore (if you can be bothered) is to accept this state of affairs, and go with the so-bad-it's-good trash approach; on that level, it almost works, or at least would do if you could see what the hell was going on.

Unfortunately, again, it seems to have been shot by someone who believes fear and suspense (not that there *is* much of either) are best created simply by turning the lights off indoors. Result—it's impossible to determine half the time (a) the difference between the killers and the good guys (b) who's alive or dead or (c) who's actually *doing* the killing; also, on several occasions, "monsters" offed five minutes ago seem to mysteriously return to life, massacring more Nordic York Dolls and their as-

sociates with renewed fervor. Or maybe they just look alike. After all, they are inbred. Or maybe they have superhuman strength. Or maybe ... when they wrote the script, they didn't give a shit. Yes, that seems the most likely option. The "plot," such as it is, *is* relatively easy to follow, although full of holes—a family hide out in their remote mountain home, afraid of a nutter they appear to be somehow related to. Luckily, they overpower and kill him, but then realize they'll have to hide there, in their basement under an old factory, for the foreseeable future, avoiding prosecution—thus being forced into bumping off and eating the occasional passing itinerant for survival, when not presumably living off whatever else is indigenous to Arctic tundra. They get away with it for 40 years (by which time the woman is very old and her kids are middle-aged grizzly-men) until, lo and behold, a bunch of rock stars and their entourage arrive to shoot a video, thus disturbing the peace and quiet and meaning they have to be picked off one by one in a variety of gruesome ways (usually beheading, though strangulation and head-splatting also figures.)

What ruins a potentially passable gore movie (aforementioned acting, dubbing and lighting aside) is the lack of any plausible explanation (if they've been living there all that time, where do they get their strength? Okay, the factory could give off radiation or something, but it's never alluded to), the lack of character focus (all, even the hero and heroine, are dull, uninteresting and expendable, with little gripping dialogue or intriguing back story), and, worst of all, the absence of any discernible structure: sure, people start going missing, and their mates, fraternal or romantic, start to notice, but rather than deriving any drama or excitement from the situation, most of the running time is taken up doing exactly that—running, randomly playing cat and mouse around the disused factory (which seems to consist of one room shot from differing angles) in the gloom, as if Helge and Ford tired of trying to discipline their wayward charges and opted for the easiest way out. Then, suddenly, a helicopter appears containing some characters who conveniently disappeared earlier (I think), the survivors are rescued, and it's over—although again, someone who could be either man or monster is shown still screaming in agony underground. Maybe he was the executive producer ...
—Darius Drewe

BRAZIL

1985
D: Terry Gilliam

In the late 1970s, David Lynch described his debut feature *Eraserhead* as "a dream of dark and troubling things." In 1984, Michael Radford saw an idea whose time had come and directed a faithful big-screen version of Orwell's *1984*. And, in 1985, Terry Gilliam, the mad animator genius of *Monty Python* who'd scored surprise cinema success as the director of 1981's *Time Bandits*, released a film that combined Lynch's dream with Radford's warning against the terrors of oppressive regimes—and, being Gilliam, also made it surprisingly funny in parts, beautifully designed and acted, and a wild and resonant piece of fantasia.

Taking place "somewhere in the 20th century," the film tells the tale of Sam Lowry, a lowly government official who falls in love with—literally—the girl of his dreams ... who may also be a dangerous terrorist involved in guerrilla actions against said government. Accepting promotion beyond his abilities in order to pursue her, he becomes involved in chaotic events that ultimately spiral to a terrifying conclusion.

Brazil is a film that I don't want to give away too much about, in case you haven't seen it—because for me, it succeeds in becoming so much more than just another remake of *1984*. As the middle segment of Gilliam's famous "Dreams Trilogy," it mixes the hideous, plastic-smiled consumer-driven dystopia of its "reality" with Sam's spectacular, mystifying reveries and nightmares, filled with symbolism and blurring the divide between the real and the imaginary until the viewer is too puzzled, and too intrigued, to stop watching.

The historic stories of the vast troubles that Gilliam ran into in simply getting the film out there—the secret screenings for critics, the full-page advert in *Variety*, the casual butchering that took place for its initial US release—have become cinematic legend, the unfortunate but determined director surely identifying more and more with his beleaguered protagonist in his increasingly desperate battles with a studio system capable of being as monolithic and callous as any dictatorial government. But, in the end, Gilliam triumphs. Maybe, ironically, Love really did conquer all.

Presenting us with a world where Orwell's omnipresent, bullying authority (massive, intimidating, Brutalist buildings, propaganda posters pasted on every available surface) crashes headlong into Rube Goldberg mechanized chaos—with government orders garbled via insects getting trapped in typewriter keys, and ducts of various levels of elegance and size intruding everywhere—Gilliam gives us a vista that succeeds at being oddly convincing even as our eyes are struggling to take in its sheer baroque complexity. And this world is peopled by fascinating characters, superbly portrayed—from Jonathan Pryce's wimpish but sympathetic Sam, via Katherine Helmond as his surface-obsessed mother, Michael Palin as cinema's happiest and scariest torturer, Peter Vaughan as the creepily avuncular public face of power, Robert De Niro's plumber-turned-Robin-Hood, Kim Greist's butch yet appealing truck-driving dream girl, to name just some—all adding to the atmosphere of this bizarre society existing just a twist away from our own.

Along the way, you'll see polka-dotted power stations, gigantic cybernetic Samurai, soaring visions of Icarus-like flight, and brutal interrogations. You'll see people literally drowned in shit and smothered in paperwork. You'll see a world that, for all of its exaggerations, you might find yourself recognizing a tad more than feels comfortable. A world that makes you laugh out loud in slightly uneasy nervousness.

You'll see a work of humane, individualist genius.
Welcome ... to *Brazil*.
"Sam, Sam ... what are we going to do with you, Sam? ..."
—Ken Shinn

CHIMERA

1989
D: Andy Morris

In the 1980s, home cameras gave way to video camcorders, and what should have been greater flexibility and freedom—but although film processing costs were removed, the less tactile format didn't lend itself as well to the amateur for the editing process, also leaving something to be desired in terms of picture quality. The image was more immediate, but less romantic. Video was therefore perfectly apt for the color-polluted pop-modernity of the 1980s, in naughty home entertainment series like *The International Red Tape* (1982) and *Electric Blue* (1982-89), in training videos, or in irksome art films like Jack Bond and Jane Arden's sci-fi shambles *Anti-Clock*.

In 1979 *Blood on Satan's Claw* scripter Robert Wynne-Simmons had been granted his directorial debut with *The Experiment*, the first British monster film shot on one-inch video tape but the editing process had not been thought through and the project still languishes in unfinished form, unseen by the public (though rumors of an obscure video release on the Club label are under investigation). The first UK horror film shot on video confirmed as securing a spot on store shelves was Lindsay Honey's *Death Shock*, which was no more than a lame collection of sex scenes linked by some routine occult cult rumblings. Things didn't improve much with Alan Briggs' no-budget *Suffer, Little Children*. If anything, it wasn't until Lindsay Shonteff's *The Killing Edge* that video was put to good use, contrarily capturing a verdant spring and the opposing bleak winter of a post-apocalyptic England.

As families took a gambit on video cameras to capture baby's very first steps or typical summer outings, the kids themselves began making films, normally using chronological shooting schedules, editing in-camera with simple results. This generation would get increasingly adventurous, but only a few youngsters had the motivation and chutzpah to go that one step further and produce a video feature. The end result may have been terrible, more often than not, but you have to appreciate the ambition of someone like Andy Morris, the teenager who shot *Chimera* in Worcester in 1988 and then the following year went one incredible step further and submitted it to the BBFC (British Board of Film Classification). It was an action that financially cost him far more than the film itself, as the Board operates on a price-per-minute charge, whether you be Warner Bros. or some teenage chancer.

With a recyclable cast of four, and a minimalist storyline stretched into what might marginally qualify as a "featurette," the results are poor, clearly amateur, and the makers have admitted that it should never have been submitted to the BBFC. Often reported as 45 minutes in length, the copy under review runs 39 minutes and 28 seconds, though I am assured that this is the released version. The film was awarded a PG rating, another killer blow to already-slim commercial prospects, but it is understood that Morris anticipated problems in the rating and so pre-cut it, perhaps too far. Despite this, it ends on a botched gory note that appears contradictory to the PG rating, no matter how unconvincing the effect may appear.

The story is slight, inspired by better films but at the same time pre-empting future genre trends. The characters are identified by functional names only, possibly influenced by Walter Hill's *The Driver*; therefore, we have The Viewer, The Screen, The Dead (not one but many) and, tellingly, The Driver. The Viewer is our female protagonist (Marcelle Perks) who rents a videocassette (the title of which is blurred and unreadable but which might be called *Pyramid*) from the local Vales Video store, encouraged by the shop assistant that it's one to "blow your mind." Returning home, she slips the cassette into the machine only for it to run a pattern that sends her to sleep.

She awakens into a parallel Worcester, a dimension where life has been all but extinguished, the survivors a peppering of zombies (mostly played by Mark Cox, but with the odd extra stunt zombie provided by director Morris), skull-faced, sharing the same head covering, a one-piece mask manufactured especially for the film. On rousing again, she finds herself in conversation with a face staring out from her television set, The Screen (Andy Morris), who informs her that she has entered a new world and that there are lessons to be learnt.

The initial exploration of the deserted streets confirms their emptiness. She continues on, sprinting into action from one location to the next—a shopping precinct, the main retail thoroughfares, a railway yard, Worcester Cathedral. All this tramping and darting around is broken up by the occasional encounter. The arrival of a car in the railway yard brings forth The Driver (Ted Murray), a detective, providing The Viewer with some hope that there are others out there, though that outlook is quickly dashed when he is revealed to be The Screen in an assumed form. The conversations are horribly stilted, with fantasy realm pretentiousness to them, but it probably all sounded good at the time to the teenage scriptwriter. In a field, a zombie armed with a shotgun takes a pot shot at The Viewer, and Marcelle performs an impressive succession of gymnastic forward flips in response, closing with a brisk kick to her assailant. Taking up the gun she blasts him, repeatedly stabs him in the head (off-screen, though

the point of view angle fully reflects the violence of the action) with a pitchfork, and then removes the mask to reveal the head of a pig; this time not a disguise, but a real pig's head cribbed from a butcher's shop.

All leads to a verbal showdown with her tormentor in a working men's club, where the bar is attended by a zombie barman. The Screen gives her the option of ruling this alternative world or instigating her own self-destruction. Stubbornly rejecting him, she backs up out of the dream and awakens on the couch. Her smile of relief is brief as she realizes that something is wrong and her face explodes in a bloody cataract; her hand reaching up towards the gory cavity with its single remaining eye, before the manikin substituting for her keels over. None too successfully, the effect is achieved with a shotgun blast at close range. The scene really ought to have been filmed somewhere other than the family lounge—for the money shot there's a cut to a fake wall covered with badly hung wallpaper, in front of which is the stunt dummy made from a casting of Marcelle's head, the resultant life-mask of which is far less convincing than Morris would claim in a subsequent "special effects" documentary, viewed by myself alongside the main attraction. What should be a grim moment is comical in effect, as, unintentionally, is much of the film.

A dissatisfied Perks set about her own edit of the film, running at a compact 26 minutes. Though the original had been submitted for professional editing by John Driscoll, Perks' cut reduced the amount of her wandering and bionic sprinting through the streets. More importantly it took out continuity errors such as a moving car in the background spoiling the feeling of isolation. Other intruders are removed—The Screen seemed to put in an appearance in a street scene, but it was uncertain whether this might have been an errant member of the public poking his body into shot, so Marcelle junked it. Fluttering pigeons in a shopping street are too lively and are also removed to add to the desolation—not only is mankind obliterated but all animal life too! The end credits differ slightly in the shorter cut, as some of the advertized businesses are no longer extant and so full addresses are unnecessary.

Marcelle Perks also shared the aforementioned effects documentary for the sake of this review, plus a series of outtakes—including a hairy moment in Oliver's Bar in the Royal Exchange, when the tripod topples and the heavy Panasonic M7 video camera smacks Marcelle in the face with an almighty crack. Suffering for one's art, even at this level.
—Paul Higson

THE COLD ROOM

1984
D: James Dearden

James Dearden remains best-known for scripting 1987's surprise hit *Fatal Attraction* but had previously shown some skill as a director, particularly with highly regarded British supporting shorts *The Contraption* (1977) and mini-classic *Panic* (1978). *The Cold Room* was adapted by Dearden from Jeffrey Caine's novel, as a feature-length production for HBO, but sadly makes a muddle of a potentially compelling and meaningful supernatural time-travel storyline. Amanda Pays plays Carla, a teenager who leaves boarding school, clutching gifts (a 1936 Berlin guidebook and a bag of weed), to join her writer father (George Segal) and meet his lover (Reneé Soutendijk). While finding her way around the divided German city, and leading a sparse existence in a run-down hotel selected by dad for its "real," "authentic" qualities, Carla begins to somehow relive the nightmarish experiences of Christa, a Berliner during the Nazi era assisting a male Jew to evade the authorities by keeping him in the hidden confined space of the title. Is Carla possessed by a spirit from the past? Is she somehow making her way back to the oppressive 1930s, flitting between the decades? Might her presents from a friendly nun and a schoolmate be having an influence? Could her birth-mother's mental illness run in the family? All of these are hinted at sketchily, but if Dearden's aim was to stir conjecture and speculation among his viewers, the whole confusing affair is treated so airily that the end result is far from satisfying. An incestuous rape scene midway merely adds tacky exploitation to the film's existing deficiencies. A considerable disappointment, all told.
—Darrell Buxton

CONSUMING PASSIONS

1988
D: Giles Foster

A few choice quotes to start with….

> "No shortcuts—just good, old-fashioned quality …"

> "Euro-Chocs. Taste of the future, yeah?"

> "I'd like to kill you. Nothing personal, of course."

> "Think how it would shorten the dole queues. We'd probably win the Queen's Award for Industry! Where do you want to be—on top of the world or drowning in shit like the rest of 'em?"

Based on the short 1973 television play *Secrets* by Michael Palin and Terry Jones, 1988's *Consuming Passions* manages to take the gruesome satire of the original and give it a whole new charge of Thatcher-era, yuppified meaning. If you've ever wondered what might happen if *Last of the Summer Wine* or an Alan Bennett play took a turn into "video nasty" territory, then this could just be the film for you.

Ian Littleton, new man at Chumley's Chocolates, causes an accident in which three employees tumble into a giant vat of the company product and are killed and added to the ingredients

before anything can be done. Initial worry turns to relief as the batch concerned proves a huge hit with the unsuspecting customers—and then to ever-darker greed and viciousness as Farris, the aggressive young businessman who's just taken the firm over, sees a quick way to soaring profits ...

This is a film which, while highly enjoyable, does feel somewhat flabby from its expansion to feature-length. A large part of the extra material comes courtesy of the very merry and extremely predatory widow Mrs. Garza—a surprisingly broad, unsubtle turn from a suitably Amazonian Vanessa Redgrave—whose sequences are undeniably amusing, but threaten to detour the piece into some forgotten Stanley Long sex comedy. Not to diss Stanley Long sex comedies, but Garza's scenes do somewhat defuse the mordant, unpleasant core of the story.

The real heart of the tale concerns the fall into darkness that awaits anyone who worships the almighty profit margin above all else. Some, like the conscience-stricken Littleton or the appalled Chumley, require some prodding before they begin to acquiesce—while others, such as Jonathan Pryce's sharp-suited Cockney wide-boy-turned-businessman Farris, embrace even the most appalling of crimes to fatten their wallets. In many ways, the story is surprisingly close to that of the 1986 *Little Shop of Horrors*—a milquetoast young employee, smitten with an appealing young lady in his boss' employ, undertakes reluctantly to do terrible things in order to win her heart—with lethal, horrific consequences. As played by (Peter's son) Tyler Butterworth and the quirkily-appealing Sammi Davis, our young lovers are a winning pair of innocents, and we do undeniably root for them—but Littleton is being dragged into a moral abyss as surely as those unfortunate men were into that mercilessly-swirling whirlpool of chocolate. The whole film ultimately aims towards the crisis point—just how much is the increasingly unhinged young employee willing to sacrifice to be a success?

Warts and all, this is a blackly comic yet finally life-affirming piece that I'd recommend to anyone. It is cast marvellously throughout—aside from those already mentioned, Freddie Jones is charmingly clueless as Chumley, Thora Hird affectionate as Littleton's "secretary," and the likes of Patrick Newell and William Rushton get to make splendid cameos, as does Andrew Sachs, finally getting to take out some of the put-upon Manuel's frustrations ....

And it has a somewhat more upbeat, if abrupt, conclusion than its inspiration. Although even there a comically unsettling note manages to intrude. In its own little way, this film manages to warn us of just how dehumanizing the drive for profit can become.

Now, who fancies a Mars bar?
—Ken Shinn

DARK TOWER

1987
D: "Ken Barnett" (Freddie Francis, Ken Wiederhorn)

Another production with a difficult-to-pin-down provenance, *Dark Tower* was filmed in Barcelona with a stellar English-speaking cast, and a "Sandy Howard presents" credit indicating this familiar wheeler-dealer somewhere in the background. Kevin Lyons' online *Encyclopedia of Fantastic Film and Television* lists the movie as a UK/US affair, since London-based Testzone Limited are noted as the copyright holder as the credits end. Michael Moriarty starred, despite also rattling off a couple of Larry Cohen quickies during the same period; Jenny Agutter was the female lead, and sizeable names like Carol Lynley, Theodore Bikel, Patch Mackenzie, and Kevin McCarthy pop up in supporting roles.

It gets off to a lively opening third with a psychic force attacking a window cleaner in his cradle, a security guard being splattered by one of those killer elevators as previously spotted in *Damien—Omen II* and *Der Lift*, and Moriarty's detective sidekick going bullet-happy, but before long it becomes all too apparent that none of the actors is receiving much in the way of direction, leaving some genuine talent floundering. Jenny, playing against type as a power-dressing go-getter typical of the era, is professional enough to handle the situation, and an actor like Moriarty will always revel in the opportunity to go wild and unfettered (he can do no wrong for me, even in a piece as uncontrolled as this is, and gives a smirking, twitchy, fun performance at times here, that almost suggests he has made it his mission to crack up whichever fellow cast member he happens to share a scene with!) Had *Dark Tower* continued in its initial vein, no matter how ragged, it could have developed into a guilty pleasure, a bit of trashy fun—but it gradually grinds to a halt, the goofy death scenes being replaced by a lot of talk and a focus on ESP abilities and half-glimpsed

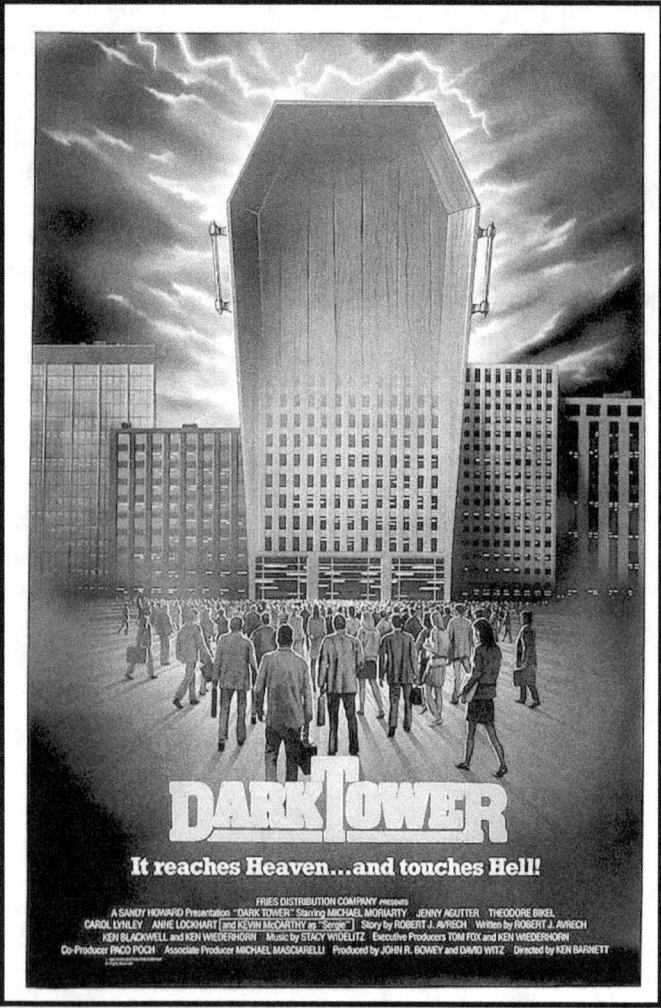

ghostly visions of the late husband whom Agutter has usurped. A lengthy episode, during which Bikel (channeling Orson Welles at his hammiest) attempts to psychoanalyze the deadly building, hardly improves matters.

Shattering glass, crumbling masonry, office machinery falling apart, all seems to inadvertently comment upon this ramshackle offering, rather than causing any kind of cogent threat within it. McCarthy is brought off the substitute's bench late on as a supposedly enigmatic figure but appears unsure about exactly what is required of him and just wanders around in a scarf and beret for a while. Nothing symbolizes more regarding his participation in this project than the arbitrary nature of his departure from it.

It's always a key sign of trouble when a movie manages to misspell the name of its star in the opening credits ...
—Darrell Buxton

DEAD & BURIED

1981
D: Gary Sherman

Gore by the seashore in this rugged, rough and ready nononsense shocker that has proved to be an enduring cult favorite among those who caught it theatrically in the early 1980s. In the UK, *Dead & Buried* was paired with second feature *The Orchard End Murder* and distributed successfully by Laurence Myers' company GTO; what fans didn't pick up on at the time was that this unusual entry in the American horror boom of the period had strong British connections, with the copyright date at the very end of the credits accompanied by the giveaway name "Barclays Mercantile Industrial Finance Limited," indicating backing from the other side of the Atlantic. Scriptwriters Ronald Shusett and Dan O'Bannon already had Anglo/American form from working on *Alien*, while director Gary Sherman had made one of the best-loved British horrors of the 1970s, *Death Line*.

It all takes place in the creepy fishing town of Potters Bluff, where the dead just won't stay that way and where local mortician and corpse restoration ace Mr. Dobbs (a winning Jack Albertson, seemingly channelling Groucho Marx) may have something to do with the condition they're in, via a mixture of voodoo, witchery, his own professional skills and a secret ingredient or two. Sheriff James Farentino strives to solve the macabre mystery but gets more than he bargained for. The use of cameras by the townsfolk is central to the disturbing plot, and photographic equipment hasn't been quite so ominous since *Peeping Tom*. The seductive Lisa Blount makes an impact as a literally drop-dead gorgeous lure for unwary male passers-by, and grabs the movie's memorable highlight when she plunges a hypo into a hapless bandaged hospital patient's exposed left eye. Questing Farentino seems pretty clueless considering he's a resident, though to be fair his inability to engage with fellow Bluffers does all make some sense by the time the final reel's parade of revelations has unspooled.
—Darrell Buxton

THE EVIL THAT MEN DO

1984
D: J. Lee Thompson

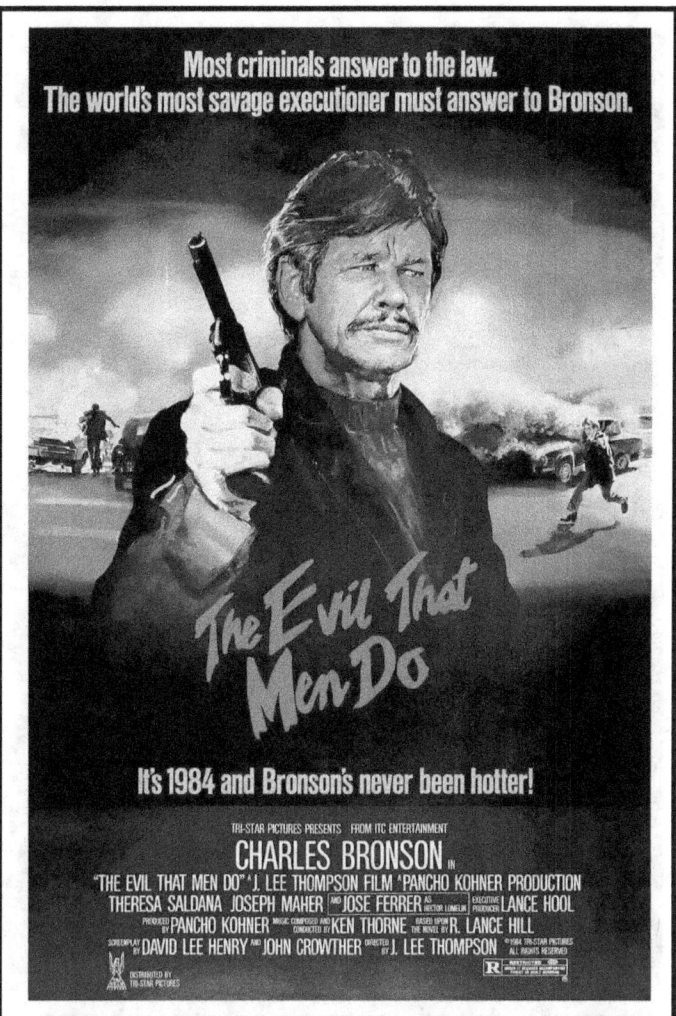

An odd kettle of fish. Coming out just as Lew Grade's ITC (Incorporated Television Company) gasped its last, *The Evil That Men Do* was the only non-Cannon film made by Charles Bronson and indeed British director J. Lee Thompson during the 1982-1989 period they worked for Golan-Globus. This adaptation of a Lance L. Hill action novel was intended for the Israeli exploitation mavericks, but instead due to the three-picture deal that Lord Grade had bestowed upon Bronson, with one picture left, this project was handed to the failing company.

It's a Mexican-United States-United Kingdom co-production, filmed in Mexico. Bronson was now in his 60s, and into those post-*Death Wish II* years of playing geriatric vigilantes with younger love interests. No change here! He plays Holland, an ex-C.I.A. assassin now enjoying life as a pensioner, until he is told that his old friend, a journalist named Hidalgo, was killed and tortured in Suriname by Clement Molloch, a crazed British medic known as "The Doctor" (played by Irish actor Joseph Maher) who uses his widespread medical knowledge to create the most severe pain. He is aided by his possibly incestuous but no less sane sister Claire (German-born Anglo-American Canadian actress Antoinette Bower, who appeared in everything from *Star Trek* and *Mission: Impossible* to playing Leslie Nielsen's wife in *Prom Night* and starring in Filipino monster flick *Superbeast*.) Maher is a very camp, very memorable hooded villain as Molloch, describing his art as "a delicate nightmarish experience of terror," and believing that torture is "a subtle and scientific speciality to be carried out with medical and scientific precision." Molloch kills Hidalgo for getting his facts wrong and claiming that Molloch killed 35 leaders; although "it is flattering," he actually only killed 20, so in a vicious scene cut from the VHS tape, Hidalgo is electrocuted while chained to a swing. Bower on the other hand is almost Thatcher-esque in her voice and mannerisms, wishing, "Hidalgo suffered a little harder." Their bodyguard is Randolph, an African American bisexual played by the great Raymond St. Jacques, the first black TV cowboy for his role in *Rawhide*.

Holland is contacted by Hector Lomelin (José Ferrer), a doctor who has been helping Molloch's victims, who gives him tapes of torture subjects describing their experiences, intended to spur Holland into action. Holland goes to Mexico, meets Lomelin, visits those who have suffered Molloch's attentions, and encounters Hidalgo's widow, Rhiana (Theresa Saldana, who had been almost murdered in 1982 by a stalker just prior to being cast in this film) and their pre-teen daughter Sarah. Holland, Rhiana and Sarah go undercover as "the Smith family" to find and hunt down Molloch and his men.

This film is full of tension, and replete with decidedly questionable moments. In one memorable scene, Miguel Angel Fuentes is squeezed to death via his testicles by Bronson. Elsewhere, a henchman is strangled with a hose. There is not as much overt horror as one would expect, but it is without doubt an exploitation film. The end is particularly gratuitous but brilliant, and gory. They discover Claire is a psycho lesbian and keep her hostage in the car boot. After accidentally killing Claire by getting involved in a high-speed car chase that results in her fatal concussion, Rhiana and Holland arrive at Molloch's hiding place. Molloch threatens to kill Sarah, Hidalgo and Rhiana's daughter, unless he sees his sister. Molloch is unaware that a bunch of former victims are present, now disfigured and looking for revenge. His henchman is shot by Holland, Sarah escapes back to her mother and the disfigured victims then gang up on Molloch, banging the car he is locked in with pickaxes and reducing him to raw meat in a matter of seconds. It is extremely gory for what was intended as a mainstream picture. The film is a typical actioner of the period, and respected journeyman director Thompson is slumming it here, but he gives it his all.
—George White

THE FANTASIST

1986
D: Robin Hardy

Where to begin? After a promising opening featuring a genuinely unpleasant and shocking murder a là José Larraz or Pete Walker, we promptly dive into this utterly lamentable mess, establishing a nonsensical plot, woefully inept dialogue that switches

from comic to dramatic without prior warning, a heroine with one of the most unconvincing fake accents ever *and* a complete lack of consistent moral center, a killer with a non-existent motive (whose identity is given away almost immediately by the name of the novel the film is taken from, as well as his inability to differentiate between his "real" voice and the one he uses to intimidate women on the phone), a ludicrous red herring with a fixation for balloons and tummy-tickling who disappears from the plot completely (known in British horror parlance as "doing a Hilda Braid"—see *Killer's Moon*!), and a hero who's such an insufferable prat you can't even feel sorry for him when his wife gets bumped off.

The horrible holiday-ad-style Celtic flute music!! The awful 1980s hairstyles!! The dull beige decor!! The lack of practically anything remotely scary, intriguing or thrilling!! The live appearance of Level 42!! And most of all, the buttock slapping!! Seriously, just when the *one* vaguely interesting twist (finally revealing the heroine to be as bonkers as the bad guy) occurs and we think we're getting somewhere, she lays down and allows him to use her bare arse as a pair of congas. Marlon Brando's *Last Tango in Paris* take on the female posterior was sane by comparison. But perhaps the most damning indictment is that this is the second feature film of Robin Hardy, director of the legendary and supposed "greatest British horror movie ever," *The Wicker Man*—which surely proves once and for all, if you ever doubted it anyway, that Anthony Shaffer was the true auteur of that production. *The Fantasist* is quite possibly the worst horror film or thriller ever made, British, Irish or otherwise. Co-funded by Lew Grade's ITC; did he learn *nothing* from *Raise the Titanic?* If you must watch a genre picture with a Dublin setting, try *The Iguana with the Tongue of Fire* instead.
—Darius Drewe

THE FIENDISH PLOT OF DR. FU MANCHU

1980
D: Piers Haggard (and Richard Quine, Peter Sellers)

Fu fu, as Joe Bob Briggs might have had it. Notorious as the perceived "bomb" that wound up Peter Sellers' career in ignominy, *The Fiendish Plot of Dr. Fu Manchu* isn't half as bad as reputed. Indeed, it's probably more typical and representative of Mr. Sellers' variable big screen output than is his feted preceding role in Hal Ashby's classic satire *Being There*. The credits reveal the star's spouse Lynne Frederick as "production executive" and oldest swinger in town, Hugh Hefner, as "executive producer," so make what you will of that; pointedly, those opening titles also hide the fact that this was a troubled production, with declared helmer Piers Haggard making way for Richard Quine, before Sellers himself took up the directorial reins. It's a brisk, watchable romp, doesn't outstay its welcome, and is arguably at least as entertaining as the lesser entries in the *Pink Panther* franchise had been up to this point.

True to form, Sellers decided to play both Fu and his nemesis Nayland Smith, upping the ante by portraying both in a state of decrepitude (the Asian master criminal is celebrating his 168th birthday as the movie opens, with a lovely twist on that traditional reveal of an organ theme actually being pumped out by an onscreen figure; the retired Smith, a literally tortured shadow of his old self, seems something of a spin on Sellers' "Chauncey Gardiner" persona from the previous year.) At one point, Fu masquerades as an antique dealer, allowing for additional acting acrobatics from the star.

The rough-and-ready screenplay throws up a selection of Goonish identities—Lady Warrington Minge, Charles Rotten, Arnold Wretch, Mavis Thing—and adds in such exotica as a gigantic, knockout-gas-emitting flowering plant cultivated by the villain, or a clockwork tarantula. The wind-up arachnid is the focus of some early fun; set loose in a museum by one of Fu's Dacoit acolytes, it does what all such objects are prone to do, malfunctioning and ramming itself against the skirting board! Although the script does trade rather desperately on "they all look the same"-style gags, a cameo by *Pink Panther* regular Burt Kwouk (extinguishing his flaming sleeve with Fu's youth-giving "Elixir Vitae" and so setting events in motion) raises a chuckle as Sellers points out his familiarity.

Helen Mirren may not care to discuss this early entry on her CV, but what a trip it must have been acting in close proximity to Sellers at this stage in her career. She plays undercover policewoman (and tap-dancing saxophonist) Alice Rage, who goes all Patty Hearst halfway through and opts to join Fu as his queen. There's solid support from the dependable likes of David Tomlinson, John le Mesurier and Stratford Johns, though imported guest star Sid Caesar is given little to work with and makes no impression.

Deposed director Haggard leapt from frying pan to fire within months, stepping in to replace Tobe Hooper on the equally problematic *Venom* soon after!
—Darrell Buxton

GORDON THE MOVIE

1982
D: Paul Nachman

"There's nothing quite like it in the whole world, I shouldn't think" remarks a muttering Gordon Robbins 25 minutes into a viewing experience which redefines the term "oddity." *Gordon the Movie* was made on a non-existent budget in 1982 and has acquired a minuscule yet enthusiastic following here and there among true devotees of weird, weeeeeeird amateur film production. The entire 57-minute mini-feature was kindly made available on YouTube several years ago, via a 2006 digitization in six heavily-pixelated and utterly washed-out chunks, and can be located online under the heading "LOST CULT SUPER 8 CANNIBALISM EPIC," which makes it sound very exciting indeed. The reality is, well, indescribable. My opening use of a dialogue quote from the movie serves as a playful introduction to this review, an attempt to steal a line from the film in order to capture its essence, but Gordon's statement in fact refers to a gristly lump of meat in a transparent plastic wrapping, which may or may not be an unidentified body part somehow obtained from the corpse of Elvis Presley and delivered to a grocer who powders his face, sports bushy fake eyebrows and rouge, and dresses like a holiday camp compère.

Gordon's nightmare visit to a dentist features POV images not unlike scenes from Terry Gilliam's *Brazil*, as a drill-wielding medic and a doll-masked nurse with artificial-looking braided hair loom large in the frame; we also cut to roving camera shots gliding across, over, and through piles of raw red meat, all accompanied by a shrill chorus of female voices warbling what may or may not be the incessantly repeated lyric "get your clothes on." Later, a hazy drunken poker session in a pub sees Gordon rambling throughout on a variety of unconnected topics including divorce and the Ark Royal. Scenes in a confessional booth have Gordon declaring his hatred of another person, this statement clearly being voiced by somebody who sounds nothing like our shuffling, shambling, scruffy, scarf-wearing title star.

"Do you remember the little red tricycle and the fish fingers you always said I'd end up looking like?"—they don't write 'em like that any more, just one snippet of yet another from-nowhere episode which sees Gordon chatting to a toffee-nosed, well-dressed "Hooray Henry" type in a dingy boozer and denying strenuously that the man is his son. The plummy-voiced type raises, in the vaguest way possible, Gordon's monopolizing of the "celebrity body part acquisition" trade, reveals that his father was "a very famous man" (thereby leaving Gordon and anyone

From Paul Nachman's Blog: "Teaser poster liberally flyposted around Bath and Bristol the week before the main poster went out for the premiere on 19th November 1982."

who has stumbled upon this item completely dazed in regard to the parentage issue!) and suggests that the shabby little fellow hunched over a pint may be able to get "a bit of him for me—a sort of heirloom." The fairground footage, the Pythonesque pub grotesques who drift through the background as Gordon sinks into a stupor, the extended and inconsequential train/car journey scenes, some inexplicable early interlude at an unidentified seafront involving a (bandaged? It's difficult to tell) convalescent in a wheelchair, the tap-dancing amid clouds of dry ice, the Tommy Cooper-style half-man/half-woman, Gordon's backstage visit to see a pop band called "Interview" and deliver some of his "special" packages to the musicians—all add to the mounting madness. Not-quite-bookend shots, away from and towards a railway tunnel entrance, at once extend the unconventionality (why frame your story symmetrically?) and suggest that the events we've sat through open-mouthed might be imagined. Before we can react, there's a brief flash of a savage razor-murder in a disused warehouse setting (very *Corruption* or *The Comeback*, this bit), a fish-eye-lens shot of a cackling Gordon seated at a piano, and an end credits card dedicating the movie to Mr. Robbins himself, "who died during its making." But wait—it isn't over yet! Dozens of mourners parade through a leafy cemetery as we are offered several minutes of footage from our star's funeral—with, inevitably, a bizarre final flourish as Gordon, or at least a lifesize glazed plaster facsimile of his head, turns towards the camera for the very last shot. End credits reveal Phil Nutman (the noted horror author and *Fangoria* correspondent) as the assistant editor, and sees director Paul Nachman identified under two different names with slight spelling variations.

There's a highly informative website devoted to whatever the hell this is. Find it at gordonthemovie.blogspot.co.uk. Content there includes details of how legendary stoner D.J. Johnnie Walker helped to promote the finished production, how Sid Vicious' mum was offered a role, and how Dilys Powell and Ken Loach were invited to the premiere only to both decline ...
—Darrell Buxton

HAUNTED HONEYMOON

1986
D: Gene Wilder

The much-loved comic actor Gene Wilder had a spotty parallel career as a director, achieving commercial success with *The Woman in Red* (1984) but receiving mixed reviews for that as well as his earlier *The Adventures of Sherlock Holmes' Smarter Brother* (1975) and *The World's Greatest Lover* (1977). His final assignment behind the cameras was *Haunted Honeymoon*, something of a love letter to the fast-talking, wise-cracking Hollywood horror comedy circa 1940. It was filmed at Elstree, with Knebworth House being used for exteriors, and is a brisk, breezy piece, if not en-

German poster for *Haunted Honeymoon*

tirely successful in its aims.

An early line of dialogue—"this is supposed to be a mystery, not a comedy"—inadvertently touches upon and inverts part of the problem, in that there's perhaps too much mystery and not enough humor in the movie itself. Wilder's direction proves variable—oddly most efficient when he's called upon to deliver the creep stuff, with some particularly impressive roving camerawork, but far less sure-handed with the funnies. He does have a tendency to hold gag shots slightly too long, killing the laugh.

Additionally, though there's plenty to enjoy here, much of the best material is stolen from superior sources. That linking corridor filled with billowing curtains is a lift from Paul Leni's 1927 *The Cat and the Canary*, the "who is the family werewolf?" schtick is borrowed from 1974's *The Beast Must Die*, and even the major showstopping routine thieves a wonderful Fred MacMurray bit of business from 1945's *Murder, He Says*, with Wilder attempting to pass off an unconscious butler's out-of-control legs as his own. The frequent sight of black gloves looming into shot betrays a giallo influence, and *Haunted Honeymoon* echoes an even earlier era of Italian shock cinema, resembling that wave of mid-'60s mansion house Gothics starring Barbara Steele (I'm not saying the sets are over-lavish but Wilder does deliver the line, "I learned to ride a bicycle in this room" at one point!)

You can tell it's a mid-1980s, British-lensed production very easily, since the ubiquitous Jonathan Pryce and Eve Ferret turn up about 20 minutes in. They're just part of a solid home-grown supporting cast including an underused Peter Vaughan and a better-utilized Jim Carter—the latter plays Montego the Magician, to whom we are introduced glowing-eyed and prestidigitating on the manor doorstep.

John Morris' grand, sweeping score, and a beautiful lighting job (cinematographer Fred Schuler) overbalance *Haunted Honeymoon*, both deserving of a better film than this frivolous bit of fluff. The set design is equally spectacular, truly capturing a "grandeur gone to seed" look worthy of a larger project. It's a little sad to witness Gilda Radner and a dragged-up Dom DeLuise soft-shoe-shuffling their way through "Ballin' the Jack" amid such out of place opulence and splendor.

Wilder clearly adores the slick source material mystery thrillers of the 1930s and early 1940s, and the same era's sponsored radio dramas to which he spends much of the running time paying homage. *Haunted Honeymoon* is an adequate time-passer, but you'd probably rather spend time with the real deal, watching Bob Hope in *The Ghost Breakers* or listening to a vintage edition of *Lights Out*.
—Darrell Buxton

HAUNTERS OF THE DEEP

1984
D: Andrew Bogle

The Children's Film Foundation had turned out a lot of variable movies by the time this supernatural tale of mines, ghost kids and crusty old doom-mongers appeared. One of the company's final productions (the writing was on the wall as soon as Maggie T pulled the plug on the Eady Levy), *Haunters of the Deep*

isn't to the same standard as the organization's best output (*The Glitterball* is my own favorite) but the combination of Cornish exteriors, less-annoying than usual child protagonists, a trace of contemporary politics and Hammer vet Andrew Keir is enough to keep a tired formula watchable.

Roche (Bob Sherman) is an American mining executive who's brought his daughter Becky (Amy Taylor) to Cornwall while he pokes around a long disused tin mine, hoping to bring it back into production. Becky strikes up a friendship with a local boy, Josh (Gary Simmons) while her dad is busy trying to get the locals fired-up about mining again, but all he does is excite the ire of the grimly pessimistic Captain Tregellis (Keir), who warns them that no good will come from opening a pit cursed by historic tragedy. Sure enough, a cave-in traps some of Roche's men underground and it's up to Becky and Josh, with the help of Keir and a ghostly child laborer, to save them.

Keir adds a bit of gravitas to what would otherwise be a well shot, atmospheric but distinctly lightweight picture. It helps that he plays the role absolutely straight (all the performances in Bogle's film are commendable) so when he says that the mine is cursed, you better believe it. This is the erstwhile Prof. Quatermass, after all. Of course, the target audience for *Haunters of the Deep* means that the chills contained within are strictly of the "PG" variety, but that's not to say that they are absent—the CFF did these kind of vaguely Gothic ghost stories rather well, and with Keir on board this at times feels like a junior Hammer movie. That's not to say the film is perfect. The screenplay, by director Bogle and fellow scripters Tony Attard and Terry Barbour, takes up quite a lot of running time explaining the history of mining in Cornwall, to the point where *Haunters of the Deep* threatens to morph into one of those contemporary Television for Schools programs. It's also very familiar fare if you've seen or recall much of the CFF's output—they seemed to do a take on the 19th century Gothic ghost story every few years, so by this point in their history it was starting to feel a bit tired. Nevertheless, Bogle injects an element of contemporary politics into the mix which helps a little, and the whole thing is shot with a strong eye for good exterior Cornish locations—*Haunters* is one of the Children's Film Foundation's best-looking movies.

Oddly, there was a brief trend for subterranean horror films in the early 1980s. The best known of these is the Canadian slasher *My Bloody Valentine* (1981), with low-budget monster movies *The Boogens* (1981), *Secrets of the Phantom Caverns/What Waits Below* (1984) and *The Strangeness* (1984) following behind. *Haunters of the Deep*, while aimed at a very different audience, holds its own in this company and offers carefully crafted atmosphere as a counterpoint to the sanguine thrills of its contemporaries. That it's largely predictable and its scares are moderated almost goes without saying, but looking beyond its self-set limitations, *Haunters of the Deep* is a well-crafted, largely effective ghost story for children, with enough about it to keep your attention too.
—Neil Pike

THE HOUSE OF USHER

1989
D: Alan Birkinshaw

The ever-busy Harry Alan Towers hit a latter-day career spike circa 1989-1990 with a glut of public domain productions aimed at the VHS rental/sell-thru markets. *The Phantom of the Opera* (starring Robert Englund) made it to theaters but was accompanied on to the video shelves by various Towers stabs at Poe, R.L. Stevenson, Agatha Christie, etc.

As often the case with this globe-trotting, deal-securing huckster, the pedigree and "country of origin" for these movies is difficult to ascertain. Possibly for a reason, though far be it from us to suggest any "creative accounting" or the like. It seems the trio of titles for which director Alan Birkinshaw (*Killer's Moon, Invaders of the Lost Gold/Horror Safari*) was hired—*The House of Usher, Masque of the Red Death, Ten Little Indians*—were lensed in South Africa, with multi-national casts. Many sources cite the movies as UK co-productions (alongside Canada, the US, South Africa, and that's before you throw Israeli partner Avi Lerner into the mix), and *The House of Usher* does at least have substantial British-based connections—besides Harry himself, there's the larger-than-life Oliver Reed and Donald Pleasence heading the cast, and some brief London location work.

All of the Towers films from this period take immense liberties with their source material (no change there, then!), and this *Usher* proves the point by featuring a wheezing, straggly-haired Pleasence as Walter Usher, coming on like a distant relative of the Femm family from *The Old Dark House* and having a very 1989 contraption bolted to his arm, a fearsome whirring drill with which he likes to make his victims "smile." This being censorious 1989, naturally we don't get to witness anything too gruesome, cutting discreetly away from Walter's DIY handiwork or from an attack by a starving rat on a strapped-down quack medic. Reed makes an inappropriate, gruff, and blustering Roderick, a far cry from Vincent Price's beautifully fey reading of the role for Roger Corman, while Romy Windsor's whiny imperilled heroine never wins you over, resulting in the central plot thrust (an attempt to lure her to the mansion and impregnate her to continue the family line) failing to engage.

You recall how Bernard Robinson used to work miracles on Hammer horrors, disguising the dimensions of sets by throwing drapes, pillars, altars, candlesticks, and the kitchen sink into strategic positions, and crafting apparently lavish and spacious arenas on which the stories could be played out? Well there's clearly a bid to try the same trick here, but the tiny stages remain evidently unsuitable and merely appear even smaller than they are through the piling-up of clutter and detritus. It's almost a relief when it all gets set ablaze towards the close.
—Darrell Buxton

THE HOUSE WHERE EVIL DWELLS

1982
D: Kevin Connor
W: Robert Suhosky
Starring: Edward Albert, Susan George, Doug McClure

Someone once remarked that "any thriller with no dialogue in its first five minutes is a movie worth your time," or words to that effect (memory tells me that it may have been a review of Roberto Faenza's *Order of Death/Copkiller* in the *New Musical Express*.) I've since considered that a pretty fair judgment—and *The House Where Evil Dwells* takes almost 12 minutes before we hear any legible spoken content at all, and just over 12 prior to English featuring on the soundtrack. Which by the NME guidelines, ought to suggest that we're in for something really special. Sadly, this isn't the case. However, that long opening prologue is certainly a striking one—fans of the great Nobuo Nakagawa or of the eerie *"Yotsuya"* horror/samurai period horror films of the 1950s will find the pre-credits sequence here to be as good an imitation of their style and aura as you'll ever see, almost a little mini-version of the form, complete with love triangle, silhouetted sex scene, erotic trinket, remote traditional dwelling place setting, and limb-and-head-lopping vengeful violence. All presented to us via none other than Kevin Connor, director of *The Land that Time Forgot*!

And the first westerner onscreen is none other than Connor's old partner in juvenile film fantasy, popular 1970s hero Doug McClure. Here he plays the uncharacteristic role of a slick property broker who procures a rented home—you've already guessed where—for businessman Edward Albert and his wife Susan George. The spirits, once mortal enemies but now seemingly spooks in cahoots, roam around the scene of their tragedy and literally step into the bodies of their modern-day equivalents, in double-exposure possession scenes from a world where *The Exorcist* never happened. Albert and George indulge in a spell of lovemaking accompanied by tinkly piano passages that would indicate that Connor had watched *Don't Look Now* a few times too many—and in a developing plot rather typical of the Thatcher/Reagan era, following George's discovery of the ivory-carved bauble depicting a female figure entwined with a horned demonic lover, our well-to-do couple then begin to argue over finances and other modern-day issues, while their ghostly Eastern counterparts egg them on to further divisive behavior. At one point a specter even looms before their bratty child at the dinner table, cueing the classic line "mommy, there's an awful face in my soup!" As McClure becomes entangled and the menage plays out once more, you could write the remainder yourself. Though having said that, a couple of silly scuttling and tree-climbing crabs, far more fitting for once of the director's family-orientated monster fantasies, make an unexpected late entrance for no particular reason—it's that kind of a movie.

The House Where Evil Dwells has, since its release, usually been considered a US production, or occasionally listed as US/Japanese. British horror scholars have pondered its provenance, though, and we're indebted to the researches of Kevin Lyons and Jonathan Rigby who in 2019 uncovered the fact that Commercial Credit Services Holdings Ltd., the company credited as

copyright holder, could be traced to the UK and is still registered with Companies House. The debate rages as to whether this can be officially classified as a "British horror film," but for completism's sake it's worthy of an entry here.
—Darrell Buxton

INCIDENT AT ROMANS COURT

1989
D: Neil Mackintosh and Howard Mackintosh

Incident at Romans Court is a 34-minute amateur horror spoof shot in eight weeks in early 1989 by the Brothers Mackintosh (Roger, Neil and Howard) of Great British Films and the Nottingham Video Group. I long imagined it to be the usual ramshackle, ad hoc, lean-to amateur effort but perhaps I should have paid more attention to the citations in the cine filmmaking community. That is not to admit this is do-it-yourself greatness, but the film does have an air of technical professionalism in the framing, lighting, props and soundtrack. There are familiar musical extracts that I perhaps should be able to identify, seemingly borrowed from British horrors of the 1960s.

The story has exorcists Marcus Bartelli (Howard Mackintosh) and Sebastian Prothero (Neil Mackintosh) called in to investigate a haunted cellar. But as they set up their equipment and make contact with the supernatural entity it defends itself by throwing them repeatedly through a portal into the English countryside miles from the haunting. The ghost-busting team are lobbed out several times before the latest in a long line of cases is solved. Spoiler Alert! The owner of the house is a ghost working with other spirits to trap and kill the pair whom the dead consider to be something of a pest. The Queen of the Ghosts wants them destroyed and commissioned the trap; but once again, finding the real house-owner, in some confusion, hidden in the cellar, they win the day.

Filmmaking talent is evident, but *Incident at Romans Court* is not particularly funny. It cannot escape the caricature performances and the humor is didactic. The film deals with the main threat, and then has something of an afterthought, as the duo investigate if the portal might still be active and take them on a far flung holiday only to end up in Skegness (a Nottingham vacationers' answer to Lancashire's Blackpool.) Not only is there something of the more recent *Doctor Who* in the premise, but both exorcists dress as if auditioning for the role of the time-traveler and companion, only more in line with the haute couture of the Davison/McCoy era.
—Paul Higson

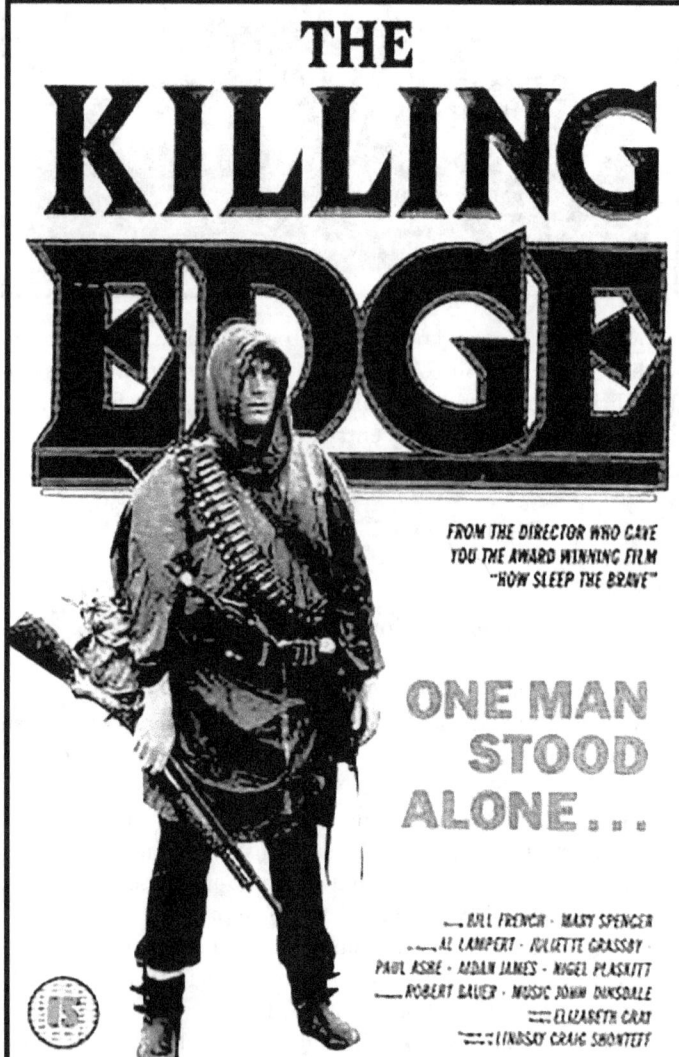

THE KILLING EDGE

1984
D: Lindsay Shonteff

The Killing Edge is Canadian-born director Shonteff's entry into the then incredibly popular post-apocalypse genre, and as such represents a rare foray into science fiction for a filmmaker better known for his straight horror, espionage thrillers and softcore smut. The picture hangs onto the coat-tails of the first wave of these films, made on the back of the twin box-office successes of *Mad Max 2* and *Escape from New York*, and which consists primarily of Italian rip-offs like Aristide Massaccesi's *2020 Texas Gladiators* (1982), Ruggero Deodato's *The Atlantis Interceptors* (1983) and Enzo G. Castellari's *The New Barbarians* (1983). Shonteff wasn't the only British-based filmmaker to have a tilt at the genre; other examples include Richard Stanley's *Hardware* (1989), Michael J. Murphy's *Death Run* (1987) and Tony Maylam's *Split Second* (1992). All of these have merit (particularly Murphy's)—which is where they differ from *The Killing Edge*, alas.

Shonteff's movie is essentially a futuristic Western following the adventures of Steve Johnson (Bill French) who survived a nuclear war that wiped out most of the British population as he happened to be in a big tunnel when the balloon went up. The plot consists of him searching for his wife and child as he attempts to avoid capture by killer robots (named Terminators!) and being used as forced labor, all the while accompanied by his son's teddy bear.

Unlike many of its spaghetti cousins, *The Killing Edge* dispenses with the dune buggies and big action set pieces, instead following its protagonist through a low-budget wasteland and chance encounters with other survivors and occasionally, one of the killer robots. The pervading cheapness, slow pace, tiny cast and lack of much action lend a bleaker tone than that of its contemporaries, however it also makes the film more of a chore to sit through. Shot on video and incredibly hard to find now, this might be Shonteff's cheapest production and while one admires his chutzpah for even attempting a genre pic on such a paltry budget, it's worth remembering that Michael Murphy shot *Death Run* on Super 8, and it's much better than this.

There are a couple of interesting bits of foreshadowing in the production worthy of note. The mention of "Terminators" is a bit of a shock—I suppose it's possible that Shonteff had picked up news of James Cameron's then-upcoming production via the trades, but it's still worth remembering that Shonteff's film was released on video almost a year before Cameron's flick debuted. Similarly, the production feels a bit like what we might have been presented with had *Threads* been directed by a genre filmmaker. That's less of a surprise, given that the BBC documentary (*QED: A Guide to Armageddon*—first broadcast in 1982) that strongly influenced Mick Jackson and Barry Hines also pre-dates the production of *The Killing Edge* and so may well have also influenced the tone of Shonteff's movie.

Shonteff was a director who happily leaned into the exploitation elements of his films—there's an element of ghoulish glee in *Night, After Night, After Night*, and he was similarly full-on with his sexploitation movies, which might explain why *The Killing Edge* feels like such a poor fit for him. Although hog-tied by what

one has to assume was a painfully tiny budget, this slightly morose, downbeat science fiction movie doesn't feel like something he'd have been drawn to if times had been better. Shonteff was a good enough director to lift the project above the absolute bottom of the 1980s direct-to-video barrel (*Death Shock*, anyone?) but it's still his weakest film and it is little surprise that it has disappeared into obscurity.
—Neil Pike

LITTLE SHOP OF HORRORS

1986
D: Frank Oz

Frank Oz's *Little Shop of Horrors* is no obscurity, but like many films made 30-40 years ago, it has a lot of competition in keeping in the public consciousness. It does have an aide-mémoire in that just as it was adapted from an off-Broadway stage production itself inspired by the original 1960 Roger Corman B-movie, that stage musical continues to be popular, even performed in schools. Musicals are difficult to get right in much the same way that anthology films are. Both genre and sub-genre are dependent on getting the right balance. In compendium movies some stories might be better than others. In musicals, just as in any pop album, there might be a couple of good songs and the rest substandard. But the combinations in getting it wrong are innumerable and I could write an exceedingly lengthy article on examples of this. There might be little innovative about the songs in *Little Shop of Horrors* but, like Richard O'Brien's *The Rocky Horror Picture Show* before it, Alan Menken's ditties are stylistically distinctly different across the running time, evenly spaced out, and perfect fits. Howard Ashman's lyric writing is tantamount to genius as the words never stray from the story, re-explore themes without repetition and don't feel confined to the tunes they occupy.

The 1986 film is fortunate to have had a 25-year gestation period and many elements theoretically came ironed out. But the musical did undergo more changes as several songs were dropped and a new number, "Mean Green Mother from Outer Space," added. Furthermore, a happier ending replaced the bleak original following poor test audience reactions to the deaths of the principal leads. I find the concessions more than agreeable. The story of a failing florist shop, in a tough New York City neighborhood, that becomes a sensation upon displaying an amazing and extremely hungry alien plant, is superbly mounted and cast. In truth, I had forgotten how good it was. It is a film with no waste. The unavoidable awareness that it is shot entirely on soundstages (Pinewood, England) is not to its detriment as that enclosure creates a level of claustrophobia, a benefit bestowed on Tobe Hooper's *Death Trap* and Ishirō Honda's *Matango: Fungus of Terror* that also had stage-bound "interior exteriors." The film also benefits hugely from the in-camera creation of effects and intrinsically constructed and well-dressed sets, with rewarding details. The several stages of the Audrey II plant monster and the puppetry continue to astonish. The speeded-up animatronic effect is the result of filming at approximately half speed to facilitate the fast dialogue that the puppet mouths could not curl the lips around. This must have been both a challenge and a nightmare for the actors who were in frame at the time.

Rick Moranis and Ellen Greene as romantic leads, Seymour and Audrey, could have been irritating comic caricatures but instead become a winning pair, despite their flaws. He is a klutz willing to become an accomplice in murder for love and she is a victim of physical abuse from an extremely violent dentist boyfriend, Orin Scrivello (played by Steve Martin). Martin's performance is choreographed to the nth detail and would be overpowering were his time not limited to the very middle of the film. But the magnificence of his physical comedy and cruel cartoon villainy cannot be denied. His scene with Bill Murray as the masochist in the dentist chair threatens another worrying movie-stealing peak with two comedy greats at their best. The warmth of the growing relationship between Seymour and Audrey beautifully counterbalances those extremes. Another constant joy is the film's Greek chorus trio of Crystal, Ronette and Chiffon (Tichina Arnold, Michelle Weeks and Tisha Campbell). They pop up throughout, on the way to school, in a typing pool, on rooftops, in glittering dresses, whatever the requirements of the number, slam-dunking the film with their hypnotic sass and sashay.

The best way to put across how good the film is would be to point to the second song, "Skid Row (Downtown)". The routine uses most of the shabby New York street set and fills it with downtown denizens; hookers, petty crooks, drunks and the generally destitute all participate. Many take up a line of lyric,

just one, for themselves. Their movements and expressions depict the pain, exhaustion and hurt of street life. They are forlorn and haunted. The camera is restless, finding new angles, and the cast stumble forwards and in and out of one another in choreography that isn't dance but is. Frank Oz exhibits his absolute mastery in this sequence, but then does so throughout. He understands emotions, character, actors, space, seeing things. *Little Shop of Horrors* is a masterpiece.
—Paul Higson

LUCIFER RISING
1980
D: Kenneth Anger

The first thing to say about Kenneth Anger's short (and most conventional) movie is that it's not really a horror film. Yes, Lucifer makes an appearance (we can tell who he is via his jacket with his name on the back) and the entire piece is dripping in ritualism, but this is essentially a film about religious devotion. It just so happens that the religion concerned is Aleister Crowley's Thelema, a complex mix of paganism, pre-Biblical Egyptian beliefs and occultism. It's best to think of Anger's films (from this period at least) as religious symbolism from a devout practitioner, and to experience them on those terms, to get the most from his unique vision.

It's usually pointless to attribute a conventional narrative to Anger's work, but *Lucifer Rising* does actually have one, albeit told exclusively through a fractured series of romanticized and surreal images and Bobby Beausoleil's soundtrack (which,

I have to admit, is startlingly good). The film is a depiction of the Aeon of Horus, a central tenet of the Book of Law, one of the key texts for Thelemites and considered as the era of light. This event is conjured by Egyptian deities Isis and Osiris (the latter played by Donald Cammell), but also includes occult ritual, as well as Judeo-Christian figures Lilith (portrayed by Marianne Faithfull) and Lucifer himself.

Like other experimental filmmakers from this period (Stan Brakhage springs to mind), Anger's works either entrance or alienate. *Lucifer Rising* is more accessible than most, but it's still to all intents and purposes surrealism, particularly if one is not familiar with Thelema or the works of Crowley. Anyone picking up a copy of the movie expecting a 28-minute version of *The Omen* (1976) or the Satanist's equivalent of *The Anarchist's Cookbook* is likely to be confused and disappointed. Instead we get a story told exclusively through symbolic and highly romanticized images and music about what is, at least to Anger, a profound religious experience. As such, *Lucifer Rising*, product of its time undoubtedly, is mesmeric—beautiful but confusing, startling yet hypnotic, and a lot more interesting to experience than a bald description of it might lead you to believe.

Long in gestation and production, *Lucifer Rising* is infamous due to the involvement, at various points, of Mick Jagger, Jimmy Page and of course, Manson Family acolyte Beausoleil, who recorded the score while in prison (for the murder of Gary Hinman, reputedly at Manson's command). The movie was partly funded by John Paul Getty, Jr., and at least some of the production was probably shot in London, hence its appearance in this tome. It took Anger 15 years to get the film completed and released, in part because much footage intended for *Lucifer Rising* ended up in his earlier *Invocation of my Demon Brother* (1969), a short with many of the same themes, which, alongside depicting Thelemite lore also played on Anger's belief that the act of filmmaking was analogous to magical ritual—the director once stating "making a movie is casting a spell." Although filming was substantially complete by 1972, Anger held the project back for almost a decade—Beausoleil's score was only recorded in 1979 and the film first arrived on the festival circuit in 1980. It was then released on home video soon after Anger sold the rights to much of his filmography in 1986.

Lucifer Rising is more closely aligned to Jodorowsky's *The Holy Mountain* (1973) than it is to, say, *Evilspeak* (1981), and any viewer expecting the likes of the latter probably went back for a refund. That said, it's one of Anger's most conventionally accessible films and the combination of complex imagery, dense themes and hypnotic score is compelling, even without an understanding of the religious belief that drives it and its singular, idiosyncratic director.
—Neil Pike

THE MAKING OF A HORROR FILM
1984
D: none credited

Purporting to show a "day in the life of Dick Randall, motion picture producer," this promotional film/documentary actually provides a lengthy look at the making of *Don't Open Till*

Christmas, the various characters that gravitated within Randall's low-budget orbit at the time and—as promised—the man himself. Randall loved taking self-parodying bit parts in the films he was involved with—witness his cameo as Caroline Munro's lecherous agent in *Slaughter High* (1985) or his scene stealing tour-de-force as a pervert caretaker in Mario Bava's *Four Times that Night* (1972). Here Randall proves to be equally entertaining merely being himself, his distinct New-Yawkese accent, Gilbert Roland moustache and carny barker persona adding up to a captivating—and very funny—screen presence.

With someone at the helm who clearly never took himself too seriously, a similarly tongue-in-cheek spirit is evident in the documentary itself. We're first introduced to Randall as he is poring over a film script, before feigning surprise at the appearance of two glamour girls dressed in Santa outfits. The ladies (one of whom is Linzi Drew) both promptly flash their boobs at Randall—you half expect Dick to turn to the camera and proclaim: "I'd buy that for a dollar!" Actor/director Edmund Purdom turns out to be surprisingly good value for money in the documentary too, far more animated here than he is in *Don't Open Till Christmas* itself! Purdom tells a tall tale about first becoming interested in the horror genre after one of his ex-wives attempted to murder him in the shower ...

Behind-the-scenes footage from Purdom's tenure seem to confirm all the stories about *Don't Open Till Christmas* being a fiasco, the rushes often appearing cringe-inducing at times. Directing the peep show murder scene, Purdom is especially hung up on coaching an acting performance out of Alison, a glamour model type who has been cast as the central attraction. "You won't be quite as nude as this," Purdom reassures her as he contemplates a Page 3 type photo of the girl. Considering all the extra attention Alison has been receiving from the director, both she and the guy playing the Santa Claus victim in the scene register as truly terrible actors. The special effects are likewise unreliable and ropey—a device used to squirt stage blood from the actor's neck prematurely runs out of the red stuff, leaving Purdom futilely asking the special effects man to "pump, pump, pump." During the same scene a crewmember can be overheard on the soundtrack moaning "old fucking pillock," an insult seemingly aimed at either the inept Santa Claus actor or a fellow technician who wandered into shot. A less complicated exterior scene shot on location at Portobello Market also descends into pure farce, with Randall seen goofing around with the locals and Purdom once again being distracted from directing the film by yet another "bird"—this time a parrot belonging to a street entertainer. The actor/director at least manages to elicit a livelier performance from the friendly squawker than he did from Alison, the parrot memorably ending up perching itself on top of Purdom's head.

The documentary is rather sketchy about any mid-production controversy, but suddenly Derek Ford is seen to be directing the film, and footage taken from the actual released version reveals the roles of the peep show girl and Santa victim played by different actors to the ones previously seen being directed by Purdom, the original actors clearly having been given the chop. The film might have a new director and a better cast at this point, but a sense of "everything that can go wrong will go wrong" persists—an explosion fills a studio with smoke, make-up adheres to a poor actor's face and a crewmember's cat eats the

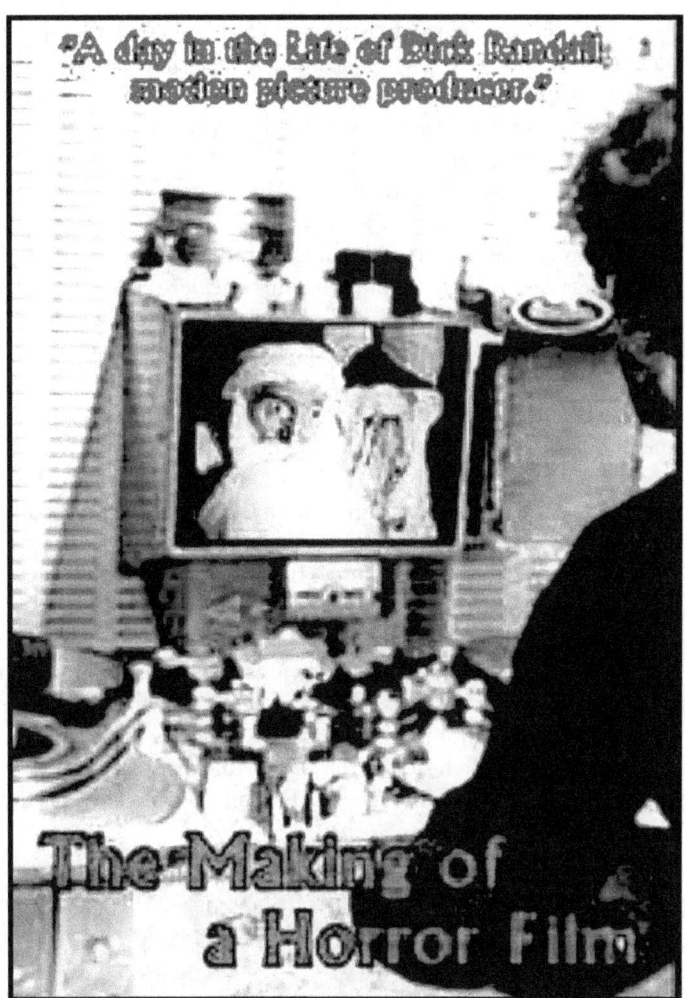

chopped liver intended to be used for a gore effect. Did all this really happen? Or is it just Dick Randall pulling our leg? As genuine stories about the making of *Don't Open Till Christmas* tend to be rather outlandish in nature anyway, it is often hard to distinguish fact from Randall wind-up at times. There are a couple of intentionally funny gags thrown into the documentary, including an appearance by a Margaret Thatcher lookalike. Explaining her presence, Randall claims that he was worried that making a violent horror film in "video nasty"-era Britain could result in his imprisonment. His answer? Hire a Thatcher impersonator and film her giving her blessing to the production, in the hope that this might guarantee an easier ride with the British censor (although Randall does admit to chickening out of trying to con the censor with this footage.)

Along the way, we're also given the dubious honor of viewing material eventually deemed too poor to be included in the final edit of *Don't Open Till Christmas*. The axed footage includes shots of Purdom talking to real policemen at the scene of a bomb scare, all filmed in cinéma vérité style (i.e. the crew chanced upon the hazardous situation, asked Purdom to mingle with the cops and opportunistically filmed the result without the knowledge of the boys in blue.) We also glimpse a deleted scene that finds Purdom and Belinda Mayne's characters stumbling upon the aftermath of another Santa murder—obviously intended as a bridge between their dinner date and her demise. Should you think the film itself had exhausted ways of bumping off blokes dressed as Santa, the documentary reveals two further murder scenes were shot but not used. The first features Santa Claus having his throat slashed with a razor; a second more imaginative variation on the theme sees Santa being strangled with a set of Christmas tree lights.

While Randall is undoubtedly the star of the show, the documentary doesn't miss the opportunity to get other equally fascinating characters on camera. Co-producer Steve Minasian is another American exploitation film wheeler-dealer, albeit a more reserved one than Randall, and talks about his background promoting *Mark of the Devil* in the States and his involvement with *The Last House on the Left* (plugging a never-made sequel to the latter in the process). Caroline Munro is less comfortable discussing blood-and-guts horror films, and perhaps sensing exactly what she has embroiled herself into here, is quick to confirm her preference for fantasy fare rather than the splatter movie approach to the genre.

Most bizarre of all is a cameo by Derek Ford's wife Valerie, who is filmed sporting an obvious wig and huge, Elton John-type outsize glasses. A softly spoken, middle-class lady, Valerie has been allocated several unseemly jobs on the production and is initially seen in a butcher's shop buying guts for the film's gore scenes. Valerie's shopping list sounds as if she is gathering the ingredients for a witch's cauldron rather than props for a movie as she asks the butcher for a sheep's eyeball, chicken entrails and

meat that looks "the nearest ... to human flesh." Valerie's next assignment—which explains why she is wearing a disguise—sees her loitering in a Soho sex shop, her mission this time being to buy a dildo for the film. At this point Valerie seems rather like the member of a dare club who has been asked to perform this sexual escapade for kicks and has gone along with it on the proviso that she can hide her identity under a wig and dark glasses. "I'm looking for a penis," Mrs. Ford casually explains "but I want a really natural sized one, these are all really rather exaggerated." A word of warning though, once you've picked yourself up off the floor from laughing at this, your imagination is stained with horrendous mental images—how exactly were the Fords planning to work this prop into the film? A gorier take on the toilet castration scene? Or something even further beyond the pale? Whatever Derek and Valerie's intentions were, the appearance of a natural sized fake penis—or a fake penis of any size—is notably absent from *Don't Open Till Christmas*, the Fords' X-rated aims clearly having hit the cutting room floor. Ultimately Valerie's brief stint as a gore and dildo wrangler is simply yet another crazy moment from the *Don't Open Till Christmas* saga.

The Making of a Horror Film is the most contradictory of promotional presskits, one that quickly gives up trying to portray the film in a good light and instead opts to milk every on-set disaster for comedic effect, casting the producer as chief stooge. An ace comedy writer asked to pen a spoof on the pitfalls of low-budget filmmaking would struggle to match the laugh-out-loud moments and eccentric characters that are on offer here. Game till the very last, the final shot in *The Making of a Horror Film* sees Dick Randall asleep in a screening room, having himself failed to stay awake during *Don't Open Till Christmas*. As the film's narrator so aptly signs off—"can't win 'em all."
—Gavin Whitaker

THE MASQUE OF THE RED DEATH

1989
D: Alan Birkinshaw

One of two versions of *Masque* to emerge in 1989—the other being a Roger Corman production with Adrian Paul and Patrick Macnee among its cast. The one we're concerned with formed part of a late-1980s partnership between producers Avi Lerner and Harry Alan Towers, with director Alan Birkinshaw, and was once described by critic and chronicler Donald C. Willis as being "just about the weirdest movie idea of Poe since the 1935 *Raven* (but not nearly as entertaining)."

Set in Bavaria, shot in South Africa, credited with having UK links by various print sources—a typical pie for globetrotting producer Towers to dig his fingers into, then. Unlike Birkinshaw's equally sidestepping take on Poe from the same year, *The House of Usher*, this is short on Brits cast-wise, but the "you can't believe they're on the same video box cover!" line-up here features that dream team of Brenda Vaccaro, Herbert Lom, and Frank Stallone—which surely compensates, at least for the type of viewer sufficiently far gone to contemplate tackling this in the first place.

It's marginally more elaborate than Birkinshaw's other work for 21st Century around this time, with an air of decadenceon-a-budget—reinforced by such elements as a chess game with human participants moving about the main hall's chequered floor, or a Fabergé egg hunt, plus, this being 1989, a troupe of "neo punk" musicians and dancers providing big-haired cabaret. Poe is rarely evoked (aside perhaps from one point where Stallone gets to morbidly muse about the transience of existence, and how we are dying from the time we take our first breath), and the remaining content is all over the place—a faux-giallo one minute, a hint of *Ten Little Indians* the next, a few splattery set piece murders. A crimson-cloaked killer in a blood-red skull mask stalks the corridors, no symbolic spirit or wraith on this occasion but a disguised flesh-and-blood maniac; their handiwork includes knifings, axings, strangulation, decapitation (via swinging timepiece pendulum, offering one further and more overt nod to Edgar Allan) and most spectacularly of all, sewing a fabric designer into a gigantic loom—albeit while lamely growling "it is time for the artist to become part of the art," a comment as familiar and as redundant as it is misplaced.

—Darrell Buxton

MISS MORISON'S GHOSTS

1981
D: John Bruce

Based on the true-life cause "The Moberly-Jourdain Incident" that briefly had Edwardian Britain in a spin, this feature-length drama for the ITV network takes an unusually scholarly approach to a semi-supernatural occurrence. Scripted by Ian Curteis (best-known as director of *The Projected Man* but with a highbrow career as actor and writer stemming from his time in Joan Littlewood's Theatre Workshop), *Miss Morison's Ghosts* presents a rounded picture of the by-then largely discredited case, in which two women claimed to have entered a loop in time during a 1901 visit to Versailles. Under the pseudonyms "Elizabeth Morison" and "Frances Lamon," the pair published the book *An Adventure*, an account of experience at the Petit Trianon where they saw the "ghosts" of Marie Antoinette and other less prominent individuals.

You really couldn't find two finer actresses than Wendy Hiller and Hannah Gordon to bring life to Curteis' interpretation of Charlotte Anne Moberly and Eleanor Jourdain. Here the duo are referred to as Miss Morison and Miss Lamont throughout, and the teleplay focuses far more on their surge through the world of academia than on the notorious Paris excursion, effectively entwining Charlotte's success in establishing St. Gilbert's College with the controversy caused by their outrageous assertions.

"What we saw did have an incoherence about it" declares Hiller at one crucial point, a line that sums up the general approach of this dramatization. One could almost retitle this production *Paranormal Inactivity*, both a comment upon the spurious nature of the original report and because Curteis and director John Bruce skirt over the Parisian visions—only a tiny fraction of the 103-minute broadcast time is devoted to the supposed spirits and shifting surroundings, yet this is all to the credit of the piece. We do not need to dwell on specters, apparitions, time-travel, as the major fascination here is the aftermath, the return of the women to Oxford and their twin battles to gain acceptance within the university environment while also attempting to convince an almost entirely skeptical community that they have encountered the fantastic ("we peeped through a curtain in time.") Religious, scholastic, and moral viewpoints are not merely a cause for wider debate here but are actually internalized within the minds of single characters as they wrestle with themselves, struggling to process the event in France against conflicting, firmly held beliefs.

Matters are not assisted by the fact that Morison and Lamont claim to have had different experiences to one another, and their own friendship begins to unravel as they fail to reach agreement—all of which works beautifully as a metaphor for their position within the college (Miss Morison is the outgoing Principal of St. Gilbert's, Miss Lamont her appointed successor, the latter frustrated as the elder woman will not stand aside and let her take immediate charge.) As in the real case, there are heavy hints dropped that the whole amazing story may have simply been the result of the companions stumbling upon a pageant rehearsal and witnessing a parade of costumed performers, though ambiguity is retained via the determination of both to express their convictions, as well as the one tantalizing loose end as Gordon insists on having heard and memorized a musical refrain which, it is later discovered, was only ever played at the court of Louis XVI and remained unpublished.

Even the stabs at lightening the tone cannot quite penetrate the determined approach to adapting this case for television. The paranormal society representative who ponders whether "we should perhaps practice clairvoyance—it would save so much on the postage!" also leads the fierce resistance against our protagonists, threatening legal action; and there's a lovely "one-upmanship" gag concerning associations with ecclesiastical dignitaries, which plays as a frivolous throwaway one-liner but has a basis in truth, as the real Eleanor Jourdain was once employed as secretary to the Archbishop of Canterbury's wife!
—Darrell Buxton

MONTY PYTHON'S THE MEANING OF LIFE

1983
D: Terry Jones

This is a real oddity. At once the most ambitious and the most frustrating of the Python troupe's films: The winner of the Grand Jury Prize at the 1983 Cannes Film Festival, a work that—however humorously—sought to explore profound philosophical questions. A film of vaulting imagination, as evidenced by Terry Gilliam's little sketch which just grew and grew, *The Crimson Permanent Assurance*—a tale of literal pirate accountants which became a supporting feature in its own right.

And perhaps emblematic of the film's fatal flaws, its towering imagination and stunning visuals are largely without laughs, one inspired jump-cutting scene showing the put-upon pen-pushers as galley-slaves. Also undeniably scrappy, with an ending which seems to appear largely because the makers had no other idea.

The laughs come more frequently in the main feature itself, but the scrappiness remains. A gaggle of bare-breasted young ladies are thrown in towards the end for no real reason, and the script's attempt to be clever by pointing out that it realizes how gratuitous this is fools no one. The occasional irritable interjections from the Greek chorus of goldfish, that seems to have very little meaning, is likely to seem more and more pertinent.

And yet meaning is there, if one wishes it, albeit usually as a joke. And this meaning flashes briefly among sketches that, perhaps due to the freedom of an "18" certificate, is often darker and bloodier than anything seen from the Pythons before.

The comedy violence of a hopelessly mismatched boys-versus-masters school rugby match which, in another astonishing edit, smashes into a gore-sodden World War One battlefield: Put-upon Catholic parents' sad decision to sell their multitude of children for scientific experiments; more bloody warfare, including bodies in slices, severed heads, and cinema's most famous missing leg during the Zulu campaign; an alarmingly proactive pair of cheery surgeons making their collections prematurely and messily from organ donor card carriers; Mr. Creosote, the world's richest, greediest, fattest and rudest man, devours his way to an explosive end; and then Death himself turns up to claim a nice group of middle-class diners at their country cottage.

After their deaths, in fact, comes perhaps the greatest horror of all. Blood and guts may shock, but when Heaven is shown to be real, and somewhere everybody ends up ... initially, that doesn't seem so bad: but then it's revealed what Heaven is—Christmas 365 days a year, every year, for all Eternity. Cozy, yes: friendly, yes. As a Tony Bennett-esque crooner who may well be God Himself declares, "it's nice and warm and everyone looks smart and wears a tie" ... but behind the coziness lies the abyss of unending forced smiles and bland terror, of the same expected presents and films on telly ("*The Sound of Music*, twice an hour, and *Jaws* 1, 2 *and* 3") forever and ever, amen. Maybe, this film whispers nervously in our ear, an unremittingly happy afterlife may well be the truest of all hells.

And yet, at the very end, the Nice Lady Presenter gives us a brief yet as worthwhile a summary of the Meaning of Life as anyone is ever likely to get. If we choose to listen.

It's a patchy film, and yet in some ways the Pythons' greatest: funny, frightening, humane, thoughtful, tuneful (the musical numbers are superb throughout), and—as that television set displaying the opening credits of an old comedy television series drifts off into the endless void—surprisingly poignant.

"Pray that there's intelligent life somewhere out in Space/'cause there's bugger-all down here on Earth! ..."
—Ken Shinn

MURDER:
THE ULTIMATE GROUNDS FOR DIVORCE

1984
D: Morris Barry

"No witnesses ... that was the rule." Morris Barry's *Murder: The Ultimate Grounds for Divorce* (1984) snuck out on video via Carey Communications in 1985 following little more than the usual trade magazine publicity. It probably requires a more in-depth study than it will get here, particularly as it is a thriller that only tangentially crosses into the horror genre. One of the problems with the film is that it is a thriller tied to four key characters, that is two couples, who spend a great amount of the screen time verbally abusing one another. Secondly, and forgive me this Spoiler Alert, but none of the four die and the only death is seen in a flashback to the murder of an acquaintance in a car park. So, having made a strong argument against its "horror" status, what am I going to do to argue its place here now?

Readily dismissed in the day and little seen since, particularly following the death of the director, Morris Barry, the film is well made and permeated by a constant level of threat and unease, goaded into place by the soundtrack and set pieces as the two couples bicker and endanger one another. The four have spent each weekend together over the last seven years and held secrets almost as long. Now on a camper van holiday 15 miles from anywhere, the aggression mounts and the memories and secrets surface. "Just how far are we from civilization?"/"Some of us are further than others."

"I must adhere," sarcastically adds Roger (Roger Daltrey), "to the time-honored tradition of the banality and stupidity ... away from mad axe men and marauding Hell's Angels." The threat instead comes from within the unit, particularly Roger himself whose behavior from the outset is overly aggressive. When the tone lifts into some friendlier territory he deliberately drags it back down again into unpleasantness. Toyah Willcox plays his partner Val, Terry Raven and Leslie Ash co-starring as the other couple Edwin and Philippa.

The blurb describes the story as a working-class *Who's Afraid of Virginia Woolf?*, but there is more than acidic banter here. The threat level is pepped up by the group members arming themselves with a gun, a knife, a mantrap and an axe. Early in the film Roger recklessly drops items from the roof close to Edwin and points a rifle at Val, which Edwin takes from him, chipping in the comment, "Every seven years the Devil loads his gun." Roger chucks petrol on to the log-fire to the chagrin of the fireside Edwin, who has to nimbly dodge the flash of flame. Close-up shots of knives and axes are accompanied by the electronic twang, ominous drone or dismaying squelch of a synthesizer compounding the dread. Edwin begins to cross-dress for fun but there may be something more to his play than that, and when Edwin brings up the car park murder with Roger it is to infer that one of them has psychopathic tendencies and is responsible for the killing.

The murder talk continues, all a game, like something from their collective childhood—"count to 10 and you're alive again." The terrorism becomes more ramped up as Roger, seemingly intent on killing his wife, pursues her across the landscape and down to the water's edge. Everything becomes a weapon and all the major props from the tent, camper van, bike and dinghy are destroyed. An abandoned house is revealed to be overhanging a collapsing cliff face when Edwin opens a door nearly falling out over the precipice. The scene recalls one in *Bloody New Year*, both films involving Hayden Pearce, an art director on this one and art director and producer on the other, who confessed to having had great fun blowing up the van.

The set-up calls to mind Colin Eggleston's *Long Weekend* only without the supernatural danger and the threat entirely human. Morris Barry (who also directed episodes of *Doctor Who*) brings it all together with great aplomb, never slacking in pace. Producer Tim Purcell also wrote the script, which is an admirable effort, heavy in dialogue, but this governs the pace, being pitched with the right ferocity. Cinematographer Charles Tookey captures everything comfortably, from high angle, to action sequences, even aerial shots. As mentioned, the music tries every electronic trick in the book, largely to good effect, dating the film nostalgically.

It's somewhat surprising that more advantage was not made of the celebrity casting, not only at the time but since. Daltrey and Toyah had significant rock and pop careers by then and Leslie Ash was every mod's dream alley shag following her role in Franc Roddam's *Quadrophenia* (in which Toyah also featured), and the three have retained their celebrity status over the subsequent decades. It's a compact thriller that occasionally runs afoul of its 1980s soundtrack but for the most part even benefits

from it. Roger Daltrey provides good menace, and Toyah goes for the gusto too, though Ash sounds a little uncertain delivering her dialogue and Terry Raven is listless and flat, explaining his infrequent invite before a camera. Filmed in Fairlight Country Park and Hastings, the film runs a sufficient 77 minutes and not the longer running time often given to it in listings.
—Paul Higson

THE NAUGHTY DREAMS OF MISS OWEN/ THE INITIANTS

1987 / 1988
D: Martin Silvearo (as Remington Steel)

You'd never believe it from the title, video cover or the majority of the running time, but 1987's *The Naughty Dreams of Miss Owen* (aka *Teenage Pussy-Cat*) is a supernatural-themed outing from Peter Kay's Strand Video label. Kay's nudity-ridden softcore productions like *Sexy Secrets of the Kissogram Girls* and *Misadventures at Megaboob Manor* were a ubiquitous sight at cheapo video shops during the 1980s and 1990s. These often hilariously inept videos capitalized on the 1980s obsession for large-breasted glamour models and Page 3 girls—like Pauline Hickey and Debee Ashby—as the videos' headliners.

Stacey Owen

Scottish model Stacey Owen is the top-heavy star of this low-rent effort, being asked to housesit for her Aunt (Cilla Blue) over a weekend. Alone in the house Stacey passes the time by taking nude swims and admiring her boobs in a mirror. Before long, an uneasy feeling that she is not alone beings to creep over poor Stacey. As it turns out her suspicions are completely correct, since a mysterious blonde (Janie Hamilton) keeps watching her from outside the house. Every time Stacey takes a dip or tucks into her breakfast, up pops blondie suggestively licking her lips and clawing at the window with her large fingernails. It would seem virtually impossible to miss an exhibition like that, yet whenever Stacey senses a presence and turns towards the sexy apparition, the woman has disappeared.

The fact that Stacy has never laid eyes on this beauty doesn't prevent her from having an erotic dream that sees the two of them share a bath and massage each other with body oil. Or was it a dream at all? Since when Stacey awakes, she discovers a wet towel and a half empty bottle of lotion. The case of the disappearing unguent deepens after a search of Auntie's house reveals several saucy photos of the figure from Stacey's dream, as well as a home video featuring in Stacey's own words, "a beautiful, huge titted young girl doing a very erotic striptease." Attempting to clear her head of this mystery woman, Stacey decides on some on-the-spot jogging, a potentially hazardous course of action. "With knockers as big as mine I have to be careful what I do," she explains in voiceover, "the vigorous bouncing of my tits however soon put all thoughts of the odd happenings out of my mind." Fortunately, Stacey manages to avoid knocking herself out with her own knockers and finally lays eyes on the person who has been peeking at her. Upon confronting the female peeping tom, Stacey discovers the woman is in fact Tracey, a friend of her Aunt and a former owner of the house. Introductions over, the two quickly become friends and spend the weekend dancing topless and trying on Auntie's lingerie, presumably stretching it out of shape in the process. Playtime comes to an abrupt halt when Auntie returns home early and as Stacey goes to open the door to her relative, Tracey disappears into thin air!! Returning to find Tracey gone, Stacey is stunned by her Aunt's revelation that she has never heard of anyone by that name. A bigger shock awaits after Stacey describes Tracey to her Aunt, only for Auntie to reveal that Tracey matches the description of Andrea, a model who died in the house three months earlier. Meaning that Stacey has spent the weekend flirting and frolicking with a ghost!!

In keeping with the censorious nature of the late 1980s, *The Naughty Dreams of Miss Owen* often feels like a retreat back to the days of the 1960s nudist film era. Any raunchy interaction between the two main characters is only hinted at in the dialogue, and what really finds favor here is asexual nudity and Stacey Owen throwing an inflatable beach ball around with similar vigor to her sun and nudist camp loving 1960s predecessors. While its contents may hark back to a tamer era, on a visual level *The Naughty Dreams of Miss Owen* is unmistakably a child of the 1980s. The Strand format of shot-on-video production values, computer generated titles, plus big boobs and even bigger hair being flung about to the sounds of MOR power ballads and electric keyboard muzak roots their videos firmly in the era. *Naughty Dreams'* supernatural angle is somewhat side-lined, prominent only for the final revelation and shots of the blonde model outstretching her large fingernails at the window—a sight that inadvertently recalls Max Schreck doing likewise in the silent horror classic *Nosferatu*!! Merely laughable on first viewing, the shots of Tracey/Andrea at the window do take on an eerie quality in light of the character being revealed to be a ghost—a fact emphasized by the shots being repeated in the video's closing moments, this time in creepy black-and-white still form. The spooky ending is—if nothing else—a totally out of the blue surprise, especially as the video's major focus on big bouncing boobs suggests it wasn't the hairs on the back of the audience's necks the filmmakers were originally aiming to make stand on end.

Not content with giving the world this unlikely marriage of the big bust fetish video and the supernatural, Strand Video had another minor brush with horror in their 1988 video *The Initiants*, also directed by Silvearo (aka "Remington Steel"). A sort of *Virgin Witch* for the video age (cover blurb: "A Satanic Orgy of Sex"), *The Initiants* sees a pair of female hitchhikers staying the night at a farmhouse only to discover their host is a warlock who has designs on involving them in a black magic orgy. Although perhaps the most shocking thing about *The Initiants* is that, for a Strand Video, the women in it have normal sized breasts for a change.

—Gavin Whitaker

ON THE THIRD DAY

1983
D: Stanley O'Toole

It's difficult to pinpoint exactly what the intention of *On the Third Day* was. A somewhat ridiculous melodrama set over an Easter weekend in Cornwall, it occasionally hints at a critique of religious hypocrisy among the chattering classes in "jam scone and a pot of tea" rural England, or a dig at "traditional family values" with secrets and infidelities being unearthed en route, but ultimately it goes nowhere. Any suggestion that this might be some kind of modern take on a Christ-like figure would also seem without substance—the closing freeze-frame shot is so terribly confusing that its apparent bid to offer a "resurrection" of sorts falls completely flat.

It's basically another of those "home invasion" affairs, only without the standard violence, class jealousy, forced sex and general depravity which that grubby subgenre usually offers. All cut-glass accents and *Daily Telegraph* attitude, it pits a headmaster/piano teacher and family against a self-proclaimed accountant (who may or may not be telling the truth about his proclaimed occupation and every other subject he discusses.) A well-to-do couple, the Hammonds (Paul Williamson, Catherine Schell) arrive back at their coastal country dwelling to realize they may have been the victims of burglary—however, further investigation reveals a clean-cut young fellow who introduces himself as Jeremy Bolt (Richard Morant), sitting calmly in their living room. He introduces himself as being a friend of a friend, and soon ingratiates himself into the household, although Mr. Hammond remains suspicious.

Bolt's unexpected arrival on Good Friday, and the events of the weekend leading to unsavory revelations and ultimate tragedy, ought to have been ripe with possibility and symbolism, but if any Biblical significance was intended it all gets rather lost in the murk. There's an awful lot of padding and unappealing "local color" here, at the expense of coherence and competent storytelling. Unnecessary interludes include heated debate during a restaurant outing (far less potent than the similar scene in Saxon Logan's *Sleepwalker* from the following year), a trek out to the visually-striking open-air clifftop Minack Theatre, a pub gag involving the village's faux-disabled barfly, and an excursion to the Trelargen Easter Fete where the horse-racing, acoustic folk tunes and amateur boxing challenges all prove rather inconsequential—the latter leads to a bruising confrontation between the headmaster and his unwelcome guest, which in a better movie might have brought things to a powerful head setting up a dramatic conclusion, but here merely fizzles out. As for the plummy-voiced discussion about the merits of The Stranglers' "Golden Brown," words fail me. There are a couple of major scenes involving gunplay—the fact that both hinge around the firing of blanks somehow sums up the deficiencies of the entire enterprise.

This was the only film to be directed by Stanley O'Toole, who as a producer and executive was responsible for several exceptional British cult movies (in particular *The Squeeze*). His heart really doesn't seem to be in it—the film's child cameo roles are filled by mini-O'Tooles, and it wouldn't surprise me to discover that he only made the picture as a means of fulfilling promises to relatives. It seems to have been available only on a scarce Karl Lorimar VHS release. Oddly, reviews at the IMDb and other examples of online coverage refer to it as a horror movie, but you'd have to stretch the definition of horror quite a way to encompass this loser. And should you be looking for an Easter-set entertainment to accompany your hot cross buns, please stick with *Rebel Without a Cause* or *The Passion of the Christ*.
—Darrell Buxton

THE OUTCASTS

1982
D: Robert Wynne-Simmons

Robert Wynne-Simmons is one of our most underappreciated fantasists, yet even following the rise of the "folk horror" movement in recent times, his name and the ways in which he set that particular trend in motion have been elbowed aside in favor of *The Wicker Man*, *Kill List*, *The VVitch* and other popular fan favorites.

The Outcasts certainly ought to be better-known, and only lack of exposure/availability prevents this from being held high as a landmark in the area of rural unease that has lately struck a chord with many. Film production in Eire, dormant for far too long, was kick-started by the establishment of the Irish Film Board in 1981 and Wynne-Simmons' bleak, supernaturally tinged tale was chosen as a key project for the relaunch of movies as a going concern in the Republic. Britain's then-new TV outlet Channel 4 became involved, assisting with funding for this and Neil Jordan's brilliantly disheveled gangland thriller *Angel*, the latter leading to a major revival in Irish cinema and setting its raw talents on the road to fame and fortune. No such luck for Wynne-Simmons, a man who had constantly toiled on the fringes and whose career ought to have been more fruitful and better critically acknowledged.

Robert's most familiar work is of course his screenplay for cult British Devil-worship classic *Blood on Satan's Claw*, and you might be forgiven upon reading a synopsis for thinking of *The Outcasts* as a close relative—it's a comparatively unconventional and more fluid/unstructured affair than *Claw*, however, despite sharing a countryside period setting and whispers of the uncanny. The story focuses upon Maura O'Donnell (Mary Ryan), described as "one of God's infirmities" and considered unfit for marriage. She encounters a Pied Piper-like figure called Scarf Michael (Mark Lally), a fiddler whose violin bow is reputed to be strung with the hair of a dead man, and who could be mortal, Satanic, or perhaps not even there at all. Evidence of Michael's powers are witnessed in the movie's most striking and memorable scene, where he conjures up frightening visions to disturb young lovers coupling in the forest—one girl finding to her disgust and terror that the lusty beau she's dallying with has somehow been replaced by an equally randy goat, on its hind legs and pinning her upright against a stone wall. Twenty-first century filmgoers who bow at the altar of "Black Phillip" from *The VVitch* may well find that their bleating horned hero has some serious competition from over three decades earlier! (*Kill List*-like straw masks also make an early appearance in *The Outcasts*.)

Unsurprisingly, Maura becomes the target of the villagers' hatred, being blamed for Michael's shenanigans as well as that season's failing potato crop. She takes up with the fantastic fiddler after his powers have assisted her in evading a rowdy mob, but in a rather confused yet somehow affecting finale, appears back outside her own family's home, viewing her father and sister within—possibly suggesting that she herself has crossed into a realm beyond, in a scene that could well have taken inspiration from the *Wurdulak* episode of 1963 anthology *Black Sabbath*.

If you most enjoy the sacrificial aspects of *The Wicker Man* or the slaughter, possession and manifestation in *Children of the Corn*, Wynne-Simmons' quieter and purposely perplexing approach may lack in appeal. On the other hand, if talk of navel-strings in the former or the intrusion of myth and legend in the latter are your bag, *The Outcasts* may prove a satisfying experience, worth making the effort to track down.
—Darrell Buxton

PANIC

1982
D: Tonino Ricci

England, as seen through the lens of the Spanish/Italian co-producers of this trashy 1982 romp (aka *Bakterion*). A scientist performing top secret research for the government gets infected. This turns him into a contagious cannibalistic being with a pizza for a face.

He travels to the nearest town on a killing spree munching his way through the usual suspects always found populating this type of stalker/thing-on-the-loose movie—a necking couple in a car, woman in shower, lone drunk—before setting his sights on a cinema and a church. Fear not, however—for "Captain Kirk" is here. No, not Shatner, but David Warbeck as a similarly named copper. Kirk hits the trail of the beast accompanied by another scientist, who happens to be a drop dead gorgeous woman from a research unit otherwise made up of old men.

The government is worried and sends in the army to seal off the village, cutting all communication and power sources—as you do when trying not to arouse panic. Surprisingly no one outside the town notices, and it takes the locals a long time to realize anything is wrong—it is set in Britain, after all ("The British are used to cuts!") Finally, they try leaving, but by this point the army have surrounded the town. If they can't neutralize the rogue pizza scientist, the government is going to drop a nuclear bomb.

A nuclear bomb? Rather drastic, not to mention bloody stupid. I'm thinking the planned American setting was changed for some reason. It's implausible that the Yanks would drop a nuclear device on themselves (at least not on purpose) but I can't see any British government being willing to do this. Hmm ... maybe the last few ...

The English setting is limited to stock footage and the usual terrible dubbing ("Xtraaaa! Xtraaaa! Reed orl abaaht it!") When the amorous couple starts undressing before attempting to get it on (pizza faced mutants permitting), you know this isn't Britain! As do all the hip dark-haired extras milling around the cinema following the monster's munch. Foreign films usually got a raw deal before they arrived on the English-speaking market—cut and spliced, laughable revoicing, dumbing down, and in some cases even re-written scripts. Sadly, *Panic* is cheesy enough anyway, with an unrealistic plot, zero tension and even less pace

There are some nice sequences that might have worked better. When the thing attacks punters in a cinema, it bursts through the screen. It carries off a blonde, who, in a twist on the usual "sex or death" theme in horror has just turned down nookie with her randy boyfriend to see the film instead. The church the creature targets is empty apart from a priest giving some young boys late night choir practice (and that's not a euphemism). It's a shame the film doesn't seem able to milk any tension as the Father does the noble thing, sacrificing himself when the grotesque horror gets hold of one of the lads trying to escape.

Sadly the finale with two "I say" Biggles types flying a bomber as a digital countdown appears on the screen, while Kirk and the bimbo hunt pizza-man in the sewers, fails to buck the "zero interest" trend. The credits end with the legend: "WHAT YOU

HAVE SEEN MIGHT REALLY HAPPEN ... PERHAPS IT ALREADY HAS!"
—Gerald Lea

A PATTERN OF ROSES

1983
D: Lawrence Gordon Clark

Helena Bonham Carter became adopted as the crinoline-clad pin up girl of choice for fans of British costume drama in the mid-1980s. A star-making role in *A Room with a View* soon led to a title lead as *Lady Jane*, and she found it hard to shake the image, becoming typecast in the likes of Zeffirelli's *Hamlet*, *Howards End*, *The Wings of a Dove* etc. Less celebrated is her latter-day participation in fantasy and macabre fare—her long relationship with Tim Burton saw her featuring prominently in his *Planet of the Apes*, *Big Fish*, *Charlie and the Chocolate Factory*, *Corpse Bride*, *Sweeney Todd: The Demon Barber of Fleet Street*, *Alice in Wonderland*, and *Dark Shadows*, and Helena's character Bellatrix Lestrange has consistently proved a highlight of the variable *Harry Potter*

is somewhat clumsy and awkward, with the parallels between 1980s teenager Tim Ingram (Stuart MacKenzie) and pre-WWI counterpart Tom (Jo Searby) being laid on thick, visual transitions from one decade to another and back handled too choppily, and Stanley Myers' bland score ranging from inappropriately jaunty refrains to generic sinister-by-numbers passages. The tale has Tim stumbling upon details of lower-class Tom's untimely death in February 1914 by way of several drawings he finds as his family's cottage is being renovated; intrigued by their sharing of the initials T.R.I., the fact that he has reached the same age at which Tom was killed, and a pencil sketch of a pretty young girl named Netty, Tim and a CND-campaigning female friend delve into the mystery—but tragic events from the past threaten to bleed into his own environment. The tumbling flow of a local weir beneath a bridge is hinted as the focus for watery disaster ("hypnotic, isn't it?"—"gives me the shivers"), but again the climax seems a little confused, a rush of edits and indistinct images failing to transmit any sense of danger or the dramatic. As for Helena, she's given disappointingly little to do in the first of her many "period" roles, but whatever scant impact this sorry piece has to offer emanates from her, already an icon in waiting. She at least looks appealing, is at ease in old-fashioned garments, delivers dialogue well and doesn't bump into the Edwardian furniture.
—Darrell Buxton

THE PHANTOM OF THE OPERA

1989

D: Rupert Julian (and Michael Armstrong; intro footage filmed in 1989)

mega-franchise. She voiced Lady Tottington in *Wallace & Gromit: Curse of the Were-Rabbit*, and by 2012 was considered of appropriate vintage to essay the raddled eccentric Miss Havisham in Mike Newell's *Great Expectations*. Perhaps most impressive was her turn in David Fincher's millennial mind-bender *Fight Club*, though her awkward, monstrously beautiful Bride in *Mary Shelley's Frankenstein* provides one of the few startling highlights of that particular misfire.

Few H.B.C. admirers are aware of her screen debut, or that it came in a made-for-television item for Channel 4. *A Pattern of Roses* was an adaptation of the children's novel by K.M. Peyton and aired just after Christmas 1983. Fittingly, it was the latest in a long line of shuddery seasonal offerings from spooky specter specialist Lawrence Gordon Clark—for many years Clark had been the mainstay behind *A Ghost Story for Christmas*, his annual take on the work of M.R. James (and Dickens), achieving contemporary critical acclaim as well as lasting praise from the generation who grew up shivering in front of these festive frighteners. Mr. Clark fared less well for the commercial channels, however—his 1979 Yorkshire TV stab at James' *Casting the Runes* was an ill-fated mess, and *A Pattern of Roses* isn't much of an improvement Shades of Clark's style remain in both, and *Pattern* in particular benefits hugely from a bleak, wintry setting and effective use of outdoor locations—trademark Clark. It's all rather slow, and short on shocks and eeriness, unfortunately, and any viewer tuning in expecting a haunting December chill would have found themselves disappointed. The whole manner of the telling

Due to Universal Pictures' failure to renew the copyright in the 1950s, their silent 1925 Lon Chaney version of *The Phantom of the Opera* was one of several early horror classics to have fallen into ownerless "public domain" status by the late 1980s. A fact that didn't escape the attention of *Don't Open Till Christmas* producers Dick Randall and Steve Minasian. With the musical version of *Phantom* still playing in the West End and Harry Alan Towers about to unleash his own slasher-film-flavored adaptation, Randall clearly thought there was life in the old Phantom yet, and decided to issue the out-of-copyright 1925 version on video. Rather than merely put out a no-frills version, Randall elected to add color tints to *Phantom* and commission Rick Wakeman to compose a modern soundtrack to the silent film. Actions that—perhaps inten-

tionally—echo the 1980s makeover that Giorgio Moroder had given to *Metropolis* a few years earlier.

Randall found himself financing a mini-*House of the Long Shadows* reunion when he hired Michael Armstrong to write and direct an introduction hosted by Christopher Lee. Armstrong had recently returned from the States and found himself making this, and writing an unfilmed script called *Enter Three Ninjas* for Randall soon after. Armstrong's atmospheric three-minute introduction to *Phantom* finds Lee exploring the damp, candlelit depths of what is meant to be the Palais Garnier, while explaining the origins of Gaston Leroux's novel and the 1925 film. In reality this introduction was shot closer to home in the UK—Armstrong recalls the filming actually taking place in the cellar of a restaurant in London. Tagged on to the opening of the video release, the introduction might have lacked the budget for authentic location shooting but is greatly enhanced by Lee's authoritative presence and Armstrong's own experience in the horror genre.

Filmed and put together in late 1989, the Randall/Wakeman/Armstrong version of *Phantom of the Opera* hit the video shelves in early 1990, just in time to be hyped as "a new masterpiece for the nineties." Wakeman's soundtrack for the film turned up the same year on his album *Phantom Power*.
—Gavin Whitaker

PINK FLOYD–THE WALL

1982
D: Alan Parker

Following three years on the heels of the original vinyl release, 1982's *Pink Floyd–The Wall* sought to bring the pomp and ambition of a concept album to the screens of the nation's fleapits. At the helm, one of the country's most stylish and successful directors, Alan Parker. On animation and looking very relaxed, the magisterial Gerald Scarfe. A cast that included Bob Geldof, Bob Hoskins, not-so-little Nell Campbell and John Scott Martin. All of the pieces were in place for this to be a remarkably good film. There was—and remains to this day—one tiny, teeny bijou problemette. The actual record that it was based on, frankly, is pretty crap.

In case you don't know, the story is the fantastically embellished autobiographical meanderings of Floyd member Roger Waters—father that he never knew, over-protective smothering mother, rotten schoolteachers, spiteful ex-wife … oh, and fantasies of being a Mosley-type fascist dictator. And, don't yer know, he's a rock star, too. Disguised under the alter ego of his fictitious counterpart, Pink.

Sometimes, searching one's soul can produce cathartic, intriguing results for both the artist and their audience. On other occasions, it can produce a pile of self-pitying rubbish. And this film plunges into the latter with a large, smelly splash.

The horrors hinted at here—Pink's apparently imminent nervous breakdown, the ever-present specter of war—are strong and valid ones. Had the narrative focused solely on them, then it could have been a work of genuine power. Regrettably, all too often they become subservient to yet more of Waters' poor-poor-me self-aggrandizing moroseness. Feel his pain! Share his suffering! Shoulder the mighty burden of being a vastly rich and popular rock musician! Flow my tears, Mr. Waters.

Pink is never allowed to become unsympathetic. From childhood, he's the brave, misunderstood loner. Even when he commits adultery with a groupie, we have to know that his horrible ex-wife beat him to the punch. He starts to feel less like some tortured soul, more like Norman Wisdom pleading with us not to laugh at him because he's a fool.

Perhaps the biggest misstep, though, is that dictator sequence. Not only because Parker, in an act of extreme foolishness, decided to hire genuine neo-Nazi bully boys as extras for the sake of realism, shocking and outraging Gerald Scarfe—but because it's the only real fantasy of Pink's that we get to view. If only we'd seen him not just as Happy Shopper Hitler, but as a postman, an astronaut, a factory worker, a mad scientist … as many other alternatives as the running time would allow … then this could have been potent and affecting, a film precursor of sorts to Kim Newman's marvellous novel *Life's Lottery*. We could have seen more of Pink's personality, his hopes and fears. We could have learned to like him. To empathize. Alas, that narrowness of options is already there in the original album and must be kept sacrosanct. It's a limiting and frankly rather nauseating duality of vision.

In fairness to the film, the cast gives it their all, the music is fine even if the lyrics are decidedly lacking, and the animated

interludes courtesy of Mr. Scarfe are powerful, terrifying stuff—I defy you not to shudder when the War Bird first morphs out of a lowering sky. As musicals go it isn't bad—but the best musicals focus on a quest, whether it's the "let's do the show right here!" approach of Rooney and Garland or Richard and Stubbs, the voyage to find a way home in *The Wizard of Oz*, the battle to save the old homestead of *The Blues Brothers*. But in the final balance, *Pink Floyd–The Wall* has a quest which goes no further than self-important navel-gazing. Effective as it can be as an audio-visual experience, in the end you're just watching the world's largest, noisiest, most expensive session on the psychiatrist's couch. Although it does end on a note of quiet hope. Which is nice.
—Ken Shinn

THE PLAGUE DOGS

1982
D: Martin Rosen

The Plague Dogs is a British animated feature produced and directed by Martin Rosen, who also adapted the screenplay from Richard Adams' novel. It was originally released in the UK in October 1982 by United Artists. It tells the story of two dogs—Snitter, a small terrier, and Rowf, a much larger black Labrador—who escape from a research center in the Lake District where they have been used as "guinea pigs" for various experiments. When the dogs escape and flee to the nearby fells, a national panic starts as it slowly emerges that the center has also been carrying out research into the bubonic plague and that the dogs may have been contaminated. *The Plague Dogs* is a borderline horror title for two reasons. Firstly, it is an extremely harrowing watch, particularly for animal lovers. Second, the plague element of the story takes the film into apocalypse territory.

To look at the vivisection angle first, the specifics are that Snitter has had brain surgery that has affected his perception of what is real and what is not, and Rowf has been involved in testing how long a dog can survive in a deep tank of water, work that has left him embittered, hostile to humans and terrified of drowning. The employees at the center—and indeed most of the humans in the film—are never seen in full, our view of them limited up to about waist height, presumably to replicate a dog's eye view. This has the effect, of course, of making the humans faceless—an implacable foe to the animals, emotionless, inscrutable, seemingly unstoppable; the stuff of nightmares, in other words.

The animation helps enormously, not because it is violent or explicit but because the animators and director clearly understand dog behavior, particularly the way they move; anyone who has ever owned a dog will recognize their actions and habits. As a consequence, the dogs become recognizable; they become believable characters in whom we are emotionally invested. That is what amplifies the horror of everything that befalls them.

The plague element introduces the idea that our heroes could ultimately be responsible for an unimaginably horrific epidemic, putting an emotional conflict at the heart of the film (as the best horrors do). The idea of an epidemic is a staple in fiction, and in the horror/sci-fi genres; a prime example is Danny Boyle's *28 Days Later ...* which, like *The Plague Dogs*, opens with truly distressing depictions of animal experimentation. Despite the title, this isn't a major element here—for one thing it is never fully established whether the dogs are plague carriers or not—but it is there and it does add to the film's horror credentials.

The Plague Dogs is a fine film: it is one of that select band of animated features—almost all of them worth watching—aimed at adults rather than children. The characterization is good, the animation—though basic by today's high standards—fits the tone and theme well, and the voice acting by the late Sir John Hurt (as Snitter) and Christopher Benjamin (as Rowf) is excellent and touching (they get solid support from a quintessentially crafty Geordie fox—"The Tod"—voiced by James Bolam.) Whether you regard it as a horror title or not, it deserves your attention.

(This review is based on the extended 103-minute version of the film)
—Daniel King

RETURN TO WATERLOO

1984
D: Ray Davies

A rare excursion into film directing by The Kinks' frontman Ray Davies, *Return to Waterloo* was a co-production between RCA Video and Channel 4 television. Broadcast on the fledgling television channel in November 1984, the film went on to enjoy a small US theatrical release in mid-1985.

Davies' film is a tricky one to try and pigeonhole, with elements of drama, musical theater, social commentary and horror all ending up on the screen. It also generally eschews dialogue, instead favoring songs—especially penned by Davies for the project—to carry and comment on the action. Davies was clearly influenced by the then new medium of the pop video, an innovation that had been especially kind to The Kinks. The cute, 1950s flavored video for their single "Come Dancing" had given the band a huge amount of exposure on early MTV and a hit on both sides of the Atlantic. Not that there is anything cute or cosily nostalgic about *Return to Waterloo*, which depicts one man's descent into paranoia and madness during a train journey to Waterloo station.

Kenneth Colley plays Davies' nameless protagonist, a man only referred to in the credits as The Traveller. On the surface The Traveller seems to be just your average middle-aged, middle-class businessman who takes the Guildford to Waterloo train to work each morning. However, it's not long before the cracks in The Traveller's life begin to be revealed. At home he leaves a depressed wife whose only other contact with the outside world appears to be writing letters to agony aunt Claire Rayner, the couple have a daughter who has mysteriously disappeared, and just before boarding the train, The Traveller picks up a tabloid bearing the headline "Rapist!—another victim," accompanied by a police identikit of the sex offender that bears a resemblance to The Traveller himself.

Once on board the train The Traveller passes the time by imagining his fellow commuters bursting into song (Davies was clearly channelling Dennis Potter's TV work here.). They represent a microcosm of 1980s Britain—ruthless businessmen serenade a new, fresh-faced member of their firm with Thatcherite chants of "why take less, when you're on the ladder, the ladder of success"; a bunch of punks, led by Slick (a young, very intense Tim Roth) are having none of it. The Traveller imagines them stomping the Thatcherite businessmen as Slick spits out the warning "the system that fed you and bred you will blow you away." The other train passengers are then beaten and dragged before Slick who sings of a fascistic future in which "we're gonna segregate the people, according to their race, and no one's gonna listen when you try to plead your case." A passionate, sadly ignored response to the musical outbursts of the businessmen and the punks is provided by an old soldier who bemoans "what has become of this land that I fought for, this country I served with pride?" as the train rolls past a graveyard.

Back in reality The Traveller's resemblance to the police identikit doesn't go unnoticed, prompting Slick to sneer that he'd like to put all rapists up against a wall and blow their heads off. As fears that he is about to be killed by the other commuters grow in The Traveller's mind, his daydreams take on a darker, more grotesque edge. He fantasizes about flying into a murderous rage, decapitating the punks with his briefcase. A *Repulsion*-style sequence sees The Traveller trying to escape the carriage only to be grabbed by zombie-like hands from under the seats (accompanied by orders of "tickets please"). In another shocking moment a blind old lady produces a knife from her handbag then casually stabs one of the punks to death. The fate of The Traveller's daughter is also cryptically alluded to in these fantasies, hinting at incestuous desire and murder with brief glimpses of

him accidentally walking into her room while she is undressed, and later shots of her dead on a mortuary slab. Surprisingly—given such themes and imagery—the film was awarded a very lenient PG certificate by the BBFC upon its video release in 1986.

At the end of the journey, reality jars ironically with The Traveller's visions. The seemingly penniless and anti-social punks are ushered into the back of a Rolls Royce by a cigar smoking music biz type, and a woman who the Traveller has been imagining as his mistress fails to materialize. As do the police, who he had continually visualized waiting at Waterloo station to arrest him. Instead The Traveller bumps into ... none other than Ray Davies himself, cameoing as a busker. The film ends with The Traveller staring right at Davies, and Davies eyeballing his own creation.

So is The Traveller really the so-called "Surrey Rapist" who may have murdered his own daughter? Or is he just a sad little man who has concocted the whole sordid scenario in order to pass the time during a humdrum train ride? It's a question the film leaves hanging over the audience's heads—an ambiguous decision, and one that doesn't appear to have been the director's original intention. Davies later claimed the film's backers became nervous about its content and asked for a more sympathetic portrayal of the lead character than he had intended. In 1997 Davies got a chance to reveal what he actually had in mind when he adapted *Return to Waterloo* as a short story for his anthology novel *Waterloo Sunset*. Davies' second take on the material is a notably nastier affair, one that sees Davies let loose from the constraints of his paymasters and leaving no doubt that the Traveller is indeed a rapist as well as a serial killer. The latter is something only fleetingly alluded to in the opening sequence of the film, which sees The Traveller stalking a blonde in the underground. In the short story version, The Traveller is free to reminisce about burying his victims in wasteland, enjoy violent sex with a female punk and, as "both the bereaved and the murderer," view his daughter's body in the morgue. Such disturbing incidents push the tale further into horror territory than the slightly compromised film version was able to venture. The story repeats the outline of the earlier film to some extent, while notably deviating from it by writing Davies himself—and the making of the 1984 film—into the plot. In a premise that mirrors the use of Freddy Krueger in *Wes Craven's New Nightmare* (1994), the print version suggests that The Traveller character actually has a life outside of the film. Davies litters the story with comments by The Traveller, mocking "a celebrity of sorts" who used to observe The Traveller on a train then tried to use him as a character in a film, only for the celebrity-turned-director to find himself being contaminated by The Traveller's own evil and sickness in the process. "He can no longer denounce me," The Traveller observes of Davies; "he is condemned."

Barely known beyond Kinks aficionados, *Return to Waterloo* is a haunting little film that sees Davies expose the nightmare landscape of 1980s Britain. Its pop video aesthetic, hangups about greedy businessmen and disillusioned young thugs, plus unlikely cameos by TV personalities Claire Rayner and Michael Fish, make *Return to Waterloo* distinct and powerful as a comment on its era. It's a film destined to linger and replay in the memory long after you've seen it, an effect it clearly had on its own director.
—Gavin Whitaker

RISE AND FALL OF IDI AMIN

1980
D: Sharad Patel

It's unlikely that any biopic of Idi Amin, no matter how trashy, could ever quite capture the true excesses of his regime in Uganda during the 1970s, but this Kenyan/British co-produced bit of sensationalism comes mighty close. Also known as *Amin: The Rise and Fall*, it's a handsomely-staged piece making the most of its sunny and opulent locations and effectively employing hundreds of extras for military scenes, but—satisfyingly for fans of the 42nd Street end of the movie biz—it focuses just as much upon Idi's penchant for murder and mayhem as it does on his power grab and the social/political situation in Africa at the time. Notorious for a genuinely shocking "severed heads in the fridge" reveal and a scene where Amin turns cannibal, wolfing down a succulent slice of an enemy (an executed appointed judge who defied him), this one resides in gleefully gory grindhouse territory, reveling in its preposterousness and achieving outrage after outrage as it progresses. A pre-*Reservoir Dogs* ear-severing, the bloody suicide-by-blade of an attractive young woman Amin has taken a passing fancy to at an evening shindig, various tortures and abuses, beatings and whippings, the on-the-spot killing of prying foreign journalists, all keep the exploitation devotee's radar alert throughout. There's even a little mini-restaging of the Israeli raid on Entebbe airport towards the finish, already the subject of three quick-off-the-mark features *Victory at Entebbe*, *Operation Thunderbolt* and *Raid on Entebbe*, though none of those depicted Idi enjoying a multiracial threesome during the attack! In one final bizarre detail, Amin's British advisor and, inevitably, eventual prisoner Denis Hills portrays himself—showing the expected deficiencies and pitfalls of placing a non-actor in a major role, but adding further strange texture to this crazy retelling of an episode in modern African history.

Joseph Olita should be commended for a wild, grandstanding performance as Amin which may play as broad and over-the-top, but which in all honesty probably comes pretty close to capturing the Ugandan dictator's brash, boastful, demigod self-promotion and self-worship. Forrest Whitaker's multiple-award-winning performance as Idi in *The Last King of Scotland* (2006) merely offered yet further proof of the cult movie fans' mantra, that the tardy mainstream invariably finds its way round to our way of thinking.
—Darrell Buxton

SECRETS OF THE PHANTOM CAVERNS (WHAT WAITS BELOW)

1984
D: Don Sharp

"The Earth is six billion years old," begins the narration, and notes that a stalagmite named Goliath is 900 thousand years old. This immediately establishes the picture's deep-time themes and, since this introduces a non-mystical genre scenario, also hints at divergent evolutionary aspects of adaptive complexity. Although Don Sharp's sci-fi horror adventure *Secrets of the Phantom Caverns* (aka *What Waits Below*) draws more of its inspiration from the hollow-Earth fantasy of Edgar Rice Burroughs' *Pellucidar* series (see *At the Earth's Core*, 1976) than from Jules Verne's much-filmed *Journey to the Center of the Earth*, but it is actually based upon the lost-continent myth of Lemuria.

The first dramatic sequence offers Robert Powell as Rupert "Wolf" Wolfsen, a lone spy in Nicaragua—where he's chased through the jungle, drives his getaway jeep through tunnels, crashes into a river and then flies by helicopter to an army camp in Belize. All this action makes the beginning seem typical of the 1980s copycat mercenary heroism and the 'Namsploitation cycle that exploded across cinema/video screens, sparked by imitators of *The Wild Geese* (1978) and *First Blood* (1982). It is a bluff that delivers some appealing familiarity before the weirdness encroaches on this Central American milieu.

From the first descent into the caves the unearthly score generates an atmosphere of disquiet and peril. Major Stevens (Timothy Bottoms) is in charge of the US military's plan to install a radio transmitter deep underground. Scientists Frieda Shelley (Anne Heywood) and Leslie Peterson (Lisa Blount) are getting in the way of a secret project. As a specialist consultant, Wolf evinces a quiet but obvious scepticism about military involvement in scientific concerns but is vocally opposed to the Americans' blatantly arrogant interference—claiming an international priority—with legitimate research.

Placement of the signals gear goes ahead but is troubled by missing men and a stolen transmitter. Aided by a local guide, Wolf leads the recovery team of civilian explorers and military support. Suspicion becomes fear when the discovery of a skeleton is soon followed by two fresh corpses (lifelike works credited to Greg Cannom). A giant snake attack heightens the claustrophobic terror. Getting nearer the astounding truth, Wolf finds a loom for weaving white hair, along with crystal daggers, and "aboriginal" bone-tools. The kidnapping of heroine Leslie brings the encounter to a crisis, with a *Doctor Who* style confrontation between ancients and moderns. However, like David Lynch's *Dune* (1984), this blood feud can only be settled by a non-lethal duel of champions in a knife fight.

Shot with exemplary production values in caverns of Tennessee and Alabama, the mix of eerie locations and matte paintings is rarely less than spectacular as background to the team's conflict with albino humanoid Lemurians, lurking about in a strange world of luminous mucus and limestone monoliths where gunshots prove to be better sonic weapons than ballistic ones. "I don't give a damn about anthropology!" warns the US army leader, informing everyone that he won't be of much use

in solving this mystery. While remaining antagonistic to intrusive outsiders, the isolated subterranean people maintain a relatively sophisticated culture, entirely unlike the subhuman creatures of later British horror movies like *The Descent* (2005). Instead, this fits into an SF niche occupied by *Warlords of Atlantis* (1978). The screaming mole men eventually cause a cave-in as the rocks overhead become part of their defence system. When they finally emerge safely, into the sunlight, the wholly sympathetic survivors choose, very wisely, to keep the secrets of the phantom caverns, and Wolf urges the military authorities to seal the cave's entrance.
—Tony Lee

SIESTA

1987
D: Mary Lambert

Proof that a stellar cast and the presence of Miles Davis as chief soundtrack contributor doesn't always lead to a good time. Shot in Spain and co-produced by the UK's then in-your-face young guns Palace Pictures, *Siesta* marked the feature debut of music video specialist Mary Lambert. Lambert had recently completed work on a promo for the Madonna hit "La Isla Bonita" and planned to use the same star and same locations for this full-length movie; Ms. Ciccone declined, uncharacteristical-

ly expressing concern about the screenplay's copious nudity and sexual content, so Ellen Barkin stepped in to play Claire, a feisty, fiery blonde who awakens in the middle of nowhere clad in a tattered red dress and inexplicably covered in bruises and blood ("it must be someone else's"). Sadly, what ought to have been the kick-off point for an intriguing heat-seared neo-noir is telegraphed virtually from the word go—I won't give the full game away but let's just say that fans of *Carnival of Souls* will realize immediately where this one is heading. It's of constant amazement that each passing generation of the cinema audience seems to be hoodwinked by the type of schtick on show here—the likes of Lucio Fulci's *Door to Silence*, M. Night Shyamalan's *The Sixth Sense* and Kim Jee-Woon's *A Tale of Two Sisters* really ought not to have fooled anybody, and seem even more openly obvious in comparison to the delicious ambiguities found within recent superior competitors such as Peter Strickland's *Berberian Sound Studio* or David Lynch's masterly *Mulholland Dr.*

Barkin does at least look stunning, unabashed and daring in a way that Madonna could clearly only dream of—within moments of the start she's naked and full-frontal, and in her later clothed form she certainly rocks rock-chick chic, though the toughness and rebellion displayed seem at odds with the vulnerability and confused state her character should emit. We're told, improbably and (as it turns out, falsely), that Ellen is a sky-diver who has been attempting maneuvers without a parachute—occasional flashes of a stunt fall pepper the already fractured narrative, and despite having had her leonine tresses hacked off by Jodie Foster in one of the story's parallel timelines it is never particularly clear which version of Claire we are following. Julian Sands pops up for his customary sucking-all-the-air-out-of-the-room performance, on this occasion dispensing a string of dreadful lewd limericks, and Alexei Sayle fares little better as a swarthy rapist cabbie. At least there's a lively and well-edited murder sequence at the explanatory climax, though it's perhaps most notable for involving a trio of A-listers in something that might have better suited a *Friday the 13th* sequel.

Director Lambert did manage to progress from this mess to better things, starting a couple of years later with her equally death-obsessed adaptation of Stephen King's *Pet Sematary*—a movie so skilled and controlled that you can barely believe it's the work of the same filmmaker.
—Darrell Buxton

SIR HENRY AT RAWLINSON END

1980
D: Steve Roberts

Written by an alcoholic, produced by an alcoholic, directed by an alcoholic, and starring an alcoholic. So, Neil Innes summed up the 1980 film version of his fellow Bonzo Vivian Stanshall's bizarre parody of the typical ancestral family saga.

As with everything Rawlinson, though, there's more than one way of interpreting that. On the one hand, rambling, un-

focused, ungainly—on the other, flooded with dizzying flashes of terror, humor, and wonder. Both the lows and the highs of the dipsomaniac psyche. With filming divided between rural locations in Gloucestershire and Knebworth House—the latter standing in for Rawlinson End itself—an atmosphere was created balanced between the idyllic and the unearthly, nestling in green nowhere, changing yet changeless as canal water.

Stanshall, assisted by director Steve Roberts, did give the slimmest thread of an underlying plot to the series of vignettes—the Rawlinsons' attempts to exorcise the ghost of Sir Henry's philandering brother Humbert, killed in flagrante delicto without his trousers. To lay the specter, Sir Henry and his family must locate it, and then put its trousers back on. All clear now?

Photographed throughout in sepia, the story unfolds like a whole series of early silent films spliced idiosyncratically together and gifted with a soundtrack. Every performance—from Denise Coffey's bumbling, nasal housekeeper Mrs. E, to Patrick Magee's fraudulent clergyman Slodden—is a masterclass in silent-movie body language, exaggerated and eloquent through gesture or expression as much as voice. And, towering above them all, Trevor Howard's magisterial, monstrous rendition of Stanshall's eternal icon, Sir Henry Rawlinson himself, to whom even Stanshall's portrayal of the affable, unsettling eccentric younger brother Hubert takes a decided second place.

The tale of the Rawlinsons and their paranormal quest leads us through many byways and diversions—from Hubert's bedroom, piled high with decomposing fruits all adding to the noble rot, to the nearby village of Concreton and its venerable pub The Fool And Bladder, where encyclopaedia-brained pub bores ("Did you know there is no proper name for the back of the knees?") and cheery local sports heroes competing in such traditional games as face-jumping and catching the javelin engage in their pastimes under the amused eye of Seth Onetooth, everybody's genial Mine Host.

But—inexorably—the real thrust of the plot heads back to Rawlinson End, wherein we wander through more bizarrerie towards a final confrontation with the beyond; via Sir Henry's small but formidable prisoner of war camp and its two bewildered inmates, derangedly gleeful cleaning staff engaging in banjolele fol-de-rol, the beautiful niece Candice wordlessly striking acrobatic and elegant erotic poses in her mini-toga like some minor goddess made flesh ... all of the way to the climactic family gathering, the ceremonial Rawlinson Roar, necessary to complete the exorcism—presided over in the dead of night by Sir Henry himself, backlit by the flames of an enormous pyre, tweed suit topped incongruously by a horned helmet and brandishing a gigantic two-handed sword as—terrifyingly—he roars. And, on perfect cue, the shade of Humbert manifests, and the ultimate struggle with the unknown plays out ...

How, best, to describe the impact of the whole? Well—take a measure of Heath Robinson, add a fifth or so of James Whale, a finger or two of *Gormenghast*, a jigger of Mack Sennett, a dash of Georges Méliès ... shake well, and garnish with a generous dusting of crushed *Wicker Man*. And then swallow the whole smoking, bubbling mess at one go for the full effect. As that suggests, it's entirely possible that this is a film which won't be to everybody's taste; but those connoisseurs willing to risk imbibing may well be pleasantly and spectacularly surprised by this strange brew. *Omnes Blotto.*
—Ken Shinn

(Walerian Borowczyk is reported to have seen *Sir Henry at Rawlinson End* in the UK in 1980. The film had a profound influence on Boro, at the time preparing his production *Docteur Jekyll et les Femmes/The Strange Case of Dr. Jekyll and Miss Osbourne*. He was inspired to cast Patrick Magee after seeing his performance as here, and also hired cinematographer Martin Bell, though firing the latter early in the *Jekyll* shoot for being slow–ed.)

SPOOKIES

1986
D: Brendan Faulkner, Thomas Doran, Eugenie Joseph

Once upon a time, an American film by the name of *Twisted Souls* might have burst forth into existence, a showcase of creative special effects of wildly varying quality that riffed off *The Evil Dead* (1981) along with any number of haunted house and slasher movies. The plot would have focused on an unbelievably disparate group of partygoers taking their revelry to a dilapidated mansion. One girl would become possessed through the use of a Ouija board and would help to unleash all manner of dangerous entities including small reptile monsters, menacing muckmen and a spider lady, among others. If finished, it might have turned a minor profit and seen all involved move onto many other things (possibly better, maybe not). However, as directed in 1984 by rookies Brendan Faulkner and Thomas Doran and written/produced by them in collaboration with Frank M. Farel, it

German VHS cover for *Spookies*

stumbled into inaction at the post-production stage, leaving the trio with an under-length piece of work still missing additional effects. At which point, the British Invasion happened all over again, just not as sweetly as when it was spearheaded by The Beatles, The Kinks, et. al.

The invader in question was one Michael Lee, best known for founding Vipco, a home video distribution company in the UK in 1979. The name was an acronym for Video Instant Picture Company but became a byword for notorious releases. Indeed, Lee's fortune was built upon the faux outrage of the "video nasty" storm in 1980s Britain. Vipco initially released the likes of Lucio Fulci's *Zombie Flesh Eaters* and Abel Ferrara's *The Driller Killer*, the latter of which boasted a scandalously graphic cover that no doubt helped to fuel the "video nasty" furore. The 1984 Video Recordings Act tightened the old censorship belt of the country and Vipco suffered accordingly. The company would rise again in 1992. In the meantime, Lee looked elsewhere for opportunities, a search that took him to America and led to a meeting with the makers of *Twisted Souls*. Frank Farel remembers Lee as having swagger but suggests that he lacked knowhow. He had roughly $500,000 to spend and was combing New York to find low-budget end filmmakers to custom build a product for him that he could then release.

Farel, Faulkner and Doran showed Lee their footage but held back on releasing the whole script. It took months for the Englishman to return with details of his own half-finished film entitled *The Anger*, a small amount of footage that Faulkner described as "painful." Unfortunately, Lee wanted the filmmakers to finish his movie first before he would finance the completion of *Twisted Souls* ... impasse.

Finally, Lee returned to the States and confirmed his wish to work with the trio on their movie but wanted "more going on." Doran's widow (he died in 2016) recalls that the Vipco man was far more interested in how to sell the film rather than any artistic aspect. He simply wanted certain things included to make it as marketable as possible. Oddly, considering his past releases, Lee also wanted as little blood as possible and no nudity, perhaps even having an eye on a "PG" certificate. It seems that he had been stung by that UK Video Recordings Act and was therefore thinking predominantly about sales in his own country rather than globally. And yet it is here that things get a little contradictory. Cecilia Doran's suggestion that it was Lee who wanted a haunted house scenario seems to fly in the face of the footage that her husband and his pals had already filmed, not to mention the unfilmed effects work they had intended to add, that of flying spirits harassing two of the cast. However, the head of Vipco undoubtedly seemed to be the most confused, on the one hand aiming for a family audience but then suggesting titles such as *Bowel Eruptor*, asking for less gore to avoid the attention of the BBFC but then demanding an *Evil Dead* influence—the film that had had its own share of troubles with the UK censors! It seems that everything was a confused mess ... and that confusion was added to with the Americans' inclusion of as many varied monsters as possible. Even before the attempt to bring the project to completion was started on a physical level, the omens were bad. Reports that their choice of location—the John Jay Estate in New York—was haunted was the least of their problems. The injection of British money hadn't helped. It had made things worse.

Doran and Faulkner divided up scenes so that they could direct the sequences in which they were personally interested, which was fair enough but does make one wonder if this added to the disjointed feel of the end result. The special effects make-up team was divided too, boasting four artists: Arnold Gargiulo, Gabriel Bartalos, Vincent J. Guastini and Nick Santeramo. They were joined by two make-up artists and a prosthetics artist. This led to very different styles which once again meant unevenness. Gargiulo took on too much and began to buckle under the pressure, his muck-men looking under par and described as "fake." Arnold was very hands on and could not delegate, became overwhelmed and was finally dismissed. Gabe Bartalos stepped up to the plate but found that he was short of funds. When Lee returned to oversee the shoot (being described as creepy), he would not free up any more cash for effects until Gabe lifted the front of the producer's car off the ground in a rage!

It is safe to say that none of the cast or crew liked Michael Lee, but the straw that broke the camel's back occurred when he tampered with the editing, first showing a rough cut to investors, not understanding that none of the footage had been edited for atmosphere or tension. When Thomas Doran was off ill, Lee had a spider sequence re-edited without telling anybody. Within two weeks, the original US crew, directors and producers all, had quit.

At this point, what we now know as *Spookies* came into being. Lee brought in a new director, Eugenie Joseph, who had previously been involved in the sex film industry. She tried to get the cast and crew back in, but loyalties lay with the original team and no one would return. And so, with a new cast and crew, indeed with a completely rewritten filmscript, shooting began again, using the still impressive Jay house with the same ludicrously cheap gravestones set in front of it. Zombies were added (odd, as Lee had initially requested the absence of that particular monster), a werecat servant, an ambiguous drifter, a young runaway, a child vampire, an evil wizard and his 50-year undead bride! Spies on set suggested that Joseph wanted to jettison all of the original footage but was unable to do so. She eventually filmed just enough to have the majority of footage, and with her 51% grafted clumsily to the rest, claimed to have saved the movie. The tale now featured a 13-year-old who ran away from home because his parents had forgotten his birthday. A passing drifter was added for a brief minute or two, advising the boy to go home and then getting slashed to death by the werecat. The boy's journey ends in nonsensical fashion as he enters the house, is thrilled to find it set up for his birthday, is shocked by a talking severed head and is chased by the werecat before being buried alive. This lack of logic is now par for the course, as the sinister wizard is killing everyone off in bizarre ways in order to revive his dead and unwilling wife. Many scenes were excised, and much of the complicated camerawork too. Close-ups filmed as reactions to effects to be added later were retained without the effects that would give them sense and reason. Nothing that was shot ended up being pieced together with any intended following shot. And then, adding insult to injury, Michael Lee insisted that the now improved muck-men should be "enhanced" with farting sound effects!

Apparently, Vestron offered $1 million for world rights but Lee demanded $2 million and lost the deal. The film limped out for a limited run in 1987 and then was released to cable television. It reached the British public on video on, you guessed it, Vipco. The resultant mess has since somehow become a cult favorite but is possibly on a par with the likes of the atrocious *Troll 2*. It is tempting to side with the original crew, who at least seemed like personable and professional types, but the sad truth is that we will never know if they had anything worthwhile on their hands even pre-Lee. The acting is inept and the footage as edited does not allow for a meaningful assessment. Ironically, a film that the British might have to argue about for part-ownership is one that nobody really wants.
—Ian Taylor

TEN LITTLE INDIANS

1989
D: Alan Birkinshaw

Although Birkinshaw's film is often cited as the fourth English language adaptation of Agatha Christie's most famous novel, it is, in fact, a version of the play that Christie herself distilled from the book and differs in critical elements from the plot of its source. Veteran producer Harry Alan Towers, who had already taken two different swings at *Ten Little Indians* (1965 under that title; and 1974's *And Then There Were None*), intended to return to the novel for this latest movie, but in the end wheeled out the same story as he had twice previously offered, shifting from the Devonshire island of the novel, and the Alpine and desert resort settings of his earlier adaptations, to a safari ranch for this effort. Although it adds a colonial feel more in keeping with the novel than we'd seen so far, familiarity with the story, and a tired sense of re-hashing old ground, results in a listless, uninvolving film.

For the two dozen folk in the world who don't know the plot, 10 people, none of them known to each other, are invited to an isolated location by an anonymous figure. Once they arrive, a recording is played, in which their unidentified host explains that the group have been selected because they all succeeded in escaping justice after being involved in actions that led to a death. Shortly after this, the invitees begin to be bumped off, and after a search of the surroundings reveals that they are alone, the survivors deduce that they are being punished for their crimes by one of their own party.

With an international cast of game exploitation pros (including Herbert Lom, in his second bash at this yarn, plus Donald Pleasence, Brenda Vaccaro and Paul L. Smith) and under the direction of Birkinshaw, one approaches this version with high hopes. Technically, the film is fine—veteran cinematographer Arthur Lavis does a nice job, giving the film a dusty, burned-out look fitting with the period colonial setting, and although the shoot is clearly low-budget, Birkinshaw does succeed in dragging every penny on to the screen. The problem centers upon some clunky dialogue from TV veteran Gerry O'Hara, and a range of highly variable performances. Lom and Pleasence display their usual talents, and perhaps more surprisingly, Frank Stallone (in a role miles from the equivalent character in both novel and stage play) is perfectly fine as the leading man. Scenery-chewing turns from Vaccaro and Smith, not to mention Neil McCarthy's foppish take on his character, undermine things, however. Similarly, Birkinshaw does a decent yet hardly inspired job. Given that writer O'Hara had been responsible for scripting and directing Campari-drenched Joan Collins softcore disco-era melodrama *The Bitch* (1979), and Birkinshaw directed the astoundingly exploitative and frequently hysterical *Killer's Moon* (1978), one might be forgiven for expecting something a bit more spicy, or at least funny. Sadly, other than a lesbian sub-plot shoehorned into the narrative before being largely forgotten, what we get is a resolutely traditional suspense film, with little actual tension, and none of the outrageousness that marks the back catalogue of most of the main protagonists.

Perhaps contributing most to the general feeling of ennui surrounding *Ten Little Indians* is the sheer familiarity of the plot to pretty much anyone likely to be attracted to it in the first place. For this, the blame could be laid in part at the feet of Christie herself. The novel, with its claustrophobic setting and spare, economic style, is one of the most important texts in the modern horror genre, influencing a whole genre of body count movies like Mario Bava's *Bay of Blood* (1970) and Sean Cunningham's *Friday the 13th* (1980). It's a grim, downbeat affair, part locked room mystery, part ghoulish murder-based satire. Christie's play completely alters the nature of the story, in particular the ending, and in doing so transforms a bleak tale into a fairly conventional murder mystery, and so that's exactly what we get here. Perfectly watchable, but disappointingly routine.
—Neil Pike

TRACK 29

1988
D: Nicolas Roeg

Bizarre as it sounds, one of the keys to understanding *Track 29*, if not director Nicolas Roeg's entire oeuvre, is to be found in the film's opening couple of minutes, via the UK children's TV cartoon show *Dangermouse* that Linda (Theresa Russell), a bored housewife, is watching as she does her aerobics. "Even time itself can be bent and twisted," the narrator tells us, "and ... two or more things can inhabit the same area at the same time, co-existing in parallel dimensions." Similarly, the use of John Lennon's "Mother" as the opening music keys us in, more explicitly, to a theme that screenwriter Dennis Potter had returned to many times in his career; indeed, *Track 29* is a reworking of his earlier *Play for Today* "Schmoedipus" from 1974. So, a film directed and written by two of the British screen's most respected and singular talents, centered on themes which are of great interest to both, should then be of great interest to us, the punters.

Linda is married to geriatrician Dr. Henry Henry (Christopher Lloyd) who, when he is not at work getting spanked by his nurse/bit on the side (Sandra Bernhard), is at home playing with his mammoth train set that seems to take up the entire first floor of his suburban home. Henry then is a man-child unable to communicate with anyone on an adult level, particularly his wife whom he ignores, especially her demands for a chance to adopt a child of her own. Linda spends most of her days with her friend Arlanda (Colleen Camp) until they have a chance meeting with a strange young Englishman, Martin (Gary Oldman). The following day Martin turns up at Linda's door, claiming to be her son whom she had been forced to give up for adoption when she was 15. Linda finds Martin's story difficult to believe but her desire for it to be true leads her to allow him into her home.

The main reason *Track 29* is a borderline title is because it asks the viewer to consider whether Martin is or isn't who he claims to be, whether he is or isn't malevolent in some way and ultimately whether he is or isn't there at all. That all this is tied into Linda's sexual frustration, and the possibility that her dalliance with Martin may lead to incest, is what pushes it close to a *Repulsion*-like psychosexual drama. Unlike *Repulsion*, however, I don't think the purpose of *Track 29* is to frighten or repel; in fact, it's hard to define what its purpose actually is.

I say that because, in my view, it is made perfectly clear that Martin (who shares his name with the very much present and very much malevolent visitor figure in Potter's *Brimstone & Treacle*) is a figment of Linda's imagination. In one sequence in

a cocktail lounge Linda is ostensibly in conversation with her son but it is made quite apparent to the viewer that she is in fact there by herself, a fact remarked on by one of the waiters. Now, that doesn't necessarily spoil or invalidate the rest of the film—after all, in *Repulsion* we're aware that most of what occurs is a projection of what is in Carol's head—but what it does do is make the film seem slight, as if it has one trick up its sleeve and little else. It's rather as if Potter and, in particular, Roeg are simply riffing on some of their standard themes, tinkering and toying with them in the same way that Henry does with his trains. And, ultimately, *Track 29* amounts to not much more than one of those same trains—it starts nowhere and after a few spins around familiar territory ends up nowhere.
—Daniel King

• • •

Wilmington, North Carolina had already provided the setting for *Blue Velvet* (1986) by the time Nicolas Roeg and company rolled into town—in the fluid world of mid-1980s cinema that particular place had become a base for Dino De Laurentiis, who had set up production facilities there for his D.E.G. studio, and so David Lynch was able to film right on Dino's new American doorstep. Had the *Blue Velvet* location scouts scanned all 50 states, mind you, they could barely have found a more suitable site to set this mom's-apple-pie-gone-wrong psycho noir. Perhaps more surprisingly, Roeg independently accessed the D.E.G. hub mere months later, with a project that only added to Wilmington's reputation as the focus of overheated, "underbelly of America/destruction of the family" film fare. What's more, the opening shot sees a hitch-hiking Gary Oldman at local landmark Cape Fear—which, in keeping with *Track 29*'s themes of confused identity and reality, is the real deal, not the "Cape Fear" of fictionalized 1962/1991 movie notoriety. The Plastic Ono Band's primal howl, "*Mother,*" plays over the scene ...

Speaking of The Beatles, George Harrison and Denis O'Brien's Handmade Films, one of the genuine success stories of the decade, backed *Track 29*, which was scripted by celebrated TV playwright Dennis Potter. In 1974 the BBC had broadcast Potter's *Play for Today*, "Schmoedipus," a small-screen drama starring Tim Curry as a stranger who turns up at the home of an unsuspecting couple, claiming to be their son, and Potter would feature variants on this type of "mysterious interloper" storyline throughout his career, often with a fantastic/angelic/satanic bent. Just before he died, controversial director Joseph Losey had done some pre-production on a potential movie version, but ultimately it was Roeg who partnered Potter in bringing *Schmoedipus*, or at least a riff on it, to cinemas. Potter had already seen his *Brimstone & Treacle* make the shift from telly to theaters, though in this case (much like Alan Clarke's *Scum*), the movie was a reaction to a BBC-imposed ban on the original *Play for Today* and a means of permitting audiences the opportunity to view the material in some form. *Track 29* isn't exactly a remake of *Schmoedipus* but is, instead, a development and expansion of that 1970s work, filtered through Potter's keenness on this particular story structure and—importantly—through the "playing with time" and "examination of sexuality" processes which had been notable aspects of the thus-far extraordinary output from Roeg. Not only does *Track 29* constitute a perfect auteurist fit for the director, but he even goes so far as to pepper it with direct self-referential quotes—Gary Oldman plays Martin as ev-

erything from a tantrum-suffering juvenile to a confident crooner, and leaves you wishing that he perhaps ought to have portrayed Johnny Rotten as well as Sid Vicious in the preceding year's *Sid and Nancy*, but there's a marked resemblance to David Bowie's Thomas Jerome Newton during the diner scene here (indeed, the entire movie has a *Man Who Fell to Earth* vibe about it); and the stunning closing shot carries strong echoes of an equally stunning, equally enigmatic pivotal moment from the early scenes of *Don't Look Now*.

Oldman's grandstanding notwithstanding, it's Theresa Russell who "holds the film together" (though that's hardly an appropriate phrase to use in describing anything with Roeg's signature on it, least of all *Track 29*)—at face value she's trapped in a loveless marriage with the older, toy train-obsessed and adulterous Christopher Lloyd, and has a secret in her past which seems to have been resolved by the unexpected visit of this odd but likeable young Englishman. But "face value" is never where it's at with Nic Roeg, and it's highly unlikely that "Martin" is real—despite him having a long introductory conversation with Russell and her best friend Colleen Camp, despite him hitching a ride with a "Mom"-tattooed trucker, despite a tellingly-naked him murdering one of the story's major players in a blood-gushing frenzy towards the climax. We're clearly shown or pushed into accepting that he is a figment at several points in the "narrative" (again, a singularly inappropriate term in discussing this director's methods!)—aside from the obvious (arrival at the house, the waiter and bartender who can't see him, etc.), why isn't Martin

involved in the closing scene? For that matter, why is Christopher Lloyd involved in it, vocally at least?! Roeg bookends the proceedings (once again, is that a valid term here?!) beautifully—as pointed out on the commentary on Indicator's 2019 Blu-ray, *Track 29* has two endings, one for viewers who depart or reach for the off-switch as the credits roll, and another entirely for those who experience the full 90 minutes and (crucially) 14 seconds; while one of the nagging questions I've always taken away from the movie is, "what if the first vehicle had stopped and picked up Martin on that rickety Cape Fear bridge at the outset?"
—Darrell Buxton

ULTIMATE CITY

1984
D: Florence Dewavrin

The year following *Sphere–The Spores of Doom* (1984), students of the National Film & Television School collected together for another fantasy offering, the 42-minute long *Ultimate City*, directed by Florence Dewavrin. We have to relegate the title to "borderline" coverage here, though, as it is not a full-blown horror. Its peripheral status stems from a dystopian vision and stray bits of bloodiness, including a scalping. The story opens in a future London, with what appears to be a couple of mutants setting upon "Hunters" who are already eyeing other targets. Several die and the surviving Hunters return to the city. One of their number is Priscilla (Annette von Klier), beautiful and faintly androgynous, the daughter of court insider Mac (Peter Porteus), who berates her over her risk-taking adventures when

Annette von Klier stars as Priscilla in *Ultimate City*.

everyone favors her to become the bride of the lunatic self-appointed King, Alexander II (Nigel Holland).

Priscilla wants no part in the court of this pantomime ruler, a pathetic trashcan Caligula, preferring instead the life of a Hunter, a group which serves the King by tracking and slaying Raels, a terrorist faction opposed to the despotic reign. Hunter Akbor (Ian Brimble) lusts after Priscilla and would risk the ire of the King to claim her as a conquest, but she has little interest in his advances also. They are alerted to the running down of a Rael and hurry to the scene, where a guard on horseback (having already shot the rebel dead) leaves him to Priscilla—she enthusiastically scalps the victim in front of a crowd. Witness to the slaying is the newly unemployed zookeeper, Antonio (David Sibley) who is returning from what constitutes a labor exchange of the future, a winding staircase of Toto Coelo rejects and a nonchalant woman behind a desk on the landing. He is vaguely concerned for the fallen man; as a protector of animals and all life, he is saddened by the public execution.

When a frog slips out of his pocket (not a euphemism!), Priscilla becomes mildly intrigued. There is little room for love and romance in this future England, where survival of the most uncaring is the rule of thumb. She does help him find employment in looking after their livestock, and a puzzle of a romance blossoms, forced into place by an incident during which bitter court advisor Ileane (Pamela Salem) gets into a girl-fight with Priscilla, Antonio interceding before Ileane can inflict any real damage. He is fired and Priscilla retreats with him to his Amphibian House apartment, in which one room is given over completely to a landscape that is a heaven for frogs.

They have sex and she awakes alone in the bed, searching the building and finding him dead in his vivarium, murdered by Akbor, who, as dim and insensitive as anyone in this future, cannot imagine love between anyone. He assumes that in the light of Antonio's death, Priscilla will fall in with his scheme to sell the frogs as valuable cuisine to the highest bidder. Off his guard, he is killed by a clearly angry Priscilla, who stabs him in the neck. Pragmatic child of dystopia that she is, she ironically comes to the conclusion that Antonio's death cannot be remedied, and does a deal with the King to take the precious amphibian delicacy in order to leave her be, fearlessly informing him that there will be consequences if she is not granted the freedom to do as she chooses—a unique standing in this society.

Dialogue is on the weak side in a script co-written by the director along with Ashley Pharoah, one of several names here involved to figure greatly in future British film and television (Pharoah would become a leading television writer on shows like *Casualty* and *Life on Mars*.) Pharoah's later abilities, though, are barely apparent here. Paul Trijbits took a producer credit and has since gone on to a substantial career in that capacity—his later films include *Hardware*, *Dust Devil*, *My Brother Tom*, *This is Not a Love Song*, *London to Brighton*, *This is England*, *Straightheads*, *Puffball* and *Tamara Drewe*, and he had a key role in the developmental New Cinema Fund at the UK Film Council. Director of Cinematography Simon Archer would go on to an extensive television career, which includes six episodes each of *Ashes to Ashes* and *Bedlam*. *Ultimate City* would appear to have launched more highly successful film luminaries than *Sphere–The Spores of Doom*. In fact, one of the assistant directors was Mike Caton-Jones, who had a particularly swift rise in film with the prominent directorial gig of *Scandal* (1989) mere years later. Pamela Salem's presence is not of particular surprise, as the film school often brought in noted and prestigious actors who could relay some of their experience to the young filmmakers. Gordon Warnecke also has a small role in the same year he would star opposite Daniel Day-Lewis in *My Beautiful Laundrette*.

The talent is buried in *Ultimate City*. The film is dogged by weak pacing, an uninteresting story, an unconvincing imagined future, a disappointing trash aesthetic in the production design and poor performances from some of the actors, particular Annette von Klier and Nigel Holland. Von Klier's accent is wildly out of place and her deep voice emphasizes an uncertainty in the delivery, whereas Holland's portrayal is over-the-top cartoon silliness, contrary to the straighter acting of others in the cast. The design hints at Jarman's *Jubilee* and *The Tempest* as well as John Waters' *Desperate Living*, L.Q. Jones' *A Boy and His Dog*, Robert Golden's *Beg!* and many other films, but possessing neither the wit nor intelligence of those works. Costume design is indistinguishable from any other ragtag post-apocalyptic brigade of beggars, the only standout detail being the plastic Stegosaurus epaulet on Priscilla's jacket. There are possible subtexts, but the film skirts these. The job agency informing Antonio that "as an ex-animal keeper you shouldn't have any problem finding work, but I can't help you" may be a political critique of unemployment in Britain at the time, but it's too thinly laid out to extrapolate from and warrant such an interpretation.

Florence Dewavrin continues to work as a film director in France and has recently been linked to a projected adaptation of a Honore de Balzac story. (My thanks to Florence for providing a copy of this film for review purposes.)
—Paul Higson

AN UNSUITABLE JOB FOR A WOMAN

1982
D: Christopher Petit

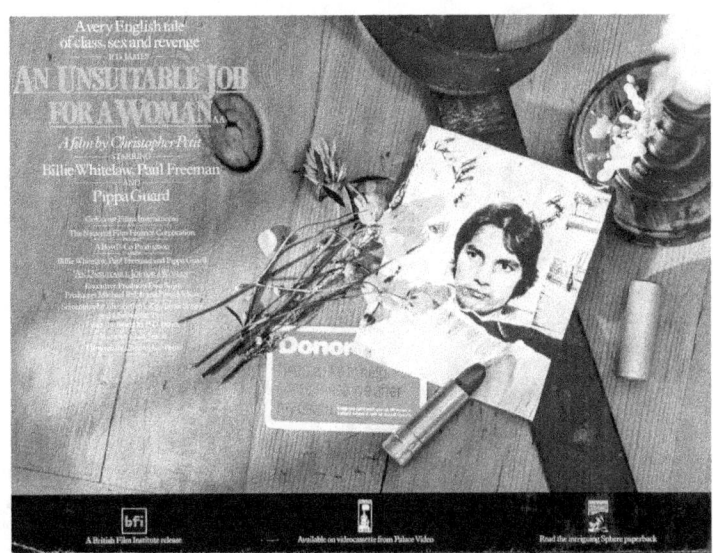

That time-old cliché, "a man of many parts," could definitely apply to Christopher Petit: As critic, director, documentarian, cut-up expert and creator of shorts so obscure one wonders if even he has seen them, he truly represents the spirit of the struggling auteur in an economically barren landscape. Yet despite his low-key background, he has made several critically lauded features with recognizable, high profile casts.

Here, in a loose adaptation of P.D. James' novel, he assembles a practical who's who of British character players, including Billie Whitelaw, Paul Freeman, David "grumpy copper" Horovitch, Elizabeth Spriggs and the redoubtable team of Pippa and Dominic Guard. While several names on that list may be more prestigious, this related pair (cousins in real life) hold the key to this unusual and unsettling film, which very nearly (but not quite) tips into horror territory via some ambiguously-placed shadows, a foreboding, dread-filled atmosphere, suggested personality transference a là Bergman's *Persona*, a dangling manikin, a close-up of one character dead underwater following their gruesome fate, and its undeniably morbid subject matter.

The opening premise sets the tone, with private investigator Cordelia Gray (Pippa, displaying an earthy, believable sexuality sadly missing from Helen Baxendale's later TV portrayal) hired by Elizabeth Leaming (Whitelaw) to investigate the suicide of the son of her employer James (Freeman). Since Cordelia's boss has *also* recently offed himself, the air is rent with the stench of death from only five minutes in. The negativity continues apace, with the elderly housekeeper (Spriggs) soon delivering one of the most hateful speeches to be found in British cinema, decrying Cordelia's generation as "arrogant, selfish and violent, with any compassion you do have seeming curiously selective, inviting punishment then screaming while punished." A good set-up for a possible genre tale, then.

Yet, while suggesting several shades of sadistic shenanigans (not only is the dead man revealed later to have been discovered in female underwear, but the fetishistic theme is further developed via a scene in which Cordelia, placing herself in his mindset, simulates auto-erotic asphyxiation with a leather belt) the film still never makes the full plunge, despite repeated threats, into full-blown horror. The reason for this is simple: Petit obviously didn't want to make a horror movie. He is, however, happy to play with several conventions of the genre—in one deftly-executed sequence, in the finest traditions of Corman, Hammer and Bava, our heroine finds herself having to escape from a pitch black and extremely dank well, Whitelaw's sudden appearance in her employer's office resembles a manifestation, and the deliberately "mwahahaha" nighttime sequence, showing Guard cowering 'neath her bedclothes at various unidentifiable "countryzoide" noises, is effective in the extreme.

Likewise, the denouement, while still horrific, is more prosaic than psychotronic; yet, despite that, the film *still* contains enough chills for fans of subtle British terror, and to qualify for borderline inclusion in this book. In true "hauntological" tradition a là *And Soon the Darkness* or *Blood on Satan's Claw*, the star of the film (aside from Pippa, red-haired, bookish and beautiful like a young Anna Massey, and Dominic, offering an older variation on his slimily sinister man-boy from *Absolution*) is its landscape. Captured in the sepia-tinted glow that imbues half the 1980s best independent productions (oh, the wonders of cheap stock), its desolate yellow country lanes and deathly still lakes provide the picture with not only a somber backdrop but its defining identity.
—Darius Drewe

WAY UPSTREAM

1987
D: Terry Johnson

Alan Ayckbourn isn't the first name that springs to mind when discussing horror—which is unfortunate, as beneath the surface of his class-conscious, observational comedy often lurks a macabre, twisted humor, plus underlying themes of suggested menace that an M.R. James or Robert Bloch might have been proud of. It's a constant subtext in his children's fantasy *Mr. A's Amazing Maze Plays* (still awaiting screen adaptation), implied in his bleak deconstruction of the Yuletide myth *Season's Greetings*, and is most obvious of all here, in a script not only laden with allegories for doom, death and the end of the world, but based around one of the most terrifying characters the small screen has witnessed.

It begins, like most of Ayckbourn's work, as a comedy of manners, initially establishing the tensions between bossy, anally-retentive novelty-manufacturing mogul Keith (Barrie Rutter) and his glamourous yet sex-starved wife June (Marion Bailey) who, presumably at the former's instigation, have hired a boat with his spineless, dithering assistant Alistair (Nick Dunning) and beautiful yet equally drippy wife Emma (Joanne Pearce), on which they intend to cruise Britain's waterways. Yet once the mysterious Vince (Stuart Wilson), an itinerant claiming to be a "victim of the system," and his brain-dead socialite shag-partner Fleur (Lizzy McInnerny) appear apparently out of nowhere, it gradually develops a darker and darker pitch, underlain by a continued threat of the supernatural and culminating in nightmares and violence.

Granted, the storyline may provide a vehicle for the playwright's obsessions—the social maneuvering of the so-called "aspirant" classes, and the difference between "thinkers" and "doers" (all very germane to life in 1980s Britain), but what reveals itself as the saga unfolds (with the six protagonists moving, either individually or collectively, towards the portentously-named "Armageddon Bridge") is sheer misanthropy, with Ayckbourn, and quite possibly director Johnson, appearing to loathe every character. Even those initially identified with by the viewer become ultimately shallow, weak or fallible: Emma and Alistair are the closest to a "hero and heroine," but the first is slow-witted, easily-led, and afraid to speak out until the (literal) point of no return has been reached, while the latter displays all the characteristics of the insipid late 1980s "New Man."

Failed Home Counties soubrette June, a redhead of little talent now resigned to life with a man she despises, initially elicits sympathy (also looking milf-tastic in sailor's cap, stockings and heels). Yet even she loses points for being vacuous enough to fall for Vince's nature-boy BDSM [bondage, dominance sadomasochism] act even after having seen what a despotic dictator he is, and how his obsessive need to refer to all the parts of the boat by their "correct" names (something, it is later intimated by Fleur, he has no actual knowledge of) far outweighs any flaws displayed by her now errant husband. And it is indeed Keith, deposed as skipper halfway and left on land to single-handedly save his factory from industrial collapse, who effects a lucky escape, alive, well, and blissfully unaware of the horrors to follow, with Vince by now not only commanding the vessel like a Hoseasons Hitler, but meting out cruel and ultimately psychotic punishment to anyone who dares show the slightest hint of insurrection. Nevertheless, it still is impossible to side with such an insufferable berk, and eventually, Keith is almost forgotten.

Rather, it's Vince's unhinged yet meticulously-calculated descent into madness and flickering evil (superbly conveyed by Wilson) that remains the film's crux, and also justifies its horror classification. For those desiring more obvious pointers, a later dream sequence involves zombified, specter-like versions of the play's protagonists appearing from underwater or inside bunk cabins, with dialogue paying direct homage to Raimi's *Evil Dead*, but that alone does not a genre picture make. Without Vince, who goes from seemingly charitably saving the crew's bacon when run aground by a mysterious vessel, to barking orders, brazen seduction, leering like a demon through windows and eventually attempting cold blooded murder—all the time grinning like a benign Angel of Death (which, of course, he may be)—within a matter of days, we would have a very dull film about couples quarrelling. Arguably, some might say Woody Allen has based half his career on that conceit, but that's perhaps to be discussed elsewhere …

Schopenhauer contended that "life without pain has no meaning." By replacing their former dynamic with order, then chaos, and finally black, frozen fear, Vince, with Fleur as his succubus, gives Keith, June, Alistair and Emma not only focus, but a reason to exist. Their primary aim, is not just to follow the trajectory of the film's title, but to seize power and prevent his further passage—by *any* means necessary. Thus the film's one major failing is his eventual demise, which, while executed with requisite drama, is left open-ended and dealt with prosaically, also leaving the fates of two other principal players unresolved. Nevertheless, the final five minutes, alluding to earlier comments made by Dunning, see events take a turn at once predictable to some and shocking to others, but either way powerful, debate-inviting, disquieting and beautiful. Put it this way: If you're a fan of *Dr. Terror's House of Horrors*, *Lost Horizon*, or even Robert Louis Stevenson's *Child's Garden of Verses*, you will be touched.

To those pining for the days when, on a weekday evening in the UK, you could turn on the TV, begin watching an unassuming play or program, and discover you were actually viewing something akin to a British horror movie, even if not aimed squarely at a genre audience, it remains a special memory indeed—its otherworldliness amplified by the fact that its cast, while all still working, have remained on the "banks" of fame rather than surfing its current, and deserve, like *Way Upstream* itself, a second float on the canals of recognition.
—Darius Drewe

WHEN THE WIND BLOWS

1986
D: Jimmy T. Murakami

> "Is there a clean white shirt, dear? Ready for the bomb?"

Protect and Survive was published in May 1980. This government pamphlet was designed to provide information to the general public concerning preparation for a nuclear attack on the UK, as well as procedure during the aftermath. The *Times* newspaper had become aware of the existence of the leaflet in late 1979 and their exposure led to the government making it generally available six months later—it seems that the details contained within may have been intended for police, fire services, and local authorities but an outcry brought the booklet to wider attention. This in turn resulted in criticism from bodies like the Campaign for Nuclear Disarmament—proper scrutiny of the guidance revealing at best a naïve outlook, at worst a bid to obfuscate and to misinform the population. Despite this, the government of the day ploughed on, with additional Home Office leaflets on Domestic Nuclear Shelters and, infamously, the series of visual briefings commissioned from Richard Taylor Animation and narrated by Patrick Allen—again, not intended for broadcast until hostilities were deemed imminent, but quickly leaked and revealed by CND and by the BBC current affairs flagship *Panorama*.

Suitably appalled by the manner in which the official line was deviating from likely reality, the popular artist and children's illustrator Raymond Briggs published his graphic novel *When the Wind Blows* in response. This 1982 work depicts a retired couple, Jim and Hilda Bloggs, with old-fashioned values, living a gentle everyday existence, and (with talk of conflict rife in the media) discussing their memories of having survived the Second World War. Their dogged insistence on following the advice of the authorities proves a masterstroke on Briggs' part, utterly destroying the pretence of *Protect and Survive* and playing up the contradictions and blatant outright lies contained within, but doing so in a deceptively mild and, at face value, non-contradictory way which only serves to paper over the author's seething enragement.

With film and television turning frequently to nuclear themes at this time, a dramatized version of *When the Wind Blows* was inevitable. American TV movie *The Day After* (1983) and the BBC's British take on the subject, *Threads* (1984) had caused a sensation, and the likes of *Special Bulletin* (1983), *Miracle Mile* (1988) and the low-key *Testament* (1983), which won a surprise Oscar nomination for its lead actress Jane Alexander, all continued to inform audiences of the folly of modern wars that could not be won.

Jimmy T. Murakami, a Dublin-based Japanese/American filmmaker and a product of the Roger Corman school (Murakami had worked on exploitation movies for Corman and directed 1980's science-fiction adventure *Battle Beyond the Stars*) had been a prominent member of the team behind *The Snowman*, Dianne Jackson's masterly adaptation of another Briggs classic. *The Snowman* was initially broadcast by Channel 4 in December 1982 and has become a Yuletide institution. You probably watch it every year—I know I do. (David Bowie, who memorably introduced *The Snowman*, returns to deliver a powerful vocal on the *When the Wind Blows* theme song.) Murakami was hired to helm *When the Wind Blows* and he and his crew made a stunning job

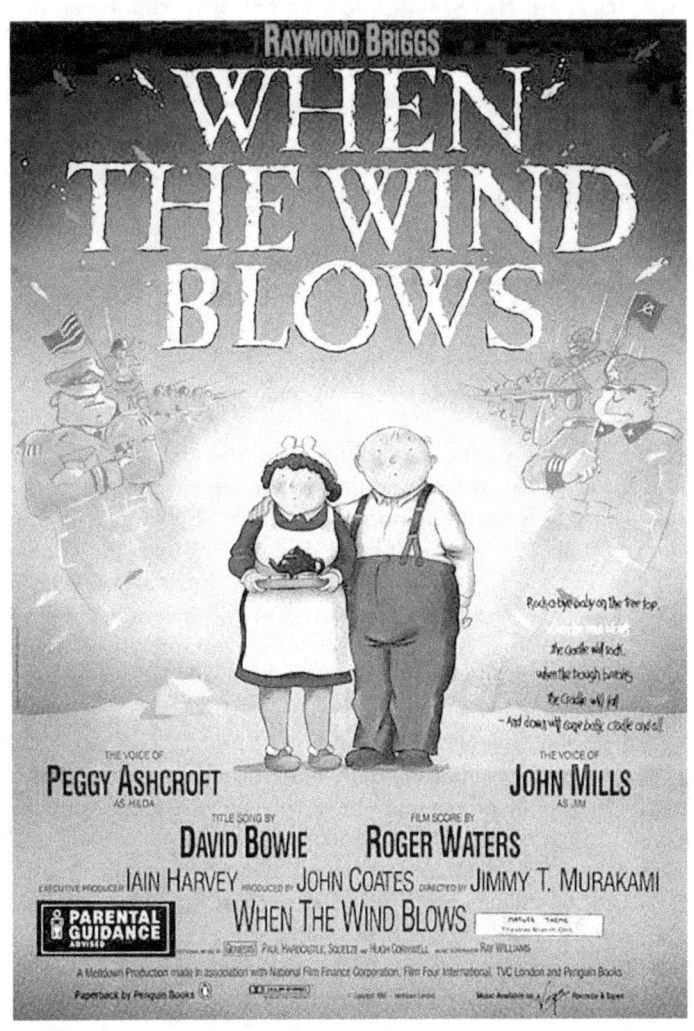

of translating Briggs' vision to the screen. He's ably assisted by a pair of superb performances by those old dependables John Mills and Peggy Ashcroft, who bring life and humor to the central characters of Jim and Hilda, thus making it all the more affecting as we witness their poorly-informed reaction to the threat of imminent war and their post-bomb descent into confusion and, eventually, radiation-caused sickness.

Briggs himself took on script duties, ensuring that the central ideas of his original work were retained. Bespectacled, balding Jim's constant repetition of the phrase "inner core or refuge" while constructing a futile "shelter" out of unhinged doors and scatter cushions bangs home the hopeless absurdity of the official line. Repetition works so effectively here, Hilda constantly fretting about the mess or the washing-up, Jim's cure for all ills being the mantra "I'll pop down to …" whichever local shop or public amenity has always solved minor inconveniences in the vanished routine past.

The animation team manages to capture the "Briggs style" effectively, with that familiar round-faced look to the main characters. As with *The Snowman*, a cozy rural environment is disrupted and we work our way to the only possible outcome, but clearly any similarities in feel and tone between the two productions quickly diverges, simply due to the variant subject matter and the author's differing intentions. It's a gruelling, agonizing ordeal watching these lovely, uncomplicated, naïve people slowly and unwittingly die. The closing 20 minutes sees them hollow-eyed, withered, covered in boils, hungry, tired, with clumps of hair falling out, yet doggedly they cling to their belief in "authority," still attempting to follow official guidance to the letter. Our final sight of them would be comical beyond belief if it weren't for the fact that every audience member will be experiencing inner rage while simultaneously crying their eyes out.
—Darrell Buxton

WHOOPS APOCALYPSE

1986
D: Tom Bussmann

The early to mid-1980s were a worrying time for those who feared the outbreak of the world's first atomic war. CND and Greenpeace saw substantial rises in membership, even as many dismissed them as misguided cranks. Public alarm over the possibility of one small incident escalating into the conflagration increased, and in 1982 Andrew Marshall and David Renwick dared to make comedy out of the fear. Their television series *Whoops Apocalypse* became an instant, talked-about success, and, for all of its satire and belly laughs, dared to show the unthinkable becoming the inevitable.

By 1986, following the likes of *Threads*, *The Day After*, Frankie's *Two Tribes* and the public release of the hidden *Protect and Survive* public information films, the concerns were arguably running higher than before. Small wonder that Marshall and Renwick were asked to re-vamp their tale for a cinema release.

And, to their credit, they elected to overhaul the original story drastically. It still tells the same tale of international relations comically—but with increasing darkness—as they fall apart until the same crisis point is reached, and a choice must be made which will affect all of humanity; their response, laudably, was not to point fingers at those in power in the East or West but at the far more intimate culprits of human foibles and blind chance. These themes were present in the original, but obvious villain figures in the corridors of power such as that evangelical Strangelove, the Deacon, were dropped. We were given a US President who is competent and trying to do the right thing, a UK Prime Minister who means well but is hopelessly insane. The only truly evil figure, the terrorist Lacrobat, is ultimately ineffectual, and his greatest triumph is a pure piece of chance that he couldn't possibly have foreseen.

Which may make the film sound remarkably somber. But it isn't. Such moments of sudden horror as Alexei Sayle coldly shooting two journalists dead to prevent them uncovering some deliberately nebulous Soviet scheme co-exists with rear admirals with innuendo-ridden names, two decrepit old servants attempting to answer phone calls very slowly, Peter Cook's Prime Minister blithely blaming unemployment on "the little pixies," Rik Mayall's foul-mouthed and completely useless S.A.S. commander—not to mention the antics of the infamous Spunky Spaniel. As we see-saw between well-endowed topless Page 3 "stunnas" strutting about warships to raise morale and Loretta Swit's President desperately fighting to prevent the worst, we are made all too aware that the original's mixture of sharp and outright crass comedy with the dread and tension of impending nuclear holocaust has been retained. Carry On Strangelove.

At times, the film can seem unfocused, a little too scattergun in its shooting to score a palpable hit with every round—yet, in the final reckoning, it's not only funny and alarming, it's also surprisingly courageous. The 1980s round of the Cold War was all too eager to split the globe into evil Commie bastards and Western imperialist warmongers, with the supporters of either side being tarred with the same lazy brush as appeasers or fascists respectively. The truth was always more painful, and more straightforward. Whichever side we took, we were all humans. And all equally capable, not so much of deliberate acts of evil, as just simply fucking things up.

Whoops Apocalypse is still there to remind us, with its striking mixture of laughter and shudders, that we are all still mortal. If you haven't seen it, then track down a copy and enjoy its odd humor.

There really is no alternative
—Ken Shinn

WILT

1989
D: Michael Tuchner

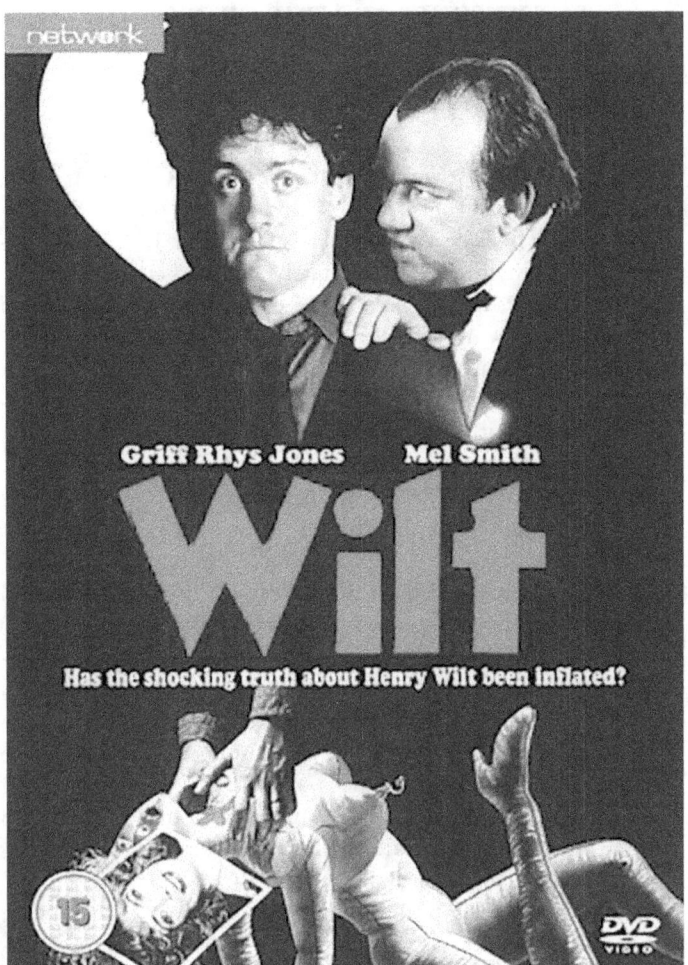

In 1976, Tom Sharpe's novel *Wilt* was first published, becoming successful enough to spawn several sequels continuing the protagonist's misadventures. As was typical of Sharpe's work its humor was a mix of the sharply satirical and the most crass and scatological. During my schooldays, Sharpe's work was popular with my classmates and myself for these very reasons—his books were the perfect blend of biting wit and the bawdiest vileness that any teenage boy could hope for.

So, when London Weekend Television threw their weight behind a feature film version in 1989, eternal fifth formers everywhere were interested. Would the sheer excess of the book be brought to the big screen? The news of the casting of renowned comedy duo Griff Rhys-Jones and Mel Smith as Henry Wilt and his unwitting enemy Police Inspector Flint boded well for a suitably funny take on the material ...

... and then the film was released.
It was immediately obvious that the book had been cruelly watered-down for the more general public. What had originally been an ultimately uplifting but scabrous tale of salvaging a precarious marriage became almost an outright rom-com. Some of the most memorable set pieces remained but were treated in a manner that verged on the embarrassed—a prime example being the buried sex doll (believed to be the corpse of Wilt's wife Eva) being recovered. In the book, the scene is cartoonish, wildly over-the-top. The film seems downright shy about it and reduces the lurid scene to little more than a cutaway gag.

In brief, *Wilt* on the big screen was all but neutered, all of Sharpe's savage, gross comedy gone. But was it at least a decent interpretation of the source?

The answer to that is yes—a qualified yes, but yes all the same. Along with the superb cast, also including such dependable character actors as Alison Steadman, Roger Lloyd-Pack, Jeremy Clyde and John Normington, the script was placed in the hands of sitcom writers Andrew Marshall and David Renwick, creators of such successful series as *Whoops Apocalypse* and *One Foot in the Grave*. While their humor was a lot less in-your-face than Sharpe's, they had a love for the bizarre and the somewhat sinister, and this helped turn *Wilt* into a cleverly different tale.

The novel lets us know what's going on from the very start—but Marshall and Renwick make the inspired choice to treat the tale as an offbeat sort-of murder mystery. Is Wilt a murderer? Just what has happened to his suddenly missing wife? Has the unassuming Wilt, as Flint suspects with mounting alarm, really disposed of the apparent victims by having them dumped at a meat pie factory? The script slyly decides to let us try to work out the solution for ourselves, and—if we haven't read the novel, or have done but are prepared to entertain the idea of an alternate version—it's a terrific approach that pays off in understated spades.

A final additional plot thread, in which there really does turn out to be a mystery serial killer on the loose, does help to add to the morbid black comedy and borderline-horror atmosphere, but ultimately contributes little other than the excuse for a very low-key action scene, and all ends happily with Wilt and Eva's love and marriage re-affirmed and Flint even becoming a sort of friend to Wilt. If you want this to be just like Sharpe's novel, then you may well exit disappointed, or even angry.

However, if you want a quality cast and two great and eccentric comedy writers turning the material into what feels at times like a Richard Curtis film gone sourly, marvellously awry, then you could do a lot worse than to take in this unassuming, quietly effective little yarn.

Just watch out for that dangerously predatory American woman.
—Ken Shinn

THE WITCHES AND THE GRINNYGOG

1983
D: Diarmuid Lawrence

A six-part ITV series aired in the run-up to Christmas 1983, *The Witches and the Grinnygog* was produced by the TVS (Television South) franchise and was based on the 1981 children's novel by Dorothy Edwards. Ultimately all rather cozy and family friendly, with a sort of "Five Delve Into Ancient Magick" feel about it, the show nevertheless has plentiful moments of unease and the unexplained. Set in a chocolate-box English village (it was shot, on film, in Titchfield and Bishop's Waltham, Hampshire), it begins with a local woman almost being run down by a passing truck, from which topples a small but weighty stone idol. She presents the figurine to her ageing father as he has always expressed a desire to add a garden gnome to his rockery—the golden-flecked gargoyle takes pride of place in the grounds of their home, but soon exhibits strange powers, causing blooms to sprout and seemingly moving its lips and speaking to the youngest member of the household. Before long, a mysterious anthropologist/witch-doctor named Mr. Twebele Alabaster (Olu Jacobs) materializes—disarmingly later displaying the ability to appear and disappear at will, without a sound or ripple—while three dotty old ladies soon follow, seemingly seeking something or someone, and accompanied by an infirm young woman who is later discovered to be a tallow manikin, though she is occasionally glimpsed alive and ambulatory.

St. Cuthbert's, a church in the area threatened with being bulldozed as part of a motorway development, is to be transferred to another site brick by brick, and so the vicar of nearby St. Edmunds, the Reverend Sogood, enlists his brood to help catalogue the reams of papers and historical materials relating to their own parish. This leads to the uncovering of a set of centuries-old diaries handwritten by Canon Alloway. As the kids peruse the Canon's notes, corresponding events and crossovers seem to be occurring around them. Did the lorry driver who mislaid the idol really see a hand moving from beneath a tarpaulin in the back of his vehicle? Why does the bundle of rags he finds there suddenly disintegrate? Might the eccentric cleaning woman Miss Bendybones have a connection with another strange lady who has vanished from a locked police cell, leaving an arcane message scrawled on the walls? And was the center of the village once a place of execution and witch-burning?

Miss Bendybones (Patricia Hayes), Mrs Ems (Sheila Grant) and Edie Possett (Anna Wing) are the three witches in *The Witches and the Grinnygog*

Particularly effective are those stray moments where the ancient and modern worlds collide—Edie (Anna Wing) remarking upon how little the area has changed but becoming bewildered by the sight of a television aerial atop her old cottage; Daisy/Marg'ret (the time-slipped young character at the heart of the tale) experiencing disturbing visions of burning flames and commenting on belching demons with "red eyes in their behinds," possibly referring to 20th century motor vehicles; a truly magical scene where Edie causes consternation in the local launderette, cramming twigs and petals into a washing machine, throwing in a caterpillar for good measure, and using this makeshift "cauldron" to produce a beautiful flowery bonnet! Even the appearance of a helicopter during the finale may well be due to spell-conjuring as opposed to anything from our known realm.

The Witches and the Grinnygog originally aired on UK television in six 25-minute instalments, but has been screened in a single movie-length edit elsewhere in the world, notably by Nickelodeon in the States (Nickelodeon also appear to have screened it in episodic format as part of their *The Third Eye* programing strand, also featuring such imported favourites as *Children of the Stones* and *Into the Labyrinth*.) As yet unavailable officially on Blu-ray or DVD, with rights issues in something of a tangle, this is definitely one for fans of cult children's telly or "folk horror" to seek out wherever possible.

—Darrell Buxton

The gargoyle living in the garden comes to life in *The Witches and the Grinnygog*

A ZED & TWO NOUGHTS

1985
D: Peter Greenaway

Two women die in a bizarre car accident involving a low-flying swan. Their respective husbands, both zoologists, try via a process of examining grief, death, and physical decay in animals to come to terms with fate, loss, humanity and their own personal destinies ... it doesn't end in a "happy-ever-after"—or maybe, viewed through a skewed prism, it does.

Writer/director Peter Greenaway's 1985 follow-up to his art-house smash *The Draughtsman's Contract* remains one of the most unique cinematic experiences of the past four decades, at once a witty, wise, vulgar, cruel, yet tender look at some weird and weighty themes, with a scientific, detached gaze that at times takes the breath away. Real life acting twins Brian and Eric Deacon seem fully in tune with the perverse material, evoking enough wry distance and yet emotional vulnerability to draw you in, and coupled with the late Sacha Vierny's extraordinary cinematography, both in terms of painterly lighting and some astounding tracking shots, and a near career-best score from Michael Nyman (the closing credits accompaniment is simply one of the finest pieces of music ever to play an audience out of a cinema), you have a film quite unlike any other. Indeed, starting with a car crash and evolving into ever more disturbing themes (the time-lapse sequences of animal decomposition, the flirting with bestiality, suicide, mutilation, mental collapse), one can see how David Cronenberg, director of the ultimate crash-themed movie, would screen this for his cast and crew before embarking on the lensing of 1988's *Dead Ringers* with Jeremy Irons; indeed, both tales bow out with remarkably similar finales (though admittedly there are less snails onscreen in David's sublime psychological drama!).

Four years later, Greenaway would direct what is probably his masterpiece, *The Cook, the Thief, His Wife & Her Lover* (see review elsewhere in this book), but whereas that was a strictly linear piece of storytelling, *Zoo* is not afraid to wander wherever it pleases—Jim Davidson as a crude zoo attendant, escaped flamingoes, Frances Barber as the deliciously weird Milo, chat-up lines from black-hatted Joss Ackland, the wheelchair-bound Felipe Arc-en-Ciel character (Wolf Kahler) and his doomed, kinked obsession with horses (don't ask!). Much as I love the Michael Gambon-starring later film, the sheer willful strangeness and visual beauty of this daring piece of work draws me back time and again. It is available in a gorgeous BFI DVD in the UK, so if you have never tried this hypnotic, exasperating, firing-on-all-cylinders slice of Greenaway genius, both a horror story and a comedy twisted beyond belief, then do so—you genuinely have not seen a film quite like this, and I don't make that statement lightly.
—Michael Wesley

APPENDIX 2: AMATEUR S.O.V. FEATURES

Access to new video technology allowed for the expansion of the "home movie" during the 1980s. Amateur filmmaking, with no intention or prospect of commercial release, had been a popular pastime throughout the world for decades, but video cameras and cassettes opened the gateway for everyone to have a go. We are sure that there must be countless examples of British horror home video from the 1980s—some of them may even lurk in your attic or beneath your stairs. The nature of the medium may have resulted in many tapes having been erased, recorded over, or simply perishing or molding with the passage of time. Fortunately, several have survived, and our "Short Films" appendix includes shot-on-video fare alongside more professional celluloid productions. The following section documents and reviews a handful of longer-form items from the amateur British scene, all coincidentally made during 1988.

NOT A LOT OF VEGETABLES

1988
D: none credited
W: none credited
Starring: Mark Adams, Paul Lambert, David Lambert, Martin Hefferan

I dare say that dozens of kids weaned on "video nasties" and other VHS treats from the rental outlets in Britain's high streets took their obsession to the next level, by creating their own camcorder epics. We've documented a few elsewhere in this book, but it's likely that most of the truly home-made, "rank amateur" productions were either erased pretty quickly or languish on eroded and unplayable cassettes stored in basements and attics.

One or two survive in digitized form, however, and the renowned *Cinemageddon* private tracker (an indispensable online resource of cult and offbeat movie fare for those lucky enough to have access) contains worldwide examples among its extensive catalogue of trash. A member of the site kindly uploaded a file which they entitled *Camcorder Atrocity*, 52 minutes of impossible-to-describe mania comprising four (unrelated?) short shockers, three of them untitled, derivation unknown.

Background details such as a *RoboCop* poster tacked to a wall, a "Freddie Starr Ate My Hamster" T-shirt, the *Neighbours* theme tune, and an ad for Iron Maiden's "*Somewhere in Time*" assist in pinpointing a date for all this childish malarkey, confirmed by a "28.5.88" graphic appearing onscreen somewhere in the midst of the fun. It's difficult to say whether the material presented here is the work of the same people—it's roughly divided into several sections. The opening chunk sees a young D.J. (whose turntable appears to have half of a seven-inch single revolving on it) and his mate smashing up bits of furniture and other nearby items in an attic, and performing an unfunny sketch about buying coffee (reading their flapping script but still managing to forget which characters they are supposed to be playing!)—inevitably all leads to a murder scene, with the record-spinner (now sporting fake plastic boobs) having ketchup sprayed all over him while his pal pretends to chop him to pieces.

We then proceed to a hand-drawn title card announcing *Not a Lot of Vegetables* ("Cheapo Films Presents ... A Budget Production...."), which turns out to be a gore-filled short by a second bunch of tykes. "This film is a warning to all those who would mess with devilry," we are informed via caption and ominous voice-over. Ouija board activity seems to prompt the possession of one boy, turning him pizza-faced and eager for blood and guts. He gruesomely disembowels his first selected kill in the back garden, excessively and rather effectively, and cuts the throat of a much younger victim in a kitchen. There's a rather neat shot of a hand punching through the Ouija board to rip the flesh off the face of the unfortunate user, and oddly we are then treated to eight minutes or so of outtakes and behind the scenes stuff, including the kids helpfully tidying up the mess they've made outside ("look mum, we even cleaned this path!"), as well as melting a fake head by pouring some unidentified liquid over it, leaving a pair of eyeballs nestling in a pile of goo.

Next up is an untitled piece, seemingly by a third bunch of lads—a spaceship, represented by a battered old can or dustbin hurled across the screen, leads to the appearance of a far-from-convincing "alien" (a juvenile in shades and a hooded garment) who strangles a teenager in the woods using an orange plastic washing line, and cuts the wrists of another. Zombie-like figures (sans make-up) stumble through the trees, their number increasing with each fresh kill, with gut-chomping and face-clawing to the fore.

Another spacecraft (possibly the plastic top from a can of whipped cream) dangles from a thread and lands atop a tiny model house. The presumed occupant of the interplanetary vehicle is a green-faced figure clad in a Megadeth T-shirt, initially revealed in a strange still-frame sequence juddering around a croquet lawn. In an attempt at a visual pun, we cut from a shot of a Chopper bicycle to one of the emerald entity pursuing a long-haired target with another chopper, a hefty axe, decapitating his prey (or at least the substituted and bewigged plastic dummy surrogate) against a tree. He pokes the eyes and rips the brains out of another plaster head and drowns someone in a bathroom sink before finishing them off by beating their brains out against the tiled wall of a shower. Naturally, two minutes of footage depicting adolescents larking about on skateboards rounds off the weirdness. Hey, we're just here to watch and document this stuff.
—Darrell Buxton

SHAKE & SHIVER

1988

In 1988, a group of students at the University of East Anglia, working under the name of Godburger Productions, set about making an independent 50-minute comedy horror film.

Taking cues from the recently popular parodies of *The Comic Strip Presents ...* shown on Channel 4 television, they decided to spoof the cartoon adventures of Scooby-Doo, turning Daphne and Velma into secret lesbian lovers, Shaggy into a chronic drug addict, Fred into a self-deluding wannabe ladies' man and Scooby himself into an alcoholic wreck of an ex-special agent.

Seeking some personal healing, they embark upon a holiday retreat at a private health farm run by an enigmatic manager known only as The Granny. Assisting her are a traumatized army veteran, a white-coated dominatrix, and a sinister drug dealer.

In what may well have been intended as homage to 1973's *Horror Hospital*, it transpires that The Granny is actually a fraudulent criminal mastermind, planning on using drugs, hypnotism and physical conditioning to create a private army of compliant keep-fit zombies from her young clientele, with only Mystery Incorporated and an undercover policeman named Dirty Garry standing in her way ...

The film was made on an amateur but skilled basis, using obviously cheap but inventive effects to provide an opening decapitation by tape measure, various melting body parts, and a Roy Ashton-like latex and tissue paper layered make-up for The Granny. More obviously rubbish special effects manifested the Meringe, a small comic-relief monster adapted from a novelty nail-through-finger joke, which was viewed on occasion against picture postcard backdrops to parody the use of back projection. A specially-composed musical score provided by the Shaggy actor provided a deliberately inane and bouncy main title theme, bursts of John Carpenter-esque sinister synthesizers, 1970s-styled funky horn workouts for Scooby's clubbing scene and sly use of an *Archers*-type reworking of the theme from *The Sweeney* for the rural crime-busting of Dirty Garry.

Exteriors and interiors were filmed in and around the city of Norwich, both in private homes belonging to the families of cast and crewmembers, and in public locations such as the now-defunct Jacquard nightclub on St. Augustine's Street and the cellars of the Louis Marchesi pub on Tombland (the building is still standing, but is now a cafe/bar.) The film was given its world premiere early in December 1988, as a weekend screening at the Cinema City cinema, also in Norwich.

And how do we know about this obscure treasure at all? We know because ... I was that Granny ...
—Ken Shinn

(Ken provided the following credits information for *Shake & Shiver*: "I believe that the directors were named Julian Kettley and Graeme Sommers, but I could be wrong. (The first names are right, but perhaps not the surnames.) Julian played Dirty Garry and Graeme played the Dealer. I played The Granny. A fellow called, I think, David Stokes played Shaggy, and the Veteran was played by one St. John Rivers. Velma was played by Pamela Mukherjee (?), Daphne by Deborah Swift (?), and the Dominatrix by Susan Ash (?). Scooby was played by one Gary Ford, if I remember correctly. It's odd, I can remember pretty much all of the first names easily, but the surnames I'm not so sure about. Should any of the cast or crew get to see this (and that would be so cool!), then they can correct my fuzzy recollections as necessary!"—ed.)

SUMMER HORROR DAY

1988
D: Martin Nike
W: Martin Nike
Starring: Martin Nike, Paul Norman Altham-Lewis, Craig Ashword, Mark Beswick, Brian T. Brewer, Michael Dobson, Phil Oldfield

There's long been a tradition of horror and science fiction fans having a go at their own mini movies. Most famously, perhaps, there were the dozens of amateur shorts featuring Dracula, the Frankenstein monster, Spider-Man, the Hideous Sun Demon and many more favorites recaptured on film by young Don Glut, later to become a keen archivist and collector highly respected on the fan circuit. The teenage Spielberg's ambitious *Firelight* entertained his pals and community a mere five years before he went legit at Universal, while over here the toils of Manchester's Delta Film Group and, further afield, the hidden gems produced by Michael J. Murphy, spearheaded the home movie scene. BBC TV's popular children's film quiz *Screen Test* spawned a junior filmmaking competition, and the young audience occasionally responded with a macabre item or two; the adult news magazine show *Nationwide* went a step further, actively and specifically seeking horror shorts for its own viewer-centered movie contest in the mid-'70s.

The video age and the availability of, and access to, recording equipment and VHS tape that could be erased and re-used, led to a boom in garage production—which only expands to this day as it is now rare to find anyone who doesn't "film" via mobile/hand-held device and automatically upload the results, of-

A victim of *Summer Horror Day*

ten transient, to YouTube. In attempting a thorough overview of the 1980s British horror scene, then, how lovely that *Summer Horror Day* surfaced during our researches—an ambitious 56-minute gorefest, filmed in Nelson, Lancashire on Super 8 (no less—no new-fangled VHS for these boys) and re-edited in a VCD "director's cut" in 2000.

Summer Horror Day being British, naturally there's very little sign of sunshine anywhere to be seen—the setting is cloudy and miserable. What we do have, however, is an energetic little romp, very basic as you'd expect, but with few slow spots and oodles of ambition, particularly in the range of gruesome, bloody effects shots and other splattery moments. The makers are indebted to *The Evil Dead* as what looks like a school exercise jotter filled with spells and incantations is found in the cellar of a suburban home (where, inevitably, we are told that the former occupants "all died mysteriously"—I guess that the Lancashire lads responsible for the movie figured we'd never buy the "Indian burial ground" concept this time out....) Tellingly, our lead characters are budding amateur filmmakers (discussing the rites laid down in the journal, one comments "Jesus Christ—what a load of bullshit!" to be met with the withering response, "it's like one of your scripts!"). Having foolishly read out loud from the book, the kids inadvertently raise a skull-faced zombie nearby (the rise of the monster corpse is preceded by a *Blue Velvet*-like extreme close-up of drops of blood on a clump of grass) and all hell breaks loose.

They don't stint on the gore, as was the case with many excitable young amateur camera-wielders in the UK, America, and especially Germany during the era. Severed hands, axings, bloody stumps, eye gouging, *Burning*-style finger severing, throat slashing, impaling, and gut chomping abound. Much of what we see is "point the camera and hope" fare but there are a handful of inventive shots achieved, with good use of close-up, filming from beneath the action, full body tracking, etc. The skull zombie (which looks as though three distinct make-up designs may have been used over the filming period) is the star of the show but there's a gaggle of slower-moving living dead who resemble a quartet of scally football hooligans as opposed to anything you might see in Romero or Fulci. In a frantic finale, our hero evades the horde, dispatches and sets alight "Deadhead the zombie" (as he's credited), encounters and swiftly decapitates a red-hooded psychopath, and manages to drive into remote countryside where, in disbelief, he is met in quick succession by car trouble and by a mechanic who miraculously materializes on the scene. Our hero smells a rat, of course—the "mechanic" is Satan's servant, here to claim his soul—and he hot-foots it into the hills, only to be met by Deadhead once again. A quick drillbit to the right eye socket and the Devil has fulfilled another bargain.

For the small but devoted band of buffs who actively seek out this kind of no-budget material, *Summer Horror Day* is well worth going out of your way to track down if you can.
—Darrell Buxton

APPENDIX 3:
UNFILMED PROJECTS

THE ANGER

The saga of the making of *Spookies* is detailed elsewhere in our book, but intertwined with that strange mess was the aborted shooting of *The Anger*. Michael Lee of video label VIPCO was attempting to get into film production in the United States, but already had a team which had begun filming a project in the UK, *The Anger*–brief footage from which was shown to the *Spookies* crew, perhaps with a view to them somehow incorporating it into the movie they were working on. Who could possibly say, where the ill-prepared and flying-by-the-seat-of-his-pants Lee was concerned?!

Vinegar Syndrome's content-packed 2019 Blu-ray release of *Spookies* featured an excellent feature-length documentary about the whole chaotic situation, during which the suggestion is made that Lee cancelled production on *The Anger* because the director was ill and had been diagnosed with a tumour. A few seconds of poor quality video remnants from a rough cut of *The Anger* turn up during the early part of *The Twisted Tale–The Unmaking of Spookies* documentary, with a male actor being attacked by what I hope is supposed to be a toy monkey come to life (this stuffed, toothy, grimacing, and highly unconvincing bundle of black fur leaps off a shelf and claws on to its hapless victim's back, the screaming guy bashing them both into a door in an attempt to rid himself of the primate menace), and a woman sitting at a table emoting in a loud "reaching the back of the stalls"manner ("please don't leave me!" she wails over and over) as the camera slowly drifts toward an oven in the background–the door of which opens to reveal a slimy green creature, looking like a badly cooked lasagne, filling the entire space. It whips out a long rubbery tongue across the room and latches around the unfortunate lady's neck, making her choke and splutter as she is strangled.

The failure to make any progress with *The Anger*, or even to integrate the tiny amount of filmed content elsewhere, would appear to be no great loss to cinema.
—Darrell Buxton

THE PIKE

The early 1980s were a boom time for pulp novels featuring bloodthirsty animals on the loose. James Herbert unleashed further outings of the rats, Shaun Hutson had his slugs and Guy N. Smith gave everyone the crabs. With the standard menagerie members already given starring roles by the time Cliff Twemlow burst on to the writing scene, the former nightclub bouncer had to resort to a freshwater fiend for his 1982 book *The Pike*. Twemlow then mined ever-deeper creature territory for a second book in 1983's *The Beast of Kane*, which tackles the problem of adopting an elk hound that turns out to be "Satan himself, fulfilling an ancient prophecy."

Twemlow gave his best shot at getting both these books on to the big screen. An early draft of *The Beast of Kane* was pitched as a potential film project to Hammer during the 1970s, only for Twemlow to receive a rejection letter from them a few weeks later. A further attempt to shunt a film adaptation of the book into production in 1982—under the title *The Dogs of Kane*—would prove equally unsuccessful. Twemlow had better luck with *The Pike*, since in contrast to the apathy shown towards *The Beast of Kane* the previous publication had begun attracting interest from the filmbiz even before it had hit the shelves. Such was the optimism surrounding cinematic ambitions for *The Pike* that Twemlow's publisher, Hamlyn, quickly slapped a "Soon to be a Major Film" blurb on to the second and third editions of the book.

Twemlow's fishy story centers on Mike Watson, a world-weary newspaper hack who receives the scoop of his life when he discovers that Lake Windermere is home to a giant, man-eating finned predator. When Mike breaks the news in the *Daily Mirror*, unscrupulous forces turn the lake into an appropriately themed tourist attraction, disregarding the obvious danger the killer pike poses to the public. With tourists ending up as dinner, it's left to Mike to gather up an eclectic bunch of people and embark on the fishing trip from hell.

After writing a screenplay treatment and composing a soundtrack, Twemlow attempted to drum up interest for the film adaptation by staging a publicity stunt at Lake Windermere on May 13, 1982. Actors of the calibre of Joan Collins and Jack Hedley were in attendance, having been penciled in as the leads. Joan seems to have first entered into Cliff Twemlow's orbit around 1981 when she was in talks to appear in *Tuxedo Warrior*, a South African action film that Twemlow had a small acting role in. While her participation in that project never came to pass, presumably a friendship between she and Twemlow struck up, resulting in her agreeing to appear in *The Pike* a year later. As well as bagging Collins and Hedley for *The Pike*, Twemlow announced that he and an actress/TV hostess called Linda Lou Allen would be taking supporting roles. On hand to cover all this were the local press as well as a crew from the BBC's *Tomorrow's World* program. Their subsequent TV piece on the event included interviews with the actors and documented the making and unveiling of a giant mechanical model of the pike itself. Described as Joan Collins' "biggest, ugliest leading man" to date, the 12-foot pike model certainly had the potential to be an impressive horror film beastie. Rumored to have cost around quarter of a million pounds to make, and operated by computer, the innovative creation was naturally the main focus of *Tomorrow's World*'s attention. Even Joan Collins was impressed by it. "I wouldn't like to be in any kind of water with him," she told *Tomorrow's World*––"it's enormous." The only bum note of the day appears to have been the raising of the subject of the book's similarities to a certain Steven Spielberg film about a shark. Twemlow rejected any *Jaws* comparison outright, claiming to *Tomorrow's World* that he first thought of the idea for his story in 1972, long before what he disdainfully referred to as "that other film."

If the crossbow Twemlow carried around with him at the publicity stunt is anything to go by, he must have fancied casting himself in the role of Ulysses Grant, a muscular Scottish hermit—nicknamed "Strongbow"—whose archery skills are called upon for the climatic pike hunt (Ulysses Grant was of course also the name of a former US President, while "Strongbow" is likely to have been Twemlow's jokey reference to the famous cider adverts.) It's a bigger surprise to discover that Twemlow wanted Joan Collins to play the book's lead female character, Emma Mannering, a rather unexceptional "hero's girlfriend" role. Especially as Diana Wynter, a far more animated female character in Twemlow's book, seems virtually tailor-made for our Joanie. Constantly complaining about her husband's sexual failings and delivering such gems as, "Maybe I can amuse myself watching the common herd make fools of themselves in the water," uber-bitch Wynter leaves quite an impression before ending up a late night snack for the pike. It's a role that positively screamed out for Joan Collins to get her claws into.

Alas for all this display of star power, pike action and good old-fashioned showmanship, the publicity stunt failed to reel in any potential investors, and this proposed Mega Joan vs. Giant Pike screen showdown failed to materialize. The only taster of what might have been is contained within the *Tomorrow's World* footage, thanks to the Beeb's crew filming staged tryouts of various scenes from the book, including the pike's attacks on a scuba driver and a fisherman. The fact that the film was never made hasn't stopped the day that Joan Collins and a giant pike rolled into town from becoming the stuff of local legend. It's an incident that people in the area still recall to this day. The Lake Windermere tourist information center is said to have added to the ballyhoo by keeping photos taken of Joan with her head in the pike's mouth on public display for many years afterwards, much to the amusement and curiosity of tourists. A further attempt at filming Twemlow's book, this time under the title *The Lake*, was announced by Ascertain Films in 2001 and appears to have briefly gone before the cameras in 2003 before shooting was abandoned.

As for the 12-foot pike model itself, like all the great oversized monsters he/it went on to terrorize Japan when the prop was sold to a robotics exhibition in the Far East. The British horror film's loss was Japan's gain, since the pike was reportedly a big hit at the exhibition, where members of the public could operate it by joystick. More recent rumors have it that the pike was later returned to the UK, either ending up with a scrap dealer or being sold to a private collector. So, if you ever happen to be at a junkyard or cleaning out a friend's garage and chance upon a life-sized model of a giant pike ... well, now you know the story of how it got there.
—Gavin Whitaker

PLASMID

Plasmid started its troubled life as a film project in 1979, until plans for the movie stalled, at which point its script was re-written into a novel, subsequently published by Star Books in June 1980. In book form, *Plasmid* is a grisly read centering around dodgy medical experiments being performed on long-term prisoners at a top-secret government research lab—the government's aim seemingly being to create a private army of supermen whose skin is adaptable to extreme weather conditions. Things predictably go wrong, and the experiments instead turn a nutjob albino prisoner into a hideous creature who escapes from the lab, setting into motion what the Star publicity blurb excitedly refers to as "a holocaust of horror." Due to the book's rather exaggerated claim that albinos possess a vampire-like fear of daylight, the creature adopts the London sewers as its hunting ground of choice. The cover of darkness makes the sewers the ideal place for a pissed off albino mutant to indulge in murder, limb tearing and a newfound taste for human flesh!!

Had the film version been made, *Plasmid* would have been the first feature-length horror movie to have been directed by Stanley Long, best known for his 1970s *Adventures of ...* sex comedy series. Despite the director's inclination towards saucy humor and a known dislike of the horror genre, Long helmed several entertaining horror film shorts around this period (later compiled into the *Screamtime* anthology) and on the basis of those mini-shockers could have probably had a decent stab at bringing *Plasmid* to the screen. Long did shoot a test featuring an actor playing the albino creature under heavy make-up; footage that—according to the few who have seen it—provided an impressive showcase for the creature (described in the book as "a warped parody of a human being"). Sadly, this was all the material destined to be shot for *Plasmid* before Long called time on the endeavor, later citing the impracticality of filming in the London sewage system as his reason for abandoning the project.

While it is clear then who would have been in the director's chair on a film version of *Plasmid*, attempting to ascertain who wrote the screenplay and spin-off novel is a far more head-scratching assignment. In the early 1990s, veteran screenwriter David McGillivray recalled penning *Plasmid* for Long, citing it in an interview as the one unfilmed script of his that he wished had been made into a movie. This was all news to Stanley Long, who claimed that McGillivray had no involvement in the project. Long maintained that the script was in fact entirely the work of his friend Jo Gannon, who had previously worked for Long as an editor on the *Adventures of ...* series. Further adding to the confusion, while the cover of the *Plasmid* novel credits Gannon as its author, a closer inspection of the book reveals it to be "a novelisation by Robert Knight based on the screenplay by Jo Gannon." Mr. Knight is in fact one of the many pseudonyms of Christopher Evans, a prolific writer of sci-fi and children's novels and an editor of several horror anthology books. Although, according to McGillivray, the *Plasmid* novel sticks fairly close to the script he claims to have penned, at times being little more than a word for word transcription of his dialogue. Long's biography gives sole credit for the original idea and script to Gannon; Long also notes that the 2005 British horror film *Creep* bears a "striking resemblance" to the unfilmed *Plasmid*.

Long's dislike of McGillivray, and attempts to erase him from the history of *Plasmid*, continued well on into the internet era, with Stanley asking an assistant to alter McGillivray and Long's Wikipedia pages, removing references to it from McGillivray's page and once more giving Jo Gannon credit for the script on Long's own page. All this over a film that was never even made, and a paperback adaptation that nobody remembers.
—Gavin Whitaker

APPENDIX 4: SHORT FILMS

Compiled by Paul Higson and Darrell Buxton

THE ANTAGONIST (1981)—Twenty-four-minute horror short directed by George Pavlou, starring Ed Bishop. Support film for *Educating Rita*'s 1983 cinema release in the UK. Mentioned by Pavlou during the *Rawhead Rex* Blu-ray commentary track.

ATTACK OF THE AT-AT (1984)—directed by Russell Smith. Amateur short, running just one minute 40 seconds. Young boy's Star Wars toy comes to life and menacingly pursues him around the house. The footage was "reworked in 2010" and released to YouTube.

AXE KILLER (198?)—directed by a young Alex Chandon, later to bring us the likes of *Bad Karma* and *Inbred*. Alex shot this at Highgate Cemetery using a Super 8 camera he had been gifted. In the October 1991 issue of *The Dark Side* magazine Alex also mentioned having filmed two sequels: "They were very basic—I don't think I need to explain the plots ..."

AXE KILLER 2 (198?)—directed by Alex Chandon.

AXE KILLER 3 (198?)—directed by Alex Chandon.

BACK FROM THE DEAD (1988)—Ten-minute Super 8 zombie/gore short, "made in Doncaster—where life is cheap!" Directed by 18-year-old horror fan Paul Mallinson.

THE BAIT (1981)—Amateur horror short directed by Arthur Smith of the Altrincham Cine Club.

THE BED (1980)—Twenty-nine-minute short helmed by Derek Vanlint (director of photography on *Alien* and *Dragonslayer*) with music by John Foxx. A young boy is tricked by his sister and her boyfriend into thinking that they have been killed—she, sucked beneath a bed by a monster, he, stabbed. The sheets of the bed then come to life and suffocate the pair. Years later, our main character is seen back at the now-empty house—it is revealed he is there on a day visit from the asylum where he is currently incarcerated.

BLACK ANGEL (1980)—As mediaeval knight Sir Maddox drowns, he sees a vision of a beautiful maiden whom he learns is being held captive by the evil Black Angel. He sets out to rescue her ... Roger Christian filmed this 25-minute fantasy, which won a huge audience when it was eventually released as the accompanying short preceding screenings of *The Empire Strikes Back*. A twist ending borrows from Ambrose Bierce's classic short story *An Occurrence at Owl Creek Bridge*. A print of *Black Angel* was rediscovered in December 2011 after decades during which it was considered a "lost" film.

THE BLACK TOWER (1987)—Twenty-three-minute avant garde short directed by John Smith. Paranoid man becomes convinced that the titular structure is following him all over London ... and beyond. At the end he ventures into the building and is apparently swallowed up—his narration on the soundtrack then being replaced by a new female voice, with the woman also seemingly spotting the building everywhere she goes.

BLOOD IS RED (198?)—Amateur camcorder-shot horror made by a teenage Matthew Edwards and his brothers. Mentioned in Matthew's 2017 book of filmmaker interviews, *Twisted Visions*.

BLOODLUST (1980)—Fourteen-minute sex/horror vampire movie from Mistral Films, directed by Russell Gay, made available by mail order for the Super 8 home viewing market. Carmilla rises from the dead to seduce a teenage victim, before presenting the girl to Count Dracula. "Vampire sex and violent death with a twist in its tail as sharp as a fiend's fangs," ran the trade ads.

THE BLOODY CHAMBER (1982)—Based on the Bluebeard-themed story by Angela Carter, this 29-minute horror short directed by Nick Lewin was released to UK cinemas as support to Walter Hill's *48 Hrs*. Rupert Everett, Suzanna Hamilton, and Terence Stamp (the latter also to cameo memorably in Neil Jordan's film of Carter's *The Company of Wolves*) headed the cast.

THE BOOK OF THE DEAD (1989)—Horror short directed by the teenage Darren Perry, still toiling away on similar fare all these years later. "An old book opens a gateway to another world."

THE BRADWICK BEAST (1988)—Twelve-minute short made by amateur filmmaker Gordon Louch, featuring family members in the cast including his son Stuart (who has revived and digitized many of his dad's films, uploading them to YouTube in recent years). This one has two children hearing a radio broadcast about a legendary local monster—the young boy goes off in search of it at a nearby farm and brings home a strange locked box. Will the beast materialize?

BROKEN GLASS (1982)—Directed by Hadi Zarbafi for Bournemouth and Poole College of Art and Design and presumed to be a short film. "Fictional drama, constructed like a puzzle, shows the horror of tampering with the supernatural."

BUTCHER MANSION (198?)—In his book of interviews with horror filmmakers, *Twisted Visions* author Matthew Edwards mentions filming amateur giallo/horror fare with his brothers via camcorder. This is one of the cited titles, along with *Blood is Red*.

CHAINSAW SCUM FUCK (1987)—Eight-minute short directed by Alex Chandon. Chainsaw-wielding maniac breaks into a house and terrorizes the teenage occupants. More effort goes into the scabrously subversive opening and closing credits (featuring expletives written in blood and a live mouse scampering around) than the main body of the movie itself!

CHIMERA (1989)—Thirty-nine-minute amateur production shot in Worcester by Andrew Morris. Said to be the first amateur film to be certified by the British Board of Film Classification (see Appendix 1 for full review.)

COLD LIGHT OF DAY (1989)—Four-minute promo, shot in one day, as an aid towards raising the budget for Fhiona-Louise's Dennis Nilsen-themed feature film. Included as a bonus extra on Arrow's Blu-ray release.

THE COTTAGE (1982)—Twenty-six-minute horror short directed by Mark Chapman, released as support to *Poltergeist* at UK cinemas in late 1982. Nicola Pagett plays a writer working at her country cottage; Ann Heffernan is the elderly visitor who claims to be a former resident and tells her about the horrific history of the property.

THE CREATURE (1987)—Five-minute film by the teenage Darren Perry, later co-director of the 2014 documentary *VHS Forever? Psychotronic People*. "A creature from another world invades a boy's room and he tries feeding it with a biscuit."

THE CREATURE PART II (1989)—Ten-minute sequel to *The Creature*.

THE CREATURE PART III: THE REVENGE (1989)– Ten-minute short, conclusion to Darren Perry's "Creature Trilogy."

CROSSROADS OF FEAR/AR GROESFFORDD OFN (1986)—Directed by Paul Turner. Running time is estimated around 40 minutes and it was made for Welsh Television. Ben Gibney, assistant director on the film: "It was shot in County Clare. The story concerned a middle-aged couple on holiday in Ireland whose caravan is assaulted by demonic forces. I never saw the finished product (and to be honest, never had much desire to)." Producer Richard Staniforth: "Sorry to be so blank but I was Cardiff-based for this shoot which took place on the West Coast of Ireland. It was very much a grab and handled by Paul Turner, who operated as the producer/director on the ground. As I say I was very tied up with the Emlyn Williams shoot *Par O Sgidiau*, which was a three-week road movie from Wales to Ireland with all sorts of problems. It was shot in Welsh for Teliesyn, a Cardiff-based production with the one-week shoot *Crossroads of Fear/Ar Groesffordd Ofn* built on at the end."

CRY WOLF! (1980)—Black-and-white spoof of werewolf lore with something of a 1950s/mad scientist vibe to it. Starring Paul Maxwell (as "Dr. Jack Russell"!), Stephen Greif and Rosalind Ayres, it was directed by Leszek Burzynski and played on UK cinema bills in 1980 supporting *Airplane!*

THE CURSE OF CORMAC (1980)—The first short film to be made by Julian Richards, later responsible for *Darklands* and *The Last Horror Movie*. Julian took two years to deliver this adaptation of a comic strip from the magazine *House of Hammer*, commencing the project at the age of just 13!

THE CURSE OF MEDUSA (1980)—Directed by Francis Williams. A comedy thriller in which a man finds himself the owner of the legendary Medusa's head, which turns all who gaze upon it to stone.

CURSE OF THE DEMON (1981)—Amateur short film entry for the BBC TV show *Screen Test*'s annual Young Filmmaker competition.

CURSED WOODS (1983)—Welsh amateur filmmaker Brian Davies made a string of horror shorts during the 1980s, under the anagrammatical "Videas Films" banner, releasing his work to the mail order VHS and DVD markets. *Cursed Woods* was his first solo venture into video production, a 20-minute short in which campers uncover evidence hidden by a murderer, and inevitably then find the psycho is on their trail.

DANCE MACABRE (1982)—Five-minute short by Sheila Graber. "A model/cut-out/cel/and live-action animation of the famous work by Saint-Saens. Portraying skeletons, ghouls, witches and the Devil Himself. The main character is a very friendly, violin playing little ghost who survives all terrors to play again another night"—*Animator Mag* archive.

DARK WATER (1980)—Gwyneth Strong and Phil Davis play a couple menaced in a swimming pool by a psychokiller during a clandestine nighttime dip. Scripted by Tony Grisoni (*Tideland*, *Red Riding*) and directed by Andrew Bogle.

DEAD END (1980)—Tracy Hyde starred in this "woman in peril in a deserted car park" 24-minute thriller directed by Alan Birkinshaw. Supported *Smokey and the Bandit II* in UK cinemas.

DEADHEAD (198?)—Amateur short directed by Justino Gaveleto. Ref: *In The Flesh* fanzine #5; "starts with a guy with a meathook in his face," progresses to show the gradual decay of the man and his head.

DEADLY CLEAVER (198?)—Geoff Woodbridge (director of 2018 feature *Some Girls Wander*) made this video horror item in the late 1980s. "The first Geoff Woodbridge film I ever saw was the (very) short *Deadly Cleaver*, a home video production reflecting his youthful Tom Savini fixation which comprised a simple gore effect and 'making of' footage"—John Martin

THE DEMON WITHIN (1982)—experienced Scottish amateur filmmaker Enrico Cocozza, active for several decades, was still at it in the early 80s. This 37-minute piece was shot in his flat, and has a young artist named Bruno "tormented by his two other selves, who manifest themselves as young boys"

DINOSAURS AND THINGS (1989)—Thirteen minutes of colourful stop-motion animated wonders from Jon Coley, shot in

'Jonamation and SuperJonamation'! Various dinosaurs, winged creatures, slithering things and bipedal behemoths attack and eat each other. And if you occasionally see the wires or the strings, that's all part of the charm. There's a flying saucer, a giant spider, and an out-of-time hippy (Coley himself?) thrown in for good measure! All filmed in stages between 1981-1989.

DO YOU BELIEVE IN FAIRIES? (1982)—David Van Day as a motocross rider who plots to steal from two little old ladies (Dora Bryan, Jean Anderson), unaware that their house is guarded by deadly fairies and killer gnomes. Scripted by Michael Armstrong and directed by Stanley Long, this short is best-known as one of the episodes in the *Screamtime* anthology feature, but has played as a stand-alone in its unedited 35-minute form.

DRACULA VS DEMON (1982)—Early work from prolific amateur Brian Davies, a 20-minute short directed in tandem with Tom Maylott. Couple walking in the woods find an ancient ring on the branch of a tree; the man puts it on, and ensuing events ultimately lead to the monster confrontation of the title.

DREAMHOUSE (1981)—Another of the trio of Stanley Long/Michael Armstrong shorts that later comprised the *Screamtime* compilation. This one sees a young couple move to a new house; the wife experiences gruesome visions, which turn out to be premonitions of forthcoming atrocities as the psychotic fiend from her nightmares shows up for real to threaten a fresh group of occupants. Featuring a memorable throat-slitting at the climax! This played on cinema bills as support to *The Exterminator* and *The Evil Dead*.

THE ERRAND (1980)—A wounded soldier on an outdoor maneuver is refused help by everyone he encounters along the way. Directed by Nigel Finch from a David McGillivray script, this half-hour short plays on contemporary Cold War fears and includes a particularly violent garrotting scene. Released as support to both *Happy Birthday to Me* and *Outland* during the early 1980s.

EVIL INSPIRATIONS (1981)—Early 1980s horror short directed by a teenage Julian Richards, later to achieve success with *Darklands* and *The Last Horror Movie*.

THE EXHUMATION (1986)—Another from Welsh amateur Brian Davies' mail order "Videas Films" crop. A recently unemployed man, depressed at losing his job, accidentally runs down and kills a khaki-clad pedestrian along a country lane. He buries the body in nearby woodland, only to later learn that his victim was carrying a substantial wad of cash. Deciding to dig up the corpse, he gets more than he bargained for.

THE FACE ON THE WALL (1986)—Directed by Roy Spence, based on a story by E.V. Lucas. In a gentlemen's club someone reminisces about the time when he was decorating and discovered a patch on the wall that was oily and would not take the paint. Gradually, it took on the dimensions of a human face ...

FEVER (1981)—Notorious entry in the amateur Young Filmmaker of the Year contest as part of the BBC children's television show Screen Test. Directed by Graham Edwards and Phil Tuppin, *Fever* featured a sick teenager lying in bed, unaware that his dressing gown has come to malevolent life and is crawling across the bedroom floor, clambering up to attempt to strangle the boy. Stephen Brotherstone and Dave Lawrence's excellent 2020 book, *Scarred for Life Volume Two: Television in the 1980s* (Lonely Water Books) includes extensive coverage on this infamous shocker, alongside details about several of the other Screen Test films (we've also mentioned a few more within this section of *Dead or Alive*.) *The Scarred For Life* readership were asked for their personal memories of the Young Filmmaker competition, adding information on half-recalled entries about a "creepy" top-hatted and caped figure in a mist-shrouded field, an invisible monster, a cemetery employee who keeps encountering a white hooded apparition that moves closer and closer with each visit, a child finding a gravestone with their own name etched into it, and an animated film about an old man driven to toppling from a high window when confronted by the eerie figure of a monk. The contest was held annually between 1973 and 1984, so it is unclear which, if any, of these films may have been made during the 1980s. Their titles may be lost in the ether.

The November 2, 1982 edition of Screen Test is on YouTube and features a Young Filmmaker entry called *Mr. Punch Beside the Sea* (a short documentary about a Yarmouth Punch & Judy show with a brief glimpse of a puppet ghost haunting Mr. Punch at the end); one of the comments beneath the clip, from a person naming themselves as "Blackpool Bootz," refers to another contest entry which they think was called "Damien," described as "very scarry (sic) at the time. Used special effects cutting film and moving chair across the room." Might this have been a scene from *Fever*?

THE GIRL WHO CRIED WOLF (1982)—Horror short filmed on Super 8 by 17-year-old Julian Richards, years before he became a professional director.

GOING TO MEET BECKY (1980)—From the age of 17, amateur filmmaker Jon Coley embarked on a series of strange shorts under the umbrella title *Other Realms*. He intended these for TV broadcast, but the quality of the work never rose above "enthusiastic home movie" level and the films remained largely unseen, until the East Anglian Film Archive and the British Film Institute made them available online. The *Other Realms* series included *Hand in Glove*, *The Fifth Minute*, *Feline Reincarnate* (all 1976); *The Cure* (1977), something of a precursor to *Creepshow*'s "Lonesome Death of Jordy Verrill" episode; *Going to Meet Becky* (1980); *Transcending Mirror Boundaries* (1981); *The Man on Platform One* (1983); and *Shadowman* (1994).

Going to Meet Becky was Coley's personal favorite, running 18 minutes (silent, with a soundtrack lifted from ambient albums by Brian Eno and Robert Fripp). A young man receives a letter from a childhood friend, imploring him to visit and recapture those golden summers they spent together as children. On arriving at her remote dwelling, he is confronted instead by some kind of insectoid alien being. Nicely shot on countryside locations and efficiently edited, though the slight story could have been told in a third of the time. Horror fans of a certain age will be pleased to catch a glimpse of the cover of a famous edition of *Radio*

Times from June 1980, featuring *Night of the Demon* (1957) and *The Ghoul* (1974) and heralding the start of that year's annual BBC2 *Horror Double Bill* season!

GOLEM (1989)—Five-minute claymation for Channel 4, an early work by Cheshire-based animator Mole Hill; "radical reinterpretation of the medieval European myth" (*Pacific Film Archive* notes, June 1989).

THE HALLOWE'EN PARTY (1983)—Amateur film shot on Super 8 by The Dover Film Society. "Comedy drama in which a rather tiresome practical joker at a Hallowe'en Party meets a violent end through the agency of Black Magic."

HEAR NO EVIL SEE NO EVIL (1980)—Guildford's amateur filmmaking society, Circle Eight, offered a tale of terror with this story about a nighttime intruder who calls upon a woman alone at home.

THE HITCH HIKER (1988)—"Home Made Films present" a spooky 10-minute short by amateur filmmaker Gordon Louch. Gordon may well have seen the 1975 amateur short by Gay Ashby, *The Girl from Green Willow*, as he employs a near-identical "urban myth" plot here. On his anniversary, a man gives a lift to a teenage girl who borrows his jacket and leaves her handbag in his car. On attempting to retrieve his garment and return the bag, he is informed that the girl died in a road accident exactly one year ago ...

HOLIDAY FOR THREE (1985)—A trio of lads in a holiday cottage dabble in a Ouija board session after returning from a night at the local pub. Directed by Clive Paton, and aka *Sting in the Tail*, it is one of the three shorts included in the jumbled anthology video release *Frightmares* (see main review.).

HORRID INTERMISSIONS (1980)—Horror short directed by Laurence Boulting and produced by Tim van Rellim.

HORRORSHOW (1987)—Five-minute short by Paul Hart-Wilden, intended as a showreel to display his filmmaking/special FX talents. This brief piece opens with a man attempting suicide by hammering nails into his head and applying an electrical charge, before another character experiences violent visions possibly induced by something nasty squirming in a bag on the table in his room. It won a fair bit of attention on the fan scene in the late 1980s and led Hart-Wilden to work on the likes of *Living Doll*, *Skinner*, and *Alone*. *Horrorshow* is available as an extra on the Mondo Macabro DVD of *Living Doll*.

THE HUNGRY GRASS (1981)—A narrated black-and-white 5-minute short from Northern Ireland, directed by Archie Reid. American visits ancestral Irish graveyard, finding it overgrown. Local myth has it that "hungry grass" sprouts where the bodies of famine sufferers lie—and the sentient plant-life is about to claim a victim, 10 years on.

INCIDENT AT ROMANS COURT (1989)—Thirty-four-minute short made by the Nottingham Video Group: A first production by this new group formed as an extension of Great British Movies (the Brothers Mackintosh: Roger, Neil and Howard.). Intended as a quickie and shot, edited and sound-tracked in eight weeks in early 1989, this comedy/drama is best described, the makers say, "as a cross between *Doctor Who* and *Ghostbusters*." It stars Howard and Neil as Marcus Bartelli and Sebastian Prothero, exorcists called in by Mr. McTaggart (Rex Mason) to rid his house of the evil spirits in the cellar. The film also features George Arme and Sharon Dawson. Described as "an enthusiastic production, splendidly lit and filmed ... with a well-recorded sound-track" (see **Appendix 1** for the full movie review).

IT CAME FROM ANOTHER WORLD (1984)—Directed by Rahul Sethi and Steve Weir, the amateur film was shot on Super 8 Kodachrome 40 and ran three minutes. Live action and model work, it is presented as a fake trailer for a giant monster movie.

KILLING TIME (1988)—Five-minute black-and-white item, directed by Ian Gamble (of Surrey), and smartly photographed in widescreen format. It tells of the demise of a young man who awakens from a dream in which a stabbing occurs during the screening of a psychedelic video. "Where does the dream stop and reality begin?" It was classified in an amateur film competition as "unsuitable for children."

THE KINVER INCIDENT (1983)—Amateur film shot on Super 8, directed by Ronald H. Smith. Competition notes: "A man lurking in a wood with a knife attempts to abduct one of two young children and is killed by their mother ... is a kind of horror story about a family picnic and a killing in the woods, lifted into the realms of semi-abstraction by perpetual use of an ultra-wide angle lens. I found it hypnotic and placed it fourth. Don Haworth placed it sixth and Alan Cleave seventh. The rest of the panel thought it more or less a pain on the eyeball." Ronald H. Smith's films (including terrorist bomb saga *Down Track* and the violent *Play Deadly*) were greatly appreciated by some but seemed to repeatedly aggravate panelists in competition because of his brutal, experimental and dark approach to telling apparently simple nihilistic tales.

LAST RESPECTS (1981)—Animated horror short running four minutes, directed by a then 14-year-old Mole Hill, and set at the funeral of a murdered gangster which "doesn't go according to plan."

THE LEGACY (1983)—Amateur one-man "horror shorts" factory Gordon Louch directed his own 17-minute version of the notorious "Black Panther" case. Teenage heiress is kidnapped and held for ransom by masked abductor; kept chained in an underground chamber, she is killed during a fightback attempt and her body is dumped in the river. The kidnapper collects an agreed sum of £50,000 but comes to a nasty end in an action-packed car chase finale, the only stray element in a piece that otherwise captures the grubbiness and mundanity of Donald Nielson's true-life crime.

THE LIFE OF PERCY (1982)—Thirty-seven-minute epic, in two parts, from prolific amateur filmmaker Gordon Louch.

Mental patient Percy Grillocks escapes and goes on a murder spree in search of pop star Alvin Shufflebottom, who killed his daughter in a car accident in 1979. Gory murders, and semi-comic characters including Alvin's manager Ray Ripoff (!), who has a poster for the 1981 British horror movie *The Appointment* tacked to the door of his office. Part Two (which seems to have been filmed separately at a later date during 1982) is less horror-orientated but has a lively Alvin vs. Percy fight scene and some nifty pitchfork-in-the-face action in the closing minutes. Not to mention Alvin's fabulous "Dennis The Menace/proto-Jesus & Mary Chain/Lieutenant Pigeon" mash-up appearance on *Top of the Pops*! Available on YouTube; Gordon's son Stuart was planning a follow-up called *The Return of Percy Grillocks!* for which a 2013 black-and-white trailer was filmed.

THE LIGHTBULB (1984)—Three-minute amateur short by Russell Smith. Two boys affected by the strange power of a red lightbulb are turned into unfeeling, unthinking zombie/automaton-like attackers.

LINDERIDGE 137 (1981)—Babysitter, pestered by mysterious telephone calls and spied on by stalker, is eventually revealed to have been murdered. East Midlands Arts-funded short that attempts to analyze the effects of the subjective camera and point of view in the contemporary slasher movie. Directed by Paul Denby. "An important essay on the codes of suspense in the horror and thriller genres"— *Monthly Film Bulletin*, February 1983 issue.

THE LOCH NESS MONSTER MOVIE (1984)—Eighteen-minute short directed by Ian Rintoul, sponsored by the Scottish Film Production Fund. A film using a blend of models, animation and live action to show the Loch Ness Monster's capture and ultimate escape from a cavalcade in Princes Street, Edinburgh. Production was by the Quinlan Film Group. Shotlist from the *Scottish Screen Archive* website: "The USA buys a portion of land in the Scottish Highlands, which includes Loch Ness. During a thunderstorm Nessie leaves the loch and is sighted on shore. The US argues in the United Nations that the monster belongs to them. Nessie is taken by truck to Edinburgh, but the truck crashes on the Forth Bridge and the monster escapes. She then terrorises Edinburgh, finally being buried in the rubble of a building she has knocked down. USA and UK restore relations. US helicopter then spots another Nessie."

THE MAGIC MAN (1984)—Award-winning 25-minute film by Roy Spence. A magician arrives at a small Irish community where graverobbers are attempting to discover the whereabouts of a deceased local's fortune. They accidentally kill the conjuror's partner/assistant and are lured into a lethal trap when the Magic Man convinces them he can converse with the dead ...

THE MAN ON PLATFORM ONE (1983)—Seventh of the eight *Other Realms* amateur shorts made by Jon Coley between 1976 and 1994. In this five-minute offering, a mysterious dark supernatural presence, "The Figure," visits a house at night and is seen at a railway bridge, seemingly connected with the death of a young woman on the tracks below.

MANIAC (1987)—Alcoholic, kleptomaniac telephone repair man turns hatchet-wielding nutcase after losing his job following a customer complaint. Nineteen-minute amateur item directed by the productive home movie horrormeister Gordon Louch. Gordon's budget-stretching ambition even extends to an impressive car stunt towards the end of this one.

THE MARK OF LILITH (1986)—Thirty-two-minute short made at the London College of Printing. Co-directed by Bruna Fionda, Polly Gladwin, and Isling Mack-Nataf. Lesbian filmmaker researching into the iconography of monstrous women becomes involved with a female vampire.

METEOR MADNESS (1980)—Vehicle for psychobilly band The Meteors; features Keith Allen as an ineffectual fancy-dress Devil who tries to disrupt a Meteors live gig. The band perform "Maniac Rockers from Hell" and several other numbers. Released as support to *Dance Craze* in 1981 and *Richard Pryor Live in Concert* in 1982.

THE MONKEY'S PAW (1984)—A 20-minute retelling of the classic W.W. Jacobs story, directed by Andrew Barker.

MONSTER (1983)—A short film directed by Alan Atkinson for the Rochdale Cine Club, a spoof documentary about the scientific investigation of the mysterious monster thought to lurk in a Northern lake.

NECRONOMICON, BOOK OF THE DEAD (1984)—A 10-minute amateur "zombies in the woods" affair, the first step into filmmaking for Chris Jones, later to make *White Angel* and *Urban Ghost Story*.

NIGHT FLIGHT (1983)—Amateur film shot on Super 8, directed by James Waugh. "Surrealist drama in which a young man kills two of the women in his life and meets his own end at the hand of the third."

NIGHTMARE (1986)—Directed by Warwick Davis, with a running time of 13 minutes. A miniature Mummy's Hand discovered in Egypt; nasty things happen when it is around. This won three top prizes at the 1986 Surrey Film Festival. "Scary, and full of exciting imagery with skilful technical trickery and a good use of Courtland Stibbe's locations." Warwick was already a professional film actor by this stage, playing Wicket the Ewok in *Return of the Jedi* and, later, the title role in *Willow*. Warwick immediately followed *Nightmare* with the short *Video Nasty*.

NIGHTSHADE (1983)—(presumed short). Directed by Tim Walter for Bournemouth and Poole College of Art and Design, it tells the myth of Leanan-sidhe, at once the muse of poets and a bloodsucking vampire.

OUT OF TOWN (1987)—Short directed by Norman Hull for Amber Valley Productions. Man gets foot stuck in a hole, passers-by won't help him. The traveler begins to exclaim that something underground is biting him—finally the earth beneath him opens up and he meets his grim fate. Starring David Morrissey.

THE PLEDGE (1981)—Hanged highwayman's rotting corpse must be cut down from the gibbet by his criminal cohorts and placed in the tomb of an archbishop, to save his soul. Impressive and grisly period piece directed by Digby Rumsey. Shown as a supporting short on the UK cinema circuit, including screenings alongside smash hit American comedy *Porky's*.

POSSESSIONS (1980)—Directed by Andrew Bogle, this BAFTA award-nominated tale of a haunted wardrobe was released to the UK cinema circuit supporting the remake of *The Postman Always Rings Twice*.

PSYCHO B (1984)—(presumed short). Directed by Nick Hunt and made for the Colchester Film Workshop, a part reproduction of the *Psycho* shower scene.

REFLECTIONS (1983)—Amateur film shot on Super 8, directed by David Felber. "Drama involving a medium, a group of young people and an assortment of sudden and violent deaths."

RETRIBUTION (1981)—Horror short directed by Gregory Dark (assistant director on *The Appointment* and the 1989 *Ten Little Indians*) which played with *Friday the 13th Part 3* on its cinema release in the UK. One scene features a murder played out in silhouette against a whitewashed wall, with a shock cut to a large fruit or vegetable being chopped on a kitchen table.

ROBOT GORILLA RAMPAGE (1989)—Amateur short directed by Jan Manthey. "Professor Bart creates a creature that is half robot and half gorilla. Naturally it grows to enormous size and goes on the rampage, etc, etc." Starring Jed Leicester, Helen Dilloway, Vic Pratt, Mark Duqueno, Jonathan Cockerell and Simon Zarywacz.

THE ROCKING HORSE WINNER (1982)—Adaptation of the D.H. Lawrence story about a rocking horse that seems to assist its rider to select the victors of forthcoming track races—with disturbing consequences.

SASQUATCH (c.1980)—Shot on Super 8 in color and presumed a short subject. An amateur film by the Frome and District Cine Club starring Ted Davies and Harry Truscott; no story details are available but there is an image of the stars just before the "monster strikes" on the Frome Film and Video Makers website archive.

SHOCK ENDING (1987)—More from Brian Davies' amateur "Videas Films" operation. Suburban murder is accidentally recorded on to a videotape, which falls into the hands of some friends of the suspected killer.

THE SHRIEK (1987)—Directed by Michael Attree. Possibly *Suspiria*-influenced? Withdrawn ballet tutor spies on his students from a distance, as he plans to prepare a "final hellish meal" to set before a Satanic idol kept hidden away in a secret room.

SON OF NORTHESCUE (1985)—"The Rochester Cine Club—a group of friendly people very interested in making films and acting—has just completed its first production, *Son of Northescue*. It was shot on Super 8 with stereo sound, and I must admit, it's rather better than my original effort. In the future, we hope to make films on standard 8 and VHS video"—L.T. Mannering, in a letter to the amateur filmmaking magazine *Movie Maker* of July 1985; the film is a sequel to a 1971 amateur vampire short called *Northescue*.

SPECIMENS (1983)—Giant robot controlled by aliens menaces a Stone Age caveman before being buried during a volcanic eruption; freed centuries later by excavation work, the mechanical monstrosity continues its quest by pursuing a pair of teenage rock'n'rollers in the 1950s. Ambitious 15-minute short by prolific Northern Irish amateur filmmaker Roy Spence.

SREDNI VASHTAR (1981)—Based on the Saki story. Young boy is persecuted by an aunt who kills his pet hen; she herself is killed in the potting shed by the boy's ferret. "Invocation to Sredni Vashtar is a shade too desperate, and the use of *'Carmina Burana'* to conjure up a primaeval force does not quite match Saki's tone."—*Monthly Film Bulletin* (September 1982).

SREDNI VASHTAR (1982)—Animated short adaptation of the Saki horror story directed by Liz Spencer (not to be confused with the Andrew Birkin film from around the same time), made while at the Hull College of Higher Education with support from the Greater London Arts Association.

SREDNI VASHTAR (1986) – another version of the Saki story, produced by Ashish Kotak and directed by Nelson Ferreira. A prize-winner in the BBC's Showcase 86 short film competition for filmmakers aged under 25.

STREET OF CROCODILES (1986)—Nightmarish animated vision from the imagination of The Brothers Quay, featuring creepy puppets and dolls, decaying cogs and machinery, etc.

A TALE OF GOTHIC HORROR (1981)—A student animation project employing tropes of the genre, directed by James Heyworth while at Goldsmiths College where he was studying Design and Applied Arts.

THE TELL-TALE HEART (1983)—Short based on the Poe story, directed by Ian Powell. Ian made "a video version as my first proper project in 1983 as part of my drama degree (shot using multi camera TV studio methods)."

Ian added:

> The project, about 20 minutes long, consisted of the narrator reading the tale in the first person with matching images and sound effects. It probably resembled something like a BBC *Supernatural* episode. It was shot on a small studio living room and bedroom set, with three actors playing 'narrator,' 'old man,' and 'police inspector,' featuring a lot of Sergio Leone-style close-ups of the character's faces, low and high angle shots as the narrator descends into madness, only to find his own image trapped under the floorboards when they are ripped up at the end. Somewhere I have a VHS

taken from the Beta cam master, which was enough to get me an interview for the National Film School directing course in 1983. I believe the lead actor was Michael Gorton. It was shot at Aberystwyth University as my directing project for a drama degree.

My biggest contribution to 1980s horror was a nearly produced feature film called *Changer*, written with SFX master Cliff Wallace, which was a mash up of *Pet Sematary*, *Altered States* and *The Emerald Forest*, set in a Gothic mansion in Canada. The director was Bob Keen, but the film got canned when he had to do the effects on *Nightbreed*. I have storyboards and production drawings, but they are not by me, so I don't have the rights to use them. It was a $5 million spectacular with lots of shape shifting special effects. I did a *Fangoria* article on it, but after two years in pre-production and about eight script drafts it finally died.

THAT'S THE WAY TO DO IT (1982)—Robin Bailey stars as a psychotic Punch & Judy man in this excellent short directed by Stanley Long, from a Michael Armstrong screenplay. Aka *Killer Punch* and released as a stand-alone and as part of the anthology feature *Screamtime*.

THE THIRD DAY (1983)—8mm amateur horror short by James Heginbotham, an entry in the annual Young Film Maker's competition for the BBC TV show *Screen Test*.

THIS UNNAMEABLE LITTLE BROOM (1985)—Eleven-minute animated marvel from The Brothers Quay. Set amid the boxed-in world inhabited by the grotesque Gilgamesh, the film uses various textures and materials including hooks, meat, dandelion fluff, decaying insects, and animal bones to create its unique universe, in which the main character sets out to ensnare Endiku, a wild man who appears to reside in a forest some way beyond the confines of Gilgamesh's environment.

THE THREE KNIGHTS (1982)—Comic 15-minute animation directed by Mark Baker. Trio of misguided knights, witch, giant, decapitations, transformations, three-headed monster all appear.

TRANSCENDING MIRROR BOUNDARIES (1981)—Sixth of the eight *Other Realms* amateur shorts directed by Jon Coley. A man is tracked down and shot dead by his twin.

TWISTED MIND (1986)—Twenty-minute amateur horror thriller directed by Gordon Louch. Wild-haired, hospitalized mental patient stabs a nurse and goes on the run, claiming further victims as he seeks the woman who ran him down in her car several months earlier.

UNHAPPY RETURNS (1982)—Thirteen-minute amateur horror short directed by Gordon Louch. Opportunist thief steals woman's handbag, containing the house keys of the absent neighbor whose cats she has agreed to feed. Upon using the keys to gain entry to the property, the burglar finds a hungry household of devious moggies …

THE VACANCY (1985)—Murder and mayhem among the aisles of a supermarket in this amateur offering from Brian Davies' "Videas Films."

VAMPIRE (1983)—More from the crazy world of amateur horror dabbler Gordon Louch, in this 21-minute comedy. Boghampton scientist and surgeon Professor Ponsonby Nutt uncovers a severed hand while metal-detecting in Transylvania; back home, he experiments on his arm in his lab but pricks himself and spills blood, causing the hand to come to life and attack him. Later, as he presides over an operation to transplant a chimpanzee's heart into a patient, Ponsonby turns into a bat, becoming a vampire who terrorizes the local woods before being staked by his undertaker friend. It was all a dream …

VAMPYR (1981)—Man reading Bram Stoker's *Dracula* sees the book fly from his grasp and flap through the air like a bat; another scene sees him on all fours, the camera tilting to give him the aspect of Count Dracula crawling up a castle wall. Not surprisingly, this vampire-themed comedy won a UK cinema circuit billing supporting Tony Scott's *The Hunger* in 1983.

VICTIMS (1985)—More serious than usual offering from amateur director Gordon Louch—20-minute short about stalker/killer upon whom the tables are turned. But is the woman who ends his activities telling the truth about herself?

VIDEO NASTY (1988)—Warwick Davis' follow-up to 1986's *Nightmare*, another amateur horror movie shot on video. The film is only three minutes long and involves a killer videotape recorder. In 2012 he screened the film to year eight and nine pupils at Sir Harry Smith Community College in Peterborough. A copy is held by the Institute of Amateur Cinematographers.

WATCH THE SPARROW BLEED (1989)—Eyeball-slicing, skull-stabbing, neck-sawing, decapitated head set ablaze, and that's just the opening scene of this enthusiastic 22-minute amateur gorefest directed by Sean Reynard.

WEREWOLF (1982)—Fun 21-minute amateur remake of *An American Werewolf in London* directed by Gordon Louch. Twenty-seven-year-old man goes to Boghampton (near Cesspool-on-Sea) to seek his father who disappeared there in 1955. Includes low-rent imitations of the Landis movie's nightmare-within-nightmare, the call home from a telephone kiosk, the warning from the dead victims, and the initial attack by a werewolf following a visit to a hostile hostelry. A transformation scene is rather more "Don Post" than "Rick Baker," although we do get a 1940s-style dissolve as wolf hair creeps over the hand of the changing unfortunate.

WHERE THE WOODBINE TWINETH (1984)—Directed by Keith Pollard for Five Arches Films of Skidby, North Humberside. Shot on 16mm Eastman Color Negative on a Bolex H16, the running time is 20 minutes. It is a costume mystery about a little girl (Elizabeth Sadler) who lives in an old house alone but for her severe Great Aunt Nell. When the girl starts talking to a doll it is as if the plaything were a real person. Sub-

This book is probably a worthwhile investment for short filmmakers, or filmmakers' of shorts should we say

sequent events, however, suggest that the fantasy has been made flesh. The final twist can actually be foreseen a minute or so in advance, though this tends to increase rather than diminish the suspense. The story was previously filmed for *The Alfred Hitchcock Hour* in 1965 and that version can be viewed on YouTube. Here the story is relocated to Edwardian England.

WINGS OF DEATH (1985)—Dexter Fletcher starred in this 20-minute short directed by Nichola Bruce and Michael Coulson, which went out as support to *A Nightmare on Elm Street* on its initial UK release. From michaelcoulson.threehumansinc.com—"In the revolting Byzantium Hotel, young heroin addict Alex relives an idyllic past before slipping into a much more terrifying world. A sinister little girl wanders the corridors, cutting open her doll "to see what's inside," while winos and junkies prowl as flesh-eating zombies ..."

YOU KNOW ME (1989)—Filmed in color with a running time of nine minutes and 19 seconds, catalogue no. 6059 in the North West Film Archive. Drama produced by Stockport Cine and Video Society, featuring members of the Woodford Players. Two women, Susan and Julie, agree to meet up, despite warnings on the radio of an escaped prisoner known as "The Strangler" being on the loose. En route, Julie's car runs out of fuel and she continues on foot, encountering a jogger and then a flasher on the way. After meeting her friend and going to the cinema, the two women return to the car with some petrol. On arrival back at home, Julie thinks she's safe, only be attacked by "The Strangler" as she enters the house.

ZOMBIE DEATHRAY (1989)—Shot on Super 8 in color and running 19 minutes, one of a number of films made circa 1990 by Richard "Rocco" Hele. Richard: "Starring Chris Krzywinski (aka Crispin Link—Chris used this pseudonym in homage to 'Cash Flagg'/Ray Dennis Steckler, we were very inspired by the sort of films covered in Jonathan Ross' *Incredibly Strange Films* TV show at the time, also Chris' acting hero was Crispin Glover), Davina Flood, Mike Sivia, Darren Thomas as Tex Rambler, Mick Elson (now a producer, recently co-executive producer of *Dredd*), Cary Dawes, Jovan Larenty (director of a Cradle of Filth video.) This film was supposed to reflect my life at the time and how it made me feel like a zombie. Stick with it for the sci-fi/horror elements. This film was screened at the London Filmmaker's Co-op." Richard was good enough to supply a number of other films that he had made with friends at Bulmershe College in Reading where they were studying film and drama or modern European literature. The other titles, *House of Strangers* (1990), *Crab Killers* (1990), *Mucus Murders* (1990) and the surviving footage of *Fiends* (1991) fall just outside our 1980s timeframe, although Richard also mentions an annual series of surreal "bees" movies. *Zombie Deathray* does not take itself particularly seriously and is quite random with ordinary lives collapsing either because of, or nothing to do with, objects falling from space. Following a car crash caused by lights from one of the objects, the surviving passenger goes on a zombie rampage.

APPENDIX 5: PROBLEM/PERIPHERAL TITLES

A brief round-up of additional titles that connect to the 1980s British horror scene while perhaps only qualifying for fringe status, due to minimal genre content, vague UK connectivity, episodic rather than "feature" format, etc.

ABSOLUTION (1978)—Anthony Shaffer-scripted tale of murder and deception in a Catholic boys' school, starring Richard Burton and Billy Connolly. Released to UK cinemas in 1981 after several years on the shelf.

THE ADVENTURES OF BARON MUNCHAUSEN (1989)—Wild Terry Gilliam-directed fantasy. Sea monster; figure of Death.

AFTER DARKNESS (1985)—Low-key horror drama starring John Hurt and Julian Sands. Filmed in Switzerland and appears to be a Swiss production but has been cited as British by some sources.

AFTER PILKINGTON (1986)—BBC *Screen Two* psychological/social drama; Miranda Richardson shifts from light comedy-of-manners into scissors-wielding attack mode.

ALICE (1988)—Czech genius Jan Svankmajer's amazing animated journey into the world of Lewis Carroll, with startling dream/nightmare images galore. Swiss/German/UK production co-funded by Channel 4.

AMAZONIA: THE CATHERINE MILES STORY (1985)—Italian jungle cannibal fare; includes London location work with shots of Trafalgar Square.

ATTACK OF THE SAUCER PEOPLE (1981)—Short science-fiction comedy by Roy Spence. Amateur filmmaker working on a UFO movie spies a genuine otherworldly craft in the skies above, and is abducted by its mean-looking occupants.

AXEL (1988)—Five-minute erotic fantasy short directed by Nigel Wingrove of Redemption Films. Angel of Death appears at the end.

BAD MANOR (1989)—little-seen short directed by Alex Chandon. Horror?

BAD TIMING (1980)—Described by the movie's own distributor Rank as "a sick film made by sick people for sick people," this typically "difficult" drama continued director Nicolas Roeg's string of riveting psychological studies. Art Garfunkel and Theresa Russell play out a sadistic, sensual, obsessive relationship seemingly leading to attempted suicide—or perhaps something more sinister?

BATMAN (1989)—Warner Bros. revival of the DC Comics' dark vigilante superhero brought this semi-forgotten character back into public consciousness, with a resulting franchise enjoying box-office success and paving the way for the later "Dark Knight" trilogy, animated series and movies. Batman graduated to a pivotal place in the so-called "shared universe" of inter-related DC Comics-based films, and was even granted a cinematic Lego incarnation. This and the immediate sequel *Batman Returns* remain high points for Bruce Wayne and his alter ego. However as helmed by Tim Burton, a true Gothic sensibility harking back to horror pictures of the 1920s and 1930s appears. A US production filmed at Pinewood utilizies several English locations.

BEHIND THE CATARACT (1987)—directed by Daniel Cannon, who (as Danny Cannon) went on to make mainstream hits *The Young Americans* and *Judge Dredd* in the 1990s. Cannon's amateur film *Sometimes* was a prize-winner in the BBC's Showcase 86 film competition; during the following year's Showcase 87 contest broadcasts, presenter Sue Robbie mentioned that "since then, he's made a full-length feature horror video, *Behind*

The Cataract," holding aloft a boxed copy of the VHS tape. Presumably few copies of this were produced, with no known official release; and its genre status is unconfirmed beyond these comments. Angela Heath-Larsen is known to have played the role of "Sister" in the production. Research ongoing on this one.

THE BELLS OF ASTERCOTE (1980)—Fifty-two-minute BBC TV production, a single drama aimed at a juvenile audience. Disappearance of a golden chalice (an ancient protector in similar vein to the Crowns from M.R. James' *A Warning to the Curious*) leads a small village community to believe that the Black Death is returning after hundreds of years, with psychosomatic cases breaking out, townies-vs-countrysiders conflict, one girl experiencing visions of the plague wiping out the local populace centuries ago, etc.

THE BLACK CAULDRON (1985)—Disney's infamous dark fantasy animated flop; based on the mythic Welsh *Chronicles of Prydain* novels by Lloyd Alexander. Reportedly, the Llechwedd slate caverns were filmed for use as a backdrop setting. Nigel Hawthorne, Freddie Jones and John Hurt provide voices.

THE BOYS IN BLUE (1983)—Remake of *Ask a Policeman*, directed by Val Guest, updated as a vehicle for comedy duo Cannon & Ball. The "headless horseman" of the original is referred to but replaced here by a fake "UFO"; dialogue reference to *Invasion of the Body Snatchers*. Footnote—the film's casting director was Valerie van Ost, memorable as a vampire in Hammer's *The Satanic Rites of Dracula* 10 years earlier.

BRADY'S BARGAIN (1983)—Short fantasy spoof (22 minutes) by noted Irish movie buffs/amateur filmmakers Roy & Noel Spence. "When greedy villager Brady captures a leprechaun in the hills, he clinches a bargain that can only lead to his own downfall"—Northern Ireland Screen Digital Film Archive. Features a rather spectacular banshee in an early scene prior to the main gold-seeking plotline.

BROTHERS AND SISTERS (1980)—Social drama directed by Richard Woolley, filmed in Leeds at the time of the "Yorkshire Ripper" investigation, and lacing events leading to the murder of a prostitute into its inspection of the British class system.

BULLSHOT (1985)—Bulldog Drummond spoof; includes a giant octopus and killer spider.

THE CABINET OF JAN SVANKMAJER (1984)—The Brothers Quay pay disturbing homage to the master Czech animator, as only they can.

CAMERON'S CLOSET (1989)—American-based monster fare directed by Armand Mastroianni. Listed as a US/UK production on the Internet Movie Database. Production company is UK-connected Smart Egg Pictures.

CARNAGE (1983)—US production directed by Andy Milligan. Possibly produced by our own Michael Lee, head of the Vipco video label. (Ref: Gavin Whitaker)

A CHRISTMAS CAROL (1980)—Fifty-five-minute TV version of the Dickens classic, made by HTV Wales and starring Sir Geraint Evans.

A CHRISTMAS CAROL (1982)—One-hundred and nine-minute opera based on the Dickens story, a UK/US co-production for Granada TV.

A CHRISTMAS CAROL (1984)—US version with George C. Scott, shot in England with strong British supporting cast.

CHRISTMAS SPIRITS (1981)—TV ghost story starring Elaine Stritch. Spooky tale of a Hollywood location scout seeking a house to be used in a horror movie and getting more than she originally bargained for ...

CRITTERS (1986)—American horror film with furry, toothy creatures invading a small town. Involvement from London-based Smart Egg Pictures.

THE DARK CRYSTAL (1982)—Jim Henson fantasy film shot in the UK, packed with bizarre creatures.

DARK ENEMY (1984)—Children's Film Unit production with "post-nuclear savagery" plot familiar to fans of Corman's *Teenage Caveman*.

DARKNESS FROM THE TREES (1981)—Twenty-two-minute short directed by Matthew Jacobs (scripter of *Paperhouse* and the 1996 *Doctor Who* TV movie), who himself describes it as "pretentious." Cast: John Rees (Old Man), David Barham (Golden Boy). A blind piano tuner lives alone until his routine is broken by a series of supernatural occurrences that lead him into a dream-like death.

THE DAY OF THE TRIFFIDS (1981)—Six-part BBC television series adapting the classic John Wyndham novel. Starring John Duttine.

DEAD END (1987)—Robbery and child kidnap feature in this over-complicated amateur short from Gordon Louch. One of the director's rare non-horror projects; a character does briefly appear in a werewolf mask, familiar from some of Gordon's other works!

DEATH FACES (1988)—Mondo-style video, said to be a UK production, directed by Countess Victoria Bloodhart and Steve White, and narrated by one Prof. Bizarro Blackstone! Features footage of the Kennedy assassination, Dillinger, Bonnie & Clyde, Hitler, plus cannibalism, car crashes, etc.

THE DECEIVERS (1988)—Pierce Brosnan infiltrates the murderous 19th century Indian Thugee cult to expose their evil. Period adventure thriller produced by Ismail Merchant.

DEPTFORD WIVES (1984)—Twenty-minute short by the Bethnal Green Women's Film Collective, seemingly riffing on *The Stepford Wives*. Dystopian tale of a world where women are forced to stay at home under constant surveillance and plan to rebel.

DIVERSION (1980)—Starring Cherie Lunghi and Stephen Moore, this supporting featurette was written and directed by James Dearden, who later expanded the idea for his smash-hit *Fatal Attraction* screenplay.

DOCTEUR JEKYLL ET LES FEMMES (1981)—Walerian Borowczyk's stunning arthouse shocker—a French/German production but set (and shot?) in London.

DOOMBEACH (1989)—Children's Film Unit production. Boy dies after swimming at a coastal resort—has the tragedy resulted from nuclear pollution leaking into the sea?

DOUBLE PIQUET (1980)— Short directed by Robert Wynne-Simmons. His website describes the plot outline thus: "A tourist at an Irish country house finds himself transported back in time to the scene of a cold-blooded murder at the card table."

THE DRUMLIN (1980)—Eighteen-minute amateur SF short from Northern Ireland, directed by Roy Spence. Giant robot (a là *The Colossus of New York*); UFO sightings; entire child population of the "Nilemah Estate" go missing; aliens demand that plans for a proposed nuclear plant should be abandoned.

EAT THE RICH (1987)—*Comic Strip* team's second theatrical venture, black comedy. Cannibalism at restaurant.

THE ELEPHANT MAN (1980)—Directed by David Lynch, starring John Hurt in his acclaimed performance as monstrously deformed real-life Victorian curiosity John Merrick.

THE EMERALD FOREST (1985)— John Boorman-directed, would be arty/highbrow jungle adventure movie; its pretensions (and its critical reception) went some way to disguising its clear lineage from the string of Italian cannibal shockers of the 1970s and early 1980s, of which it occasionally seems reminiscent in an upmarket, palatable way.

ERIK THE VIKING (1989)—Nordic fantasy involving members of the *Monty Python* team. Sea monster.

EUREKA (1983)—Stunning opening sequence of this Nicolas Roeg film plays like a Poe tale, as a gold prospector hits it rich but his wife's life-force seems to be drained away at the moment of his lucky strike (both *The BFI Companion To Horror* and the *Monthly Film Bulletin* allude to Poe in reference to the movie.). Voodoo and extreme violence also feature in one of Roeg's most demanding, controversial, and brilliant movies.

THE EXERCISE (1985)—BBC *Play For Today*, starring Ian Hart. Military cadets on a training exercise in the Welsh hills find events taking a sinister turn.

THE EXPERIMENT (1979/80)—Unfinished (?) creature feature directed by Robert Wynne-Simmons, shot on one-inch videotape. Appears to have had an obscure, unconfirmed 1981 video release in a 58-minute version. 1979 novel by John Urling Clark and Robin Beresford Evans, published by Sphere, states, "Now a nerve-twisting shock movie" on its cover and provides tantalizing further details: "The Video Film Partnership in association with Amaranth ... starring Vivien Wolf as the doctor, Helen Gill as the wife, Richard Marner as the Nazi Scientist." Research ongoing on this one ...

THE FALLS (1980)—Peter Greenaway's three-hour-plus feature debut, made up of 92 short sections each detailing the lives of different victims of the VUE (Violent Unknown Event), which has killed much of the population and left some survivors becoming obsessed with birds or even mutating into them.

FAUST (1980)—Eighty-minute version of the Faust legend, based on Triple Theatre Action's long-running touring stage production. Directed by Steven Rumbelow, starring Brian Abbott and Monica Buford.

FEVERHOUSE (1985)—Fifty-minute experimental film set in a gloomy old hospital, with nurses murdering and neglecting patients. Directed by Howard Walmsley of the band Biting Tongues, who contributed the soundtrack.

FIRST TRANSMISSION (1982)—Controversial 4-hour compilation video release by "Thee Temple Ov Psychick Youth" (including members of uncompromising industrial music legends Throbbing Gristle); includes disturbing rituals, Satanism, castration, cult leader Jim Jones, etc.

FLASH GORDON (1980)—Sam J. Jones stars as the legendary interplanetary hero. Directed by Mike Hodges.

FORBIDDEN SUN (1989)—Greek-set thriller co-written by Robin Hardy, typically mixing his usual concerns, sex, violence, and ancient rituals. Aka *Bulldance*.

FRANKENSTEIN'S GREAT AUNT TILLIE (1983)—Donald Pleasence, Yvonne Furneaux, and Aldo Ray star in this poor Mexican horror-comedy set in Mucklefugger, Transylvania. Some sources claim British production involvement.

THE FRUIT MACHINE (1988)—Comic thriller with fantasy touches, set in and around a gay community. Psycho character.

THE GHOST DOWNSTAIRS (1982)—Hour-long Faustian drama directed by Andrew Gosling for B.BC.2, starring Cyril Cusack. Based on the novel by Leon Garfield.

GHOST IN THE WATER (1982)—Two youngsters seek information about the life and death of a long-deceased girl named Abigail Parkes, leading to one of them almost becoming possessed by Abigail's spirit. Fifty-five-minute production for BBC television, based on Edward Chitham's novel.

THE GHOST SONATA (1980)—Donald Pleasence stars in Philip Saville's feature-length version of the August Strindberg dark fantasy, made for the BBC.

GHOST STORIES (1983)—Directed by Nick Hamlyn. Experimental (short?) film, dark interiors, ghost stories told.

GHOST STORIES FROM THE PICKWICK PAPERS (1987)—The spooky side of Charles Dickens' tales is the focus of this animated production, made in Dublin.

GOVAN GHOST STORY (1989)—Hour-long drama for BBC Scotland. Unemployed docker's memories of his upbringing and working life are stirred by the ghost of a battered child.

GREEN-EYED MONSTER (1989)—One-off ITV drama aimed at a children's audience. Young girl's jealousy manifests itself as an evil power, signified by her glowing green eyes. She even sets the family home ablaze; at the end, the new baby is revealed to also have glowing green eyes, hinting at a future propensity for similar mayhem to come.

HANNIBAL THE CANNIBAL (1982)—Amateur short film entry for the BBC TV show *Screen Test*'s annual Young Filmmaker competition.

THE HAUNTING OF M (1980)—Elegant, subtle ghost story, set and filmed in Scotland. US production directed by Anna Thomas.

THE HAUNTING PASSION (1983)—Canadian TV movie starring Jane Seymour as a young wife who begins an affair with a ghost. ITC Entertainment are named as one of the production companies.

HELLCATS: MUD WRESTLING (1983)—Sexploitation featurette in which female mud-wrestlers appear. Top billed is an American lady grappler known as "Queen Kong"; one of the wrestlers appears briefly in a vampire costume.

HIGHLANDER (1986)—Directed by Russell Mulcahy. "Immortals," warriors battling throughout the centuries; decapitations.

THE HOUND OF THE BASKERVILLES (1988)—Feature-length episode of Granada TV's celebrated *The Return of Sherlock Holmes* series, starring Jeremy Brett.

INCIDENTS IN AN EXPANDING UNIVERSE (1985)—Shot on Super 8, this 45-minute film is an early work by Richard Stanley, which the director has stated is set in the same universe as his later feature *Hardware*. The story takes place in a totali-

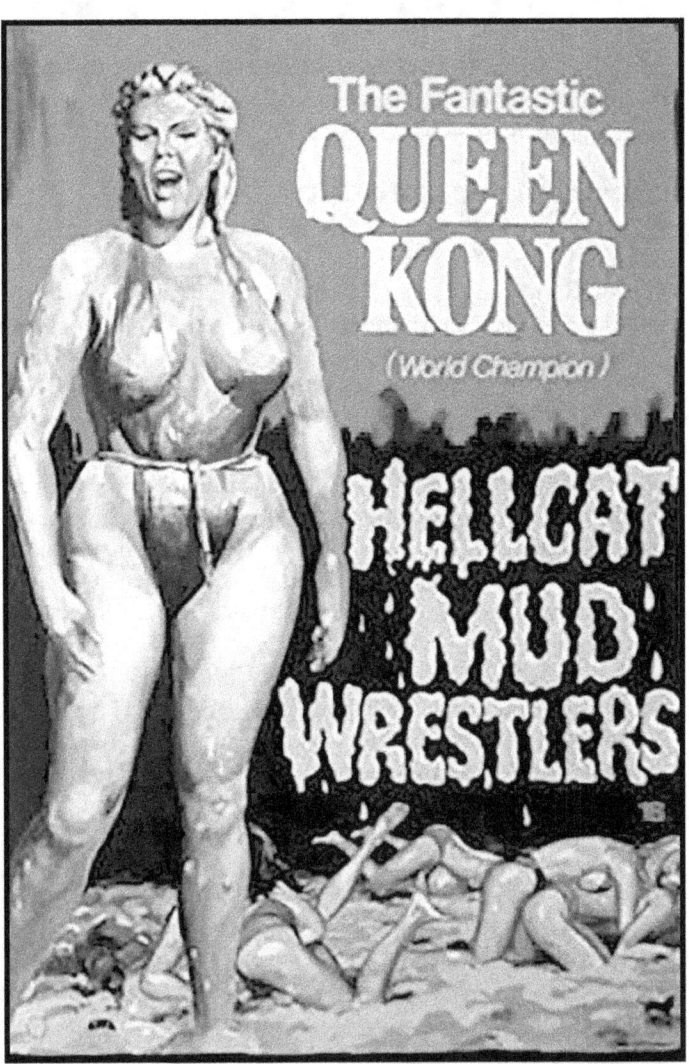

tarian 2037 where a soldier and a sculptress attempt to survive and form a relationship, against a backdrop of raging war and nuclear fallout.

INDIANA JONES AND THE TEMPLE OF DOOM (1984)—Second of the Spielberg/Lucas "Indiana Jones" series, US production filmed at Elstree Studios. Sacrificial thugee cult; gory removal of victim's heart; voodoo; snapping crocodiles; consumption of "chilled monkey brains" a là *Faces of Death*.

INN OF THE FLYING DRAGON (1981)—Swedish/Irish vampire film based on a Le Fanu story, from the makers of *Victor Frankenstein*.

INVASION UFO (1980)—Episodes from Gerry Anderson's live action TV series from the 1970s were later compiled into this rather confusing feature edit.

IT COULDN'T HAPPEN HERE (1987)—Movie starring pop duo the Pet Shop Boys; Joss Ackland appears as a priest and as an insane killer.

IT'S AN ILL WIND (1983)—Amateur film shot on Super 8, made by the Albany Cine Club. "Black comedy in which all the principal characters meet sudden and violent ends—the only one to benefit being the local undertaker."

JAMES BONK IN MATT BLACKFINGER (1988)—Short film made for Channel 4 by Akiko Hada, a James Bond spoof using toys, including Godzilla, in the role of Agent 0017.

THE JEALOUS MIRROR (1982)—Directed by Astrid Frank, and if you think her much sought-after *Red* (1976) is difficult to see ... Mark Wynter was in both films and reports that lighting cameraman, Robert Krasker, was also shared with the earlier production. It was classified a short film ("so less than 40 minutes") but "to my knowledge it was not released, certainly not in the UK—oh, the plot concern was me as suitor to Glynis Barber. I arrive at her flat with champagne. In opening it the cork pings on to the glass of her tall dressing mirror. Several large cracks appear in the mirror. She tapes them up. On subsequent visits my shape and face is horribly distorted, and my suit appears far too large on my frame. Hence the mirror proves to be jealous of its owner's liaison. I have no positive recall of the outcome, but I vaguely remember the mirror causes me to go slightly bonkers. But I lived to tell the tale and here I am telling it. And I end the relationship. Who wouldn't? At the time of filming I was in *Charley's Aunt* at The Adelphi and appearing in a late-night Rodgers and Hart cabaret review with Dylis Watling at Quaglino's. No wonder I was going bonkers!" Roger, over and out. Marco!

JOHNNY AND THE DEVIL (1988)—Claymation fantasy short directed by Alison Pook.

KEN AND THE LOCH NESS MONSTER (1983)—Amateur short film entry for the BBC TV show *Screen Test*'s annual Young Filmmaker competition.

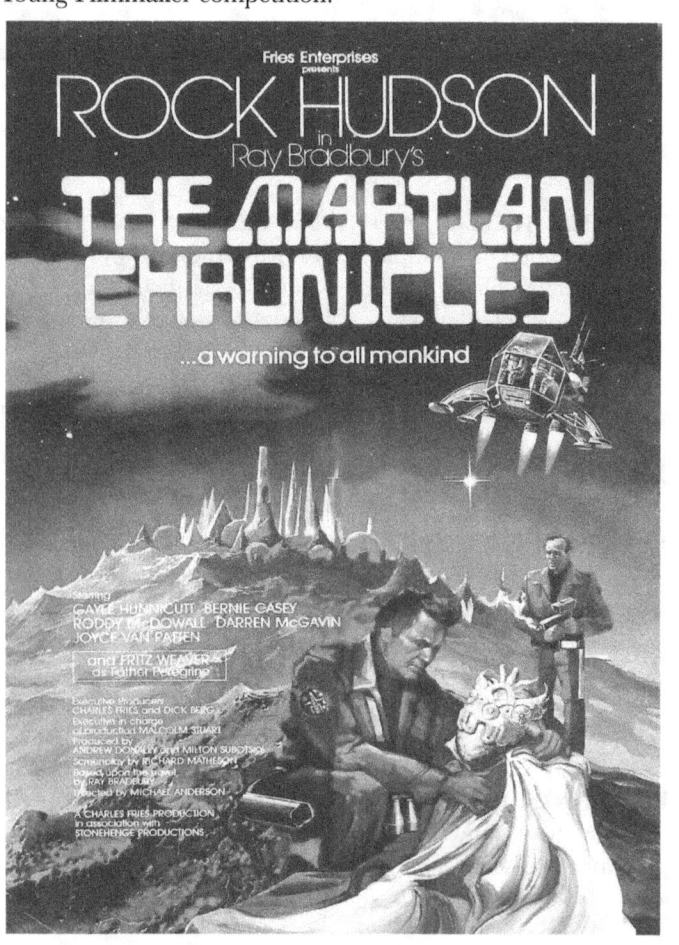

KNIGHTS ELECTRIC (1980)—Twenty-four-minute short directed by Barney Broom, played with *Brimstone & Treacle* in some UK cinemas. Punky gang of hoodlums pester and threaten young women at a fairground but are thwarted at every turn by a possibly supernatural quartet of Gary Numan lookalikes, who seem to appear from nowhere at opportune moments.

KRULL (1983)—Sword and sorcery fantasy. Giant "Crystal Spider" attack; monstrous, lobster-like armored "Slayers" appear; transformations occur and ultimate confrontations with "The Beast" surface, etc.

LABYRINTH (1986)—Jim Henson fantasy, with David Bowie as the baby-napping Goblin King.

LABYRINTH OF THE BLUD DEVILS (1985)—Twenty-two-minute amateur fan short based on TV's *Doctor Who*. Directed by Eric Davies.

LABYRINTH OF THE BLUD DEVILS 2 (1988)—Fourteen-minute amateur short based on *Doctor Who*. Directed by Eric Davies.

LABYRINTH OF THE BLUD DEVILS 3 (1989)—Third entry in the amateur *Doctor Who*-based series, this one running 43 minutes. Directed by Ian Taylor.

LITTLE SWEETHEART (1988)—John Hurt stars in US/UK thriller co-produced by the BBC. Bank-embezzling couple on the run get more than they bargained for when they encounter a nine-year-old blonde moppet with "bad seed" tendencies. Aka *Poison Candy*.

LORCA AND THE OUTLAWS (1984)—UK/Australian SF, also known as *Starship* and *2084*. Mining company controls its disgruntled and rebellious workforce via the use of killer androids. Directed by Roger Christian.

MACBETH (1983)—Production of "the Scottish play" for the *BBC Television Shakespeare* project, starring Nicol Williamson in the title role, with Jane Lapotaire as Lady Macbeth.

THE MAGIC SHOP (1983)—Directed by Ian Emes. Short based on H.G. Wells' story about a magic store in London where customers see many strange tricks; the shop vanishes when they leave.

MARIA MARTEN OR MURDER IN THE RED BARN (1980)—Jane Howell's retread of the old barnstormer made famous by Tod Slaughter, produced for BBC television in three 55-minute instalments and screened between Christmas and New Year.

THE MARTIAN CHRONICLES (1980)—Three-part UK/US mini-series based on Ray Bradbury's science fiction short story collection, filmed at Shepperton Studios and on location in Malta and the Canary Islands.

MEDIAEVIL (1983)—Four-minute experimental cut-up largely composed of images and dialogue from James Whale's

Frankenstein, interlaced with images of childbirth, a body-building Arnold Schwarzenegger, etc. Shown at Leicester Short Film Festival 2002.

MEMOIRS OF A SURVIVOR (1981)—Dystopian drama based on Doris Lessing's novel; starring Julie Christie. Feral youth roaming the subways; portal to Victorian times.

THE MEN FROM ITC: GHOST OF A CHANCE (1989/2016)—Forty-seven-minute fan film, comic tribute to the heroes of those great ITC series of circa 1970. It seems Roger Moore may be killing off a number of fictional characters in order to reign supreme on TV. Each death sees the victim go to "ITC Heaven" where they are kitted out with a Marty Hopkirk-style white suit. Filming commenced on this project in 1989 and was resumed more than a quarter of a century later!

METAMORPHOSIS (1987)—Feature-length TV version of Steven Berkoff's Kafka stage adaptation, starring Tim Roth and Berkoff himself.

MOONDIAL (1988)—Six-part children's TV series based on novel by Helen Cresswell. Girl travels back in time under the influence of a strange sundial, finds herself considered a ghost by the young Victorian kitchen-boy she encounters and befriends in the past. Masked chanting children, hints of vaguely occult ceremonies, Jacqueline Pearce as an evil and possibly supernatural governess. Released in the mid-1990s as a 113-minute feature edit on VHS.

MR. JOLLY LIVES NEXT DOOR (1987)—From the Channel 4 TV show *The Comic Strip Presents ...*, starring Adrian Edmondson and Rik Mayall, directed by Stephen Frears. Riotous comedy which features cartoon violence galore, including gory murders committed by axe-wielding hitman Peter Cook.

MURDER ON THE MOON (1989)—Brigitte Nielsen and Julian Sands star in this feature-length TV production. With outposts established on the moon following a nuclear war on Earth, Russian and American officials join forces to investigate a murder.

MY COUSIN, THE GHOST (1986)—Hong Kong horror comedy directed by Wu Ma. Man sells his restaurant in Britain, returns to Hong Kong; turns out to be a zombie. Stephen Jones' *Essential Monster Movie Guide* lists this as a Hong Kong/UK production.

THE NAKED CELL (1988)—A young woman with an addiction to sex is abducted, imprisoned and tortured by unknown captors. Starring Victoria Jeffrey as "The Prisoner"; directed by John Crome.

THE NATURE OF THE BEAST (1988)—Tiger-like creature rumored to be roaming northern moors. "The lurking nastiness on the moors is in danger of becoming a catch-all metaphor for unemployment and social and industrial decay"— *Monthly Film Bulletin* (December 1988)

NIGHT CLUB (1983)—Amateur film shot on 16mm, directed by Colin Jones and Reg Lancaster. "Suspense drama built around a mysterious wooden club with supernatural properties and a young mother's encounter with a burglar."

NIGHTMARE (1984)—Alex Chandon (*Bad Karma/Cradle of Fear*) made this Super 8 short at the age of 15. Ref: *The Dark Side* (October 1991). Presumably it is a horror-themed movie?

THE NIGHTMARE MAN (1981)—Four-part serial for BBC television, from David Wiltshire's novel *Child of Vodyanoi*. Brutal murders hit a remote Scottish island, with the added fear among the locals that the perpetrator may not be from this Earth ...

A NIGHTMARE ON ELM STREET (1984)—First of the long-running Freddy Krueger franchise, from Smart Egg Pictures; often referred to as a British production in early trade reports. UK-based Smart Egg were also involved in later franchise entries including the 1980s releases *A Nightmare on Elm Street Part 2: Freddy's Revenge* (1985), *A Nightmare on Elm Street 3: Dream Warriors* (1987), *A Nightmare on Elm Street 4: The Dream Master* (1988), and *A Nightmare on Elm Street: The Dream Child* (1989).

NIGHTMARES (1992)—Video anthology of three student shorts, of which *Oilman* and *False Profit* date from the late 1980s. Packaged and promoted as a horror film but none of the three shorts contain any significant genre content.

OH WHAT THE HELL (1984)—Directed by Ben Harrison. Safety training film in which the Devil and his assistants from the Department of Danger guide careless people into having accidents in the office, factory or warehouse. Written by and starring Rowan Atkinson. Also featuring George A. Cooper, Jim Broadbent, Diana Weston and Gordon Gostelow.

OLIVIA (1983)—Horror mystery from the prolific German director Ulli Lommel, partially filmed in London, as one character is involved in dismantling London Bridge, prior to its move to Arizona.

ORPHEUS IN THE UNDERWORLD (1983)—Two-hour BBC production of the Offenbach operetta, starring Denis Quilley and Honor Blackman.

OUT OF ORDER (1981)—Thirty-three-minute short features a cameo by Bob Monkhouse. "A married couple bond each anniversary by tormenting someone to death"—IMDb.

OUTLAND (1981)—Sean Connery starred in Peter Hyams' ambitious "space Western," relocating the plot of *High Noon* to Jupiter's moon Io. Plenty of splattery gore and enough use of special make-ups, bladder effects, etc. to rival the contemporary likes of *An American Werewolf in London*.

THE PHANTOM OF THE OPERA (1988)—Animated version from Dublin-based company Emerald City, the producers of *Ghost Stories from the Pickwick Papers*.

THE PHANTOM OF THE OPERA (1989)—Robert Englund behind the mask this time, in a Harry Alan Towers (UK?) production filmed in Hungary.

PHASE ONE (1982)—Nine-minute SF short by Roy Spence. Astronaut discovers alien race.

PLAY DEADLY (1984)—Amateur film shot on Super 8, directed by Ronald H. Smith. Competition notes: "For the second year running I found myself almost alone in voting for a film by Ronald H. Smith. Apart from the fact that the wide-angle lens as a constant device has now been abandoned, there is a great deal of similarity between the two. The stories are violent, far from likeable and not even very clever when written down on paper. But when told by Mr. Smith through camerawork and cutting and action closely related to music, I find them compulsive—all the more so, perhaps, but why?"

PRECIOUS BANE (1989)—BBC adaptation of Mary Webb's novel. Rural community, rumors of witchcraft, heroine with harelip is wrongly accused of murder.

PRECIOUS JEWELS (1982)—Directed by "Bos." Fifty-four-minute rape terror drama starring Kathy Green, Amanda Blackburn and "Gypsy" David Cooper. Made for JP Films. Video Catalogue number: Market MAV044, and subsequently banned by the BBFC for its tone, a preoccupation with bondage, sexual terrorism and rape.

PRISONERS OF THE LOST UNIVERSE (1983)—Cut-rate Flash Gordon wannabe directed by Terry Marcel. "Leprous zombies"—*Monthly Film Bulletin*, June 1984. "Dead monk-like creatures"—Donald C. Willis.

RAGNAROK (1982)—Animated SF/fantasy anthology feature written by Alan Moore. Basic pulp yarn; includes a talking Tyrannosaurus as one of the key characters!

RAIDERS OF THE LOST ARK (1981)—Steven Spielberg and George Lucas combined forces for this tribute to 1930s/1940s adventure serials, the first of their *Indiana Jones* movies; thrills and spills lead to horrific climax as spirits from the opened "Ark of the Covenant" cause faces to melt and heads to explode. Big-budget US production filmed on location worldwide, with interiors shot at our own Elstree Studios.

THE REFLECTING SKIN (1990)—Arty horror drama directed by Philip Ridley; some reference sources give a 1989 production date for this late-1990 cinema release.

RESURRECTED (1989)—David Thewlis stars in drama about a returning Falklands War veteran, once presumed dead. "It's possible to read Kevin as a ghost whose appearance helps to trigger off malign forces ... his stiff gait and strange, muffled figure give him all the appearance of a zombie ... such a reading is also encouraged by lines of dialogue like, 'Do you believe in ghosts? Perhaps that's what I am,' Kevin's habit of saying things like, 'When I was dead,' and the eerie scene in which he listens to the tape of a séance in which his mother had tried to reach him"— *Monthly Film Bulletin*, October 1989.

RETURN TO OZ (1985)—Fairuza Balk stars as Dorothy in this bleak and creepy "family entertainment" lifted from several L. Frank Baum novels, set in and around a demolished Emerald City/Yellow Brick Road. Crammed with nightmarish fantasy characters, notably the terrifying "Wheelers." Filmed at Elstree and on UK locations.

RICHARD III (1983)—Production for the *BBC Television Shakespeare* project, directed by Jane Howell and starring Ron Cook in the title role.

ROBIN HOOD AND THE SORCERER (1984)—Feature-length edition of the HTV television series *Robin Of Sherwood*; sorcerer invokes "powers of the Lords Of Darkness," possession, visions of rotting and hanged corpses.

ROBIN HOOD: THE SWORDS OF WAYLAND (1984)—Further film-length HTV drama, Robin (Michael Praed) and his men versus the Abbess of Ravenscar (Rula Lenska), head of the coven The Cauldron Of Lucifer.

SEAN CONNERY'S EDINBURGH (1982)—Twenty-eight-minute travelogue with Connery as onscreen narrator detailing the history of the Scottish capital. Some brief macabre/Gothic imagery, and a mention about the crimes of Burke and Hare.

THE SECRET OF THE BLACKBIRDS (1983)—Russian feature version of Agatha Christie's *A Pocketful of Rye*, shot in London. Murders galore, poisoning, strangulation, shooting.

SHADOW ON THE EARTH (1988)—Influenced by a TV screening of *Invaders From Mars*, youngsters suspect that their neighbor is an alien. Comedy drama made for BBC2.

SHOCK TREATMENT (1981)—Sequel to *The Rocky Horror Picture Show*.

THE SIGN OF FOUR (1983)—Ian Richardson as Sherlock Holmes in this companion piece to Douglas Hickox's *Hound of the Baskervilles*.

THE SIGN OF FOUR (1987)—Granada TV's adaptation for their long-running Holmes series starring Jeremy Brett. This one also features John Thaw and Ronald Lacey.

SPHINX (1981)—Egyptology-themed adventure romp of the old school, directed by Franklin J. Schaffner. Murder, imperiled heroine (Lesley-Anne Down), treasure-filled tomb, etc.

THE SQUIFFY MAN (1983)—Amateur film shot on 16mm, directed by Keith Pollard for Five Arches Films. Competition notes: "… is a kind of avant-garde extravaganza which features a vampire, a man in a black mask, a heroine who walks around in her nightdress clutching a doll and pretty well anything else you can name short of a kitchen sink. It's superbly photographed and, as far as I could make out, utterly meaningless. I found it quite enjoyable as a filmic folly but most of the other judges were positively hostile and Barry Brown went so far as to say that he was angry to note from a credit title that 'money was granted to allow this film to be made'." Fantasy about a young girl's encounters with various strange characters.

STALK AND SLASH (1989)—Blue Seal Award Winner at the Institute of Amateur Cinematographers in 1989; it was directed by a Michael Coleman of Staffordshire. But unless the story surprises or features a member of Guns N' Roses picking a flower, then it seems safe to assume this is the work of a young horror fan inspired by the modern serial killer subgenre. The IAC wasn't too keen on psycho horror, which suggests that there must have been some technical skill involved. (Paul Higson).

A SUMMER GHOST (1987)—Hour-long drama for Channel 4, directed by Robert Wynne-Simmons. Family moves into house where a murder was once committed; adolescent daughter begins to fantasize stories about the events, dreaming of a red-cloaked woman and seeing visions of the victim.

SUPERGIRL (1984)—Faye Dunaway as witch villainess "Selena"; huge, demon-like monster at climax.

THE SUPERGRASS (1985)—Ronald Allen as vampire-like police chief in this feature-length, theatrically released production from Peter Richardson and *The Comic Strip*.

A SWARM IN MAY (1983)—Directed by Colin Finbow and made by the Children's Film Unit. Drama set in boys' school,

features beekeeper's restless spirit who is exorcised when his abandoned methods are taken up again by one of the pupils.

SWORD OF THE VALIANT (1984)—Stephen Weeks' remake of his earlier *Gawain and the Green Knight*.

TAKING TIGER MOUNTAIN (1982)—Bill Paxton takes an early starring role in this experimental, existential post-apocalyptic drama filmed and set in Wales. Cannibalism and mutant rats are mentioned, disease and chaos are rampant and Paxton is drugged, brainwashed and programed to assassinate a pimp in this bleak new world where prostitution is rife. Shot during the 1970s, this took years to be assembled and screened; the Vinegar Syndrome label issued a version on Blu-ray in 2019, bringing it to wider attention.

TERRORE AD AMITYVILLE PARK (1984)—Norman J. Warren's film *Prey* (1977), with additional scenes filmed by Ferruccio Casacci in Italy involving a mummy!

THE 13TH DAY OF CHRISTMAS (1985)—Episode of the Granada TV series *Time For Murder*, given a stand-alone VHS video release in the US. Scripted by former newsreader Gordon Honeycombe and starring Patrick Allen, it tells of a seasonal get-together disrupted by the appearance of the hosts' psychotic and violent son.

THUNDER ROCK (1985)—Charles Dance and Kathleen Byron in a TV movie version of Robert Ardrey's supernaturally-themed play about a lighthouse keeper haunted by visions of lost souls.

TIME BANDITS (1981)—Directed by Terry Gilliam. Ogre, minotaur; David Warner appears as "Evil." There is much dark fantasy amid the typical Gilliam spectacle and absurdity.

French poster for *Time Bandits*

TIME MASTERS (1982)—French animated fantasy directed by René Laloux, set on planet of giant hornets. BBC co-production with other European partners.

TOWERS OF BABEL (1981)—Black comedy short starring Sheila Steafel and Ken Campbell. Residents of a London apartment block are perturbed by a strange odor emanating from one flat and the absence of the couple who live there. Rotting corpse revealed in brief gruesome close-up.

TRAILERS (1986)—Award-winning 17-minute animation by Dartford-based Allan Burgoyne. Described by the maker as, "an anarchic, satirical comedy which makes fun out of films like *Gremlins*, *Plan 9 from Outer Space* and *Bambi*" and consisting of short cameo gems with titles like "*The Homicidal Hamster from Hell*."

TURNAROUND (1987)—Norwegian film scripted by our own David McGillivray and Ray Selfe, features many familiar faces among the cast (Ed Bishop, Gayle Hunnicutt, Eddie Albert, etc.) Tale of a motorcycle gang who disrupts a boy's party; his magician grandfather takes revenge by forcing the bikers to endure his "haunted" house filled with strange illusions and tricks. Sometimes referred to as a British production and advertised on posters and video covers as a supernatural/possession movie (which it is not!).

THE UNBORN (1980)—BBC *Playhouse* TV play directed by Michael Custance.

VEC VIDENO (1987)—Yugoslavian horror movie partly-backed by the UK-linked Smart Egg Pictures. "Piano teacher deeply traumatised by the events of his childhood"—IMDb.

THE VICTOR (1985)—Directed by Derek Hayes and Phil Austin, an excellent 14-minute animated film concerning a stressed young man in an increasingly nightmarish scenario, the conclusion of which is that he is a soldier participating in a program to turn him into the ultimate killing machine. The film closes with actual footage of US Army volunteers trying and failing to tackle sections of an exercise course. Highly rated at the time, with much respect for the animation team.

VINCENT PRICE'S DRACULA (1982)—Documentary hosted by Price, with some dramatized scenes and clips from various vampire movies.

VOICE OVER (1981)—Ian McNeice stars as radio scriptwriter working on a serial involving a vampire-hunter. A knife murder occurs at the end.

WARTIME (1987)—Reeltime *Doctor Who* spin-off with John Levene reprising his role as Warrant Officer Benton, on a mission to deliver radioactive material to U.N.I.T. headquarters but distracted by ghostly visions of his late father and brother.

THE WEB (1987)—Seventeen-minute stop-motion short directed by Joan Ashworth, based on Mervyn Peake's *Titus Groan*. Low on plot but high on strangeness and dimly lit ambience, as long-legged spiders scuttle about the interior of Gormenghast and we witness a dramatic violent conflict between the characters Flay and Swelter.

WILLOW (1988)—Big-budget fantasy shot at Elstree. Executive producer George Lucas, directed by Ron Howard, starring Warwick Davis. Evil sorceress, troll, vicious black-maned dog-creatures, two-headed monster The Eborsisk, duels in magic and a spell to transform people into swine.

THE WOLVES OF WILLOUGHBY CHASE (1988)—Gothic melodrama aimed at older children.

THE WORST WITCH (1986)—Seventy-minute fantasy involving witches and Halloween, made for Central TV. Fairuza Balk, Diana Rigg and Tim Curry head the cast.

THE YOB (1988)—Pretentious video director and football hooligan have their personalities swapped in a scientific experiment. *The Comic Strip Presents ...* comedy owing much to Cronenberg's *The Fly* and Fuest's *The Final Programme*.

Z FOR ZACHARIAH (1984)—Post-apocalyptic drama filmed for the BBC's *Play For Today*, based on Robert C. O'Brien's novel.

THE ZIP (1988)—Eleven-minute short with Denis Lawson discovering a zip fastener in his chest. He pulls the zipper, and another version of him emerges from inside his body. Directed by Jo Ann Kaplan, from a Michel Parry script. Music by *Xtro* director Harry Bromley Davenport.

ZOMBIE BRIGADE (1986)—Australian zombie movie with involvement from Smart Egg Pictures.

APPENDIX 6:

HAMMER: THE 1980s

Having dominated the British fear film landscape since the mid-1950s, the popular "Hammer Horror" brand had unceremoniously ground to a halt by the time their Dennis Wheatley adaptation *To the Devil a Daughter* emerged into an unreceptive marketplace. Theories abound as to why the legendary House of Horror could apparently no longer compete, but maybe things had just run their natural course.

Enter Roy Skeggs and Brian Lawrence, long-time company associates with a vision and a willingness to step up and continue with the Hammer name once long-time helmsmen the Carreras family had given up the ghost. Lawrence and Skeggs managed to keep the Hammer flame flickering for a brief period in the early 1980s, but via the small screen rather than through cinema.

Having dabbled with television previously—1958's *Tales of Frankenstein*—aborted following its pedestrian pilot "*The Face in the Tombstone Mirror*"; 1968's rather better-received *Journey to the Unknown*—Hammer lit up the Saturday night ITV schedules with the strong and meaty *Hammer House of Horror*, albeit to be followed by something of a damp squib in the flabby shape of *Hammer House of Mystery and Suspense*.

Although we're not covering television in depth, aside from our TV movies appendix, therefore omitting *Sapphire & Steel*, *Tales of the Unexpected*, *West Country Tales*, *Rentaghost* and other fondly recalled small-screen spookers from our survey, the story of 1980s British terror would be incomplete without a nod to Hammer. In the States, episodes of *Hammer House of Horror* were doubled up and packaged as feature "movies" for US consumption, and the later *Mystery and Suspense* stories, screened under the *Fox Mystery Theater* banner overseas, were tailored for 90-minute slots including the requisite commercial breaks. So a book on "British horror films" of the era really needs to acknowledge them—plus, quality-wise (at least as far as the 1980 crop of shows go) Hammer were back in a big way, right up there with the best that the new breed of home-grown horrormeisters had to offer.

HAMMER HOUSE OF HORROR

During 1979 and 1980, the Rank cinema circuit began to run revival screenings of Hammer horror movies—some on those fabled "Sunday one-day-only" shows, others in week-long slots pairing the likes of *Countess Dracula* and *Hands of the Ripper*. As many reading this book will already be aware, BBC2's generation-changing "Horror Double Bills" and the ITV regions' Friday night programming permitted we horror-hungry tykes to catch up on many of the British shockers we'd read about in our well-thumbed volumes by Denis Gifford, Alan Frank and the rest, so the opportunity to get to see Hammer on the big screen at my local Odeon was one not to be passed up. Especially since—as I was beginning to gather from obsessive perusal of those aforementioned tomes—the well was running dry.

So, the announcement that Hammer (albeit in name only for the time being) were back in business, with a series of shuddersome small-screen Saturday night spookers, couldn't have arrived at a more apposite time for us 1970s monster kids. *Hammer House of Horror*—that simple, no-nonsense title said it all—aired during the gloomy autumn and winter months towards the end of 1980, and if students of contemporary TV terror had grown used to the quietness and subtlety of the Beeb's *A Ghost Story for Christmas*, the clever combination of science fiction and classic scare tropes which defined *Sapphire & Steel*, or the sick humor of the twist-reliant, Roald Dahl-hosted *Tales of the Unexpected*, what a thrill to see that we could rely on Hammer to ramp up the "grisly" quotient.

As someone who had learned the names of Terence Fisher, Jimmy Sangster, Freddie Francis and company by rote (if only the education system set exams in this stuff! Far more interesting than logarithms or trigonometry), I must confess having felt mild disappointment back then that few if any of the "old guard" seemed to be involved in this fresh venture. Mere moments into series opener "Witching Time", however, and all was forgiven—could this show actually exceed its promise, and capture the vintage vibe of classic Hammer, while nodding towards the contemporary fashionable cynicism and slasher-inspired violence on offer in cinemas and on new-fangled videocassette?

Hammer House of Horror seems to have appealed mightily to junior siblings/nephews/acquaintances too—those of us who

were weaned on 1970s telly for our fright fix sagely compared and contrasted this sprightly upstart with the traditional Christopher Lee/Peter Cushing chillers to which we were by now well accustomed, but do bear in mind that there was a whole new audience experiencing these shows. To this day I find myself enjoying lively, nostalgic conversations with younger pals who know little of Hammer's heyday but have memories of "the black fingernail" from "The Two Faces of Evil" or "that one about the cannibal cult" ("The Thirteenth Reunion") seared into their consciousness.

"Witching Time" kicked the series off to a sublime start—what better way to bridge the grand costume drama approach of the old school with this exciting new endeavor than a sexy tale about a time-traveling sorceress? Patricia Quinn cemented her genre credentials, having already done her level best to steal *The Rocky Horror Picture Show* from under the noses of the supposed leads, dominating proceedings here as the seductive Lucinda Jessop, magically transported to the modern day to evade the fate of witch trial execution and bidding to supplant Prunella Gee in the affections of soundtrack-composing hubby Jon Finch.

Perky Julia Foster starred in "The Thirteenth Reunion," as an investigative journalist prying too far into the goings-on at a slimming center, the Chesterton Clinic. Participants who put on the pounds rather than shedding them, mysterious deaths, missing bodies and odd behavior from a shady funeral firm appear in this episode. All leads to a climactic surprise revealing this as a classier British cousin of René Cardona's exploitation epic *Survive!*

Estate agent Norman Shenley (a perfectly cast Denholm Elliott) is the focus of "Rude Awakening," a fondly remembered "reoccurring nightmare" scenario in which the nervy property broker seems to be having a dreamworld affair with his gorgeous secretary (whose scanty, provocative outfits are progressively trouser-rousing), with the downside that he is confronted with accusations that he has murdered his wife on Friday the 13th and is constantly assailed by visions of menace and death. The brief shot where an ambulatory suit of armor lumbers towards Elliott at a remote country house remains one of the enduring visual highlights of the show's entire run.

Low points for the series include the muddled "Growing Pains," where a research scientist's adopted son gives everyone the creeps, "Visitor from the Grave," a revival of the creaky old post-*Les Diaboliques* plot that Jimmy Sangster had already milked to death two decades previously, and "The Mark of Satan," a disappointing stab at Satanic conspiracy lifted only by a sympathetic supporting performance by one of the darlings of the Ken Russell set, Georgina Hale.

"The Two Faces of Evil" featured a messy yet very effective plot that took some following, though rewardingly so to the patient viewer; it certainly has its merits, and improbably managed to concoct a classic scare motif out of bright yellow oilskins! On balance, a major high spot within the entire run. "Guardian of the Abyss" and "Children of the Full Moon" hark back to the traditional Hammer methodology, the former featuring an ancient mirror and plans for sacrificial rites—all-grown-up Rosalyn Landor, the little girl at the focus of Hammer masterpiece *The Devil Rides Out*, stars in this one, not only providing a further link to the company's golden age but giving a decent account of herself in the process. "Children of the Full Moon," meanwhile, has a Brothers Grimm ambience in its "strange house in the woods" setting and (anticipating the following year's major horror cinema trend) latent lycanthropy. "Charlie Boy" maintains the old-fashioned feel, with a plot about voodoo and a curse-carrying African idol. "Carpathian Eagle," perhaps representative of the series as a whole, gives a welcome starring role to popular TV personality of the day Suzanne Danielle, and mixes slasher antics with familiar reincarnation/prophecy devices to considerable effect.

Which ultimately brings us to perhaps the two best-known offerings from this short but never-to-be-forgotten run.

"The Silent Scream"—Peter Cushing's celebrated return to the Hammer fold, with a cold, calculating turn reflecting recent roles he'd taken in everything from *Shock Waves* to *Star Wars* during the late 1970s. If the "electric prison" plot thrust is largely stolen (from the superb 1961 Vernon Sewell quickie programer *House of Mystery*) then at least the script's Pavlovian spin on events gives the cast and director plenty to work with, and the pet shop setting lends an air of "normality" papered over the barely suppressed madness here. And, obvious or not, the visual punchline is undeniably staggering.

"The House That Bled to Death"—Hammer's playful spin on *The Amityville Horror*, the type of thing they could never have done as a movie but which was perfect for the nighttime small-screen arena. At once a joyous low-rent spoof of the modern-day haunted house yarn (prefiguring *Poltergeist* and 1992 TV sensation *Ghostwatch* by staging such a story in an ordinary, everyday neighborhood) and a vicious supportive comment on the widely-held belief that reports of the urban uncanny were no more than elaborate and avaricious hoaxing, "House" certainly lives up to its title—I've referred above to various moments in *Hammer House of Horror* as being particularly indelible, and am sure that I barely need go on here; you're all already thinking "childrens' birthday party" in relation to this one, aren't you?
—Darrell Buxton

• • •

Mention *Hammer House of Horror* to anyone who has an interest in the genre and more than likely the first thing out of their mouth will be enthusiastic recollection of "The House That Bled to Death," one of the most memorable episodes of any series shown on the television. Created in 1980 by Hammer Films in association with Cinema Arts International and ITC Entertainment, the whole thing ran for 13 episodes between September and December of 1980.

Trapped by the unfashionable Gothic template on which they had founded their success, the late 1970s saw Hammer fail miserably with their last four films—*The Legend of the 7 Golden Vampires* (1974), *Shatter* (1974), *To the Devil a Daughter* (1976) and *The Lady Vanishes* (1979)—in part because films such as *The Texas Chain Saw Massacre* (1974), *La Bête* (1975) and *Carrie* (1976) were proving that the viewers' tastes and preferences were becoming more visceral, challenging and interestingly demanding, something Hammer had lost sight of as far back as 1966, with *The Plague of the Zombies* becoming their watershed moment.

By the time Hammer had belatedly offered up the dire remake of Hitchcock's *The Lady Vanishes*, everyone had moved on.

Seeing potential, Brian Lawrence and Roy Skeggs gave us *Hammer House of Horror*—the company's second TV series, the first being *Journey to the Unknown* (1968), a rather underwhelming contribution to the telly schedules mainly due to its science fiction and fantasy themes, something that *Out of the Unknown* (1965-1971) did much better. This time, however, the move to the small screen was a masterstroke.

The attraction of the new series, apart from the reputation that Hammer had gained as purveyors of classic (and classy) horror, is that the episodes often starred familiar British names of TV and film. One of the quintessential Hammer actors, Peter Cushing, appeared in a true gem ("The Silent Scream") while in others we had such stars as Denholm Elliott, Diana Dors, Warren Clarke, Jon Finch, and Anthony Valentine, as well as future *James Bond* actor Pierce Brosnan in one of his very first screen roles. And, with directorial duties performed by people responsible for other Hammer productions, such as Peter Sasdy (*Taste the Blood of Dracula, Hands of the Ripper*), Don Sharp (*The Kiss of the Vampire, Rasputin the Mad Monk*), and Alan Gibson (*Dracula A.D. 1972, The Satanic Rites of Dracula*), the stamp of quality was assured.

Inevitably, given Hammer's reputation and background, the storylines were based upon themes familiar to fans of the films: haunted houses, cannibals, ghosts, demons, werewolves, possession, human sacrifice, etc. Yes, in some respects, Hammer was all about "does exactly what it says on the tin," but that didn't really matter. Plus, the televisual medium is compact, which requires taut storylines and screenwriting; creating impact and atmosphere within a small space (both physically and thematically) within the constraints of the limited budgets of television drama. In other words, then, it was all about distilling the essence of whatever dramatic theme was being used that week, and heightening it.

Hammer House of Horror was broadcast at the tail end of a gogglebox era in which genre series reigned supreme and were regular items on TV listings, spanning the 1950s, 1960s, and 1970s—classics such as *A Ghost Story for Christmas, Mystery and Imagination, Beasts,* and *Tales of the Unexpected*. As has been said elsewhere, horror is a very difficult genre to capture successfully on TV, as budgetary paucity sometimes means that often essential "special effects" prove to be anything but special. On the other hand, such limitations often bring out the best in technicians, whenever they're called upon to fall back on ingenuity. That's an aspect which Hammer was famous for: Reusing sets for different films by rearranging them or employing the same location for several productions shot back to back. And what they were particularly good at was creating atmosphere, which translated well to the claustrophobic limits of the television screen.

One could easily say that *Hammer House of Horror* represented the swansong of a much-loved and well-known brand name that, in its heyday, had consistently produced some of the best examples of genre filmmaking. But, just like the Hammer production process itself, the company was adaptable, and utilized the increasingly popular television medium to its advantage. The series was well received and, although only lasting the single flurry, it has since been rerun several times and has attained cult status. A second series was mooted, script editor Anthony Read even writing an episode in anticipation of a new run being green-lit. However, the original backers, ITC, were not prepared to continue with it; undaunted, Hammer eventually found new partners from America, though a stipulation as part of the deal was that the horror elements should be very diluted for US consumption. Also, the decision was made to continue under these conditions, the word "Horror" was to be dropped from the title, and *Hammer House of Mystery and Suspense* limped into existence.

Luckily, with the advent of new media, fresh life has been breathed into the original 1980 series, with a modern generation of viewers coming on board and old fans tasting once again the frisson of fear that sent delicious shivers of fright up their spines. The entire series was released on DVD by ITV on October 14, 2002 and by Synapse in the US on September 11, 2012. October 23, 2017 saw the Network label release a sparkling Blu-ray collection; Imprint in Australia added informative commentaries by the likes of Mark Gatiss, Kim Newman, Jonathan Rigby and Kevin Lyons to their version of the set on October 21, 2020.
—Johnny Mains

WITCHING TIME
Broadcast September 13, 1980
D: Don Leaver W: Anthony Read Starring: Jon Finch, Patricia Quinn, Prunella Gee, Ian McCulloch, Lennard Pearce, Margaret Anderson

A composer and his wife reside at isolated Woodstock Farm. He is convinced that she is having an affair, and matters are complicated when a 17th-century witch unexpectedly enters their domestic turmoil. The man's wife then fights for his very soul, to wrest him back from the clutches of the malignant sorceress.

THE THIRTEENTH REUNION
Broadcast September 20, 1980
D: Peter Sasdy W: Jeremy Burnham Starring: Michael Latimer, Julia Foster, Dinah Sheridan, Richard Pearson, Norman Bird, Warren Clarke

During a journalistic investigation into a new slimming company called "Think Thin," a woman finds out some shocking truths behind the facade. Bizarre occurrences, fatalities and other secrets are just waiting to be uncovered—but will their revelation lead to her death?

RUDE AWAKENING
Broadcast September 27, 1980
D: Peter Sasdy W: Gerald Savory Starring: Denholm Elliott, Lucy Gutteridge, James Laurenson, Pat Heywood, Gareth Armstrong

An estate agent experiences extremely realistic and vivid dreams, so much so that upon waking he doesn't know what is real life and what isn't. Suggestions that he has killed his spouse add to his confusion.

GROWING PAINS
Broadcast October 4, 1980
D: Francis Megahy W: Nicholas Palmer Starring: Gary Bond, Barbara Kellerman, Norman Beaton, Tariq Yunus, Geoffrey Beevers

A couple, a diplomat and her scientist husband, adopt a boy after the tragic death of their only son, but very soon weird things start to happen. Is the arrival of the new family member connected in any way?

THE HOUSE THAT BLED TO DEATH
Broadcast October 11, 1980
D: Tom Clegg W: David Lloyd Starring: Nicholas Ball, Rachel Davies, Brian Croucher, Patricia Maynard, Milton Johns, George Tovey

A couple buy an old house so that they can restore it to its former glory. However, it comes with a notorious past—it was the scene of a brutal murder. Unsettling phenomena start to happen, culminating at their daughter's birthday party when blood gushes out of a burst pipe. The family flees, but even then, there is more to all of this than meets the eye.

CHARLIE BOY
Broadcast October 18, 1980
D: Robert Young W: Bernie Cooper, Francis Megahy Starring: Leigh Lawson, Marius Goring, Angela Bruce, Frances Cuka, Michael Culver, Jeff Rawle

Owners of an African fetish object come to realize that it is possessed of evil powers.

THE SILENT SCREAM
Broadcast October 25, 1980
D: Alan Gibson W: Francis Essex Starring: Peter Cushing, Brian Cox, Elaine Donnelly, Anthony Carrick, Terry Kinsella, Robin Browne

The proprietor of a pet shop is not all he seems to be. In fact he's a former guard at a Nazi concentration camp, who is intent on continuing to experiment on humans as he did in his former life. His latest guinea pigs are a convict recently released from prison and the ex-prisoner's wife.

CHILDREN OF THE FULL MOON
Broadcast November 1, 1980
D: Tom Clegg W: Murray Smith Starring: Diana Dors, Christopher Cazenove, Celia Gregory, Victoria Wood, Robert Urquhart

Getting lost one night while driving, a couple comes across an old mansion, which turns out to be a kind of hospice—run by a woman who says that the children she cares for are actually werewolves. After staying the night, the man is told it was just a dream, but his wife has suddenly become pregnant and is acting strangely ...

CARPATHIAN EAGLE
Broadcast November 8, 1980
D: Francis Megahy W: Bernie Cooper, Francis Megahy Starring: Suzanne Danielle, Anthony Valentine, Siân Phillips, Barry Stanton, Jeffrey Wickham, Pierce Brosnan

A series of grisly murders have taken place, which all involve the victims having their hearts cut out. A young woman believes that

she is the one committing the crimes, albeit under the control of the spirit of a murderess, which possesses her. A police detective is assigned the puzzle of the murders.

GUARDIAN OF THE ABYSS
Broadcast November 15, 1980
D: Don Sharp W: David Fisher Starring: Ray Lonnen, Barbara Ewing, John Carson, Rosalyn Landor, Paul Darrow

An artifact (a scrying mirror) attracts a woman who is on the run from devil worshipers, thus endangering the life of an antiques dealer who has the object in question. As part of the sect's practices, human sacrifice is an essential requirement.

VISITOR FROM THE GRAVE
Broadcast November 22, 1980
D: Peter Sasdy W: John Elder Starring: Kathryn Leigh Scott, Gareth Thomas, Simon MacCorkindale

A woman attacked by a would-be rapist while her husband is away manages to shoot the intruder dead—but that's just the start of her problems, as he returns from the grave to pursue her.

THE TWO FACES OF EVIL
Broadcast November 29, 1980
D: Alan Gibson W: Ranald Graham Starring: Gary Ray-

mond, Anna Calder-Marshall, Philip Latham, Jenny Laird, Brenda Cowling

While driving on their way to their holiday destination, a family pick up a mysterious hitchhiker. Subsequently the car crashes—but which of the two men in the car is the one who died?

THE MARK OF SATAN
Broadcast December 6, 1980
D: Don Leaver W: Don Shaw Starring: Peter McEnery, Emrys James, Georgina Hale, Peter Birrel, Conrad Phillips

A mortuary worker has come to believe that he has been specially chosen by the Devil to do his work on Earth. His colleagues, however, think he's delusional—but what if he's telling the truth?

HAMMER HOUSE OF MYSTERY AND SUSPENSE

Coming along at the fag-end of the classic Hammer era, it is hard to review *Hammer House of Mystery and Suspense* as part of that great lineage. Mainly because of the lack of recognizable Hammer stars (i.e. Christopher Lee and Peter Cushing) and secondly because this series doesn't capture those unique, vivid visuals that Hammer were known for.

In 1980, Hammer Film Productions had one of its latter-day successes with the *Hammer House of Horror* television series, co-produced and financed by Lew Grade's ITC. This was an anthology collection of hour-long shockers that had been a big hit with audiences and was seemingly assured of a second season. Until the gigantic iceberg hit. Due to the huge box-office flop of Grade's *Raise the Titanic*, ITC pulled out of financing that second season, leaving Brian Lawrence and Roy Skeggs, masterminds of the *Hammer House of Horror* concept, to look elsewhere.

In the end, four years after the first show, *Hammer House of Mystery and Suspense* arrived on UK screens. Slightly different in format and with new bedfellows/backers on board, the series ran from September to December 1984. The success of *Hammer House of Horror* was the effective condensing of the key Hammer traits into a powerful 50-60 minute episode. Here is where *Hammer House of Mystery and Suspense* differs.

In the search for fresh finance, Hammer struck a deal with 20th Century Fox television and the demands from them were very different to the deal with Lew Grade. Firstly, every episode was now 70 minutes, in effect making them TV movies, which in most cases brought an unnecessary amount of padding. Secondly, the necessity of an American "name" in a lead or key role (something of a throwback to the days of their 1950s cinema program-fillers). And finally, the shows were to skew more towards mystery and crime rather than the supernatural horror that Hammer was best known for. In fact, the show even aired in the US under the title *Fox Mystery Theater*.

So instead of Peter Cushing, we get Dirk Benedict ("Face" from *The A-Team* and the original Starbuck in *Battlestar Galactica*.) Instead of great televisual horror, we get a series of crime/mysteries with a bit of a supernatural element thrown in. It makes you wonder why they bothered branding it "Hammer" at all.

A returning trait from *Hammer House of Horror* is the quality of the people behind the camera and penning the pages. Featuring familiar names like Val Guest (director of Hammer's *The Quatermass Xperiment*, *The Abominable Snowman* and a dozen other Hammer films), John Hough (director of *Twins of Evil*) and Peter Sasdy (*Taste the Blood of Dracula*) each directing three episodes, plus Paul Annett (*The Beast Must Die*) and Cyril Frankel (*The Witches*) chipping in with one each, alongside first time Hammer directors Gabrielle Beaumont (director of a bunch of *Star Trek: The Next Generation* episodes and *Beastmaster III*!) and Alan Cooke (*The Mind Of Mr. Soames*). The series also brought scriptwriters like Brian Clemens (*Captain Kronos–Vampire Hunter*), Jeremy Burnham (*The Horror of Frankenstein*), Don Houghton (*Dracula A.D. 1972*) and John Peacock (*To the Devil a Daughter*) back into the Hammer fold for its last hurrah.

Picking out some of the best over the series, "Black Carrion" really feels like it has a strong Hammer influence; even then it is like a Hammer directed by Jesús Franco, wild and unpredictable. Accomplished director John Hough brings the tale of a journalist and a 1960s pop expert who are investigating an immensely popular act that disappeared at the height of their fame. They track down their quarry, the Verne Brothers, to the deserted and brilliantly named village of Briars Frome. People are going missing, cars are being run off the road and it all ties back to the village and the Verne Brothers. Hough pads out the running time a little but of all the episodes, this is one that feels most like a full feature.

Another John Hough-directed tale is the "Czech Mate" episode, which couldn't be further from the Hammer blueprint if it tried! Seemingly channeling the success of *Tinker Tailor Soldier*

Spy (1979) and *Smiley's People* (1982), both starring Alec Guinness, rather than a direct Hammer influence, "Czech Mate" is a taut, suspense filled thriller. Hough reunites with *Straw Dogs* star Susan George for the first time since 1974's *Dirty Mary Crazy Larry* and the bulk of the story is put on George's shoulders. She plays the ex-wife of John (Patrick Mower), who invites her to Prague and then disappears, leaving her alone, without her passport and penniless. This is a good tense tale that ramps up the suspense of a woman adrift in a communist country at the height of the Cold War, with a suitably dark ending.

Other highlights include "The Late Nancy Irving" (director, Peter Sasdy) which features a really great, atmospheric build up, which the ending can only fail to live up to. Nancy Irving is an American pro golfer who, after witnessing a car crash, wakes up in an infirmary, hooked up to a drip. Told she has a rare anaemic condition she starts to think something is awry when she has no visitors and seems to be getting weaker by the day.

The series also brought Val Guest out of retirement for his last directing credits. Of the three he directed "In Possession" is the standout. The plot of a couple being haunted by spirits is handled very well and benefits from taking itself and the premise very seriously. Another Guest-directed episode is a cracking idea that sadly fails to deliver, "Child's Play" stars Mary Crosby (*Dallas*) and Nicholas Clay (*Excalibur*) and is about a couple who wake up to find themselves trapped in their home and beset by supernatural forces.

Brian Clemens' "The Sweet Smell of Death," starring Dean Stockwell and Shirley Knight, is a disappointment with a fairly predictable murder mystery plot while "A Distant Scream" suffers mainly from giving everything away in the opening 10 minutes! "Mark of the Devil" sees Dirk Benedict cursed with an ever-growing tattoo (something probably not as terrible a fate today as it was then!) with so-so results, while "Last Video and Testament" seems lacking in both "Mystery" and "Suspense" as we watch a husband get revenge on his cheating wife and her lover. "Paint Me a Murder" was a hokey idea in 1984, never mind now, while "And the Wall Came Tumbling Down" manages to drag a few spooky scenes out of its limp script.

"The Corvini Inheritance" hauls the stalker storyline out of retirement with fairly good results—David McCallum and Jan Francis impress as the auction house security guard and the woman being terrorized by a mystery prowler. It overstays its welcome slightly but is one of the better episodes. Last and by all means least is "Tennis Court," the tale of a haunted tennis court ... needless to say, it doesn't serve an ace.

Not the blood-curdling scream that you would have hoped for in the final work of pre-makeover, pre-*The Woman in Black/Let Me In* Hammer—but not a silent whimper either.
—Adam J. Marsh

MARK OF THE DEVIL

D: Val Guest W: Brian Clemens Starring: Dirk Benedict, Jenny Seagrove, George Sewell

Gambling addict kills a tattooist to obtain stake money for a poker session—he leaves the card table a richer man but notices a tiny inkspot has appeared on his chest. As time passes, the mark begins to spread ...

Italian DVD for *Hammer House of Mystery and Suspense*

LAST VIDEO AND TESTAMENT

D: Peter Sasdy W: Roy Russell Starring: Deborah Raffin, Oliver Tobias, Shane Rimmer

Electronics expert plans to use his knowledge of the field to take revenge on his unfaithful wife and her lover, as they plot against him.

CHILD'S PLAY

D: Val Guest W: Graham Wassell Starring: Mary Crosby, Nicholas Clay, Debbie Chasan

A couple discover their home has become encased behind impenetrable walls and are subjected to further weird and inexplicable occurrences as they seek a way out.

THE CORVINI INHERITANCE

D: Gabrielle Beaumont W: David Fisher Starring: David McCallum, Jan Francis, Terence Alexander

Young woman living alone in a flat is terrorized by a ski-masked stalker and turns to her security guard neighbor for assistance.

IN POSSESSION

D: Val Guest W: Michael J. Bird Starring: Carol Lynley, Christopher Cazenove, Judy Loe

Couple preparing to leave their UK home experience visions of the murder of an elderly woman by the victim's husband. A memorable twist makes this one of the best of the series.

PAINT ME A MURDER
D: Alan Cooke   W: Jesse Lasky, Jr., Pat Silver   Starring: Michelle Phillips, James Laurenson

Struggling painter fakes his own death; his wife begins to release his unknown, unseen works on to the lucrative art market. Further twists naturally ensue.

A DISTANT SCREAM
D: John Hough   W: Martin Worth   Starring: David Carradine, Stephanie Beacham, Stephen Greif

Lovers holiday on the Cornish coast but appear to be being followed by a strange old man who turns out to have a weird, fantastical connection with the pair.

BLACK CARRION
D: John Hough   W: Don Houghton   Starring: Season Hubley, Leigh Lawson, Norman Bird

A journalist and a music expert join forces to attempt to trace the hitmaking duo The Verne Brothers, seemingly unseen since 1963. Researches lead them to a small out-of-the-way village containing secrets galore ...

THE LATE NANCY IRVING
D: Peter Sasdy   W: David Fisher   Starring: Cristina Raines, Marius Goring, Simon Williams

Female golf professional witnesses a car crash, awakens in hospital where she is told she was involved in the accident and is also suffering from a rare form of anaemia, requiring regular blood transfusions ...

CZECH MATE
D: John Hough   W: Jeremy Burnham   Starring: Susan George, Patrick Mower, Peter Vaughan

Atypical espionage thriller ... a woman is persuaded to accompany her ex-husband behind the Iron Curtain but soon finds herself alone and in peril.

THE SWEET SCENT OF DEATH
D: Peter Sasdy   W: Brian Clemens   Starring: Dean Stockwell, Shirley Knight, Michael Gothard

American Ambassador's wife finds red roses mysteriously appearing at her isolated country home and begins to suspect she is the focus of a murderer's attentions.

AND THE WALL CAME TUMBLING DOWN
D: Paul Annett   W: Dennis Spooner, John Peacock   Starring: Barbi Benton, Gareth Hunt, Peter Wyngarde

Plans to demolish a church in a run-down part of London are disrupted by on-site deaths and other strange happenings. Could this all be connected with witchcraft and satanic practices from centuries earlier?

TENNIS COURT
D: Cyril Frankel   W: Andrew Sinclair   Starring: Peter Graves, Hannah Gordon, Ralph Arliss

Couple inherit a house with an indoor tennis court on the grounds adjacent to the property. The court seems to exert a sinister force, somehow linked with the death of an airman during World War Two.

APPENDIX 7:

MICHAEL J. MURPHY

The history of the British horror movie is peppered with mavericks, individuals working outside the accepted systems yet driven to create a lasting and substantial body of work. From cinema's earliest days, pioneers have shown the way forward, and the tradition continues into the 21st century as the increased availability and usage of new technologies allow budding film artists to bypass the standard pathways, crafting work that can reach an audience while retaining a considerable level of creative control.

Sitting at the heart of this diverse movement, Michael J. Murphy may well have taken inspiration from those who had gone before, but this unsung hero of British film may equally have set the agenda—unwittingly and unheralded—for the future of the culture. If "everyone's a filmmaker" these days, then Murphy as much as anyone paved the way, picking up a camera and going out and doing it. His crowning glory was in gaining prominent video release for his 1982 double bill *The Last Night* and *Invitation to Hell*, the vivid box art a familiar sight among the Clint Eastwood, Burt Reynolds, Charles Bronson and Sylvester Stallone epics it fought for shelf space in the UK's videotape rental emporiums.

In this section of *Dead or Alive* we will endeavor to tell Michael's story, via his enthusiastic low-budget films, through the eyes of his inner circle, and by way of the admiration he garnered from a small yet devoted bunch of supporters and fans. Wayne Maginn of DVD label Sarcophilous Films re-issued *The Last Night* and *Invitation to Hell* on disc—Wayne was kind enough to pen a loving tribute to Mr. Murphy for our limited first edition of this book, and this is reprinted here. Reminiscences from his time working on Mike's productions are provided by close friend Phil Lyndon. Murphy cranked out films from his teenage years in the mid-1960s right to the end of his life, with *The Return of Alan Strange* in 2015—one of his final artistic deeds, mere weeks before his untimely passing, was to provide a hugely informative and entertaining foreword for our first edition. Mike wrote it in March 2015 but didn't make it to see his words hit print just two months later. We're proud to offer you the chance to read that piece once again here.

Thanks are due to Philip Lyndon, Stephen Longhurst, Patrick Olliver, Wayne Maginn, Paul Higson, Mike Peter Reed and all who are endeavoring to archive Mr. Murphy's works and promote his output to an ever-expanding and increasingly appreciative audience. And to M.J.M. himself, for embodying the striving spirit of the British horror scene during the 1980s and beyond. Years ahead of his time. We miss him.

Original Foreword to the 2015 edition by Michael J. Murphy

I was bitten by the filmmaking bug at an early age, saving whatever money I could get hold of to buy my first standard 8mm movie camera in the mid-1960s, when I was in my teens. With overly ambitious ideas and thinking of myself as the next Cecil B. DeMille, I made a handful of mini epics with the help of school friends, family and local actors. They were all feature-length, in color and with full soundtracks. I even shot one in "Cinemascope!" These no-budget efforts were shown to local audiences and because of my teenage tendency to indulge in blood, gore, and semi-nudity (on the screen, that is!), they helped me to gain employment as a trainee film director at the Elstree Film Studios of Associated British Picture Corporation. Training there made me aware of the difficulties of breaking into the British film industry. In the late 1960s, film production was in decline. The power of the unions made it close to impossible to produce low-budget films that stood any chance of some form of distribution, so, somewhat disillusioned, I left the studio and got a "proper" job, continuing to make my own 16mm films as an expensive hobby—showing them for charity fund-raising and entering them into various film competitions.

Then in the late 1970s the commercial availability of VHS and Betamax video recorders created a revolution in the way we watched television, giving the public the choice of viewing what they wanted, at a time convenient to themselves. By 1980 video libraries were opening up everywhere and there was an

Michael J. Murphy

insatiable demand for tapes on their shelves. With the major film companies holding back on video releases of their cinema productions, and the authorities unable to control the flood of foreign and uncensored sexploitation films, the gates were opened for the independent filmmaker.

Although I was a few years late, in 1982 I elected to steer away from what I considered to be more intelligent, artistic thrillers or dramas. I decided to go back to my teenage leanings, towards sensationalism and titillation. Although never a major player in the field, I managed to produce 11 features in the 1980s. About half of these fitted into the horror genre and were aided by the likes of Mary Whitehouse, and the *Daily Mail* campaign against so-called "video nasties." As with many other films of the period, what was intended as low-budget fodder for the video libraries became notorious because of the adverse publicity—while many superior and well-crafted offerings were overlooked.

As the decade proceeded the major distributors had opened up their back catalogues and were releasing their productions on to the lucrative video market. The era of the highly publicized, often inferior, exploitation movie was drawing to a close. The smaller distributors, often run by entrepreneurial business types who had very little interest in the product they were selling, were struggling to compete. A few survived into the 1990s, but the glory days were over.

The book you hold in your hands, a study of over one hundred British horror movies, is a valuable and informative insight into the decade that was revolutionary in the history of British cinema!

Tributes

As the initial UK limited edition of "Dead or Alive" went to press, the sad news arrived that Michael J. Murphy had died, during the afternoon of April 10, 2015. We would like to dedicate our book to Michael. His independent, go-out-and-do-it approach to moviemaking was decades ahead of its time, and we hope that the contents of the book will at last confirm Mike's true place in the history of British cinema.

Wayne Maginn, a keen supporter of Mr. Murphy's work, and head of Sarcophilous Films, the DVD label that released a superb special edition of Mike's celebrated duo *Invitation to Hell* and *The Last Night*, here offers his own personal tribute to the director:

Michael J. Murphy, Britain's greatest independent filmmaker, is no longer with us. The seemingly unstoppable director finally took his bow just prior to this book's publication.

As a kid Mike was so profoundly mesmerized by cinema that he started making films in his teens and was still at it in his 60s. That childhood flame always burned bright within him.

A gracious, funny, talented and warm-hearted guy, he had been making films ever since he laid his hands on a small 8mm camera, his amateur career spanning an incredible half a century. Yet, somehow, he managed to remain tucked away in some small corner of the British movie industry producing film after film, with his name barely recognized or uttered as part of its illustrious history.

The man had a pretty alarming lack of interest in his own significance too, always preferring to look forward to new projects rather than back on past labors. Attempting to archive materials to preserve his legacy was an awkward task at times, but Mike was always happy to help and very generous with his time. However, when I mentioned paying for transfers of his old films, he was not keen—finding it hard to consider someone spending their money on "old rope" when it would be best invested in a new project!

In March of 2015, we discussed me visiting before the summer was upon us, as he said he was later likely to be starting work on yet another new film. Sadly, it was never to be.

After finishing *The Return of Alan Strange* (2015), a film that even *feels* as if Mike is tying up some loose ends, one could be forgiven for believing this to be an intentional swansong of sorts. But that was never his intention. His zest for filmmaking was relentless. But that was Mike—he was hard working and ambitious, passionate about his task as much as he was keen to help people, and he was never going to quit. Or at least it was never going to be out of choice, despite what he had mentioned occasionally in recent years.

If we can't look forward to his next film though, then perhaps it is finally that time to start looking back at the incredible body of work he left for us in almost 50 years of filmmaking, and ensuring his legacy prospers. And for those of us who were privileged to know him and become his friends, we have such memories.

Mike ... my friend ... what a true inspiration you were to those who knew you or admired your work. That many had still never heard of you to this day was as frustrating as it was a fun secret for those "in-the-know" to share and enjoy. It was like you had your own little cult and were content with that!

Time to revisit the wealth of fantastic personal adventures you captured on celluloid (and digital) and ensure your legacy lives on.

Much love to you, my friend. You will be sorely missed but always championed ...
—Wayne Maginn

Phil Lyndon, a close friend and filmmaking colleague of Michael J. Murphy, kindly offered us these reminiscences for this new edition of "Dead or Alive":

My reminiscences start when M.J.M. was casting for *Death Run* in 1987. Patrick Olliver who had appeared in *Bloodstream* and *Legend of a Hero* was down to play The Messiah—leader of a post apocalyptic rebel society. I had acted with Pat in Am Dram in Portsmouth and he suggested M.J.M. see me. M.J.M. recruited his casts largely from Am Dram at the time.

I was cast as Yob 1. I spent time also doubling as masked guards and mutants (many of us did! My brother appeared as a rebel and numerous mutants too, killed about four times in total.) I had an interest in old horror films and classic TV, so M.J.M. and I often talked about his days on *The Avengers*, *The Saint*, late Hammer films etc. I wound up dubbing the character Hero too on *Death Run* (a London waiter and Chippendale-type dancer M.J.M. had found in a restaurant.) Back then it was all shot on film with no live sound, we lip synch dubbed everything. I was impressed with M.J.M.'s knowledge of old-school effects—liquid latex mutant make-up, hollowed arrows propelled down fishing line into someone's chest, plaster casts of actors' head for decapitation scenes etc ...

Avalon was next and I spent a lot of time with M.J.M. creating sets and models and appeared as a camp wizard dressed in blue velvet. I used to joke that when M.J.M. was making a fantasy film no one in his road had any curtains left hanging in their front rooms! There was a carpet shop at the end of M.J.M.'s road and we would use inner carpet tubes (giant loo rolls) covered in paper maché for tree trunks, for fencing and columns.

For one fantasy film he constructed a model castle from sanitary products, nicknamed Tampon Towers.

He was masterful in many areas, not just writing, shooting and editing but make-up, model making, in-camera effects and was a great stills photographer too. Props and helmets would be often made of fiberglass or modeling clay, wooden duplicates of metal weapons would double up in fight scenes. *Avalon* saw a stop frame dragon that we compared to the *Clangers* soup dragon ... he also shared to me years later that the werewolf he created in *Bloodstream* reminded him more of a womble. M.J.M. was always realistic and self-effacing about his work.

I went on to play Mike the manager in *Torment* and Father Daniel in *Moonchild*, then The Master in *Atlantis*. *Torment* and *Moonchild* were filmed in the way he loved to film—hire a farmhouse, set the story predominantly there, take the cast there for two weeks and film by day and socialize at night, the wine flowing freely. At this time there was a repertory group feel to the cast. Something M.J.M. didn't fully condone, I think he liked some new blood included, though he was fortunate he had some strong actors in Patrick, Debbie, Neil, Judith and myself who could work quickly and not fuck up too much—£25 to pro-

Murphy and the makeshift outdoor blue screen he rigged up with the help of cast and crew.

cess every three mins. of film stock. In retrospect M.J.M.'s days watching TV being filmed gave him the discipline to film quickly.

There was a period I lost touch with M.J.M. He had some distribution success late 1980s and films like *The Rite of Spring*, *Road to Nowhere* and *Second Sight* saw him pulling in some "pro" actors probably recruited from ads in *The Stage*.

I came back on the scene when M.J.M. had sold a lot of equipment, now in a digital age and celebrating a DVD release of *Invitation to Hell*. I helped him with the "Making of" feature and director's commentary. He wanted to make a new film but believe it or not didn't even own a camera. *ZK3* saw a small cast and crew self-finance a holiday/shoot to his beloved Paxos in Greece, returning to shoot *Nekros*. He had shot *Roxi* there too. These films saw myself, Judith and June back in front of the camera (Jude and June's partners Chris and Mark crewing) and I instigated getting Patrick back in the fold. M.J.M. was due to return to Paxos with Patrick in the lead of a planned film *Pornophobia* but M.J.M. unexpectedly died after an infection led to sepsis.

As I had helped M.J.M. with the preproduction on *ZK3* and *Nekros*, and meeting regularly, we decided "Murlin Films" would change to "Murlyn"—fate our surnames allowed this change.

At his funeral M.J.M. spoke on a giant video screen, an interview no one had previously seen, his coffin was carried by some of his actors and I spoke along with June and Jude. We asked the hearse to pass down his road and stop at the house. A place we had socialized and filmed in, the garage and garden that had seen gladiators fight, zombies rise from coffins, mutants attacked with flaming torches, model mountains built, love scenes enacted, the home of Murlin/Murlyn and M.J.M.'s home since birth.
—Phil Lyndon

MICHAEL J. MURPHY: THE 1980s FILMS

Death in the Family
The Cell
Invitation to Hell
The Last Night
Quälen
Bloodstream
Death Run
Avalon
Moonchild
Torment

DEATH IN THE FAMILY

1981
D: Michael J. Murphy
W: none credited
Starring: Caroline Aylward, Russell Hall, Peri Tastsidis, Shirley Carol Aston, Jeanne Griffin

Several poisonings, a bludgeoning, incest, a couple of bombs, a dismembered burnt arm in a rock pool and a knifing, all in a package only 51 minutes in length. In fact, there are more bodies than there are cast members in this one ... and still you reach the end and you can't rightly declare Michael J. Murphy's *Death in the Family* a fully-fledged horror film. It is too bright, too in love with the sunshine and holiday location for that, too fond of blue skies, the rented villa and the blue waters. It zips by, over before you know it, with so little in the way of opening and closing titles, that it does feel unfinished or like a long extract, in storytelling terms, it is clearly complete and satisfactory.

Certainly, if this was alone on a ticket one would have felt cheated, but it would never have appeared on a program alone in 1981 when it was made, and it never saw the inside of a movie theater anyway. Hats off to Richard Ault, a fellow Michael J. Murphy enthusiast, who realized he had this film in the "bottom of a drawer," a hitherto unrecorded, certainly forgotten, video release on the Neon Video label in September 1983. Murphy was unaware of the release until we brought it to his attention 23 years on. Having worked with Des Dolan towards the release of *Invitation to Hell* and *The Last Night*, Dolan had borrowed the 16mm master print of *Death in the Family* from Murphy, theoretically in order to make a master video print. However, nothing more was heard from Dolan on the subject and Murphy assumed that it was unsellable. Neon was Des Dolan hiding behind a managing director Ron Gale as, by that time, he had wronged so many people in the industry that if anyone knew Des was involved, they wouldn't have touched the Neon product with a bargepole.

In my previous coverage of the title in the online magazine, *The Zone*, on the Pigasus Press website, we stated that the film ran 90 minutes shot on 16mm, this information provided by Murphy, though it is hard to tell how this considerably shorter film might have been otherwise padded out. It is unlikely it would have worked out as well without the introduction of other characters. Additional plotting around so few players would have been the death of it, or am I underestimating Michael J. Murphy?

The film opens with Oliver (Russell Hall) at the villa receiving his sister, Debbie (Caroline Aylward), then receiving her some more in the pushed together single beds upstairs! Their new stepmother Shirley (Shirley Carol Aston) shows up the next day, but father Max (Rick Arthur) is still absent. Mary (Jeanne Griffin) is the suspicious housekeeper sifting through their things to prove that Oliver has been on the island longer than he claims. She fails to register any surprise upon catching the siblings in a slobbery clinch in the bedroom window. Beachside, Shirley and the step kids discover the aforementioned charred limb in the shallows and recognize Max's ring on the finger. The police discover that the family yacht is reduced to smithereens. This incident initially assessed by the authorities to have been no more than accidental, the incestuous two begin to make accusatory suggestions against the stepmother, particularly after spotting her with a young Greek beau at the marina.

They plot her demise. Mary tells Shirley about the interfamilial tryst and Shirley challenges them about it. In a pique, she broaches the sleeping arrangements, Oliver responding, "We're not hurting anyone. We're just protecting ourselves from people like you." The murder plot begins in earnest, but it is Mary who is the inadvertent victim of a violent bludgeoning in the shower. "Make sure you hit her around the neck, so it looks like it happened during a car crash," urges his sister.

The young Greek man is Yannis (Peri Tastsidis), the son of Max's partner, who very nearly scuppers their plans with a visit at the moment when Debbie, in a black wig disguise, is on her way to buy cyanide from the silver jewellery factory, their new tactic being to slip it into Shirley's lemon tea. Shirley is already participating in a trademark Murphy bondage scene, tied to a chair, having threatened to call the police suspecting Mary's murder when blood began pumping back up out of the shower plughole. It is only a death postponed for Shirley, her corpse set up for a suicide tableau, but not before she has begun to plant suspicions between the kissing sister and brother.

Yannis is foolish enough to return with findings that he will only relate to Shirley. His evidence is that the burnt arm in the crab pool belonged not to Max but his own father, so you really don't feel too bad if the lusty young Greek's priority in the wake of his father's death is to try and get Debbie into those pushed together twin beds. So, a knife in the gut it is for him.

In a final twist it is Oliver who planned and executed the first murder, of their father, and Debbie and dad who engineered all the subsequent killings, persuading Oliver to conduct all of the dirty work so that all the evidence incontrovertibly points to him. Max and Debbie leave predicting Oliver will poison himself rather than face the judicial system, which he does, but not before flicking one final switch, having anticipated their game and planted a remote-control bomb in her suitcase. It is death all round like a great Russian opera.

There are an astonishing number of twists and turns in this film given the brisk running time and the limit of cast members. The action almost entirely takes place inside and around the villa and it is to Murphy's great credit as a scriptwriter and director that, despite having gone to the trouble of shooting abroad, you can't criticize this confinement and failure to take greater advantage of the locations as he did in other shoots in Greece and Portugal. But given some of his past experiences getting footage in the can and ruined shoots, factoring in a working holiday with restricted time abroad, his focus on a small story, cast and locations is sensible in order to complete the film which again was made on a budget that wouldn't cover Oliver Reed's bar bill.

The film has very little in the way of credits, naming only the actors, and the composer of the score, Philip Love, which may well be Murphy again. The video release does not even credit a director, so it is at least nice to identify Michael's participation in print. Murphy is particularly good in this type of thriller territory, though there would appear to be some bleeding of plots from one film to another. It makes chasing up his 1970s films more important than ever, and let's not forget that he would return to Greece and themes of murder in the family for his 2004 film *Roxi*. One can only hope that at some point a gracious benefactor might fund the rescue of the early M.J.M.s and that wishful thinking may bring a box set of the Murphy Euro thrillers, incorporating *Death in the Family*, *Secrets* (1977) and *Almost a Movie* (1978).
—Paul Higson

THE CELL

1982
D: Michael J. Murphy
W: none credited
Starring: Carol Aston, Russell Hall, Manley Alexander

In 17th century Russia, a condemned prisoner, a student from Kiev, lies in a cell awaiting his death sentence. As an unmarried man, under an old custom, he is permitted a visit from a prostitute on his final night. Preferring to talk with this young woman, he protests his own innocence and hears how she herself committed murder following the fiery demise of her daughter while liaising with a customer who kept her tied up. In the morning he is taken to a place of execution and decapitated with a double-edge blade—the gruff gaoler who has been keeping guard overnight discovers the whore dead in his cell.

Just 13 minutes long, but a fine example of Michael J. Murphy's amateur work. The copy under review carries an onscreen statement before the film reading "Movie Maker—10 Best competition. 4 Star Award," indicating some deserved recognition in competition. *The Cell* is one of Murphy's most accomplished efforts and would have made a worthy supporting programer short had there been the chance of it gaining any sort of cinema circuit release. Sadly, it languished in utter obscurity for decades until being unearthed by Michael's keen devotees. Though talky, it is never less than engaging and attention-grabbing—the three main performances are above average for this director, the prison set is authentically gloomy with a sense of horrible history about it, the concept of the overnight visit adds a salacious touch to the grimness, and Murphy overlays a couple of brief flashback shots to good effect. The climax contains a superb if derivative edit, from the shock of an offscreen decapitation to an image of wine being poured into a receptacle as the viewer's consciousness is still recovering from the sight of the swinging, deadly axe. A handful of Murphy regulars fill out the crowd during the execution scene.
—Darrell Buxton

INVITATION TO HELL

1982
D: Michael J. Murphy
W: Carl Humphrey
Starring: Becky Simpson, Joseph Sheahan, Colin Efford, Stephen Longhurst, Russell Hall, Catherine Rowlands (credited as "Rolands"), Tina Barnett

A young virgin, Jacky (Becky Simpson), travels to a costume party—venue, a North Devon farmhouse—hosted by her college chum, Laura (Catherine Rowlands). That evening she's drugged and taken to a Black Mass ceremony. The morning after, she awakens with claw-like scratches on her hips and makes a failed attempt to escape, fearing for her own life—will the clutches of Satan prove to have too strong a pull?

Shot in five days on a micro budget of £1,000, this film was released in 1983, during the infamous "video nasties" crusade, on VHS by Scorpio Video. *Invitation to Hell* is not to be confused with the 1984 Wes Craven TV movie, with Robert Urich.

Director Michael J. Murphy is a DIY filmmaker who has made heaps of cheap films like *Bloodstream*, *Tristan*, *Death Run* and the inevitable *Wicker Man* clone *The Rite of Spring*, most of which fall into the horror, science fiction and fantasy categories. Despite its padded script (from "Carl Humphrey," the director's pseudonym) and terrible acting, the film does contain much of merit. It has a jarringly effective synth score, an atmospheric and versatile location and a few strikingly graphic death scenes, reminiscent of many of the banned films of the time. Equally eye-

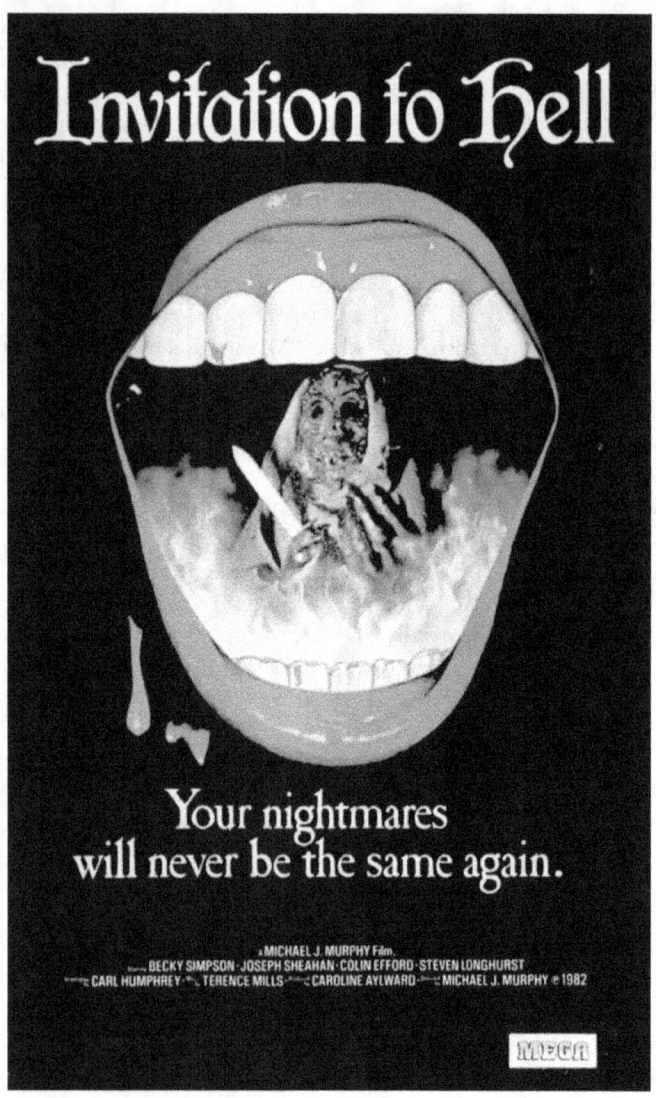

> Leaves a putrid taste in one's mouth. One of the all-time lowest points in British Horror.
> —Nigel Burrell, *Flesh & Blood*

UK critics, even those "in the know," have never quite got it when no-budget, amateur, even semi-pro fare is laid before them. It's so easy to be scathing, with substandard performances, poor photography, illiterate scripting and entry-level direction being fish in a barrel to the would-be-witty, almost encouraging a string of sub-Wildean *bon mots* as they chortle their way through some no-hoper production. For example, responses to the work of the notorious Richard Driscoll during the past 30 years are very revealing; certainly no one regards him as a talent, we all howl with derision as his misguided epics play out before us, many recognize him as "Britain's Ed Wood" without even necessarily having seen a complete work by the man. And yet ... there's something there, some indefinable world-view, an innate and admirable skill in luring major screen stars to appear before his camera, a chutzpah in defying the authorities and mercilessly ripping off Hollywood, often to little or no financial gain, yet he does it anyway, seemingly compelled to crank out disaster after disaster, lifting chunks of off-cuts from one project and splicing them haphazardly into another (which probably makes him more like "Britain's Fred Olen Ray," I'd say.) Nobody else is doing what Richard Driscoll does, and for that alone he is to be marveled at.

In a book all about the 1980s British horror movie, it's vital that we mark the momentous changes battering the industry at that time. Videotape as a means of mass exhibition being a major shift,

catching are the opening credits—featuring a Celtic font over a red-colored flame. Furthermore, the film carries a Norman J. Warren or Pete Walker feel—just think of *Satan's Slave* or any occult-themed Brit horrors of the 1970s. A must for any hardcore retro British horror fan, like myself, and a perfect pizza and beer film for a group of friends.

After decades of scarce availability with gray market bootlegs, *Invitation to Hell* finally got an official uncut release on DVD by Sarcophilous Films in 2008, as a double bill special edition with *The Last Night*, bunched together with "making of" documentaries, trailers, commentaries and slideshows of over 100 photos—including poster and video images—for both films. Limited to 1,000 numbered units worldwide, yet essential for collectors and champions of the obscure.
—Jason D. Brawn

THE LAST NIGHT

1982
D: Michael J. Murphy
W: none credited
Starring: Steve Longhurst, Catherine Rowlands, David Bruhl, Colin Efford

> Threadbare
> —Jonathan Rigby, *English Gothic*.

of course; but what of video as an outlet for the gifted artisan, a chance to level the arena and permit your next-door-neighbor's home movies to compete for shelf space with Stanley Kubrick?

Step forward Michael J. Murphy. Like Spielberg, Michael embarked on ambitious feature-length projects while still in his teens; through the 1970s he continued his spare-time craft, but the video boom gave him his break—in the desperate rush by chancer operations to acquire shelf-filling product, Murphy benefited when the Scorpio label made his *Invitation to Hell* and *The Last Night* available to intrepid rental customers. The innovations offered by this release were manifold; the combined running length of the twin offerings was just in excess of 90 minutes (was *Movie Movie* an inspirational precedent?), here were British titles that had never threatened to get near cinema screens or broadcast television, and Murphy's treatment of the standard terror tropes were often brutal and upsetting; *Invitation* features a startling moment where a sex scene (essential to the plot, something near-unique in itself!) is brusquely interrupted by an horrific carving-knife-rammed-through-the-throat showstopper, while *The Last Night* ventures into murkier waters still with a bout of overt necrophilia. Murphy makes a virtue of the home-made status of *The Last Night* by staging the action in and around a provincial theater, the am-dram nature of the play-within-a-film *Murder in the Dark* handily disguising any deficiencies amid the movie's cast. The basic plot has two dangerous hardened criminals invading the theater during a performance by The Prestidge Players, grimly bumping them off one by one in the slasher fashion of the day—the extraordinary conceit which lifts the film above much of its competition sees the savage murders taking place while an audience ("19 so far—that's three more than Tuesday") watches the stage production—leading, ingeniously, to the Prestidge cast numbers dwindling before their very gaze, leaving the wilier of our George-and-Lenny duo (Steve Longhurst) having to hastily live on his wits and assume direction of the live show, lest the gradual disappearance of the players should alert ticket holders to the backstage (and, audaciously, onstage) carnage. Murphy also revels in his unorthodox truncation, abruptly and stunningly closing the proceedings by bloodily wrecking a birthday celebration as the gore-drenched party girl herself (Catherine Rowlands) staggers into the dressing room area to confront a bunch of appalled revelers.

"Putrid" it may be, but *The Last Night* is also daring, forward thinking, revolutionary, and an ahead-of-its-time example of the future of "film production for all." Advocates of so-called "Free Cinema," rejoice! Michele Soavi's classic late-period giallo *Stagefright* (1987) masters the stark confines and rampant avarice of the "actors trapped in a theater" set-up, but Murphy's approach to the theme is a "poor man's version" in budgetary and resource terms only, at its finest very nearly achieving the sour cynicism of its Italian successor. Exit, pursued by threadbare ...
—Darrell Buxton

QUÄLEN

1983
D: Michael J. Murphy (as "Michael Melsack")
W: Michael J. Murphy
Starring: Stephen Longhurst, Catherine Rowlands, David Slater, Wendy Young

The release together on videocassette of two 16mm films, *Invitation to Hell* (1982) and *The Last Night* (1982), each running less than 50 minutes and made on a scant budget, was certain to draw the attention of barrow boy film producers looking for a quick turnaround on a small investment. The two films directed by Michael J. Murphy had been made for £1,000 and £2,000 respectively, and unknown to Murphy a third of his films had scored a video release, as *Death in the Family* (1981), of similar length and budget, this time filmed in Greece, had snuck out too, though to much less attention. Any chancer producer worth his salt ought to have been asking, "Who on Earth is this scrimping outsider filmmaker shooting films abroad on a budget of a grand? And more importantly, how can we get him on board?"

Entrepreneur Des Dolan had niftily latched on to the distribution of films on home video, doing so with the necessary showmanship and gusto. He was behind a number of labels, most prominently Go Video, garnering a certain infamy with notorious atrocity exhibitions like *Cannibal Holocaust* and *S.S. Experiment Camp*. If he could land himself a filmmaker who could turn out decent films on a negligible wad of notes, then he might be able to rack himself up a highly profitable library of in-house productions cheaper than the cost of buying them in. *Inseminoid* had been made for half a million pounds and promoted at twice the cost, yet here was someone who might be able to push out a saleable product at a fraction of the price.

Dolan engaged Murphy to make a movie for him, Dolan stumping up most of the budget for the film. Murphy as usual kept the costs down by multi-tasking in a number of technical roles including camerawork and editing. Murphy had abandoned an opportunity to work in the film industry proper following an apprenticeship in the union-constricted ABPC studio and, homesick, had returned to Portsmouth, continuing his feature filmmaking as an expensive hobby, setting himself remarkable challenges, taking the production of many of his films abroad to Greece and Portugal for the shoot. The film Murphy would make for Dolan was *Quälen* (with an umlaut over the letter "a") which according to the title card, translates as "to torment; torture; frighten to death." Shooting took place in Devon on this occasion.

Murphy already had a troupe of players and friends to dip into for the cast and supporting crew but again the main technical duties would fall upon Michael himself under several pseudonyms. This time there was little allusion to a theatrical release, and it was intended that it concentrate on the new home video market, which was already cutting into cinema attendances. Videocassettes were cheap to produce but sold hard to the fresh crop of video store owners. The recommended retail price for each copy of *Commando* in the UK in 1985 was a whopping £79.99, which would require a lot of renting before recouping the cost. A lesser title costing several thousand could sell to store owners a lot cheaper, make its money back quickly and return the original budget sooner to the producer. How could it fail?

Murphy's common themes are of cross and double-cross, and of ghastly phantoms with the *Scooby-Doo*/Jimmy Sangster touch, ever-likely revealed as a masked villain attempting to propel a family member to an early grave. No change here. Returning from *The Last Night* and *Invitation to Hell* was Stephen Longhurst as Neville Harmer, heir to a large estate and son to an overbearing father, Alfred (Al Greer), a bitter, wheelchair-bound old sod who takes every opportunity to belittle his kin. He makes unkind remarks about Neville's beloved Vicky, played by Catherine Rowlands, also returning from the earlier films. The son threatens to depart. "You can't leave here, you come with the house; we're fixture and fittings."

The aggrieved Neville leaves him stranded during one of their circuits of the grounds (that include a lake and sawmill). Father releases the brakes on the wheelchair but loses control of it, hurtling down the path and into the lake to drown, the final splash closer in spirit to Chuck Jones than a credible death scene.

A guiltless Neville looks forward to the inheritance, marrying Vicky and selling off the estate. But father has put a clause in the will, which determines that in order to retain the bequest he must remain in residence on the place at least 11 months in the year, or the property will transfer to a distant relative. The estate threatens to become a prison for him and his new wife. The estate is co-managed by the faithful, spinsterish Dorothy (Wendy Young), but Vicky complains about not having enough to do, clearly eyeing up Dorothy's job for herself. Vicky finds a locked bedroom and Dorothy informs her that access is forbidden by Neville. Neville provides the background to the room's tragic history. In the 1880s an ancestor had become romantically linked to a local girl below his standing, and his disapproving father arranged for her to be removed, hiring thugs to gang rape and thereby dishonor her, an act that results in her being drowned in the lake. Witnessing the murder from his window, the son throws himself to his death. Rumors began that the house was haunted and on one night as punishment, Neville was locked in the room ...

He throws a party but the phantoms bop in and out of view; a wheelchair pushed by a rotten corpse in the cellar, a putrescent face dripping maggots outside the window. The culmination of this is a scene reminiscent of the revivification of zombie "Orville" in Bob Clark's film *Children Shouldn't Play with Dead Things*, as Neville finds the horrible decaying corpse rising from its wheelchair in the shadow-bedecked lounge. The corpse chases him across the estate to the accursed room where he becomes entangled in curtains and is thrown from the window.

Having been out for the evening Vicky returns home and goes down the cellar to collect a bottle of wine, turning to encounter the phantom, approach it, smile at it and kiss it, in a possible nod to the cut-and-paste kiss between Vulnavia and Phibes in the ad campaigns for *The Abominable Dr. Phibes*. The fake ghoul is the groundsman, Patrick (David Slater, also returning from the previous two films) and with no will, the declared stipulations would not arise, and the lovers can sell up and make off with the lot.

While out walking the dog, Dorothy finds Neville, who is not quite dead, though the fall has rendered him a paraplegic, neatly setting up a circular doomed pattern of injuries and punishments and clauses. Neville, previously admonished by his crippled father for his weakness, ironically becomes a stronger person in his disabled form, suspecting the plot against him and becoming as vengeful and as scheming as the conspirators. He has Vicky and Patrick sign a new will with an identical codicil that would condemn his wife to the property upon his death. In an impressive set piece while the house is empty, Neville leaves his chair and crawls upstairs and around the rooms to find evidence of the fraudulent haunting played upon him. The lovers discover that the props have been uncovered and disturbed, and suspect Dorothy as she is the only other able-bodied person with access upstairs. Vicky interrogates Dorothy who, realizing that she has been drugged, flees, beseeching help from Patrick who has just returned. Instead they both give chase and in an astonishing sequence Vicky collects a pickax, runs alongside Dorothy who is struggling to ride her bicycle hard enough, and embeds the sharp end in her face. The timing is so spot-on that it continues to provide a jolt no matter how many times you see it. Most of Murphy's films have a "money-shot" shock moment of this nature and impact.

The body ends up in the lake. Neville offers a bonus to a pair of mill employees to put Patrick out of action. They spring an attack on him, breaking his arm in a mantrap that will permanently destroy his judo ambitions and make him less attractive to the wife. Neville plants the worms of suspicion in Patrick's mind, suggesting that Vicky hired the thugs and that he may be next! Patrick has seen what Vicky is capable of and agrees to go with a pay-off from Neville, while Neville is in no doubt that Dorothy's sudden "holiday" took her only as far as the grave. The showdown between the lead couple is inevitable, and is another well-devised sequence that sees Vicky try to kill Neville first with poison and then a knife, the battle moving from house to garden, with increasing tension and uncertainty as to who, if either, might survive the struggle. Neville even grabs an opportunity to phone Patrick, currently spending one last night in a lodge elsewhere on the estate. But Vicky stabs Neville during the call and proceeds to take his body down to the lake, rowing out to the middle. Patrick arrives searching the property for them and ventures into the haunted room from where he can see them on the water; Neville, yet again not quite finished, grabs Vicky and pulls them both under the surface where they drown. Meanwhile the room around Patrick jumps into supernatural activity and he is thrown from the window to his death.

It is a densely plotted story for a handful of characters, quite common to Murphy's work prior to and following *Quälen* as he explores variations on themes, always looking for a way to surprise the viewer. The switch from straight thriller narrative into supernatural twist would resurface over 20 years later in *Skare* (2007), where an absurdist tale of murder and cannibalism would end with a similar paranormal outburst in a room, again based on events recorded in an earlier century in flashback. In *Quälen* though, as with the disabling of father and son and the fates of various lovers, the turn of a tale from a sham spooking into a real haunting is cyclical; Murphy as cinematic Keats. In his other work narratives and histories would be repeated within a film, sometimes chronologically, sometimes on different levels as in *The Last Night* where it took a post-modernist approach, taking place on two distinct planes, the play performed before a live audience and the reality of what was occurring in the siege and murder—cast in order of disappearance, as author Simon Brett might have it.

Quälen is the work of a skilled draughtsman as much as it is that of a scriptwriter. But for all the intrinsic thought put into it, it is still an exceedingly low-budgeted film and that unfortunately shows. Props, like the portrait of the father, and some of the effects look cheap. Performances can be rep in tone and fight sequences unconvincing. That should not detract from the accomplishments of Murphy and company on what was achieved at short notice and with little money. The rising of the phantom in the lounge is atmospherically shot, and *Quälen* moves at a trot, as is always so with Murphy.

A Dolan-Melsack Film, Murphy forewent his usual company name of Murlin to see how this partnership might develop, a possible new approach of investment and as a director/writer for hire. The film did not do well though, turning up in Spain on the Continental Video label having been dubbed into Spanish, and then in America under the title *The Hereafter* in English, but with image quality poor. Murphy never saw any money from the film and Dolan didn't return his calls, leading Murphy into a revenge plot of his own, his next film *Bloodstream*, about the murder of a film producer and his cohorts. Murphy returned to funding his own movies and making money from them where he could in cable, international markets and eventually DVD

—Paul Higson

BLOODSTREAM

1985
D: Michael J. Murphy
W: Carl Humphries
Starring: Patrick Olliver, Jacqueline Logan, Catherine Rowlands, Mark Wells, Stephen Longhurst

The videocassette home entertainment boom led to a scrabble for material to sate rental customers' new appetites. It was initially an exciting time for independent filmmaker Michael J. Murphy, who had been making a film a year on average out of

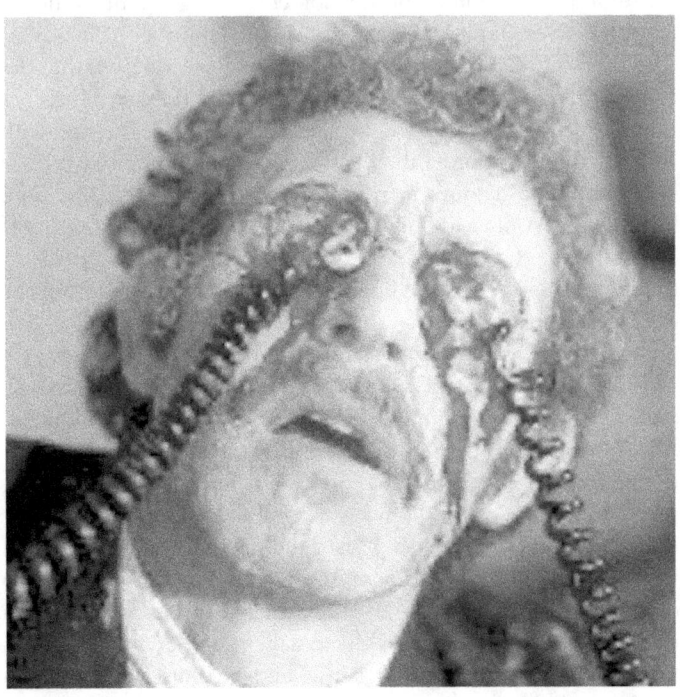

Bloodstream

his own pocket and from his love for movies. His first three feature films of the 1980s had been given a video release, *Death in the Family* on the Neon label followed by the more popular *Invitation to Hell* and *The Last Night* (which Murphy had self-funded, both shot on 16mm) on Scorpio. *Invitation to Hell* had a second, solo outing on Senator, though this was without the authority of the maker and he was to see no money from either the legitimate or unlawful issue.

His ability to turn out a film on a budget well under the common expectation of production cost brought him to the attention of Des Dolan, the head honcho at a number of labels including Go Video, notorious for unleashing several titles that became branded "video nasties." Dolan helped finance Murphy's next feature-length horror *Quälen*, and the film was finished with a Castilian dub, apparently then receiving contemporary release only in Spain. So, four in a row saw cassette marketplace action, but Murphy confessed finagling details of business did not interest him as much as the process of creating stories with a camera, that he was naïve and that little money was recuperated from the dishonest distribution.

Murphy vented his frustrations through his next movie *Bloodstream* (1985), his first film since 1969 to be shot on Super 8, and his last in that format. "*Bloodstream* was very self-indulgent. I had been badly treated by distributors and took my revenge by making a film about them and their family members being murdered in the most vile ways possible ... even burnt their pet dog." Shooting on Super 8 limited the saleability of the project. Further stacking the odds against a release was the intention to deliberately go out and make a "video nasty," at a time when there had been a purge on the less salient end of tape distribution with the Video Recordings Act, and with strict classification of the medium imminent. The post-modern context of Murphy's film was never going to excuse it from the wrath of any censor if it made it that far. Nobody was going to risk submitting a film like *Bloodstream* to the BBFC at the time, even if the story inadvertently supported the stance of the righteous brigade; that a steady diet of gory horror was an unrestrained Open University course creating couch potato psychopaths. *Bloodstream* stands unique in the output of the day; the "video nasty" phenomenon being a peculiarly British affair, and *Bloodstream* the only British film to directly address the sub-category while remaining a narrative horror in itself.

Bloodstream has never had an official English language release, and neither did Murphy entertain one. He was dissatisfied with the quality of the movie but more importantly, he felt that he had gone too far with the revenge motif. To take it out on the producers and distributors was one thing, but to extend the killing to the innocent members of their families could be read as a sinister, disturbing and threatening response, and Murphy did not want to be misunderstood in his wish-fulfilment flight of fancy. It is an outcast even in this outsider filmmaker's career. It does not bear the Murlin name of most of his movies, instead labeled a "Custom F.V. production made in association with Carma Productions," the latter another deliberate misspelling; a sly "reap and ye shall sow" message hurled at industry conmen.

Bloodstream is a curio and a half. For a project so personal, it was also Murphy's most ambitious for some time, with a large cast and a great amount of additional planning, as he shot not only the main story but a series of vignettes of traditional and not-so-classic horror film themes and sub-genres, which would be seen as extracts from home video rental titles within the film. Possibly Murphy was uncertain how much longer he could continue to splash the cash to make his little films, and so he is here accounting for as many as possible lest he never get around to them—setting the template for Tarantino's *Kill Bill* duo, dare we suggest? *Bloodstream*'s stung protagonist, filmmaker and horror aficionado Alistair Bailey (Patrick Olliver) bides many an hour in his armchair watching movies that respectively feature a masked serial killer, zombies, a mummy, a vampire, demonic possession, a werewolf, a cannibal feast and a hunchbacked jester with a captive girl in a torture dungeon (in true poverty row fashion, more *Guru, the Mad Monk* than Quasimodo.) The cannibal dinner appears to be inspired by *The Folks at Red Wolf Inn* (1972), with improved table manners, though perhaps let down by the small talk; example, an airy enquiry concerning the nature of the repast is met by the response "rump, my dear ... you're eating your husband's arse!"

Bailey has just delivered a new film called *Bloodstream* to independent producer and distributor William King (Mark Wells) at his Soho Square offices. King admits that quality is not a priority, a view seconded by his associate Simon (Steve Longhurst) who adds that the company's acquisitions are intended for the "curry brigade," just a bit of "blood and tits" after a night on the sup. We get a taste of the second *Bloodstream*, the movie within the movie, in the opening sequence as a couple separate and the male half bursts into gory metamorphosis (a possible bow to the body horror transformations of *Xtro*, *The Beast Within*, *The Incredible Melting Man* and perhaps even *The Company of Wolves*.)

King cites Clause 27, small print in their contract, that stipulates that, "if at any time I am not satisfied with the progress of the production I am entitled to amend our agreement or render the contract null and void" and refuses to stump up the completion money for the film. This does not stop him from stealing the work and selling it on the moment that he has driven Bailey from his offices. We hear him planning a trip to the European Video Convention and later learn that the video has shifted 20,000 tapes in Canada alone.

King's secretary, Nikki (Jacqueline Logan), cannot avoid overhearing all about the dodgy dealing that takes place in the King offices and contacts Bailey. She has a plan to get Bailey his money back, while putting paid to King and the coterie that colludes with him in living off King's exploitation of others. The plan is murder, and Bailey will commit the killings, the victims to include King, his immediate family, and the deceitful co-stars.

Womanizer and ex-porn star Greg (David Slater) will be done in while powerlifting on a cheapjack gym set, the murder seemingly modeled on a tableau from *Happy Birthday to Me* (1981). A hedge trimmer and an electric carving knife will be used on Simon and Mrs. King (Wendy Young) respectively, and despite the meager trappings, nudity highlights the bath-time slaying of the daughter Lisa (Samantha Page). Distrustful actress Judy (Catherine Rowlands) is silenced with a knife in the mouth. The most disturbing moment, though, is when the family dog Cleo (Boo) interferes with the killing of Simon in the garden. Bailey tethers her to a tree and pours petrol over her before burning her alive. Clearly, it is only water splashed across the cuddly mutt, but the image of the petrol can emptied over the anxious animal is distressing. The torching is just off-screen, but there is often one shocking and highly effective moment of horror in each Michael J. Murphy film, and this takes the biscuit here.

Meanwhile Nikki is rejigging contracts in the office, hopefully allowing Bailey to emerge from the scheme rich based on existent deals. She also intends to make the murders appear to be the actions of King himself, the forthcoming adverse publicity promising even greater revenue on their tawdry back catalogue. Alas, for Nikki, her financial surprise for Bailey is no longer important, as the gruesome killing spree has scrambled all reason. He rewards her for her greed by making her his next victim. When we last see Bailey, he is in a cell promising us, the viewer, "Just wait till I get out of here. I'm going to make a bloody marvellous film."

Bloodstream had been reported as lost, or at least unlikely ever to be seen, but was fortunately made available again (along with an English language version of *Quälen*) by Stephen Longhurst, the actor who appeared in eight Murphy films. This was his fourth for Murphy in a row, taking the role of Simon, added to the kill list because, as Nikki remarks, "we both know what a little shit he is." There has never been an official release of the film, and the version available may not pass everyone's quality control standards but does not impair viewing. The editing and camerawork are at times a bit ragged for a Murphy film, and the sets and effects are often poor, though this is as a result of trying to do too much on too tiny a budget. During a witch-burning sequence the pyre has been topped up with palettes.

The movies within the film are supposed to look so-so (indeed, Bailey the character will criticize them), but on a clearly rushed and over-ambitious production much else shows clear haste too; take the thrown-together posters, very amateur in design, that deck the walls of the King offices promoting previous fictional releases with titles like *Sucked to Death*, *Cobra Kill!*, *The Virgin*, *The Lust Machine*, *Return of Lucifer* and *Awaken Zombie*. The film abounds in fake titles, with which geeks like me have always been fascinated, imagining a sham alternative universe of film a là Stephen Romano's inventive *Shock Festival* creations, so we are delighted with the set visit to *Kongarilla* (a title that sounds completely ripe for Asylum Pictures, maybe Murphy could have sold it to them.) To continue the catalogue, the fake videocassettes in the movie bear titles that include *Path to Hell*, *Son of Mummy*, *Zombie Lust*, *Cry Werewolf*, *Gut Feelings*, *Dead Sex*, and *Lightning Strike*. Though, as I have speculated, I suspect Murphy was banging these clips out to compensate for a predicted future failure to tackle them. *Lightning Strike*, also excerpted, is a post-apocalyptic action romp, a sub-genre that Murphy would get around to for real with *Death Run* soon after.

Bloodstream is not one of Murphy's best flicks despite its importance, even as an outsider film, because of the ironic stance that it takes. The meta-movie was to owe a far greater debt to *Hollywood Boulevard* (1975) but few directors explored ironic cinema as so far ahead of the trend. His earlier *The Last Night* was a tidier and more effective example of his post-modern exploration, and the later *Second Sight* (1992) is the most successful of his investigations into dissections of the creative arts. In the Murlin acting stable, Patrick Olliver was Murphy's answer to Oliver Reed, but here his role is ill fitting, unlike some of the later villains and protagonists he essayed in such an accomplished manner for the director. *Bloodstream* may be too adventurous for its stretched resources and is subsumed by an avalanche of bargain basement detail. On the plus side it is never dull, and that one moment of pure horror—the dog burning—was more jaw-dropping than anything most horror films at the time were actually capable of producing.
—Paul Higson

DEATH RUN

1987
D: Michael J. Murphy
W: Michael J. Murphy
Starring: Rob Bartlett, Wendy Parsons, Debbi Stevens, Eddie Kirby, Patrick Olliver, Stephen Longhurst, Phil Lyndon

As this micro-budget, post-nuke actioner unwound I found myself wondering if it was to become the first film I'd ever have to review without actually having sat all the way through to the end. So atrocious is it in just about every conceivable sphere that only professionalism and a perverse curiosity kept me going. After it had finished and I lay on the floor with a wet towel over my head, I began to gather my thoughts, such as they are.

The story is a familiar one: Clean-cut couple adrift in a post-apocalypse nightmare. Pretty soon they fall into the clutches of a gang of mean bikers armed with flails. Turns out the bikers are themselves in thrall to the charismatic but thoroughly evil Messiah who routinely forces his prisoners to undergo "The Run," a sort of ground-level zipline with people trying to kill you. Our hero is earmarked for The Run, but he and his girlfriend are helped to escape and then to turn the tables ...

So far so good. But then the problems start. The acting is terrible, worse even than in early 1980s TV commercials. But

then, I said to myself, the guy who plays "Hero"—so named to distinguish him from the male lead, who is a total wet wipe—actually wasn't so awful. Okay, he couldn't deliver dialogue or emote but then this is an action thriller; what's required of him is to be beefy. Think of those lunks in all the Italian post-nuke movies—he's no worse than them and they all have the luxury of being dubbed. Along similar lines, the leading lady Barbara isn't that bad either, certainly compared to the ill-fated love interest Jennifer. The point is, you have to put these things in context, and everything is relative.

The production design is awful, particularly the make-up and costumes, being of school play standard. For example, the mutants, and there are plenty of them, are wrapped up in bed sheets with crap plastered over their faces, including what appears to be balloons that inflate—excuse me, swell up—to indicate the appalling radiation sickness of the sufferer. The look for the gentleman is "street punk" (ripped denim/leather, shirtless, dirty smears on the faces); while it's "heavy metal prostitute" for the lady (P.V.C. skirts, lingerie, dirty smears on the faces.).

But, then again, despite the fight scenes being laughably bad (never have a I seen a kick to the goolies be delivered with so little conviction), some of the gore effects are nonetheless pretty good, especially the throat-slittings, stabbings and arrows in the face, and there are plenty—you can't ask for much more in a film of this type. We've all seen desperately dull action flicks which skimp on the violence simply because it's easier and cheaper not to bother; well, for all his faults, Murphy *does* bother and it's that level of commitment which makes his films endearing.
—Daniel King

AVALON

1989
D: Michael J. Murphy
W: Carl Humphries
Starring: Patrick Olliver, Stephen Harris, Debbi Stevens, Rob Bartlett, Abigail Blackmore

A pumped-up, leather-and-studs clad Merlin battles sultry blonde witch-queen Morgana for possession of Excalibur, in Michael J. Murphy's lusty Arthurian romp.

Ever noticed how the so-called fantasy "epics" often contain lengthy interludes where their warriors and spellcasters sit around chatting, or tramping through the forest from one castle to the next? From the would-be weighty/significant (*Excalibur*)

to the juvenile (*Krull*), they all seem to bank on their audience exiting the theater chattering about, "that bit with the spider" or "the scene where they fight the two-headed monster," relying on this to cover up any longueurs, flaws, deficiencies, or holes in the budget. The *Monty Python* team were quick to spot such falsity, and their *Monty Python and the Holy Grail*, *Jabberwocky* and the like therefore stand up against any competition, no matter how financially-inflated, in terms of visual spectacle and ambition, making a virtue of comparative cheapness.

You do get the impression that Michael Murphy must have looked at *Willow* or the *Robin of Sherwood* TV series and come to the same conclusion. Despite lack of, well, everything, Mike was never phased by limitation and, alongside his regular dips into the world of horror, was never averse to attempting a historical costumer—*Avalon* brings Arthurian myth into the Murphy orbit and is as entertaining as movies costing several hundred times more.

Avalon displays a light comic approach to the material, which proves a perfect fit. The quest begins as confident Owen (Harris) and enthusiastic, youthfully raw Kieran (Bartlett) vow to assist pretty Clotilde (Blackmore) in seeking her lost love Edwin. Along the way, they encounter Murphy-regular Patrick Olliver in whiskery wizard get-up ("I am Merlin the Magician. Maybe you have heard of me?"); one quick spell and Merlin has transformed himself into something out of *Mad Max 2*, far more appropriate for the fight ahead. Joining them as they journey towards "the Isle of the Dead—where souls wait in limbo," the quartet fends off an army of raised-from-the-grave, sword-wielding zombies—this scene is a little lackluster, but is compensated for by later tournament combat at Morgana's court, and by the mysterious appearance of a gloopy, swamp-dwelling beast resembling one of *Doctor Who*'s 1970s Sea Devils ("all slimy, like a sewer") who turns out to be a significant figure. Clotilde has been kidnapped by now and assimilated into the assortment of handmaidens attending the evil queen, her memory wiped, and her personage threatened by a pair of exceedingly camp male Morgana acolytes (Phil Lyndon and Stephen Longhurst, having a ball!) Can good defeat the forces of darkness before the entire production funds are exhausted?

Murphy livens up the sword-and-sorcery routine with a curveball every so often—what about that three-way love scene between Kieran, one of Morgana's all-too-willing saucepots, and a deadly poisonous snake, for example? Or the scrap between our heroic trio and a triumvirate of doppelgangers? ("Very clever—very clever" remarks Merlin, and it's hard not to agree.). There's even a stop-motion fire demon brought into play towards the climax—not exactly to Harryhausen standard, but its mere presence and the attendant scope of Murphy's vision all serve to add to the tapestry.
—Darrell Buxton

MOONCHILD

1989
D: Michael J. Murphy
W: Steve Newcombe
Starring: Judith Holding, Patrick Olliver, Philip Lyndon, Catherine Rowlands

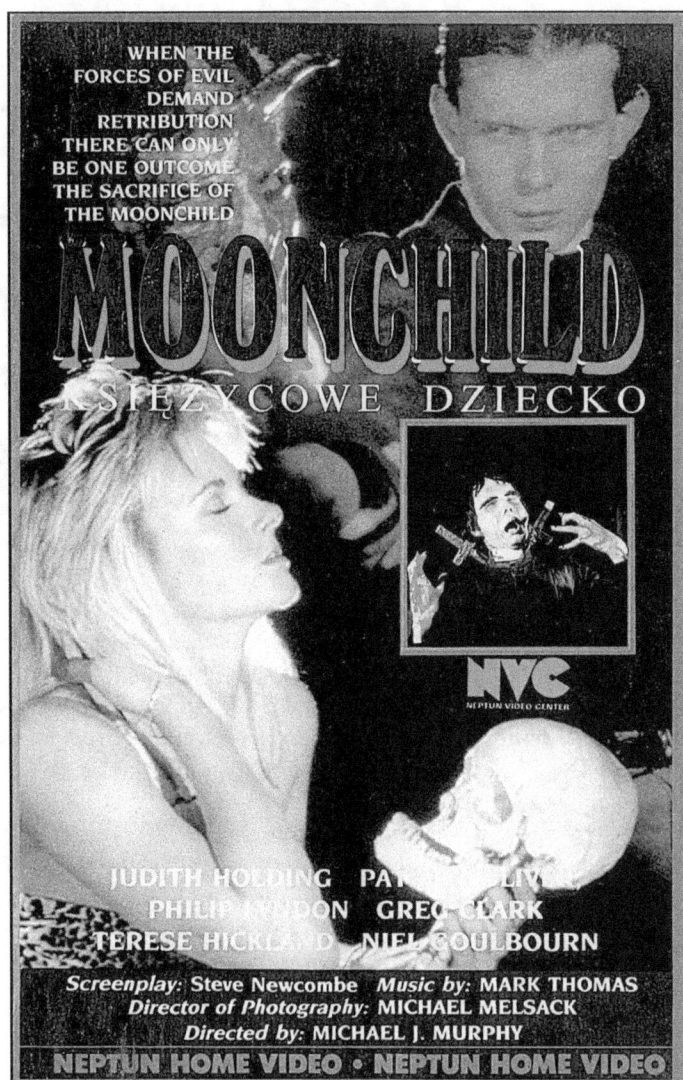

Sarah (Judith Holding) is a young woman arriving in a pastoral English village at the height of summer where she has been employed as a personal assistant to Professor Lucan (Patrick Olliver), an authority on the occult. Lucan is suffering from an unspecified debilitating illness, reliant on a Zimmer frame, and later a wheelchair. He is putting together his latest tome and as Sarah types up his notes, she becomes informed of, and unnerved by, his findings on ritual practices.

As the new girl in the village she becomes popular among the young men. The local priest, Daniel (Philip Lyndon), takes a platonic interest, while Morris dancing local pet store assistant Tony (Greg Clark), a pleasant-seeming fellow, is regarded by the increasingly paranoid Sarah as conspiring against her. Both at least are infinitely more preferable company than Steve (Alan Jansen), nephew of the neighborhood nurse, Kelly (Therese Hickland). Steve is a cocky runt who perceives the perfect night out to be a violent squabble with other locals before a bit of the old carnal trampolining. If his thuggery is supposed to impress Sarah into bed, on this occasion it fails. She begins to trust only the priest and the gardener, Davies (Neil Goulbourn), who is the quintessence of country life, complete with thick ooh-arr accent and well run-in clothes, plucking dead birds and chortling knowingly.

Sarah discovers that Lucan's last assistant has been deposited in a local sanatorium, and a visit reveals that she too is named

Scene from *Moonchild*

Sarah (Catherine Rowlands), is blonde, hails from the same part of London and shares a birth date down to the year. That birthday is also only a few days away. The panic and the bad dreams heighten and an outsider friend, Jan (June Bunday, credited as "Jessica Day") goes missing on leaving the village. The viewer has seen her graphically murdered.

As Lucan writes and narrates, he provides exposition. "It is impossible for the AntiChrist to return without the presence of the Moonchild. However, when the roles are analyzed the interdependency of Moonchild and AntiChrist becomes clear. The purity of her birth complements the foulness of his own ... he needs to feel her innocence to externalize his own corruption. There is no corruption without innocence. No evil without good. Now it is possible to understand her role as catalyst."

The day comes, and as anyone familiar with classic paranoia horror plotting will know, Sarah is clearly going to seek protection with the wrong person, one possessed by the devil "Alus." Further revelations unfold, and it is now on the genuine protectors to race to her rescue before the fall of the blade.

The formulaic plot at least manages to engage throughout. Several of the strongest actors in Murphy's repertory company, Olliver, Holding and Goulbourn take key roles and the majority of the film is dependent on performance, dialogue and solid technique, giving it a professionalism that had often previously been scotched in his movies by over-enthusiastic attempts at spectacle, requiring complicated action sequences and innumerable effects, unconvincing on Murphy's tight budgets.

Miss Holding is no conventional film beauty, but this makes a change from the unfeasibly gorgeous heroines usually imperiled in occult thrillers. More important is the natural delivery she gives the dialogue, helping us warm to her. Most of the male leads come out on the appreciable side too, particularly Patrick Olliver, who has a great voice perfectly suited to the horror genre. Neil Goulbourn provides a memorable character role and you could imagine him propping up the leads in a Hammer film. Sadly, there are a couple of poor performances, the most comic-bookish is by Alan Jansen, as immensely irritating asshole Steve. "She was messing me around, so I packed her in, beat up her new guy and slept with her best friend," is typical Steve.

It's perhaps unfair to criticize the dialogue, as strong research into the supernatural has clearly been undertaken. The device of feeding the occult threat to Sarah through her transcription duties is successfully incorporated, though one is suspicious that the occult passages have been plagiarized. The inclusion of Hughes Mearns' *Antigonish* without credit reaffirms these doubts. For those who don't recognize it by name, the poem runs: "Yesterday upon the stair, I met a man who wasn't there/He wasn't there again today, I wish, I wish he'd go away."

Murphy's use of Mearns' verse beats James Mangold's employment of it in his Hollywood hit *Identity* by 14 years. In *Moonchild*, the use of the poem is blatantly to echo the uncanny effect that the wonderful ditty always has, and (unlike the Mangold film) bears no true relevance to the plot, but it's perfect that the recital fell to Olliver and his mellifluous tones.

The film does not set out to be a constant gore-fest but it does have periodic episodes of graphic horror that are managed to superior effect. The bloody mayhem does its job, is unsettling, and there is nothing coy about it, with mutilated legs here and a torn-open chest there. A shocking throat-slitting does raise a rare gasp and is all the more impressive when you consider that the budget and shooting schedule wouldn't have permitted too many takes. The gruesome slaying is committed in so leisurely a manner that it appals in unusual fashion. It reminds one of the similarly shocking throat slashing found in Stanley Long's 1981 short *Dreamhouse* (later incorporated into

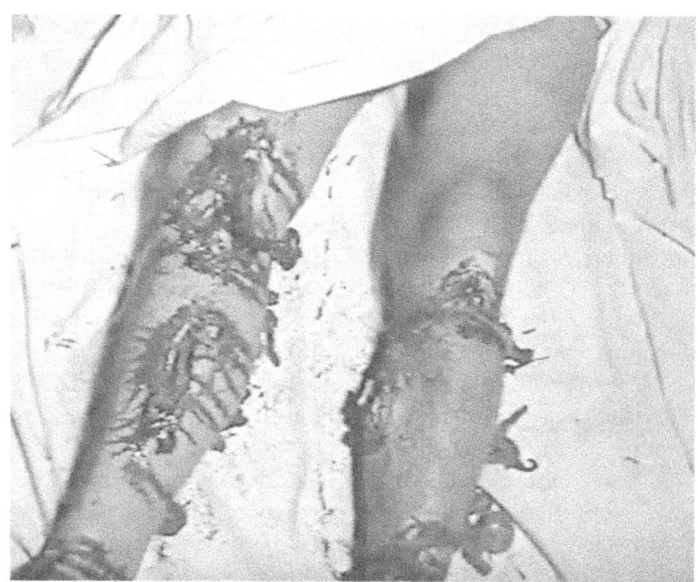

SPFX scene from *Moonchild*

the compendium horror *Screamtime*) and I suspect that Murphy may have intentionally attempted to reproduce that moment. The rituals in Sarah's nightmares are the oddest in a British film since Vernon Sewell's *The Curse of the Crimson Altar* in 1968, again a possible influence.

The final visit to the sanatorium utilizes a quick tempo score, as Sarah and Tony amble through the grounds while the frantic "other" Sarah races through corridors and appears at portals in the building before throwing herself out of one of

the windows. It is another ambitious sequence that works above and beyond Murphy's resources. *Moonchild* may ultimately be let down by budgetary limitations, but for the most part holds your attention, looks good, and surely, features the first Morris dancing hero in screen history!
—Paul Higson

This review by the author is based on his original 2003 review of the film at "The Zone" website, Pigasus Press, reproduced with kind permission by editor, Tony Lee)

TORMENT

1989
D: Michael J. Murphy
W: Leo Golding
Starring: Debbi Stevens, Rob Bartlett, Philip Lyndon, Catherine Rowlands

No sooner had the indefatigable Michael J. Murphy completed shooting *Moonchild* in the summer of 1989 than he was back with yet another fresh project. September of that year brought about *Torment*, probably in more ways than one given Mr. Murphy's astounding output during this era.

Through the British musical journey from rock'n'roll to punk and beyond, our cinema had just about kept pace with the changing youth trends and had offered almost as many cult classic pop offerings, as it had horror, science fiction or crime thrillers. Rely on Michael to present something we'd never experienced previously,—a movie about a low-rent Bonnie Tyler-like female vocalist, object of a stalker's murderous obsession, who flips the tables on Mister Unstable, kidnapping and torturing him partly in revenge for the savage murders of her friends/family/entourage, partly because she herself is out of her mind on pills and booze supplied by management—all leading to an utterly extraordinary closing scene which, I kid you not, appears to blatantly borrow from the finale of Bunuel's *Un Chien Andalou*! (as indeed did *Star Wars* spin-off *Rogue One* some years later.).

Murphy has always excelled in sniping at the pressures of showbiz in its various forms, via a psychotic prison escapee directing a provincial stage play in *The Last Night*, the anguished authors of *ZK3* and *Second Sight* hallucinating (or are they?) Jimmy Sangster-esque plots against them, or the camp bitchiness of the 1960s small-screen cult stars who somehow convinced millions of viewers of their macho status in *The Return of Alan Strange*. Here it's Debbi Stevens in a very 1980s hairdo and fashions as chart hitmaker Anna, encountering a crazy and possessive fan in what initially appears to be a roll-your-eyes, "seen it all before" plotline. Never underestimate M.J.M., however—the stringent demands the music industry makes upon Anna, coupled with the discovery that Mat (Bartlett), the handyman hunk with whom she is enjoying a carefree fling, is also the guy chopping his way through those closest to her, drives Anna to entrap, bind, and menace him; no feminist turnabout a là Michael Winner's *Dirty Weekend*, though, as Stevens' behavior eventually goes even beyond the boundaries of the ensnared male killer, taking persecution to excess by depriving her naked and tied captive of sustenance, bumping off her own manager when he calls unexpectedly, and then heading down to a nearby beach with the dying Mat for that aforementioned Bunuelian closing sequence, where the demented homicidal couple, entwined by insanity, lie waiting for the engulfing tide to end their mutual misery.

As with the majority of Michael's films, *Torment* has been rarely seen—this and his 1992 production *Second Sight* did pick up a few airings on the late, lamented cable TV channel HVC and have popped up here and there occasionally since, but it's a great pity that Murphy's unique spins on horror's basest concepts remain largely unknown.
—Darrell Buxton

Dario Argento poses with editor Darrell Buxton

ABOUT THE EDITOR

Darrell Buxton previously edited *The Shrieking Sixties–British Horror Films 1960-1969*, a critically acclaimed title from Midnight Marquee Press, nominated for a British Fantasy Society award in 2011. He also co-edited the Rondo-nominated *Unsung Horrors* and *Into the Velvet Darkness: A Celebration of Vincent Price*, among others.

Darrell is a familiar presence at film societies, festivals, and special movie events around the United Kingdom, as well as being an experienced interviewer and writer. He hosts the regular and popular "Fright Club" screenings at Derby QUAD arts center, and has published several collections of his introductions from these shows.

A contributor to the Headpress publications *Creeping Flesh: The Horror Fantasy Film Book* and *Offbeat: British Cinema's Curiosities, Obscurities and Forgotten Gems*, Darrell has also written for *Samhain*, *Giallo Pages*, *We Belong Dead* and other noted fanzines/small press movie journals.

His efforts in tracking hidden treasures from horror cinema's buried past brought about the rediscovery and Blu-ray release of Saxon Logan's film *Sleepwalker* (1984) and helped to revive interest in the career of maverick director Michael J. Murphy.

Darrell co-wrote the screenplay for the feature film *Ouijageist* (2018), directed by John R. Walker, and contributed to the script of *5G Zombies* (2020).

Visit www.midmar.com for a complete list of our titles on film history!

www.ingramcontent.com/pod-product-compliance
Lightning Source LLC
Chambersburg PA
CBHW081353070526
44583CB00020B/2547